AP Precalculus

JM EDU

PREFACE

Joseph Pak was born and raised in South Korea and moved to the United States during his teenhood. Joseph graduated from high school in Texas, where he discovered his knack for studying mathematics. He received his Bachelor's degree in mathematics at the University of Texas at Austin. Subsequently, Joseph passed a content examination(135 Mathematics 8–12), which certified him to work as a mathematics instructor at Texas Public High School.

Joseph has been teaching U.S. mathematics to students in Seoul, South Korea, for over a decade, during which time he realized a desperate need for high–quality workbooks for his students. He has been researching and developing exquisite content for his workbooks to educate his students more effectively, and to mostly alleviate the hardships students often encounter when trying to tackle new concepts in mathematics.

After years of extensive research in math education, Joseph proudly presents this comprehensive workbook, carefully designed to help students excel in their AP Precalculus GPA and confidently prepare for the AP Precalculus Exam. Key features include:

1. 5-Step Systematic Approach: Concept → Example → Check Point → Review Exercise → Chapter Test ensures a step–by–step mastery of precalculus.

2. Clear Explanations: Simplified, detailed guidance for understanding complex topics and mastering problem–solving strategies.

3. Self-Study Ready: Structured problems allow independent learning and effective practice.

4. **Critical Thinking Focus**: Creative, concept—based problems enhance critical thinking and problem—solving skills.

5. **Exam Success**: A proven resource for achieving top scores on the AP Precalculus Exam and excelling in class.

This workbook is your ultimate guide to AP Precalculus success!

Author's Words:

A well—structured workbook plays a critical role in students' learning experience. It serves as a very influential guide for students. I hope this book helps you realize all your inner—inquisitivity in learning mathematics, as well as contribute to the advancement of U.S. mathematics at large.

As a final note, I am thrilled that you've chosen this book to help you on this journey, and please do not hesitate to reach out to us to share your challenges, concerns, and successes. Wish you all the best of luck!

Joseph Pak
JM EDU
B.A. Mathematics —University of Texas at Austin, 2006

1. AP Precalculus AP Exam Format

Section I: Multiple Choice

- **Total**: 40 Questions | 2 Hours | 62.5% of Exam Score
  - **Part A**: 28 Questions | 80 Minutes | 43.75% of Exam Score
    - Calculator Not Permitted
  - **Part B**: 12 Questions | 40 Minutes | 18.75% of Exam Score
    - Graphing Calculator Required

Section II: Free Response

- **Total**: 4 Questions | 1 Hour | 37.5% of Exam Score
  - **Part A**: 2 Questions | 30 Minutes | 18.75% of Exam Score
    - Graphing Calculator Required

    Question 1 Function Concepts

    Question 2 Modeling a Non-Periodic Context
  - **Part B**: 2 Questions | 30 Minutes | 18.75% of Exam Score
    - Calculator Not Permitted

    Question 3 Modeling a Periodic Context

    Question 4 Symbolic Manipulations

2. AP Precalculus Course Overview

Units	Exam Weighing
Unit 1: Polynomial and Ration Function	30-40%
Unit 2: Exponential and Logarithmic Functions	27-40%
Unit 3: Trigonometric and Polar Functions	30-35%
Unit 4: Functions Involving Parameters, Vectors, and Matrices	Not assessed on the AP Exam

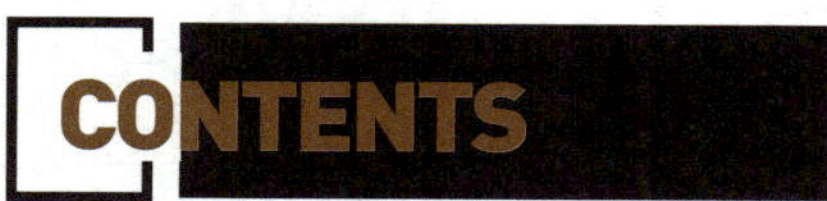

CONTENTS

Unit I Polynomial and Rational Functions

Unit II Exponential and Logarithmic Functions

Unit III Trigonometric and Polar Functions

Unit IV Functions Involving Parameters, Vectors, and Matrices

Solutions Manual

Unit I

Polynomial and Rational Functions

1. Relations and Functions
2. Rates of Change
3. Polynomial Functions of Higher Degree
4. Division of Polynomials
5. Real Zeros of Polynomial Functions
6. Rational Functions
7. Transformations of Functions
8. Unit I Test

1 Relations and Functions

01 Definition of Relations and Functions

1. Relations are a collection of ordered pairs,$(x,\ y)$points.
2. Functions are a special type of relation, one that pairs one x values with only one y value.
3. Functions and relations can be described by various forms to include equations, graphs, sets, tables, and mapping. Refer to the followings below.

Equations: $y=x^2-1$ or $f(x)=x^2-1$

Function Notation: $y=f(x)$

Sets: $\{(0,\ -1),\ (1,\ 0),\ (2,\ 3),\ (3,\ 8)\}$

Graphs:

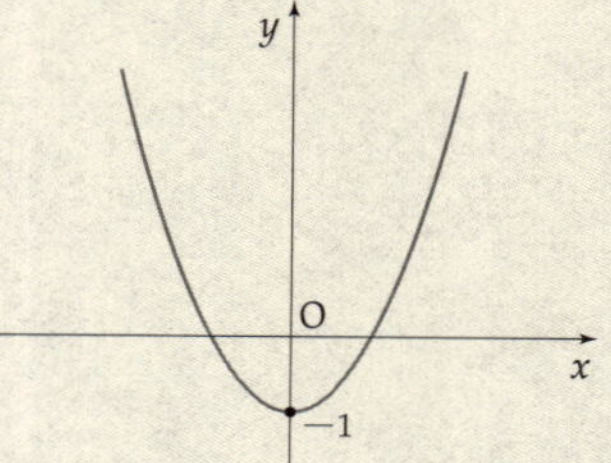

Tables:

x	y
0	−1
1	0
2	3
3	8

Mapping:

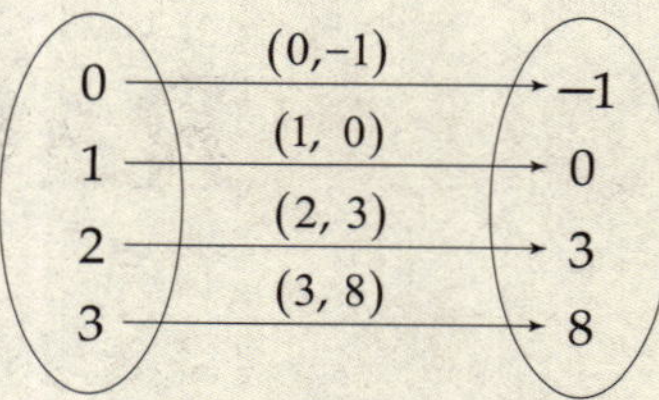

4. Domain: The set of values of the independent variable (often the $x-$values) for which the function is defined.
5. Range: The set of the corresponding values of the dependent variable (often the $y-$values).

Example 1

Let f be the function given by $f(x)=x^2-3x+5$. What is the value of $f(2)$?

Solution

$f(2)=2^2-3\cdot2+5=3$

$f(2)=3$

Check Point 1

Solutions_Page 2

Let f be the function given by $f(x)=2x^3-5x^2+1$. What is the value of $f(-2)$?

Example 2

What is the domain and range of the following relation?

$\{(-2, 3), (-1, 5), (0, 7), (1, 5)\}$

Solution

The domain is the set of all $x-$coordinates in the given points. So, the domain is: $\{-2, -1, 0, 1\}$. The range is the set of all $y-$coordinates in the given points. Since 5 is repeated, we only list it once in the range. So, the range is: $\{3, 5, 7\}$

Domain: $\{-2, -1, 0, 1\}$
Range: $\{3, 5, 7\}$

Check Point 2

Solutions_Page 2

Determine the domain and range of the following relation: $(0, 3)$, $(-1, 3)$, $(2, 4)$, $(3, 3)$.

02 Implied Domain of Basic Functions

1. If f is defined by a function, the implied domain consists of all real number for which the function is defined.
2. Polynomial function $y=a_nx^{n+}a_{n-1}x^{n-1}+\cdots+a_0$: Domain is all real numbers.
3. Rational Function $y=\frac{1}{x}$: Domain is all real numbers except $x=0$.
4. Radical Function $y=\sqrt{x}$: Domain is all real numbers such that $x\geq0$.

Example 3

What is the domain of the function $f(x)=\dfrac{1}{(x-1)(x-2)}$?

Solution

The denominator $(x-1)(x-2)=0$ when $x=1$ and $x=2$.
So the function is defined for all real numbers x except for $x=1$ and $x=2$.
Therefore, the domain of the function f is all real numbers except $x=1$ and $x=2$.
In interval notation, the domain is $(-\infty,\ 1)\cup(1,\ 2)\cup(2,\ \infty)$.

$(-\infty,\ 1)\cup(1,\ 2)\cup(2,\ \infty)$

Check Point 3

Solutions_Page 2

What is the domain of the function $g(x)=\dfrac{2x+4}{2x^3+x^2-6x}$?

Example 4

What is the domain of the function $f(x)=\sqrt{2x+1}$?

Solution

The function is defined when $2x+1\geq 0 \rightarrow x\geq -\frac{1}{2}$.
Therefore, the domain of the function f is all real numbers x such that $x\geq -\frac{1}{2}$.

In interval notation, the domain is $\left[-\frac{1}{2},\infty\right)$.

$\left[-\frac{1}{2},\infty\right)$

Check Point 4

Solutions_Page 2

What is the domain of the function $g(x)=2\sqrt{3x+1}-5$?

Review Exercise

01 If $f(x)=2x-1$, which of the following equals $f(1)+2f(2)$?

02 If $f(x)=\frac{a}{x-1}+x-1$ and $f(2)=2f(-1)$, then what is the value of a?

03 If $f(x)=3-2x^2$ and $x<0$, for what value of x is $f(x)=0$?

04 For which of the following functions f does $f(2)=0$?

I. $f(x)=x^2-4$

II. $f(x)=x^2+x-6$

III. $f(x)=\frac{x-2}{x^2-4}$

(A) I only
(B) II only
(C) I and II only
(D) II and III only

05 If $f(x)=ax^2+bx+c$ such that $f(0)=-1$ and $f(-1)=3$, what is the value of $a-b$?

06 If $f(x)=2+\sqrt{\frac{x}{2}-4}$, which of the following CANNOT be a value of $f(x)$?

(A) 6
(B) 4
(C) 2
(D) 0

07 $$f(x)=\frac{1}{\sqrt{x^2-4}}$$

What is the domain of the function f?

(A) $-2\le x\le 2$
(B) $x\le -2$ or $x\ge 2$
(C) $-2<x<2$
(D) $x<-2$ or $x>2$

Review Exercise

08 $f(x)=\frac{\sqrt{2x+1}}{x^2+x}$

What is the domain of the function f?

(A) $-1<x\leq-\frac{1}{2}$

(B) $-1<x\leq-\frac{1}{2}$ or $x<-1$

(C) $-\frac{1}{2}\leq x<0$

(D) $-\frac{1}{2}\leq x<0$ or $x>0$

09 Which of the following functions has all real numbers for its domain?

(A) $f(x)=\sqrt{x+2}$

(B) $f(x)=|x+2|$

(C) $f(x)=\frac{x^2-4}{x+2}$

(D) $f(x)=\frac{1}{x+2}$

10

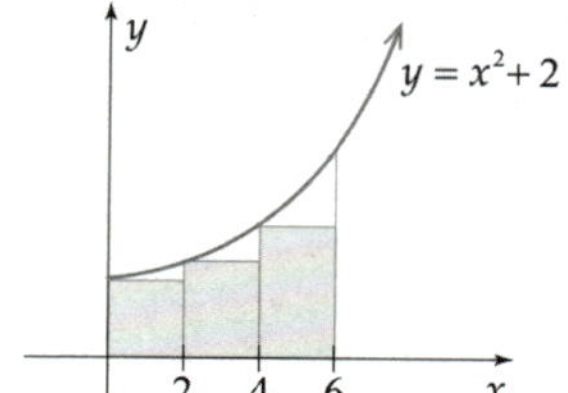

Figure NOT drawn to scale.

The figure above shows a portion of the graph of $y=x^2+2$. what is the sum of the areas of the three inscribed rectangles shown above?

2 Rates of Change

01 Average Rate of Change

Generally, when the value of x in function $y=f(x)$ changes from a to b, the value of y changes from $f(a)$ to $f(b)$ The change in x, $b-a$, is expressed as Δx and the change in y, $f(b)-f(a)$, is expressed as Δy. And the ratio of Δy to Δx, $\frac{\Delta y}{\Delta x}=\frac{f(b)-f(a)}{b-a}$ is called the **average rate of change** of function $y=f(x)$ when the value of x changes from a to b.

1. The average rate of change over the interval $[a, b]$ is $\frac{\Delta y}{\Delta x}=\frac{f(b)-f(a)}{b-a}$.
2. The average rate of change represents the slope of the line AB.
3. We read Δ as "delta" which is a Greek word meaning "difference."

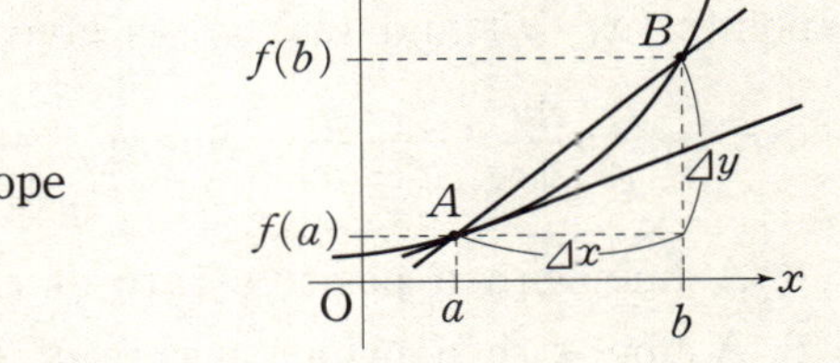

Example 1

x	-2	-1	0	1	2	3
$f(x)$	12	7	1	-2	0	2

The table above gives value of a polynomial function f at selected x. What is the average rate of change of f over the closed interval $-2\leq x\leq 3$?

Solution

The average rate of change of f over $-2\leq x\leq 3$ is

$$\frac{\Delta y}{\Delta x}=\frac{f(3)-f(-2)}{3-(-2)}=\frac{2-12}{5}=-2$$

$\frac{\Delta y}{\Delta x}=-2$

Check Point 1

Solutions_Page 4

x	-2	-1	0	1	2	3
$f(x)$	12	7	1	-2	0	2

The table above gives value of a polynomial function f at selected x. What is the average rate of change of f over the closed interval $-1 \leq x \leq 2$?

02 Rate of Change in Linear Function

The **average rate of change of the line** is commonly referred to as the slope of the line. The slope, usually denoted by the letter m, of a line passing through the points (x_1, y_1) and (x_2, y_2) is given by

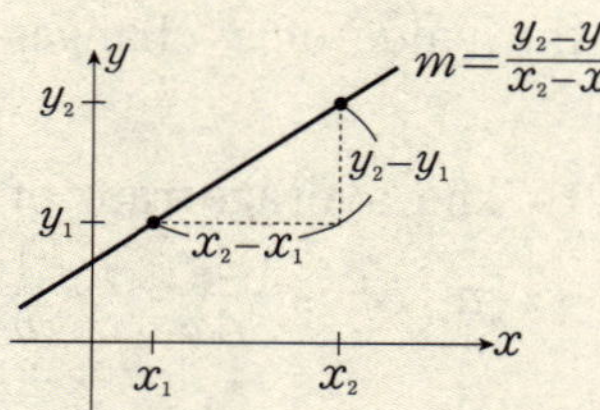

$$m=\frac{\Delta y}{\Delta x}=\frac{y_2-y_1}{x_2-x_1}, \text{ where } x_2-x_1 \neq 0$$

1. A line with a **positive rate of change increases** from left to right.
2. A line with a **negative rate of change decreases** from left to right.

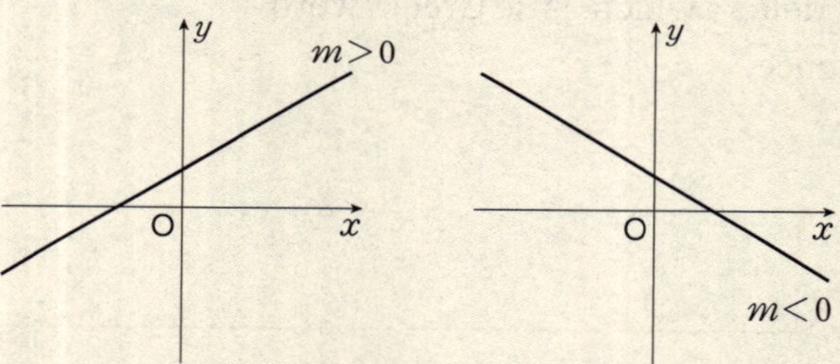

✔ In general, a graph with a constant rate of change r is positive if the graph is increasing and negative if the graph is decreasing. Refer to the graph below.

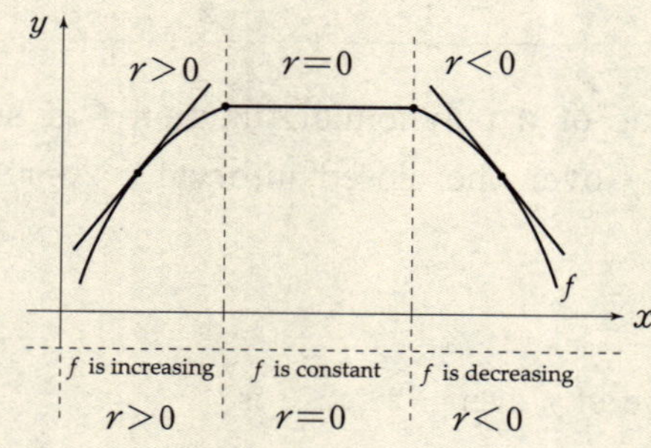

Example 2

Find the rate of change of the line that passes through the points (1, 5) and (5, 7).

Solution

Let $(x_1, y_1)=(1, 5)$ and $(x_2, y_2)=(5, 7)$.
The rate of change(slope) of the line is

$$m=\frac{\Delta y}{\Delta x}=\frac{y_2-y_1}{x_2-x_1}$$
$$=\frac{7-5}{5-1}=\frac{2}{4}=\frac{1}{2}$$

$\frac{\Delta y}{\Delta x}=\frac{1}{2}$

Check Point 2

Solutions_Page 4

Determine the rate of change of the line that passes through the points (−4, −1) and (2, 35).

03 Rate of Change in Quadratic Function

1. Rate of Change

The average rate of change of a quadratic function is not constant but rather varies across different intervals. One key property is that **the average rate of change** of a quadratic function **increases constantly** as we move away from a certain point. The graph below gives a visual representation of the slope.

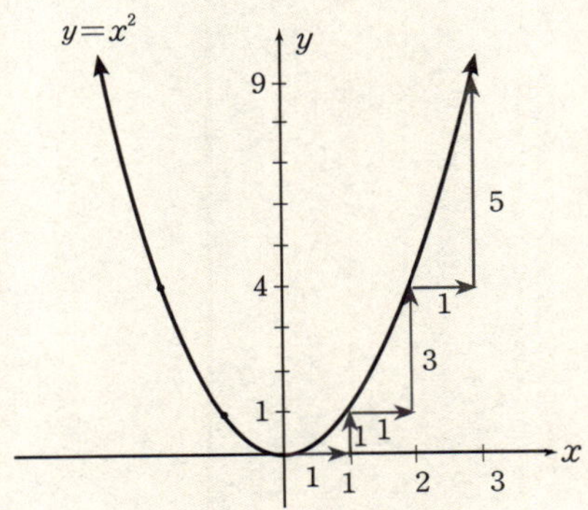

x	y	Average rate of change
0	0	
		1
1	1	+2
		3
2	4	+2
		5
3	9	+2
		7
4	16	

(1) As x increases by 1 from a certain point, specially (0, 0) in the figure above, the average rate of change constantly increases by 2.

(2) The rate of change is positive for $x>0$ and negative for $x<0$ in the figure above. The sign of the rate of change in a quadratic function depends on whether the parabola opens upward(concave up) or downward(concave down).

2. Definition of Concavity

(1) The graph of f is **concave up** if the **rate of change continually increases.**

(2) The graph of f is **concave down** if the **rate of change continually decreases.**

(3) A point where the concavity of the graph changes from concave up to down or vice versa is called a **point of inflection.**

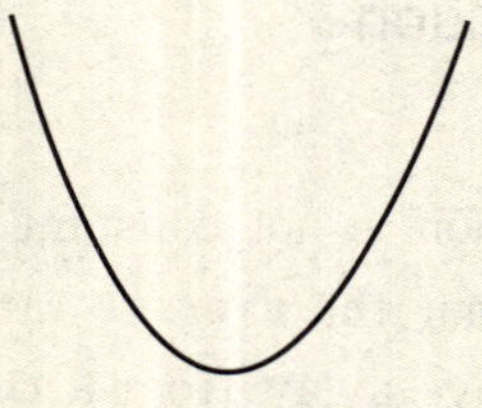

Concave up

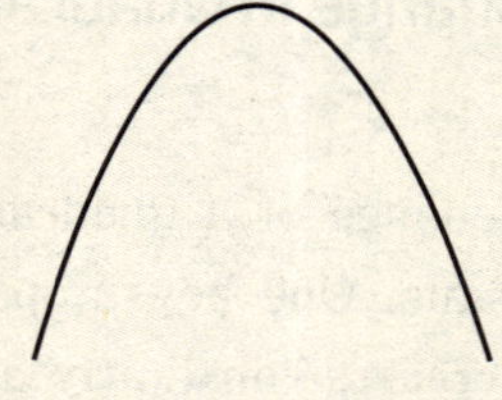

Concave down

Example 3

x	-1	0	1	2	3
$f(x)$	-2	-3	-2	1	6

The table above gives value of a polynomial function f at selected x. Determine whether f is linear or quadratic. If quadratic, state whether the graph of the parabola would be concave up or concave down.

Solution

x	-1	0	1	2	3
$f(x)$	-2	-3	-2	1	6

Changes in x: $+1$, $+1$, $+1$, $+1$

Changes in $f(x)$: -1, $+1$, $+3$, $+5$ $\Rightarrow$ (1)

Changes in the changes: $+2$, $+2$, $+2$ $\Rightarrow$ (2)

(1): The rate of change is NOT constant.
(2): The rate of change is INCREASING constantly.

The average rates of change are not constant, but the rate of change is constantly increasing by 2 as shown above. Therefore, the function f is quadratic, and its graph of parabola would be concave up.

Quadratic and concave up

Check Point 3

Solutions_Page 4

x	0	1	2	3	4
$f(x)$	2	0	1	5	12

The table above provides values of a polynomial function f at specific x values. Determine if f is linear or quadratic. If it is quadratic, specify whether the parabola's graph is concave up or concave down.

Review Exercise

01

x	0	1	2	3	4
$f(x)$	3	2	3	6	11

The table gives the value of a function f for selected intervals of x. Which of the following describes the rate of change of the graph of f in the interval $0 \le x \le 4$?

(A) The rate of change of f is constant and positive.

(B) The rate of change of f is constant and negative.

(C) The rate of change of f is increasing.

(D) The rate of change of f is decreasing.

02

x	$0<x<2$	$2<x<4$	$4<x<6$	$6<x<8$
Rate of change of f	Increasing	2	decreasing	-2

The table describes the rate of change of a function f for selected intervals of x. The function f is defined for $0 \le x \le 8$. On which of the following intervals is the graph of f concave up?

(A) $0<x<2$

(B) $2<x<4$

(C) $4<x<6$

(D) $6<x<8$

For questions 03−04, refer to the following graph.

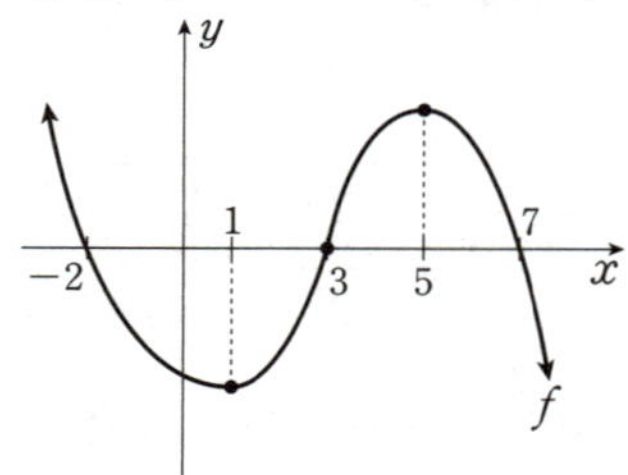

03 On which of the following intervals is the rate of change increasing?

(A) $-2<x<3$

(B) $1<x<5$

(C) $3<x<7$

(D) $1<x<7$

04 Which of the following statements about the rate of change of f over the interval $1<x<5$ is true?

(A) The rate of change is increasing.

(B) The rate of change is decreasing.

(C) The rate of change is positive.

(D) The rate of change is negative.

05 "The rate of change of f is negative and increasing"

The statement above is characteristics of the rates of change of the function f on interval $2<x<4$. Which of the following is true about f on interval $2<x<4$?

(A) The graph of f is increasing and concave up.
(B) The graph of f is increasing and concave down.
(C) The graph of f is decreasing and concave up.
(D) The graph of f is decreasing and concave down.

For questions 06–07, refer to the following graph.

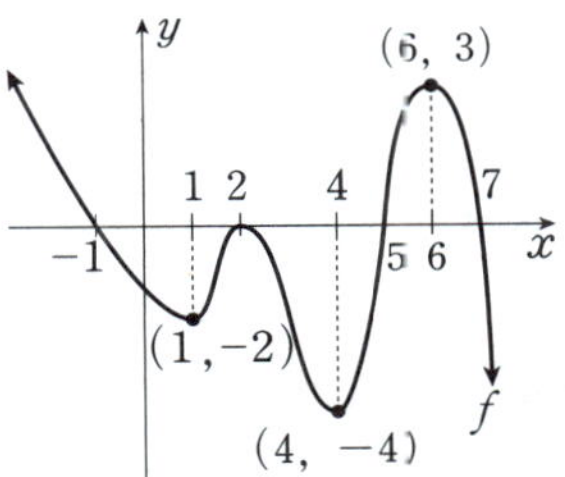

06 On which of the following interval is the average rate of change of f greatest?

(A) $-1<x<1$
(B) $1<x<2$
(C) $2<x<4$
(D) $4<x<6$

07 On which of the following intervals is the rate of change negative?

(A) $-1<x<2$
(B) $2<x<4$
(C) $4<x<5$
(D) $5<x<7$

Review Exercise

08

x	$0 \le x \le 1$	$1 \le x \le 4$	$4 \le x \le 6$	$6 \le x \le 10$
Average Rate of change	-8	-3	5	10

The table gives the rate of change of a function f for selected intervals of x. On which of the following interval does the function decreases the most?

(A) $0 \le x \le 1$

(B) $1 \le x \le 4$

(C) $4 \le x \le 6$

(D) $6 \le x \le 10$

09 The function f is given by $f(x) = x^2 - 2x + 3$. Which of the following of f is true?

(A) The graph of f has a positive rate of change for all x.

(B) The graph of f has a negative rate of change for all x.

(C) The graph of f exhibits an increasing rate of change for all x.

(D) The graph of f exhibits a decreasing rate of change for all x.

10 The function f is given by $g(x) = -2x^2 - 8x + 5$. Which of the following of the graph of f is true?

(A) For $x > -2$, the graph of g has a positive rate of change, and for $x < -2$, the graph of g has a negative rate of change.

(B) For $x > -2$, the graph of g has a negative rate of change, and for $x < -2$, the graph of g has a positive rate of change.

(C) For $x > -2$, the graph of g exhibits a decreasing rate of change, and for $x < -2$, the graph of g exhibits an increasing rate of change.

(D) For $x > -2$, the graph of g exhibits an increasing rate of change, and for $x < -2$, the graph of g exhibits a decreasing rate of change.

11 For the function f, the rate of change is positive for $x<4$ and negative for $x>4$. Which of the following is true?

(A) The graph of f has a maximum at $x=4$.

(B) The graph of f has a minimum at $x=4$.

(C) The graph of f is concave down for $x<4$ and is concave up for $x>4$.

(D) The graph of f is concave up for $x<4$ and is concave down for $x>4$.

12 For the function f, the rate of change is increasing for $x<4$ and decreasing for $x>4$. Which of the following is true?

(A) The graph of f has a maximum at $x=4$.

(B) The graph of f has a minimum at $x=4$.

(C) The graph of f is concave down for $x<4$ and is concave up for $x>4$.

(D) The graph of f is concave up for $x<4$ and is concave down for $x>4$.

3 Polynomial Functions of Higher Degree

01 Definition of Polynomial Functions

A standard form of polynomial function of x with degree n is written as

$$f(x)=a_nx^n+a_{n-1}x^{n-1}+\cdots+a_1x+a_0$$

where a_n, a_{n-1}, $\cdots$, a_1, a_0 are real numbers $a_n\neq0$, and n is non−negative integer.

1. The name of polynomial function is determined by the value of n. (Refer to the example below)
2. Each monomial (a_nx^n, $a_{n-1}x^{n-1}$, $\cdots$, a_1x, a_0) is called a term. Especially, a_nx^n is a leading term and a_0 is a constant term or constant.
3. The constants a_n, a_{n-1}, $\cdots$, a_1 are called coefficients of each terms. and a_n is called a leading coefficient of the function.

02 Names of Polynomial Functions by Degree

The following names are assigned to polynomials according to their degree:

Degree	Name	Function Examples
$n=0$	Constant function	$f(x)=6$
$n=1$	Linear function	$f(x)=2x-1$
$n=2$	Quadratic function	$h(x)=x^2+3x+2$
$n=3$	Cubic function	$g(x)=-4x^3-3x+5$
$n=4$	Quartic function	$y=3x^4+x^3$
$n=5$	Quintic function	$y=x^5-2x^4+3x^2-5$

In general, the functions with degree 3 or higher are called polynomial functions of higher degree.

Example 1

Write the function in standard form and then find the leading coefficient and constant term.

① $f(x)=4x-5+3x^2$ ② $f(x)=4x-5x^3+6-x^2$

Solution

① $f(x)=4x-5+3x^2$

→ $f(x)=3x^2+4x-5$: A polynomial function with degree 2 or a quadratic function.

Leading coefficient: 3 Constant term: -5

② $f(x)=4x-5x^3+6-x^2$

→ $f(x)=-5x^3-x^2+4x+6$: A polynomial function with degree 3 or a cubic function.

Leading coefficient: -5 Constant term: 6

Check Point 1

Solutions_Page 6

Write the function in standard form and then find the leading coefficient and constant term.

① $g(x)=5+2x^2-3x^4$ ② $h(x)=x+5x^2+6x^3-1$

03 Power Functions

In this section, we will study fundamental features of the graphs of the polynomials functions. First, let us take a look at the power function $f(x)=x^n$, the simplest form of polynomial function.

$f(x)=x^n$

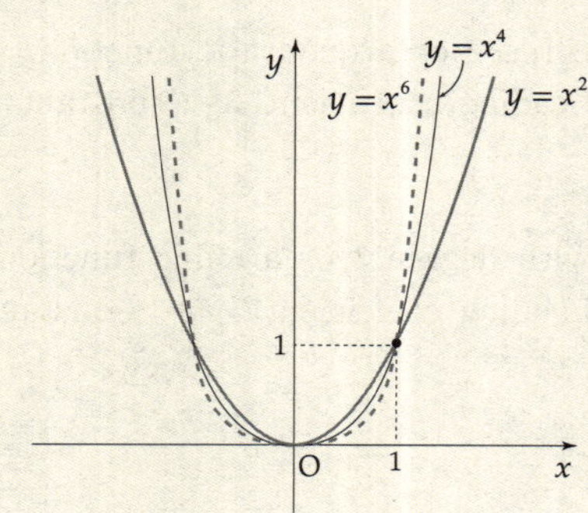 	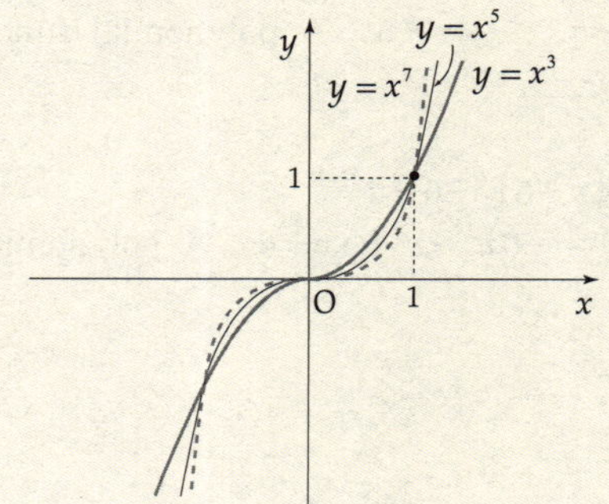
Graphs with an even number of n are similar to each other. ✔ The larger the value of n the flatter the graph near the x−axis. ✔ The graphs touch the x−axis at the x−intercept.	Graphs with an odd number of n are similar to each other. ✔ The larger the value of n the flatter the graph near the x−axis. ✔ The graphs pass through the x−axis at the x−intercept.

04 End Behavior of Polynomial Functions

We will now discuss about the ending behavior of polynomial functions. Whether the graph of a polynomial function eventually increases or decreases is completely determined by the degree n and its leading coefficient a_n, This process is called leading term test or leading coefficient test.

The graph of the polynomial function $f(x)=a_nx^n+a_{n-1}x^{n-1}+\cdots+a_1x+a_0$ eventually increases or decreases in the following manner.

	n=even	n=odd
$a_n>0$	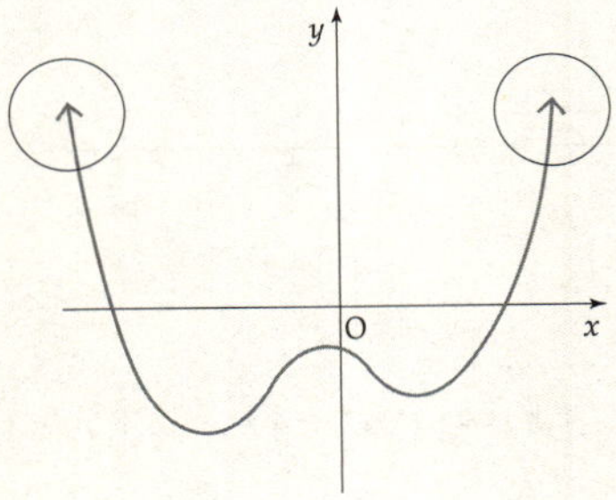	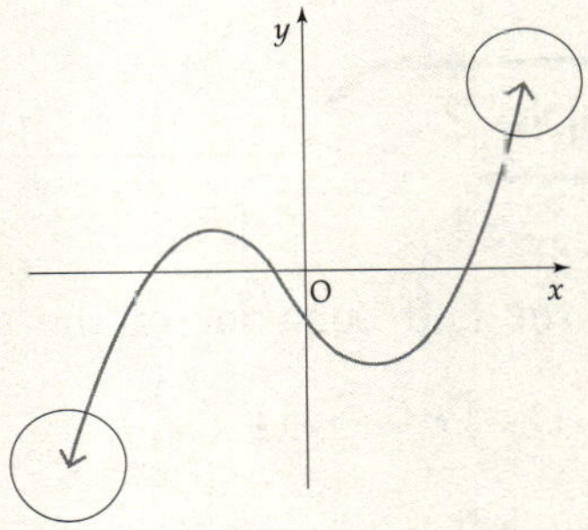
	As $x\to\infty$, $f(x)$ increases As $x\to-\infty$, $f(x)$ increases	As $x\to\infty$, $f(x)$ increases As $x\to-\infty$, $f(x)$ decreases
$a_n<0$	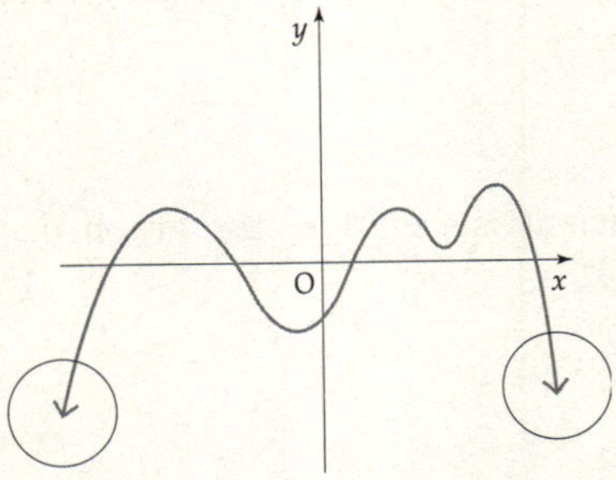	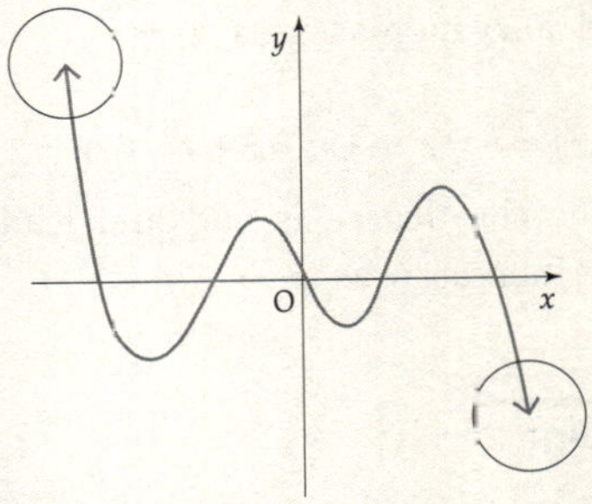
	As $x\to\infty$, $f(x)$ decreases As $x\to-\infty$, $f(x)$ decreases	As $x\to\infty$, $f(x)$ decreases As $x\to-\infty$, $f(x)$ increases

1. When the input values of a nonconstant polynomial function increase without bound, the output values will either increase or decrease without bound. The corresponding mathematical notation is

$$\lim_{x\to\infty} f(x)=\infty \text{ or } \lim_{x\to\infty} f(x)=-\infty$$

2. When the input values of a nonconstant polynomial function decrease without bound, the output values will either increase or decrease without bound. The corresponding mathematical notation is

$$\lim_{x\to-\infty} f(x)=\infty \text{ or } \lim_{x\to-\infty} f(x)=-\infty$$

Example 2

Describe the end behavior of the graph.

① $f(x)=x^4-4x^3-3x+1$

② $h(x)=-2x^3+4x^2-x+7$

Solution

① $f(x)=x^4-4x^3-3x+1 \rightarrow n=4,\ a_n=1$

Since the degree is even and leading coefficient is positive, the graph increases as $x\rightarrow\infty$ and also increases as $x\rightarrow-\infty$

② $h(x)=-2x^3+4x^2-x+7 \rightarrow n=3,\ a_n=-2$

Since the degree is odd and leading coefficient is negative, the graph decreases as $x\rightarrow\infty$ but increases as $x\rightarrow-\infty$

Check Point 2

Solutions_Page 6

Describe the end behavior of the graph.

① $f(x)=4x^3-x$

② $f(x)=-x^4+2x^2-4x-3$

05-1. Zeros of Polynomial Functions

Recall that finding the zeros of a function is equivalent to finding the x-intercept of the function. In order to find zeros, we just let $f(x)=0$ and solve the equation for x by factoring. If the equation is not factorable, then we will have to use some other techniques, which we will discuss in subsequent sections.

> Finding zeros of Polynomial Function $f(x)=a_nx^n+a_{n-1}x^{n-1}+\cdots+a_1x+a_0$
> 1. Substitute $f(x)=0$, $a_nx^n+a_{n-1}x^{n-1}+\cdots+a_1x+a_0=0$.
> 2. Factor the equation in the form of $(x-a)(x-b)(x-c)=0$.
> 3. $x=a$, $x=b$, $\cdots$, $x=c$ are the zeros of the function.
> 4. $(a, 0)$, $(b, 0)$, $(c, 0)$ are x-intercept of the graph of $f(x)$.
> 5. The function $f(x)$ has, at most, n real zeros.

Example 3

Find the zeros of the function $f(x)=x^3-x$.

Solution

$x^3-x=0$ → Let $f(x)=0$

$x(x^2-1)=0$ → Remove common factor x

$x(x-1)(x+1)=0$ → Factor the quadratic

$x=0$, $x-1=0$, or $x+1=0$

$x=0$, $x=1$, or $x=-1$

So the zeros of f are 0, 1, and -1

Check Point 3

Solutions_Page 6

Find the zeros of the function.

① $f(x)=x^3+x^2-12x$

② $f(x)=3x^3-x^2+6x-2$

05-2. Multiplicity of a Zero

If f is a polynomial function and $(x-a)^r$ is a factor of f, then $(x-a)^r$ produces a repeated zero $x=a$ and we say a is a zero of **multiplicity** r.

Example 4

Find the zeros of the function $g(x)=x^4+x^3-2x^2$.

Solution

$x^4+x^3-2x^2=0$ → Let $f(x)=0$

$x^2(x^2+x-2)=0$ → Remove common factor x^2

$x^2(x-1)(x+2)=0$ → Factor the quadratic

$x^2=0$, $x-1=0$, or $x+2=0$

$x=0$, $x=1$, or $x=-2$

So the zeros of f are 0(multiplicity 2), 1, and -2

Check Point 4

Solutions_Page 6

Find the zeros of the function.

① $g(x)=4x^4-16x^2$

② $h(x)=2x^3-4x^2+2x$

06 Graph of Polynomial Functions.

Now we are ready to sketch a graph of simple polynomial functions. Here are some steps to draw a polynomial function.

1. Apply the leading term(coefficient) test to find out whether the graph eventually increases or decreases.
2. Find the zeros of the function by factoring.
3. For the factor of $(x-a)^r$ and $r>1$, the graph touches the x-axis if r is even and passes through the x-axis if r is odd.
4. If necessary, plot a few additional points between zeros to sketch more precise graph.
5. Sketch the graph.

Example 5

Sketch the graph of $f(x)=x^4+x^3-6x^2$.

Solution

End behavior: Degree is 4(even) and leading coefficient is 1(positive).
By leading term test, the graph <u>increases</u> as $x \to \infty$
and also <u>increases</u> as $x \to -\infty$

Zero: $x^4+x^3-6x^2=0$
$x^2(x^2+x-6)=0$
$x^2(x+3)(x-2)=0 \to x=0,\ x=-3$ or $x=2$

So the zeros are -3, 0, and 2

Multiplicity of zero: For $x=-3$ and $x=2$(multiplicity 1), the graph passes through the x-axis.
For $x=0$(multiplicity 2), the graph touches the x-axis.

Additional Points: $f(-2)=-16$ and $f(1)=-4$

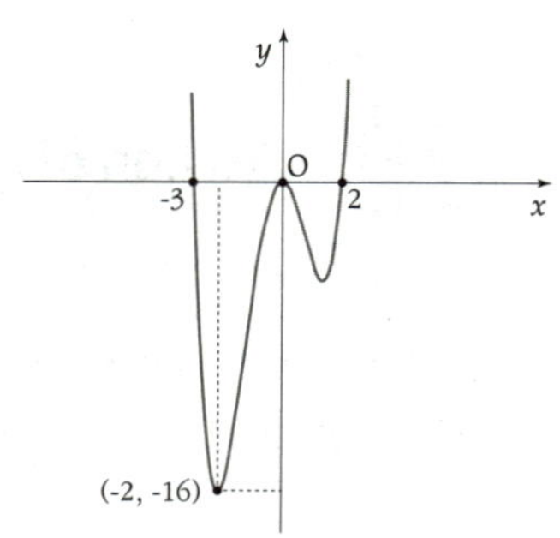

Check Point 5

Solutions_Page 6

Sketch the graph of the function.

① $f(x)=(x-1)(x+1)^2(x-2)$ ② $g(x)=-x^5-x^4$

07 Properties of Polynomial Function

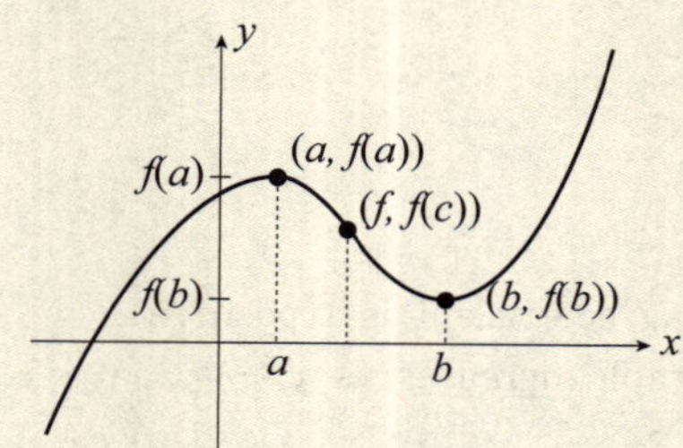

$f(a)$: local maximum
$f(b)$: local minimum
$(c,\ f(c))$: point of inflection

1. A polynomial function switches between increasing and decreasing at points where it has local(relative) maxima or minima. The endpoints of a polynomial function can be considered local minimum or maximum if the function is defined on a closed interval.

2. The greatest local maximum is called the absolute(global) maximum, and the least local minimum is called the absolute(global) minimum.
3. Between two distinct real zeros of a polynomial function, there must be at least one local maximum or minimum.
4. Polynomial functions of an even degree will have either a global maximum or a global minimum.
5. If f is a polynomial function of degree n, then f has at most $n-1$ turning points.
6. Points of inflection occur where the rate of change of the function changes, indicating a shift in concavity.
7. Points of inflection mark where the graph transitions from concave up to concave down, or vice versa.

08 Even and Odd Function

1. Even Function: A polynomial function $f(x)$ is considered even if it satisfies the property $f(-x)=f(x)$ for all x in its domain. Geometrically, this means that the graph of the function is symmetric about the $y-$axis.
2. Odd Function: A polynomial function $f(x)$ is considered odd if it satisfies the property $f(-x)=-f(x)$ for all x in its domain. Geometrically, this means that the graph of the function has rotational symmetry of 180 degrees about the origin.

Review Exercise

01 Describe the end behavior of the graph.

(1) $f(x)=-3x^4+x^2+x-4$

(2) $f(x)=4x^3-2x^2-5x+1$

(3) $g(x)=\frac{x^2}{4}-x^5-2x^4$

02 Which of the following must be true about the graph of the function

$h(x)=-4+2x-6x^2+\frac{2x^4}{3}$?

I. It eventually increases as x increases. II. It eventually increases as x decreases. III. It eventually decreases as x increases. IV. It eventually decreases as x decreases.

(A) I and II only
(B) I and III only
(C) II and III only
(D) II and IV only

03

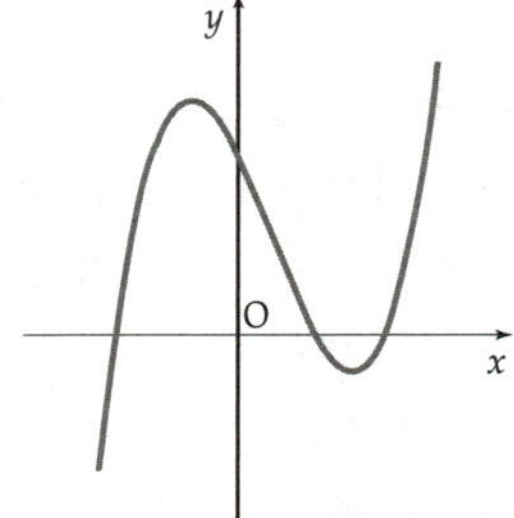

If the graph above represents the graph of $f(x)=ax^3+bx^2+cx+d$, then which of the following must be true?

(A) $a>0$ and $d>0$
(B) $a<0$ and $d>0$
(C) $a>0$ and $d<0$
(D) $a<0$ and $d<0$

04 Find the zeros of the function.

(1) $f(x)=x^3-9x$

(2) $f(x)=-2x^4+10x^3-8x^2$

(3) $g(x)=x^3-4x^2-x+4$

(4) $h(x)=x^4-5x^2+4$

05 Sketch the graph of the function.

(1) $f(x)=(x-1)(x+2)(x-3)$

(2) $f(x)=-2x^4+8x^2$

(3) $h(x)=-2x^5-x^4+6x^3$

(4) $f(x)=-x^3(x+2)(x-3)$

(5) $h(x)=x^3-5x^2-2x+10$

06

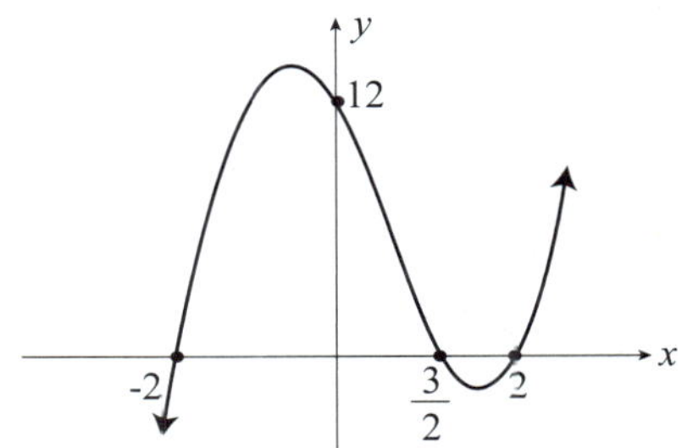

What is the smallest possible degree that the polynomial whose graph is shown above can have?

Review Exercise

07 The polynomial function f is given by $f(x)=(2x+1)^3(3x-1)$. Which of the following is true about f?

(A) f is a polynomial of degree 4 with a leading coefficient 6.
(B) f is a polynomial of degree 4 with a leading coefficient 24.
(C) f is a polynomial of degree 3 with a leading coefficient 6.
(D) f is a polynomial of degree 3 with a leading coefficient 24.

08 The polynomial function g is given by $g(x)=ax^2+bx+c$, where $a\neq0$ and b and c are positive constant. Which of the following statements about the graph of g is true?

(A) The graph of g has both a global maximum and a global minimum.
(B) The graph of g has either a global maximum or a global minimum, but not both.
(C) The graph of g has neither a global maximum nor a global minimum.
(D) With the information given above, we cannot determine the presence of a global maximum or global minimum for the function g.

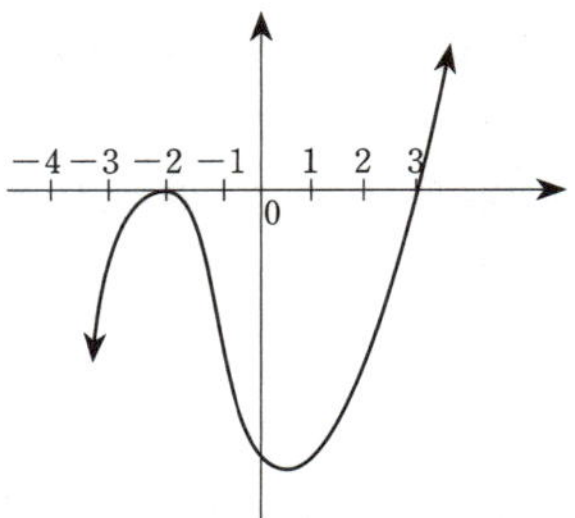

Figure not drawn to scale.

09 The graph of polynomial function f is given above. Which of the following could be the equation of f?

(A) $f(x)=(x-3)(x+2)$
(B) $f(x)=(x-3)(x+2)^2$
(C) $f(x)=(x-3)^2(x+2)$
(D) $f(x)=(x-3)^2(x+2)^2$

10 Suppose the function $g(x)$ is a polynomial of degree 4 where $x\neq0$. If g can be written as $g(x)=\dfrac{f(x)}{x}$, which of the following must be true about the degree of $f(x)$?

(A) $f(x)$ is a polynomial of degree 3.
(B) $f(x)$ is a polynomial of degree 4.
(C) $f(x)$ is a polynomial of degree 5.
(D) The degree of the function f cannot be determined from the information given above.

11 Let f be a polynomial function.

If both $\lim_{x\to\infty} f(x)=\infty$ and $\lim_{x\to-\infty} f(x)=\infty$, which of the following must true about f?

(A) The degree of f is even and the leading coefficient of f is positive.

(B) The degree of f is odd and the leading coefficient of f is positive.

(C) The degree of f is even and the leading coefficient of f is negative.

(D) The degree of f is odd and the leading coefficient of f is negative.

12 Let g be a polynomial function. If degree of g is odd and the leading coefficient is negative, which of the following must true about g?

(A) $\lim_{x\to-\infty} g(x)=\infty$ and $\lim_{x\to\infty} g(x)=\infty$

(B) $\lim_{x\to-\infty} g(x)-\infty$ and $\lim_{x\to\infty} g(x)=\infty$

(C) $\lim_{x\to-\infty} g(x)=\infty$ and $\lim_{x\to\infty} g(x)=-\infty$

(D) $\lim_{x\to-\infty} g(x)=-\infty$ and $\lim_{x\to\infty} g(x)=-\infty$

13 If $\lim_{x\to\infty} h(x)=-\infty$ and $\lim_{x\to-\infty} h(x)=\infty$, which of the following could be the function of $h(x)$?

(A) $h(x)=x^3-4x+1$

(B) $h(x)=-x^4+5x^2-x$

(C) $h(x)=x^6-x^4-5x^3$

(D) $h(x)=-4x^5+3x^2-2$

14 The graph of g is given by $g(x)=x^3-4x^2+4x$. Which of the following is true?

(A) g has a local maximum between $x=-2$ and $x=0$.

(B) g has a local minimum between $x=-2$ and $x=0$.

(C) g has a local maximum between $x=0$ and $x=2$.

(D) g has a local maximum between $x=0$ and $x=2$.

4 Division of Polynomials

In the previous section, we were able to find the zeros of polynomial functions by factoring. However, some of the polynomials are really tough to factor. Polynomial divisions, long division and synthetic division, can be used to factor these complicated polynomials.

01 Long Division

We will discuss how to divide polynomials by using long division. It closely resembles the division of integers.

$$\begin{array}{r} 212 \\ 13\overline{)2759} \\ \underline{26} \\ 159 \\ \underline{13} \\ 29 \\ \underline{26} \\ 3 \end{array} \quad \Longrightarrow \quad \begin{array}{rl} 2x^2+x+2 & \blacktriangleright \text{ Quotient} \\ x+3\overline{)2x^3+7x^2+5x+9} & \blacktriangleright \text{ Dividend} \\ \underline{2x^3+6x^2} & \blacktriangleright \ (x+3)\times 2x^3 \\ x^2+5x+9 & \blacktriangleright \text{ Subtract} \\ \underline{x^2+3x} & \blacktriangleright \ (x+3)\times x \\ 2x+9 & \blacktriangleright \text{ Subtract} \\ \underline{2x+6} & \blacktriangleright \ (x+3)\times 2 \\ 3 & \blacktriangleright \text{ Remainder} \end{array}$$

The result above can be summarized as

$2759=(13)\cdot(212)+3$ $\qquad$ $2x^3+7x^2+5x+9=(x+3)\cdot(2x^2+x+2)+3$

So, Dividend $=$ (Divisor) $\cdot$ (Quotient) $+$ Remainder

Division Algorithm

Let $f(x)$ and $d(x)$ be polynomials with degree of d, $d\neq 0$, less than or equal to the degree of f. Then there exist a quotient $q(x)$ and remainder $r(x)$ such that

$$\underbrace{f(x)=d(x)\cdot q(x)+r(x)}_{\text{Polynomial Form}} \Leftrightarrow \underbrace{\frac{f(x)}{d(x)}=q(x)+\frac{r(x)}{d(x)}}_{\text{Fraction Form}}$$

Example 1

Divide $6x^3-11x^2-2x-1$ by $2x-1$.

Solution

$$\begin{array}{r} 3x^2-4x-3 \\ 2x-1\overline{)6x^3-11x^2-2x-1} \\ \underline{6x^3-3x^2\quad\quad\quad\;} \\ -8x^2-2x-1 \\ \underline{-8x^2+4x\quad\;} \\ -6x-1 \\ \underline{-6x+3} \\ -4 \end{array}$$

Dividend: $6x^3-11x^2-2x-1$

Divisor: $2x-1$

Quotient: $3x^2-4x-3$

Remainder: -4

Polynomial Form: $6x^3-11x^2-2x-1=(2x-1)\cdot(3x^2-4x-3)-4$

Fraction Form: $\dfrac{6x^3-11x^2-2x-1}{2x-1}=3x^2-4x-3-\dfrac{4}{2x-1}$

$\dfrac{6x^3-11x^2-2x-1}{2x-1}=3x^2-4x-3-\dfrac{4}{2x-1}$

Solutions_Page 10

Check Point 1

Divide using long division.

① $\dfrac{x^3-6x^2+3x-4}{x+2}$　　② $(x^4-5)\div(x^2+2)$

02 Synthetic Division

There is a shortcut for long division, which is a lot simpler and easier. It is called synthetic division. It is very useful method when dividing polynomials; however it can be only used when divisor is linear.

$$\frac{2x^3+7x^2+5x+9}{x+3} \Rightarrow$$

	2	7	5	9
		+	+	+
−3	↓	−6↓	−3↓	−6↓
×	2	1	2	3

Quotient → $2x^2$ $1x$ 2

Quotient: $2x^2+x+2$
Remainder: 3

Polynomial Form $2x^3+7x^2+5x+9=(x+3)\cdot(2x^2+x+2)+3$

Fraction Form $\frac{2x^3+7x^2+5x+9}{x+3}=2x^2+x+2+\frac{3}{x+3}$

Example 2

Divide $x^4-4x^3+x^2+2x-3$ by $x-2$.

Solution

	1	−4	1	2	−3
		+	+	+	+
2	↓	2↓	−4↓	−6↓	−8↓
	1	−2	−3	−4	−11

Quotient: x^3-2x^2-3x-4
Remainder: -11

Polynomial Form: $x^4-4x^3+x^2+2x-3=(x-2)\cdot(x^3-2x^2-3x-4)-11$

Fraction Form: $\dfrac{x^4-4x^3+x^2+2x-3}{x-2}=x^3-2x^2-3x-4-\dfrac{11}{x-2}$

$$\frac{x^4-4x^3+x^2+2x-3}{x-2}=x^3-2x^2-3x-4-\frac{11}{x-2}$$

Check Point 2

Solutions_Page 10

Divide using synthetic division

① $\dfrac{x^2-4x+1}{x-3}$

② $\dfrac{x^3+4x^2-9x+2}{x+3}$

03 Remainder Theorem

Let the quotient and remainder be $q(x)$ and R, respectively. The remainder theorem states that $f(a)=R$ when a polynomial $f(x)$ is divided by $(x-a)$. Here is an explanation.

$$\frac{f(x)}{(x-a)}=q(x)+\frac{R}{(x-a)}$$

$$f(x)=(x-a)q(x)+R$$

$$f(a)=(a-a)q(x)+R \quad \rightarrow \text{Substitute } a \text{ for } x$$

$$f(a)=0\cdot q(x)+R \quad \rightarrow f(a)=R$$

In a similar manner, when $f(x)$ is divided by $(ax+b)$, the remainder is $f\left(-\frac{b}{a}\right)$.

1. $\dfrac{f(x)}{(x-a)} \Rightarrow f(a)=R$

2. $\dfrac{f(x)}{(ax+b)} \Rightarrow f\left(-\dfrac{b}{a}\right)=R$

Example 3

Find the remainder when $x^4-4x^3+x^2+2x-3$ is divided by $x-2$.

Solution

Let $f(x)=x^4-4x^3+x^2+2x-3$.
Then, $f(2)=R \rightarrow f(2)=(2)^4-4(2)^3+(2)^2+2(2)-3=-11$.

The remainder is -11

Check Point 3

Solutions_Page 11

Find the remainder when $6x^3-11x^2-2x-1$ is divided by $2x-1$.

04 Factor Theorem

Factor theorem is a special case of remainder theorem. The theorem states that a polynomial $f(x)$ has a factor $(x-a)$ if and only if $f(a)=0$. Here is an explanation.

$$f(a)=0 \text{ means that the } \frac{f(x)}{(x-a)}=q(x)+\frac{0}{(x-a)}.$$

$$\text{Then, } f(x)=(x-a)q(x) \rightarrow (x-a) \text{ is factors of } f(x).$$

$\frac{f(x)}{(x-a)} \Rightarrow q(x)$	$\Leftrightarrow$	$f(a)=0$ $f(x)=(x-a)\cdot q(x)$ $(x-a)$ is a factor of $f(x)$

Example 4

① Verify that $x-3$ is a factor of x^3-2x^2-5x+6.
② Let $x+2$ is a factor of $3x^3+2x^2-x+b$. Find the value of b.

Solution

① Let $f(x)=x^3-2x^2-5x+6$; then $f(3)=(3)^3-2(3)^2-5(3)+6=0$.
Therefore, $x-3$ is a factor of x^3-2x^2-5x+6.

② Let $f(x)=3x^3+2x^2-x+b$.
Since $x+2$ is a factor of $3x^3+2x^2-x+b$,
$f(-2)=3(-2)^3+2(-2)^2-(-2)+b=0$
$-14+b=0 \rightarrow b=14$.

$b=14$

Check Point 4

Solutions_Page 11

① Verify that $x+5$ is a factor of $x^3-21x+20$.
② Use factor theorem to find b if a factor of the polynomial $2x^3-15x^2+24x+b$ is $x-2$.

Review Exercise

01 Divide using long division.

(1) $\dfrac{6x^3+4x^2-7x-1}{2x^2-1}$

(2) $(x^3+x^2-x+1)\div(x^2-2x-1)$

(3) $\dfrac{12x^4+6x^3+16x^2+12x-7}{2x^2+3}$

(4) $(x^5-1)\div(x^3-2)$

02 Divide using synthetic division.

(1) $\dfrac{x^3-4x^2-2x+9}{x-4}$

(2) $\dfrac{x^5-2x^3-1}{x-2}$

(3) $\dfrac{3x^3+5x^2-\frac{1}{2}x+4}{x+1}$

(4) $(2x^2-5x+1)\div(2x-1)$

03 Use remainder theorem to find the remainder when $f(x)=x^3-4x^2+5x-1$ is divided by $x-2$.

04 Use factor theorem to find b if a factor of the polynomial $x^4-2x^3+bx^2+4$ is $x+2$.

05 Verify the given factors of the polynomial and then find the remaining linear factors of the polynomial.

	Polynomial	Factor(s)
(1)	$2x^3-x^2-5x-2$	$(x-2)$

	Polynomial	Factor(s)
(2)	$x^4+x^3-11x^2-9x+18$	$(x-1)$, $(x+3)$

06 What is the remainder when the polynomial

$p(x)=3x^{150}+5x^{100}-4x^{75}-7x^{25}-10$

is divided by $x+1$?

07 When x^3+ax^2+bx+3 is divided by $(x-1)$ and $(x+1)$, the remainder is 2 and 8, respectively. What is the value of $a+b$?

08 If a polynomial $2x^3+kx^2-5x-2$ is divisible by $x+1$, then it is also divisible by

(A) x^2-x-2
(B) x^2+3x-2
(C) x^2-1
(D) $2x^2-x-1$

5 Real Zeros of Polynomial Functions

01 The Rational Zero Theorem

Here is a way to find the rational zeros of the polynomial function with higher degree.

Let $f(x)=a_n x^n+a_{n-1}x^{n-1}+\cdots+a_1x+a_0$ with integral coefficients.
Given $f(x)$, we look for the values that satisfy $f(x)=0 \Rightarrow$ find zeros of the function.

$$\text{Possible rational zeros: } \pm\frac{p}{q}=\pm\frac{\text{factors of constant term, } a_0}{\text{factors of leading coefficient, } a_n}$$

Having formed a list of possible rational zeros, use a trial−and−error method to determine the actual zero of the polynomial function. Tnen, divide $f(x)$ by linear factors using synthetic division to find remaining zeros.

Example 1

Find the rational zeros of the function.

① $f(x)=x^3-x^2-4x+4$ ② $f(x)=3x^3+5x^2-26x+8$

Solution

① The possible rational zeros of $f(x)=x^3-x^2-4x+4$ are $\pm\frac{p}{q}=\pm\frac{1,\ 2,\ 4}{1}=\pm1,\ \pm2,\ \pm4$.

We look for the zero using a trial−and−error method.
$f(1)=(1)^3-(1)^2-4(1)+4=0 \ \rightarrow\ x-1$ is a factor of $f(x)$
Now, divide $f(x)$ by $x-1$ using synthetic division.

$$\begin{array}{r|rrrr} & 1 & -1 & -4 & 4 \\ 1 & & 1 & 0 & -4 \\ \hline & 1 & 0 & -4 & \boxed{0} \end{array} \quad \rightarrow \quad \begin{aligned} &x^3-x^2-4x+4 \\ &=(x-1)(x^2-4) \\ &=(x-1)(x-2)(x+2) \end{aligned}$$

Therefore, $f(x)=(x-1)(x-2)(x+2)$ and the rational zeros are $x=1$, $x=2$, and $x=-2$.

Alternate Solution

Since x^3-x^2-4x+4 is a factorable polynomial,

$$\begin{aligned} x^3-x^2-4x+4 &= x^2(x-1)-4(x-1) \\ &= (x-1)(x^2-4) \\ &= (x-1)(x-2)(x+2) \quad \rightarrow f(x)=(x-1)(x-2)(x+2) \end{aligned}$$

Therefore, the rational zeros of $f(x)$ are $x=1$, $x=2$, and $x=-2$.

The zeros are $x=1$, $x=2$ and $x=-2$

② The possible rational zeros of $f(x)=3x^3+5x^2-26x+8$ are

$$\pm\frac{p}{q}=\pm\frac{1,\ 2,\ 4,\ 8}{1,\ 3}=\pm1,\ \pm2,\ \pm4,\ \pm8,\ \pm\frac{1}{3},\ \pm\frac{2}{3},\ \pm\frac{4}{3},\ \pm\frac{8}{3}.$$

We look for the zero using a trial−and−error method.

$f(1)=3(1)^3+5(1)^2-26(1)+8=-10\neq0$

$f(-1)=3(-1)^3+5(-1)^2-26(-1)+8=36\neq0$

$f(2)=3(2)^3+5(2)^2-26(2)+8=0 \quad \rightarrow \quad x-2$ is a factor of $f(x)$.

Now, divide $f(x)$ by $x-2$ using synthetic division.

$$\begin{array}{r|rrrr} 2 & 3 & 5 & -26 & 8 \\ & & 6 & 22 & -8 \\ \hline & 3 & 11 & -4 & \boxed{0} \end{array} \qquad \begin{aligned} &3x^3+5x^2-26x+8 \\ \rightarrow &=(x-2)(3x^2+11x-4) \\ &=(x-2)(x+4)(3x-1) \end{aligned}$$

Therefore, $f(x)=(x-2)(x+4)(3x-1)$ and the rational zeros are $x=2$, $x=-4$, and $x=\frac{1}{3}$.

The zeros are $x=2$, $x=-4$ and $x=\frac{1}{3}$

Check Point 1

Solutions_Page 13

Find the rational zeros of the function.

① $f(x)=x^3-3x^2-4x+12$

② $f(x)=2x^3-7x^2+2x+3$

02 Fundamental Theorem of Algebra

A polynomial function with degree n has n complex zeros(real+non−real or imaginary). Some of these zeros may be repeated.

For example, $f(x)=x^4-16$ has four zeros.

Because

$$x^4-16=0$$
$$(x^2-4)(x^2+4)=0$$
$$(x-2)(x+2)(x^2+4)=0$$

$$\Rightarrow \quad x-2=0 \rightarrow x=2, \quad x+2=0 \rightarrow x=-2, \quad x^2+4=0 \rightarrow x^2=-4 \rightarrow x=\pm 2i$$

So four zeros are $x=2$, $x=-2$, $x=2i$, and $x=-2i$.
$x=2$, $x=-2$ are real zeros and $x=2i$, $x=-2i$ are imaginary zeros.

Example 2

Find all the zeros of the function.

① $f(x)=x^3-x^2+x-1$ ② $f(x)=x^3+x-10$

Solution

① $f(x)=x^3-x^2+x-1 \rightarrow$ there are three zeros.
Since x^3-x^2+x-1 is a factorable polynomial,

$$x^3-x^2+x-1=x^2(x-1)+(x-1)$$
$$=(x-1)(x^2+1) \quad \rightarrow \quad f(x)=(x-1)(x^2+1)$$

$$f(x)=0 \rightarrow (x-1)(x^2+1)=0$$
$$x-1=0 \text{ or } x^2=-1 \rightarrow x=1 \text{ or } x=\pm i$$

The three zeros are $x=1$, $x=i$, and $x=-i$.

Note: If quadratic factor (x^2+1) has no real zeros, then such factor is said to be irreducible.

② $f(x)=x^3+x-10$ → there are three zeros.

The possible rational zeros $\pm\frac{p}{q}=\pm\frac{1,\ 2,\ 5,\ 10}{1}=\pm1,\ \pm2,\ \pm5,\ \pm10$.

Using a trial-and-error method, $f(2)=(2)^3+(2)-10=0$.
Now, divide $f(x)$ by $x-2$ using synthetic division.

$$\begin{array}{c|cccc} & 1 & 0 & 1 & -10 \\ 2 & & 2 & 4 & 10 \\ \hline & 1 & 2 & 5 & \boxed{0} \end{array} \quad \rightarrow \quad \begin{aligned} &x^3+x-10 \\ &=(x-2)(x^2+2x+5) \rightarrow f(x)=(x-2)(x^2+2x+5) \end{aligned}$$

$x-2=0$ → $x=2$

Using the quadratic formula,

$$x^2+2x+5=0 \rightarrow x=\frac{-2\pm\sqrt{2^2-4(1)(5)}}{2(1)}=-1\pm2i$$

The three zeros are $x=2$, $x=-1-2i$ and $x=-1+2i$.

Check Point 2

Solutions_Page 14

Find all the zeros of the function $f(x)=x^3+2x^2-2x-12$.

03 Complex Conjugate Zeros

Let a and b be real numbers and $b\neq0$. If $a+bi$ is a zero of the function $f(x)$, then its complex conjugate $a-bi$ is also a zero of $f(x)$.

For example, $2+i$ is a zero of the function $f(x)$, then $2-i$ is also a zero of $f(x)$.

Example 3

Write a third-degree polynomial function with a leading coefficient a whose zeros are $1+2i$ and 2. (a is non-zero integer)

Solution

Since $1+2i$ is a zero, $1-2i$ is also a zero.

$$\begin{aligned} f(x) &= a(x-(1+2i))(x-(1-2i))(x-2) \\ &= a((x-1)-2i)((x-1)+2i)(x-2) \\ &= a((x-1)^2-(2i)^2)(x-2) \\ &= a(x^2-2x+5)(x-2) \\ &= a(x^3-4x^2+9x-10) \end{aligned}$$

→ If
$a=1$; $f(x)=x^3-4x^2+9x-10$
$a=2$; $f(x)=2x^3-8x^2+18x-20$
$a=3$; $f(x)=3x^3-12x^2+27x-30$
$a=-1$; $f(x)=-x^3+4x^2-9x+10$
⋮

The particular function is depend on a.

Tips: When we find a polynomial with 2 non−real zeros, we could use following technique.

Let two zeros be $\alpha=1+2i$ and $\beta=1-2i$.
Sum of zeros: $(1+2i)+(1-2i)=2$.
Product of zeros $(1+2i)\cdot(1-2i)=1-4i^2=5$.

A function with two zeros α and β can be written as

$$\begin{aligned} f(x) &= a(x-\alpha)(x-\beta)) \\ &= a(x^2-(\alpha+\beta)x+(\alpha\cdot\beta)) \\ &= a(x^2-2x+5). \end{aligned}$$

With the third zero 2, $f(x)=a(x^2-2x+5)(x-2)=a(x^3-4x^2+9x-10)$.

$f(x)=a(x^3-4x^2+9x-10)$

Check Point 3

Solutions_Page 14

Write a third−degree polynomial function with leading coefficient 1 and with the given zeros.

① -1, 2 and 3.

② -1, $2i$, and $-2i$.

04 Descarte's Rule of Signs

Let $f(x)=a_nx^n+a_{n-1}x^{n-1}+\cdots+a_1x+a_0$ with real coefficients and $a_0\neq0$.

1. The number of <u>positive</u> real zeros of $f(x)$ is either equal to the number of sign changes between successive terms of $f(x)$ or is less than that number by an even integer.
2. The number of <u>negative</u> real zeros of $f(x)$ is obtained by applying same rule to $f(-x)$.

Example 4-1

Describe the possible zeros of $f(x)=2x^4+4x^3-x^2-6x+1$.

Solution

$f(x)=2x^4+\overbrace{4x^3-x^2}^{+\ to\ -}\overbrace{-6x+1}^{+\ to\ -}$ → Two sign changes

$f(-x)=2(-x)^4+4(-x)^3-(-x)^2-6(-x)+1$

$f(-x)=\underbrace{2x^4-4x^3}_{+\ to\ -}\underbrace{-x^2+6x}_{+\ to\ -}+1$ → Two sign changes

Using Descarte's rule of signs, the following number of zero combinations are possible.

Positive	Negative	Imaginary
2	2	0
2	0	2
0	2	2
0	0	4

By the fundamental theorem of algebra, polynomial function of degree four has always four zeros in total.

Example 4–2

Describe the possible zeros of the function $f(x)=4x^3-x^2-3$ using Descarte's rule of sings and then find all the zeros.

Solution

$f(x)=\overbrace{4x^3-x^2}^{+\ to\ -}-3$ → One sign change

$f(-x)=4(-x)^3-(-x)^2-3$

$f(-x)=-4x^3-x^2-3$ → No sign changes

The number of possible zero combinations:

Positive	Negative	Imaginary
1	0	2

p: factors of 3; q: factors of 4

The possible rational zero: $\pm\frac{p}{q}=\pm\frac{1,\ 3}{1,\ 2,\ 4}=\pm1,\ \pm3,\ \pm\frac{1}{2},\ \pm\frac{3}{2},\ \pm\frac{1}{4},\ \pm\frac{3}{4}$.

Since there is no negative zero, we look for a zero from positive numbers.

$f(1)=4(1)^3-(1)^2-3=0$ → $x-1$ is a factor of $f(x)$

$$\begin{array}{r|rrrr} & 4 & -1 & 0 & -3 \\ 1 & & 4 & 3 & 3 \\ \hline & 4 & 3 & 3 & \boxed{0} \end{array}$$

→ $4x^3-x^2-3=(x-1)(4x^2+3x+3)$

$x=1$ and $4x^2+3x+3=0$ → $x=\frac{-3\pm\sqrt{3^2-4(4)(3)}}{2(4)}=\frac{-3\pm\sqrt{39}i}{8}$.

The zeros are $x=1$ and $x=-\frac{3}{8}\pm\frac{\sqrt{39}i}{8}$

Check Point 4

Solutions_Page 14

Describe the possible zeros of the function $f(x)=x^4+2x^3+x+2$ using Descarte's rule of sings and then find all the zeros.

05 Polynomial Inequalities

To solve a polynomial inequality problem, follow these general steps:

1. Transform the inequality into standard form: Move all terms to one side of the inequality to set the polynomial expression greater than or less than zero.
2. Factor the polynomial: If possible, factor the polynomial expression to identify the roots (zeros) of the polynomial.
3. Analyze the intervals: Use the zeros to divide the number line into intervals. Test a value from each interval in the polynomial to determine whether it is positive or negative in that interval.
4. Determine the solution: Based on the analysis of intervals, determine the regions where the polynomial is positive or negative according to the inequality.
5. Write the solutions: Express the solution in interval notation or as a union of intervals.

Example 5

Solve the inequalities.

① $(x+2)(x-3)<0$ ② $x^2-4x-5\geq 0$

Solution

① $(x+2)(x-3)<0$ → The zeros are $x=-2$, and $x=3$.

We need to identify the interval(s) with a negative sign.

Let's use test values such as $x=-3$, $x=0$, and $x=4$. Then, we can proceed as follows:

$x=-3$; $(-3+2)(-3-3)>0$

$x=0$; $(0+2)(0-3)<0$

$x=4$; $(4+2)(4-3)>0$

The solution set is $\{x|-2<x<3\}$ or $(-2, 3)$.

$\{x|-2<x<3\}$ or $(-2, 3)$

② $x^2-4x-5\geq 0$

$(x+1)(x-5)\geq 0$ → The zeros are $x=-1$, and $x=5$.

We need to identify the interval(s) with a positive sign.

Let's use test values such as $x=-2$, $x=0$, and $x=6$. Then, we can proceed as follows:

$x=-2$; $(-2+1)(-2-5)>0$

$x=0$; $(0+1)(0-5)<0$

$x=6$; $(6+1)(6-5)>0$

The solution set is $\{x|x\leq -1$ or $x\geq 5\}$ or $(-\infty, -1]\cup[5, \infty)$. Remember that -1 and 5 are included in the solution set because the polynomial is equal to or greater than 0.

$\{x|x\leq -1$ or $x\geq 5\}$ or $(-\infty, -1]\cup[5, \infty)$

Check Point 5

Solutions_Page 15

Solve the inequalities.

① $2x^2-3x<2$

② $x^3-x^2-2x\geq 0$

Review Exercise

Solutions_Page 15

01 Find the rational zeros of the function.

(1) $g(x)=x^4-x^3-2x-4$

(2) $f(x)=x^3-10x^2+31x-30$

(3) $g(x)=3x^3+x^2-22x-24$

(4) $h(x)=6x^4-17x^3+10x^2+7x-6$

02 Find all the zeros of the function $f(x)=x^4+3x^3+2x^2-3x-3$.

03 Use the given zero to find remaining zeros of the function.

(1) $f(x)=2x^3-x^2+2x-1$
Zero: i

(2) $f(x)=x^3-5x^2+11x-15$
Zero: $1-2i$

04 Write a polynomial function with the leading coefficient 1 and with the given zeros.

(1) Zeros: 1, -2, $3+2i$

(2) Zeros: 2(multiplicity 2), $-1-3i$

Review Exercise

05 Find a third−degree polynomial function that has zeros -2, 1, and 3 and in which the coefficient of x^2 is -5.

06 $f(x)=2x^5-3x^4-7x^3+8x^2-11x+12$
Determine the possible number of positive and negative real zeros of the function above using Descarte's rule of signs.

07 Describe the possible zeros of the function $f(x)=x^3+2x^2+3x+6$ using Descarte's rule of signs and then find all the zeros.

08

x	$f(x)$
-2	0
-1	6
0	4
1	0

Suppose f is a polynomial function with degree 3. Based on the table above, which of the following could be f?

(A) $f(x)=x(x-2)(x+2)$
(B) $f(x)=(x-1)\left(x-\frac{1}{2}\right)(x+2)$
(C) $f(x)=(x-2)(x-1)(x+2)$
(D) $f(x)=(x-1)\left(x-\frac{1}{2}\right)\left(x+\frac{1}{2}\right)$

09 Solve the inequalities.

(1) $(x+5)(2x-3)(4-x)\leq 0$

(2) $6x^2+2>3-x$

(3) $4x^3+9x\leq 12x^2$

(4) $x^3-4x^2-4x+16\geq 0$

10 The function h is a polynomial of degree 5. If $h(2)=h(4)=0$, which of the following must be true?

(A) $h(-2)=0$
(B) h has at least 2 complex zeros.
(C) h has at least 3 more real zeros besides $x=2$ and $x=4$.
(D) h can be written as $h=(x-2)(x-4)\cdot f(x)$, where $f(x)$ is a polynomial of degree 3.

11 If $(x-2)$, $(x+5)$ and $(x+i)$ are factors of the polynomial g, what is the least possible degree of g?

12 The function h is given by
$h(x)=x^3-4x^2-4x+16$.
Find the interval of x where $h<0$.

6 Rational Functions

01 Definition of Rational Function

A rational function is any function which can be written as

$$f(x)=\frac{p(x)}{q(x)}$$

where $p(x)$ and $q(x)$ are polynomials and $q(x)\neq 0$. For example, $f(x)=\frac{1}{x}$, $f(x)=\frac{2x-1}{x-3}$, and $y=\frac{(x+3)(x-2)}{x^2-4}$ are rational functions. The domain of a rational function is the set of all real numbers except the values that make the denominator zero. Now, let's check the terminologies and basic concepts we need to know from the graph.

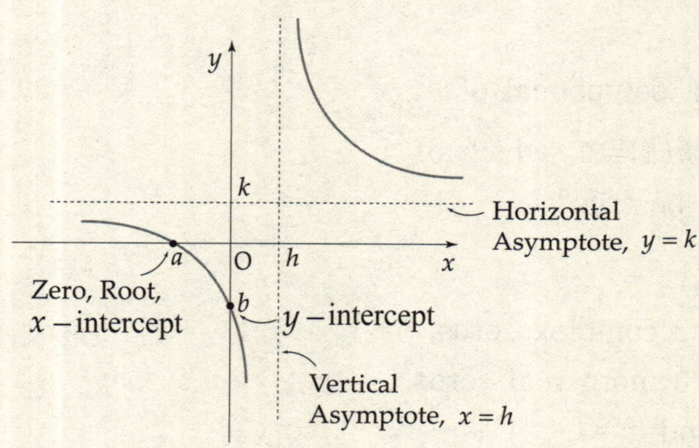

1. Vertical Asymptote: $x=h \Rightarrow f(x) \to \infty$ or $f(x) \to -\infty$ as $x \to h$.
2. Horizontal Asymptote: $y=k \Rightarrow f(x) \to k$ as $x \to \infty$ or $x \to -\infty$.
3. Domain: $(-\infty,\ h)\cup(h,\ \infty)$ or all real numbers except for $x=h$.
4. Range: $(-\infty,\ k)\cup(k,\infty)$ or all real numbers except for $y=k$.
5. Zero, Root, $x-$intercept: $x=a$.
6. $y-$intercept: $x=b$

How to Graph a Rational Function

1. Identify vertical and horizontal asymptotes.
2. Find x-intercept and y-intercept, if any.
3. If necessary, plot a few additional points (usually points between vertical asymptotes).
4. Sketch the graph.

02 Graph of $y=\frac{c}{x}$, $(c\neq0)$

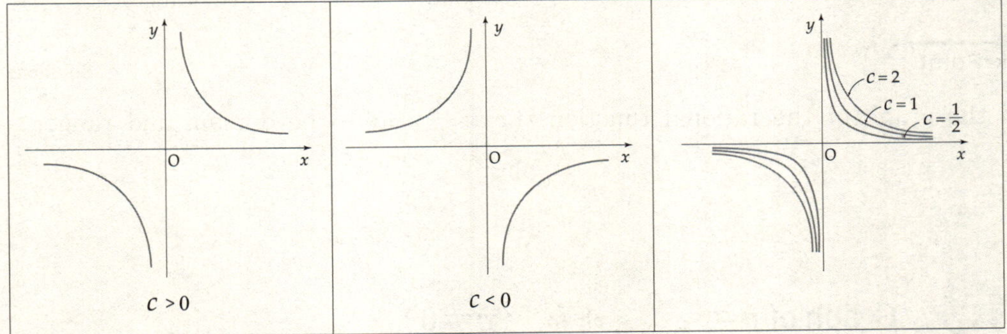

1. Vertical Asymptote: $x=0$.
2. Horizontal Asymptote: $y=0$.
3. Domain: All real numbers except for $x=0$.
4. Range: All real numbers except for $y=0$.
5. As $|c|$ gets larger, the graph moves further away from the origin.

Example 1

Sketch the graph of the rational function $f(x)=\frac{2}{x}$. State the domain and range.

Solution

Vertical Asymptote: $x=0$

Horizontal Asymptote: $y=0$

Additional Points(s):

$f(1)=\frac{2}{1}=2 \rightarrow (1,\ 2)$

$f(-1)=\frac{2}{-1}=-2 \rightarrow (-1,\ -2)$

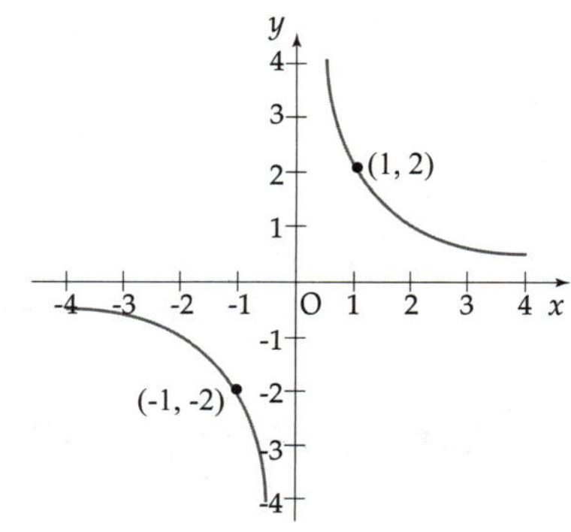

Domain: $(-\infty,\ 0)\cup(0,\ \infty)$, Range: $(-\infty,\ 0)\cup(0,\ \infty)$

Check Point 1

Solutions_Page 20

Sketch the graph of the rational function $f(x)=\frac{3}{x}$. State the domain and range.

03 Graph of $y=\frac{c}{x-h}+k$, $(c\neq 0)$

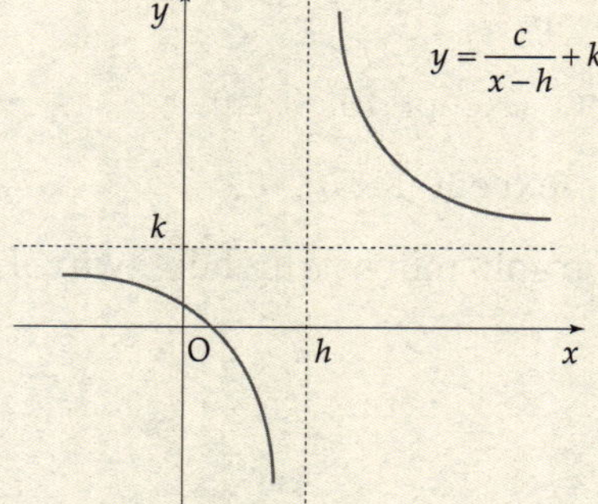

1. Shift the graph of $y=\frac{c}{x} \rightarrow h$ units horizontally and k units vertically.

2. Vertical Asymptote: $x=h$.

3. Horizontal Asymptote: $y=k$.

4. Domain: All real numbers except for $x=h$.

5. Range: All real numbers except for $y=k$.

Example 2

Sketch the graph of the rational function $f(x)=-\frac{2}{x+1}+1$. State the domain and range.

Solution

Graph $y=-\frac{2}{x}$ first and then shift it 1 unit to the left and 1 unit up.

Vertical Asymptote: $x+1=0$, $x=-1$

Horizontal Asymptote: $y=1$

x-intercept: $0=-\frac{2}{x+1}+1 \rightarrow x=1$

y-intercept: $f(0)=-\frac{2}{(0)+1}+1=-1 \rightarrow y=-1$

Additional Point(s):

$f(-2)=-\frac{2}{(-2)+1}+1=3 \rightarrow (-2, 3)$

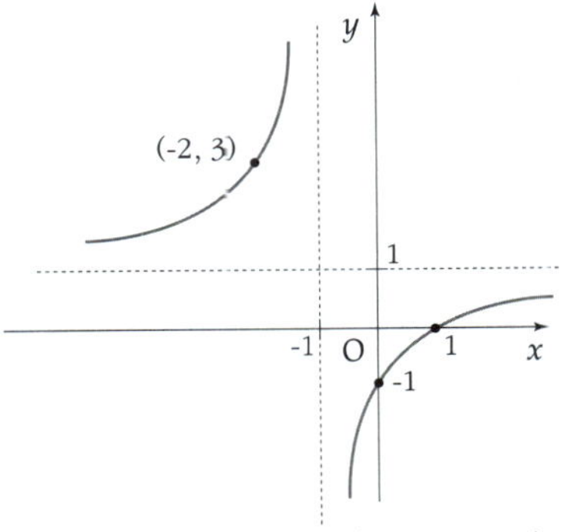

Domain: $(-\infty, -1)\cup(-1, \infty)$, Range: $(-\infty, 1)\cup(1, \infty)$

Check Point 2

Solutions_Page 20

Sketch the graph of the rational function. State the domain and range.

① $f(x)=\frac{2}{x+3}$

② $g(x)=3+\frac{4}{x-2}$

04 Asymptotes and Holes of $f(x)=\frac{p(x)}{q(x)}$

Let $f(x)=\frac{p(x)}{q(x)}=\frac{a_nx^n+a_{n-1}x^{n-1}+\cdots+a_1x+a_0}{b_mx^m+b_{m-1}x^{m-1}+\cdots+b_1x+b_0}$

where $a_n\neq0$, $b_m\neq0$, and the degree of $p(x)$ is 1 or greater.

(1) Vertical asymptotes occur where $q(x)=0$, but $p(x)\neq0$.

(2) Horizontal asymptotes follow three rules below.

(a) If $n<m$, horizontal asymptote is at $y=0$.

(b) If $n=m$, horizontal asymptote is at $y=\frac{a_n}{b_n}$.

(c) If $n>m$, there is no horizontal asymptote.

(3) Holes occur where $q(x)=0$ and $p(x)=0$.

Example 3

Sketch the graph of the function $f(x)=\frac{x-2}{2x+3}$. State the domain and range.

Solution

Vertical Asymptote: $2x+3=0 \rightarrow x=-\frac{3}{2}$

Horizontal Asymptote: $n=1$ and $m=1 \rightarrow y=\frac{1}{2}$

Hole: No hole exists.

$x-$intercept: $0=\frac{x-2}{2x+3} \rightarrow x-2=0 \rightarrow x=2$

$y-$intercept: $f(0)=\frac{(0)-2}{2(0)+3}=-\frac{2}{3} \rightarrow y=-\frac{2}{3}$

Additional Point(s):

$f(-2)=\frac{(-2)-2}{2(-2)+3}=4 \rightarrow (-2,\ 4)$

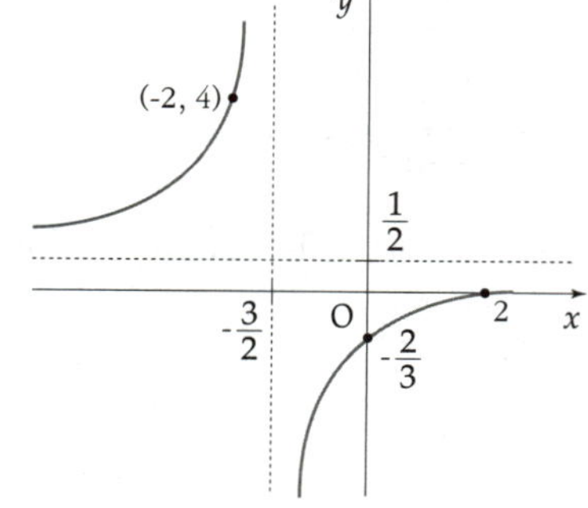

Domain: $\left(-\infty,\ -\frac{3}{2}\right)\cup\left(-\frac{3}{2},\ \infty\right)$, Range: $\left(-\infty,\ \frac{1}{2}\right)\cup\left(\frac{1}{2},\ \infty\right)$

Check Point 3

Solutions_Page 21

Sketch the graph of the rational function. State the domain and range.

① $g(x)=\dfrac{1}{2x-3}$　　② $h(x)=\dfrac{3x-2}{1-2x}$

05 Slant(Oblique) Asymptotes

Let $f(x)=\dfrac{p(x)}{q(x)}=\dfrac{a_n x^n+a_{n-1}x^{n-1}+\cdots+a_1x^1+a_0}{b_m x^m+b_{m-1}x^{m-1}+\cdots+b_1x^1+b_0}$, where $a_n\neq 0$ and $b_m\neq 0$.

If $n=m+1$, $f(x)$ can be expressed using long division in the from

$$f(x)=\underbrace{ax+b}_{\text{Slant Asymptote}}+\frac{R}{q(x)}.$$

The line $y=ax+b$ is a slant asymptote for the graph of f.

Example 4

Sketch the graph of the function $f(x)=\dfrac{x^2-1}{x-2}$. State the domain.

Solution

$f(x)=\dfrac{x^2-1}{x-2}$ → $f(x)=\dfrac{(x-1)(x+1)}{x-2}$

Since $n=m+1$, there exists a slant asymptote.

$$\begin{array}{r|l} & x+2 \\ \hline x-2 & x^2 \qquad -1 \\ & x^2-2x \\ \hline & 2x-1 \\ & 2x-4 \\ \hline & 3 \end{array}$$

→ $\dfrac{x^2-1}{x-2}=x+2+\dfrac{3}{x-2}$

Slant Asymptote: $y=x+2$
Vertical Asymptote: $x-2=0 \rightarrow x=2$
Hole: No hole exists.

x-intercept: $0=\dfrac{(x-1)(x+1)}{x-2} \rightarrow 0=(x-1)(x+1) \rightarrow x=1,\ x=-1$

y-intercept: $f(0)=\dfrac{(0)^2-1}{(0)-2}=\dfrac{1}{2} \rightarrow y=\dfrac{1}{2}$

Additional Point(s): $f(3)=\dfrac{(3)^2-1}{(3)-2}=8 \rightarrow (3,\ 8)$

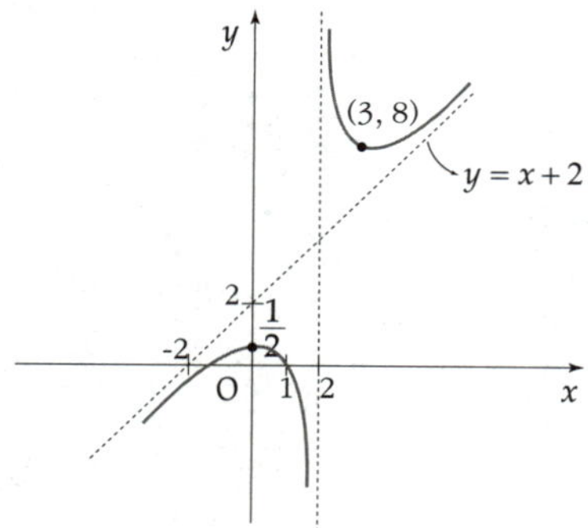

Domain: $(-\infty,\ 2)\cup(2,\ \infty)$

Check Point 4

Solutions_Page 21

Sketch the graph of the function $f(x)=\dfrac{x^2+1}{x+1}$. State the domain.

06 Rational Functions and Limits

1. In a rational function f with a horizontal asymptote at $y=b$, where b is a constant, the output values approach b as the input values increase or decrease indefinitely. The corresponding mathematical notation is

$$\lim_{x\to\infty} f(x)=b \text{ or } \lim_{x\to-\infty} f(x)=b$$

2. In a rational function f, near a vertical asymptote at $x=a$, the denominator of the rational function approaches zero, causing the function's values to increase or decrease without bound. The corresponding mathematical notation is

(1) $\lim_{x \to a^+} f(x)=\infty$ or $\lim_{x \to a^+} f(x)=-\infty$ for x values near a and greater than a.

(2) $\lim_{x \to a^-} f(x)=\infty$ or $\lim_{x \to a^-} f(x)=-\infty$ for x values near a and less than a.

3. If a rational function f has a hole at $x=a$, its location can be found by examining output values near a. If these values approach L, the hole is situated at the point (a, L). It is noted that

$$\lim_{x \to a^-} f(x)=\lim_{x \to a^+} f(x)=\lim_{x \to a} f(x)=L$$

07 Rational Inequalities

To solve a rational inequality problem, follow these general steps:

1. Transform the inequality into standard form: Move all terms to one side of the inequality to set the rational expression greater than or less than zero.
2. Find the critical points: Identify the values of x that make both the denominator and numerator of the rational expression equal to zero.
3. Analyze the intervals: Use the critical points to divide the number line into intervals. Test a value from each interval in the original inequality to determine whether the rational expression is positive or negative in that interval.

4. Determine the solution: Based on the analysis of intervals, determine the regions where the rational expression is positive or negative according to the inequality.
5. Write the solutions: Express the solution as a union of intervals where the inequality is true. Use interval notation to represent the solution set.

Example 5

Solve the inequalities.

① $\dfrac{x-2}{x+3} \le 0$ ② $x > \dfrac{1}{x}$

Solution

① $\dfrac{x-2}{x+3} \le 0$ → The zero is $x=2$, and it is undefined at $x=-3$.

We need to identify the interval(s) with a negative sign.

Let's use test values such as $x=-4$, $x=0$, and $x=3$. Then, we can proceed as follows:

$$x=-4;\ \frac{-4-2}{-4+3} > 0$$

$$x=0;\ \frac{0-2}{0+3} < 0$$

$$x=3;\ \frac{3-2}{3+3} > 0$$

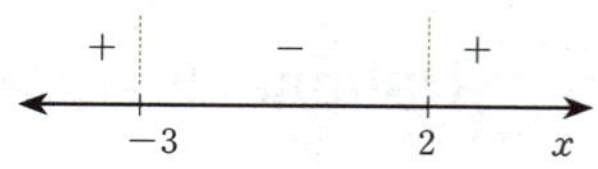

The solution set is $\{x \mid -3 < x \le 2\}$ or $(-3, 2]$.

$\{x \mid -3 < x \le 2\}$ or $(-3, 2]$

②
$$x > \frac{1}{x}$$

$$x - \frac{1}{x} > 0$$

$$\frac{x^2-1}{x} > 0$$

$\dfrac{(x+1)(x-1)}{x} > 0$ → The zeros are $x=-1$ and $x=1$, and it is undefined at $x=0$.

We need to identify the interval(s) with a positive sign.

Let's use test values such as $x=-2$, $x=-0.5$, $x=0.5$, and $x=2$.
Then, we can proceed as follows:

$$x=-2;\ \frac{(-2+1)(-2-1)}{-2}<0$$

$$x=-0.5;\ \frac{(-0.5+1)(-0.5-1)}{-0.5}>0$$

$$x=0.5;\ \frac{(0.5+1)(0.5-1)}{0.5}<0$$

$$x=2;\ \frac{(2+1)(2-1)}{2}>0$$

− + − +
−1 0 1 x

The solution set is $\{x|-1<x<0 \text{ or } x>1\}$ or $(-1, 0)\cup(1, \infty)$.

$\{x|-1<x<0 \text{ or } x>1\}$ or $(-1, 0)\cup(1, \infty)$

Check Point 5

Solutions_Page 22

Solve the inequalities.

① $\dfrac{2x-3}{2+x}\leq 0$

② $\dfrac{2}{x-2}>\dfrac{1}{x+1}$

Review Exercise

01 Sketch the graph of the function. State the domain and range.

(1) $f(x)=-\frac{1}{2x}-2$

(2) $h(x)=-\frac{3}{2x-3}+1$

02 Sketch the graph of the function. State the domain and range.

(1) $f(x)=\frac{x-1}{3x+2}$

(2) $g(x)=\frac{1}{x^2-4}$

(3) $h(x)=\frac{3+x-2x^2}{x^2+3x+2}$

(4) $f(x)=\frac{2}{x^2+1}$

03 Sketch the graph of the function. State the domain.

(1) $f(x)=\frac{x^2-4x+3}{x-2}$

(2) $f(x)=\frac{2x^3-3x^2-2x}{2x^2+3x+1}$

04 $y=\frac{x^2-x-6}{2x^2-8}$

Which of the following could be the asymptotes(s) of the function above?

I. $x=2$ II. $x=-2$ III. $y=0.5$

(A) I only

(B) I and II only

(C) I and III only

(D) II and III only

05 If $r(x)=\dfrac{5x+k}{x-3}$, for what value of k does the graph of r NOT have a vertical asymptote?

06 Which of the following functions have a zero at $x=3$ and exactly two asymptotes, at $y=1$ and $x=-1$?

(A) $f(x)=\dfrac{x-3}{x-1}$

(B) $f(x)=\dfrac{x-3}{x^2-1}$

(C) $f(x)=\dfrac{x^2-4x+3}{x-1}$

(D) $f(x)=\dfrac{x^2-4x+3}{x^2-1}$

07 Find the range of the function defined by $g(x)=\dfrac{1}{2x+1}-3$.

08 Solve the inequalities.

(1) $\dfrac{1}{x}-2<0$

(2) $\dfrac{2-x}{x+1}\leq 0$

(3) $\dfrac{3}{x-3}>\dfrac{4}{x+1}$

(4) $\dfrac{x^3-x}{x^2-x-12}\geq 0$

09 The rational function f is given by $f(x)=\dfrac{p(x)}{q(x)}$, where p and q are polynomial functions. If the graph of f has a slant asymptote of $y=3x+1$ and $p(x)=3x^4-5x^2+1$, which of the following must be true?

(A) q has degree of 2 with leading coefficient 1

(B) q has degree of 2 with leading coefficient 3

(C) q has degree of 3 with leading coefficient 1

(D) q has degree of 3 with leading coefficient 3

Review Exercise

10 The rational function f is given by $f(x)=\dfrac{4x^3-5x+1}{2x^3+1}$. Which of the following statements must be true?

(A) As x increases without bound, f increases without bound.

(B) As x decreases without bound, f decreases without bound.

(C) As x increases without bound, f approaches 2.

(D) As x decreases without bound, f approaches -2.

11 The rational function f is given by $f(x)=\dfrac{p(x)}{q(x)}$ where p and q are polynomial functions. If the degree of p is greater than q, which of the following must be the value of $\lim\limits_{x\to\infty} f(x)$?

(A) 0

(B) ∞

(C) $-\infty$

(D) The value of $\lim\limits_{x\to\infty} f(x)$ cannot be determined from the information given above.

12 The rational function f is given by $f(x)=\dfrac{(ax-2)(x^b+1)}{2x^3-4x-1}$, where a and b are positive integers. What is the value of $a+b$ so that the graph of f has a horizontal asymptote at $y=3$?

13 The rational function $f(x)=\dfrac{x^2-9}{x^2-1}$. On what intervals of x is $f(x)<0$?

(A) $-3<x<-1$ or $1<x<3$

(B) $x<-3$ or $-1<x<1$

(C) $-1<x<1$ or $x>3$

(D) $x<-3$ or $x>3$

7 Transformations of Functions

01 Transformation of Function

Suppose $y=f(x)$ defines any function and $h>0$, $k>0$.

1. The function $g(x)=f(x)+k$ represents a vertical translation of the graph of f by k units.

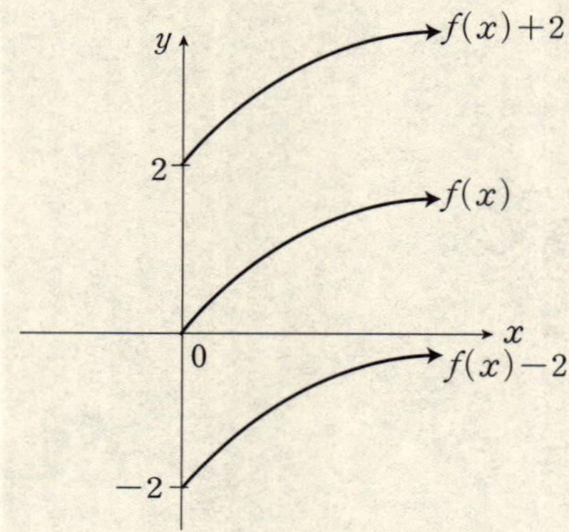

2. The function $g(x)=f(x+h)$ represents a horizontal translation of the graph of f by $-h$ units.

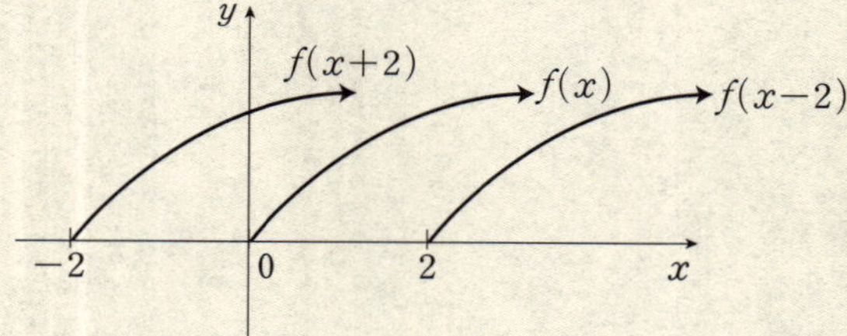

3. The function $g(x)=af(x)$, where $a\neq0$, causes a vertical dilation of the graph of f by a factor of a. If $a<0$, it also reflects the graph over the x−axis.

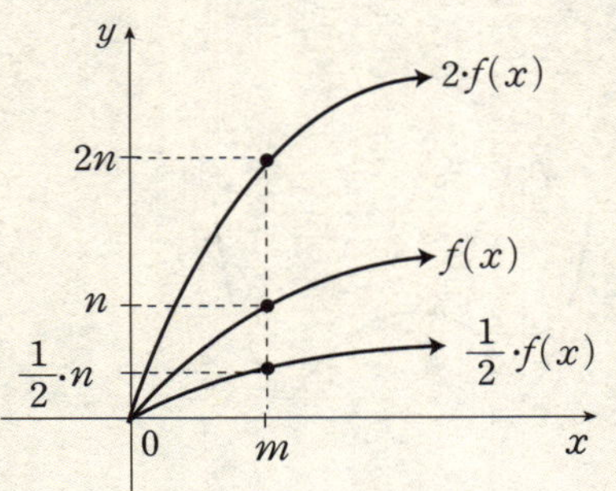

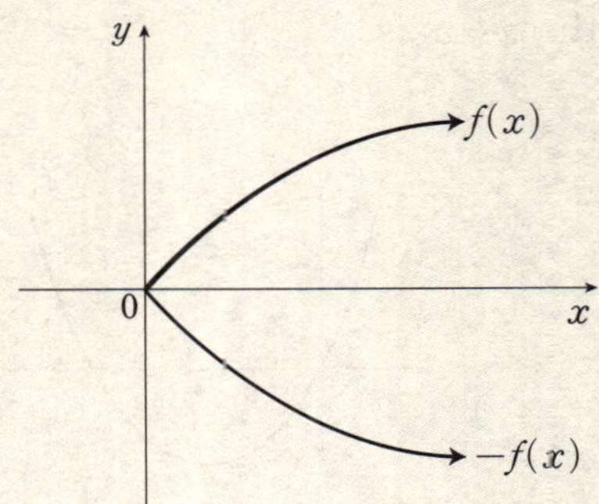

4. The function $g(x)=f(bx)$, where $b\neq0$, causes a horizontal dilation of the graph of f by a factor of $\frac{1}{b}$. If $b<0$, it reflects the graph over the y−axis.

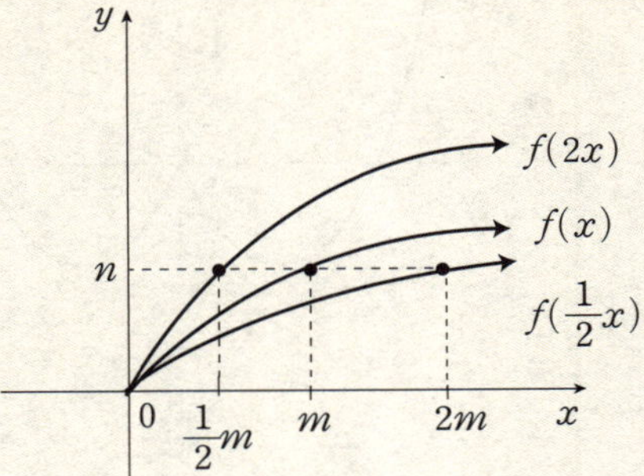

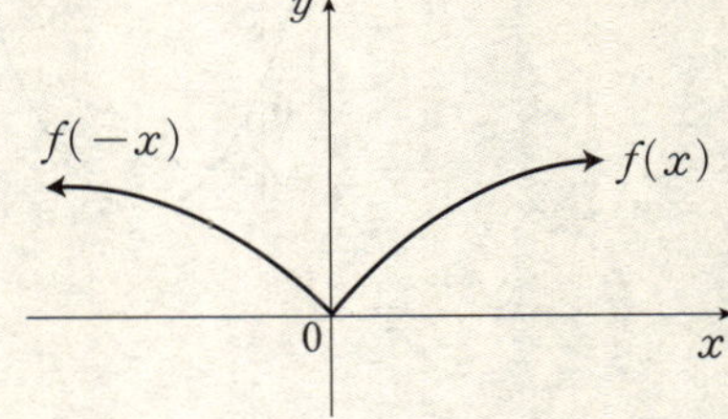

5. Absolute Value Transformation

(1) $g(x)=|f(x)|$: Reflect the portion of the graph below the $x-$axis across the $x-$axis.

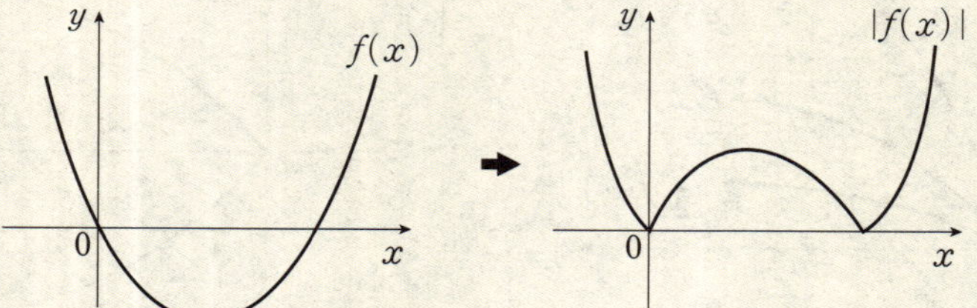

(2) $g(x)=f(|x|)$: Duplicate the graph on the right side of the $y-$axis and mirror it onto the left side of the $y-$axis.

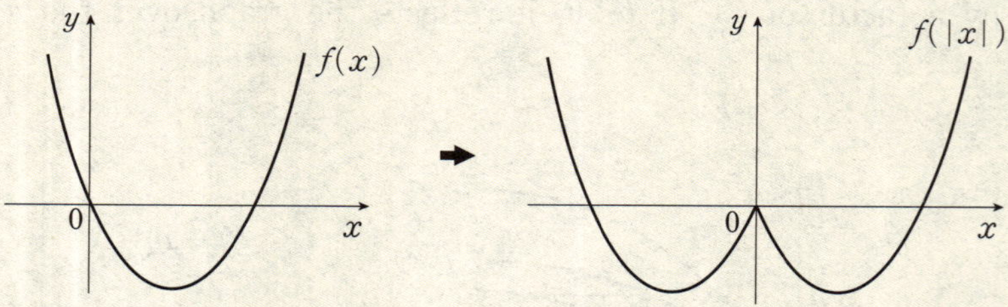

02 Multiple Transformations

Transformations are applied in the following order if a function has multiple transformations.

1. Horizontal translation
2. Horizontal or Vertical dilations
3. Reflections over the $x-$ and/or $y-$axis
4. Vertical translation

Example 1

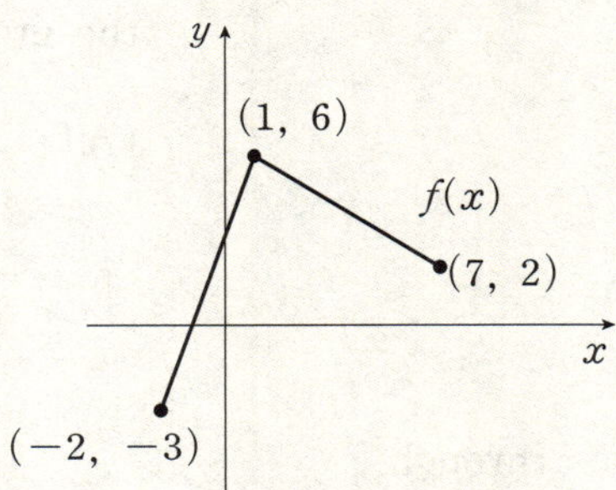

Given the graph of $f(x)$ above, sketch the graph of the following functions.

① $f(x+2)-1$ ② $-f(2x)+3$

Solution

① Translate 2 units to the left ⇒ Translate 1 unit down.

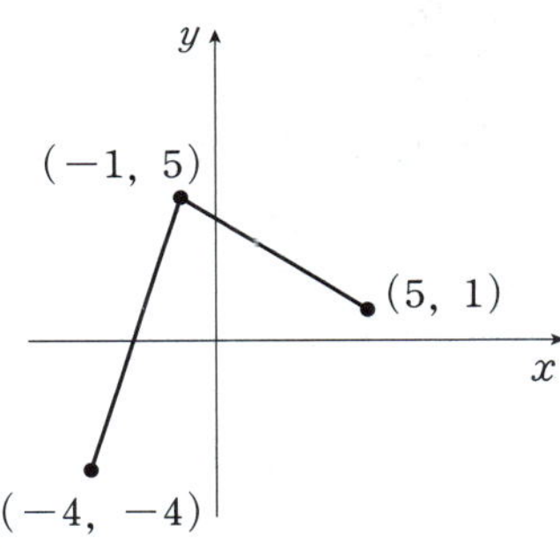

② Shrink horizontally by a factor of $\frac{1}{2}$

⇒ Reflects the graph over the x−axis

⇒ Translate 3 units up.

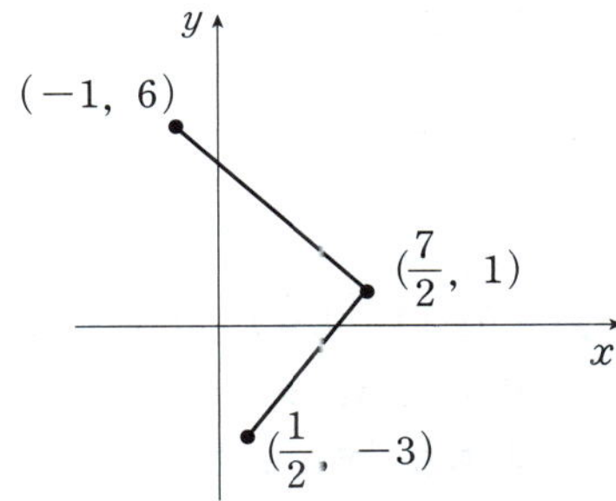

Review Exercise

01 Which of the following functions transforms $y=f(x)$ by shifting it 2 units to the left and 3 units up?

(A) $y=f(x+3)+2$
(B) $y=f(x-3)+2$
(C) $y=f(x-2)+3$
(D) $y=f(x+2)+3$

02 The graph of $y=f(x)$ passes through the point $(-2, 4)$. If the graph of $y=f(x)$ is shifted 2 units to the right and 1 unit down, which point must it go through?

(A) $(0, 0)$
(B) $(0, 3)$
(C) $(-4, 3)$
(D) $(-4, 5)$

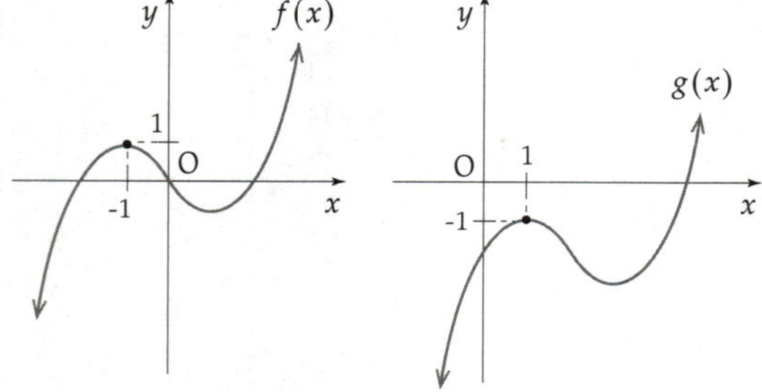

03 The graph of f and g are shown above. Which of the following statements is true?

(A) $g(x)=f(x-2)+2$
(B) $g(x)=f(x+2)+2$
(C) $g(x)=f(x-2)-2$
(D) $g(x)=f(x+2)-2$

04 A function h has the property that $h(x)=h(x-1)$ for all x. Which of the following could be a portion of the graph of h?

(A)
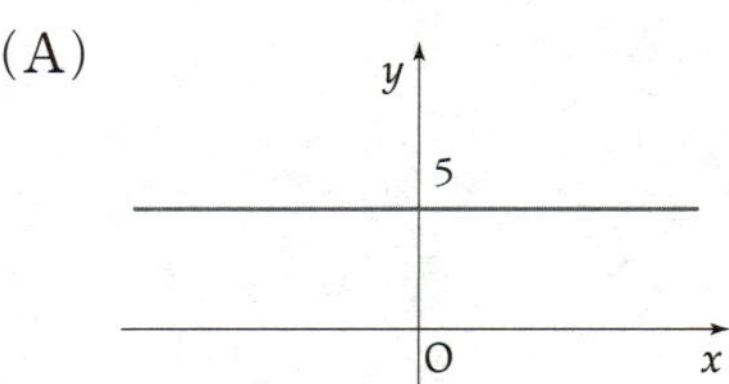

(B)
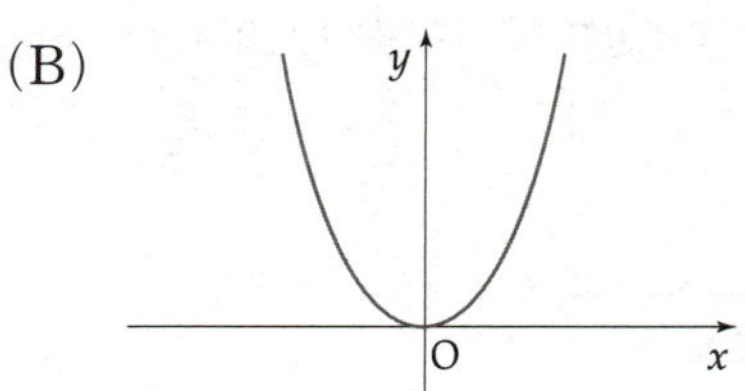

(C)
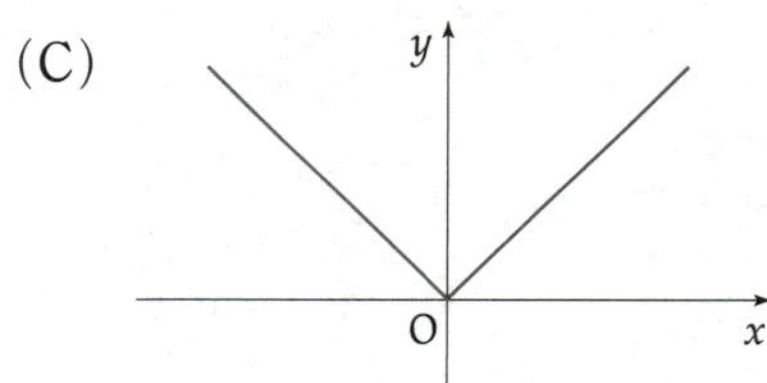

(D)
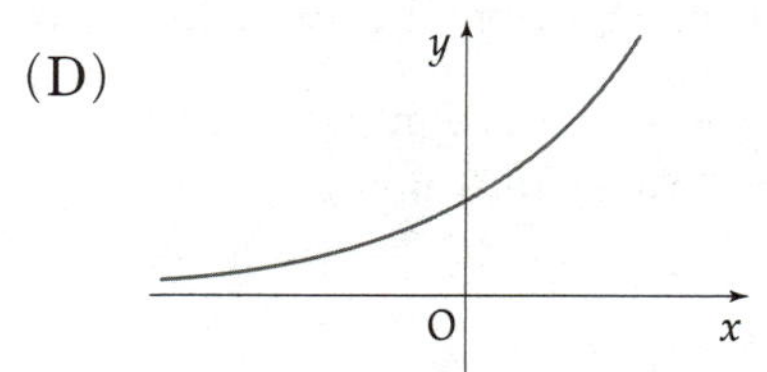

05 Which of the following translation of the graph of $f(x)=x^2$ would result in the graph of $f(x)=x^2+4x+m$, where m is a real number such that $m>4$?

(A) 2 units to the right and $m+4$ units down

(B) 2 units to the left and $m-4$ units up

(C) 4 units to the left and $m-2$ units down

(D) 4 units to the right and $m+2$ units up

06 What is the equation of the function $g(x)$ whose graph can be obtained by transforming the graph of $y=\sqrt{x}$ vertically stretched by a factor of 3, reflected in the $y-$axis, and then translated 2 units down?

(A) $g(x)=3\sqrt{x-2}$

(B) $g(x)=-3\sqrt{x+2}$

(C) $g(x)=3\sqrt{-x-2}$

(D) $g(x)=3\sqrt{-x}-2$

07

x	0	1	2	3
$f(x)$	-2	3	4	-1

The table gives the value of a function f for selected intervals of x. The graph of g is the result of a vertical dilation of f by the factor of 4, followed by reflection over the $y-$axis, and then a translation of 3 units down. What is the value of $g(-2)$?

08 The function f and g are defined as $g(x)=2f(2x+1)$. Which of the following is true?

(A) g is the result of a horizontal translation of f of 1 unit to the left, followed by a vertical dilation by the factor of 2, and then a horizontal dilation by a factor of 2.

(B) g is the result of a horizontal translation of f of 1 unit to the left, followed by a vertical dilation by the factor of 2, and then a horizontal dilation by a factor of 0.5.

(C) g is the result of a horizontal translation of f of 0.5 unit to the left, followed by a vertical dilation by the factor of 2, and then a horizontal dilation by a factor of 0.5.

(D) g is the result of a horizontal translation of f of 0.5 unit to the left, followed by a vertical dilation by the factor of 2, and then a horizontal dilation by a factor of 2.

Unit I Test

01 Which of the following is true about the function $f(x)=-2x^3+5x^2-4x+1$?

(A) $f(x) \to \infty$ as $x \to \infty$; $f(x) \to \infty$ as $x \to -\infty$.
(B) $f(x) \to -\infty$ as $x \to \infty$; $f(x) \to \infty$ as $x \to -\infty$.
(C) $f(x) \to -\infty$ as $x \to \infty$; $f(x) \to -\infty$ as $x \to -\infty$.
(D) $f(x) \to \infty$ as $x \to \infty$; $f(x) \to -\infty$ as $x \to -\infty$.

02 Which of the following must be true about the graph of the function $f(x)=-x^4+5x^3+x$?

I. It eventually increases as x increases
II. It eventually increases as x decreases
III. It eventually decreases as x increases
IV. It eventually decreases as x decreases

(A) I and II only
(B) I and III only
(C) II and IV only
(D) III and IV only

03 For the function f, the rate of change is positive for $x<4$ and negative for $x>4$. Which of the following is true?

(A) The graph of f has a local maximum at $x=4$.
(B) The graph of f has a local minimum at $x=4$.
(C) The graph of f is concave down for $x<4$ and is concave up for $x>4$.
(D) The graph of f is concave up for $x<4$ and is concave down for $x>4$.

04 For the function f, the rate of change is increasing for $x<4$ and decreasing for $x>4$. Which of the following is true?

(A) The graph of f has a maximum at $x=4$.
(B) The graph of f has a minimum at $x=4$.
(C) The graph of f is concave down for $x<4$ and is concave up for $x>4$.
(D) The graph of f is concave up for $x<4$ and is concave down for $x>4$.

05 The polynomial function f is given by $f(x)=a_nx^n+a_{n-1}x^{n-1}+\cdots+a_1x+a_0$. If $\lim_{x\to\infty} f(x)=\infty$ and $\lim_{x\to-\infty} f(x)=-\infty$, which of the following statements must be true?

(A) The value of n is even and the value of a_n is positive.
(B) The value of n is even and the value of a_n is negative.
(C) The value of n is odd and the value of a_n is positive.
(D) The value of n is odd and the value of a_n is negative.

06 Find the zeros of the function. Then, sketch the graph of the function.

(1) $f(x)=(x-1)(x+1)^2(x-2)$ (2) $g(x)=2x^3-3x^2-8x+12$

07 Divide $8x^3+6x^2+3x-4$ by $2x-1$ using long division.

Unit I Test

08 Divide x^5-5 by $x+3$ using synthetic division.

09 What is the remainder when the polynomial $g(x)=4x^{2017}-3x^{2010}+2x-1$ is divided by $x-1$?

10 When x^4+ax^2-x+b is divided by $(x+2)$ and $(x+3)$, the remainder is 16 and 77, respectively. What is the value of $a+b$?

11 Find the value of b if $x-2$ is a factor of $bx^4-15x^3+27x^2-10x$.

12 $x+2$ and $x-3$ are factors of the polynomial $P(x)=6x^4-7x^3-37x^2+8x+12$. Find the remaining linear factors of $P(x)$.

13 If a polynomial $2x^3+ax^2-5x-2$ is divisible by $(x+1)$, then it is also divisible by

(A) x^2-x-2
(B) x^2+3x-2
(C) x^2-1
(D) $2x^2-x-1$

14 Find all the zeros of the function.

(1) $g(x)=4x^3-7x^2+x-6$

(2) $g(x)=x^4+x^3-x^2-4x-12$

15 The polynomial function f is given by $f(x)=2x^3+4x^2-18x-36$. Which of the following is true about the graph of f?

(A) The graph of f does not intersects the x-axis.
(B) The graph of f intersects the x-axis at one point.
(C) The graph of f intersects the x-axis at two points.
(D) The graph of f intersects the x-axis at three points.

16 $2+i$ is one of the zeros of the function $f(x)=x^3-6x^2+13x-10$. Find the remaining zeros of the function f.

Unit I Test

17 Write a third degree polynomial function with the leading coefficient 3 and zeros 1 and $-1+i$.

18 How many integers are in the solution set of $x^2-3x-10<0$?

19 Suppose the following three statements are true about the function f. Which of the following function could be f?

I. The vertical asymptote of $f(x)$ occurs at $x=-2$. II. The horizontal asymptote of $f(x)$ occurs at $y=2$. III. $f(x)$ has only one zero.

(A) $f(x)=\dfrac{2x-1}{2x+4}$

(B) $f(x)=\dfrac{2x+2}{x^2-1}$

(C) $f(x)=\dfrac{2x^2-2}{x^2+x-2}$

(D) $f(x)=\dfrac{2x^2-4}{x^2+3x+2}$

20 The rational function h is given by $h(x)=\frac{(x-1)(x+2)f(x)}{(x-1)^2(x+2)^2}$, where f is a polynomial function. If the polynomial function f is given by $f(x)=3x^2-4$, which of the following statements about h must be true?

(A) The graph of h has a horizontal asymptote at $y=0$.
(B) The graph of h has a horizontal asymptote at $y=3$.
(C) The graph of h has a horizontal asymptote at $y=-4$.
(D) The graph of h does not have any horizontal asymptotes.

21 Which of the following is an asymptote of $f(x)=\frac{2x^2-32}{x^2-7x+12}$?

(A) $x=-3$
(B) $x=3$
(C) $y=0$
(D) $y=1$

22

$$y=\frac{2x^2+1}{x^3-x^2-x}$$

How many asymptotes does the above function have?

(A) 1 (B) 2 (C) 3 (D) 4

23 Graph the function $y=\frac{x^2-x-2}{x^2+4x+3}$. State the domain and range.

Unit I Test

24

$$y=\frac{3x^3+2x^2-3x-2}{2x^2+x-3}$$

Find the equation of the slant asymptote and the vertical asymptote of the above function.

25 If $f(x)=\frac{x^2-4}{x-2}$, what value does f approach as x approaches 2?

(A) -2
(B) 2
(C) 4
(D) -4

26 Which of the following expressions approaches 4 as x increases without bound?

(A) $\frac{4x+1}{2x}$

(B) $\frac{4x+4}{x+1}$

(C) $\frac{8x^2+1}{2x-1}$

(D) $\frac{1-4x}{x}$

27 If $f(x)=\frac{x^2-16}{x-2}$, for what values of x is $f(x)\geq 0$?

(A) $2<x\leq 4$
(B) $x\leq -4$ or $x\geq 4$
(C) $-4\leq x<2$ or $x\geq 4$
(D) $-4\leq x<2$

28 If $f(x)=x^3+1$ and the function g is equivalent to f translated 2 units to the right and 3 units down, what is the value of $g(1)$?

(A) 1
(B) -1
(C) 3
(D) -3

memo

Unit II Exponential and Logarithmic Functions

1. Arithmetic and Geometric Sequence
2. Exponential Functions
3. Composition of Functions and Inverse Functions
4. Logarithmic Functions
5. Properties of Logarithms
6. Exponential and Logarithmic Equations
7. Application of Exponentials and Logarithms
8. Competing Function Model Validation
9. Semi-log Plots
10. Unit II Test

1 Arithmetic and Geometric Sequence

01 Definition of Sequence

A sequence is a list of ordered numbers where it has a first number, a second number, a third number and so on. A sequence is usually written as

$$a_1,\ a_2,\ a_3,\ \cdots,\ a_n.$$

and each number is called the term(also called a member or an element) of a sequence. For example, a_1 is first term, a_2 is second term, and a_n is n^{th} term. We say a sequence is finite if it has a limited number of terms(a_1, a_2, a_3, $\cdots$, a_n) and infinite if it has an unlimited number of terms(a_1, a_2, a_3, $\cdots$, a_n, a_{n+1}, $\cdots$). For instance, 1, 3, 5, 7 is a finite sequence and 1, 3, 5, 7, $\cdots$, 99, $\cdots$ is an infinite sequence.

Example 1

Write the first three terms and $(n+1)^{th}$ term of the sequence $a_n=2n+1$.

Solution

$a_n=2n+1$

1st term: $a_1=2(1)+1=3$ 　 2nd term: $a_2=2(2)+1=5$

3rd term: $a_3=2(3)+1=7$ 　 $(n+1)^{th}$ term: $a_{n+1}=2(n+1)+1=2n+3$

$a_1=3,\ a_2=5,\ a_3=7,\ a_{n+1}=2n+3$

Check Point 1

Solutions_Page 36

Write the first three terms and $(n+1)^{th}$ term of the sequence.

① $a_n=n^2-n+3$ 　 ② $a_n=\dfrac{n^3}{(2n-1)^2}$

02 Arithmetic Sequence

An arithmetic sequence is a sequence in which the difference between any two consecutive terms is constant. This constant is called the common difference and is denoted by d. Now, let's derive a formula for an arithmetic sequence.

2, 5, 8, 11, ⋯ → Each term after the first is found by adding 3 to the preceding term.

1st term:	$a_1=2=2+3(0)$	$\rightarrow a_1=a_1+d(0)$	$0d$ is added
2nd term:	$a_2=5=2+3(1)$	$\rightarrow a_2=a_1+d(1)$	$1d$ is added
3rd term:	$a_3=8=2+3(2)$	$\rightarrow a_3=a_1+d(2)$	$2d$ is added
4th term:	$a_4=11=2+3(3)$	$\rightarrow a_4=a_1+d(3)$	$3d$ is added
⋮	⋮	⋮	
n^{th} term:	$a_n=2+3(n-1)$	$\rightarrow a_n=a_1+d(n-1)$	$(n-1)d$ is added

Notice that $d=5-2=8-5=11-8=3$. In other words, the common difference is $d=a_2-a_1=a_3-a_2=a_4-a_3=\cdots=a_n-a_{n-1}$.

There is also a formula for arithmetic sequence that can be an alternative.
When a_k is given, the nth term is $a_n=a_k+(n-k)d$.

The nth Term of an Arithmetic Sequence:

1. Given $a_n=a_1+(n-1)d$
2. Given $a_n=a_k+(n-k)d$

Common Difference: $d=a_n-a_{n-1}$

Example 2

Write a formula for the nth term and the 8th term of the sequence, 1, 5, 9, 13, ⋯.

Solution

1, 5, 9, 13, ⋯ → $a_1=1$ and $d=4$.
$a_n=a_1+(n-1)d=1+(n-1)(4)=4n-3$
So $a_n=4n-3$ and $a_8=4(8)-3=29$.

$a_n=4n-3,\ a_8=29$

Check Point 2

Solutions_Page 36

Write a formula for the nth term and the 10th term of the sequence.

① 2, 5, 8, 11, ⋯ ② 4, 1, −2, −5, ⋯

Example 3

Find the first term and the formula for the nth term of the arithmetic sequences.

① $a_6=20,\ d=2$ ② $a_5=-6,\ a_{10}=-21$

Solution

① $a_6=20,\ d=2,\ a_n=a_1+(n-1)d$
$a_6=a_1+(6-1)(2),\ 20=a_1+10,\ a_1=10$
$a_n=10+(n-1)(2)=2n+8,\ a_n=2n+8$

$a_1=10,\ a_n=2n+8$

② $a_5=-6,\ a_{10}=-21,\ a_n=a_1+(n-1)d$
$a_5=a_1+(5-1)d,\ -6=a_1+4d$ and $a_{10}=a_1+(10-1)d,\ -21=a_1+9d$

Now, solve the system.

$$\begin{array}{rl} & -6=a_1+4d \\ - & -21=a_1+9d \\ \hline & 15=-5d \end{array}$$

$15=-5d \rightarrow d=-3$ ⇒ Substitute $d=-3$ into $-6=a_1+4d$

$-6=a_1+4(-3)$, $a_1=6$
$a_n=6+(n-1)(-3)=-3n+9$, $a_n=-3n+9$

Alternative solution

$a_n=a_k+(n-k)d$
$a_{10}=a_5+(10-5)d$, $-21=-6+5d$, $d=-3$
Now, substitute $d=-3$ into $a_5=a_1+(5-1)d$.
$-6=a_1+(5-1)(-3)$
$-6=a_1-12$, $a_1=6$ and $a_n=6+(n-1)(-3)=-3n+9$, $a_n=-3n+9$

$a_1=6$, $a_n=-3n+9$

Check Point 3

Solutions_Page 36

Find the first term and a formula for the nth term of the arithmetic sequence.

① $a_{12}=38$, $d=4$　　② $a_{12}=10$, $a_4=-38$

03 Geometric Sequence

A geometric sequence is a sequence in which the ratio of any two consecutive terms is constant. This constant is called the common ratio and denoted by r.

3, 6, 12, 24, ⋯ → Each term after the first is found by multiplying 2 to the preceding term.

1st term:	$a_1=3=3\times(2)^0$	$\rightarrow a_1=a_1\times(r)^0$	r^0 is multiplied
2nd term:	$a_2=6=3\times(2)^1$	$\rightarrow a_2=a_1\times(r)^1$	r^1 is multiplied
3rd term:	$a_3=12=3\times(2)^2$	$\rightarrow a_3=a_1\times(r)^2$	r^2 is multiplied
4th term:	$a_4=24=3\times(2)^3$	$\rightarrow a_4=a_1\times(r)^3$	r^3 is multiplied
⋮	⋮	⋮	⋮
n^{th} term:	$a_n=3\times(2)^{n-1}$	$\rightarrow a_n=a_1\times r^{n-1}$	r^{n-1} is multiplied

Notice that $r=6\div3=12\div6=24\div12=2$. In other words, the common ratio is $r=a_2\div a_1=a_3\div a_2=a_4\div a_3=\cdots=a_n\div a_{n-1}$.
There is also a formula for geometric sequence that can be an alternative. When a_k is given, the nth term is $a_n=a_kr^{n-k}$.

The nth Term of a Geometric Sequence:

1. $a_n=a_1 r^{n-1}$
2. $a_n=a_k r^{n-k}$

Common Ratio: $r=\dfrac{a_n}{a_{n-1}}$

Example 4

Write a formula for the nth term and the 8th term of the sequence 2, 4, 8, 16, ⋯.

Solution

2, 4, 8, 16, ⋯ → $a_1=2$ and $r=2$

$a_n=a_1r^{n-1}$, $a_n=2(2)^{n-1}$, $a_8=2(2)^{8-1}=256$

$a_n=2(2)^{n-1}$, $a_8=256$

Check Point 4

Solutions_Page 36

Write a formula for the nth term and the 10th term of the sequence.

① 3, 9, 27, 81, ⋯

② −5, 10, −20, 40, ⋯

Example 5

Find the first term and the formula for the nth term of the geometric sequence.

① $a_5=72$, $r=3$

② $a_4=1$, $a_7=\dfrac{1}{8}$

Solution

① $a_5=72$, $r=3$, $a_n=a_1r^{n-1}$

$a_5=a_1(3)^{5-1}$, $72=a_1(3)^4$, $a_1=\frac{8}{9}$

$a_n=\frac{8}{9}(3)^{n-1}$

$a_1=\frac{8}{9}$, $a_n=\frac{8}{9}(3)^{n-1}$

② $a_4=1$, $a_7=\frac{1}{8}$, $a_n=a_1r^{n-1}$

$a_4=a_1r^{4-1}$, $1=a_1r^3$ and $a_7=a_1r^{7-1}$, $\frac{1}{8}=a_1r^6$

Now, solve the system: $\frac{a_1r^6}{a_1r^3}=\frac{\frac{1}{8}}{1}=\frac{1}{8}$, $r^3=\frac{1}{8}$, $r=\frac{1}{2}$. So we have

$a_n=a_1r^{n-1}$

$a_4=a_1r^{4-1}$, $1=a_1\left(\frac{1}{2}\right)^3$, $a_1=8$. Therefore, $a_n=8\left(\frac{1}{2}\right)^{n-1}$.

Alternative solution

$a_n=a_kr^{n-k}$, $a_7=a_4r^{7-4}$, $\frac{1}{8}=1\cdot r^3$, $r=\frac{1}{2}$

Now, substitute $r=\frac{1}{2}$ into $a_4=a_1r^3$.

$1=a_1\left(\frac{1}{2}\right)^3$, $1=\frac{1}{8}a_1$, $a_1=8$. Therefore, $a_n=8\left(\frac{1}{2}\right)^{n-1}$.

$a_1=8$, $a_n=8\left(\frac{1}{2}\right)^{n-1}$

Check Point 5

Solutions_Page 36

Find the first term and a formula for the nth term of the geometric sequence.

① $a_2=3$, $r=-2$ ② $a_3=10$, $a_6=1250$

04 Recursive Sequence

Sometimes, sequences are defined recursively. This type of sequence always comes with the first few terms and a formula.

Example 6

Let $a_1=1$, $a_2=2$, $a_n=a_{n-2}+2a_{n-1}$, where $n\geq3$. Find the first 5 terms of the sequence.

Solution

$a_1=1$ and $a_2=2$

$n=3$; $a_3=a_{3-2}+2a_{3-1}=a_1+2a_2=1+2(2)=5 \rightarrow a_3=5$

$n=4$; $a_4=a_{4-2}+2a_{4-1}=a_2+2a_3=2+2(5)=12 \rightarrow a_4=12$

$n=5$; $a_5=a_{5-2}+2a_{5-1}=a_3+2a_4=5+2(12)=29 \rightarrow a_5=29$

So the first 5 terms are 1, 2, 5, 12, 29

Check Point 6

Solutions_Page 37

Where $n\geq3$, find the first 5 terms of the sequence.

① $a_1=6$, $a_2=-2$, $a_n=a_{n-1}-a_{n-2}$

② $a_1=6$, $a_2=4$, $a_n=\dfrac{a_{n-1}-n}{2}+\dfrac{3a_{n-2}}{4}$

Review Exercise

Solutions_Page 37

01 Find the 10th term of the sequence 15, 9, 3, -3, $\cdots$.

02 The fourth term of an arithmetic sequence is 24, and the eighth term is 8. What is the first term of this sequence?

03 Find the 8th term of each sequence 200, 100, 50, 25, $\cdots$.

04 The third term of a geometric sequence is 5, and the sixth term is 625. What is the first term of this sequence?

Review Exercise

05 If $a_1=10$ and $a_n=a_{n-1}-4n-1$, what is the value of a_4?

06 For set $\{-1, 1, 7, 25\}$, which of the following number should be added to each of the terms so that the resulting numbers form consecutive terms of a geometric sequence?

(A) 0 (B) 1
(C) 2 (D) 3
(E) 4

07 If the first term of an arithmetic sequence is 2 and fifth terms of sequence 14, what is the value of the first term of the sequence to exceed 600?

08

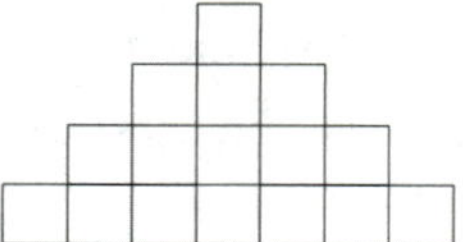

In Figure above, the first row has 1 square. If 2 additional squares are added to each new row after the first, how many squares will be in the 100th row?

09 A sequence is recursively defined as follows

$$a_1=2,\ a_{n+1}=\begin{cases}2a_n-2, & \text{if } a_n \text{ is odd}\\ a_n+3, & \text{if } a_n \text{ is even}\end{cases}$$

for $n\geq 1$. What is the sum of the first five terms?

10 A ball is dropped from a height of 243 *ft* above the ground. If the ball rebounds two−thirds of the distance it has fallen, how high does the ball rebound on the fifth bounce?

11 Consecutive terms of a sequence have the values 81, 27, 9, and 3. Of the following, which describes the sequence?

(A) The terms could be part of an arithmetic sequence with a common ratio of −54.

(B) The terms could be part of an arithmetic sequence with a common ratio of 3.

(C) The terms could be part of a geometric sequence with a common ratio of $\frac{1}{3}$.

(D) The terms could be part of a geometric sequence with a common ratio of 3.

12 Consecutive terms of a sequence have the values −3, 3, 9, and 15. Of the following, which describes the sequence?

(A) The terms could be part of an arithmetic sequence with a common difference of 6.

(B) The terms could be part of an arithmetic sequence with a common difference of −1.

(C) The terms could be part of a geometric sequence with a common ratio of −1.

(D) The terms could be part of a geometric sequence with a common ratio of 3.

Review Exercise

13 For an arithmetic sequence a_n, if $a_8 - a_4 = 16$, what is the value of $a_{21} - a_{15}$?

14 For a geometric sequence g_n, if $g_8 \div g_4 = 16$, what is the value of $g_{21} \div g_{15}$?

15 The fourth term of a sequence is 8 and the seventh term is 1. Which of the following must be true?

(A) If the sequence is arithmetic, the eighth term could be 0.5.

(B) If the sequence is geometric, the first term could be 32.

(C) If the sequence is arithmetic, the first term could be 32.

(D) If the sequence is geometric, the sixth term could be 2.

memo

2 Exponential Functions

01 Properties of Exponents

We already talked about calculating polynomials using law of exponents in Algebra 2. In this section, we will discuss over exponential function and their graphs. Let us review the properties of exponents first.

1. Basic Law of Exponents

Let $a>0$, $b>0$ and m, n be real numbers.

(1) $a^m \cdot a^n = a^{m+n}$ (2) $a^m \div a^n = \frac{a^m}{a^n} = a^{m-n}$ (3) $(a^m)^n = a^{mn}$

(4) $(ab)^m = a^m b^m$ (5) $\left(\frac{a}{b}\right)^m = \frac{a^m}{b^m}$ $(b \neq 0)$

Example 1 – 1

① $2^3 \cdot 2^4 = 2^{3+4} = 2^7 = 128$ ② $\frac{3^5}{3^3} = 3^{5-3} = 3^2 = 9$

③ $(2^2)^3 = 2^{2\times3} = 2^6 = 64$ ④ $(4x^2)^3 = 4^3 \cdot x^{2\times3} = 64x^6$

⑤ $\left(\frac{2x^3}{5}\right)^2 = \frac{2^2 \cdot x^{3\times2}}{5^2} = \frac{4x^6}{25}$

2. Zero and Negative Exponents

Let $a \neq 0$ and m be positive number.

(1) $a^0 = 1$ (2) $a^{-m} = \frac{1}{a^m}$

Note 0^0 and 0^m is not defined.

Example 1 – 2

① $5^0 = 1$, $(-5)^0 = 1$ ② $5^{-3} = \frac{1}{5^3} = \frac{1}{125}$

3. Radicals ⇒ Rational Exponents

Let $a>0$, $n\geq 2$, and m, n be integers.

(1) $\sqrt[n]{a}=a^{\frac{1}{n}}$ (2) $\sqrt[n]{a^m}=a^{\frac{m}{n}}$ (3) $\frac{1}{\sqrt[n]{a^m}}=\frac{1}{a^{\frac{m}{n}}}=a^{-\frac{m}{n}}$

Example 1 - 3

① $\sqrt[4]{2}=2^{\frac{1}{4}}$ ② $\sqrt[3]{9}=\sqrt[3]{3^2}=3^{\frac{2}{3}}$ ③ $\frac{1}{\sqrt{125}}=\frac{1}{\sqrt{5^3}}=\frac{1}{5^{\frac{3}{2}}}=5^{-\frac{3}{2}}$

4. Transformation of Exponents

Let $a>0$, $b>0$ and m, n, r be real numbers.

(1) If $a^m=b^n$, then

$(a^m)^{\frac{1}{m}}=(b^n)^{\frac{1}{m}} \Rightarrow a=b^{\frac{n}{m}}$

$(a^m)^{\frac{1}{n}}=(b^n)^{\frac{1}{n}} \Rightarrow b=a^{\frac{m}{n}}$

(2) If $a^m=b^n=k$, then

$a^m=k \Rightarrow (a^m)^{\frac{1}{m}}=(k)^{\frac{1}{m}} \Rightarrow a=k^{\frac{1}{m}}$

$b^n=k \Rightarrow (b^n)^{\frac{1}{n}}=(k)^{\frac{1}{n}} \Rightarrow b=k^{\frac{1}{n}}$

Check Point 1

Solutions_Page 40

Simplify the expression.

① $(a^4)^2\times(a^2)^{-3}\times a^5\div a^3$

② $(xy^2z^2)^2\div x^3y\times(x^3z)^3\times y^5z^3$

③ $\frac{(8ab)^3}{a^4}\times\frac{b^2}{16a^4}\div\frac{(4b)^3}{32}$

④ $\frac{3a^4}{b}\div(9ab)^2\times\sqrt{81a^3b^4}$

02 Definition of Exponential Function

A basic exponential function f with base a has the form

$$f(x)=a^x \ (a>0, \ a\neq 1)$$

and the domain is considered to be the set of all real numbers.

$f(x)=3^x$, $g(x)=\left(\frac{1}{2}\right)^x$, and $y=5\cdot 3^{x-2}$ are examples of exponential functions.

03 The Graph of $f(x)=a^x$ $(a>0, \ a\neq 1)$

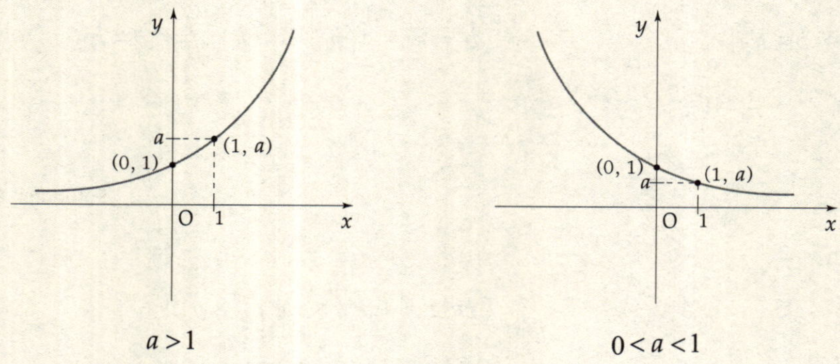

1. The graph passes through the point $(0, 1)$ and $(1, a)$.
2. The horizontal asymptote is x−axis($y=0$).
3. When $a>1$, y increases as x increases.
   When $0<a<1$, y decreases as x increases.
4. The graph is one−to−one, so it has an inverse function.
5. Domain: $(-\infty, \infty)$; Range: $(0, \infty)$.

Example 2

Sketch the graph of the function $f(x)=2^x$ and $f(x)=\left(\frac{1}{2}\right)^x$.

Solution

x	$f(x)=2^x$	$f(x)=\left(\frac{1}{2}\right)^x$
-2	$2^{-2}=\frac{1}{4}$	$\left(\frac{1}{2}\right)^{-2}=(2^{-1})^{-2}=2^2=4$
-1	$2^{-1}=\frac{1}{2}$	$\left(\frac{1}{2}\right)^{-1}=(2^{-1})^{-1}=2$
0	$2^0=1$	$\left(\frac{1}{2}\right)^0=1$
1	$2^1=2$	$\left(\frac{1}{2}\right)^1=\frac{1}{2}$
2	$2^2=4$	$\left(\frac{1}{2}\right)^2=\frac{1}{2^2}=\frac{1}{4}$
3	$2^3=8$	$\left(\frac{1}{2}\right)^3=\frac{1}{2^3}=\frac{1}{8}$

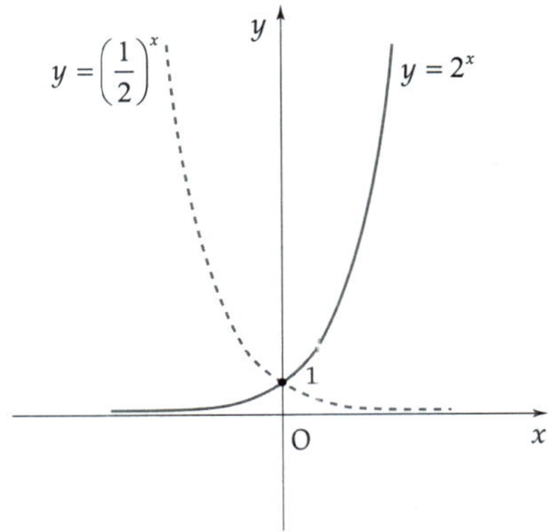

Check Point 2

Solutions_Page 40

Sketch the graph of the function.

① $f(x)=4^x$

② $f(x)=\left(\frac{1}{4}\right)^x$

04 Translation of the Graph

1. To graph $y=a^{x-h}+k$, shift the graph of $y=a^x$ horizontally h units and vertically k units.
2. The equation of horizontal asymptote is $y=k$.

Example 3

Sketch the graph of $y=2^x$ and $y=2^{x-3}+1$.

Solution

In order to graph $y=2^{x-3}+1$, first graph $y=2^x$ and then shift it 3 units to the right and 1 unit up.

The equation of horizontal asymptote is $y=1$.
Domain of $y=2^{x-3}+1$: $(-\infty, \infty)$
Range of $y=2^{x-3}+1$: $(1, \infty)$

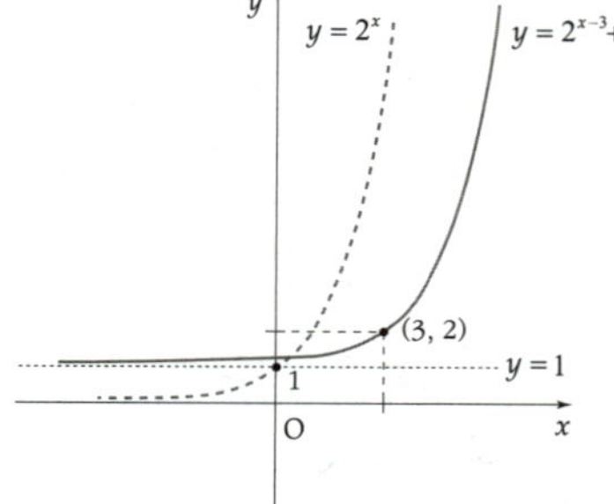

Check Point 3

Solutions_Page 41

Sketch the graph of the function.

① $f(x)=2^x+3$

② $g(x)=2^{x-1}+4$

05 Symmetry of the Graph

1. About the x-axis: $-f(x)=a^x \Rightarrow f(x)=-a^x$
2. About the y-axis: $f(x)=a^{-x} \Rightarrow f(x)=\left(\frac{1}{a}\right)^x$
3. About the origin: $-f(x)=a^{-x} \Rightarrow f(x)=-\left(\frac{1}{a}\right)^x$

Example 4

Sketch the graph of $y=2^x$, $y=-2^x$, $y=2^{-x}$, and $y=-2^{-x}$. Then discuss the symmetry of the graphs.

Solution

Given $y=2^x$,

$y=2^{-x} \Rightarrow$ Symmetric about the y-axis

$y=-2^x \Rightarrow$ Symmetric about the x-axis

$y=-2^{-x} \Rightarrow$ Symmetric about the origin

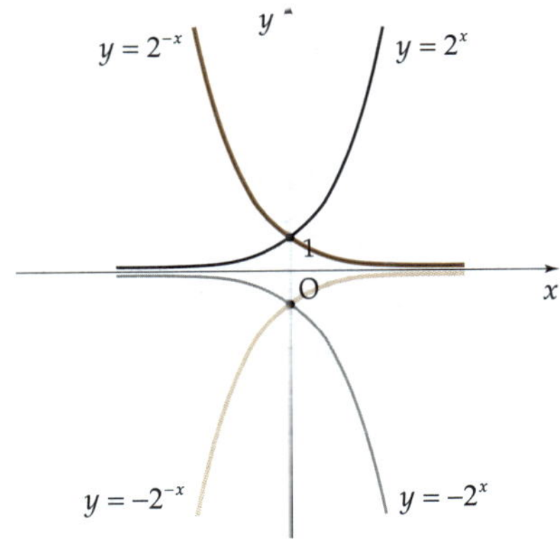

Check Point 4

Solutions_Page 41

Sketch the graph of the function $y=-2^x+3$.

06 Change in Linear and Exponential Functions

1. Changes in Linear Functions

(1) In linear functions, the rate of change(slope) remains constant throughout the function's domain.

(2) Changes in a linear function result in a straight−line movement either upwards(if the slope is positive) or downwards(if the slope is negative).

(3) Linear function of the form $y=mx+b$ are similar to arithmetic sequences of the form

$a_n=a_1+(n-1)d$, which can also be written as $a_n=a_0+dn$.

$$y=mx+b \iff a_n=a_0+dn$$

$$y=a_n,\ b=a_0,\ m=d,\ x=n$$

2. Changes in Exponential Functions

(1) In exponential functions, the rate of change is not constant: it grows or decays rapidly depending on the value of the base.

(2) Changes in an exponential function result in exponential growth (if the base is greater than 1) or exponential decay(if the base is between 0 and 1).

(3) Exponential function of the form $y=a\cdot b^x$ are similar to geometric sequences of the form $g_n=a_1\cdot r^{n-1}$, which can also be written as $g_n=a_0\cdot r^n$

$$y=a\cdot b^x \iff g_n=a_0\cdot r^n$$

$$y=g_n,\ a=a_0,\ b=r,\ x=n$$

07 Relationship Between Exponential Functions and Limits

Exponential function $y=a\cdot b^x(a>0,\ a\neq1)$ often involve limits when analyzing their behavior at extreme values of x.

1. For $b>1$, $\lim_{x\to\infty}(a\cdot b^x)=\infty$ and $\lim_{x\to-\infty}(a\cdot b^x)=0$

2. For $0<b<1$, $\lim_{x\to\infty}(a\cdot b^x)=0$ and $\lim_{x\to-\infty}(a\cdot b^x)=\infty$

Example 5

For the given function $f(x)=3\cdot2^x$, evaluate each of the following.

(1) $\lim_{x\to\infty}f(x)$ (2) $\lim_{x\to-\infty}f(x)$

Solution

(1) As x approaches infinity, 2^x grows exponentially. Therefore,

$\lim_{x\to\infty}f(x)=\lim_{x\to\infty}3\cdot2^x=\infty$.

$\lim_{x\to\infty}f(x)=\infty$

(2) As x approaches negative infinity, 2^x approaches 0 because the negative exponent indicates a reciprocal of an exponentially growing number. Therefore,

$\lim_{x\to-\infty}f(x)=\lim_{x\to-\infty}3\cdot2^x=0$.

$\lim_{x\to-\infty}f(x)=0$

Check Point 5

Solutions_Page 41

For the given function $f(x)=3\cdot\left(\frac{1}{4}\right)^x$, evaluate each of the following.

(1) $\lim_{x\to\infty}f(x)$ (2) $\lim_{x\to-\infty}f(x)$

Review Exercise

01 Simplify the expression.

(1) $(x^2)^3 \times (xy^2)^4 \times x^3y$

(2) $(ab^3)^4 \div (b^6)^{\frac{1}{2}} \times a^4b \div (a^2b)^2$

(3) $(2x)^4 \times (8x^2y)^2 \div \left(\frac{xy^4}{16}\right)^{-3}$

(4) $xy^3 \div \sqrt{81x^{-2}y^4} \times \sqrt{(9y^3)^3}$

02 Sketch the graph of the function

(1) $f(x)=3^x$

(2) $f(x)=-\left(\frac{4}{3}\right)^x$

(3) $y=-4^{-x}$

03 Sketch the graph of the function.

(1) $f(x)=3^{x-2}$

(2) $g(x)=3^x-2$

(3) $y=3^{x+2}+\frac{3}{2}$

04 Sketch the graph of the function.

(1) $f(x)=-3^{x+1}-2$

(2) $g(x)=2^{-x}+1$

(3) $y=-\left(\frac{1}{2}\right)^{-x-3}+1$

05 Find all values of a that satisfies the following.

(1) $2^{3a+1}=32$

(2) $3^{a+4}=27^{3-2a}$

(3) $5^{-2}=\dfrac{5^{\frac{1}{x}}\times 25^{\frac{2}{x}}}{25^{-\frac{3}{x}}}$

(4) $\dfrac{2^{b+3}}{32^{\frac{b}{5}}}=\dfrac{4^{2b+3}}{8^{-b}}$

06 If $4^x+4^x+4^x+4^x=4^{2x+3}$ for all x, then what is the value of x?

07 If $f(x)=m^x$ for all real number x and $m>1$, then $f(a+b)=$?

(A) $f(a)+f(b)$
(B) $f(a)\cdot f(b)$
(C) $f(ab)$
(D) $f(m^a)+f(m^b)$

08 If the graph of the exponential function $y=a^{x-1}+2$ passes through the points $(2,\ 4)$ and $\left(m,\ \frac{9}{4}\right)$, what is the value of m?

Review Exercise

09 The function f is modeled by $f(x)=8\cdot16^{2x+1}$. Which of the following expressions could also define $f(x)$?

(A) 2^{8x+7}

(B) 4^{4x+3}

(C) 8^{4x+3}

(D) $16^{2x+0.5}$

10 The function $g(x)=81\cdot\left(\frac{1}{9}\right)^{x-1}$ can be written as $g(x)=3^k$. What is the value of k in terms of x?

11 A certain species of fish in a lake grows exponentially. The population $P(t)$ at time t(in years) is modeled by the function $P(t)=200(1.02)^t$. What will be the population after 10 years?

Time(days)	Amount(mg)
0	200
1	160
2	128
3	102.4

12 The table above shows the amount of a certain chemical in a solution over time. Assuming the amount of the chemical decreases exponentially, which of the following is the exponential function $C(t)$ that models the amount of the chemical, where t is the time in days?

(A) $C(t)=200(1.008)^t$

(B) $C(t)=200(1.08)^t$

(C) $C(t)=200(0.08)^t$

(D) $C(t)=200(0.8)^t$

13 The function h is given by $h(x)=4^x$.

(1) If the function g is modeled by $g(x)=\frac{h(x)}{16}$, which of the following statements is true?

(A) The graph of g is the result of translating h horizontally to the right by 2 units.

(B) The graph of g is the result of translating h horizontally to the left by 2 units.

(C) The graph of g is the result of translating h vertically up by 16 units.

(D) The graph of g is the result of translating h vertically down by 16 units.

(2) If the function f is modeled by $f(x)=2^{2x-2}$, which of the following statements is true?

(A) The graph of f is the result of translating h horizontally to the right by 2 units.

(B) The graph of f is the result of translating h horizontally to the right by 1 unit.

(C) The graph of f is the result of translating h vertically down by 2 units.

(D) The graph of f is the result of translating h vertically down by 1 unit.

14 For the function g, the value of $g(x)$ increases by 1.5% for every increase in the value of x by 1. Which of the following equations represents the function g?

(A) $g(x)=0.015x+10$

(B) $g(x)=1.5x+10$

(C) $g(x)=10(1.015)^x$

(D) $g(x)=10(2.5)^x$

15 Suppose the population of a certain bird species decreases linearly. Which of the following statements must be true about the population of the bird species?

(A) Each year, the population of the bird species increases by 50 compared to the previous year.

(B) Each year, the population of the bird species decreases by 50 compared to the previous year.

(C) Each year, the population of the bird species increases by 5% compared to the previous year.

(D) Each year, the population of the bird species decreases by 5% compared to the previous year.

Review Exercise

Linear Function: $y=2-x$

Exponential Function: $y=0.5^x-0.25$

16 Which of the following is true about two functions given above?

(A) The exponential function is greater than the linear function for all x

(B) The exponential function is less than the linear function for all x

(C) The exponential function is greater than the linear function on the interval $0<x<2$

(D) The exponential function is less than the linear function on the interval $0<x<2$

17 The function f is given by $f(x)=4\cdot 5^x$. Which of the following statements is true about the graph of f?

(A) The graph of f increases exponentially and $\lim_{x\to\infty} f(x)=\infty$.

(B) The graph of f decreases exponentially and $\lim_{x\to\infty} f(x)=0$.

(C) The graph of f increases linearly and $\lim_{x\to\infty} f(x)=\infty$.

(D) The graph of f decreases linearly and $\lim_{x\to\infty} f(x)=-\infty$.

18 Determine the horizontal asymptote of the exponential function $g(x)=2\cdot 0.5^x$.

memo

3 Composition of Functions and Inverse Functions

01 Composition of Functions

Given two functions $f: X \rightarrow Y$ and $g: Y \rightarrow Z$, we can define a new function where X is the domain and Z is the range by matching the element X to $g(f(x))$, as shown below. This function is called the composition of function g with function f and is defined as

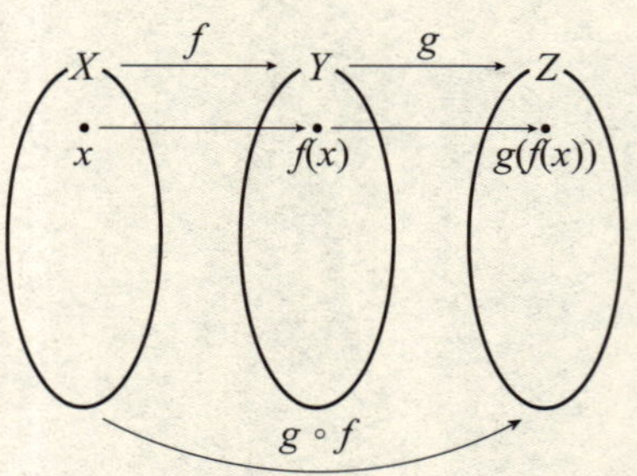

$$g \circ f = (g \circ f)(x) = g(f(x))$$

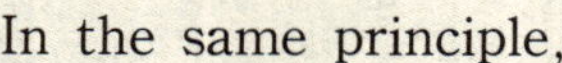

In the same principle,

1. $f \circ g = (f \circ g)(x) = f(g(x))$
2. $f \circ f = (f \circ f)(x) = f(f(x))$
3. $f \circ g \circ h = (f \circ g \circ h)(x) = f(g(h(x)))$

Concept Check

Given $f(x) = \sqrt{x+1}$ and $g(x) = \dfrac{1}{x-1}$,

1. $g \circ f = (g \circ f)(x) = g(f(x)) = g(\sqrt{x+1}) = \dfrac{1}{\sqrt{x+1}-1}$
2. $f \circ g = (f \circ g)(x) = f(g(x)) = f\left(\dfrac{1}{x-1}\right) = \sqrt{\dfrac{1}{x-1}+1}$

   ✔ Notice that $f \circ g \neq g \circ f$.

3. $(g \circ f)(3)$

   Method 1: $(g \circ f)(x) = \dfrac{1}{\sqrt{x+1}-1}$, $(g \circ f)(3) = \dfrac{1}{\sqrt{3+1}-1} = \dfrac{1}{2-1} = 1$

   Method 2: $(g \circ f)(3) = g(f(3)) = g(\sqrt{3+1}) = g(2) = \dfrac{1}{2-1} = 1$

Example 1

Given $f(x)=3x-1$ and $g(x)=2x^2$, find each of the following.

① $g \circ f$　　② $f \circ g$　　③ $(g \circ f)\left(\frac{1}{3}\right)$

Solution

① $g \circ f = g(f(x)) = g(3x-1) = 2(3x-1)^2 = 2(9x^2-6x+1) = 18x^2-12x+2$

② $f \circ g = f(g(x)) = f(2x^2) = 3(2x^2)-1 = 6x^2-1$

③ **Method 1**: $g \circ f = 2(3x-1)^2$, $(g \circ f)\left(\frac{1}{3}\right) = 2\left(3\left(\frac{1}{3}\right)-1\right)^2 = 2(1-1)^2 = 0$

Method 2: $(g \circ f)\left(\frac{1}{3}\right) = g\left(f\left(\frac{1}{3}\right)\right) = g\left(3\left(\frac{1}{3}\right)-1\right) = g(0) = 2(0)^2 = 0$

Check Point 1

Solutions_Page 46

Given $f(x)=\frac{1}{2}x^2-2$ and $g(x)=2x$, find each of the following.

① $f \circ g$　　② $g \circ f$

③ $(f \circ g)(2)$　　④ $(g \circ g \circ f)(-1)$

02 Composition of Functions and its Domain

The domain of $g \circ f$ is set of all x in the domain of f for which $f(x)$ is in the domain of g, as shown below.

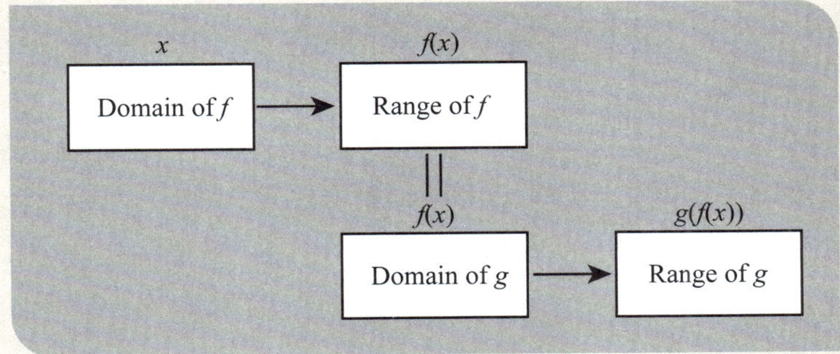

Finding the domain of the function $g \circ f = g(f(x))$ consists of three steps:

1. Find the domain of the function $f(x)$.
2. Construct the function $g(f(x))$ and find the domain of this new function.
3. The domain of the function $g(f(x))$ is the set of numbers common to the domain of both $f(x)$ and the new function constructed from $g(f(x))$.

Concept Check

Given $f(x)=\frac{1}{x+2}$ and $g(x)=\frac{1}{x-1}$, the domain of $g \circ f = g(f(x))$ can be found as follows:

1. The domain of $f(x)=\frac{1}{x+2}$ is all real numbers except $x=-2$.

2. $g \circ f = g(f(x)) = g\left(\frac{1}{x+2}\right) = \frac{1}{\frac{1}{x+2}-1} = -\frac{x+2}{x+1}$

   and the domain of $g \circ f \Rightarrow y=-\frac{x+2}{x+1}$ is all real numbers except $x=-1$.

   $f(x)=\frac{1}{x+2}$ -2 x $y=-\frac{x+2}{x+1}$ -1 x

3. The domain of $g \circ f = g(f(x))$ is set of numbers common to the domain of both $f(x)=\frac{1}{x+2}$ and $y=-\frac{x+1}{x+2}$, which is all real numbers except $x=-2$ and $x=-1$.

Example 2

Given $f(x)=\sqrt{x-1}$ and $g(x)=2x$, find each of the following and their domains.

① $f\circ g$ ② $f\circ f$

Solution

① $f\circ g=f(g(x))=f(2x)=\sqrt{2x-1}$

Domain of $g(x)=2x$: All real numbers.

Domain of $f\circ g \Rightarrow y=\sqrt{2x-1}$: $\left\{x \mid x\geq\frac{1}{2}\right\}$

$g(x)=2x$ $y=\sqrt{2x-1}$ x $\frac{1}{2}$

Domain of $f\circ g$: $\left\{x \mid x\geq\frac{1}{2}\right\}$

② $f\circ f=f(f(x))=f(\sqrt{x-1})=\sqrt{\sqrt{x-1}-1}$

Domain of $f(x)=\sqrt{x-1}$: $\{x \mid x\geq1\}$

Domain of $f\circ f \Rightarrow y=\sqrt{\sqrt{x-1}-1}$:

For $\sqrt{\sqrt{x-1}-1}$ to be defined, we must have

$\sqrt{x-1}-1\geq0$, $\sqrt{x-1}\geq1$

$x-1\geq1$, $x\geq2$: $\{x \mid x\geq2\}$

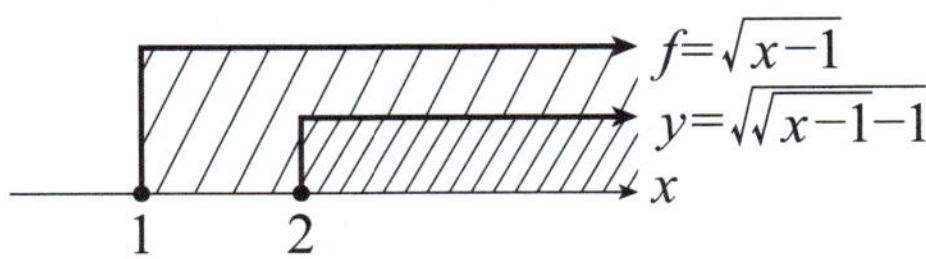

Domain of $f\circ f$: $\{x \mid x\geq2\}$

Check Point 2

Solutions_Page 46

Given $f(x)=\frac{2}{x}$ and $g(x)=2x+5$, find each of the following and their domains.

① $f\circ g$ ② $g\circ f$ ③ $f\circ f$

03 The Definition of Inverse

The inverse of f, which is denoted by f^{-1}, can be formed by interchanging input (x−values) and output(y−values) of the function. As a result, the domain of f is equal to the range of f^{-1} and the range of f is equal to the domain of f^{-1}. The graph of f^{-1} is a reflection of the graph of f about the line $y=x$.

Concept Check

Let a set of ordered pairs of f be $\{(1, -3), (2, 0), (3, 1)\}$.

f: $\{(1, -3), (2, 0), (3, 1)\}$	f^{-1}: $\{(-3, 1), (0, 2), (1, 3)\}$
Domain of f: $\{1, 2, 3\}$ →	Domain of f^{-1}: $\{-3, 0, 1\}$
Range of f: $\{-3, 0, 1\}$ →	Range of f^{-1}: $\{1, 2, 3\}$

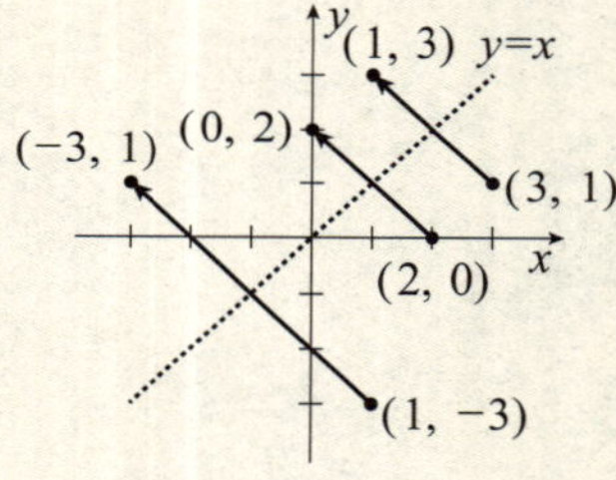

Given a function f, its inverse f^{-1} does not always become a function. f^{-1} is a function if and only if f is a one−to−one function. A function is one−to−one if each value of input corresponds to exactly one value of output. If the one−to−one function is continuous, it always either increases or decreases.

Concept Check

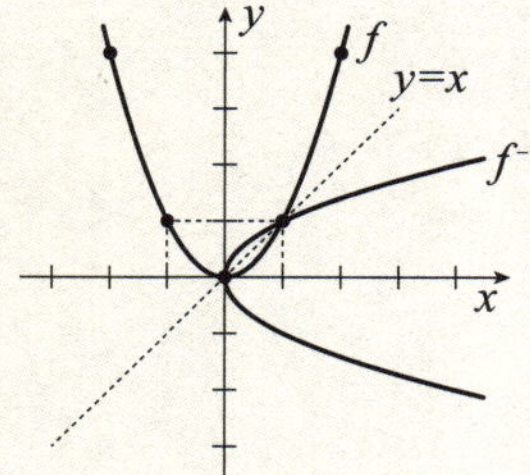

f is NOT one–to–one
→ f^{-1} is NOT a function.

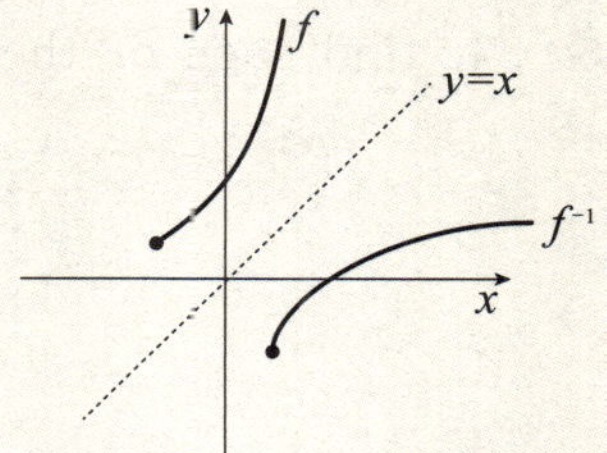

f is one–to–one
→ f^{-1} is a function.

In summary, if the function $f: X \to Y$ is a one–to–one function,

1. Its inverse function $f^{-1}: Y \to X$ exists
2. $y=f(x) \Leftrightarrow x=f^{-1}(y)$

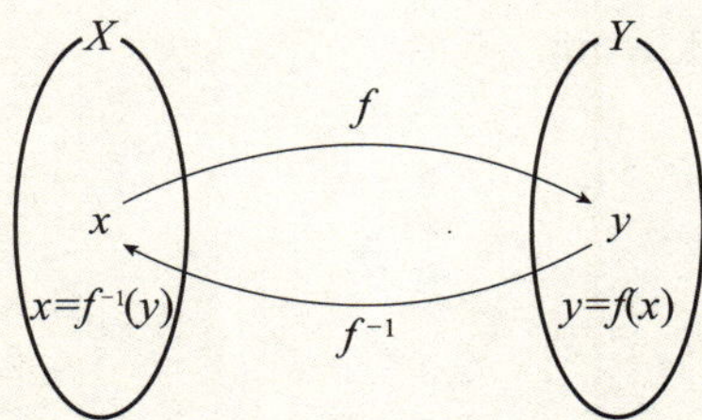

Concept Check

Given $f(x)=3x-2$, find $f(4)$ and $f^{-1}(4)$.

$y=f(x) \Leftrightarrow x=f^{-1}(y)$

1. Since $f(4)$ is the value of y when $x=4$,

   $3(4)-2=10 \to f(4)=10$

2. Since $f^{-1}(4)$ is the value of x when $y=4$,

   $4=3x-2,\ x=2 \to f^{-1}(4)=2$

Example 3

Given $f(x)=5x+4$, find each of the following.

① $f(-1)$ ② $f^{-1}(3)$ ③ $f^{-1}(2b-1)$

Solution

① $f(-1)=5(-1)+4=-1$

② $3=5x+4$, $-1=5x$

$x=-\frac{1}{5}$, $f^{-1}(3)=-\frac{1}{5}$

③ $2b-1=5x+4$, $2b-5=5x$

$x=\frac{2b-5}{5}$, $f^{-1}(2b-1)=\frac{2b-5}{5}$

Check Point 3

Solutions_Page 47

Given $g(x)=2\sqrt{x-1}+1$, find each of the following.

① $g(5)$ ② $g^{-1}(5)$ ③ $g^{-1}(a)$

04 Properties of Inverse Function

If we have a one-to-one function $f: X \to Y$ and its inverse function $f^{-1}: Y \to X$, then

1. $(f^{-1})^{-1}=f$
2. $(f^{-1}\circ f)(x)=x$ and $(f\circ f^{-1})(x)=x$

Concept Check

1. Since $y=f(x) \Leftrightarrow x=f^{-1}(y) \Leftrightarrow y=(f^{-1})^{-1}(x)$, $(f^{-1})^{-1}=f$
2. $(f^{-1}\circ f)(x)=f^{-1}(f(x))=f^{-1}(y)=x$

   $(f\circ f^{-1})(y)=f(f^{-1}(y))=f(x)=y$. By replacing y with x, $(f\circ f^{-1})(x)=x$

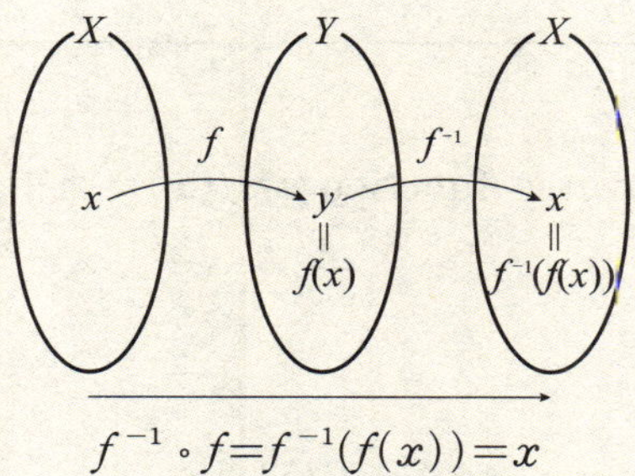

$$f^{-1}\circ f=f^{-1}(f(x))=x$$

Example 4

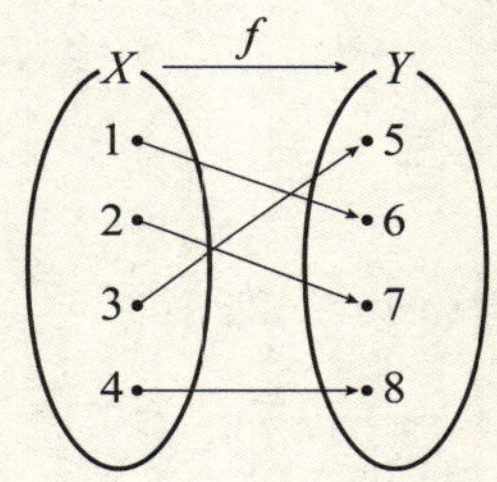

Given the function f as shown above, find each of the following.

① $f(2)$ ② $f^{-1}(5)$ ③ $(f^{-1}\circ f)(3)$

④ $(f\circ f^{-1})(8)$ ⑤ $(f^{-1})^{-1}(4)$

Solution

① $f(2)=7$

② $f^{-1}(5)=3$

③ Since $(f^{-1}\circ f)(x)=x$, $(f^{-1}\circ f)(3)=3$

④ Since $(f^{-1}\circ f)(x)=x$, $(f\circ f^{-1})(8)=8$

⑤ Since $(f^{-1})^{-1}=f$, $(f^{-1})^{-1}(4)=f(4)=8$

Check Point 4

Solutions_Page 47

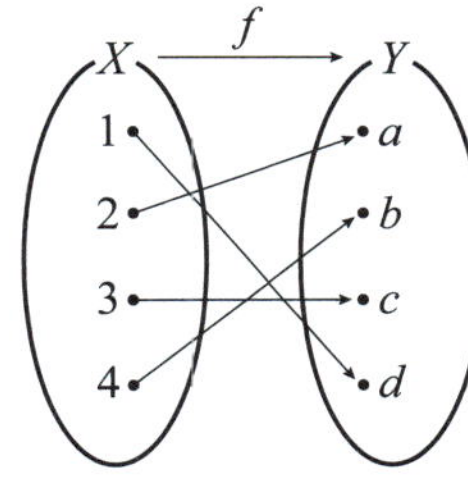

Given the function f as shown, find each of the following.

① $f(3)$ ② $f^{-1}(b)$

③ $f^{-1}(d)$ ④ $(f^{-1})^{-1}(4)$

⑤ $(f^{-1}\circ f)(4)$ ⑥ $(f\circ f^{-1})(a)$

Example 5

Show that $g(x)=\frac{x-1}{3}$ is inverse function of $f(x)=3x+1$.

Solution

If g is inverse of f, $(f\circ g)(x)=x$ and $(g\circ f)(x)=x$.

$(f\circ g)(x)=f(g(x))=f\left(\frac{x-1}{3}\right)=3\left(\frac{x-1}{3}\right)+1=(x-1)+1=x$

$(g\circ f)(x)=g(f(x))=g(3x+1)=\frac{(3x+1)-1}{3}=\frac{3x}{3}=x$

Therefore, g is inverse of f

Check Point 5

Solutions_Page 47

Show that $g(x)=\frac{1-2x}{4}$ is inverse function of $f(x)=-2x+\frac{1}{2}$.

05 Finding an Inverse of f

In general, when representing a function, we write the elements of the domain as x and the elements of the range as y. Therefore, in the inverse function $x=f^{-1}(y)$, x and y are interchanged and represented by $y=f^{-1}(x)$.
Use the following procedure to find the inverse function.

1. Check if the function f is a one-to-one function.
2. Replace f with y.
3. Interchange x and y.
4. Solve the resulting equation for y.

Example 6

Find the inverse of f and then determine whether the inverse is a function.

① $f(x)=\dfrac{x-2}{4}$ ② $f(x)=x^2+1$

Solution

① $f(x)=\dfrac{x-2}{4}$, $y=\dfrac{x-2}{4}$

$x=\dfrac{y-2}{4}$, $4x=y-2$

$4x+2=y$, $f^{-1}(x)=4x+2$

$f^{-1}(x)$ is a function because $f(x)$ is a one-to-one function.

② $f(x)=x^2+1$, $y=x^2+1$

$x=y^2+1$, $x-1=y^2$

$\pm\sqrt{x-1}=y$, $f^{-1}(x)=\pm\sqrt{x-1}$

$f^{-1}(x)$ is NOT a function because $f(x)$ is NOT a one-to-one function.

Check Point 6

Solutions_Page 47

Find the inverse of f and then determine whether the inverse is a function.

① $f(x)=\sqrt{x-3}+1$ ② $f(x)=\sqrt[3]{x}+1$

Example 7

Find the inverse function of f then sketch the graph.

① $f(x)=\dfrac{3x+1}{2}$ ② $f(x)=2\sqrt{x}+1$

Solution

① $f(x)=\dfrac{3x+1}{2}$, $y=\dfrac{3x+1}{2}$

$x=\dfrac{3y+1}{2}$, $2x=3y+1$

$2x-1=3y$, $\dfrac{2x-1}{3}=y$

$f^{-1}(x)=\dfrac{2x-1}{3}$

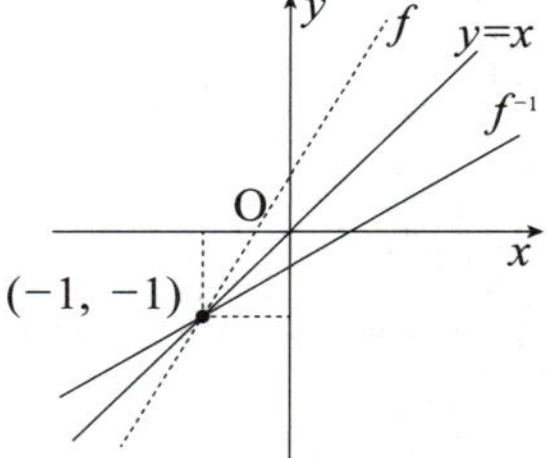

② $f(x)=2\sqrt{x}+1$, $y=2\sqrt{x}+1$

$x=2\sqrt{y}+1$, $x-1=2\sqrt{y}$

$\dfrac{x-1}{2}=\sqrt{y}$, $\dfrac{(x-1)^2}{4}=y$

$f^{-1}(x)=\dfrac{(x-1)^2}{4}$ where $x\geq 1$

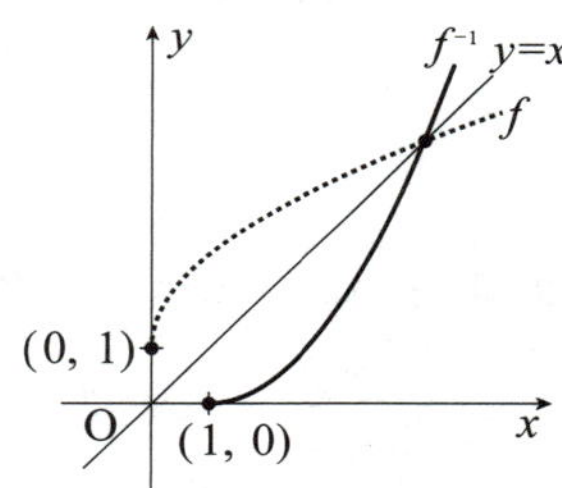

Check Point 7

Solutions_Page 48

Find the inverse function of f then sketch the graph.

① $f(x)=-4x-3$ ② $f(x)=\dfrac{2-3x}{3}$

③ $f(x)=x^2-3$, $x\geq 0$ ④ $f(x)=\sqrt{x-2}$

Review Exercise

01 Given $f(x)=2x-1$, $g(x)=\dfrac{1}{x-1}$, and $h(x)=\sqrt{3x+2}$, find each of the following.

(1) $(f \circ g)(-4)$

(2) $(g \circ h)\left(\dfrac{2}{3}\right)$

(3) $g \circ f$ and its domain

(4) $g \circ h$ and its domain

02 Given $f(x)=4x-a$ and $g(x)=-2x+5$, answer the following questions.

(1) If $(f \circ g)(2)=4$, what is the value of a?

(2) If $(g \circ g)(b)=-11$, what is the value of b?

03 Given $f(1-4x)=\dfrac{3x-2}{4}$,
find each of the following.

(1) $f(x)$

(2) $f(4a-1)$

04 Given $f\left(\dfrac{3x+1}{2}\right)=2x+5$,
what is the value of $f(2)+f(5)$?

05 Let $f(x)=3x-2$ and $g(x)=kx+2$. If $f\circ g=g\circ f$, what is the value of k?

06 Given $f(x)=-3x+4$ and $g(x)=4x-1$, find the function h that satisfies each of the following.

(1) $f\circ h=g$

(2) $h\circ g=f$

Review Exercise

07

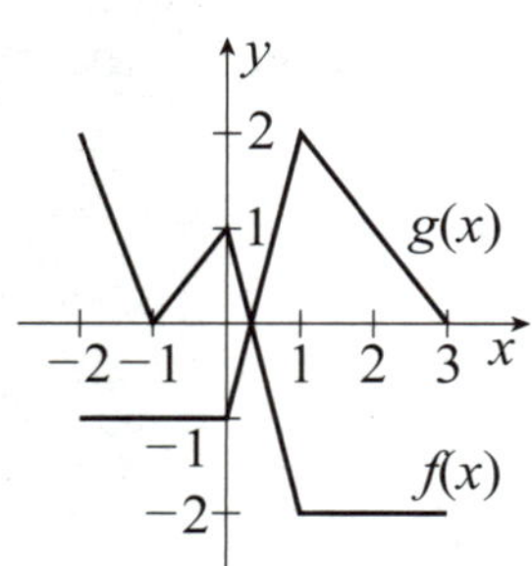

In the graphs of f and g shown above, find each of the following.

(1) $(f \circ g)(0)$

(2) $(g \circ f)(2)$

08 Given $f(x)=\frac{1+x}{x-2}$, find each of the following.

(1) $f^{-1}(3)$

(2) $f^{-1}(k)$ in terms of k

09 Show that g is inverse function cf f.

(1) $f(x)=2x-1,\ g(x)=\frac{x+1}{2}$

(2) $f(x)=\sqrt{x-4},\ g(x)=x^2+4$ where $x\geq0$

10 Find the inverse function of f then sketch the graph.

(1) $f(x)=4-x^2,\ x\geq0$

(2) $f(x)=\frac{2}{x}$

11 If $f(x)=5x+2$ and $f^{-1}(a)=4$, what is the value of a?

12 If $f(x)=3\sqrt{bx-2}+1$ and $f^{-1}(2)=1$, what is the value of b?

13 Suppose that $f(x)=ax+b$. If the graph of f^{-1} passes through two points $(2, -3)$ and $(10, 1)$, what is the value of $a+b$?

14 A coffee shop sells iced tea that comes in different concentrations. The concentration of tea syrup in the mixture, C, as a function of the amount of water, W, added is given by $C(W)=\frac{100}{W+2}$.
What is the inverse function $W(C)$, and what does it represent?

(A) $W(C)=\frac{100}{C}-2$; it represents the amount of water needed to achieve a certain concentration of tea syrup.

(B) $W(C)=\frac{C}{100}-2$; it represents the amount of syrup needed to achieve a certain concentration of tea.

(C) $W(C)=2-\frac{100}{C}$; it represents the amount of water needed to achieve a certain concentration of tea syrup.

(D) $W(C)=\frac{100}{W+2}$; it represents the amount of water needed to achieve a certain concentration of tea syrup.

4 Logarithmic Functions

01 Definition of Logarithmic Function

In algebra 2, we studied the concept of an inverse function. If a function always increases or decreases without bounds, it is said to be one−to−one, and that function must have an inverse function. In the first section of this chapter, we learned the graphs of exponential functions, $y=a^x$. By looking at the graph of the exponential function, you will see that it is one-to-one so that it has an inverse function, $x=a^y$. In the function $x=a^y$, y is called the logarithm of x and it is written as $y=\log_a x$, which is called a logarithmic function with base a.

exponent

$$y=\log_a x \iff a^y=x$$

base

"log" is abbreviation of "logarithm."

Example 1

Write each equation in exponential or logarithmic form.

① $\log_2 16=4$

② $\log_{25} 5=\frac{1}{2}$

③ $3^5=243$

④ $2^{-5}=\frac{1}{32}$

Solution

① $\log_2 16=4$

The base is 2 and the exponent is 4.

So $2^4=16$.

② $\log_{25} 5=\frac{1}{2}$

The base is 25 and the exponent is $\frac{1}{2}$.

So $25^{\frac{1}{2}}=5$.

③ $3^5=243$

The base is 3 and the exponent is 5.

So $\log_3 243=5$.

④ $2^{-5}=\frac{1}{32}$

The base is 2 and the exponent is -5.

So $\log_2\left(\frac{1}{32}\right)=-5$.

Check Point 1

Solutions_Page 51

Write each equation in exponential or logarithmic form.

① $\log_2 64=6$

② $\log_5\left(\frac{1}{25}\right)=-2$

③ $2^3=8$

④ $9^0=1$

Example 2

Evaluate the expression $\log_4 64$.

Solution

Let $\log_4 64=x$.

$4^x=64$ → Definition of logarithm

$4^x=4^3$ → $64=4^3$

$x=3$ → If $a^m=a^n$, then $m=n$

$\log_4 64=3$

Check Point 2

Solutions_Page 51

Solve for x

① $\log_3 9=x$

② $2\log_{\frac{1}{2}} 32=x$

③ $\log_{\sqrt{2}} 4=x$

02 The Graph of $f(x)=\log_a x$ ($a>0$, $a\neq1$)

1. Definition of Logarithmic Function with Base a

For $a>0$ and $a\neq1$,

(1) $y=\log_a x \iff x=a^y$.

(2) Read the function $f(x)=\log_a x$ as log base a of x.

(3) The function $f(x)=\log_a x$ is a inverse function of $f(x)=a^x$.

2. The property of the graph of $f(x)=\log_a x$ $(a>0,\ a\neq 1)$

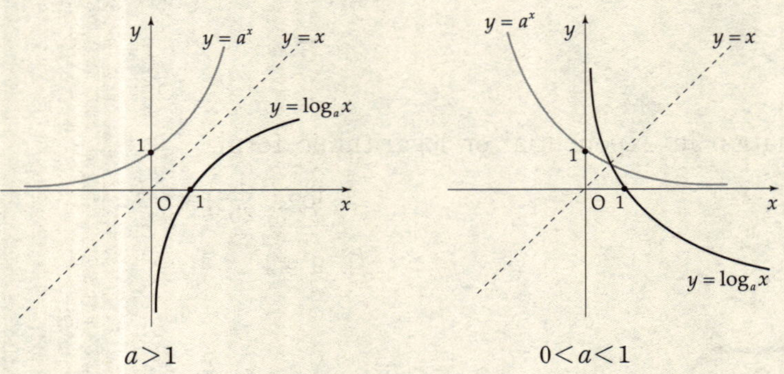

(1) The graph passes through the point $(1,\ 0)$ and $(a,\ 1)$.

(2) The vertical asymptote is $y-$axis $(x=0)$.

(3) When $a>1$, y increases as x increases.

When $0<a<1$, y decreases as x increases.

(4) The graph is one-to-one, so it has an inverse function.

(5) The graph is reflection of graph of $f(x)=a^x$ about the line $y=x$.

(6) Domain: $(0,\ \infty)$; Range: $(-\infty,\ \infty)$.

3. The relationship between the graph of $f(x)=\log_a x$ and $f(x)=\log_{\frac{1}{a}} x$.

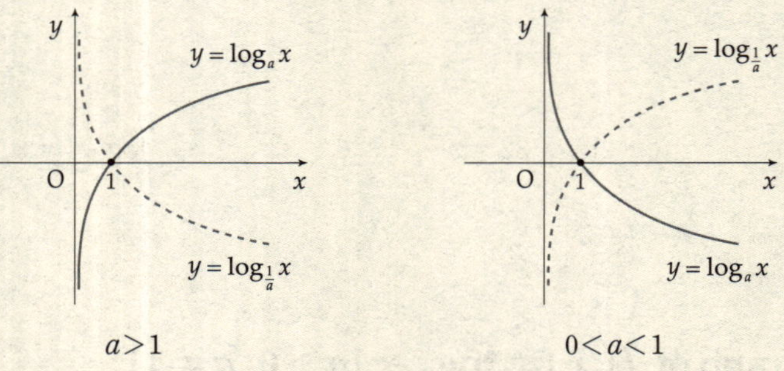

(1) The graph $f(x)=\log_a x$ and $f(x)=\log_{\frac{1}{a}} x$ are symmetric about $x-$axis each other.

Example 3-1

Sketch the graph of the function $f(x)=2^x$ and $f(x)=\log_2 x$.

Solution

x	$f(x)=2^x$	x	$f(x)=\log_2 x$
-2	$2^{-2}=\frac{1}{4}$	$\frac{1}{4}$	$\log_2\left(\frac{1}{4}\right)=-2$
-1	$2^{-1}=\frac{1}{2}$	$\frac{1}{2}$	$\log_2\left(\frac{1}{2}\right)=-1$
0	$2^0=1$	1	$\log_2 1=0$
1	$2^1=2$	2	$\log_2 2=1$
2	$2^2=4$	4	$\log_2 4=2$
3	$2^3=8$	8	$\log_2 8=3$

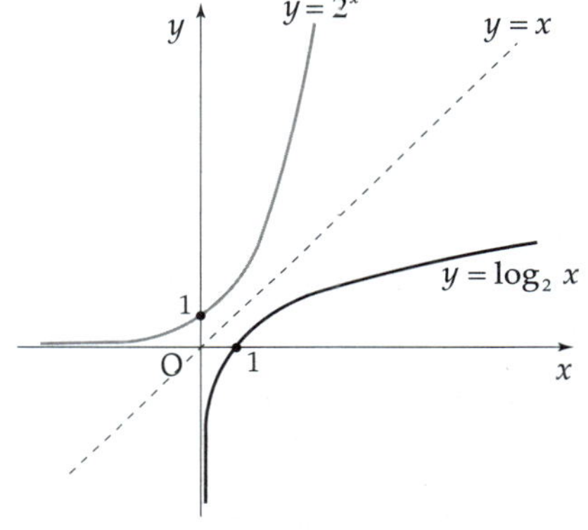

Example 3–2

Sketch the graph of the functions $f(x)=\log_3 x$ and $f(x)=\log_{\frac{1}{3}} x$.

Solution

x	$f(x)=\log_3 x$	$f(x)=\log_{\frac{1}{3}} x$
$\frac{1}{9}$	$\log_3\left(\frac{1}{9}\right)=-2$	$\log_{\frac{1}{3}}\left(\frac{1}{9}\right)=2$
$\frac{1}{3}$	$\log_3\left(\frac{1}{3}\right)=-1$	$\log_{\frac{1}{3}}\left(\frac{1}{3}\right)=1$
1	$\log_3 1=0$	$\log_{\frac{1}{3}} 1=0$
3	$\log_3 3=1$	$\log_{\frac{1}{3}} 3=-1$
9	$\log_3 9=2$	$\log_{\frac{1}{3}} 9=-2$

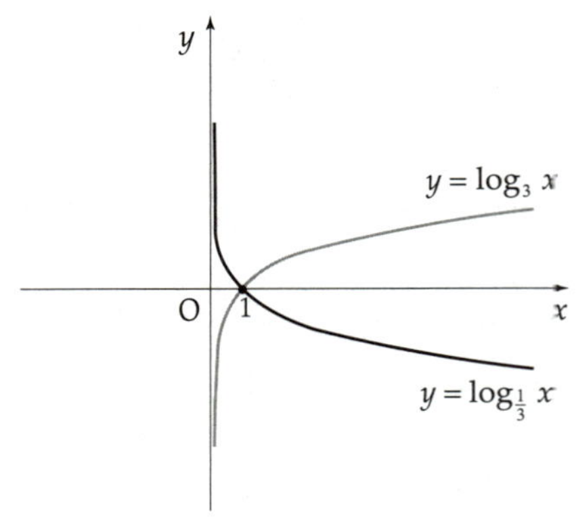

Check Point 3

Solutions_Page 52

Sketch the graph of the function.

① $f(x)=\log_5 x$ ② $f(x)=\log_{\frac{1}{4}} x$

03 Translation of the Graph

1. To graph $y=\log_a(x-h)+k$, shift the graph of $y=\log_a x$ horizontally h units and vertically k units.
2. The equation of vertical asymptote is $x=h$.

Example 4

Sketch the graph of $y=\log_2 x$ and $y=\log_2(x-1)+2$.

Solution

In order to graph $y=\log_2(x-1)+2$, first graph $y=\log_2 x$ and then shift it 1 unit to the right and 2 units up.

The equation of vertical asymptote is $x=1$.

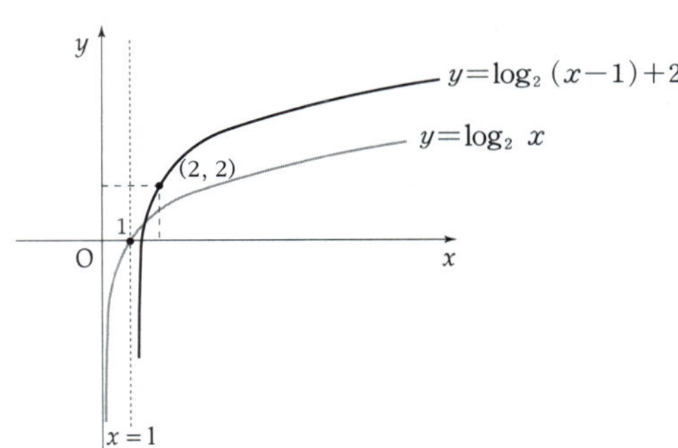

Check Point 4

Solutions_Page 52

Sketch the graph of the function.

① $f(x)=\log_2 x+1$

② $f(x)=\log_4(x+1)$

04 Symmetry of the Graph

1. About the $x-axis$: $-f(x)=\log_a x \Rightarrow f(x)=-\log_a x \Leftrightarrow f(x)=\log_a\left(\frac{1}{x}\right)$.
2. About the $y-axis$: $f(x)=\log_a(-x)$.
3. About the origin: $-f(x)=\log_a(-x) \Rightarrow f(x)=-\log_a(-x) \Leftrightarrow f(x)=\log_a\left(-\frac{1}{x}\right)$.

✔ The reason $-\log_a x=\log_a \frac{1}{x}$ and $-\log_a(-x)=\log_a\left(-\frac{1}{x}\right)$ is explained in the properties of logarithms in the next section.

Example 5

Sketch the graph of $y=\log_2 x$, $y=-\log_2 x$, $y=\log_2(-x)$, and $y=-\log_2(-x)$. Then discuss the symmetry of the graphs.

Solution

Given $y=\log_2 x$,

$y=\log_2(-x)$ $\Rightarrow$ Symmetric about the $y-$axis
$y=-\log_2 x$ $\Rightarrow$ Symmetric about the $x-$axis
$y=-\log_2(-x)$ $\Rightarrow$ Symmetric about the origin

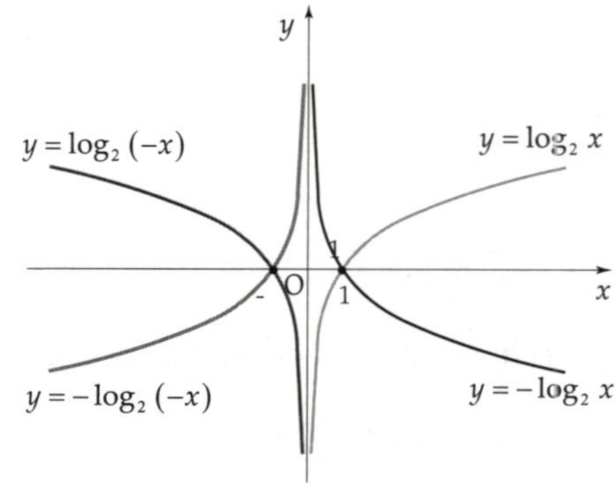

Check Point 5

Solutions_Page 53

Sketch the graph of $f(x)=-\log_2(x+4)$.

05 Relationship Between Logarithmic Functions and Limits

Logarithmic function $y=\log_a x(a>1)$ often involve limits when analyzing their behavior at extreme values of x

1. Limit as x Approaches Infinity:

   (1) $\lim_{x\to\infty}(\log_a x)=\infty$

   (2) As x increases, $\log_a x$ increases without bound, but more slowly compared to polynomial or exponential functions.

2. Limit as x Approaches Zero from the Right:

   (1) $\lim_{x\to 0^+}(\log_a x)=-\infty$

   (2) As x approaches zero from the right, $\log_a x$ decreases without bound.

Example 6

For the given function $f(x)=2\log_3 x$, evaluate each of the following.

(1) $\lim_{x\to\infty} f(x)$ (2) $\lim_{x\to 0^+} f(x)$

Solution

(1) As x approaches infinity, $\log_3 x$ increases without bound. Therefore,

$$\lim_{x\to\infty} f(x)=\lim_{x\to\infty}(2\log_3 x)=\infty.$$

$\lim_{x\to\infty} f(x)=\infty$

(2) As x approaches zero from the right, $\log_3 x$ decreases without bound. Therefore,

$$\lim_{x\to 0^+} f(x)=\lim_{x\to 0^+}(2\log_3 x)=-\infty.$$

$\lim_{x\to 0^+} f(x)=-\infty$

Check Point 6

Solutions_Page 53

For the given function $f(x)=-\log_2 x$, evaluate each of the following.

(1) $\lim_{x\to\infty} f(x)$ (2) $\lim_{x\to 0^+} f(x)$

Review Exercise

01 Write the logarithmic equation in exponential form.

(1) $\log_2 32=5$

(2) $\log_{11} 1=0$

(3) $\log_{25} 5=\frac{1}{2}$

(4) $\log_6 \left(\frac{1}{216}\right)=-3$

(5) $\log_{\frac{2}{3}} \left(\frac{8}{27}\right)=3$

(6) $\log_{\frac{1}{2}} 16=-4$

02 Write the exponential equation in logarithmic form.

(1) $7^2=49$

(2) $16^0=1$

(3) $25^{\frac{3}{2}}=125$

(4) $3^{-4}=\frac{1}{81}$

03 Solve for x.

(1) $\log_4 64=x$

(2) $\log_{64} 4=x$

(3) $\frac{2}{3}\log_4 x=-2$

(4) $\frac{1}{10}\log_{\frac{1}{3}} x=-\frac{3}{5}$

(5) $\log_2(\log_4 x)=-1$

(6) $x=\log_{\frac{1}{5}} 25-2$

04 Sketch the graph of the function.

(1) $y=\log_3 x$

(2) $y=\log_{\frac{1}{2}} x$

(3) $y=\log_4(-x)$

05 Sketch the graph of the function.

(1) $f(x)=\log_2(x+3)$

(2) $g(x)=\log_3 x-2$

(3) $y=\log_4(x-1)+4$

Review Exercise

06 Sketch the graph of the function.

(1) $g(x)=\log_3(-x)-2$

(2) $y=-\log_{\frac{2}{3}}(x-3)+5$

07 Find the base b such that $\log_b 4=-\frac{2}{3}$.

08 Evaluate $\log_{2\sqrt{2}}\left(\frac{1}{64}\right)$.

09 Solve the equation $y=2\log_3(3x-1)-1$ for x in terms of y.

x	y
1	2
2	4
3	8

10 The table above shows the values of x and their corresponding y values for the function $y=2^x$. Which of the following represents the correct values for $\log_2 y$?

(A) $\log_2 2=2$, $\log_2 4=4$, $\log_2 8=8$
(B) $\log_2 2=0.5$, $\log_2 4=1$, $\log_2 8=1.5$
(C) $\log_2 2=1$, $\log_2 4=2$, $\log_2 8=3$
(D) $\log_2 2=0$, $\log_2 4=1$, $\log_2 8=2$

11 Which of the following is equal to 3?

(A) $3\log_3 6$
(B) $-\frac{1}{4}\log_4\left(\frac{1}{64}\right)$
(C) $\frac{1}{2}\log_4 128$
(D) $-\frac{3}{2}\log_5 \frac{1}{25}$

12 If $a=\dfrac{\log_4 5}{2}$, which of the following is true?

(A) $4^a=5\cdot 2$

(B) $4^a=\dfrac{5}{2}$

(C) $4^{2a}=5$

(D) $4^a=5^2$

13 Which of the following tables indicates that f is a logarithmic function given $y=f(x)$?

(A)

x	1	2	3	4
y	5	10	15	20

(B)

x	1	2	3	4
y	3	6	12	24

(C)

x	5	10	20	40
y	1	2	3	4

(D)

x	3	9	15	21
y	1	2	3	4

14 If the function h is given by $h(x)=2^{3x}-2$, which of the following expression is equal to $h^{-1}(x)$

(A) $\dfrac{1}{3}\log_2(x+2)$

(B) $\dfrac{1}{3}\log_2 x+2$

(C) $\log_2 x+\dfrac{2}{3}$

(D) $\log_2(3x+2)$

15 If the function f is given by $f(x)=\log_3(\log_2 x)$, what is the expression for $f^{-1}(x)$ in terms of x?

16 For the function $f(x)=-\dfrac{1}{2}\log_3 x$, which of the following must be true?

(A) The graph of f increases without bound as x increases without bound.

(B) The rate of f increases without bound as x increases without bound.

(C) As x approaches zero from the right, the graph of f decreases without bound.

(D) The graph of f is always concave down.

Review Exercise

x	$y=5^x$	$y=\log_5 x$
1	A	B
5	C	D

17 The table above provides values for x and their corresponding values for the functions $y=5^x$ and $y=\log_5 x$. What is the value of $A+B+C+D$?

18 If the exponential function f is given by $f(x)=4^x$, which of the following could be a table of values for the inverse function of f?

(A)

x	$f^{-1}(x)$
3	64
5	1024

(B)

x	$f^{-1}(x)$
64	3
1024	5

(C)

x	$f^{-1}(x)$
-2	$\frac{1}{16}$
-4	$\frac{1}{256}$

(D)

x	$f^{-1}(x)$
$-\frac{1}{16}$	2
$-\frac{1}{256}$	4

19 The exponential function f is given by $f(x)=4^x-12$. Determine the domain of the inverse function of f.

20 The function g is an increasing function where each time the output value increases by 1, the corresponding input values triples. Which of the following could define g?

(A) $g(x)=3x$
(B) $g(x)=x^3$
(C) $g(x)=3^x$
(D) $g(x)=\log_3 x$

21 The function f is given by $f(x)=a\log_b(2x-c)$, where a, b, and c are all positive constants greater than 1. Which of the following intervals is the domain of the function f?

(A) (c^a, ∞)
(B) $\left(\frac{c}{2}, \infty\right)$
(C) $(-\infty, 2c)$
(D) $(-\infty, c^a)$

22 The logarithmic function f is given by $f(x)=2\log_4(x-2)+1$. Which of the following is true about the graph of f?

(A) The graph of f is increasing at an increasing rate over the given domain.

(B) The graph of f is increasing at an decreasing rate over the given domain.

(C) The graph of f is decreasing at an increasing rate over the given domain.

(D) The graph of f is decreasing at an decreasing rate over the given domain.

23 Which of the following is true about the graph of $f(x)=2\log_5(x+1)-2$?

(A) $\lim_{x\to -1^+} f(x)=-1$ and $\lim_{x\to\infty} f(x)=-2$

(B) $\lim_{x\to -1^+} f(x)=-\infty$ and $\lim_{x\to\infty} f(x)=-2$

(C) $\lim_{x\to -1^+} f(x)=-1$ and $\lim_{x\to\infty} f(x)=\infty$

(D) $\lim_{x\to -1^+} f(x)=-\infty$ and $\lim_{x\to\infty} f(x)=\infty$

5 Properties of Logarithms

01 Properties of Logarithms

Assume $a>0$, $a\neq 1$, $m>0$, $n>0$, and t is real number.

1. $\log_a a=1$ and $\log_a 1=0$ → Definition of Logarithm
2. $\log_a(mn)=\log_a m+\log_a n$ → Product Property
3. $\log_a\left(\frac{m}{n}\right)=\log_a m-\log_a n$ → Quotient Property
4. $t\log_a m=\log_a m^t$ → Power Property
5. $a^{\log_a m}=m$ → Inverse Property

Note The logarithm with base 10 is called the **common logarithm** and it usually is denoted by **log m**, which is equal to **log_10 m**.

Proof

1. Since $a^1=a$, where base is a and exponent is 1, $\log_a a=1$.
   Since $a^0=1$, where base is a and exponent is 0, $\log_a 1=0$.
2. Let $\log_a m=x$ and $\log_a n=y$. Then $a^x=m$ and $a^y=n$. So $mn=a^x\cdot a^y=a^{x+y}$.
   This implies that $\log_a(mn)=x+y=\log_a m+\log_a n$.
3. Let $\log_a m=x$ and $\log_a n=y$. Then $a^x=m$ and $a^y=n$. So $\frac{m}{n}=\frac{a^x}{a^y}=a^{x-y}$.
   This implies that $\log_a\left(\frac{m}{n}\right)=x-y=\log_a m-\log_a n$.
4. Let $\log_a m=x$. Then $a^x=m$, $(a^x)^t=(m)^t$, $a^{xt}=m^t$.
   This implies that $\log_a m^t=xt=t\log_a m$.
5. If $a^{\log_a m}=m$,
   then $\log_a a^{\log_a m}=\log_a m$, $\log_a m\cdot\log_a a=\log_a m$, $\log_a m=\log_a m$,
   which proves $a^{\log_a m}=m$.

Example 1

Evaluate the logarithm.

① $\log_6 6$ ② $\log_5 1$ ③ $\log 10$

④ $\log_2 8+2\log_3 9$ ⑤ $\log_3\left(\frac{1}{81}\right)-3\log_2\left(\frac{1}{64}\right)$ ⑥ $2^{\log_2 5}$

Solution

① $\log_6 6=1$

② $\log_5 1=0$

③ $\log 10=\log_{10}10=1$

④ $\log_2 8+2\log_3 9$
$=\log_2 2^3+2\log_3 3^2$
$=3\log_2 2+2\cdot 2\log_3 3$
$=3+4=7$

⑤ $\log_3\left(\frac{1}{81}\right)-3\log_2\left(\frac{1}{64}\right)$
$=\log_3 3^{-4}-3\log_2 2^{-6}$
$=-4\log_3 3-3\cdot(-6)\log_2 2$
$=-4+18=14$

⑥ $2^{\log_2 5}=5$

✔ Be careful with following calculations.

(1) $\log_a(m+n)\neq\log_a m+\log_a n$

(2) $\log_a(mn)\neq\log_a m\times\log_a n$

(3) $\frac{\log_a m}{\log_a n}\neq\log_a m-\log_a n$

(4) $\log_a m\cdot\log_a n\neq\log_a m+\log_a n$

(5) $(\log_a m)^n\neq n\log_a m$

Check Point 1

Solutions_Page 59

Evaluate the logarithm.

① $\log_4 4+\log_9 1$ ② $\log_2 8+\log_4 2$ ③ $\log_5\sqrt{25}-\frac{1}{2}\log_3 27$

02 Change of Base Formula

Assume $a>0$, $a\neq1$, and $b>0$.

1. $\log_a b=\dfrac{\log_m b}{\log_m a}$ $(m>0,\ m\neq1)$
2. $\log_a b=\dfrac{1}{\log_b a}$ $(b\neq1)$

Proof

1. Let $\log_a b=x$. Then $a^x=b$, $\log_m a^x=\log_m b$, $x\log_m a=\log_m b$.

   So $x=\dfrac{\log_m b}{\log_m a}$, $\log_a b=\dfrac{\log_m b}{\log_m a}$.

2. Let $\log_a b=x$. Then $a^x=b$, $\log_b a^x=\log_b b$, $x\log_b a=1$.

   So $x=\dfrac{1}{\log_b a}$, $\log_a b=\dfrac{1}{\log_b a}$.

For example,

1. $\log_2 3=\dfrac{\log_4 3}{\log_4 2}=\dfrac{\log_5 3}{\log_5 2}$ → Base could be any positive number, but 1
2. $\log_2 3=\dfrac{1}{\log_3 2}$

03 Natural Logarithm and its Properties

The number e is called Euler's number and it is approximately 2.71828. We will talk more about Euler's number in the section of Application of Exponentials and Logarithms. The logarithm with base e is called the natural logarithm and it usually is denoted by $\ln m$, which is equal to $\log_e m$.

Assume $m>0$, $n>0$, and t is real number.

1. $\ln e=1$, $\ln 1=0$
2. $\ln(mn)=\ln m+\ln n$
3. $\ln\left(\frac{m}{n}\right)=\ln m-\ln n$
4. $t\ln m=\ln m^t$
5. $e^{\ln m}=m$
6. $\log_n m=\frac{\ln m}{\ln n}$ $(n\neq1)$

For example,

1. $\ln 10=\ln(2\times5)=\ln 2+\ln 5$
2. $\ln\left(\frac{5}{2}\right)=\ln 5-\ln 2$
3. $\ln 9=\ln 3^2=2\ln 3$
4. $e^{\ln 6}=6$
5. $\log_2 3=\frac{\ln 3}{\ln 2}$

Example 2

Expand the logarithmic expression.

① $\log_2(8y^3)$ ② $\log_3\left(\frac{y^3}{9x^4}\right)$

Solution

① $\log_2(8y^3)=\log_2 8+\log_2 y^3=\log_2 2^3+3\log_2 y=3\log_2 2+3\log_2 y=3+3\log_2 y$

② $\log_3\left(\frac{y^3}{9x^4}\right)=\log_3 y^3-\log_3 3^2-\log_3 x^4=3\log_3 y-2\log_3 3-4\log_3 x=3\log_3 y-2-4\log_3 x$

Check Point 2

Solutions_Page 59

Expand the logarithmic expression.

① $\log_3\left(\frac{x}{9}\right)$ ② $\ln\left(\frac{ab^4}{\sqrt{c}}\right)$ ③ $\log_4 \sqrt[4]{256x^3}$

Example 3

Write the expression as a single logarithm.

① $2\log(x-4)+3\log y-\log x$ ② $4-2\ln a-\frac{2}{3}\ln b$

Solution

① $2\log(x-4)+3\log y-\log x$

$=\log(x-4)^2+\log y^3-\log x=\log\left(\frac{y^3(x-4)^2}{x}\right)$

② $4-2\ln a-\frac{2}{3}\ln b$

$=4\ln e-\ln a^2-\ln b^{\frac{2}{3}}=\ln e^4-\ln a^2-\ln\sqrt[3]{b^2}=\ln\left(\frac{e^4}{a^2\sqrt[3]{b^2}}\right)$

Check Point 3

Solutions_Page 59

Write the expression as a single logarithm.

① $\log_2 3-\log_2 x$ ② $2\log_5 2+4\log_5 x$

③ $5\log 2-\frac{1}{2}\log a-\frac{5}{2}\log b$ ④ $\ln a-\frac{1}{2}(3\ln b+4)$

Review Exercise

01 Evaluate the logarithm.

(1) $\frac{1}{2}\log_3\left(\frac{1}{3}\right)+2\log_5 25$

(2) $\log\left(\frac{1}{1000}\right)-\log\left(\frac{1}{10}\right)+2\log\left(\frac{1}{100}\right)$

(3) $\log_3\sqrt{27}+\frac{1}{2}\log_3 3-\log_3\sqrt[3]{9}$

(4) $2\ln e^3+\ln 25+2\ln 2$

(5) $2^{\log_2 4-\frac{1}{2}\log_2 64}$

(6) $5^{\log_5 60-\log_5 3-1}$

02 Use calculator to evaluate the logarithm.

(1) $\log_2 5$

(2) $\log_{\frac{1}{3}}\left(\frac{7}{9}\right)$

03 Expand the logarithmic expression.

(1) $\log_2(16x^2y)$

(2) $\log_4\left(\frac{y^2}{16x}\right)$

(3) $\log_e\sqrt{\frac{ab^2}{4}}$

(4) $\ln\left(\frac{\sqrt[3]{ab^5}}{2}\right)$

Review Exercise

04 Write the expression as a single logarithm.

(1) $2(\log_4 x - \log_4 z)$

(2) $3\log_2 x + \frac{3}{2}\log_2 y + 3$

(3) $\frac{1}{2}(\log_a(x^2 - x - 2) - \log_a(x-2) - 2\log_a x)$

05 Find the value of the logarithmic expression given that $\log_a 2 = 0.64$, $\log_a 3 = 1.12$, and $\log_a 5 = 1.64$

(1) $\log_a 90$

(2) $\log_a\left(\frac{12}{25}\right)$

(3) $\log_a \sqrt{108}$

06 If $\log_b \sqrt{a} = c$, then what is $2\log_b a^3$ in terms of c?

07 If $\log_7(\log_5(\log_2 k))=0$, what is the value of k?

08 If $\log_k 2=a$, $\log_k 3=b$, and $\log_k 5=c$, write $\log_k\left(\frac{108}{25}\right)$ in terms of a, b, and c.

09 For all positive real numbers m, $\frac{\log_2 m^5}{\log_4 m^5}=?$

(A) 2

(B) $\frac{1}{2}$

(C) $2m$

(D) $\frac{m}{2}$

10 What is the value of $9^{\log_3 5}$?

11 What is the value of

$\log_4 6\times\log_6 8\times\log_8 10\times\log_{10} 16$?

12 The function f is given by $f(x)=\ln x$. Which of the following expression is equal to $3f(a)-0.5f(b)$, where a and b are both positive integers?

(A) $\ln\frac{a^3}{\sqrt{b}}$

(B) $\frac{\ln a^3}{\ln\sqrt{b}}$

(C) $\frac{3}{2}\ln\frac{a}{b}$

(D) $\ln\sqrt{\frac{a^3}{b}}$

Review Exercise

13 If the function f is given by $f(x)=\log_4 x$, then which of the following expression is equal to $f(x^2)+f\left(\frac{x}{16}\right)$?

(A) $\frac{(\log_4 x)^3}{2}$

(B) $\frac{3}{2}\log_4 x$

(C) $(\log_4 x)^3-2$

(D) $3\log_4 x-2$

14 If $\ln a-\frac{1}{2}\ln b=2\left(\ln m-\frac{1}{2}\ln n\right)+3\ln k$, where a, b, m, n, and k are all positive constants, which of the following expressions is equal to a?

(A) $\frac{m^2k^3\sqrt{b}}{n}$

(B) $\frac{m^2k^3}{n\sqrt{b}}$

(C) $\frac{k^3\sqrt{bm}}{n}$

(D) $\frac{k^3}{n}\sqrt{\frac{m}{b}}$

15 If the function f is given by $f(x)=\log x^4$ and $g(x)=\frac{x}{10}$, then which of the following expression is equal to $f(g(x))$?

(A) $\left(\frac{\log x}{10}\right)^4$

(B) $(\log x-1)^4$

(C) $4\log x-4$

(D) $(\log x-10)^4$

16 If the logarithmic expression $\log_3\left(\frac{27^{2m}}{81^n}\right)$ is equivalent to the expression $am+bn$, what is the value of $a+b$?

17 The function f and g are given by $f(x)=\log_5 x$ and $g(x)=2\log_5(x^2)$, respectively. Which of the following describes a transformation where the graph of g is the image of the graph of f?

(A) A vertical dilation by a factor of 2

(B) A vertical dilation by a factor of 4

(C) A horizontal dilation by a factor of $\frac{1}{2}$

(D) A horizontal dilation by a factor of $\frac{1}{4}$

18 The function f and g are given by $f(x)=\log_2 x$ and $g(x)=\log_2(2x)$, respectively. Which of the following describes a transformation where the graph of g is the image of the graph of f?

I. A vertical dilation by a factor of 2

II. A horizontal dilation by a factor of $\frac{1}{2}$

III. Vertical translation of 1 unit up

(A) I only

(B) II only

(C) III only

(D) II and III only

19 If the function f is given by $f(x)=2\log_4(4x-1)-1$, what is the expression for $f^{-1}(x)$ in terms of x?

20 If the function g is given by $g(x)=2\ln x+\frac{1}{2}\ln x$, which of the following expression is equal to $g^{-1}(x)$

(A) e^{2x+5}

(B) e^{5x+2}

(C) $e^{\frac{2x}{5}}$

(D) $e^{\frac{5x}{2}}$

21 The function y is given by $y=4\cdot 3^{x+1}$. If the value of $a+b$ is equal to $\log k$ in the equation $\log y=ax+b$, what is the value of k?

6 Exponential and Logarithmic Equations

In this section, we will solve various types of exponential and logarithmic equations. Literally, exponential equations are equations that involve a variable in an exponent and logarithmic equations are equations that involve the logarithm of a variable or variable expression. We apply two crucial strategies for solving exponential and logarithmic equations. They are One-to-One Property and Power Property.

01 Exponential Equations

1. One-to-One Properties
   (1) Assume $a>0$ and $a\neq 1$
   If $a^m=a^n$, then $m=n$.
   (2) Assume $a>0$, $a\neq 1$, $b>0$, and $b\neq 1$.
   If $a^m=b^m$, then $a=b$ or $m=0$.

2. Power Property
   Assume $a>0$, $a\neq 1$, $m>0$, $n>0$, and t is real number.
   $\log_a m^t = t\log_a m$

Strategies for Solving Exponential Equations

1. Isolate the exponential term on one side of the equation.
2. Use properties of exponents to solve for the variable.
3. If number 2 is not possible, take the logarithm on each side of the equation to bring down the exponent.

✔ The best choice for the base of log operation is the base of the exponential expression itself. However, we can also use the common base of 10, or the natural base of e (denoted by ln) and still have the same answers. Consider the equation $2^x=5$.

$2^x=5$		$2^x=5$		$2^x=5$
$\log_2 2^x=\log_2 5$		$\log 2^x=\log 5$		$\ln 2^x=\ln 5$
$x\log_2 2=\log_2 5$	or	$x\log 2=\log 5$	or	$x\ln 2=\ln 5$
$x=\log_2 5$		$x=\dfrac{\log 5}{\log 2}$		$x=\dfrac{\ln 5}{\ln 2}$

Using the calculator, we can see that all three value are equal ($x\approx 2.322$).

4. Then solve for the variable.

Example 1

Solve the equation.

① $3(2^{x-2})=48$ ② $3^{2x}=6$ ③ $(\sqrt{2})^x=8\cdot 2^{2x}$

Solution

① $3(2^{x-2})=48$

$2^{x-2}=16$	→ Divide by 3
$2^{x-2}=2^4$	→ $16=2^4$
$x-2=4$	→ One-to-one property
$x=6$	→ Solve for x

$x=6$

② $3^{2x}=6$

$\log_3 3^{2x}=\log_3 6$	→ Take the log with base 3 on each side
$2x\cdot\log_3 3=\log_3 6$	→ Power property
$2x\cdot\log_3 3=\log_3 6$	→ $\log_3 3=1$
$x=\dfrac{\log_3 6}{2}$	→ Divide each side by 2

$x=\dfrac{\log_3 6}{2}$

③ $(\sqrt{2})^x=8\cdot 2^{2x}$

$\left(2^{\frac{1}{2}}\right)^x=2^3\cdot 2^{2x}$	→ $\sqrt{2}=2^{\frac{1}{2}}$ and $8=2^3$
$2^{\frac{x}{2}}=2^{3+2x}$	→ Property of exponents
$\dfrac{x}{2}=3+2x$	→ One-to-one property
$x=-2$	→ Solve for x

$x=-2$

Check Point 1

Solutions_Page 63

Solve the equation.

① $5^{x-4}=125$ ② $64^{2x+1}=\dfrac{1}{256}$

③ $4^x-2=10$ ④ $e^{0.1x}-7=-4$

02 Logarithmic Equations

1. One-to-One Properties

(1) If $\log_a m = \log_b m$, then $a=b$ or $m=1$.
(2) Assume $m>0$ and $n>0$.
If $\log_a m = \log_a n$, then $m=n$.

Strategies for Solving Logarithmic Equations

1. Isolate the logarithmic terms on one side of the equation and then combine them as a single logarithm.
2. Write the equation in exponential form.
3. Solve for the variable.
4. Check for extraneous solutions.

Example 2

Solve the equation. Check for extraneous solutions.

① $\log(-3x-1)=\log(-4x-6)$ ② $\log_2(x+1)-4=0$

③ $\log_3 x^2=4$ ④ $\log_2 x+\log_2 (x-1)=1$

Solution

① $\log(-3x-1)=\log(-4x-6)$

$-3x-1=-4x-6$ → One-to-one Property

$x=-5$ → Solve for x

Check the solution

$\log(-3(-5)-1)=\log(-4(-5)-6)$

$\log(14)=\log(14)$

Solution checks!

$x=-5$

② $\log_2(x+1)-4=0$

$\log_2(x+1)=4$ → Isolate the logarithmic term

$x+1=2^4$ → Change to exponential form

$x=15$ → Solve for x

Check the solution

$\log_2(15+1)-4=\log_2 16-4=4-4=0$

Solution checks!

$x=15$

③ $\log_3 x^2=4$

$x^2=3^4$ → Change to exponential form

$x^2=81$ → $3^4=81$

$x=9$ or $x=-9$ → Solve for x

Check the solution: $x=9$

$\log_3 9^2=\log_3 81=4$

Solution checks!

Check the solution: $x=-9$

$\log_3(-9)^2=\log_3 81=4$

Solution checks!

$x=\pm 9$

Be careful with following calculation!

$\log_3 x^2=4$

$2\log_3 x=4$ → Power property

$\log_3 x=2$ → Divide by 2

$x=3^2$ → Change to exponential form

$x=9$ → Solve for x

✔ We need to be aware of the fact that the domain of $\log_3 x^2$ is all nonzero real numbers

④ $\log_2 x+\log_2(x-1)=1$

$\log_2 x(x-1)=1$ → Product property

$x(x-1)=2$ → Change to exponential form

$x^2-x-2=0$ → Expand

$(x-2)(x+1)=0$ → Factor

$x=2$ or $x=-1$ → Solve for x

Check the solution: $x=2$

$\log_2 2+\log_2(2-1)=1+\log_2 1=1+0=0$

Solution checks!

Check the solution: $x=-1$

$\underbrace{\log_2(-1)}_{\text{Undefined}}+\underbrace{\log_2(-1-1)}_{\text{Undefined}}\neq 1$

$x=-1$ is an extraneous solution. Therefore, the only solution is $x=2$.

$x=2$

Check Point 2

Solutions_Page 63

Solve the equation. Check for extraneous solutions.

① $4+\log_2(x+1)=6$

② $\log_2(x+1)-\log_2(x-2)=1$

③ $\log_4(2x+1)=\log_4 5+\log_4(-x-4)$

④ $\ln\sqrt{x-4}-3=1$

Review Exercise

Solutions_Page 63

01 Solve the equation.

(1) $2^{2x-3}-32=0$

(2) $3^{x+1}-9\sqrt{27}=0$

(3) $e^{3x-1}-8=2$

(4) $\left(\frac{1}{4}\right)^{1-4x}=4\sqrt[4]{4}$

(5) $2^{x^2-4x}=\left(\frac{1}{2}\right)^{x+2}$

(6) $\left(\frac{2}{3}\right)^{x^2+3x}=\left(\frac{3}{2}\right)^{2x+6}$

02 Solve the equation. Check for extraneous solutions.

(1) $\log_4(4x-2)=\log_4(x+7)$

(2) $\ln(3x-5)=2$

(3) $\log(x^2-3x)=1$

(4) $\log_3(2x-1)+\log_3(x-2)=2$

03 If $2^{m-1}=n$, what is the value of m in terms of n?

(A) $\ln n-\ln 2+1$

(B) $\ln\left(\frac{n}{2}\right)+1$

(C) $\frac{\ln n}{\ln 2}+1$

(D) $\frac{\ln n+1}{\ln 2}$

(E) $\frac{\ln 2}{\ln n+1}$

04 If a and b are both nonzero real numbers and $1.24^a=4.25^b$, what is the value of $\frac{a}{b}$?

05 Find the solution to the equation $4^{2x+3}-2=4$.

06 If $\log_4(\log_3(\log_2 k))=\frac{1}{2}$, what is the value of k?

07 If $a \cdot 3^b = 15$ and $a \cdot 27^b = 60$, what is the value of b?

08 Find the solution(s) to the equation $9^x - 3^x - 6 = 0$.

09 Solve the equation.

(1) $3^{2x+1} - 3^{2x} = 18$

(2) $\log_3 x + \log_3 (x-2) - 1 = 0$

10 Solve the inequality.

(1) $4^{x+1} > 8^x$

(2) $\log_2 (x^2 - 3x) < 2$

(3) $5^{2x-1} \leq 125^{x-2}$

11 In how intersections do the graph of $y = \log_5 (5x+6)$ and $y = 2\log_5 x$ have?

(A) Zero

(B) One

(C) Two

(D) Infinitely many

Review Exercise

12 Which of the following is the x coordinate(s) of the point(s) of intersection of $y=\ln x$ and $y=\ln(x+2)+\ln(x+6)$?

(A) 3

(B) 4

(C) 3 and 4

(D) There are no intersection points.

13 The function f is given by $f(x)=\log(x-3)+\log(x+2)$. What are all the values of x for which the graph of f is less than $\log 14$?

(A) $-4<x<3$

(B) $-4<x<5$

(C) $3<x<5$

(D) There are no values of x.

14 The function f is given by $f(x)=\ln(3x+14)-\ln(x^2+5x-10)$. What are all the values of x for which $f(x)<0$?

(A) $x<-6$

(B) $x>4$

(C) $x<-6$ or $x>4$

(D) There are no values of x.

memo

7 Application of Exponentials and Logarithms

Application is generally classified as exponential growth and decay. Exponential growth and decay apply to any situation, frequently in business, biology, chemistry, and social science. First, let's find out how to find the balance in the account that earns compound interest.

01 Investment Earning

Investment earning is one of the most familiar examples of exponential growth. Let us derive the formula for investment earning using exponential function.

A: balance or total amount

P: initial investment

r: an annual interest rate

t: number of years

n: number of compoundings per year

(1) The interest is compounded once a year

Year		Balance at the end of each year
0	$P=P$	$A=P$
1	$P_1=P+P\cdot r=P(1+r)$	$A=P(1+r)$
2	$P_2=P_1+P_1(r)=\underline{P_1}(1+r)$ $=\underline{P(1+r)}(1+r)=P(1+r)^2$	$A=P(1+r)^2$
3	$P_3=P_2+P_2(r)=\underline{P_2}(1+r)$ $=\underline{P(1+r)^2}(1+r)=P(1+r)^3$	$A=P(1+r)^3$
⋮	⋮	⋮
t	$P_t=P(1+r)^t$	$A=P(1+r)^t$

(2) The interest is compounded n times per year

In this case, the balance after one compounding period is

$$A=P+\frac{P\cdot r}{n}=P\left(1+\frac{r}{n}\right)$$

Thus, the balance after one year with n compoundings is $A=P\left(1+\frac{r}{n}\right)^n$ and after t years, it is $A=P\left(1+\frac{r}{n}\right)^{nt}$

(3) The interest is compounded continuously

$A=P\left(1+\frac{r}{n}\right)^{nt}$ We let $k=\frac{n}{r} \Rightarrow n=kr$

$A=\left(1+\frac{r}{kr}\right)^{krt}$ Substitute kr for n

$A=P\left(1+\frac{1}{k}\right)^{krt}$ Simplify

$A=P\left[\left(1+\frac{1}{k}\right)^k\right]^{rt}$ Apply property of exponents

$\left(1+\frac{1}{k}\right)^k$ approaches 2.7182818⋯ as $k\to\infty$.

We define this number as e and it is called Euler's number.

Finally, formula for continuous compounding is $A=Pe^{rt}$.

Memorize as formulas!

1. The interest is compounded once a year: $A=P(1+r)^t$
2. The interest is compounded n times per year: $A=P\left(1+\frac{r}{n}\right)^{nt}$
3. The interest is compounded continuously: $A=Pe^{rt}$

✔ Euler's number $e\approx 2.71828$

Example 1

Mr. Smith is investing $1,200 for 15 years at a 5.5% annual interest rate. What will be the balance if it is compounded

① Yearly ② Quarterly ③ Monthly ④ Continuously

Solution

① Yearly

$A=P(1+r)^t$

$A=1200(1+0.055)^{15}=\$2,678.97$

② Quarterly ($n=4$)

$A=P\left(1+\frac{r}{n}\right)^{nt}$

$A=1200\left(1+\frac{0.055}{4}\right)^{(4)(15)}=\$2,722.91$

③ Monthly ($n=12$)

$A=P\left(1+\frac{r}{n}\right)^{nt}$

$A=1200\left(1+\frac{0.055}{12}\right)^{(12)(15)}=\$2,733.10$

④ Continuously

$A=Pe^{rt}$

$A=1200e^{(0.055)(15)}=\$2,738.26$

✔ The more times per year it is compounded, the more interest the investor earns.

Check Point 1

Solutions_Page 67

Assume Rick borrowed \$10,000 at 6% interest annually. What will be the amount after 20 years if the interest is compounded

① Annually ② Quarterly ③ Monthly ④ Continuously

Example 2

Suppose Mr. Smith invested \$3,500 in a bank account at 5% interest compounded continuously.

① How long will it take to double the initial investment?

② How long will it take to triple the initial investment?

③ If Mr. Smith instead invests \$7,000, how long will it take to double?

Solution

① We need use the formula $A=Pe^{rt}$ to solve for t and the amount A becomes \$3,500×2=\$7,000.

$7000=3500e^{0.05t}$, $2=e^{0.05t}$

$\ln 2=\ln e^{0.05t}$, $\ln 2=0.05t \ln e$

$\ln 2=0.05t$, $t=\frac{\ln 2}{0.05} \approx 13.86$

It takes about 13.86 years

② The amount A becomes \$3,500 × 3 = \$10,500.

$10500=3500e^{0.05t}$

$3=e^{0.05t}, \ln 3=\ln e^{0.05t}$

$\ln 3=0.05t \ln e,\ \ln 3=0.05t$

$t=\dfrac{\ln 3}{0.05} \approx 21.97$

It takes about 21.97 years

③ The amount A becomes \$7,000 × 2 = \$14,000.

$14000=7000e^{0.05t},\ 2=e^{0.05t}$

$\ln 2=\ln e^{0.05t},\ \ln 2=0.05t \ln e$

$t=\dfrac{\ln 2}{0.05} \approx 13.86$

It also takes about 13.86 years

✔ Regardless of how much the initial amount is, it takes the same time for the initial amount to double.

Check Point 2

Solutions_Page 67

① How long will it take the initial investment of \$1,000 to double if the interest is 5% and compounded continuously?

② Jason invests \$7,500 in an account that pays 6% interest per year, compounded semi-annually(twice a year). How long will it take for the amount to be \$10,000?

02 Basic Exponential Growth and Decay

Just like we have studied from investment earning, we can use the general form of an exponential function to describe exponential growth or decay. The modeled function is usually stated in the problem. Otherwise, we will have to find ourselves. Through several types of examples, we will discuss how to solve exponential growth or decay problems.

Example 3

Suppose that the population of L.A. increases at a rate of 1.4%. If the current population is 4 million, what will be the population in 20 years?

Solution

$A=Pe^{rt}$, where

P: The initial population t: The time in years

r: The rate A: The future population after t years

$A=Pe^{rt}$

$A=4e^{0.014\times 20}=5.293$

The population of L.A. would be approximately 5.293 million after 20 years

Check Point 3 Solutions_Page 67

Suppose that the number of bacteria in a culture is counted as 250 at the beginning of experiment. If the number of bacteria increases at a rate of 9% per hour, what is the expected number of bacteria present in the culture after 1 day?

Example 4

A certain medicine has a half-life of 12 hours. If a patient is given 20 mg in his blood stream, after how many hours does the patient have 1 mg remaining in his bloodstream?

Note Half-life is the time required for a quantity to reduce to half its initial value.

Solution

$A=Pe^{rt}$, where

P: The initial amount of medicine in patient's bloodstream

t: The time in hours r: The rate

A: The amount of medicine in patient's bloodstream after t hours

$A=Pe^{rt}$

$10=20e^{r\times 12}$ → Half-life is 12 hours

$\frac{1}{2}=e^{12r}$, $\ln\left(\frac{1}{2}\right)=\ln e^{12r}$

$\ln\left(\frac{1}{2}\right)=12r\cdot\ln e$, $r=\frac{1}{12}\ln\left(\frac{1}{2}\right)$

So the equation is $A=20e^{\frac{1}{12}\ln\left(\frac{1}{2}\right)\cdot t}$.

Now, we can determine the time for 1 mg remaining in the bloodstream by substituting 1 for A.

$1=20e^{\frac{1}{12}\ln\left(\frac{1}{2}\right)\cdot t}$

$\frac{1}{20}=e^{\frac{1}{12}\ln\left(\frac{1}{2}\right)\cdot t}$, $\ln\left(\frac{1}{20}\right)=\ln e^{\frac{1}{12}\ln\left(\frac{1}{2}\right)\cdot t}$

$\ln\left(\frac{1}{20}\right)=\frac{1}{12}\ln\left(\frac{1}{2}\right)\cdot t\ \ln e$, $t=\dfrac{12\ln\left(\frac{1}{20}\right)}{\ln\left(\frac{1}{2}\right)}=51.86$

It takes about 51.86 hours

Check Point 4

Solutions_Page 67

A certain radioactive isotope has a half-life of 1,600 years. How many years would it take for an initial quantity of 5 grams to decays to 1 gram?

Review Exercise

01 Charles invests \$2,000 in an account that pays 5.5% interest per year, compounded semiannually. How long will it take for the investment to be \$3,000?

02 A man deposited \$8,000 in a savings account for which the interest is compounded continuously. If the balance will triple in 20 years, what is the annual interest rate for this account?

03 How long will it take an investment to increases in value of 25% if the interest rate is 3.5% compounded quarterly?

04 Mr. Johnson deposited \$500 in a savings account that pays him 4% interest compounded continuously. How long does it take to reach \$600?

05 Suppose that the number of bacteria in a culture is 20 at the beginning of experiment. If the number of bacteria increases at a rate of 40% per hour, what is the expected number of bacteria present in the culture after 8 hours?

06 If the value of a new truck was \$28,000 5 years ago, and by now the value was halved. If the value of this car had decreased by the same percent each year, what is the annual percent decrease during the last 5 years?

07 A town with an initial population of 5,000 increases exponentially. After five years, the population has grown by 20%.

(A) What will the population be after 10 years?

(B) How long will it take for the population to double in size?

08 A culture of bacteria contains 125,000 bacteria at 10A.M. If the culture has 850,000 at 2P.M., how many bacterial will there be at 8 P.M.?

09 If 10 grams of a certain radioactive isotope decays to 2 grams in 1,200 years, what is the half-life of this isotope?

10 A fossilized bone of Native American contains 40% of its original carbon-14 content. Assuming that the half-life of carbon-14 is 5,730 years, approximately how old is the bone?

11 If the number of bacteria in a culture are 10 and is growing by 60% per hour, in how many hours will the number of bacteria first exceed 1,000?

8 Competing Function Model Validation

01 Scatterplot and Regression Model

1. **Scatterplot**: A scatterplot is a type of graph used to display the relationship between two quantitative variables. Each point on the scatterplot represents an observation in the data set, with one variable plotted along the x-axis and the other along the y-axis. Scatterplots are essential for visualizing data patterns, trends, and potential correlations between variables.

2. **Three Regression Models**

(1) Linear Regression: $y=mx+b$
Linear regression models the relationship between two variables by fitting a straight line to the data. The slope m indicates the rate of change of the dependent variable y with respect to the independent variable x.

(2) Quadratic regression: $y=ax^2+bx+c$
Quadratic regression models the relationship between two variables using a parabolic curve. The coefficients a, b, and c determine the shape and position of the parabola.

(3) Exponential regression: $y=a\cdot b^x$
Exponential regression models the relationship between two variables using an exponential function. The base b indicates the growth(if $b>1$) or decay(if $0<b<1$) rate, and the coefficient a represents the initial value.

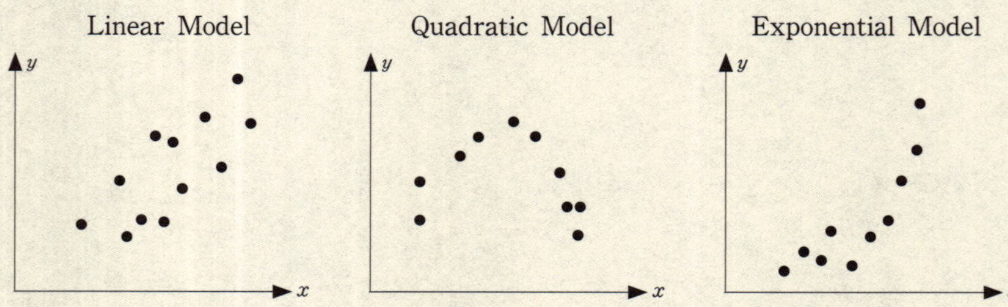

3. Comparison of Models

(1) Linear Model

- Fits data with a constant rate of change.
- Best for straight-line patterns.

(2) Quadratic Model

- Fits data with a variable rate of change, forming a parabola.
- Best for curved patterns with a single peak.

(3) Exponential Model

- Fits data with multiplicative growth or decay.
- Best for rapidly increasing or decreasing patterns.

Example 1

Hours Studied (x)	Test Score (y)
1	60
2	62
3	74
4	80
5	87
6	88

The following table shows the number of hours studied and the corresponding scores obtained by a group of students in a math test. Use linear regression to find the equation of the best-fit line and predict the score for a student who studies for 7 hours.

Solution

Using the calculator, the equation of the best−fit line using linear regression is $y=6.314x+53.067$. Now predict the test score for 7 hours of study:

$$y=6.314(7)+53.067=97.265$$

So, the predicted score is $97.265 \approx 97$. 97

Check Point 1

Solutions_Page 70

Time in seconds (x)	Height in meters (y)
0	4
1	11
2	15
3	17
4	14
5	8

The table above shows the height of a projectile at different times after it is launched. Use quadratic regression to determine the equation that models the height of the projectile as a function of time. Then, use the equation to predict the height of the projectile at 5.5 seconds

02 Residual Plot and Linear Model

Residuals are the differences between observed values and the values predicted by the model. By examining the pattern of the residuals, we can determine if the model is appropriate for the data.

1. Residuals

(1) Residual=Observed Value−Predicted Value

(2) They measure the deviation of data points from the regression line.

(3)

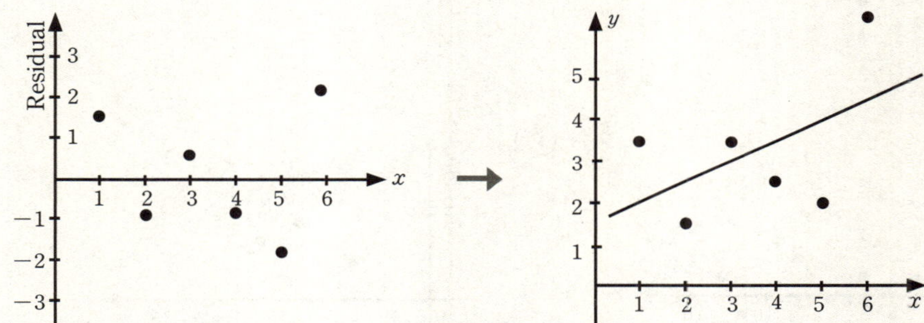

If the residual plot shows no pattern, then the linear model is appropriate.

(4)

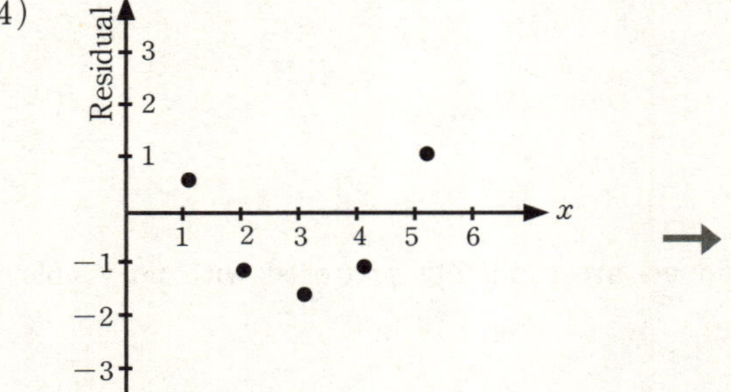

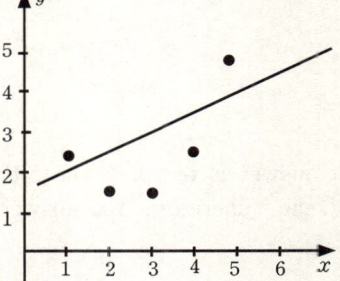

If the residual plot shows a pattern, then the linear model is not appropriate.

(5) Positive residuals indicate that the model underestimated the actual value. On a residual plot, positive residuals appear above the horizontal axis(zero line).

(6) Negative residuals indicate that the model overestimated the actual value. On a residual plot, negative residuals appear below the horizontal axis(zero line).

Example 2

Which of the following residual plots is appropriate for a linear model?

(A)

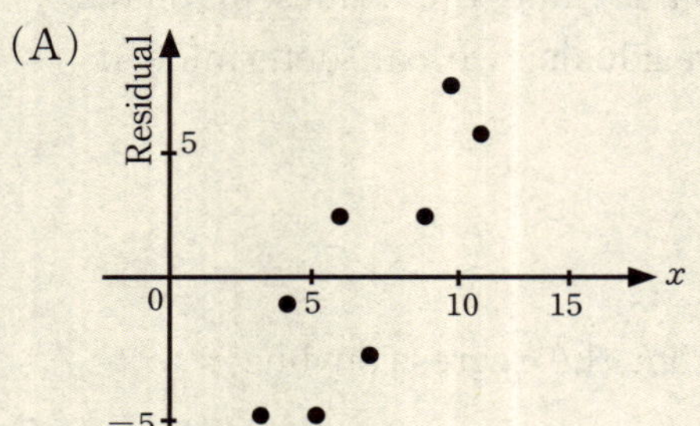

(B)

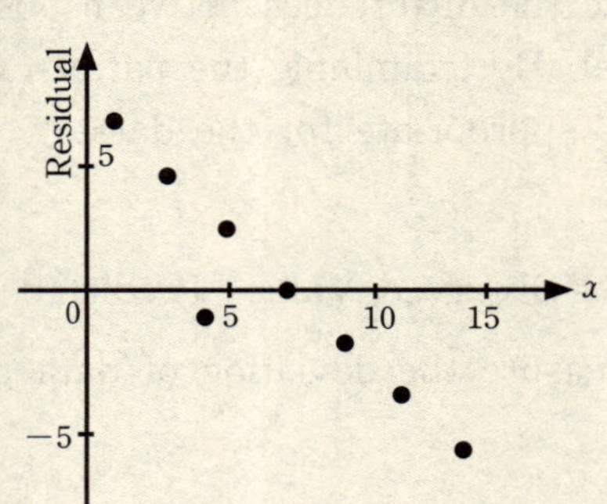

(C)

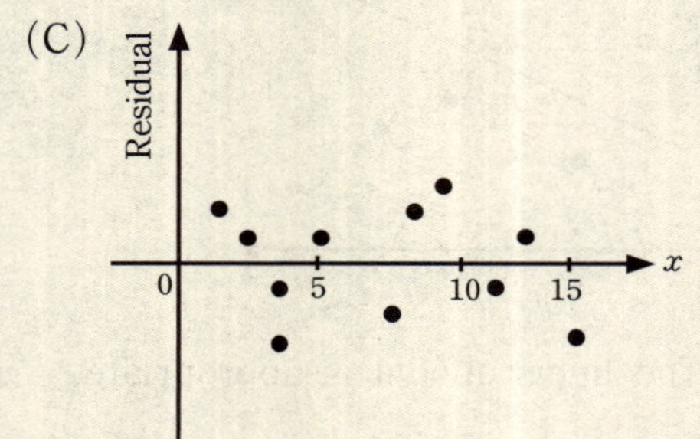

(D)

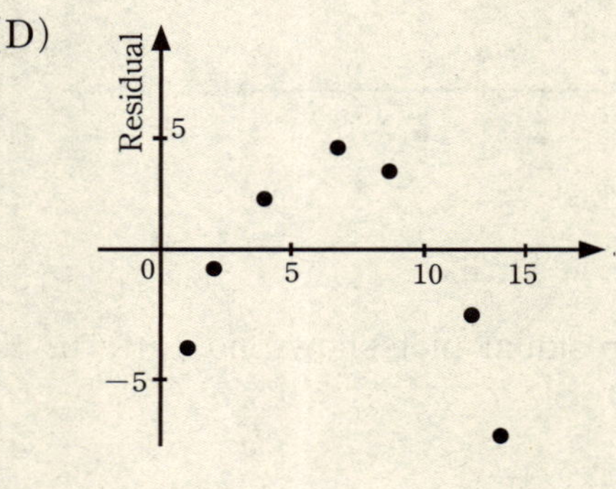

Solution

The correct answer is the plot where the residuals are randomly scattered with no visible pattern or trend. Therefore, the answer is (C).

(C)

Review Exercise

Solutions_Page 70

Time in hours(x)	Population(y)
0	100
1	180
2	324
3	583
4	1049

01 The following table shows the population of a bacteria culture over several hours. Use exponential regression to determine the equation that models the population growth.

(1) Write the exponential equation that models the population growth.

(2) Predict the population of the bacteria culture at 5 hours.

Weight(pounds)(x)	Mileage(mpg)(y)
2000	30
2500	28
3000	25
3500	22
4000	20

02 A car dealership wants to predict the mileage(miles per gallon) of cars based on their weight(in pounds). The following table shows the weights of several cars and their corresponding mileages.

(1) Use linear regression to determine the equation that models the relationship between car weight and mileage.

(2) Predict the mileage of a car that weighs 3200 pounds.

Review Exercise

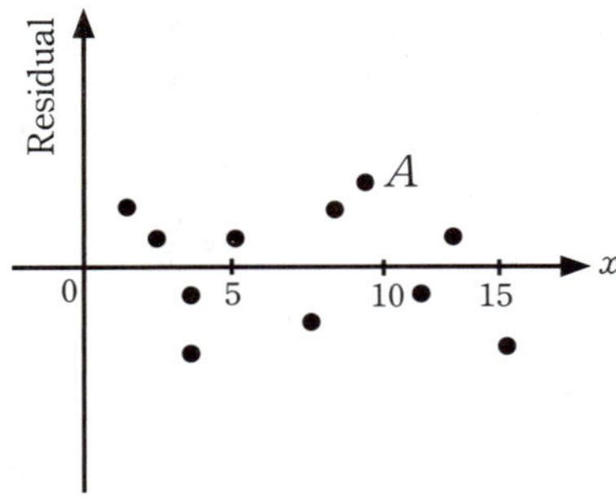

03 The students calculated a linear regression $y=mx+b$ with the number of years of experience as the input values and salary as the output values. The given residual plot has a point labeled A at coordinates (9, 1500). What does point A indicate in the context?

(A) The observed salary for 9 years of experience is \$1,500 higher than the predicted salary.

(B) The observed salary for 9 years of experience is \$1,500 lower than the predicted salary.

(C) The predicted salary for 9 years of experience is \$1,500.

(D) The residual is \$1,500, which means the prediction is perfect.

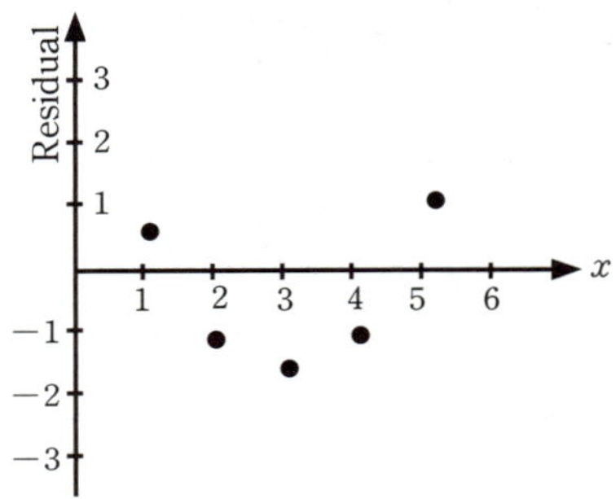

04 The residual plot above is created from the data set. Based on the residual plot, which of the following statements is true?

(A) The residual plot shows no apparent pattern, indicating that the linear regression model is appropriate for the data.

(B) The residual plot shows a curved pattern, indicating that the linear regression model is not appropriate for the data.

(C) The regression equation would overestimate at $x=6$.

(D) We would not know whether the regression equation underestimates or overestimates for a certain data point.

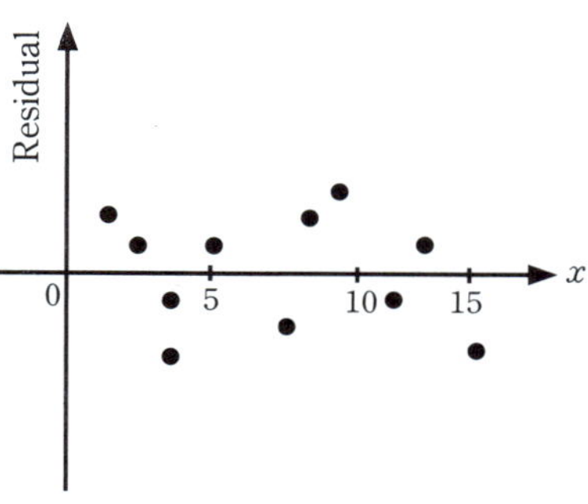

05 Students in a AP Precalculus class are constructing a model for a data set. The residual plot for their linear regression model is given. Which of the following is the best conclusion?

(A) The exponential model is appropriate because the residuals show a pattern.
(B) The exponential model is appropriate because the residuals show no pattern.
(C) The exponential model is not appropriate because the residuals show a pattern.
(D) The exponential model is not appropriate because the residuals show no pattern.

memo

9 Semi-log Plots

01 Semi-log Plots

A semi−log plot is a type of graph that uses a logarithmic scale for one axis (usually the y−axis) and a linear scale for the other axis(usually the x−axis). This type of plot is particularly useful for visualizing data that spans several orders of magnitude, such as exponential growth or decay.

1. Axes

(1) Linear Scale: One axis, typically the x−axis, uses a standard linear scale.

(2) Logarithmic Scale The other axis, typically the y−axis, uses a logarithmic scale, which means that equal distances on this axis represent equal ratios of change.

2. Exponential Functions

(1) When plotting an exponential function of the form $y=a\cdot b^x$, the graph will appear as a straight line. This is because the logarithmic transformation linearizes the exponential relationship.

(2) The slope of this line represents the growth rate of the function.

(3) For instance, let's take a look at the graph of $y=2\cdot 6^x$ on a semi−log plot.

x	0	1	2	3	4
y	2	12	72	432	2592
$\log y$	0.301	1.079	1.857	2.635	3.414

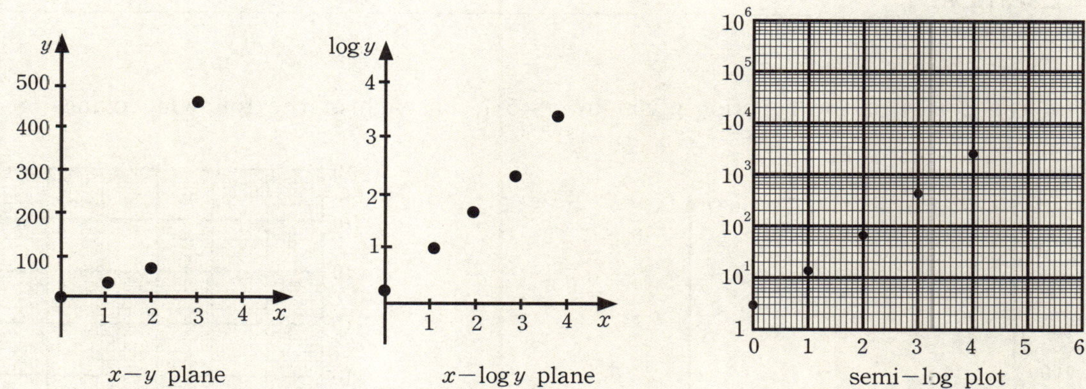

For an exponential function, it appears exponential on an $x-y$ plane but linear on an $x-\log y$ plane or semi−log plot.

3. Logarithmic functions of the form: Logarithmic functions of the form $y=\log_b x$ can also be plotted on semi−log graphs, but they do not produce straight lines. Instead, they retain their logarithmic shape.

4. Interpreting Semi−Log Plots

(1) If the data forms a straight line on a semi−log plot, it indicates an exponential relationship.

(2) The intercept with the y−axis(if the x−axis is linear and the y−axis is logarithmic) represents the initial value a in the exponential function $y=a\cdot b^x$.

Example 1

Plot the points of the function given by $y=5\cdot7^x$ on each of the following planes.

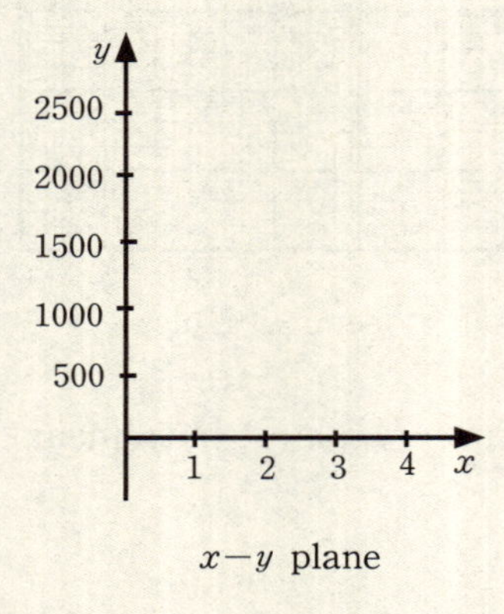

$x-y$ plane

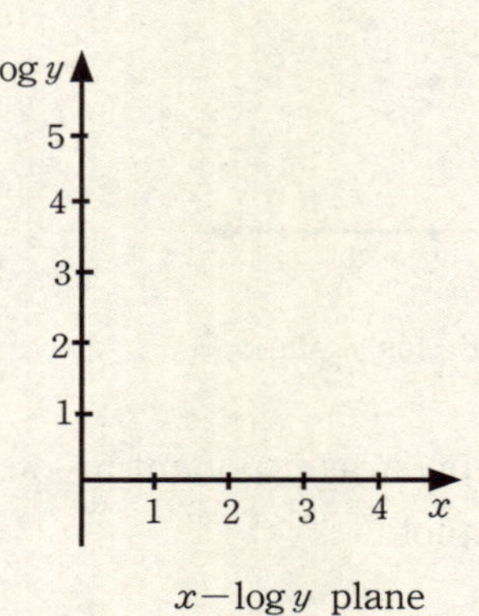

$x-\log y$ plane

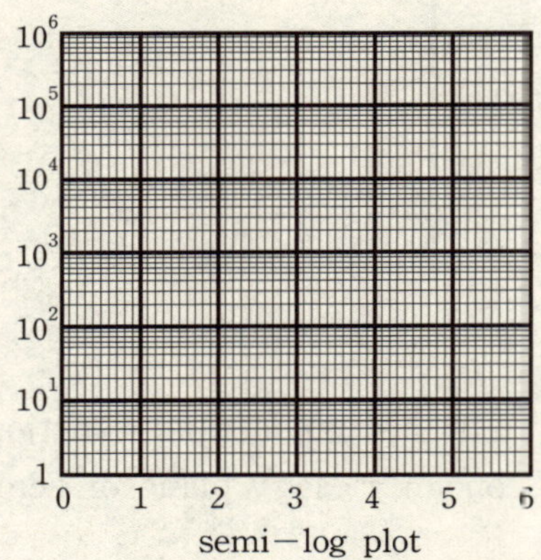

semi−log plot

Solution

x	0	1	2	3	4
y	5	35	245	1715	12005
$\log y$	0.699	1.544	2.389	3.234	4.079

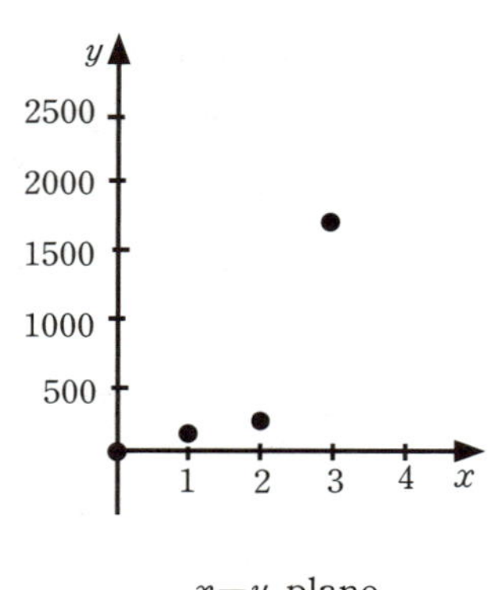

$x-y$ plane

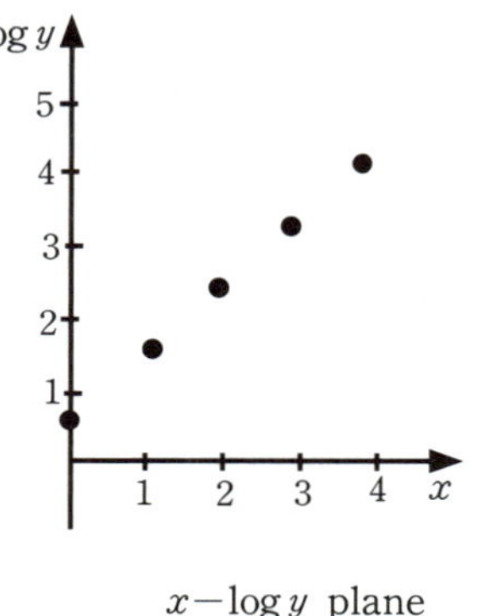

$x-\log y$ plane

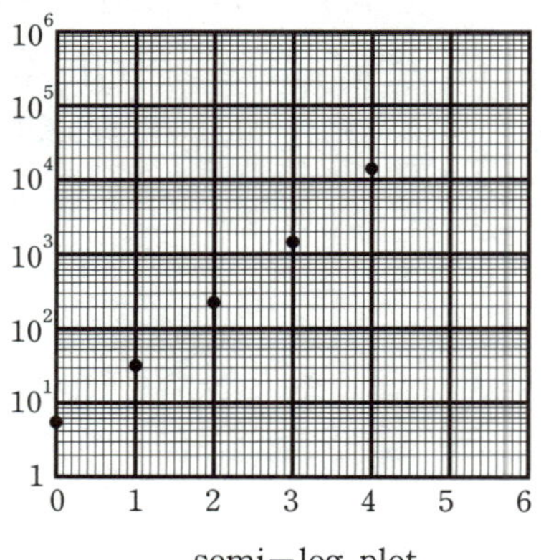

semi−log plot

Check Point 1

Solutions_Page 71

Plot the points of the function given by $y=3300\cdot\left(\frac{1}{6}\right)^x$ on each of the following planes.

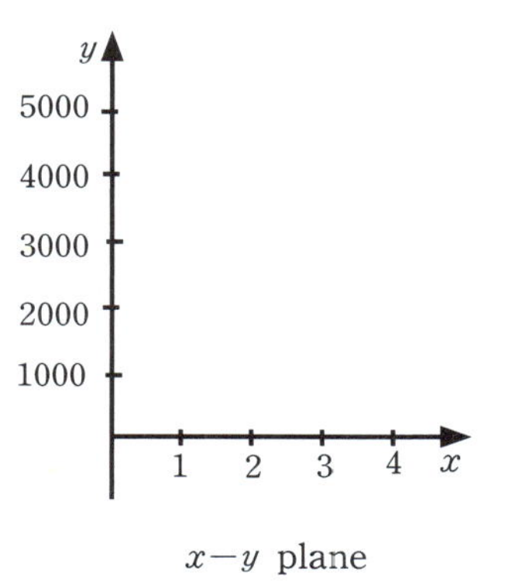

$x-y$ plane

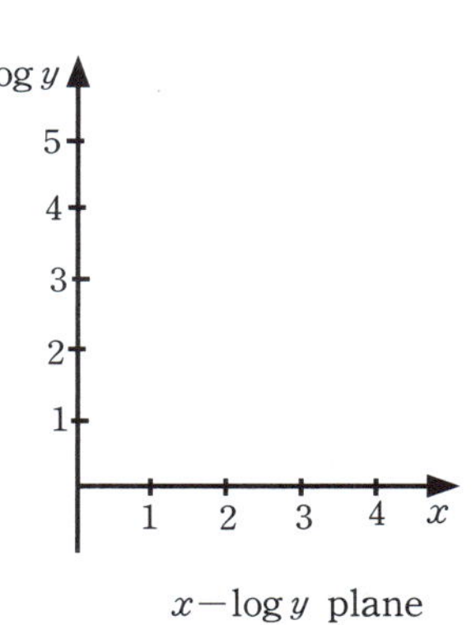

$x-\log y$ plane

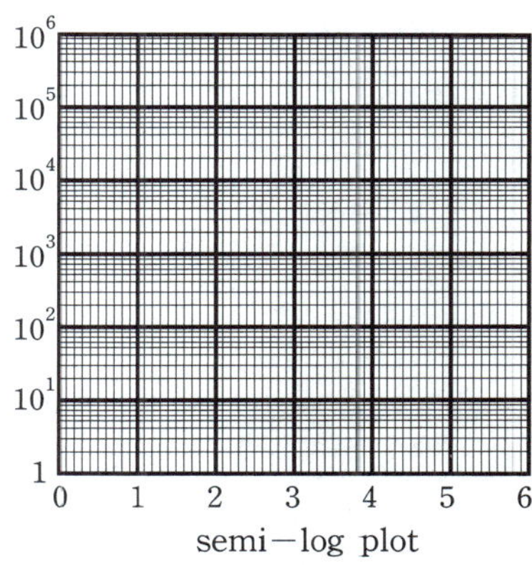

semi$-$log plot

Review Exercise

01 In a semi−log plot, which of the following functions appear linear with slope log2?

(A) $f(x)=2x$
(B) $f(x)=x^2$
(C) $f(x)=2^x$
(D) $f(x)=\log_2 x$

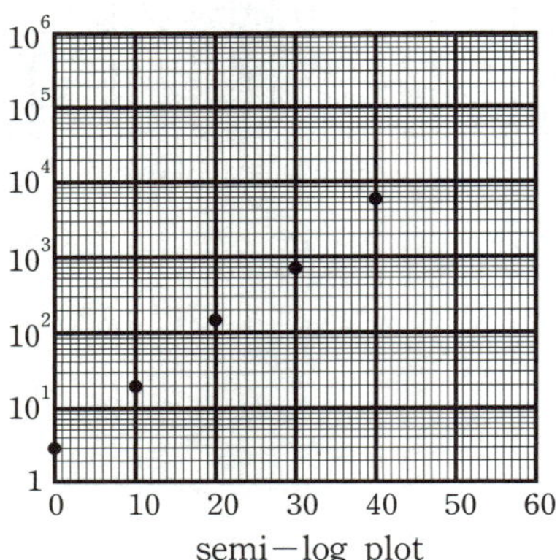

semi−log plot

02 The semi−log plot of points from the function $f(x)$ is given above. Which of the following tables could represent $f(x)$?

(A)

x	0	10	20	30	40
$f(x)$	2	11	12	85	160

(B)

x	0	10	20	30	40
$f(x)$	30	110	205	280	350

(C)

x	0	10	20	30	40
$f(x)$	3	20	130	850	5800

(D)

x	0	10	20	30	40
$f(x)$	30	200	1050	1800	2500

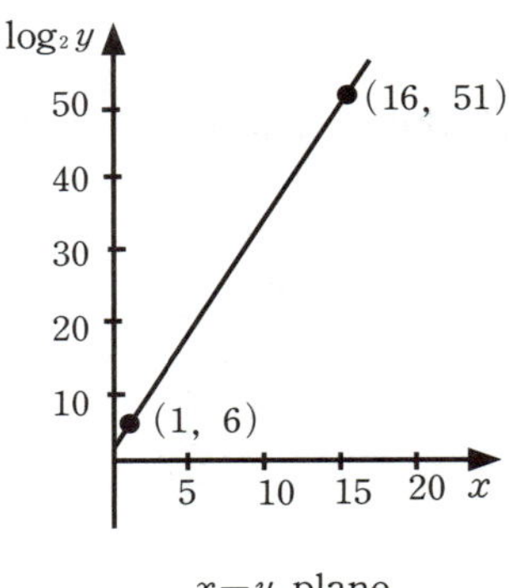

$x-y$ plane

03 Which of the following equations represents the graph above?

(A) $f(x)=3x+3$
(B) $f(x)=3x^2+8$
(C) $f(x)=8\cdot 2^{3x}$
(D) $f(x)=\log_2 x+3$

04 Which of the following represents the graph of exponential function?

I.

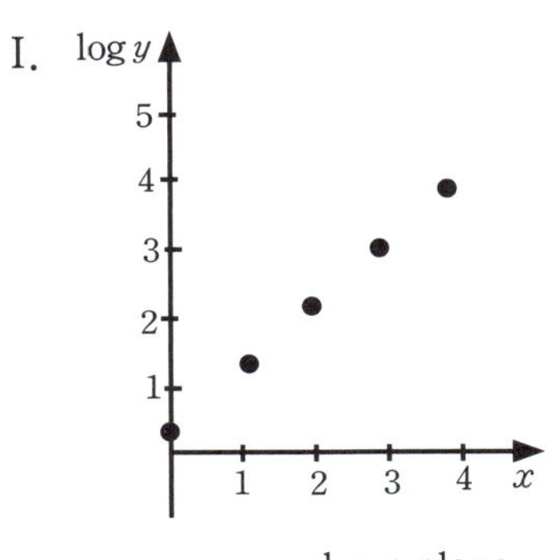

$x-\log y$ plane

II.

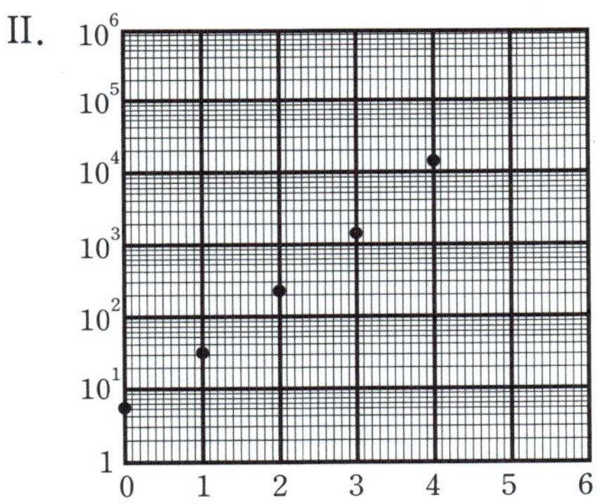

(A) I only

(B) II only

(C) Both I and II

(D) Neither I nor II

05 The function g is given by $g(x)=5\cdot 4^x$. If $\ln(g(x))=ax+b$, what is the value of $a+b$?

(A) $\ln 9$

(B) $\ln 20$

(C) $\ln 4\cdot\ln 5$

(D) $\ln 4^5$

x	1	3	5	7	9
$\log y$	4	8	12	16	20

06 The table above gives selected values of $(x, \log y)$. If $y=h(x)$, which of the following statements is true about the function f?

(A) The function h is exponential because both the values of x and $\log y$ are linear.

(B) The function h is logarithmic because both the values of x and $\log y$ are linear.

(C) The function h is linear because both the values of x and $\log y$ are linear.

(D) The function h can be both exponential and logarithmic because both the values of x and $\log y$ are linear.

Review Exercise

Time(hours)	Population
0	50
2	200
4	800
6	3200
8	12800

07 The table above shows the population of a bacterial culture over several hours. Plot the data on a semi−log plot below and determine the exponential function that models the population growth.

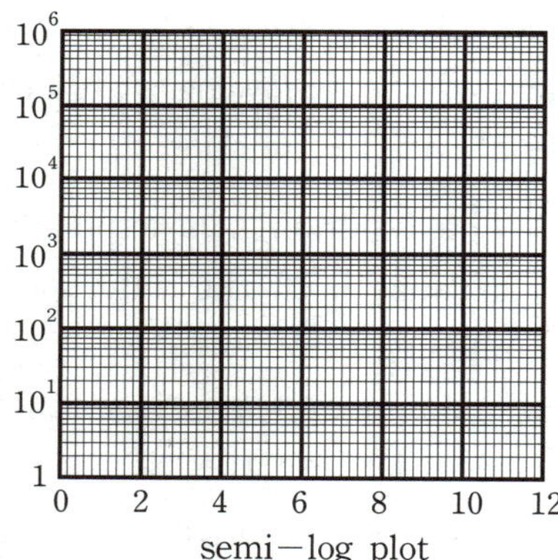

semi−log plot

memo

Unit II Test

01 Sketch the graph of the function $f(x)=\left(\frac{1}{3}\right)^x-2$.

02 Find the function resulted when the graph of the function $y=4^x$ is reflected about the x-axis and shifted 2 units to the right.

03 Write the logarithmic equation in exponential form.

(1) $\log_5 25=2$

(2) $\log_{\frac{1}{3}} 27=-3$

04 Write the exponential equation in logarithmic form.

(1) $4^{-3}=\frac{1}{64}$

(2) $\left(\frac{1}{25}\right)^{\frac{1}{2}}=\frac{1}{5}$

05 Solve for x.

(1) $\frac{1}{2}\log_3 x = -1$

(2) $\log_x 27 = \frac{3}{2}$

06 Sketch the graph of the function $g(x) = -\log_2(x) - 4$.

07 Find the function resulted when the graph of the function $y = \ln x$ is reflected about the $y-$axis and shifted 1 unit to the left and 2 units up.

08 Solve the equation for x in terms of y.

(1) $y = \frac{1}{2}\log_2(x+4)$

(2) $y = 2 + \frac{3}{2}\log_{\frac{1}{2}}(2-x)$

Unit II Test

09 Evaluate the logarithm.

(1) $\frac{1}{2}\log_6 9 - 2\log_6 6 + \log_6 2$

(2) $\ln e^{-2} + \ln\left(\frac{1}{e^4}\right) + 4\ln 1$

(3) $2^{\log_2 6 + 2\log_2 4 - \log_2 5}$

(4) $e^{-\frac{1}{2}\ln 3 + \ln 12}$

10 All of the following are equal EXCEPT

(A) $\log 1000$

(B) $-\log_2 \frac{1}{8}$

(C) $\log_5 15$

(D) $-\log_4\left(\frac{1}{64}\right)$

11 Expand the logarithmic expression.

(1) $\log(2\sqrt{x}y^5)$

(2) $\ln\left(\frac{ab^3}{\sqrt{c}}\right)^3$

12 Write the expression as a single logarithm.

(1) $\log_3 5+2\log_3 x-\frac{1}{3}\log_3 y$

(2) $\frac{2}{3}(\ln(4a^2-1)-\ln(2a+1)+2\ln a)$

13 Find each logarithmic expression in terms of x, y, and z given that $\log_a 2=x$, $\log_a 3=y$, and $\log_a 5=z$.

(1) $\log_a\left(\frac{1}{75}\right)^2$

(2) $\log_a \sqrt[3]{180}$

14 Solve the equation.

(1) $-5^{5x-4}+10=4$

(2) $e^{10-4x}-9=15$

(3) $\log_3(4x-1)=\log_3(2x+1)-\frac{1}{2}\log_3 9$

(4) $-\log_4(x-1)+\log_4 x=\frac{1}{2}$

Unit II Test

15 If a and b are both nonzero real numbers and $4^a=6^b$, what is the value of $\frac{a}{b}$?

16 Find the solutions to the equation $6\cdot4^x+2^x-15=0$.

17 If $16^{k-1}=5$, then what is 4^{2k+1}?

18 How many years will it take for an initial investment of \$500 to double if the annual interest rate is 12%, compounded monthly?

19 The current value of a certain car is \$18,000. If it decreases in value at a rate of 15% annually, what will the car's value be in 4 years?

20 The value of the coin, made in memory of the Athens Olympics 15 years ago, is now doubled. If the value of the coin had increased by the same percent each year, what is the annual percent increase during the last 15 years?

21 The third term of an arithmetic sequence is -2, and the eleventh term is $-\frac{1}{6}$. What is the first term of this sequence?

22 The third term of a geometric sequence is $\frac{1}{32}$, and the eighth term is -1. What is the first term of this sequence?

Unit II Test

23 When a certain piece of machinery is initially purchased, its value is 50,000 dollars. If the machinery loses 12% of its value each year, when will the machinery's value be 25,000 dollars?

(A) Between 2 years and 3 years after its initial purchase
(B) Between 3 years and 4 years after its initial purchase
(C) Between 5 years and 6 years after its initial purchase
(D) Between 6 years and 7 years after its initial purchase

24 The population of a certain type of algae in a pond is 200 at the beginning of an experiment. If the population of the algae increases at a rate of 7% per day, which of the following equations models the population P of the algae after t days?

(A) $P(t)=0.07t+200$
(B) $P(t)=7t+200$
(C) $P(t)=200(1.07)^t$
(D) $P(t)=200(1.7)^t$

25 The terms of the increasing arithmetic sequence P are positive. The terms of the increasing geometric sequence Q are positive. The values of the first terms of both sequences are the same, and the values of the fifth terms of both sequences are the same. Which of the following statements describes the values of the third terms of the sequences?

(A) The third term of the arithmetic sequence is less than the third term of the geometric sequence.
(B) The third term of the arithmetic sequence is greater than the third term of the geometric sequence.
(C) The third term of the arithmetic sequence is equal to the third term of the geometric sequence.
(D) The relationship between the values of the third terms cannot be determined from the given information.

26 If $2^n+2^{n+1}=k$, where n and k are both positive integers, which of the following expressions in terms ok k represents $2^{n-1}+2^{n+2}$?

(A) k (B) $\frac{3k}{2}$ (C) $2k$ (D) $\frac{5k}{2}$

27 The function f is given by $g(x)=12\cdot\left(\frac{1}{3}\right)^x$. Which of the following statements is true about the graph of g?

(A) The graph of g increases exponentially and $\lim_{x\to\infty} f(x)=\infty$.

(B) The graph of g decreases exponentially and $\lim_{x\to\infty} f(x)=0$.

(C) The graph of g increases linearly and $\lim_{x\to\infty} f(x)=\infty$.

(D) The graph of g decreases linearly and $\lim_{x\to\infty} f(x)=-\infty$.

28 Given $f(x)=\frac{2}{x-2}$, $g(x)=4x-1$, and $h(x)=\sqrt{2x+1}+3$, find each of the following.

(1) $(f\circ g)(2)$ (2) $(g\circ h)(0)$

29 The function f is given by $f(x)=3x+1$ and the function g is given by $g(x)=\frac{x-3}{2}$. If $f(x)=g(h(x))$, which of the following represents the function $h(x)$?

(A) $h(x)=6x-1$

(B) $h(x)=6x+5$

(C) $h(x)=-x-1$

(D) $h(x)=-x+1$

Unit II Test

30 If $f(x)=\log_2(x-2)$ and $g(x)=2x^2+1$, what are all value of a such that $f(g(a))=0$?

(A) 1 only

(B) -1 and 1

(C) 2 only

(D) -2 and 2

31

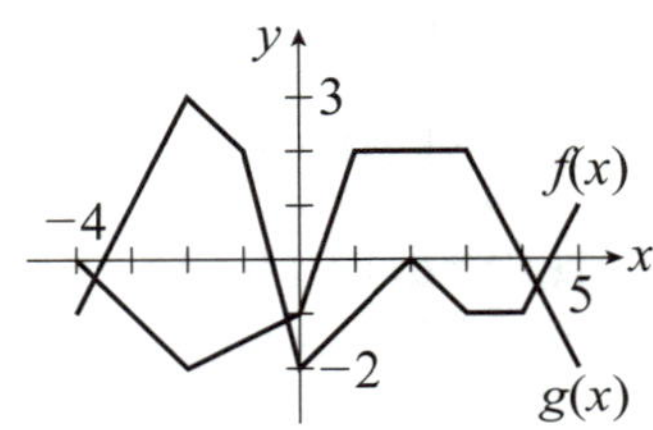

In the graphs of f and g shown above, find each of the following.

(1) $(f \circ g)(0)$

(2) $(g \circ f)(-1)$

32 If $g(x)=x+3k-1$ and $g=g^{-1}$, what is the value of k?

33 If the function $f(x)=\frac{ax+b}{x-c}$ has its inverse function $f^{-1}(x)=\frac{5x+1}{x-3}$, what is the value of $a+b+c$?

34 Suppose that $h(x)=ax+b$. If the graph of h^{-1} passes through two points $(-4, 6)$ and $(8, 3)$, what is the value of $a+b$?

35 If $1-4^{2y}=x$, which of the following expressions is equal to y in terms of x?

(A) $y=\log_4(1-x)^2$

(B) $y=\log_4(x-1)^2$

(C) $y=\log_4\sqrt{1-x}$

(D) $y=\log_4\sqrt{x-1}$

36 Which of the following is NOT equal to the others?

(A) $\ln e^2$

(B) $\log_3 9$

(C) $-\log_{0.5} 4$

(D) $\log_4 8$

Unit II Test

37 The logarithmic function f is given by $f(x)=2\log(x-4)+1$. Determine the range of the inverse function of f.

38 The function f is an increasing function where each time the output value increases by 1, the corresponding input values doubles. Which of the following could define f?

(A) $f(x)=2x+2$
(B) $g(x)=x^2$
(C) $g(x)=2^x$
(D) $g(x)=\log_2 x$

39 The exponential function f is given by $f(x)=2\cdot 3^{x-1}$. Which of the following is true about the graph of f?

(A) The graph of f is increasing at an increasing rate over the given domain.
(B) The graph of f is increasing at an decreasing rate over the given domain.
(C) The graph of f is decreasing at an increasing rate over the given domain.
(D) The graph of f is decreasing at an decreasing rate over the given domain.

40 Which of the following is true about the graph of $f(x)=2^x+\log_2 x$?

(A) $\lim_{x\to 0^+} f(x)=1$ and $\lim_{x\to\infty} f(x)=2$

(B) $\lim_{x\to 0^+} f(x)=-\infty$ and $\lim_{x\to\infty} f(x)=2$

(C) $\lim_{x\to 0^+} f(x)=1$ and $\lim_{x\to\infty} f(x)=\infty$

(D) $\lim_{x\to 0^+} f(x)=-\infty$ and $\lim_{x\to\infty} f(x)=\infty$

41 If the function f is given by $f(x)=1-\log_4(4x-8)$, which of the following expression is equal to $f^{-1}(x)$

(A) $4^{1-x}+8$

(B) $4^{1-x}+2$

(C) $4^{-x}+8$

(D) $4^{-x}+2$

42 If the function f is given by $f(x)=\log_2 x$, then which of the following expression is equal to $f(4x)+f\left(\frac{x^2}{8}\right)$?

(A) $3\log_2 x-1$

(B) $\log_2 4x-3$

(C) $\log_2 4x-1$

(D) $3\log_2 x-3$

Unit II Test

43 

Average Temperature (°F)	Electricity Consumption (kWh)
40	1200
50	1100
60	900
70	850
80	750
90	600

A company wants to predict the monthly electricity consumption(in kilowatt–hours, kWh) of its office based on the average monthly temperature(in degrees Fahrenheit). The table above shows the observed data for six months. Predict the electricity consumption for a month with an average temperature of $75^{\circ}F$ using linear regression to determine the equation that models the relationship between average monthly temperature and electricity consumption.

44

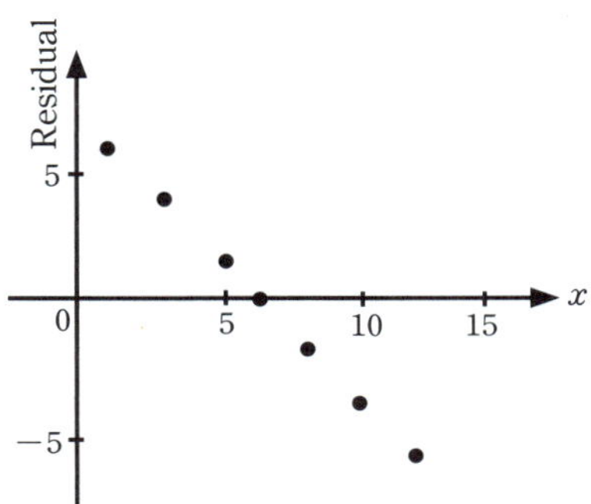

Students are constructing a model for a data set. The residual plot for their linear regression model is given. Which of the following is the best conclusion?

(A) The linear model is appropriate because the residuals show a pattern.
(B) The linear model is appropriate because the residuals show no pattern.
(C) The linear model is not appropriate because the residuals show a pattern.
(D) The linear model is not appropriate because the residuals show no pattern.

45 In a semi−log plot, which of the following functions appear linear with y−intercept $\log 8$?

(A) $f(x)=2^{x+3}$
(B) $f(x)=4^{x+2}$
(C) $f(x)=8^{x}$
(D) $f(x)=\log_8 x$

Unit II Test

46 In a certain region, a thermometer is taken from indoors to the outdoors. The temperature reading of the thermometer after t minutes can be described by the function $A(t)=24-15\cdot 2^{-\frac{1}{15}t}$. Which of the following statements is true according to this model?

(A) After approximately 15 minutes, the thermometer's reading reaches 0°C.
(B) The thermometer's reading is 15°C when it is initially placed outdoors.
(C) Over a long period, the thermometer's reading will approach 24°C.
(D) Initially, the thermometer's reading increases, but after a certain point, it will start to decrease.

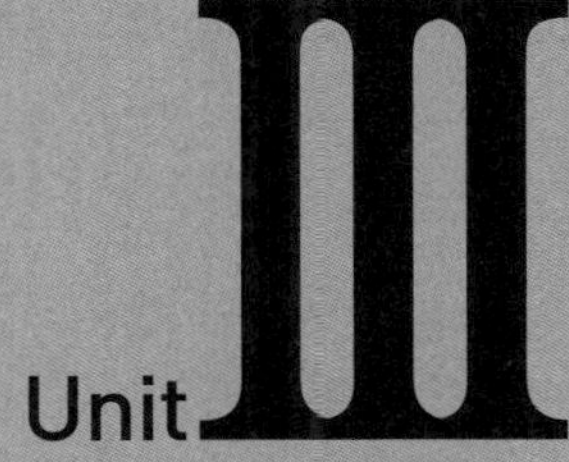

Unit III

Trigonometric and Polar Functions

1. Angles and Their Measure
2. Trigonometric Functions of Angles
3. Graphs of Trigonometric Functions
4. Inverse Trigonometric Functions
5. Real-Life Problems with Trigonometry
6. Fundamental Trigonometric Identities
7. Trigonometric Equations and Identities, Part I
8. Trigonometric Equations and Identities, Part II
9. Polar Coordinates and Equations
10. Polar Form of a Complex Numbers
11. Unit III Test

1 Angles and Their Measure

01 Definition of Angles

An angle is determined by rotating one of two rays that share a fixed endpoint known as the vertex. Angles are usually labeled with Greek letters θ and read as "theta". The starting position of the ray is the initial side and the ending position after rotation is the terminal side.

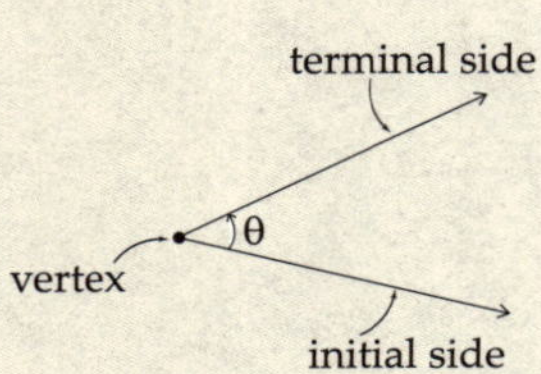

An angle with its vertex at the origin and its initial side along the positive $x-$axis is said to be in a standard position. Positive angles are generated by counterclockwise direction and negative angles by clockwise direction.

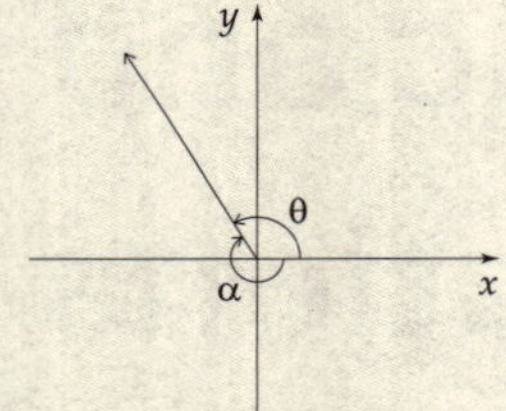

(1) Angles θ and α are in standard position.

(2) θ is positive angle.

(3) α is negative angle.

Recall that there are four quadrants, as shown in the figure. The angle is called a quadrant angle when the terminal side of the angle lies right on one of the axes.

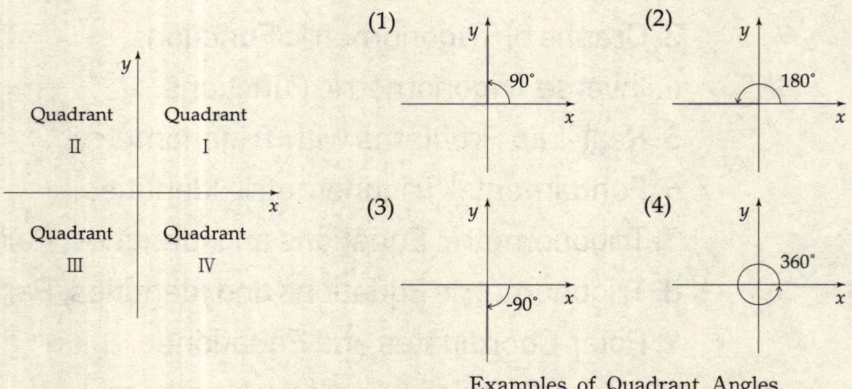

Examples of Quadrant Angles

02 Degree Measure

We already learned about the degree measure, represented by the symbol.

It is a unit of angular measure equal to $\frac{1}{180}th$ of a straight angle. Each degree is subdivided into 60 minutes and each minute is subdivided into 60 seconds.

(1) 1 degree$(1°)=60$ minutes$(60')$

(2) 1 minute$(60')=60$ seconds$(60'')$

Example 1

① Convert $24.315°$ to the degrees, minutes, seconds form.

② Convert $15°6'38''$ to the decimal form.

Solution

① $24.315°=24°+(0.315\times60)'$ → Multiply the decimal portion of the degree by 60

$=24°+18.9'$ → Simplify

$=24°+18'+(0.9\times60)''$ → Multiply the decimal portion of the minute by 60

$=24°+18'+54''$ → $24.315°$ can be written as $24°18'54''$

$24.315°=24°18'54''$

✓ We say that $24.315°$ is decimal degree form and $24°18'54''$ is DMS form.

② $15°6'38''=15°+\left(6'\times\frac{1°}{60'}\right)+\left(38''\times\frac{1°}{3600''}\right)$ → $1°=60$ min$=3600$ sec

$=15.1106°$ → $15°6'38''$ can be written as $15.1106°$

$15°6'38''=15.1106°$

Check Point 1-1

Solutions_Page 80

Rewrite the angle in DMS form.

① $38.755°$

② $-58.12°$

Check Point 1-2

Solutions_Page 80

Rewrite the angle in decimal form to the nearest thousandth.

① $27°35'42''$ ② $-34'26''$

03 Radian Measure

Another way to measure angles is in radians. To define a radian, we can use a central angle of a circle, as shown in figure. One radian is the measure of an angle θ when the radius is equal to the length of a corresponding arc. 180° is equal to π radian.

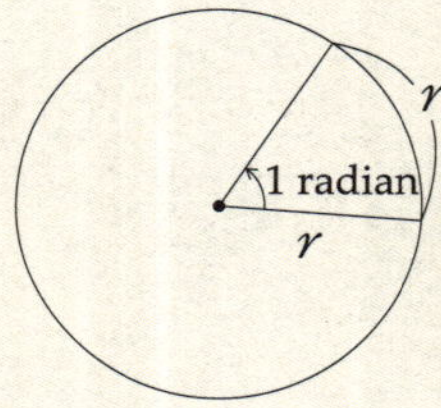

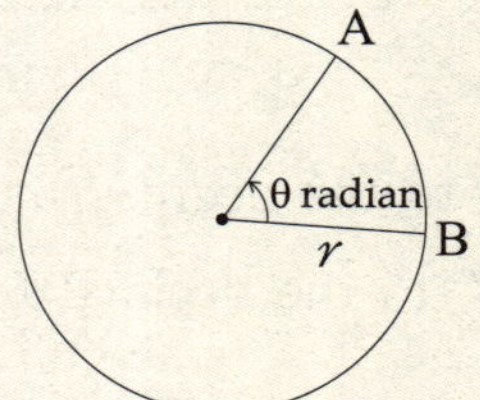

1. $\theta \text{ rad} = \dfrac{\overset{\frown}{AB}}{r}$
2. $\pi \text{ rad} = 180° \rightarrow 1 \text{ rad} = \dfrac{180°}{\pi},\ 1° = \dfrac{\pi \text{ rad}}{180}$
3. To convert degrees to radians $\rightarrow$ (Measure of degree) $\times \dfrac{\pi \text{ rad}}{180°}$
4. To convert radians to degrees $\rightarrow$ (Measure of radian) $\times \dfrac{180°}{\pi \text{ rad}}$

Degree	0°	30°	45°	60°	90°	180°	270°	360°
Radian	0	$\frac{\pi}{6}$	$\frac{\pi}{4}$	$\frac{\pi}{3}$	$\frac{\pi}{2}$	π	$\frac{3\pi}{2}$	2π

When no units of angle measure are specified, it is indicative of radian measure. For example, if we write $\theta = \pi$, we mean that $\theta = \pi$ radians.

Example 2

① Rewrite 225° in radian measure.

② Rewrite $\frac{3\pi}{4}$ in degree measure.

Solution

① $225^\circ = 225^\circ \times \frac{\pi}{180^\circ} = \frac{5\pi}{4}$ → Multiply by $\frac{\pi}{180^\circ}$

$225^\circ = \frac{5\pi}{4}$

② $\frac{3\pi}{4} = \frac{3\pi}{4} \times \frac{180^\circ}{\pi} = 135^\circ$ → Multiply by $\frac{180^\circ}{\pi}$

$\frac{3\pi}{4} = 135^\circ$

Check Point 2–1

Solutions_Page 80

Rewrite the angle in radian measure.

① 150° ② 315°

Check Point 2–2

Solutions_Page 80

Rewrite the angle in degree measure.

① $\frac{13\pi}{6}$ ② $\frac{7\pi}{11}$

04 Coterminal Angles

Two angles are called coterminal angles if they have the same initial and terminal side. If α is the measure of an angle, then all angles measuring

1. $\alpha^\circ = \alpha^\circ \pm (360^\circ \times n)$, if measured in degree
2. $\alpha = \alpha \pm (2\pi \times n)$, if measured in radian

where n is an integer.

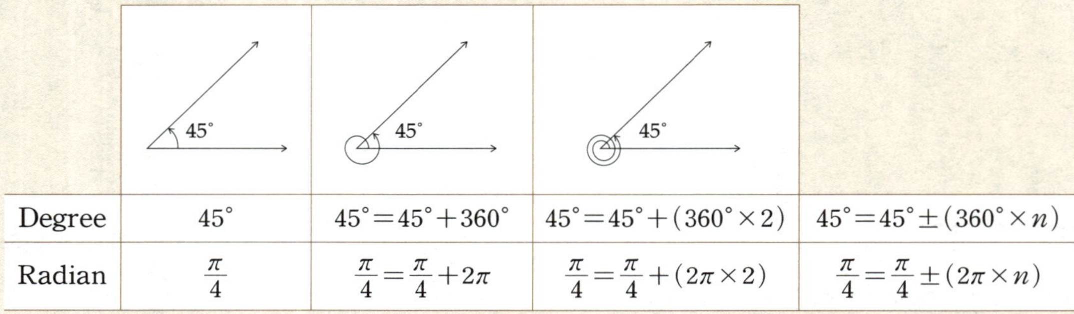

Degree	45°	$45^\circ = 45^\circ + 360^\circ$	$45^\circ = 45^\circ + (360^\circ \times 2)$	$45^\circ = 45^\circ \pm (360^\circ \times n)$
Radian	$\frac{\pi}{4}$	$\frac{\pi}{4} = \frac{\pi}{4} + 2\pi$	$\frac{\pi}{4} = \frac{\pi}{4} + (2\pi \times 2)$	$\frac{\pi}{4} = \frac{\pi}{4} \pm (2\pi \times n)$

Example 3

Find three coterminal angles(two positive and one negative) for the given angle.

① 60° ② $\frac{\pi}{3}$

Solution

① Coterminal angles of 60° would be $60^\circ + 360^\circ = 420^\circ$, $60^\circ + (360^\circ \times 2) = 780^\circ$, or $60^\circ - 360 = -300^\circ$.

$60^\circ = 420^\circ = 780^\circ = -300^\circ$

② Coterminal angles of $\frac{\pi}{3}$ would be $\frac{\pi}{3}+2\pi=\frac{7x}{3}$, $\frac{\pi}{3}+(2\pi\times 2)=\frac{13\pi}{3}$, or $\frac{\pi}{3}-2\pi=-\frac{5\pi}{3}$.

$\frac{\pi}{3}=\frac{7\pi}{3}=\frac{13\pi}{3}=-\frac{5\pi}{3}$

Check Point 3

Solutions_Page 80

Find two coterminal angles(one positive and one negative) for the given angle.

① $270°$

② $-47°$

③ $\frac{5\pi}{7}$

④ -5

05 Arc Length and Area of Sector

In Geometry, we learned how to find the arc length and the area of a sector of a circle when the measured central angle is in degree. We also can find the arc length and the area of the sector using radian measure.

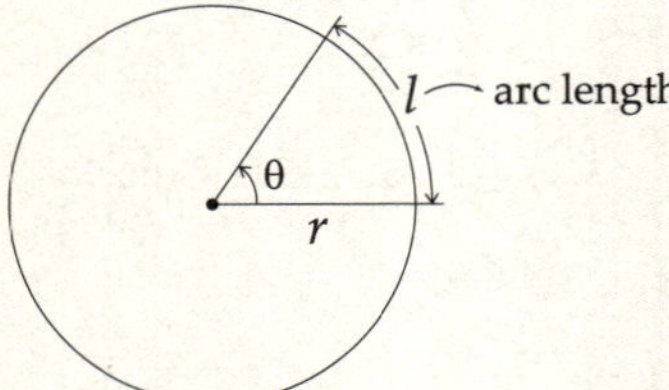

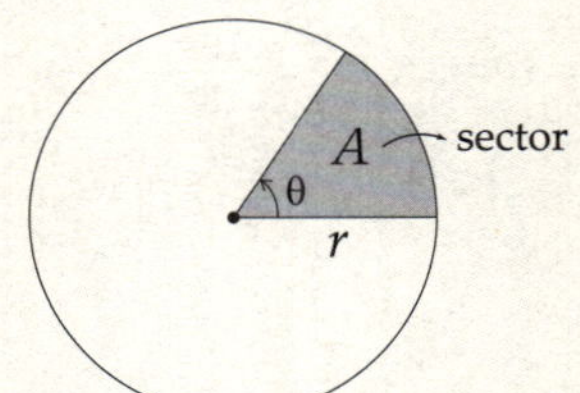

1. Arc length

$l=2\pi r\times\frac{\theta°}{360°}$ → If measured in degree

$l=2\pi r\times\frac{\theta}{2\pi}=r\theta$ → If measured in radian

2. Area of a sector

$A=\pi r^2\times\frac{\theta°}{360°}$ → If measured in degree

$A=\pi r^2\times\frac{\theta}{2\pi}=\frac{1}{2}r^2\theta=\frac{1}{2}rl$ → If measured in radian

Example 4

A circle has a radius 8 and arc is intercepted by a central angle of 120°, as shown on the right. Find the arc length and the area of the sector.

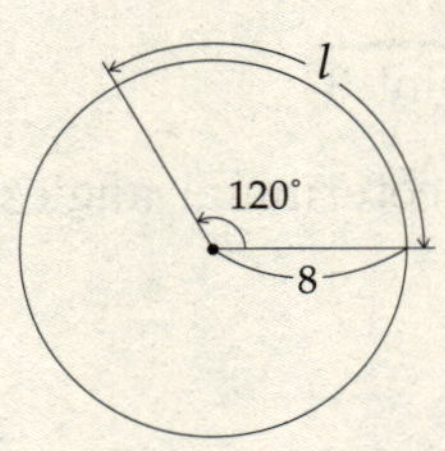

Solution

Are length $l=2\pi r\times\frac{\theta^\circ}{360^\circ}=2\pi(8)\times\frac{120^\circ}{360^\circ}=\frac{16\pi}{3}$

Area of sector $A=\pi r^2\times\frac{\theta^\circ}{360^\circ}=\pi(8)^2\times\frac{120^\circ}{360^\circ}=\frac{64\pi}{3}$

Alternate Solution

$120^\circ=120^\circ\times\frac{\pi}{180^\circ}=\frac{2\pi}{3}$ → Convert degree to radian

Are length $l=r\theta=8\times\frac{2\pi}{3}=\frac{16\pi}{3}$

Area of sector $A=\frac{1}{2}r^2\theta=\frac{1}{2}(8)^2\left(\frac{2\pi}{3}\right)=\frac{64\pi}{3}$ or $A=\frac{1}{2}rl=\frac{1}{2}(8)\left(\frac{16\pi}{3}\right)=\frac{64\pi}{3}$

Arc length $l=\frac{16\pi}{3}$

Area of sector $A=\frac{64\pi}{3}$

Check Point 4

Solutions_Page 80

Find the arc length and the area of the sector of the given circle.

①

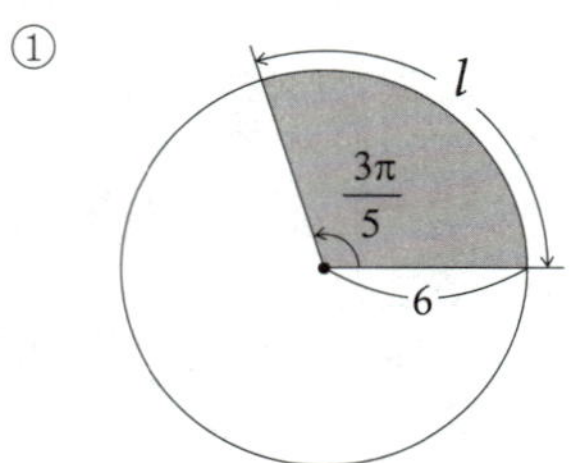

②

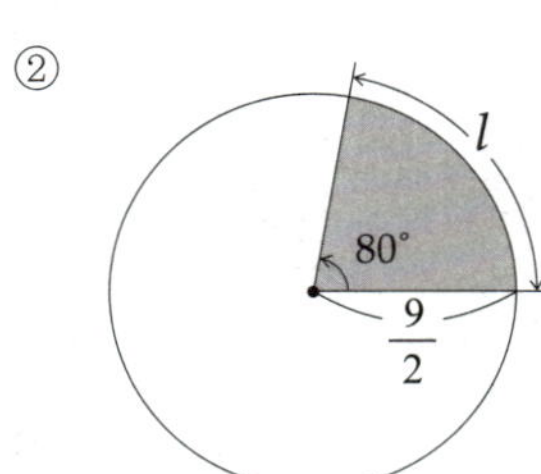

06 Linear and Angular Speeds

The length of arc can be used to analyze the motion of a particle moving at a constant speed along a circular path. Linear speed(denoted as v) measures how fast the particle moves, and angular speed(denoted as w) measures how fast the angle changes.

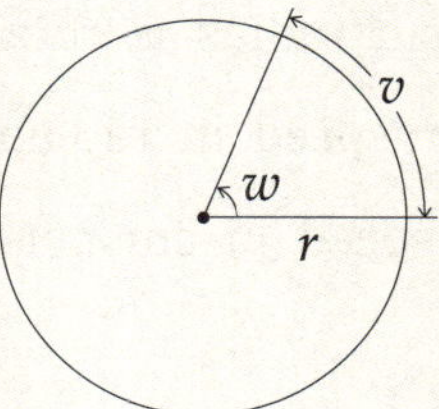

1. Linear Speed $v=\frac{l}{t}$
2. Angular Speed $w=\frac{\theta}{t}$
3. $l=r\theta$, $\theta=wt$, $v=\frac{l}{t}=\frac{r\theta}{t}=\frac{rwt}{t}$ $\rightarrow$ $v=rw$

l : Arc length
θ: Angle in radian that corresponds to the arc length
t: Time traveled

Example 5

A wheel with a 20 feet radius makes 4 revolutions in 5 minutes. Find the linear speed in feet per minute, and the angular speed of the wheel in radians per minute.

Solution

Know that linear speed is equal to arc length of 4 revolutions divided by time, 5 minutes. Arc length of 4 revolutions: $4\times2\pi(20)=160\pi\ ft$. So the linear speed is

$$v=\frac{160\pi\ ft}{5\ \text{min}}=32\pi\ ft/\text{min}$$

Angular speed is equal to total angles rotated in 4 revolutions divided by total time, 5 minutes. Total angles rotated in 4 revolutions: $4\times 2\pi = 8\pi\ rad$. So the angular speed is

$$w=\frac{8\pi\ rad}{5\ \text{min}}=1.6\pi\ rad/\text{min}$$

The linear speed $v=32\pi\ ft/\text{min}$
The angular speed $w=1.6\pi\ rad/\text{min}$

Check Point 5

Solutions_Page 80

A circle with a 5 cm radius is rotating at 20 rpm(revolutions per minute).

① Find the angular speed in radians per second.

② Find the linear speed in cm per second.

Review Exercise

Solutions_Page 81

01 Rewrite the angle in DMS form.

(1) $21.26°$

(2) $135.465°$

02 Rewrite the angle in decimal form to the nearest thousandth.

(1) $37°51'16''$

(2) $265°25'45''$

03 Rewrite the angle in radian measure or degree measure.

(1) $\frac{11\pi}{4}$

(2) $-\frac{15\pi}{6}$

(3) $495°$

(4) $-300°$

Review Exercise

04 Find three coterminal angles (two positive and one negative) for the given angle.

(1) $\frac{5\pi}{6}$

(2) $-\frac{9\pi}{4}$

(3) $495°$

(4) $-300°$

05 Find the missing values.

(1)

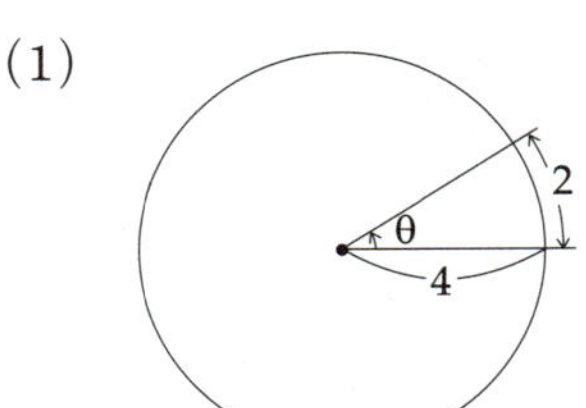

(2)

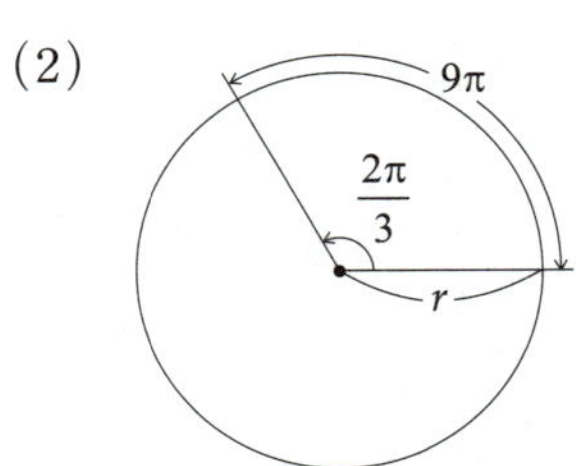

06 Find the area of the sector of the circle with given information.

(1)

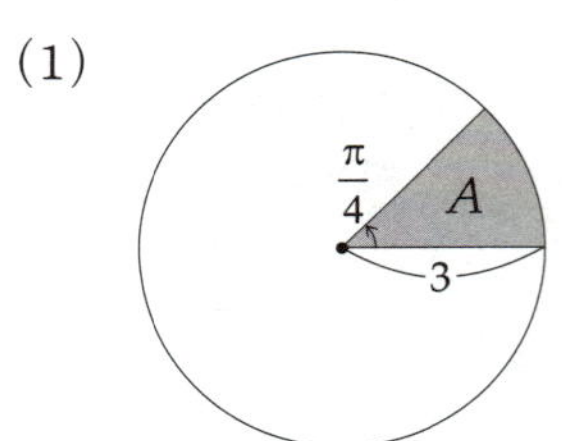

(2)

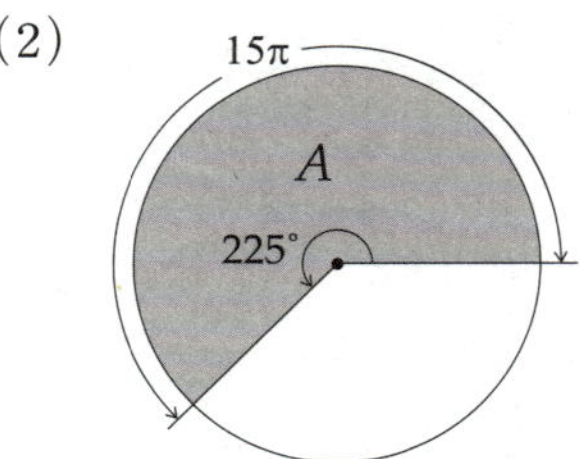

07 Find the length of a pendulum if it swings through an angle of $\frac{7\pi}{12}$, and the tip sweeps out an arc of 8 inches.

09 If a sector of a circle has an arc length of 8π inches and an area of 26π square inches, what is the central angle in radian measure?

08 A central angle of two concentric circles is 2 radians. If the radius of the larger circle is twice the radius of the smaller circle, what is the ratio of the area of the larger sector to the area of the smaller sector?

10 A tire with a 2 *ft* radius is rotating at a rate of 40 miles per hour.
(1 mile=5280 feet)

(1) How many revolutions per minute does this tire make?

(2) What is the angular speed of the tire in radians per minute?

2 Trigonometric Functions of Angles

In this chapter, we will study one of the most important topics in Pre−Calculus, trigonometry, and its widely applied applications. The word trigonometry means measurement of triangles. Simply saying, it deals with relationships among the sides and angles of triangles.

01 The Unit Circle

The unit circle is a circle whose radius is 1 and whose center is at the origin of a rectangular coordinate system. The following discussion sets the stage for defining the trigonometric functions using the unit circle. Let $P(x, y)$ be the intersection of the terminal side. Then a right triangle with angle θ and two legs(x and y) is created as shown in Figure.

We define six trigonometric functions as follows.

Word	Symbol	Definition
Sine	sin	$\sin\theta=\frac{y}{1}=y$
Cosine	cos	$\cos\theta=\frac{x}{1}=x$
Tangent	tan	$\tan\theta=\frac{y}{x}$
Secant	sec	$\sec\theta=\frac{1}{x}=\frac{1}{\cos\theta}$
Cosecant	csc	$\csc\theta=\frac{1}{y}=\frac{1}{\sin\theta}$
Cotangent	cot	$\cot\theta=\frac{x}{y}=\frac{1}{\tan\theta}$

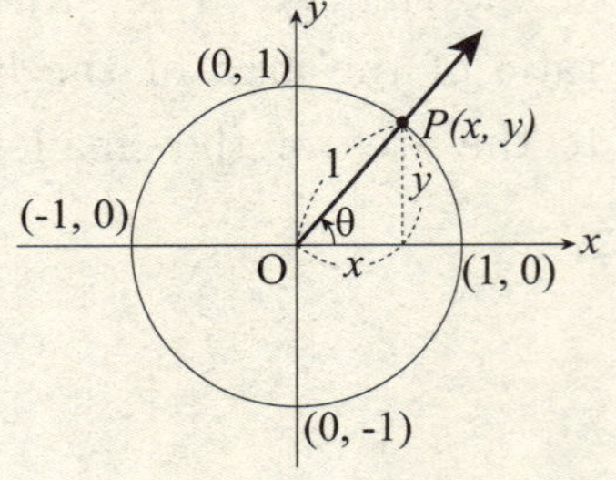

Since we use the unit circle in these definitions of the trigonometric functions, they are sometimes referred to as circular functions.

Example 1

Find the six trigonometric function of the angle θ on the unit circle.

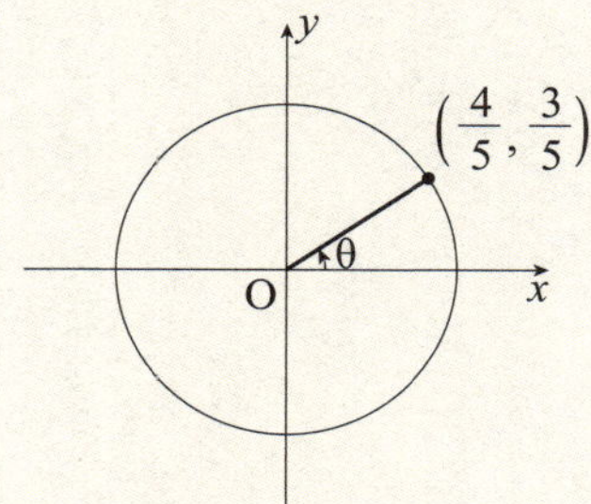

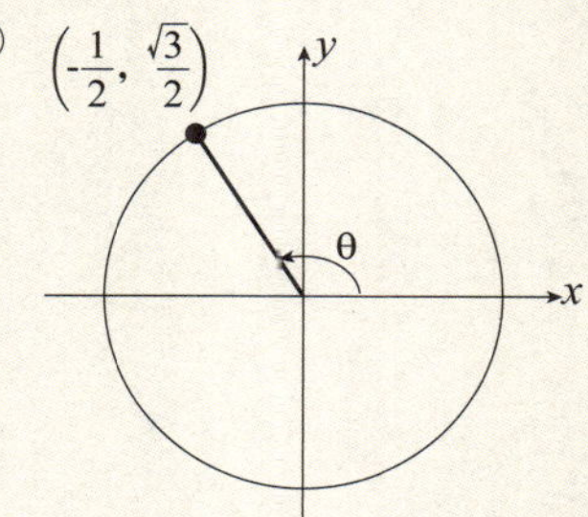

Solution

The value can be obtained by using the definition of the trigcnometric function from the unit circle.

① $\sin\theta = y = \frac{3}{5}$ $\qquad$ $\csc\theta = \frac{1}{\sin\theta} = \frac{5}{3}$

$\cos\theta = x = \frac{4}{5}$ $\qquad$ $\sec\theta = \frac{1}{\cos\theta} = \frac{5}{4}$

$\tan\theta = \frac{y}{x} = \frac{\frac{3}{5}}{\frac{4}{5}} = \frac{3}{4}$ $\qquad$ $\cot\theta = \frac{1}{\tan\theta} = \frac{4}{3}$

$\sin\theta = \frac{3}{5}$, $\cos\theta = \frac{4}{5}$, $\tan\theta = \frac{3}{4}$, $\csc\theta = \frac{5}{3}$, $\sec\theta = \frac{5}{4}$, $\cot\theta = \frac{4}{3}$

② $\sin\theta = y = \frac{\sqrt{3}}{2}$ $\qquad$ $\csc\theta = \frac{1}{\sin\theta} = \frac{2}{\sqrt{3}} = \frac{2\sqrt{3}}{3}$

$\cos\theta = x = -\frac{1}{2}$ $\qquad$ $\sec\theta = \frac{1}{\cos\theta} = -\frac{2}{1} = -2$

$\tan\theta = \frac{y}{x} = \frac{\frac{\sqrt{3}}{2}}{-\frac{1}{2}} = -\sqrt{3}$ $\qquad$ $\cot\theta = \frac{1}{\tan\theta} = -\frac{1}{\sqrt{3}} = -\frac{\sqrt{3}}{3}$

$\sin\theta = \frac{\sqrt{3}}{2}$, $\cos\theta = -\frac{1}{2}$, $\tan\theta = -\sqrt{3}$, $\csc\theta = \frac{2\sqrt{3}}{3}$, $\sec\theta = -2$, $\cot\theta = -\frac{\sqrt{3}}{3}$

✔ When defining the trigonometric function from the unit circle, we define the value using the coordinates of the point in the coordinate plane, not the length of the side of the triangle. Therefore, we can define the trigonometric function value even if it is not an acute angle, and the value of the trigonometric function may be negative.

Check Point 1

Solutions_Page 82

Find the six trigonometric functions of the angle θ on the unit circle.

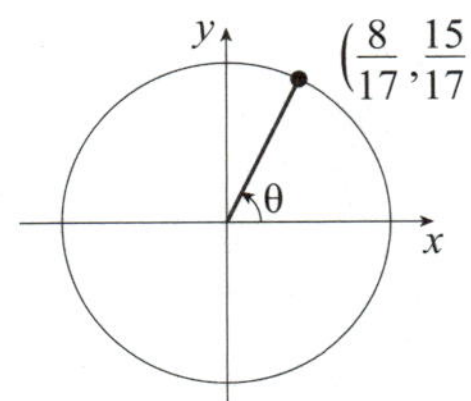

②

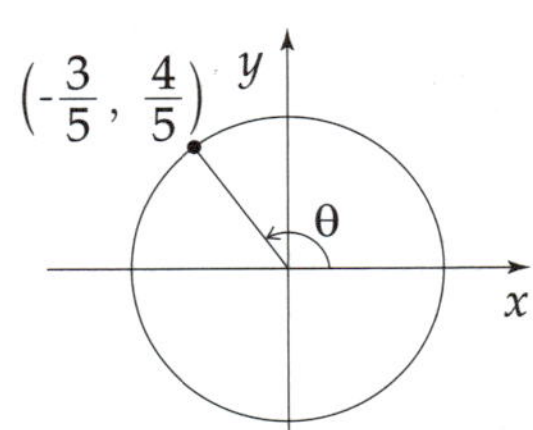

02 Trigonometric Functions with Quadrant Angles

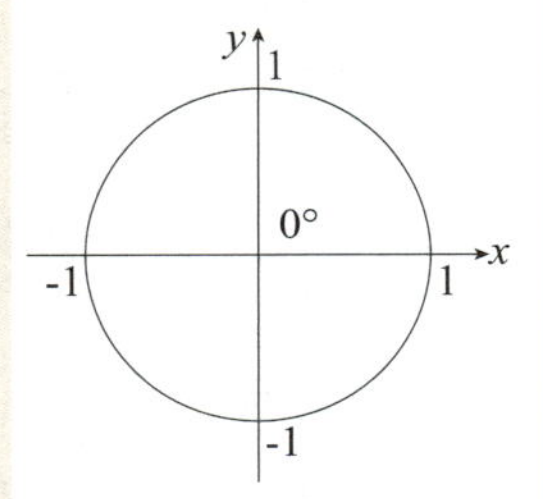	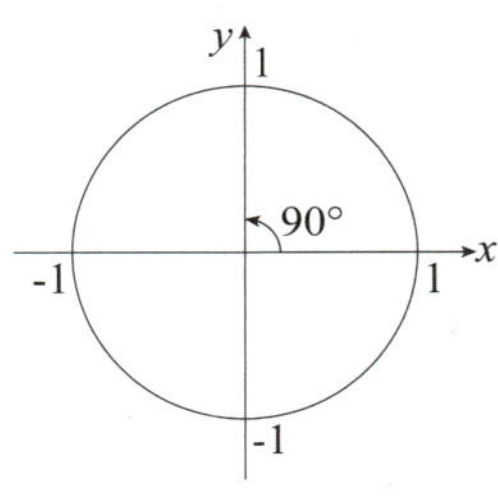	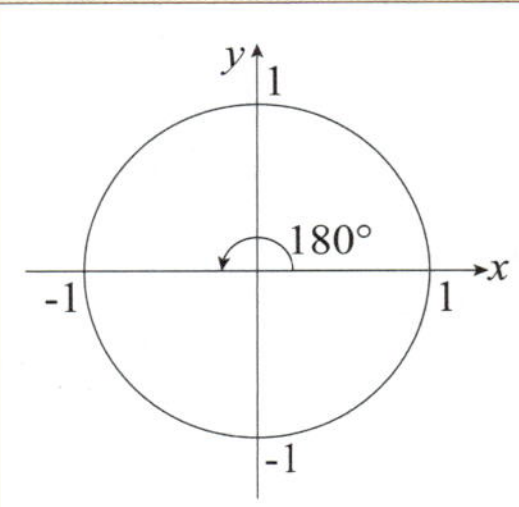	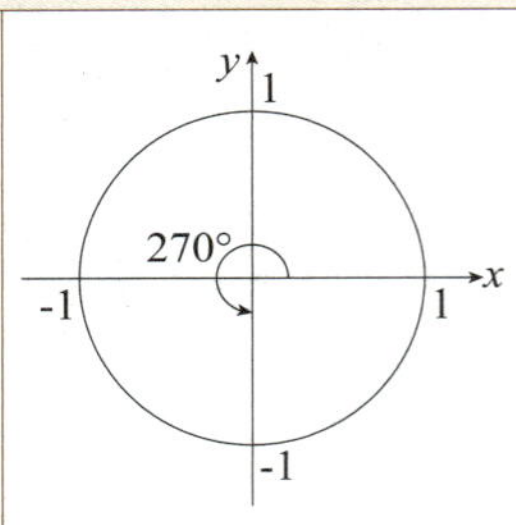
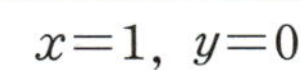 $x=1,\ y=0$	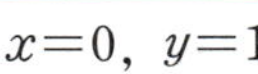 $x=0,\ y=1$	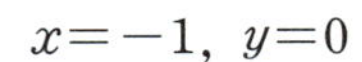 $x=-1,\ y=0$	$x=0,\ y=-1$

θ (deg)	$0°$	$90°$	$180°$	$270°$
θ (rad)	0	$\frac{\pi}{2}$	π	$\frac{3\pi}{2}$
$\sin\theta=y$	0	1	0	-1
$\cos\theta=x$	1	0	-1	0
$\tan\theta=\frac{y}{x}$	$\frac{0}{1}=0$	$\frac{1}{0}=\text{undef}$	$\frac{-1}{0}=0$	$\frac{-1}{0}=\text{undef}$

undef=undefined

03 Special Triangles

$45°-45°-90°$ Triangle	$30°-60°-90°$ Triangle
	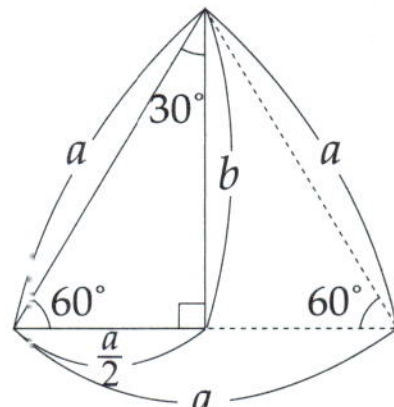
By Pythagorean theorem, $b^2=a^2+a^2$ $b^2=2a^2$ $b=\sqrt{2}a$ So the ration of $a:a:b=1:1:\sqrt{2}$	Given a equilateral triangle with side a, we bisect the triangle and use Pythagorean theorem to find the ratio. $\left(\frac{a}{2}\right)^2+b^2=a^2$ $b^2=a^2-\frac{a^2}{4}=\frac{3a^2}{4}$ $b=\frac{\sqrt{3}a}{2}$ So the ration of $\frac{a}{2}:b:a=1:\sqrt{3}:2$

The trigonometric functions of special angles are as follows:

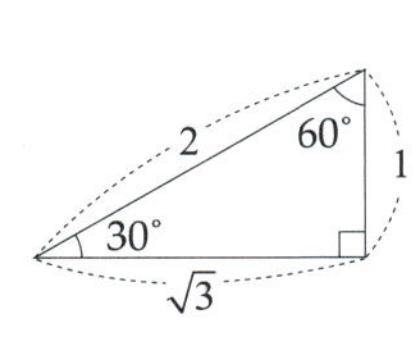

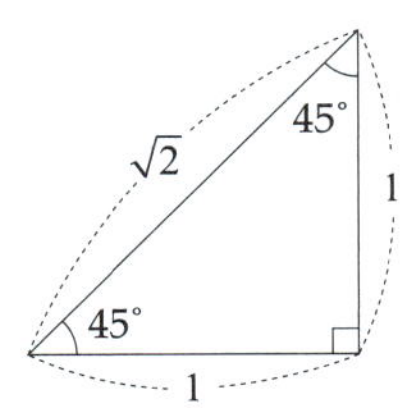

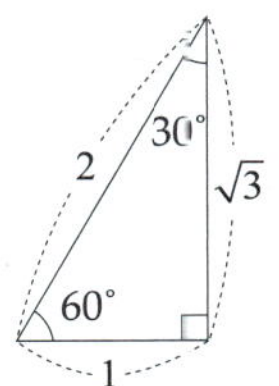

θ (deg)	$30°$	$45°$	$60°$
θ (rad)	$\frac{\pi}{6}$	$\frac{\pi}{4}$	$\frac{\pi}{3}$
$\sin\theta$	$\frac{1}{2}$	$\frac{1}{\sqrt{2}}$	$\frac{\sqrt{3}}{2}$
$\cos\theta$	$\frac{\sqrt{3}}{2}$	$\frac{1}{\sqrt{2}}$	$\frac{1}{2}$
$\tan\theta$	$\frac{1}{\sqrt{3}}$	1	$\sqrt{3}$

04 Trigonometric Functions with Non-Unit Circle

Solving trigonometric values in a unit circle reduces the calculation burden and easy to understand. However, it is not necessary to evaluate the trigonometric values on the unit circle basis.

Unit Circle

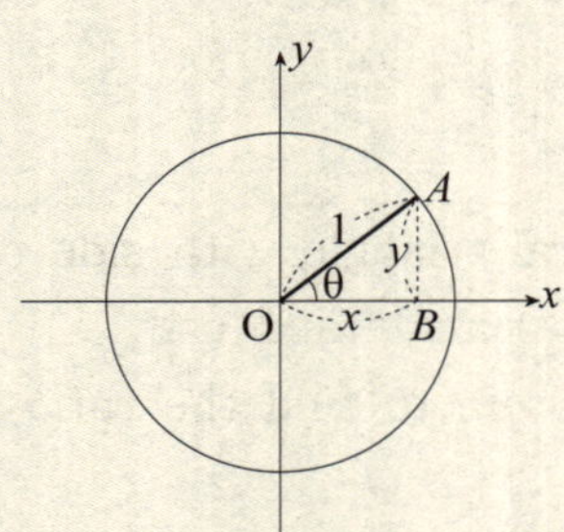

Non−Unit Circle

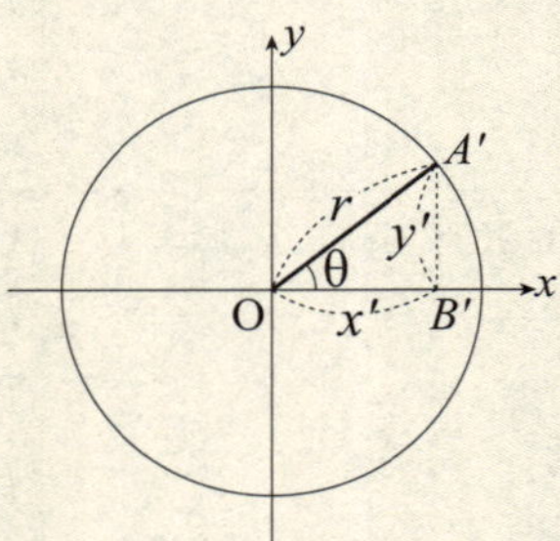

In the Figure above, given an angle of equal size, ΔOAB and ΔOA′B′ are similar triangles. So we have

$$\sin\theta=\frac{y}{1}=\frac{y'}{r},\ \cos\theta=\frac{x}{1}=\frac{x'}{r},\ \text{and}\ \tan\theta=\frac{y}{x}=\frac{y'}{x'}$$

To conclude, if the magnitude(size) of the angle is constant, the value of the trigonometric function is the same regardless of the size of the right triangle. Consider the following example given an angle $\theta=30°$.

Unit Circle

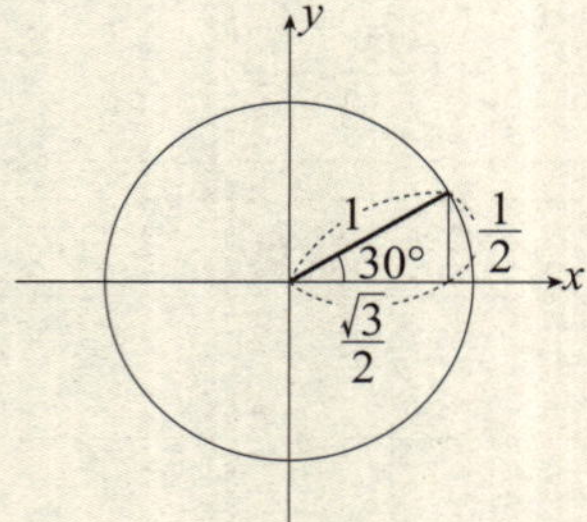

$\sin 30°=y=\frac{1}{2}$

$\cos 30°=x=\frac{\sqrt{3}}{2}$

Non−Unit Circle

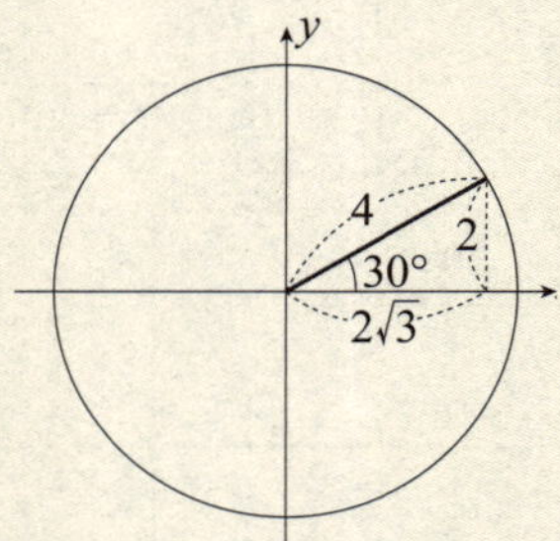

$\sin 30°=\frac{2}{4}=\frac{1}{2}$

$\cos 30°=\frac{2\sqrt{3}}{4}=\frac{\sqrt{3}}{2}$

$$\tan 30° = \frac{y}{x} = \frac{\frac{1}{2}}{\frac{\sqrt{3}}{2}} = \frac{1}{\sqrt{3}} = \frac{\sqrt{3}}{3} \qquad \tan 30° = \frac{2}{2\sqrt{3}} = \frac{1}{\sqrt{3}} = \frac{\sqrt{3}}{3}$$

Once again, the value of the trigonometric function is determined by the angle, not by the size of the triangle. To find the value of a trigonometric function, it is usually best to use the ratios of special triangles instead of unit circles. However, it is easier to use a unit circle for quadrant angles.

05 Reference Angle

The value of the trigonometric functions greater than 90° or less than 0° can be determined from reference angle. Reference angle, also known as the reference number, is the acute angle α formed by the terminal side of angle θ and the x-axis, as shown in Figure.

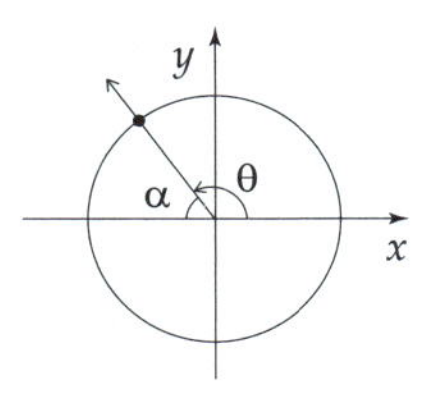	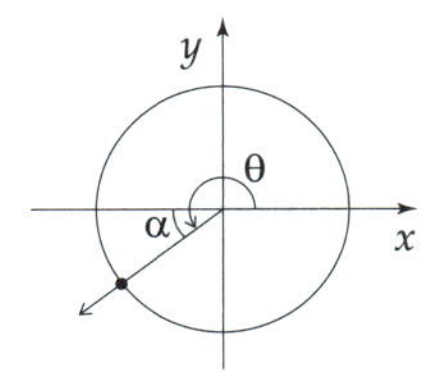	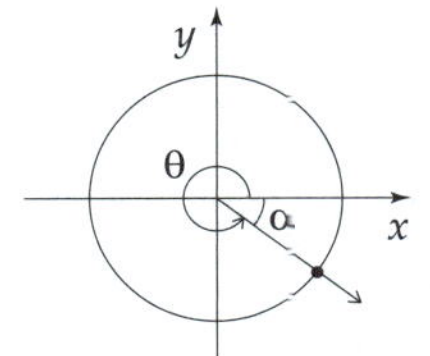
$\alpha = 180° - \theta$	$\alpha = \theta - 180°$	$\alpha = 360° - \theta$

Example 2

Find the reference angle for $\theta = 150°$.

Solution

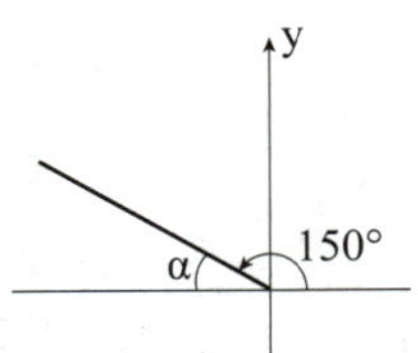

The reference angle is $\alpha=180°-150°=30°$.

Check Point 2

Solutions_Page 82

Find the reference angle for each angle.

① $\theta=225°$ ② $\theta=\frac{5\pi}{3}$

Example 3

Find the six trigonometric functions at the angle $\theta=135°$.

Solution

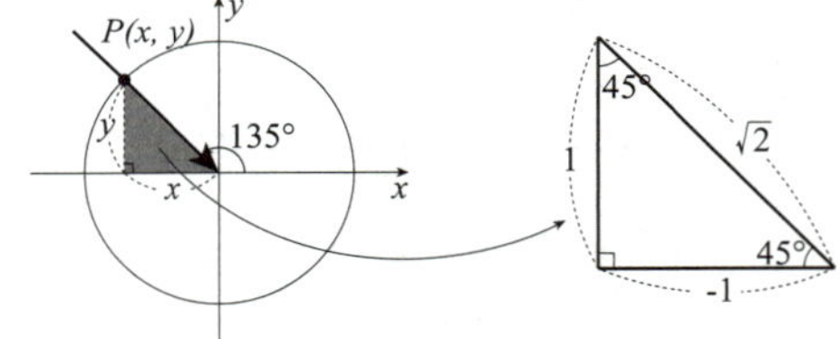

The reference angle is $\alpha=180°-135°=45°$.
We can simply use the triangle on the right to define six trigonometric functions.
Note that the value of x is negative.

$\sin 135°=\frac{1}{\sqrt{2}}=\frac{\sqrt{2}}{2}$ $\csc 135°=\frac{1}{\sin 135°}=\frac{\sqrt{2}}{1}=\sqrt{2}$

$\cos 135°=\frac{-1}{\sqrt{2}}=-\frac{\sqrt{2}}{2}$ $\sec 135°=\frac{1}{\cos 135°}=\frac{\sqrt{2}}{-1}=-\sqrt{2}$

$\tan 135°=\frac{1}{-1}=-1$ $\cot 135°=\frac{1}{\tan 135°}=-1$

$\sin 135°=\frac{\sqrt{2}}{2}$, $\cos 135°=-\frac{\sqrt{2}}{2}$, $\tan 135°=-1$, $\csc 135°=\sqrt{2}$, $\sec 135°=-\sqrt{2}$, $\cot 135°=-1$

✔ The value of the trigonometric function at 45 degrees and the value of the trigonometric function at 135 degrees are the same except for the sign of some values.

Check Point 3

Solutions_Page 83

Find the six trigonometric functions at each angle.

① $\theta=300^\circ$　　② $\theta=\frac{4\pi}{3}$　　③ $\theta=-\frac{5\pi}{4}$

06 The Signs of Trigonometric Functions

The signs of trigonometric functions are depend on what quadrant the terminal side with angle θ lies

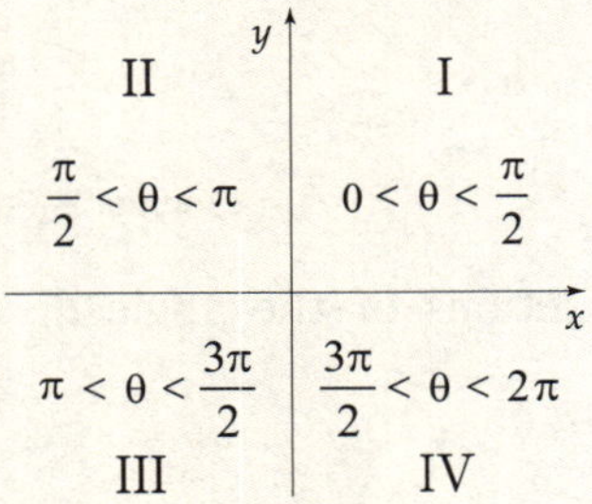

II: $\frac{\pi}{2}<\theta<\pi$	I: $0<\theta<\frac{\pi}{2}$
III: $\pi<\theta<\frac{3\pi}{2}$	IV: $\frac{3\pi}{2}<\theta<2\pi$

Quadrant	I	II	III	IV
Signs	$x>0,\ y>0$	$x<0,\ y>0$	$x<0,\ y<0$	$x>0,\ y<0$
$\sin\theta=y$	+	+	−	−
$\cos\theta=x$	+	−	−	+
$\tan\theta=\frac{y}{x}$	+	−	+	−

Tips to memorize

All − San − Ta − Clause

All − Students − Take − Calculus

Example 4

Given that $\sin\theta=-\frac{1}{3}$ and $\tan\theta>0$, find $\cos\theta$ and $\cot\theta$.

Solution

Since $\sin\theta<0$ and $\tan\theta>0$, θ lies in Quadrant III as shown in figure.

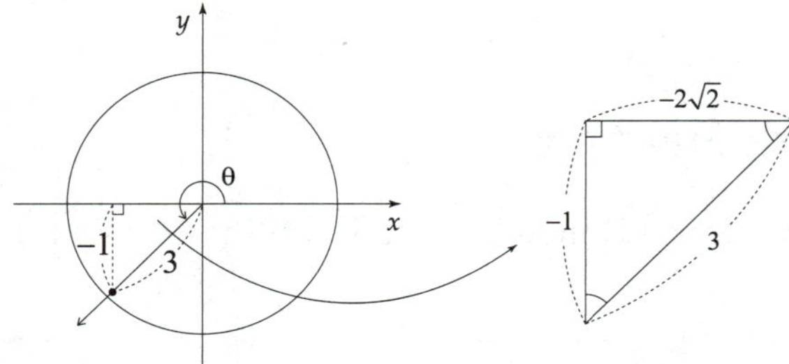

$x^2+y^2=r^2$ → Pythagorean theorem

$x^2+(-1)^2=3^2$, $x^2=9-1=8$, $x=-2\sqrt{2}$.

$\cos\theta=-\frac{2\sqrt{2}}{3}$, $\cot\theta=\frac{-2\sqrt{2}}{-1}=2\sqrt{2}$.

$\cos\theta=-\frac{2\sqrt{2}}{3}$, $\cot\theta=2\sqrt{2}$

Check Point 4

Solutions_Page 83

Using the given information, find the rest of trigonometric functions of the angle θ.

① $\cos\theta=\frac{4}{5}$, $\cot\theta=\frac{4}{3}$

② $\csc\theta=\frac{7}{5}$, $\cot\theta<0$

Review Exercise

Solutions_Page 84

01 Let each points be on the circle that corresponds to θ. Find the six trigonometric functions of the angle θ.

(1)

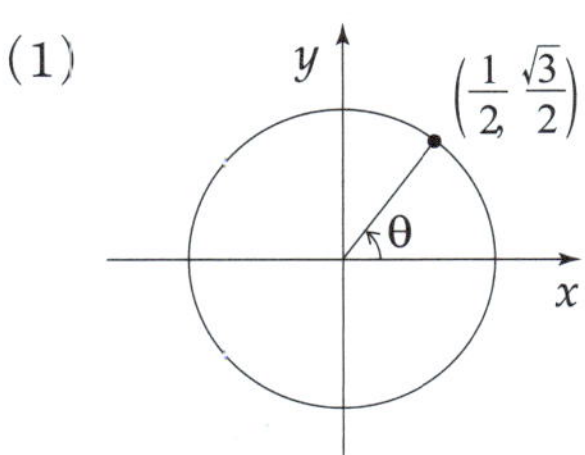

(2)

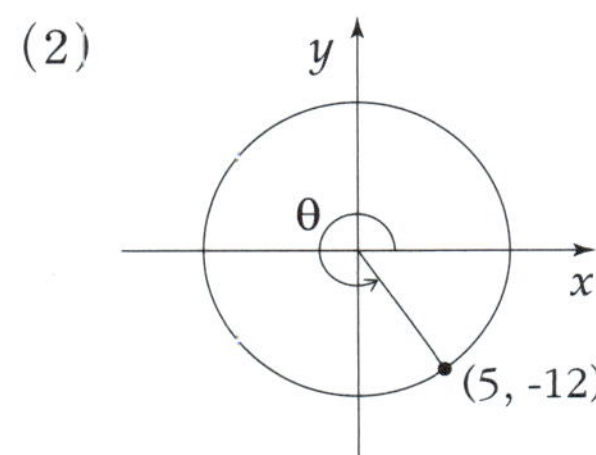

02 Find the reference angle for each angle.

(1) $\theta=-120°$

(2) $\theta=\dfrac{17\pi}{6}$

03 Find the six trigonometric functions at each angle.

(1) $\theta=\dfrac{\pi}{3}$

(2) $\theta=\dfrac{5\pi}{4}$

(3) $\theta=90°$

(4) $\theta=-180°$

Review Exercise

04 Using the given information, find the rest of trigonometric functions of the angle θ.

(1) $\sin\theta=\frac{1}{2}$, $\tan\theta=\frac{1}{\sqrt{3}}$

(2) $\cos\theta=\frac{2}{3}$, $\tan<0$

(3) $\sec\theta=-3$, $\sin\theta<0$

(4) $\cot\theta=-\frac{2}{\sqrt{5}}$, $\sec\theta>0$

05 State the quadrant in which θ lies.

(1) $\cot\theta<0$ and $\sec\theta\tan\theta<0$

(2) $\sin\theta\cos\theta>0$ and $\cos\theta\tan\theta<0$

06

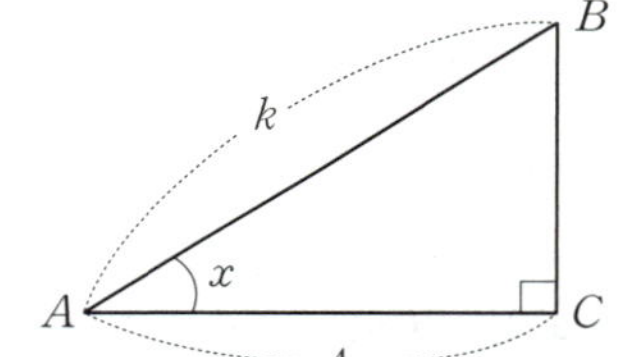

If $\sin x=\frac{1}{2}$ in Figure above, what is the value of k?

07

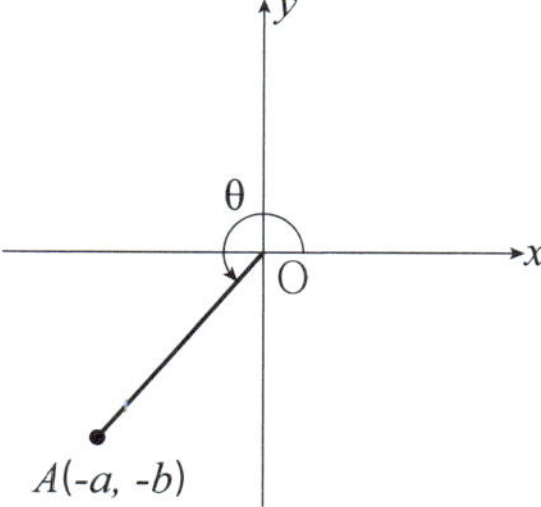

In Figure above, find the six trigonometric function of the angle θ in terms of a and b.

08 If $\cos\theta = m$ and $0 < \theta < \frac{\pi}{2}$, find $\tan\theta + \csc\theta$ in terms of m.

09 If $\sin x = k$ and $0 < x < \frac{\pi}{2}$, find each of the following in terms of k.

(1) $\cos x$

(2) $\tan(\pi - x)$

(3) $\sec(x + \pi)$

(4) $\csc(2\pi - x)$

10

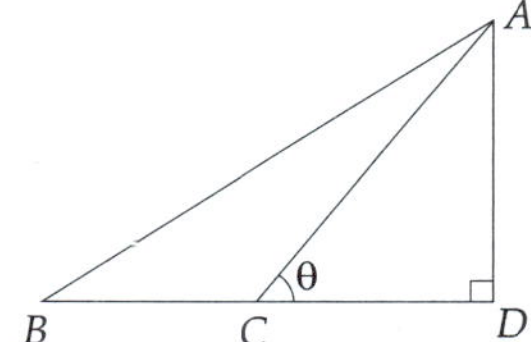

In Figure above, if $\overline{AB} = 8$, $\overline{BC} = 2$, and C is the midpoint of $\overline{BD}$, then what is the value of $\sin\theta$?

Review Exercise

11

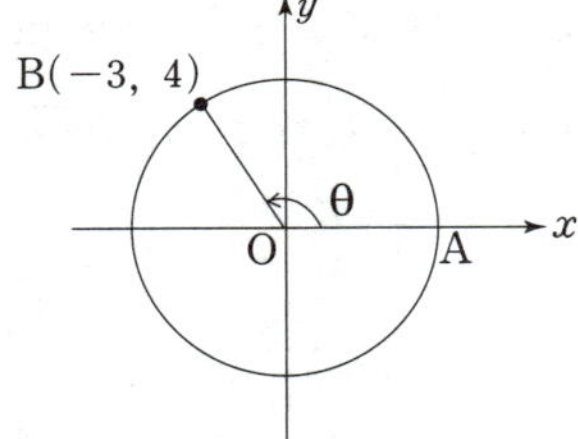

The diagram above shows a circle in the xy−plane, centered at the origin. The angle θ is in standard position, with two points A and B on the circle. (The unit of the radius is centimeters)

(1) What is the value of $\sin\theta+\cos\theta$?

(2) What is the slope of the terminal side OB?

(3) If the particle rotates around the circle counterclockwise at 4 revolutions per minute, what is the linear speed of the particle in centimeters per second?

12 In the xy−plane, the terminal ray of angle θ in standard position intersects a circle of radius r at the point $(-4\sqrt{3}, -4)$. What is the value of $r\theta$? (θ is in radian)

13

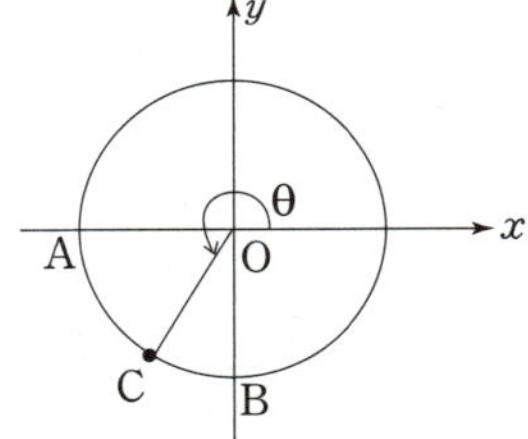

The diagram above shows a unit circle in the xy−plane. The measure of angle AOC is twice as large as the measure of angle BOC.

(1) What are the coordinates of point C?

(2) What is the slope of the terminal side OC?

(3) What is the value of $\sin\angle AOC \times \cos\angle BOC$?

14

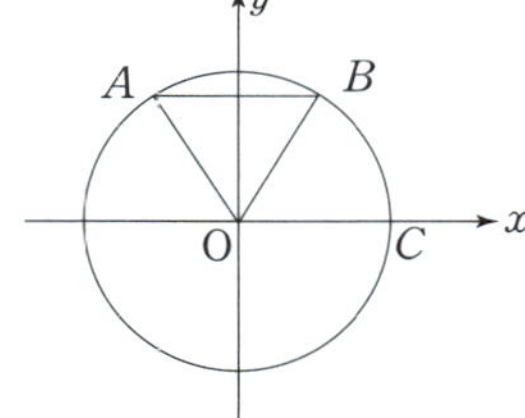

The diagram above shows a circle of radius 4 in the xy−plane, where AOB is an equilateral triangle, and the chord AB is parallel to the x−axis.

(1) What is the distance between two points A and B?

(2) What is the value of $\sin \angle COB - \sin \angle COA$

15 If $\cos \alpha = -\cos \beta$ and $\sin \alpha = \sin \beta$ where $0 < \alpha < \frac{\pi}{2}$ and $0 < \beta < 2\pi$, what does α equal to in terms of β?

(A) β

(B) $\frac{\pi}{2} - \beta$

(C) $\pi - \beta$

(D) $\pi + \beta$

16

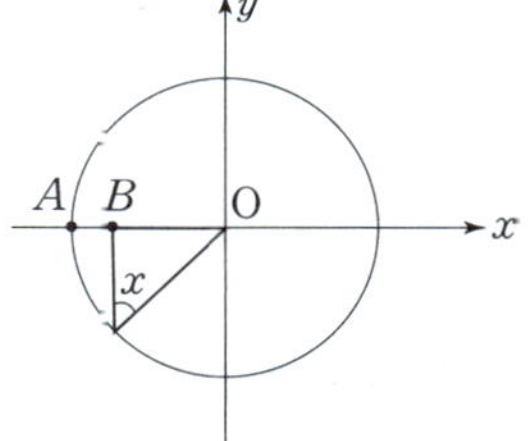

The diagram above shows a unit circle in the xy−plane. Which of the following expressions is equal to the length of AB?

(A) $\sin x$

(B) $\cos x$

(C) $1 - \sin x$

(D) $1 - \cos x$

17

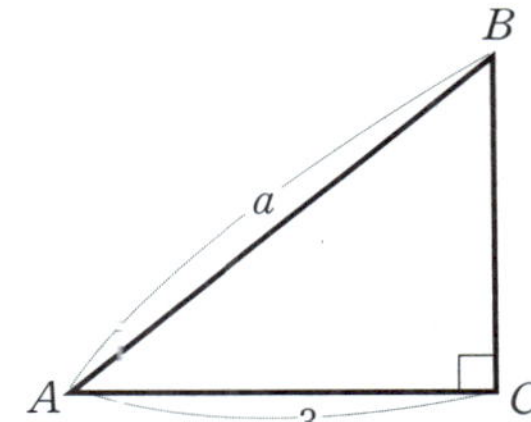

A right triangle is given above.
If $\sin A = h$, which of the following expressions represents the length of side BC in terms of h?

(A) $\frac{3h}{\sqrt{1-h^2}}$

(B) $\frac{9h}{\sqrt{1-h^2}}$

(C) $3\sqrt{h^2-1}$

(D) $9\sqrt{h^2-1}$

3 Graphs of Trigonometric Functions

01 Graph of Sine and Cosine Functions

In this part, we will study techniques for sketching the graphs of the sine and cosine function. The curves are periodic with period 2π and its graph repeats a cycle indefinitely in the positive and negative directions. The amplitude of the graph, defined as half the difference between the maximum and minimum values of the function, is 1. Let us take a look at the properties of the graphs.

1. Graph of $f(x)=\sin x$ and $f(x)=\cos x$

x	0	$\frac{\pi}{6}$	$\frac{\pi}{4}$	$\frac{\pi}{3}$	$\frac{\pi}{2}$	$\frac{3\pi}{4}$	π	$\frac{5\pi}{4}$	$\frac{3\pi}{2}$	$\frac{7\pi}{4}$	2π
$\sin x$	0	$\frac{1}{2}$	$\frac{\sqrt{2}}{2}$	$\frac{\sqrt{3}}{2}$	1	$\frac{\sqrt{2}}{2}$	0	$-\frac{\sqrt{2}}{2}$	-1	$-\frac{\sqrt{2}}{2}$	0
$\cos x$	1	$\frac{\sqrt{3}}{2}$	$\frac{\sqrt{2}}{2}$	$\frac{1}{2}$	0	$-\frac{\sqrt{2}}{2}$	-1	$-\frac{\sqrt{2}}{2}$	0	$\frac{\sqrt{2}}{2}$	1

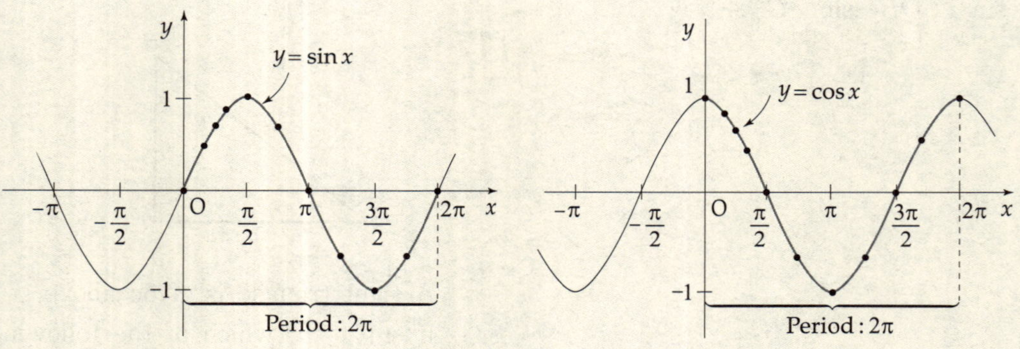

Range: $-1 \le y \le 1$ Range: $-1 \le y \le 1$

✔ The sine curve is symmetric about the origin, whereas the cosine curve is symmetric about the y−axis. These indicates that the sine function is odd and the cosine function is even.

(1) Domain: $(-\infty,\ \infty)$

(2) Range: $\{y \mid -1 \le y \le 1\}$

(3) Amplitude: 1

(4) Period: 2π

Note:
(1) The sine and cosine functions are both known as sinusoidal functions.
(2) The frequency of a sinusoidal function indicates the number of complete cycles the function completes within a unit interval, usually per unit of time. The frequency is the reciprocal of the period.

02 Graph of $f(x)=a\sin(bx)$ and $f(x)=a\cos(bx)$

The properties of the graph $f(x)=a\sin(bx)$ and $f(x)=a\cos(bx)$ are as follows.

(1) Domain: $(-\infty,\ \infty)$

(2) Range: $\{y \mid -|a| \le y \le |a|\}$

(3) Amplitude: $|a|$

(4) Period: $\dfrac{2\pi}{|b|}$ (5) Frequency $\dfrac{1}{\text{Period}}$

✔ It helps to sketch the graphs of the sine and cosine function better and easier if we find the critical points, which are x−intercepts, maximum point, and minimum point. Refer to the Figure below.

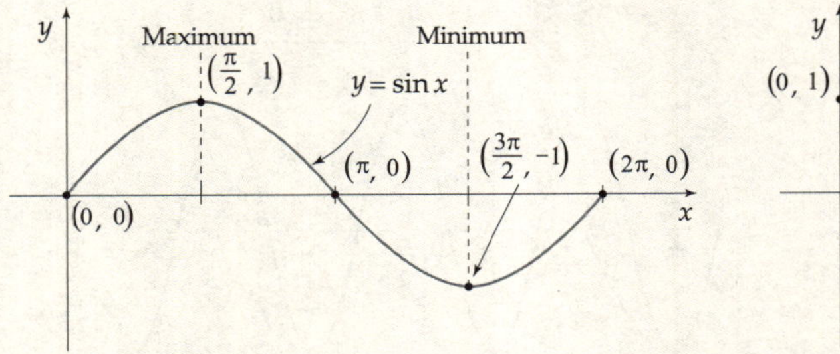

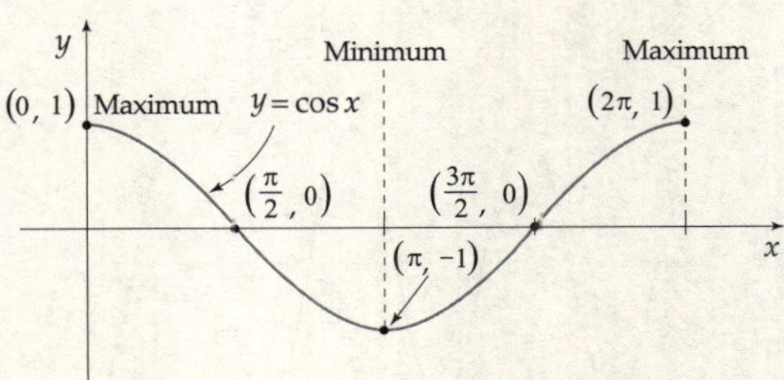

Example 1

Sketch the graph of each function.

① $y=2\sin x$ ② $y=\frac{1}{2}\cos x$

③ $y=2\sin(2x)$ ④ $y=-\cos(2x)$

Solution

① $y=2\sin x$

x	0	$\frac{\pi}{2}$	π	$\frac{3\pi}{2}$	2π
$2\sin x$	0	2	0	-2	0

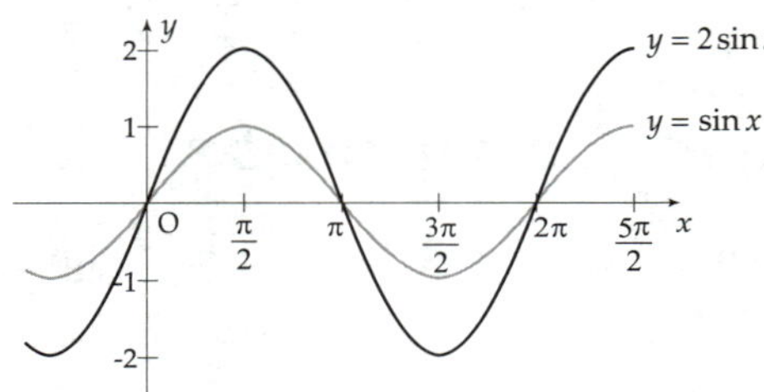

Domain: $(-\infty, \infty)$
Range: $\{y \mid -2 \le y \le 2\}$
Amplitude: 2
Period: $\frac{2\pi}{1}=2\pi$

② $y=\frac{1}{2}\cos x$

x	0	$\frac{\pi}{2}$	π	$\frac{3\pi}{2}$	2π
$\frac{1}{2}\cos x$	$\frac{1}{2}$	2	$-\frac{1}{2}$	0	$\frac{1}{2}$

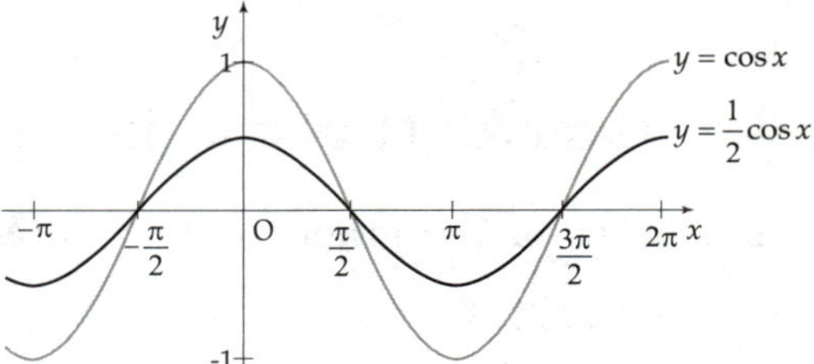

Domain: $(-\infty, \infty)$
Range: $\left\{y \mid -\frac{1}{2} \le y \le \frac{1}{2}\right\}$
Amplitude: $\frac{1}{2}$
Period: $\frac{2\pi}{1}=2\pi$

③ $y=2\sin(2x)$

x	0	$\frac{\pi}{4}$	$\frac{\pi}{2}$	$\frac{3\pi}{4}$	π
$2\sin(2x)$	0	2	0	-2	0

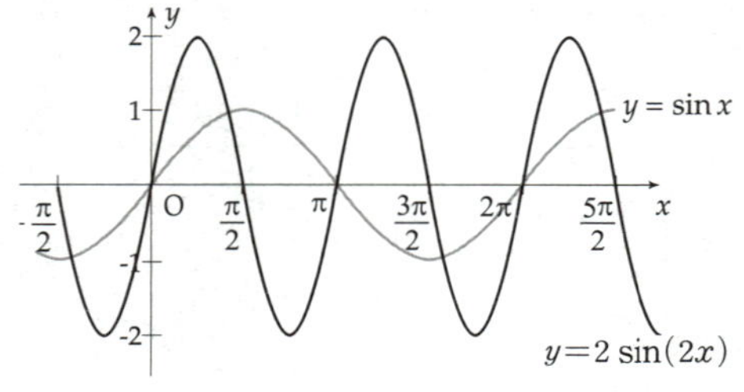

④ $y=-\cos(2x)$

x	0	$\frac{\pi}{4}$	$\frac{\pi}{2}$	$\frac{3\pi}{4}$	π
$-\cos(2x)$	-1	0	1	0	-1

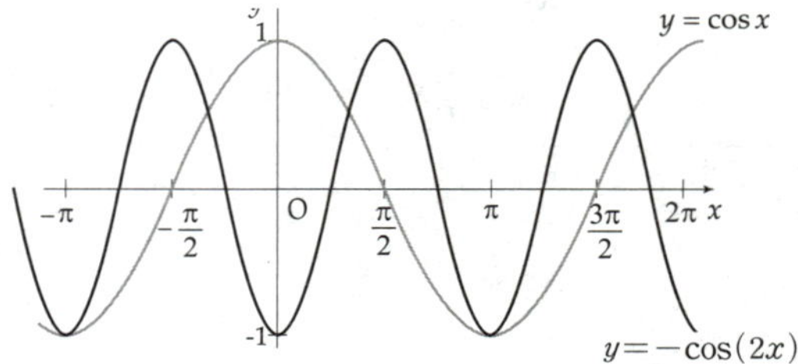

Domain: $(-\infty, \infty)$
Range: $\{y \mid -2 \le y \le 2\}$
Amplitude: 2
Period: $\frac{2\pi}{2}=\pi$

Domain: $(-\infty, \infty)$
Range: $\{y \mid -1 \le y \le 1\}$
Amplitude: 1
Period: $\frac{2\pi}{2}=\pi$

Check Point 1

Solutions_Page 90

Sketch the graph, including two full periods, of the function. Identify the domain, range, amplitude, and period of the function.

① $y=\frac{1}{2}\sin x$ ② $y=\cos(3x)$ ③ $y=-3\cos\frac{x}{2}$

03 Graph of $f(x)=a\sin b(x-h)+k$ and $f(x)=a\cos b(x-h)+k$

In order to graph $f(x)=a\sin b(x-h)+k$ or $f(x)=a\cos b(x-h)+k$, first graph $f(x)=a\sin(bx)$ or $f(x)=a\cos(bx)$ and then

(1) Shift it h units to the right if $h>0$, or to the left if $h<0$

(2) Shift it k units up if $k>0$, or down if $k<0$

Example 2

Sketch the graph of $y=2\sin 2\left(x-\frac{\pi}{4}\right)+1$.

Solution

We first graph $y=2\sin(2x)$ and then shift it $\frac{\pi}{4}$ units to the right and 1 unit up.

x	0	$\frac{\pi}{4}$	$\frac{\pi}{2}$	$\frac{3\pi}{4}$	π	$\frac{5\pi}{4}$
$2\sin x$	0	2	0	-2	0	
$2\sin 2\left(x-\frac{\pi}{4}\right)$		0	2	0	-2	0
$2\sin 2\left(x-\frac{\pi}{4}\right)+1$		$0+1=1$	$2+1=3$	$0+1=1$	$-2+1=-1$	$0+1=1$

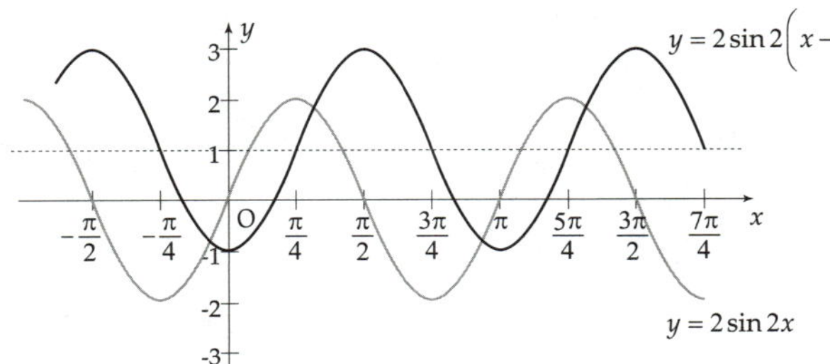

Domain: $(-\infty, \infty)$
Range: $\{y \mid -1 \le y \le 3\}$
Amplitude: 2
Period: $\frac{2\pi}{2}=\pi$

Check Point 2

Solutions_Page 90

Sketch the graph, including two full periods, of the function. Identify the domain, range, amplitude, and period of the function.

① $y=-2\cos(4x)-1$ ② $y=\frac{3}{2}\sin 2\left(x+\frac{\pi}{2}\right)$

04 Graph of Tangent Function

Now, we will study techniques for sketching the graphs of the tangent function. This curve is periodic with period π and its graph also repeats a cycle indefinitely in the positive and negative directions. However, unlike the curves of sine and cosine, the tangent curve does not have amplitude, but it has vertical asymptotes. Let us take a look at the properties of the graph.

1. Graph of $f(x)=\tan x$

x	$-\frac{\pi}{2}$	$-\frac{\pi}{4}$	0	$\frac{\pi}{4}$	$\frac{\pi}{2}$	$\frac{3\pi}{4}$	π	$\frac{3\pi}{2}$
$\tan x$	undef	-1	0	1	undef	-1	0	undef

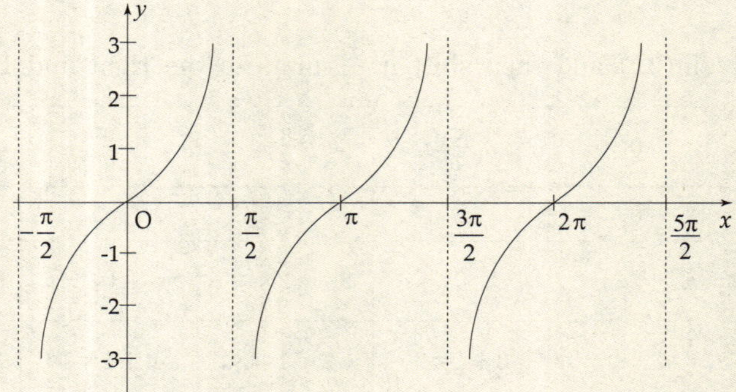

(1) Domain: All real numbers except for $y=\frac{\pi}{2}+n\pi$ $(n \in Z)$

(2) Range: $(-\infty, \infty)$

(3) No amplitude exists thus; no maximum or minimum value exist.

(4) Period: π

(6) Equation of vertical asymptotes: $x=\frac{\pi}{2}+n\pi$ $(n \in Z)$

✔ It helps to sketch the graphs of the tangent function better and easier if we find the critical values, which are $x-$intercepts, vertical asymptotes, and mid$-$point of these two values. Refer to the Figure below.

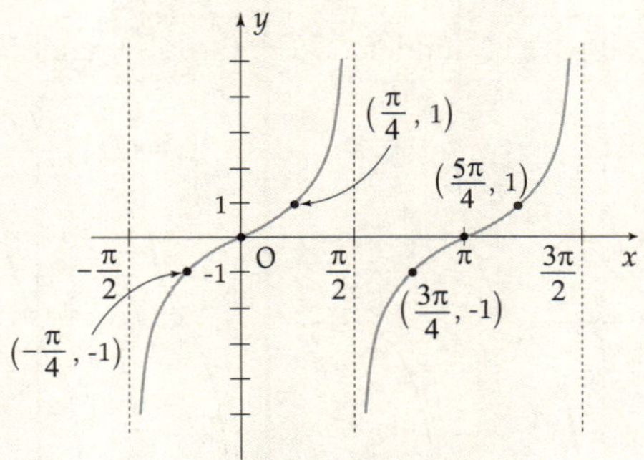

2. Graph of $f(x)=a\tan b(x-h)+k$

(1) Shift h units of the graph of $f(x)=a\tan(bx)$; to the right if $h>0$, or to the left if $h<0$

(2) Shift k units of the graph of $f(x)=a\tan(bx)$; upward if $k>0$, or downward if $k<0$

(3) No minimum or maximum value exist

(4) Period is $\frac{\pi}{|b|}$

(5) Equation of vertical asymptotes $x=\left(\frac{\pi}{2}+n\pi\right)\cdot\frac{1}{b}+h$ $(n \in Z)$

Example 3

Sketch the graph of each function.

① $y=\tan(2x)$ ② $y=2\tan(2x)$ ③ $y=\tan 2\left(x-\frac{\pi}{8}\right)+1$

Solution

① $y=\tan(2x)$

x	$-\frac{\pi}{4}$	$-\frac{\pi}{8}$	0	$\frac{\pi}{8}$	$\frac{\pi}{4}$
$\tan(2x)$	undef	-1	0	1	undef

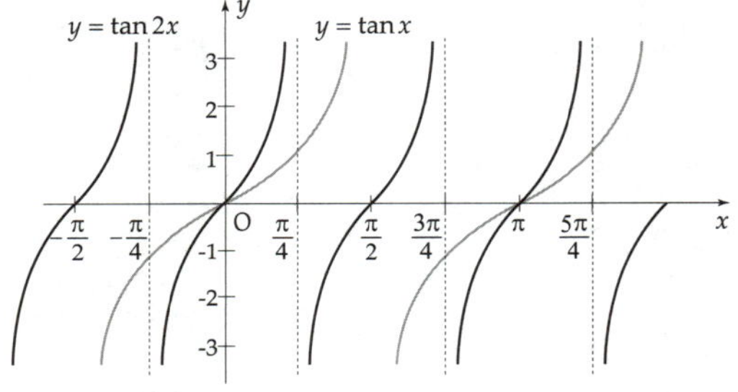

Equation of Asymptote:

$x=\left(\frac{\pi}{2}+n\pi\right)\cdot\frac{1}{2}=\frac{\pi}{4}+\frac{n\pi}{2}\quad(n\in Z)$

Domain: All real numbers except

$x=\frac{\pi}{4}+\frac{n\pi}{2}\quad(n\in Z)$

Range: $(-\infty,\infty)$

Period: $\frac{\pi}{2}$

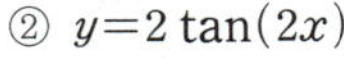

② $y=2\tan(2x)$

x	$-\frac{\pi}{4}$	$-\frac{\pi}{8}$	0	$\frac{\pi}{8}$	$\frac{\pi}{4}$
$2\tan(2x)$	undef	-2	0	2	undef

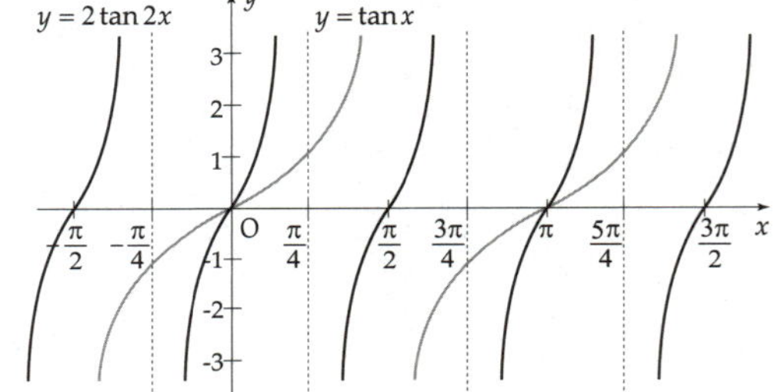

Equation of Asymptote:

$x=\left(\frac{\pi}{2}+n\pi\right)\cdot\frac{1}{2}=\frac{\pi}{4}+\frac{n\pi}{2}\quad(n\in Z)$

Domain: All real numbers except

$x=\frac{\pi}{4}+\frac{n\pi}{2}\quad(n\in Z)$

Range: $(-\infty,\infty)$

Period: $\frac{\pi}{2}$

③ $y=\tan 2\left(x-\frac{\pi}{8}\right)+1$

We first graph $y=\tan(2x)$ and then shift it $\frac{\pi}{8}$ units to the right and 1 unit up.

x	$-\frac{\pi}{4}$	$-\frac{\pi}{8}$	0	$\frac{\pi}{8}$	$\frac{\pi}{4}$	$\frac{3\pi}{4}$
$\tan(2x)$	undef	-1	0	1	undef	
$\tan 2\left(x-\frac{\pi}{8}\right)$		undef	-1	0	1	undef
$\tan 2\left(x-\frac{\pi}{8}\right)+1$		undef	$-1+1=0$	$0+1=1$	$1+1=2$	undef

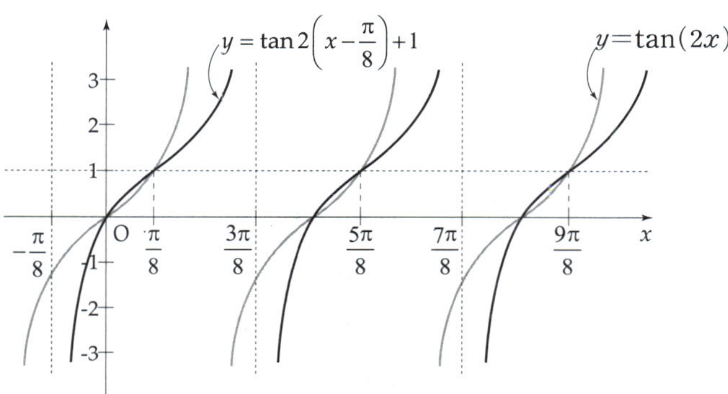

Equation of Asymptote:

$x=\left(\frac{\pi}{2}+n\pi\right)\cdot\frac{1}{2}+\frac{\pi}{8}=\frac{3\pi}{8}+\frac{n\pi}{2}\ (n\in Z)$

Domain: All real numbers except $x=\frac{3\pi}{8}+\frac{n\pi}{2}\ (n\in Z)$

Range: $(-\infty,\infty)$

Period: $\frac{\pi}{2}$

Check Point 3

Solutions_Page 90

Sketch the graph, including two full periods, of the function. Identify the domain, range, period, and equation of vertical asymptotes of the function.

① $y=3\tan\left(\frac{x}{3}\right)$ ② $y=-\tan\left(2x-\frac{\pi}{2}\right)+1$

05 Graph of Cosecant, Secant, and Cotangent Functions

Cosecant, secant, and cotangent function are reciprocals of sine, cosine, and tangent functions. For example, at a given value of x, the value of $\csc x$ is the reciprocal of $\sin x$ and $\csc x$ has vertical asymptote if $\sin x=0$. Same theories applies to $\sec x$. So, the easiest way to sketch the graph of a cosecant and secant functions is to first sketch its reciprocal functions. Then, sketch the graph along the asymptote starting at the maximum and minimum values.

For the cosecant graph, sketch in the same way as graphs for sine and cosine.

Here are summary of the graph of $y=\csc x$, $y=\sec x$, and $y=\cot x$.

1. $y=\csc x=\dfrac{1}{\sin x}$

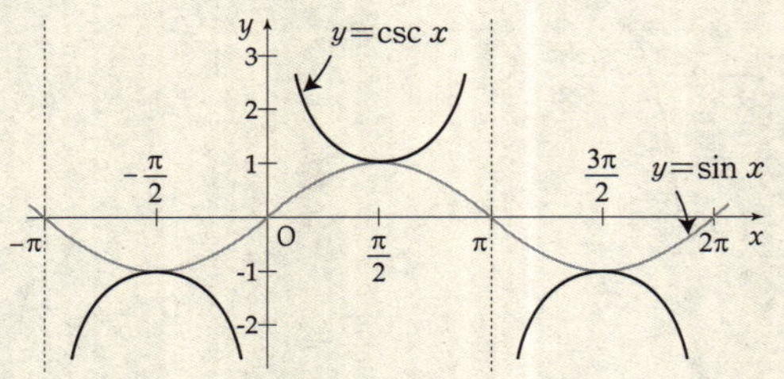

Domain: All real numbers except $x=n\pi$ $(n\in Z)$

Range: $(-\infty,\ -1]\cup[1,\ \infty)$

Equation of Asymptote: $x=n\pi(n\in Z)$

Period: 2π

Symmetry: origin

2. $y=\sec x=\dfrac{1}{\cos x}$

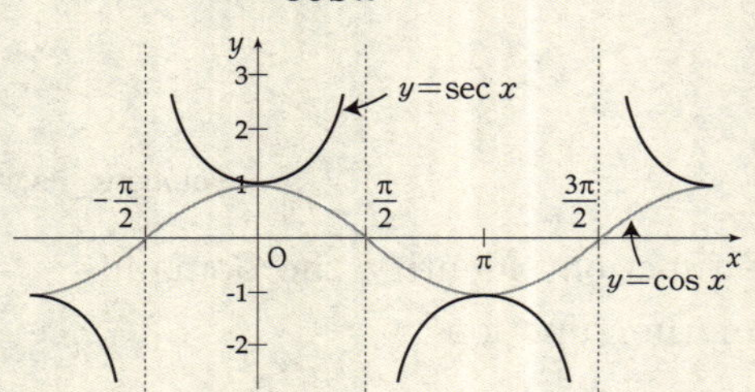

Domain: All real numbers except $x=\dfrac{\pi}{2}+n\pi$ $(n\in Z)$

Range: $(-\infty,-1]\cup[1,\infty)$

Equation of Asymptote: $x=\dfrac{\pi}{2}+n\pi$ $(n\in Z)$

Period: 2π

Symmetry: $y-$axis

3. $y=\cot x=\dfrac{1}{\tan x}$

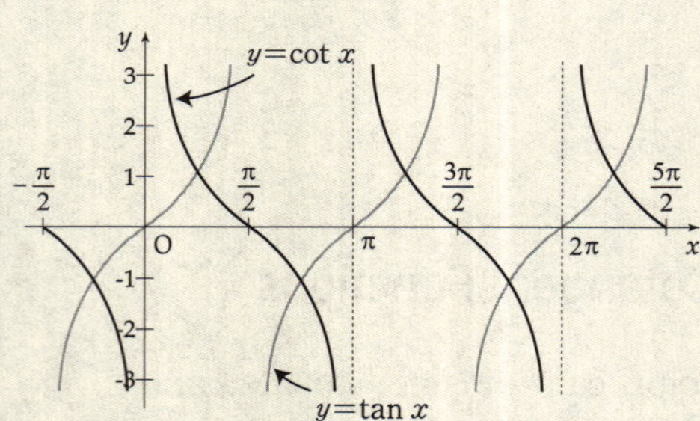

Domain: All real numbers except $x=n\pi$ $(n\in Z)$

Range: $(-\infty,\infty)$

Equation of Asymptote: $x=n\pi(n\in Z)$

Period: π

Symmetry: origin

Example 4–1

Sketch the graph of $y=2\csc\left(x-\dfrac{\pi}{4}\right)$

Solution

First, sketch the graph of its reciprocal $y=2\sin\left(x-\frac{\pi}{4}\right)$. Then, sketch the graph $y=2\csc\left(x-\frac{\pi}{4}\right)$ along the asymptote starting at the maximum and minimum values.

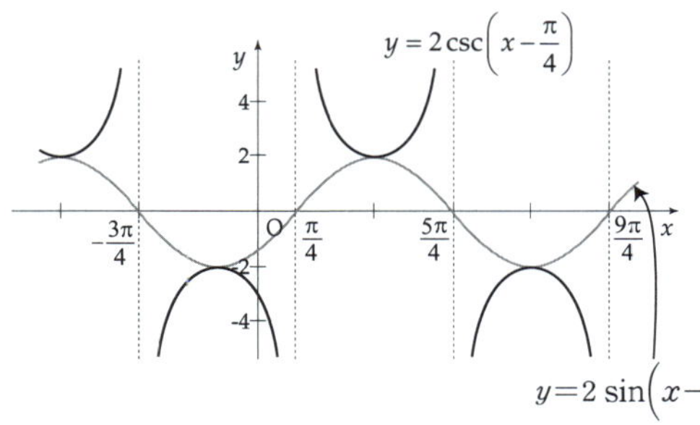

Domain: All real numbers except $x=\frac{\pi}{4}+n\pi$ $(n\in Z)$

Range: $(-\infty,\ -2]\cup[2,\ \infty)$

Equation of Asymptote: $x=\frac{\pi}{4}+n\pi$ $(n\in Z)$

Period: $\frac{2\pi}{1}=2\pi$

Example 4–2

Sketch the graph of $y=\cot(2x)-1$.

Solution

To graph $y=\cot(2x)-1$, first sketch the graph of $y=\cot(2x)$ and then shift it 1 unit down.

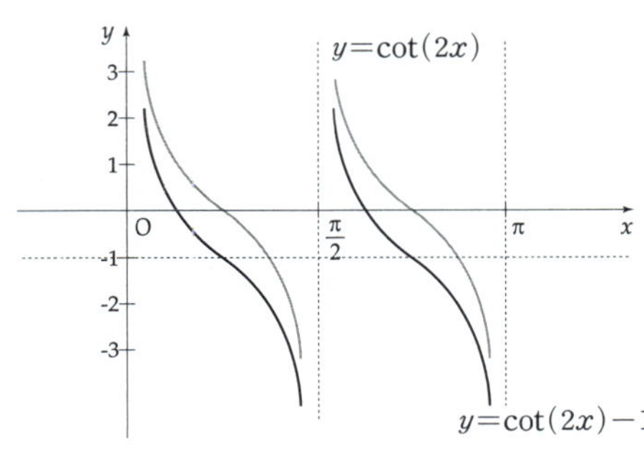

Domain: All real number except $x=\frac{n\pi}{2}(n\in Z)$
Range: $(-\infty,\ \infty)$

Equation of Asymptote: $\frac{n\pi}{2}(n\in Z)$

Period: $\frac{\pi}{2}$

Check Point 4

Solutions_Page 91

Sketch the graph, including two full periods, of the function. Identify the domain, range, period, and equation of vertical asymptotes of the function.

① $y=\sec(\pi x)$ ② $y=-2\cot\left(\frac{\pi x}{2}\right)-1$ ③ $y=-\csc(2x-\pi)$

Review Exercise

01 What is the amplitude of the graph of $f(x)=3-2\cos\left(x+\frac{\pi}{2}\right)$?

02 What is the period of the graph of $f(x)=5\sin 2(x-\pi)-1$?

03 Find the amplitude and period of the function $f(x)=\frac{1}{\pi}\cos\left(\frac{x}{\pi}\right)$.

04 What is the range of the graph of $f(x)=1-\frac{1}{2}\sin(x-2)$?

05

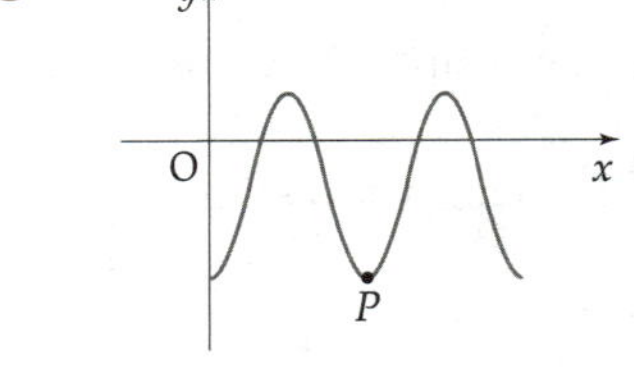

The graph above shows a portion of the graph of $g(x)=-2\cos(4x)-1$. Find the coordinates of the point P.

06 At what value of x, does the graph of $f(x)=1-\cos(2x)$ has a maximum value?

(A) $\frac{\pi}{6}$ (B) $\frac{\pi}{4}$

(C) $\frac{\pi}{2}$ (D) $\frac{3\pi}{4}$

07 If the graph of the function $y=2\cos x$ is shifted $\frac{\pi}{4}$ units to the left and 4 units up, which of the following could be the equation of the shifted graph?

(A) $y=2\cos\left(x+\frac{\pi}{4}\right)-4$

(B) $y=2\cos\left(x+\frac{\pi}{4}\right)+4$

(C) $y=-2\cos\left(x-\frac{\pi}{4}\right)+4$

(D) $y=-2\cos\left(x+\frac{\pi}{4}\right)-4$

08 For which of the following values of x is it always true that $\sin x < \cos x$?

(A) $0 < x < \frac{\pi}{4}$

(B) $\frac{\pi}{4} < x < \frac{\pi}{2}$

(C) $\frac{\pi}{2} < x < \frac{3\pi}{4}$

(D) $\frac{3\pi}{4} < x < \pi$

09 As x increases on the interval $\left(\frac{\pi}{2}, \pi\right)$, which of the following functions also increases?

(A) $f(x) = \sin x$

(B) $f(x) = \cos x$

(C) $f(x) = \tan x$

(D) $f(x) = \cot x$

10

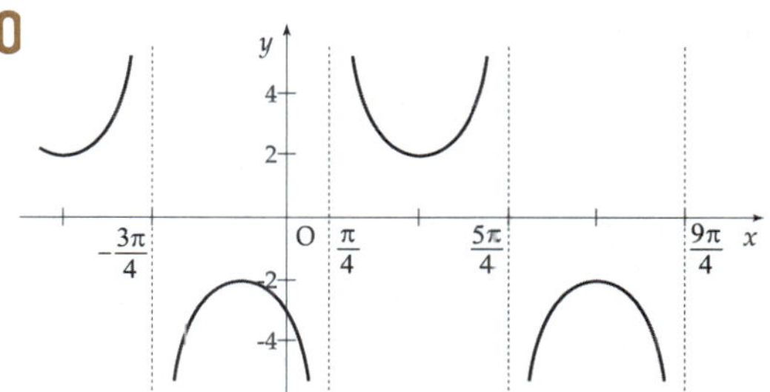

Which of the following could be a function of the graph in Figure above?

(A) $y = 2\csc\left(x - \frac{\pi}{4}\right)$

(B) $y = -2\csc\left(x - \frac{\pi}{4}\right)$

(C) $y = 2\sec\left(x - \frac{\pi}{4}\right)$

(D) $y = -2\sec\left(x + \frac{\pi}{4}\right)$

11

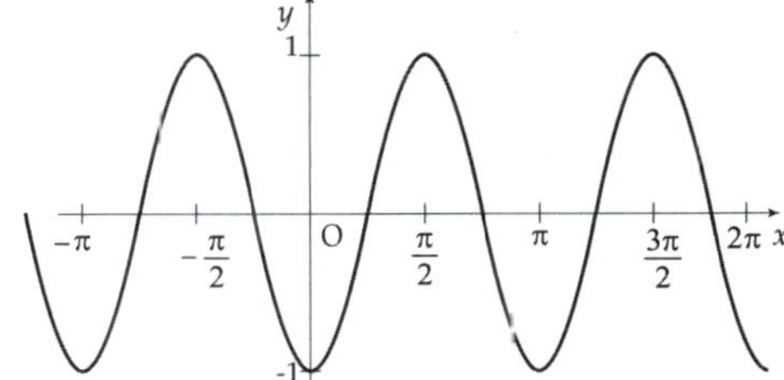

The graph shown above is a function of the form $y = a\cos(bx)$. Find the value of $a + b$.

Review Exercise

12 The function $y=2\sin(2x)$ is graphed in the $xy-$plane. If $y=1$, which of the following is true about the value of x on the interval $0<x<2\pi$?

(A) There are no value of x on $0<x<2\pi$ for which $y=1$.

(B) There are 2 value of x on $0<x<2\pi$ for which $y=1$.

(C) There are 4 value of x on $0<x<2\pi$ for which $y=1$.

(D) There are 6 value of x on $0<x<2\pi$ for which $y=1$.

13 The function f is given by $h(x)=\sin x$. If angle x is in the second quadrant and angle y is greater than x but less than π, which of the following is correct?

(A) $h(x)<h(y)$

(B) $h(x)=h(y)$

(C) $h(x)>h(y)$

(D) It is not possible to determine which of $f(x)$ and $f(y)$ is larger based on the information given above alone.

14 The function f is given by $f(x)=\tan x$. If angle x is in the third quadrant and angle y is greater than x but less than $\frac{3\pi}{2}$, which of the following is correct?

(A) $f(x)<f(y)$

(B) $f(x)=f(y)$

(C) $f(x)>f(y)$

(D) It is not possible to determine which of $f(x)$ and $f(y)$ is larger based on the information given above alone.

15 In the graph of the function $f(x)=\cos x$ for $0\le x\le 2\pi$ in the $xy-$plane, which of the following is true about the value of f?

(A) The value of f gives the horizontal distance from the $x-$axis for $0\le x\le 2\pi$.

(B) The value of f gives the horizontal displacement from the $x-$axis for $0\le x\le 2\pi$.

(C) The value of f gives the vertical distance from the $x-$axis for $0\le x\le 2\pi$.

(D) The value of f gives the vertical displacement from the $x-$axis for $0\le x\le 2\pi$.

16 At what value of x does the graph of $f(x)=\frac{1}{2}+\frac{3}{4}\cos\left(2x-\frac{\pi}{2}\right)$ reach its maximum value?

(A) 0

(B) $\frac{\pi}{4}$

(C) $\frac{\pi}{2}$

(D) $\frac{3\pi}{4}$

17 The function f is given by $f(x)=\sin\left(\frac{x}{2}\right)$. On which of the following interval is the graph of f is increasing and concave up?

(A) $0<x<\pi$

(B) $\pi<x<2\pi$

(C) $2\pi<x<3\pi$

(D) $3\pi<x<4\pi$

18

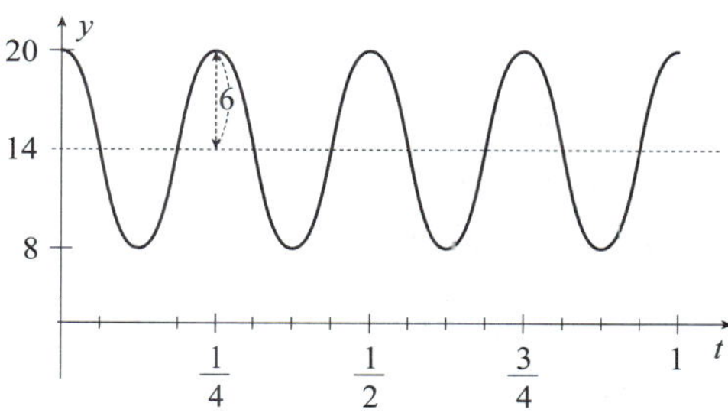

The figure shows the graph of a periodic function f in the xy—plane. What is the frequency of f?

19 Which of the following is true about the relationship between the graphs of $f(x)=\sin x$ and $g(x)=\cos x$ in the xy—plane?

(A) $f(x)=g\left(x+\frac{\pi}{2}\right)$

(B) $g(x)=f\left(x+\frac{\pi}{2}\right)$

(C) $f(x)=g(x+\pi)$

(D) $g(x)=f(x+\pi)$

Review Exercise

20 The function f is given by $f(x)=\tan x$. Which of the following is true about the function $g(x)=|f(x)|$?

(A) g is an odd function.

(B) g is an even function.

(C) g is both odd and even.

(D) g is neither odd nor even.

21

x	0	2	4	6	8
y	12	8	4	8	12

The table provides selected values of the sinusoidal function $f(x)$ with a period of 8. If $f(x)$ is expressed as $f(x)=a\cos(bx)+c$, what is the value of abc?

22 The function f is given by $f(x)=\tan(2x-\pi)$. Which of the following statements about the vertical asymptotes of the graph of f is true?

(A) The vertical asymptotes of the graph of f occur at $x=\frac{\pi}{2}+\pi n$, where n is an integer.

(B) The vertical asymptotes of the graph of f occur at $x=\frac{\pi}{4}+\frac{\pi n}{2}$, where n is an integer.

(C) The vertical asymptotes of the graph of f occur at $x=\frac{\pi}{2}+\frac{\pi n}{2}$, where n is an integer.

(D) The vertical asymptotes of the graph of f occur at $x=\frac{\pi}{4}+\pi n$, where n is an integer.

23

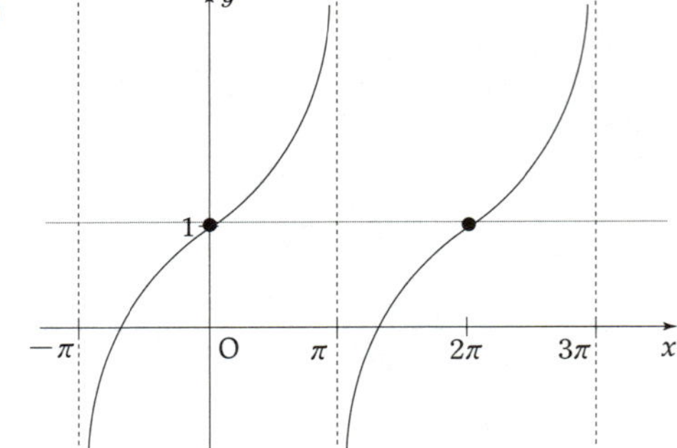

The figure above is the graph of the function f given by $f(x)=\tan(bx)+c$. What is the value of of $b+c$?

24 The function f is given by $f(x)=\csc x$. Which of the following statements about the vertical asymptotes of the graph of f is true?

(A) The vertical asymptotes occur at $x=\frac{\pi}{2}+2\pi n$, where n is any integer.

(B) The vertical asymptotes occur at $x=\frac{\pi}{2}+\pi n$, where n is any integer.

(C) The vertical asymptotes occur at $x=2\pi n$, where n is any integer.

(D) The vertical asymptotes occur at $x=\pi n$, where n is any integer.

25 The function f is given by $f(x)=3\cot(2x-\pi)$. Which of the following statements about the domain of the graph of f is true?

(A) The set of all real numbers x, except $x=\frac{\pi}{2}+\frac{\pi n}{2}$, where n is any integer.

(B) The set of all real numbers x, except $x=\frac{\pi}{2}+\pi n$, where n is any integer.

(C) The set of all real numbers x, except $x=\frac{\pi n}{2}$, where n is any integer.

(D) The set of all real numbers x, except $x=\pi n$, where n is any integer.

26 The function f is given by $f(x)=2-\frac{3}{2}\sin x$. Which of the following is the range of the graph of f?

(A) $-2\leq y\leq 2$

(B) $-0.5\leq y\leq 2.5$

(C) $-0.5\leq y\leq 1.5$

(D) $0.5\leq y\leq 3.5$

27 The function f is given by $f(x)=1+2\sec(x+\pi)$. Which of the following is the range of the graph of f?

(A) $[-1, 3]$

(B) $(-\infty, -1]\cup[3, \infty)$

(C) $[-2, 2]$

(D) $(-\infty, -2]\cup[2, \infty)$

4 Inverse Trigonometric Functions

01 Inverse Sine and Cosine Functions

We learned that the inverse function of a given function exists if and only if the function is a one-to-one function. Since we know that the graphs of $y=\sin x$ and $y=\cos x$ have repeating peaks and troughs(or maximum and minimum), they are not one-to-one functions. However, if we restrict the domain of the function as shown in Figure below, the restricted function is one-to-one and then it has its corresponding inverse function.

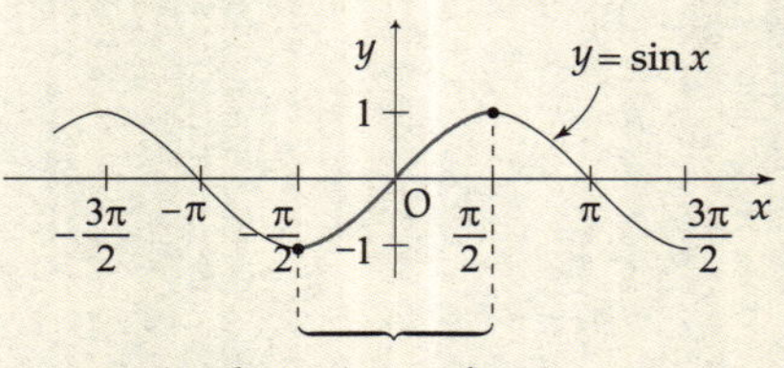

sin x has an inverse function on this interval.

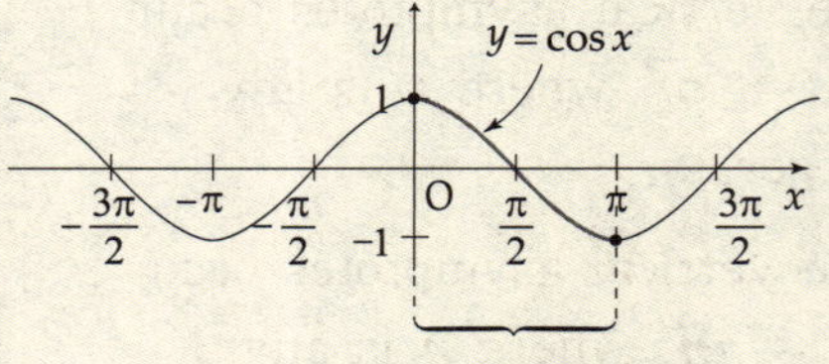

cos x has an inverse function on this interval.

The inverse function is the inverse of this restricted portion of each function.

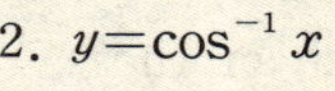

The inverse sine function is written as $y=\sin^{-1} x$ or $y=\arcsin x$.

1. $y=\sin^{-1} x$

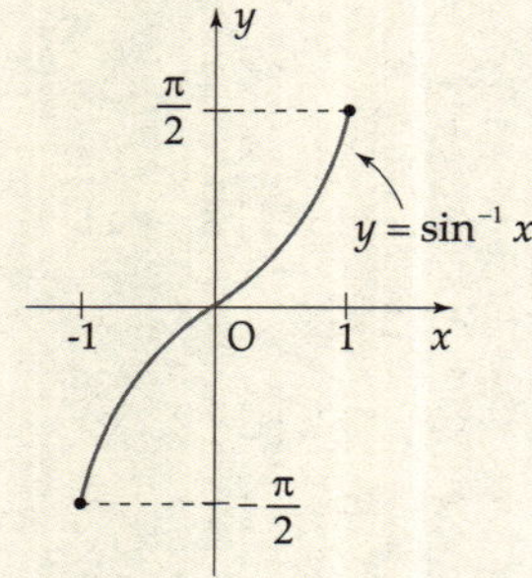

(1) $y=\sin^{-1} x$ if and only if $x=\sin y$

(2) Domain: $[-1,\ 1]$

(3) Range: $\left[-\frac{\pi}{2},\ \frac{\pi}{2}\right]$

2. $y=\cos^{-1} x$

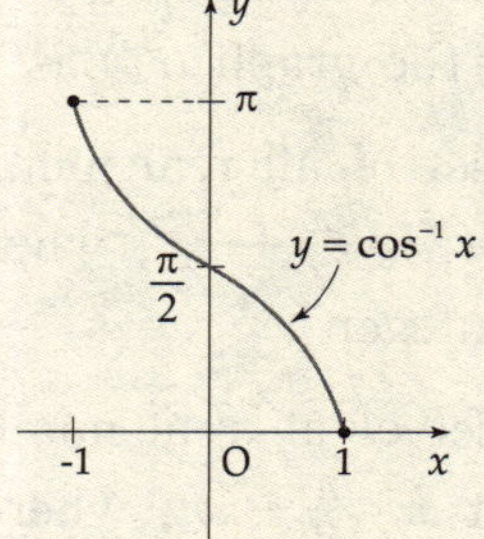

(1) $y=\cos^{-1} x$ if and only if $x=\cos y$

(2) Domain: $[-1,\ 1]$

(3) Range: $[0,\ \pi]$

Example 1

Find the value of each expression.

① $\sin^{-1}\dfrac{1}{2}$　　② $\cos^{-1}\left(-\dfrac{1}{\sqrt{2}}\right)$　　③ $\sin^{-1}\sqrt{2}$

Solution

① Let $\sin^{-1}\dfrac{1}{2}=y$. Then $\dfrac{1}{2}=\sin y$.

The question is asking for the angle y whose sine is $\dfrac{1}{2}$ in the range of $\left[-\dfrac{\pi}{2}, \dfrac{\pi}{2}\right]$.

Since $\sin\dfrac{\pi}{6}=\dfrac{1}{2}$, $\sin^{-1}\dfrac{1}{2}=\dfrac{\pi}{6}$

$\sin^{-1}\dfrac{1}{2}=\dfrac{\pi}{6}$

② Let $\cos^{-1}\left(-\dfrac{1}{\sqrt{2}}\right)=y$. Then $-\dfrac{1}{\sqrt{2}}=\cos y$ in the range of $[0, \pi]$.

Since $\cos\dfrac{3\pi}{4}=-\dfrac{1}{\sqrt{2}}$, $\cos^{-1}\left(-\dfrac{1}{\sqrt{2}}\right)=\dfrac{3\pi}{4}$.

$\cos^{-1}\left(\dfrac{1}{\sqrt{2}}\right)=\dfrac{3\pi}{4}$

③ We cannot evaluate $\sin^{-1}\sqrt{2}$ because there is no angle whose sine is $\sqrt{2}$. Remember that the domain of the inverse sine function is $[-1, 1]$.

$\sin^{-1}\sqrt{2}=\text{Undefined}$

Check Point 1

Solutions_Page 96

Find the value of each expression.

① $\arccos\dfrac{1}{2}$　　② $\sin^{-1}\left(-\dfrac{1}{2}\right)$　　③ $\cos^{-1}\dfrac{\sqrt{2}}{2}$　　④ $\sin^{-1}(-1)$

02 Inverse Tangent Function

Similarly, we can define an inverse tangent function by restricting the domain of $y=\tan x$ to the interval $\left(-\frac{\pi}{2},\ \frac{\pi}{2}\right)$.

$y=\tan x$

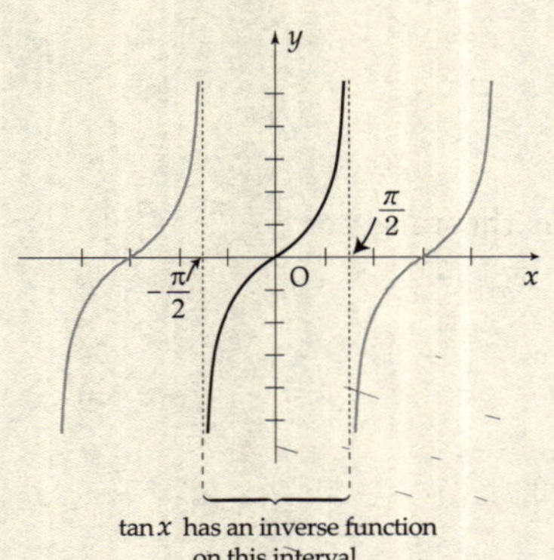

→

$y=\tan^{-1} x$

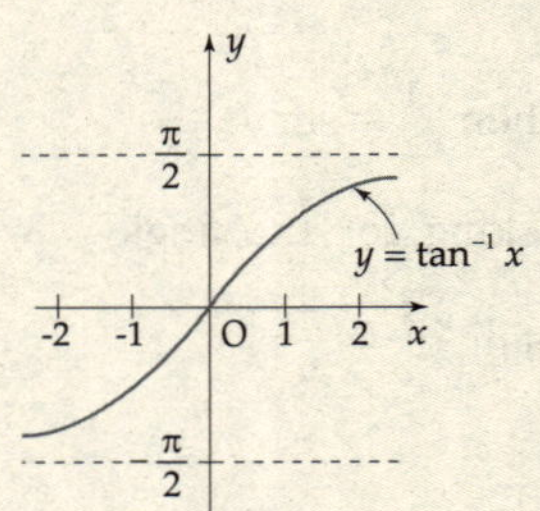

(1) $y=\tan^{-1}x$ if and only if $x=\tan y$

(2) Domain: $(-\infty,\ \infty)$

(3) Range: $\left(-\frac{\pi}{2},\ \frac{\pi}{2}\right)$

Example 2

Find the value of $\tan^{-1}(\sqrt{3})$.

Solution

Let $\tan^{-1}\sqrt{3}=y$. Then $\sqrt{3}=\tan y$ in the range of $\left[-\frac{\pi}{2},\ \frac{\pi}{2}\right]$

Since $\tan\frac{\pi}{3}=\sqrt{3}$. $\tan^{-1}(\sqrt{3})=\frac{\pi}{3}$.

$\tan^{-1}(\sqrt{3})=\frac{\pi}{3}$

Check Point 2

Solutions_Page 96

Find the value of each expression.

① $\tan^{-1}(-1)$

② $\arctan\left(-\frac{1}{\sqrt{3}}\right)$

03 Composition of Functions

In Algebra 2, we learned that one of the important properties of inverse function is

$$f(f^{-1}(x))=x \text{ and } f^{-1}(f(x))=x.$$

The following equations are always true in the restricted domains.

1. $\sin(\sin^{-1}x)=x$ and $\sin^{-1}(\sin x)=x$
2. $\cos(\cos^{-1}x)=x$ and $\cos^{-1}(\cos x)=x$
3. $\tan(\tan^{-1}x)=x$ and $\tan^{-1}(\tan x)=x$

Don't just memorize properties above. Instead, learn how to solve compositions of trigonometric and inverse trigonometric function problems through various examples.

Example 3

Find the value of each expression.

① $\sin^{-1}\left(\sin\frac{7\pi}{6}\right)$ ② $\tan\left(\tan^{-1}\frac{3}{5}\right)$ ③ $\sin\left(\cos^{-1}\frac{1}{3}\right)$

Solution

① First, $\sin\frac{7\pi}{6}=-\frac{1}{2}$ and then $\sin^{-1}\left(\sin\frac{7\pi}{6}\right)=\sin^{-1}\left(-\frac{1}{2}\right)$.

Now if we let $\sin^{-1}\left(-\frac{1}{2}\right)=y$, then $-\frac{1}{2}=\sin y$ in the range of $\left[-\frac{\pi}{2}, \frac{\pi}{2}\right]$.

Since $\sin\left(-\frac{\pi}{6}\right)=-\frac{1}{2}$, the answer is $-\frac{\pi}{6}$.

$\sin^{-1}\left(\sin\frac{7\pi}{6}\right)=-\frac{\pi}{6}$

② Let $\tan^{-1}\frac{3}{5}=y$. Then $\tan y=\frac{3}{5}$ in the range of $\left(-\frac{\pi}{2}, \frac{\pi}{2}\right)$.

Now, draw a triangle with angle y whose tangent is $\frac{3}{5}$.

So $\tan\left(\tan^{-1}\frac{3}{5}\right)=\tan y=\frac{3}{5}$.

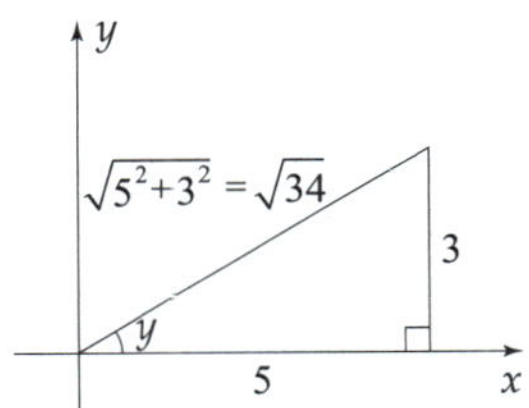

$\tan\left(\tan^{-1}\frac{3}{5}\right)=\frac{3}{5}$

③ Let $\cos^{-1}\frac{1}{3}=y$. Then $\cos y=\frac{1}{3}$ in the range of $[0,\ \pi]$.

Draw a triangle with angle whose cosine is $\frac{1}{3}$.

So $\sin\left(\cos^{-1}\frac{1}{3}\right)=\sin y=\frac{2\sqrt{2}}{3}$.

$\sin\left(\cos^{-1}\frac{1}{3}\right)=\frac{2\sqrt{2}}{3}$

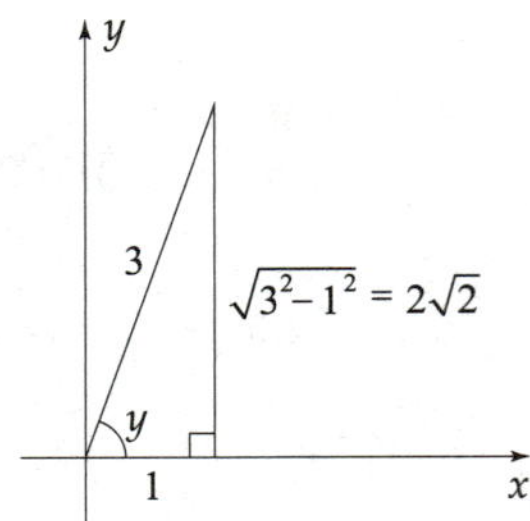

Check Point 3

Solutions_Page 96

Find the value of each expression.

① $\arcsin\left(\cos\frac{\pi}{4}\right)$

② $\cos^{-1}\left(\cos\frac{11\pi}{6}\right)$

③ $\sin(\arctan\sqrt{3})$

④ $\tan\left(\sin^{-1}\left(-\frac{1}{5}\right)\right)$

⑤ $\sin\left(\cos^{-1}\frac{1}{\sqrt{3}}\right)$

Review Exercise

Solutions_Page 97

01 Find the value of each expression.

(1) $\sin^{-1}\frac{\sqrt{3}}{2}$

(2) $\arctan(-\sqrt{3})$

(3) $\cos^{-1} 1$

(4) $\arcsin(-4)$

02 Write θ as a function of x.

(1)

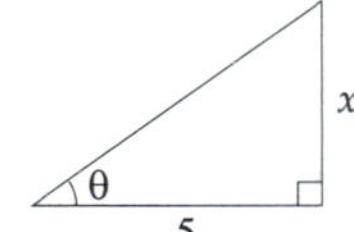

(2)

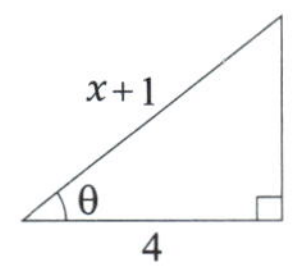

03 Find the value of each expression.

(1) $\arcsin\left(\sin\frac{5\pi}{3}\right)$

(2) $\sin\left(\cos^{-1}\frac{5}{13}\right)$

(3) $\cos^{-1}(\sin(3\pi))$

(4) $\sin(\tan^{-1}(-2))$

04 Find the algebraic expression in terms of x equivalent to each expression. $(x>0)$

(1) $\sec(\sin^{-1} x)$

(2) $\cos\left(\tan^{-1}\frac{1}{x}\right)$

Review Exercise

05

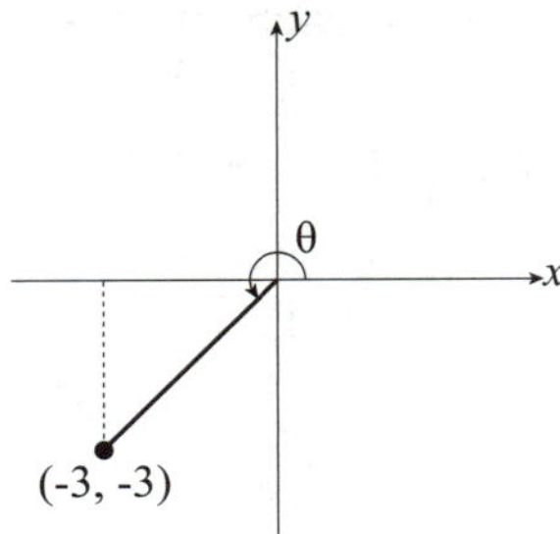

In Figure above, what is the radian measure of angle θ?

06 If $\tan x = \frac{2}{5}$ and $\pi \leq x < \frac{3\pi}{2}$,

then what is the value of $\cos x$ rounded to three decimal places?

07 The function f is given by $f(x) = 2\sin(2x)$ for $-\frac{\pi}{4} \leq x \leq \frac{\pi}{4}$.

Find the domain of the inverse of f.

08 The function f is given by $f(x) = \frac{1}{2}\cos(2\pi x)$ for $0 \leq x \leq \frac{1}{2}$.

Find the domain of the inverse of f.

09

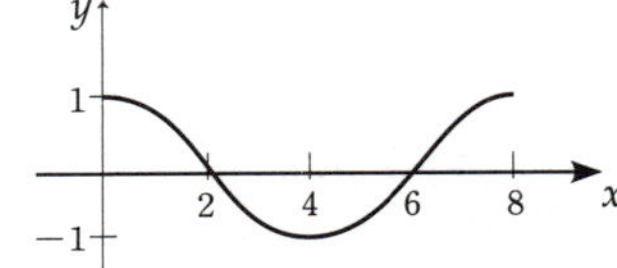

The graph of the sinusoidal function f is given in the xy-plane. Determine the length of the largest interval of x-values over which the inverse function of f can be defined.

10 The function f is given by $f(x) = 2\sin(\pi x)$ for $-\frac{1}{2} \leq x \leq \frac{1}{2}$.
Which of the following is equal to the inverse of f?

(A) $\pi \arcsin\left(\frac{x}{2}\right)$

(B) $\frac{1}{\pi}\arcsin\left(\frac{x}{2}\right)$

(C) $\pi \arcsin(2x)$

(D) $\frac{1}{\pi}\arcsin(2x)$

11

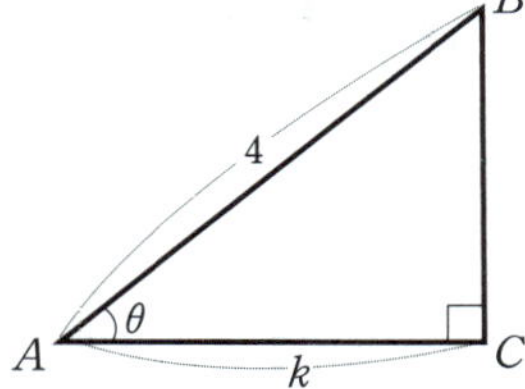

A right triangle is shown above. If the function h gives the value of θ as a function of k, which of the following could define $h(k)$?

(A) $h(k)=\sin^{-1}\frac{\sqrt{16-k^2}}{4}$

(B) $h(k)=\cos^{-1}\frac{\sqrt{16-k^2}}{4}$

(C) $h(k)=\sin^{-1}\frac{4}{\sqrt{16-k^2}}$

(D) $h(k)=\cos^{-1}\frac{4}{\sqrt{16-k^2}}$

12

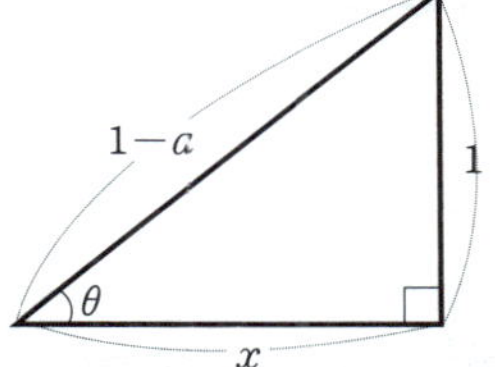

A right triangle is shown above. Which of the following expresses θ as a function of a?

(A) $\theta=\sin^{-1}(1-a)$

(B) $\theta=\sin^{-1}\left(\frac{1}{\sqrt{a(a-2)}}\right)$

(C) $\theta=\cos^{-1}\left(\frac{\sqrt{a(a-2)}}{1-a}\right)$

(D) $\theta=\cos^{-1}(1-a)$

5 Real-Life Problems with Trigonometry

01 Applications involving Right Triangles

In this section, we will demonstrate how trigonometry can be used to solve real life problems, in which they are mostly in the fields of navigation, surveying, and astronomy. The main problem generally was to determine an inaccessible distance or unknown angle.

Example 1-1

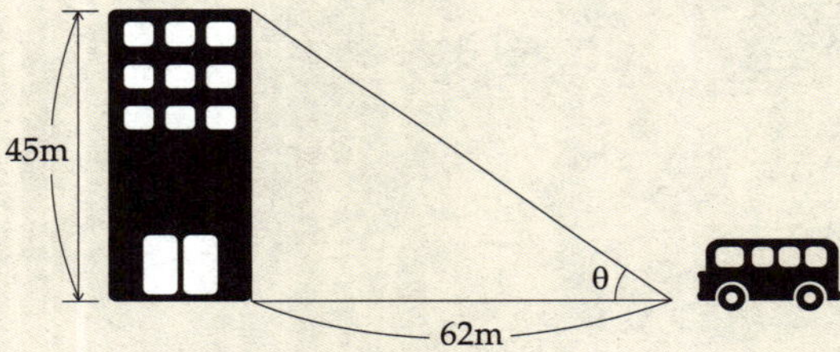

A bus is 62 meter from the base of a building 45 meters high, as shown in Figure above. Find the angle of elevation from the bus to the top of the building.

Solution

$\tan\theta = \frac{45}{62} \rightarrow \theta = \tan^{-1}\frac{45}{62} = 35.97°$

So the angle of elevation from the bus to the top of the building is approximately 35.97°.

35.97°

Example 1–2

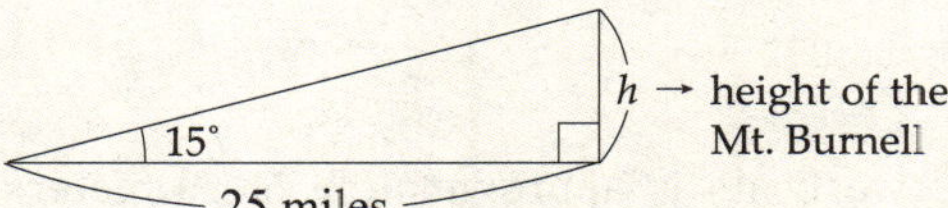

David is standing 25 miles away from Mt. Burnell. If the top of the Mt. Burnell makes an angle of 15°, as shown in Figure above, what is the height of Mt. Burnell?

Solution

$\tan 15° = \frac{h}{25} \rightarrow h = 25 \tan 15° = 6.7$

So Mt. Burnell is approximately 6.7 miles high.

6.7 miles

Example 1–3

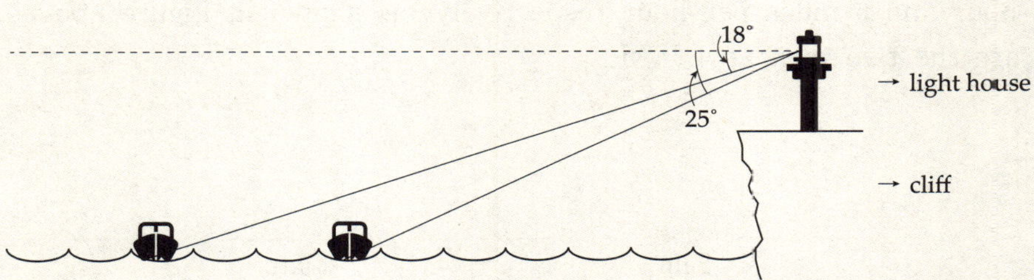

A light house on a 50 meter high cliff makes angles of depression 18° and 25° with two boats respectively, as shown in Figure above. If the light is located 10 meters above the lighthouse, what is the distance between the two boats?

Solution

From the figure below, we need to find $\overline{AB}$ and $\overline{AB} = \overline{AC} - \overline{BC}$.

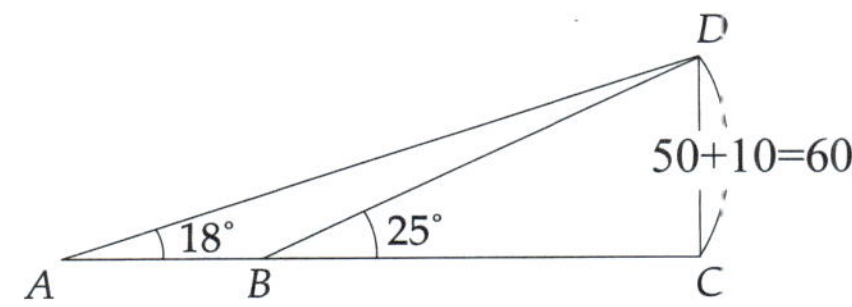

$\tan 18° = \frac{60}{\overline{AC}} \rightarrow \overline{AC} = \frac{60}{\tan 18°} = 184.66$

$\tan 25° = \frac{60}{\overline{BC}} \rightarrow \overline{BC} = \frac{60}{\tan 25°} = 128.67$

$\overline{AB} = \overline{AC} - \overline{BC} = 184.66 - 128.67 = 55.99$

So the distance between the two boats is approximately 55.99 meters.

55.99 meters

Example 1–4

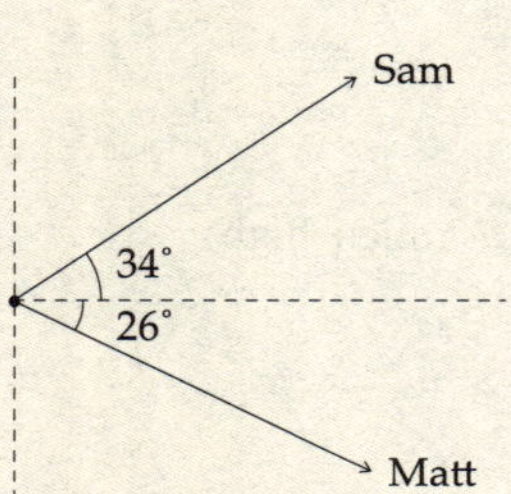

At noon, Sam and Matt start to walk from the same point with the speed of 8 miles per hour and 5 miles per hour respectively, as shown in Figure above. How far away are the two men at 4 P.M.?

Solution

	Sam	Matt
Speed	8 mph	5 mph
Distance Traveled	$8 \times 4 = 32$ miles	$5 \times 4 = 20$ miles

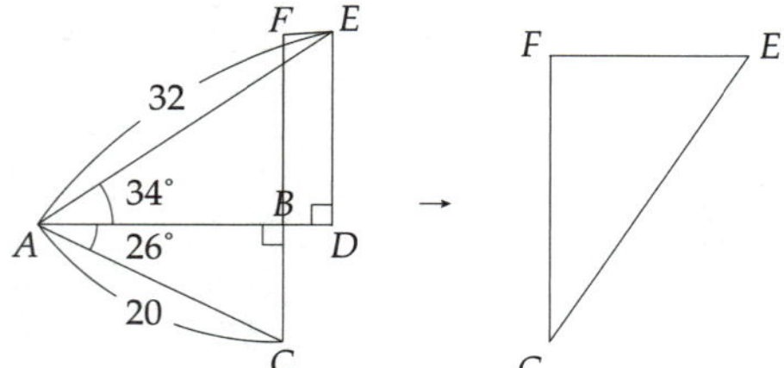

$\cos 34° = \frac{\overline{AD}}{32} \rightarrow \overline{AD} = 32 \cos 34° = 26.53$

$\cos 26° = \frac{\overline{AB}}{20} \rightarrow \overline{AB} = 20 \cos 26° = 17.98$

In a similar manner,

$\overline{DE} = 32 \sin 34° = 17.89$ and $\overline{BC} = 20 \sin 26° = 8.78$.

Now, $\overline{FE} = \overline{BD} = \overline{AD} - \overline{AB} = 26.53 - 17.98 = 8.55$ and $\overline{FC} = \overline{DE} + \overline{BC} = 17.89 + 8.78 = 26.67$.

By the Pythagorean theorem, $\overline{EC}=\sqrt{8.55^2+26.67^2}=28$. So the distance between Sam and Matt is 28 miles.

28 miles

Check Point 1

Solutions_Page 99

① When the angle of elevation of the sun from the ground is 16°, a post casts a 14 meters long shadow on level ground. What is then the height of the post?

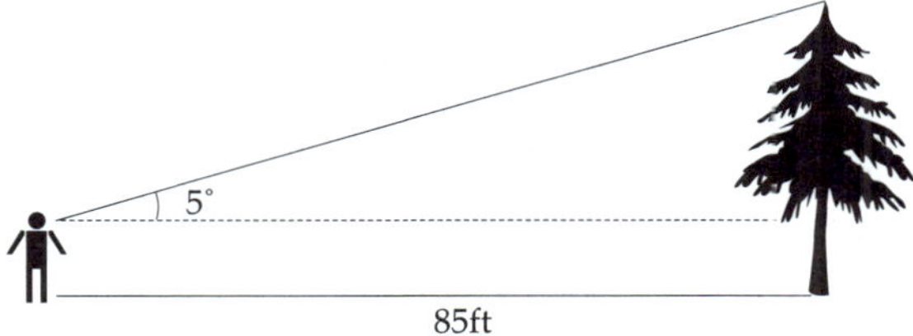

② Mrs. Jones is 5 feet tall and is looking at the top of a tree 85 feet away, as shown in the Figure above. What is the height of the tree?

③ A surveyor measures the angle of elevation of a building from level ground at 14°. If he walks 30 meters away from the building, where the angle of elevation from the ground is now 8°, what is the height of the building?

④ A 6 foot tall person starts to walk directly towards a vertical cliff that is 45 feet tall. Find the distance the person traveled if the angle of elevation from his eye level to the top of the cliff changes from 15° to 20°.

02 Simple Harmonic Motion

The trigonometric functions are ideally suited for modeling periodic behavior called simple harmonic motion. The graphs of sine and cosine functions, for example, tells us that these functions themselves exhibit periodic behavior.

When we model with simple harmonic motion, we use $f(t)=a\sin(wt)$ or $f(t)=a\cos(wt)$. The amplitude($|a|$) of the motion is the maximum displacement of the objects. The period$\left(p=\frac{2\pi}{w}\right)$ is the time required to complete one cycle. A cycle is one complete vibration of an object. The frequency$\left(f=\frac{1}{p}=\frac{w}{2\pi}\right)$ is the number of cycles per unit of time. Note that the hertz(symbol: Hz) is the derived unit of frequency in the International System of Units(SI) and is defined as one cycle per second.

Example 2-1

The displacement of a mass suspended by a spring is modeled by the function $f(t)=-6\sin(8\pi t)$, where f is measured in inches and t in seconds. Find the amplitude, period, and frequency of the motion of the mass.

Solution

From the formulas for amplitude, period, and frequency, we have the amplitude is $|a|=|-6|=6$ inches, the period is $p=\frac{2\pi}{w}=\frac{2\pi}{8\pi}=\frac{1}{4}$ seconds, and the frequency is $f=\frac{1}{p}=\frac{8\pi}{2\pi}=4$ cycles per seconds.

$|a|=6$ in, $p=\frac{1}{4}$ sec, $f=4$ Hz

Example 2–2

Suppose that an object attached to a spring is compressed 4 inches from its rest position and then released. If it returns to the same position after $\frac{3}{2}$ seconds, find an equation that relates the displacement y of the object from its rest position after time t seconds. Assume no friction.

Solution

When the object is released at $t=0$, the displacement of the object from the rest position is $y=4$ inches. So, since the displacement at $t=0$ is a maximum, it would be better to use the cosine function $y=a\cos(wt)$ to describe the motion.

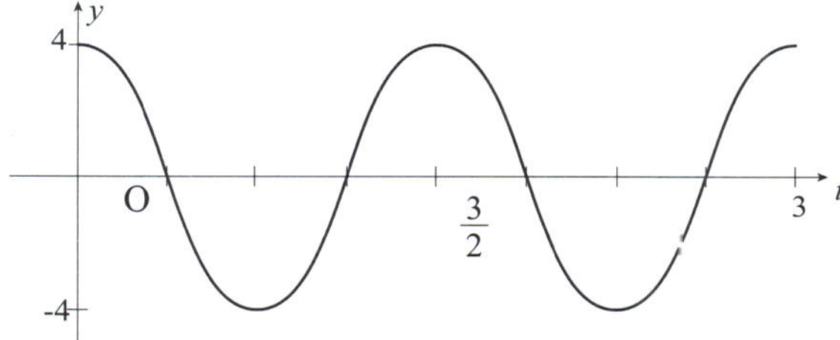

Knowing that the amplitude is 4 and the period is $\frac{3}{2}$, we have $a=4$ and $p=\frac{2\pi}{w}=\frac{3}{2}$, $w=\frac{4\pi}{3}$.

Therefore, putting it together, we get $y=4\cos\left(\frac{4\pi}{3}t\right)$.

$y=4\cos\left(\frac{4\pi}{3}t\right)$

Check Point 2

Solutions_Page 100

① The displacement of a mass suspended by a spring is modeled by the function $f(t)=3\cos(3\pi t)$, where f is measured in centimeters and t in seconds. Find the amplitude, period, and frequency of the motion of the mass.

② A mass is suspended from a spring. The spring has compressed a distance of 6 cm from its rest position and then released. It is observed that the mass returns to the compressed position after 0.5 seconds. Assume no friction.

(A) Find a function that models the displacement of the mass.

(B) What is the displacement of the mass 1.2 seconds after it is released?

Review Exercise

01 A surveyor determines the angle of elevation of a building from level ground to be 45°. If the surveyor moves 20 feet towards the building, then the measure of the angle of the elevation becomes 60°. Find the height of the building.

02 An airplane is flying at an altitude of 12,000 feet. If an airplane must approach a runway at an angle of depression of 17°, at what horizontal distance from the runway should the airplane start to descend?

03 A 6-foot tall person stands 20 feet from a post. If this person casts an 8 feet long shadow which ends at exactly the same point as the shadow of the post, how tall is the post?

04 Steven drives his racing car, with a constant speed of 80 miles per hour, due east at 11 A.M. At 3 P.M. Steven changes his direction to N50°E and arrives at his destination at 5 P.M. Find the directed distance Steven traveled by his racing car.

05 A 5 foot tall woman is 8 miles from the base of a mountain and her angle of elevation to the top of the mountain is $8°$. If she moves 3 miles closer to the mountain, what will be her angle of elevation to the top of the mountain?

06

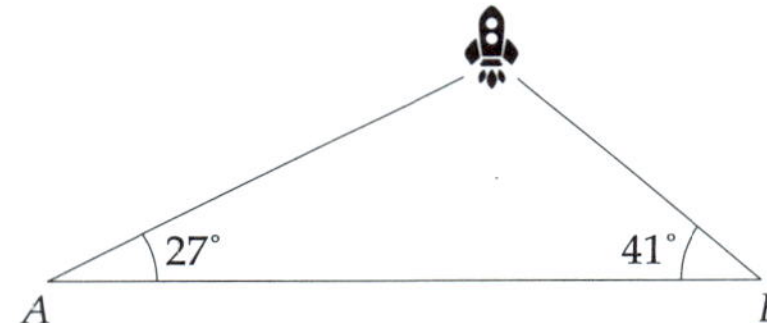

A rocket is launched vertically upward at 3 miles per second, as shown in Figure above. After 6 seconds later, what will be the distance between A and B?

07

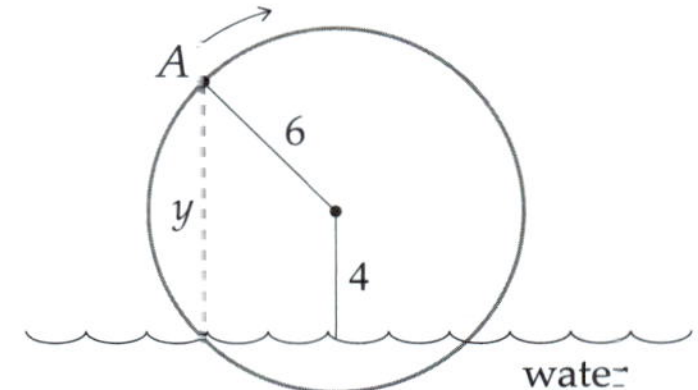

Suppose that the waterwheel in Figure above rotates clockwise at 8 revolutions per minute. If the point A is on the rim of the wheel at its greatest height after 2 seconds, find the equation that represents the distance y of the point A from the surface of the water in terms of the number of seconds t?

Review Exercise

08

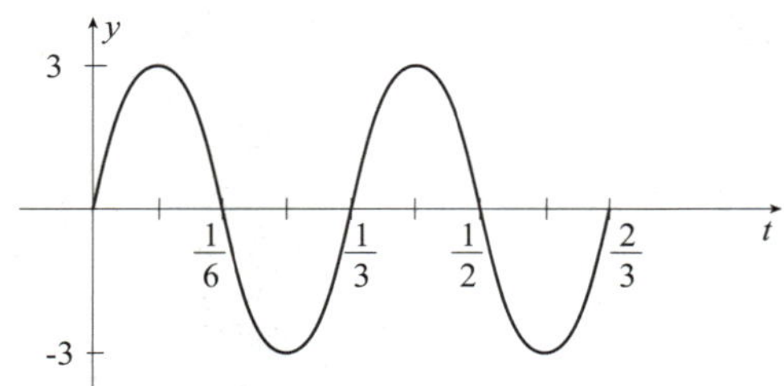

A mass attached to a coiled spring is in simple harmonic motion. The graph above gives its displacement $y(t)$ from equilibrium at time t. Find the function y.

09 A boat floating in a lake is bobbing in simple harmonic motion. Its displacement above the bottom of the horizontal lake is modeled by
$y=-0.4\cos\left(\frac{2\pi}{5}t\right)+20$,
where y is measured in meters and t in seconds. Find the maximum displacement of the boat above the bottom of the lake and frequency of the motion of the boat.

10 A mass oscillates in simple harmonic motion at the end of a spring attached to a wall. The mass is released at time $t=0$ at its maximum distance of 20 centimeters from the wall and it oscillates between its maximum distance and a minimum distance of 8 centimeters. If the mass oscillates 4 cycles per second, find each of the following.

(1) The amplitude of the motion.

(2) The period of the motion.

(3) The function that describes this motion.

(4) The total distance the mass travels in 2 seconds.

11 The daily high temperatures in a certain city are described by a sinusoidal function over time in the xy-plane. The peak daily high temperature is 90 degrees, and the lowest is 60 degrees. Based on these temperatures, what is the most appropriate value for the amplitude of the sinusoidal function?

(A) 15

(B) 22.5

(C) 30

(D) 37.5

12 The water level in a coastal area varies throughout the day and can be modeled by a sinusoidal function in the xy-plane. During a 24-hour period, the highest water level is 10 meters, and the lowest water level is 2 meters. The line $y=h$, where h is a constant, represents the midline of the sinusoidal graph. What is the value for h?

13 In a particular greenhouse, the temperature is modeled by a sinusoidal function f with respective to time t over a 24-hour period. During this period, the highest temperature recorded is 90 degrees Fahrenheit, and the lowest temperature is 60 degrees Fahrenheit. Which of the following would best define f?

(A) $f(x)=15\sin\left(\frac{\pi(t-2)}{12}\right)+75$

(B) $f(x)=15\sin\left(\frac{\pi(t-2)}{12}\right)+60$

(C) $f(x)=15\sin\left(\frac{\pi(t-2)}{24}\right)+75$

(D) $f(x)=15\sin\left(\frac{\pi(t-2)}{24}\right)+60$

14 The concentration of a certain chemical in a lake is modeled by the sinusoidal function $g(t)=84-160\cos\left(\frac{2\pi}{365}t\right)$, where t represents the number of days since the beginning of the year. Which of the following intervals is the concentration g increasing and concave down?

(A) $0<t<91$

(B) $92<t<182$

(C) $183<t<273$

(D) $274<t<365$

Review Exercise

15 A Ferris wheel has a diameter of 50 meters and completes one full revolution every 4 minutes. The lowest point of the Ferris wheel is 5 meters above the ground. Assume a rider boards the Ferris wheel at its lowest point at $t=0$. The height $h(t)$ of the rider above the ground as a function of time t (in minutes) can be modeled by a sinusoidal function. Which of the following equations best represents the height of the rider at any time t?

(A) $h(t)=30-25\sin\left(\frac{\pi}{2}t\right)$

(B) $h(t)=30-25\cos\left(\frac{\pi}{2}t\right)$

(C) $h(t)=30-25\sin\left(\frac{\pi}{4}t\right)$

(D) $h(t)=30-25\cos\left(\frac{\pi}{4}t\right)$

16

Time(hours)	Temperature(°C)
0	10
4	14
8	18
12	22
16	18
20	14
24	10

The table above shows the temperature T(in degrees Celsius) recorded at different times t(in hours) throughout a day in a certain city. The temperature can be modeled by a sinusoidal function. Which of the following equations best represents the temperature $T(t)$ as a function of time t?

(A) $T(t)=6\sin\left(\frac{\pi}{12}t\right)+16$

(B) $T(t)=12\sin\left(\frac{\pi}{12}t-\frac{\pi}{2}\right)+16$

(C) $T(t)=6\sin\left(\frac{\pi}{12}t-\frac{\pi}{2}\right)+16$

(D) $T(t)=6\cos\left(\frac{\pi}{12}t-\frac{\pi}{2}\right)+16$

17 A ball on a spring is pulled 6 centimeters below its rest position and then released. The period of the motion is 6 seconds. If D(in centimeters) represents the displacement of the ball and t(in seconds) represents the time after the ball is released, which of the following equations describes the motion of the ball?

(A) $D=6\sin\left(\frac{\pi}{3}t\right)$

(B) $D=-6\sin(3\pi t)$

(C) $D=6\cos(3\pi t)$

(D) $D=-6\cos\left(\frac{\pi}{3}t\right)$

6 Fundamental Trigonometric Identities

In this section, we will study fundamental identities. An identity is a statement that describes relation between two expressions that hold for all values of the variables. It is a very useful tool in evaluating trigonometric functions, simplifying trigonometric expressions, and solving trigonometric equations. Make sure you understand the following identities and memorize them.

01 Reciprocal Identities

1. $\sin\theta=\dfrac{1}{\csc\theta} \Leftrightarrow \csc\theta=\dfrac{1}{\sin\theta}$

2. $\cos\theta=\dfrac{1}{\sec\theta} \Leftrightarrow \sec\theta=\dfrac{1}{\cos\theta}$

3. $\tan\theta=\dfrac{1}{\cot\theta} \Leftrightarrow \cot\theta=\dfrac{1}{\tan\theta}$

02 Quotient Identities

1. $\tan\theta=\dfrac{\sin\theta}{\cos\theta}$

2. $\cot\theta=\dfrac{\cos\theta}{\sin\theta}$

Proof

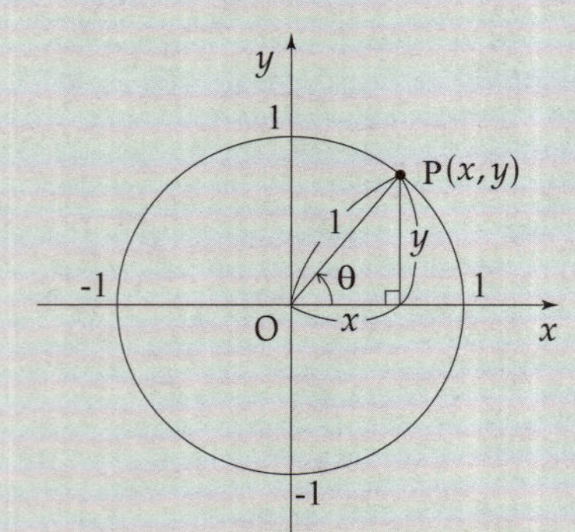

1. $\sin\theta=y=\dfrac{1}{\frac{1}{y}}=\dfrac{1}{\csc\theta} \rightarrow \csc\theta=\dfrac{1}{\sin\theta}$

$\cos\theta=x=\dfrac{1}{\frac{1}{x}}=\dfrac{1}{\sec\theta} \rightarrow \sec\theta=\dfrac{1}{\cos\theta}$

$\tan\theta=\dfrac{y}{x}=\dfrac{1}{\frac{x}{y}}=\dfrac{1}{\cot\theta} \rightarrow \cot\theta=\dfrac{1}{\tan\theta}$

2. $\tan\theta=\dfrac{y}{x}=\dfrac{\sin\theta}{\cos\theta}$ and $\cot\theta=\dfrac{1}{\tan\theta}=\dfrac{1}{\frac{\sin\theta}{\cos\theta}}=\dfrac{\cos\theta}{\sin\theta}$

03 Pythagorean Identities

1. $\sin^2\theta+\cos^2\theta=1$ 2. $1+\tan^2\theta=\sec^2\theta$ 3. $1+\cot^2\theta=\csc^2\theta$

✔ Know that $(\sin\theta)^2$, $(\cos\theta)^2$, and $(\tan\theta)^2$ are written as $\sin^2\theta$, $\cos^2\theta$, and $\tan^2\theta$.

Proof

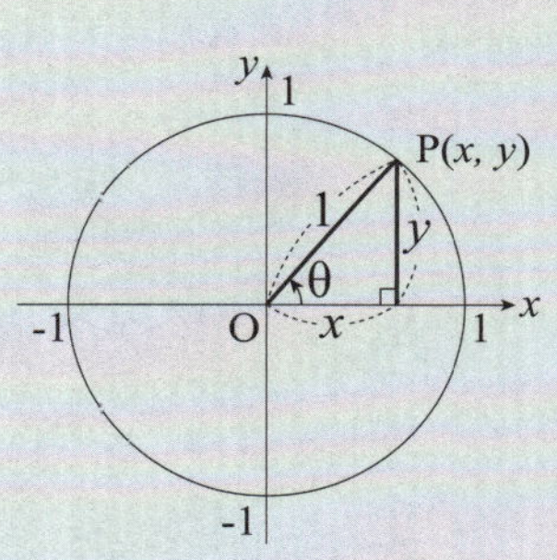

1. $\sin^2\theta+\cos^2\theta=y^2+x^2=1$
2. Divide $\sin^2\theta+\cos^2\theta=1$ by $\cos^2\theta$

$$\frac{\sin^2\theta}{\cos^2\theta}+\frac{\cos^2\theta}{\cos^2\theta}=\frac{1}{\cos^2\theta}$$

$$\left(\frac{\sin\theta}{\cos\theta}\right)^2+1=\left(\frac{1}{\cos\theta}\right)^2 \rightarrow \tan^2\theta+1=\sec^2\theta$$

3. Divide $\sin^2\theta+\cos^2\theta=1$ by $\sin^2\theta$

$$\frac{\sin^2\theta}{\sin^2\theta}+\frac{\cos^2\theta}{\sin^2\theta}=\frac{1}{\sin^2\theta} \rightarrow 1+\cot^2 x=\csc^2\theta$$

Example 1-1

Using trigonometric identities, find $\cos\theta$ and $\tan\theta$ if $\sin\theta=\frac{4}{5}$ and θ is in Quadrant II.

Solution

Since $\sin^2\theta+\cos^2\theta=1$, $\cos^2\theta=1-\sin^2\theta=1-\left(\frac{4}{5}\right)^2=\frac{9}{25}$ and $\cos\theta=\pm\frac{3}{5}$.

However, $\cos\theta<0$ when θ lies in Quadrant II. So $\cos\theta=-\frac{3}{5}$.

Now, $\tan\theta=\dfrac{\sin\theta}{\cos\theta}=\dfrac{\frac{4}{5}}{-\frac{3}{5}}=-\dfrac{4}{3}$.

$\cos\theta=-\frac{3}{5}$, $\tan\theta-\frac{4}{3}$

Example 1–2

$$\cos\theta=\frac{3}{4},\ \tan\theta<0$$

Use the given information above and trigonometric identities to find the six trigonometric functions.

Solution

By Pythagorean identity,

$\sin^2\theta+\cos^2\theta=1$, $\sin^2\theta=1-\cos^2\theta=1-\left(\frac{3}{4}\right)^2=\frac{7}{16}$, $\sin\theta=\pm\frac{\sqrt{7}}{4}$.

Since $\cos\theta>0$ and $\tan\theta<0$, θ lies in Quadrant IV. So, $\sin\theta=-\frac{\sqrt{7}}{4}$.

$\sin\theta=-\frac{\sqrt{7}}{4}$ $\qquad$ $\csc\theta=\frac{1}{\sin\theta}=-\frac{4}{\sqrt{7}}=-\frac{4\sqrt{7}}{7}$

$\cos\theta=\frac{3}{4}$ $\qquad$ $\sec\theta=\frac{1}{\cos\theta}=\frac{4}{3}$

$\tan\theta=\frac{\sin\theta}{\cos\theta}=\frac{-\frac{\sqrt{7}}{4}}{\frac{3}{4}}=-\frac{\sqrt{7}}{3}$ $\qquad$ $\cot\theta=\frac{1}{\tan\theta}=-\frac{3}{\sqrt{7}}=-\frac{3\sqrt{7}}{7}$

$\sin\theta=-\frac{\sqrt{7}}{4}$ $\quad$ $\cos\theta=\frac{3}{4}$ $\quad$ $\tan\theta=-\frac{\sqrt{7}}{3}$

$\csc\theta=-\frac{4\sqrt{7}}{7}$ $\quad$ $\sec\theta=\frac{4}{3}$ $\quad$ $\cot\theta=-\frac{3\sqrt{7}}{7}$

Check Point 1

Solutions_Page 103

Use the given information and trigonometric identities to find the six trigonometric functions.

① $\cos\theta=\frac{1}{\sqrt{2}}$, $\tan\theta<0$ $\qquad$ ② $\sin\theta=\frac{1}{2}$, $\cos\theta<0$

③ $\tan\theta=-2$, $\cos\theta>0$ $\qquad$ ④ $\sec\theta=4$, $\sin\theta>0$

04 Identities for Negatives

1. $\sin(-\theta) = -\sin\theta$ $\csc(-\theta) = -\csc\theta$
2. $\cos(-\theta) = \cos\theta$ $\sec(-\theta) = \sec\theta$
3. $\tan(-\theta) = -\tan\theta$ $\cot(-\theta) = -\cot\theta$

Remember the sine and tangent functions are odd functions, and the cosine function is even function.

Proof

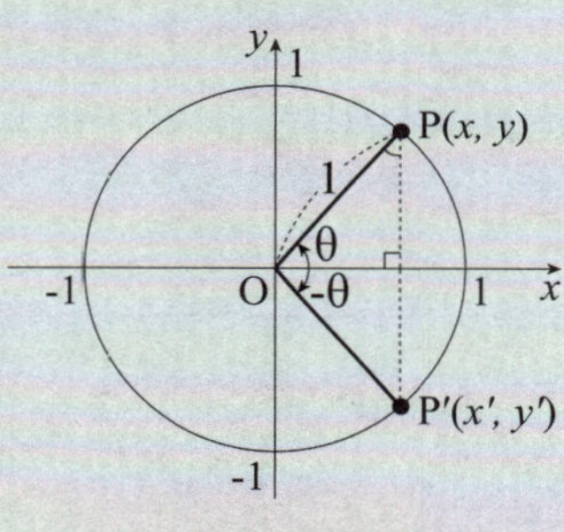

$x' = x$ and $y' = -y$

1. $\sin(-\theta) = y' = -y = -\sin\theta$
   $\rightarrow \csc(-\theta) = -\csc\theta$
2. $\cos(-\theta) = x' = x = \cos\theta$
   $\rightarrow \sec(-\theta) = \sec\theta$
3. $\tan(-\theta) = \dfrac{y'}{x'} = \dfrac{-y}{x} = -\tan\theta$
   $\rightarrow \cot(-\theta) = -\cot\theta$

Example 2

Evaluate each trigonometric function using identities for negatives.

① $\sin\left(-\frac{7\pi}{3}\right)$ ② $\cos\left(-\frac{3\pi}{4}\right)$

Solution

① $\sin\left(-\frac{7\pi}{3}\right) = -\sin\frac{7\pi}{3} = -\sin\frac{\pi}{3} = -\frac{\sqrt{3}}{2}$.

② $\cos\left(-\frac{3\pi}{4}\right) = \cos\frac{3\pi}{4} = -\frac{\sqrt{2}}{2}$.

$\sin\left(-\frac{7\pi}{3}\right) = -\frac{\sqrt{3}}{2}$

$\cos\left(-\frac{3\pi}{4}\right) = -\frac{\sqrt{2}}{2}$

Check Point 2

Solutions_Page 104

Evaluate each trigonometric function using identities for negatives.

① $\tan\left(-\frac{\pi}{6}\right)$　　② $\sec\left(-\frac{5\pi}{3}\right)$

05 Cofunction Identities

1. $\sin\left(\frac{\pi}{2}-\theta\right)=\cos\theta$　　$\cos\left(\frac{\pi}{2}-\theta\right)=\sin\theta$
2. $\tan\left(\frac{\pi}{2}-\theta\right)=\cot\theta$　　$\cot\left(\frac{\pi}{2}-\theta\right)=\tan\theta$
3. $\sec\left(\frac{\pi}{2}-\theta\right)=\csc\theta$　　$\csc\left(\frac{\pi}{2}-\theta\right)=\sec\theta$

Proof

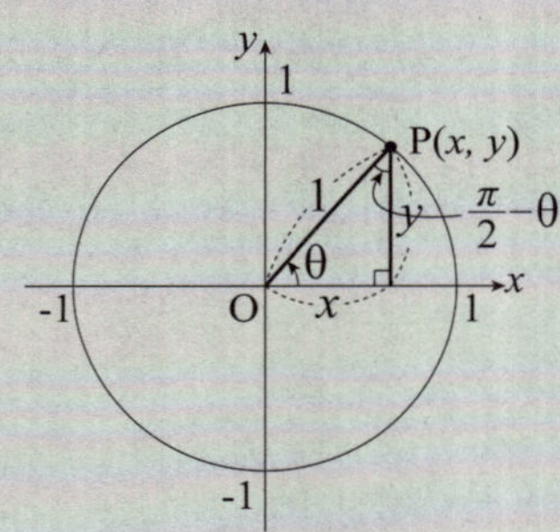

1. $\sin\left(\frac{\pi}{2}-\theta\right)=x=\cos\theta$ and $\cos\left(\frac{\pi}{2}-\theta\right)=y=\sin\theta$
2. $\tan\left(\frac{\pi}{2}-\theta\right)=\frac{x}{y}=\cot\theta$ and $\cot\left(\frac{\pi}{2}-\theta\right)=\frac{y}{x}=\tan\theta$
3. $\sec\left(\frac{\pi}{2}-\theta\right)=\frac{1}{y}=\csc\theta$ and $\csc\left(\frac{\pi}{2}-\theta\right)=\frac{1}{x}=\sec\theta$

Example 3

Evaluate each trigonometric function using cofunction identities.

① $\sin\frac{\pi}{6}$　　② $\tan\frac{\pi}{3}$

Solution

① $\sin\frac{\pi}{6}=\cos\left(\frac{\pi}{2}-\frac{\pi}{6}\right)=\cos\frac{\pi}{3}=\frac{1}{2}$　　$\sin\frac{\pi}{6}=\frac{1}{2}$

② $\tan\frac{\pi}{3}=\cot\left(\frac{\pi}{2}-\frac{\pi}{3}\right)=\cot\frac{\pi}{6}=\sqrt{3}$

$\tan\frac{\pi}{3}=\sqrt{3}$

Check Point 3

Solutions_Page 104

① $\cos\frac{\pi}{3}$ ② $\csc\frac{\pi}{6}$

Example 4

Simplify the expression.

① $\dfrac{1-\sin^2\theta}{\cos\theta}$ ② $\sin\left(\frac{\pi}{2}-\theta\right)-\cot\theta\sin\theta$

③ $\cos\theta+\cos\theta\tan^2\theta$ ④ $\dfrac{1}{1+\sin\theta}+\dfrac{1}{1-\sin\theta}$

Solution

① $\dfrac{1-\sin^2\theta}{\cos\theta}=\dfrac{\cos^2\theta}{\cos\theta}$ → $\sin^2\theta+\cos^2\theta=1$

$=\cos\theta$

$\dfrac{1-\sin^2\theta}{\cos\theta}=\cos\theta$

② $\sin\left(\frac{\pi}{2}-\theta\right)-\cot\theta\sin\theta=\cos\theta-\dfrac{\cos\theta}{\sin\theta}\sin\theta$ → $\sin\left(\frac{\pi}{2}-\theta\right)=\cos\theta$, $\cot\theta=\dfrac{\cos\theta}{\sin\theta}$

$=\cos\theta-\cos\theta=0$

$\sin\left(\frac{\pi}{2}-\theta\right)-\cot\theta\sin\theta=0$

③ $\cos\theta+\cos\theta\tan^2\theta=\cos\theta(1+\tan^2\theta)=\cos\theta\sec^2\theta$ → $1+\tan^2\theta=\sec^2\theta$

$=\cos\theta\dfrac{1}{\cos^2\theta}=\dfrac{1}{\cos\theta}=\sec\theta$ → $\sec\theta=\dfrac{1}{\cos\theta}$

$\cos\theta+\cos\theta\tan^2\theta=\sec\theta$

④ $\dfrac{1}{1+\sin\theta}+\dfrac{1}{1+\sin\theta}=\dfrac{1-\sin\theta}{1-\sin^2\theta}+\dfrac{1+\sin\theta}{1-\sin^2\theta}$

$=\dfrac{2}{1-\sin^2\theta}=\dfrac{2}{\cos^2\theta}=2\sec^2\theta$ → $\sin^2\theta+\cos^2\theta=1$

$\dfrac{1}{1+\sin\theta}+\dfrac{1}{1-\sin\theta}=2\sec^2\theta$

Check Point 4

Solutions_Page 104

Simplify the expression.

① $\sin\left(\frac{\pi}{2}-\theta\right)\sec\theta$ ② $\frac{1-\cos^2\theta}{\cos^2\theta-1}$ ③ $\frac{\sin^2\theta}{1-\cos\theta}-\cos\theta$ ④ $\sin\theta\sec\theta+\cos\theta\csc\theta$

Example 5

Factor the expression.

① $\sin^2\theta-1$ ② $2\cos^2\theta-\cos\theta-6$ ③ $\sec^2\theta-2\tan\theta$ ④ $2\sin^2 x-\cos x-1$

Solution

① The expression has the form a^2-b^2. Let $\sin\theta=A$.

$\sin^2\theta-1=A^2-1^2=(A-1)(A+1)$
$=(\sin\theta-1)(\sin\theta+1)$

$\sin^2\theta-1=(\sin\theta-1)(\sin\theta+1)$

② The expression has the form ax^2-bx^2+c. Let $\cos\theta=A$.

$2\cos^2\theta-\cos\theta-6=2A^2-A-6=(2A+3)(A-2)$
$=(2\cos\theta+3)(\cos\theta-2)$

$2\cos^2\theta-\cos\theta-6=(2\cos\theta+3)(\cos\theta-2)$

③ Using Pythagorean identity $\sec^2\theta=1+\tan^2\theta$,

$\sec^2\theta-2\tan\theta=(1+\tan^2\theta)-2\tan\theta$
$=\tan^2\theta-2\tan\theta+1$ → Let $\tan\theta=A$
$=A^2-2A+1=(A-1)^2$
$=(\tan\theta-1)^2$

$\sec^2\theta-2\tan\theta=(\tan\theta-1)^2$

④ Using Pythagorean identity $\sin^2 x+\cos^2 x=1$,

$2\sin^2 x-\cos x-1=2(1-\cos^2 x)-\cos x-1$
$=-2\cos^2 x-\cos x+1$ → Let $\cos x=A$
$=-2A^2-A+1=-(2A-1)(A+1)$
$=-(2\cos x-1)(\cos x+1)$

$2\sin^2 x-\cos x-1=-(2\cos x-1)(\cos x+1)$

Check Point 5

Solutions_Page 105

Factor the expression.

① $\cos^2 x - \cos x - 2$

② $\tan^3\theta - 4\tan\theta$

③ $\cos^2\theta\sec^2\theta - \cos^2\theta$

④ $2\cot^4\theta + 4\cot^2\theta + 2$

06 Verifying Trigonometric Identities

To verify that a given statement is an identity, we prove that two expressions are equal. However, unfortunately, there is no set of rules that can be used in verifying trigonometric identities, and the process is learned best by lots of practices.

Here are some tips for verifying trigonometric identities.

1. Choose which side to work with, usually a more complicated side.
2. Show that one side can be transformed into the other by using various trigonometric techniques we have learned.
3. When there are no simple conversions that can be used to reach the other side of the equation, convert the entire expression to an expression that contains only sines and cosines.
4. Sometimes, it helps to work with each side separately and reach the same results.

By working through several examples, you will have a sense for what is appropriate in verifying trigonometric identities.

Example 6

Verify the identity.

① $\sec\theta-\sin\theta\tan\theta=\cos\theta$

② $\dfrac{1}{1-\cos\theta}+\dfrac{1}{1+\cos\theta}=2\csc^2\theta$

③ $\sec\theta\csc\theta=\sin\theta\sec\theta+\cos\theta\csc\theta$

④ $\dfrac{1-\cos\theta}{\cos\theta}=\dfrac{\tan^2\theta}{1+\sec\theta}$

⑤ $\sec^4\theta-\tan^4\theta=\sec^2\theta+\tan^2\theta$

Solution

① Work on left side to reach right side.

$$\sec\theta-\sin\theta\tan\theta=\frac{1}{\cos\theta}-\sin\theta\frac{\sin\theta}{\cos\theta}=\frac{1-\sin^2\theta}{\cos\theta}=\frac{\cos^2\theta}{\cos\theta}=\cos\theta.$$

The identity is verified

② Work on left side to reach right side.

$$\frac{1}{1-\cos\theta}+\frac{1}{1+\cos\theta}=\frac{1+\cos\theta}{1-\cos^2\theta}+\frac{1-\cos\theta}{1-\cos^2\theta}=\frac{2}{1-\cos^2\theta}=\frac{2}{\sin^2\theta}=2\csc^2\theta$$

The identity is verified

③ Since right side is more complicated, we will work on right side to reach left side.

$$\begin{aligned}\sin\theta\sec\theta+\cos\theta\csc\theta&=\sin\theta\frac{1}{\cos\theta}+\cos\theta\frac{1}{\sin\theta}\\&=\frac{\sin\theta}{\cos\theta}+\frac{\cos\theta}{\sin\theta}=\frac{\sin^2\theta+\cos^2\theta}{\cos\theta\sin\theta}\\&=\frac{1}{\cos\theta\sin\theta}=\sec\theta\csc\theta\end{aligned}$$

The identity is verified

④ For this example, let us work with each side separately.

Left side:

$$\frac{1-\cos\theta}{\cos\theta}=\frac{1}{\cos\theta}-\frac{\cos\theta}{\cos\theta}=\sec\theta-1$$

Right side:

$$\frac{\tan^2\theta}{1+\sec\theta}=\frac{\sec^2\theta-1}{1+\sec\theta}=\frac{(\sec\theta-1)(\sec\theta+1)}{1+\sec\theta}=\sec\theta-1$$

The identity is verified because both sides are equal to $\sec\theta-1$

⑤ Work on left side to reach right side.

$$\begin{aligned}\sec^4\theta-\tan^4\theta&=(\sec^2\theta-\tan^2\theta)(\sec^2\theta+\tan^2\theta)\\&=1\cdot(\sec^2\theta+\tan^2\theta)=\sec^2\theta+\tan^2\theta\end{aligned}$$

The identity is verified

Check Point 6

Solutions_Page 105

Verify the identity.

① $\sec\theta-\cos\theta=\sin\theta\tan\theta$

② $\sin^2\theta-\cos^2\theta=1-2\cos^2\theta$

③ $\tan\theta+\cot\theta=\sec\theta\csc\theta$

④ $-\cot^2\theta=(1+\csc\theta)(1+\csc(-\theta))$

⑤ $\sin\theta(1+\cot^2\theta)=\csc\theta$

⑥ $\cot\theta=\dfrac{\sin\left(\frac{\pi}{2}-\theta\right)}{\sin\theta}$

Review Exercise

01 Using the given information, $\sec\theta=-\frac{5}{2}$ and $\sin\theta>0$, find the rest of the six trigonometric functions.

02 Simplify the expression.

(1) $\dfrac{\cot\theta+1}{\tan\theta+1}$

(2) $\dfrac{\sin(-\theta)}{1+\cos(-\theta)}-\dfrac{\sin(-\theta)}{1-\cos(-\theta)}$

(3) $\dfrac{1}{\cos^2\theta}-\sin\theta\sec\theta\tan\theta$

(4) $\dfrac{\cos\theta-1}{\sin\theta}+\dfrac{\sin\theta}{\cos\theta-1}$

03 Which of the following is equal to $\tan x-\tan(-x)+\sec x-\sec(-x)$?

(A) $2\tan x$

(B) $2\sec x$

(C) $2\tan x+2\sec x$

(D) $2\tan x-2\sec x$

(E) 0

04 Factor $1+\cos^2\theta-\sin\theta$.

05 For all x, what is the value of $e^{\frac{\sin(x)}{\cos(x)}}\cdot e^{\frac{\sin(-x)}{\cos(-x)}}$?

06 For $0 \le x < \frac{\pi}{2}$, which of the following is NOT equal to 1?

(A) $\cos(2x)\sec(2x)$

(B) $\sqrt{\sin^2 x + \cos^2 x}$

(C) $\frac{1}{\cos^2 x} - \frac{\sin^2 x}{\cos^2 x}$

(D) $\sin\left(\frac{\pi}{2} - x\right) - \cos x$

(E) $\frac{\sec x}{\cos x} - \frac{\tan x}{\cot x}$

07

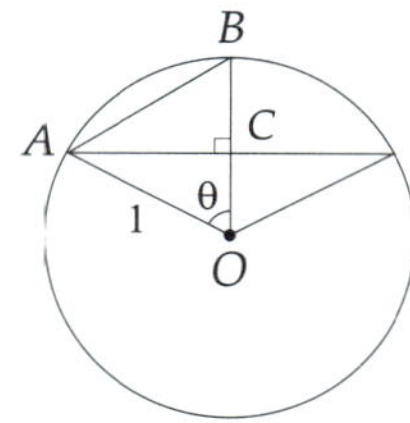

In Figure above, which of the following is equal to the distance from A to B?

(A) $\sqrt{2-2\cos\theta}$

(B) $2\cos\theta$

(C) $\sqrt{2-2\sin\theta}$

(D) $\sqrt{2+2\sin\theta}$

(E) $2\sin\theta$

08 Verify the identity.

(1) $\sin\theta + \cos\theta = \frac{\tan\theta + 1}{\sec\theta}$

(2) $\frac{1}{\sec\theta - \tan\theta} = \sec\theta + \tan\theta$

(3) $-\frac{\sin\theta}{1+\cos\theta} = \frac{\cos\theta - 1}{\sin\theta}$

(4) $2\cot\theta = \frac{\sin\theta}{1-\cos\theta} - \frac{\sin\theta}{1+\cos\theta}$

(5) $\frac{\sin\theta}{1-\cos\theta} = \frac{1}{\csc\theta - \cot\theta}$

Review Exercise

(6) $\sin\theta\cos\theta = \dfrac{1}{\tan\theta + \cot\theta}$

(7) $\sin\theta(\cos^4\theta - 2\cos^2\theta + 1) = \sin^5\theta$

(8) $\sec^5\theta\tan^3\theta$
$= \sec^6\theta(\sec\theta\tan\theta) - \sec^4\theta(\sec\theta\tan\theta)$

(9) $\dfrac{\cot\theta - \tan\theta}{\cot\theta + \tan\theta} = \cos^2\theta - \sin^2\theta$

(10) $3\csc^2\theta - 3\csc^2\theta\cos^2\theta - \cos^2\theta - \sin^2\theta$
$= 2$

09 If $\sin^2\left(\frac{1}{m}\right) + \sin^2\left(\frac{1}{n}\right) + \sin^2\left(\frac{1}{k}\right) = 2.47$, what is the value of $\cos^2\left(\frac{1}{m}\right) + \cos^2\left(\frac{1}{n}\right) + \cos^2\left(\frac{1}{k}\right)$?

10 Which of the following expressions could represent $-\dfrac{\sin x}{\cos^2 x - 1}$?

(A) $\sin x$
(B) $\cos x$
(C) $\sec x$
(D) $\csc x$

11 If $0 \le x < \frac{\pi}{2}$ and $\cos x = \frac{4}{5}$, then what is the value of $\tan^2 x + 1$?

12 For $0<x<\frac{\pi}{2}$, which of the following expressions are equal to 1?

I. $\sec(2x)\csc(2x)$

II. $\sec^2 x-\left(\frac{\sin x}{\cos x}\right)^2$

III. $2\sin^2 x+\cos(2x)$

(A) I only
(B) II only
(C) I and II only
(D) II and III only

13

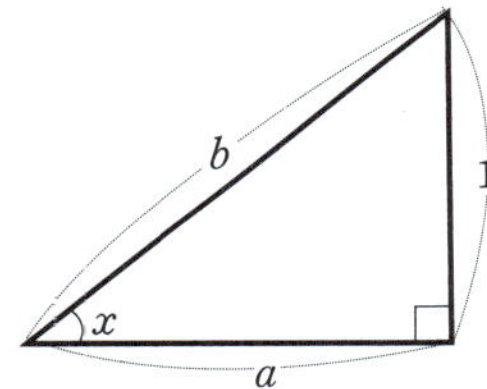

A right triangle is given above. Which of the following expressions could be $a+b$?

(A) $\sin x+\cos x$
(B) $\tan x+\sec x$
(C) $\frac{1+\sin x}{\cos x}$
(D) $\frac{1+\cos x}{\sin x}$

14 For all x, which of the following expressions represents $2^{\sin x\cdot\cos x}\cdot 2^{\sin(-x)\cos(-x)}$?

(A) 1
(B) $2^{\sin(2x)}$
(C) $2^{2\sin x}$
(D) $2^{\sin^2 x\cos^2 x}$

7 Trigonometric Equations and Identities, Part I

01 Trigonometric Equations

A trigonometric equation is an equation that contains trigonometric functions. To solve the trigonometric equation, use standard algebraic techniques, such as factoring and substitution using trigonometric identities. The first step in solving a trigonometric equation is to isolate the trigonometric term in the equation. For example, to solve $\sqrt{2}\cos x-1=0$, we first solve for $\cos x$ as follows.

$\sqrt{2}\cos x-1=0$ → Original Equation

$\sqrt{2}\cos x=1$ → Add 1 to both sides

$\cos x=\dfrac{1}{\sqrt{2}}$ → Divide both sides by $\sqrt{2}$

Now we look for the angle x such that cosine of x is equal to $\dfrac{1}{\sqrt{2}}$. We know that $\cos x$ has a period of 2π and the angle x lies in Quadrant I and IV since $\cos x>0$. Thus, the solutions in the interval $[0,\ 2\pi)$ are $x=\dfrac{\pi}{4}$ and $x=\dfrac{7\pi}{4}$. There are infinitely many solutions if the interval of x is not bounded. This type of solutions

are called the general solutions and they can be written as $x=\dfrac{\pi}{4}+2\pi n,(n\in Z)$ and

$x=\dfrac{7\pi}{4}+2\pi n,(n\in Z)$.

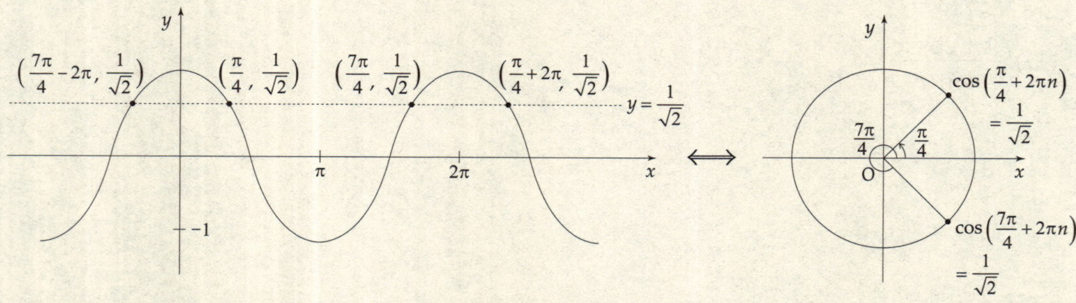

Now, through several examples, we will learn how to solve trigonometric equations.

Example 1–1

Solve $3\sin x+1=\sin x$.

Solution

$3\sin x+1=\sin x$ → Original equation

$2\sin x=-1$ → Isolate $\sin x$ term

$\sin x=-\frac{1}{2}$ → Divide each side by 2

Since $\sin x$ has a period of 2π, the solutions in the interval $[0,2\pi)$ are $x=\frac{7\pi}{6}$ and $x=\frac{11\pi}{6}$.

The general solutions are $x=\frac{7\pi}{6}+2\pi n(n\in Z)$ and $x=\frac{11\pi}{6}+2\pi n\ (n\in Z)$.

In the interval $[0,\ 2\pi)$, $x=\frac{7\pi}{6}$ and $x=\frac{11\pi}{6}$

The general solutions are $x=\frac{7\pi}{6}+2\pi n$ and $x=\frac{11\pi}{6}+2\pi n\ (n\in Z)$

Example 1–2

Solve $2\cos^2 x-\cos x-1=0$.

Solution

This trigonometric equation is a quadratic type $ax^2+bx+c=0$. To solve the equation, we factor just like we do for quadratic equation or, if this is not possible, we use the Quadratic Formula.

$2\cos^2 x-\cos x-1=0$ → Original equation

$(2\cos x+1)(\cos x-1)=0$ → Factor

$2\cos x+1=0$ or $\cos x-1=0$

$\cos x=-\frac{1}{2}$ or $\cos x=1$

Since $\cos x$ has a period of 2π,

(1) For $\cos x=-\frac{1}{2}$,

The solutions in the interval $[0,\ 2\pi)$ are $x=\frac{2\pi}{3}$ and $x=\frac{4\pi}{3}$

The general solutions are $x=\frac{2\pi}{3}+2\pi n(n\in Z)$ and $x=\frac{4\pi}{3}+2\pi n(n\in Z)$.

(2) For $\cos x=1$,

The solutions in the interval $[0,\ 2\pi)$ is $x=0$. The general solution is $x=2\pi n\ (n\in Z)$.

In the interval $[0,\ 2\pi)$, $x=\frac{2\pi}{3}$, $x=\frac{4\pi}{3}$ and $x=0$

The general solutions are $x=\frac{2\pi}{3}+2\pi n$, $x=\frac{4\pi}{3}+2\pi n$, and $x=2\pi n\ (n\in Z)$

Check Point 1

Solutions_Page 109

Find all solutions of the equation in the interval $[0,\ 2\pi)$ and then find the general solution of the equation.

① $\sqrt{2}\sin x+1=0$

② $\sqrt{3}\sec x+2=0$

③ $\sin^2 x=\sin x$

④ $\tan x-2\tan x\cos x=0$

Example 2

Solve $2\sin(2x)-\sqrt{3}=0$.

Solution

This trigonometric equation involves multiple angles $2x$. For this type of equation, we first solve for $2x$ and then divide each side by 2.

$$2\sin(2x)-\sqrt{3}=0 \quad \rightarrow \text{Original equation}$$

$$2\sin(2x)=\sqrt{3} \quad \rightarrow \text{Isolate } \sin(2x) \text{ term}$$

$$\sin(2x)=\frac{\sqrt{3}}{2} \quad \rightarrow \text{Divide each side by 2}$$

To find the solutions in the interval $[0,\ 2\pi)$, we first fine the solutions in the interval $[0,\ 4\pi)$.

$$2x=\frac{\pi}{3},\ 2x=\frac{2\pi}{3},\ 2x=\frac{7\pi}{3},\ \text{and } 2x=\frac{8\pi}{3}.$$

Dividing these results by 2, we obtain the solutions in the interval $[0,\ 2\pi)$

$$x=\frac{\pi}{6},\ x=\frac{\pi}{3},\ x=\frac{7\pi}{6},\ \text{and } x=\frac{4\pi}{3}.$$

Now the general solutions can be written as

$$2x=\frac{\pi}{3}+2\pi n \ (n\in Z) \ \rightarrow \ x=\frac{\pi}{6}+\pi n \ (n\in Z) \text{ and}$$
$$2x=\frac{2\pi}{3}+2\pi n \ (n\in Z) \ \rightarrow \ x=\frac{\pi}{3}+\pi n \ (n\in Z).$$

In the interval $[0,\ 2\pi)$, $x=\frac{\pi}{6}$, $x=\frac{\pi}{3}$, $x=\frac{7\pi}{6}$, and $x=\frac{4\pi}{3}$

The general solutions are $x=\frac{\pi}{6}+\pi n$ and $x=\frac{\pi}{3}+\pi n$ $(n\in Z)$

Check Point 2

Solutions_Page 110

Find all solutions of the equation in the interval $[0,\ 2\pi)$ and then find the general solution of the equation.

① $\sin(2x)=1$

② $\sin x(2\cos(2x)+1)=0$

Example 3

Solve $3+3\sin x-2\cos^2 x=0$.

Solution

In this particular trigonometric equation, we need to convert $\cos^2 x$ to $\sin^2 x$ using Pythagorean identity.

$3+3\sin x-2\cos^2 x=0$ → Original equation

$3+3\sin x-2(1-\sin^2 x)=0$ → $\cos^2 x=1-\sin^2 x$

$2\sin^2 x+3\sin x+1=0$ → Simplify

$(2\sin x+1)(\sin x+1)=0$ → Factor

$2\sin x+1=0$, $\sin x=-\frac{1}{2}$ or $\sin x+1=0$, $\sin x=-1$

Since $\sin x$ has a period of 2π,

(1) For $\sin x=-\frac{1}{2}$,

The solutions in the interval $[0,\ 2\pi)$ are $x=\frac{7\pi}{6}$ and $x=\frac{11\pi}{6}$

The general solutions are $x=\frac{7\pi}{6}+2\pi n$ $(n\in Z)$ and $x=\frac{11\pi}{6}+2\pi n$ $(n\in Z)$.

(2) For $\sin x=-1$,

The solutions in the interval $[0,\ 2\pi)$ is $x=\frac{3\pi}{2}$.

The general solution is $x=\frac{3\pi}{2}+2\pi n\ (n\in Z)$.

In the interval $[0,\ 2\pi)$, $x=\frac{7\pi}{6}$, $x=\frac{11\pi}{6}$ and $x=\frac{3\pi}{2}$

The general solutions are $x=\frac{6\pi}{7}+2\pi n$, $x=\frac{11\pi}{6}+2\pi n$, and $x=\frac{3\pi}{2}+2\pi n\ (n\in Z)$

Check Point 3

Solutions_Page 110

Find all solutions of the equation in the interval $[0,\ 2\pi)$ and then find the general solution of the equation.

① $1+\sin x-2\cos^2 x=0$

② $\tan^2 x=3-2\sec^2 x$

02 Sum and Difference Identities

Let us derive the sum and difference identities for sine from the following figure.

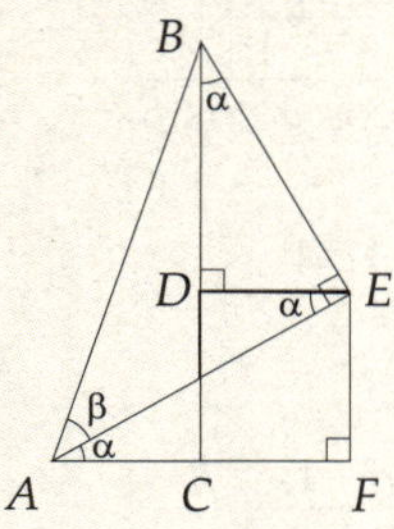

Draw two triangles ΔABC and ΔAEF. Then, draw $\overline{BE}$ perpendicular to $\overline{AE}$, and $\overline{DE}$ perpendicular to $\overline{BC}$.

$$\sin(\alpha+\beta)=\frac{BC}{AB} \quad \rightarrow \text{Definition of sine}$$

$$=\frac{EF+BD}{AB} \quad \rightarrow \text{BC=DC+BD=EF+BD}$$

$$=\frac{EF}{AB}+\frac{BD}{AB} \quad \rightarrow \text{Separate the fraction}$$

$$=\frac{EF}{AE}\cdot\frac{AE}{AB}+\frac{BD}{BE}\cdot\frac{BE}{AB} \quad \rightarrow \text{Multiply } \frac{AE}{AE} \text{ and } \frac{BE}{BE}$$

$$\sin(\alpha+\beta)=\sin\alpha\cos\beta+\cos\alpha\sin\beta \quad \rightarrow \text{Definition of sine and cosine}$$

Thus, $\sin(\alpha-\beta)=\sin(\alpha+(-\beta))$

$$=\sin\alpha\cos(-\beta)+\cos\alpha\sin(-\beta) \quad \rightarrow \text{Apply sum identity}$$

$$\sin(\alpha-\beta)=\sin\alpha\cos\beta-\cos\alpha\sin\beta \quad \rightarrow \text{Apply identities for negative}$$

Now, let us derive the sum and difference identities for cosine.

$$\cos(\alpha+\beta)=\frac{AC}{AB} \quad \rightarrow \text{Definition of cosine}$$

$$=\frac{AF-DE}{AB} \quad \rightarrow \text{AC=AF-CF=AF-DE}$$

$$=\frac{AF}{AB}-\frac{DE}{AB} \quad \rightarrow \text{Separate the fraction}$$

$$=\frac{AF}{AE}\cdot\frac{AE}{AB}-\frac{DE}{BE}\cdot\frac{BE}{AB} \quad \rightarrow \text{Multiply } \frac{AE}{AE} \text{ and } \frac{BE}{BE}$$

$$\cos(\alpha+\beta)=\cos\alpha\cos\beta-\sin\alpha\sin\beta \quad \rightarrow \text{Definition of sine and cosine}$$

Thus, $\cos(\alpha-\beta)=\cos(\alpha+(-\beta))$

$=\cos\alpha\cos(-\beta)-\sin\alpha\sin(-\beta)$ → Apply sum identity

$\cos(\alpha-\beta)=\cos\alpha\cos\beta+\sin\alpha\sin\beta$ → Apply identities for negative

Finally, $$\tan(\alpha+\beta)=\frac{\sin(\alpha+\beta)}{\cos(\alpha+\beta)}=\frac{\sin\alpha\cos\beta+\cos\alpha\sin\beta}{\cos\alpha\cos\beta-\sin\alpha\sin\beta}\cdot\frac{\frac{1}{\cos\alpha\cos\beta}}{\frac{1}{\cos\alpha\cos\beta}}$$

$$=\frac{\frac{\sin\alpha}{\cos\alpha}+\frac{\sin\beta}{\cos\beta}}{1-\frac{\sin\alpha\sin\beta}{\cos\alpha\cos\beta}}=\frac{\tan\alpha+\tan\beta}{1-\tan\alpha\tan\beta}$$

and $$\tan(\alpha-\beta)=\tan(\alpha+(-\beta))=\frac{\tan\alpha+\tan(-\beta)}{1-\tan\alpha\tan(-\beta)}=\frac{\tan\alpha-\tan\beta}{1+\tan\alpha\tan\beta}$$

Here are the sum and difference identities. Make sure to memorize them!

Sum and Difference Identity

1. $\sin(\alpha\pm\beta)=\sin\alpha\cos\beta\pm\cos\alpha\sin\beta$
2. $\cos(\alpha\pm\beta)=\cos\alpha\cos\beta\mp\sin\alpha\sin\beta$
3. $\tan(\alpha\pm\beta)=\dfrac{\tan\alpha\pm\tan\beta}{1\mp\tan\alpha\tan\beta}$

Example 4-1

Find the exact value of $\sin\frac{5\pi}{12}$.

Solution

Noting that $\frac{5\pi}{12}=\frac{\pi}{6}+\frac{\pi}{4}$, apply the sum identity for sine.

$$\sin\frac{5\pi}{12}=\sin\left(\frac{\pi}{6}+\frac{\pi}{4}\right)=\sin\frac{\pi}{6}\cos\frac{\pi}{4}+\cos\frac{\pi}{6}\sin\frac{\pi}{4}$$
$$=\frac{1}{2}\cdot\frac{\sqrt{2}}{2}+\frac{\sqrt{3}}{2}\cdot\frac{\sqrt{2}}{2}=\frac{\sqrt{2}+\sqrt{6}}{4}.$$

If you are still not familiar with radian measure, first convert the angle to degree measure.

$$\frac{5\pi}{12}\times\frac{180^\circ}{\pi}=75^\circ.$$

$$\sin 75^\circ=\sin(45^\circ+30^\circ)=\sin 45^\circ \cos 30^\circ+\cos 30^\circ \sin 45^\circ$$

$$=\frac{1}{2}\cdot\frac{\sqrt{2}}{2}+\frac{\sqrt{3}}{2}\cdot\frac{\sqrt{2}}{2}=\frac{\sqrt{2}+\sqrt{6}}{4}.$$

$\sin\frac{5\pi}{12}=\frac{\sqrt{2}+\sqrt{6}}{4}$

Example 4–2

Find the exact value of $\cos 100^\circ\cos 55^\circ+\sin 100^\circ\sin 55^\circ$.

Solution

By applying the difference identity for consine,

$\cos 100^\circ\cos 55^\circ+\sin 100^\circ \sin 55^\circ=\cos(100^\circ-55^\circ)=\cos(45^\circ)=\frac{\sqrt{2}}{2}$.

$\cos 100^\circ \cos 55^\circ+\sin 100^\circ \sin 55^\circ=\frac{\sqrt{2}}{2}$

Check Point 4

Solutions_Page 110

Find the value of each expression.

① $\sin 105^\circ$

② $\cos\frac{7\pi}{12}$

③ $\sin 100^\circ \cos 35^\circ+\cos 100^\circ \sin 35^\circ$

④ $\cos\frac{\pi}{12}\cos\frac{\pi}{4}+\sin\frac{\pi}{12}\sin\frac{\pi}{4}$

⑤ $\tan\frac{11\pi}{12}$

⑥ $\dfrac{\tan\frac{\pi}{8}-\tan\frac{3\pi}{8}}{1+\tan\frac{\pi}{8}\tan\frac{3\pi}{8}}$

Example 5–1

Using difference identity for sine, verify the cofunction identity $\sin\left(\frac{\pi}{2}-\theta\right)=\cos\theta$.

Solution

$$\sin\left(\frac{\pi}{2}-\theta\right)=\sin\frac{\pi}{2}\cos\theta-\cos\frac{\pi}{2}\sin\theta$$
$$=1\cdot\cos\theta-0\cdot\sin\theta=\cos\theta$$

The identity is verified

Example 5–2

Find all solutions of the equation in the interval $[0, 2\pi)$ and then find the general solutions of the equation $\sin\left(x+\frac{\pi}{3}\right)+\sin\left(x-\frac{\pi}{3}\right)=1$.

Solution

$$\sin\left(x+\frac{\pi}{3}\right)+\sin\left(x-\frac{\pi}{3}\right)=1$$
$$\left(\sin x\cos\frac{\pi}{3}+\cos x\sin\frac{\pi}{3}\right)+\left(\sin x\cos\frac{\pi}{3}-\cos x\sin\frac{\pi}{3}\right)=1$$
$$2\sin x\cos\frac{\pi}{3}=1,\ 2\sin x\cdot\frac{1}{2}=1,\ \sin x=1$$

So the only solution in the interval $[0, 2\pi)$ is $x=\frac{\pi}{2}$

and general solution is $x=\frac{\pi}{2}+2\pi n\ (n\in Z)$.

$x=\frac{\pi}{2};\ x=\frac{\pi}{2}+2\pi n\ (n\in Z)$

Check Point 5

Solutions_Page 111

Find all solutions of the equation in the interval $[0, 2\pi)$ and then find the general solutions of the equation $\sin\left(x+\frac{\pi}{4}\right)+\sin\left(x-\frac{\pi}{4}\right)=1$.

Review Exercise

Solutions_Page 111

01 Find all solutions of the equation in the interval $[0, 2\pi)$ and then find the general solution of the equation.

(1) $2\cos^2 x + \cos x = 0$

(2) $4\sin^2 x - 1 = 0$

(3) $3\tan(3x) + \sqrt{3} = 0$

(4) $\tan^2 x - 2\tan x - 3 = 0$

(5) $\sec x \tan x - 4\sin x = 0$

(6) $2\sin^2(3x) + \sin(3x) - 1 = 0$

(7) $\tan^3 x = 3\tan x$

(8) $3\tan^4 x - 10\tan^2 x + 3 = 0$

Review Exercise

02 Find the exact value of the expression.

(1) $\sin\frac{\pi}{12}$

(2) $\tan\frac{11\pi}{12}$

(3) $\cos 51^\circ \cos 6^\circ + \sin 51^\circ \sin 6^\circ$

(4) $\sin\frac{\pi}{4}\cos\frac{\pi}{12}+\cos\frac{\pi}{4}\sin\frac{\pi}{12}$

03 Find the exact value of the expression if $\sin\alpha=\frac{3}{5}$ and $\cos\beta=-\frac{1}{2}$.
(both α and β lies in Quadrant II)

(1) $\sin(\alpha+\beta)$

(2) $\cos(\alpha+\beta)$

(3) $\tan(\alpha+\beta)$

04 Referring to the following Figure below, write each of the following.

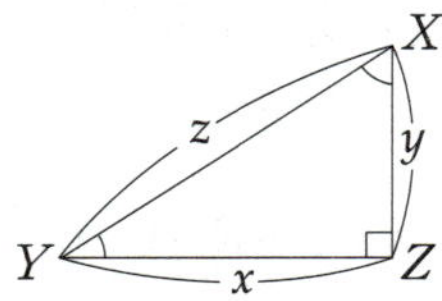

(1) $\sin(X+Y)$

(2) $\cos(X+Y)$

05 Prove the identity

$\tan\left(\frac{\pi}{2}+x\right)=-\cot x.$

06 Prove the indentity

$\cos\left(x-\frac{\pi}{4}\right)+\cos\left(x+\frac{\pi}{4}\right)=\sqrt{2}\cos x.$

07 Find all solutions of the equation $\sin(2x)\cos x - \cos x \sin x = 0$ in the interval $[0, 2\pi)$.

08 Find the exact value of the expression.

(1) $\cos\left(\sin^{-1}\left(\frac{2}{3}\right) - \tan^{-1}\left(\frac{1}{2}\right)\right)$

(2) $\sin(2\arctan(-2))$

09 Write $\cos(\sin^{-1}a + \tan^{-1}b)$ as an algebraic expression in a and b, where $-1 \le a \le 1$ and b is any real number.

10 Using the sum and difference identities, write the expression $\sin(3x)$ in terms of $\sin x$ and $\cos x$

11 The graph of f is defined by $f(x) = 2\sin x + 1$ and the graph of g is defined by $g(x) = -2$. How many points of intersection exist between the graph of f and g?

(A) None

(B) One

(C) Two

(D) Infinitely many

Review Exercise

12 If $3\sin x - 2\cos^2 x = 0$, then which of the following could be x?

(A) $\frac{\pi}{12}$

(B) $\frac{\pi}{6}$

(C) $\frac{\pi}{4}$

(D) $\frac{\pi}{3}$

13 Find the point of intersection of the graphs $y = 3 - \tan^2 x$ and $y = 2\sec^2 x$ in the interval $0 < x < \pi$.

14 Which of the following represents the complete set of solutions to the equation $2\tan x - 8 = 0$?

(A) $x = \arctan\frac{1}{4} + \pi n$, where n is any integer.

(B) $x = \arctan\frac{1}{4} + 2\pi n$, where n is any integer.

(C) $x = \arctan 4 + 2\pi n$, where n is any integer.

(D) $x = \arctan 4 + \pi n$, where n is any integer.

15

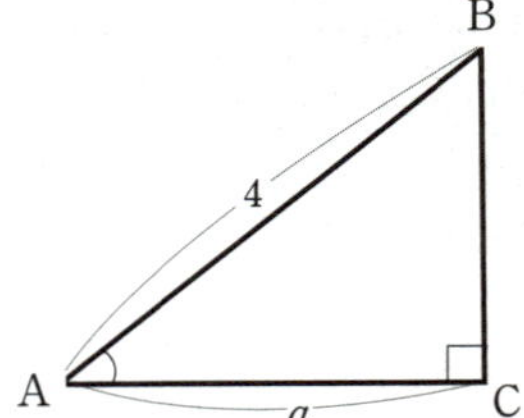

A right triangle is given above. If the measure of angle A is $\frac{7\pi}{12}$, what is the value of a?

16

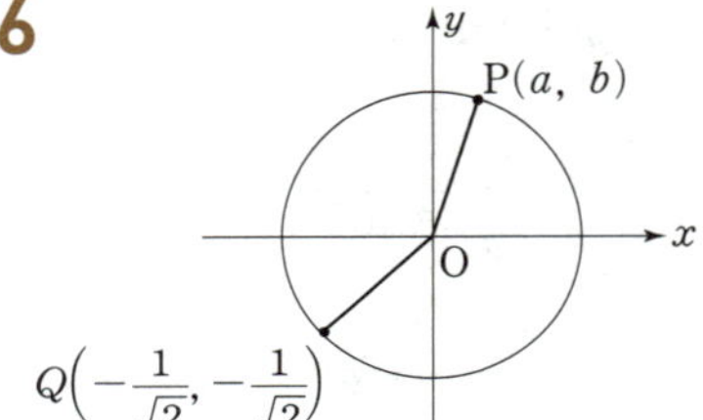

The diagram above shows a unit circle in the xy−plane. Write the expression $\sin\angle\text{POQ}$ in terms of a and b.

17 If $0 \le x < 2\pi$ and $\tan\left(-\frac{\pi}{4}\right) = \cos\left(x - \frac{\pi}{2}\right)$, then what is the value of x?

memo

8 Trigonometric Equations and Identities, Part II

01 Double-Angle Identities

1. $\sin(2\theta)=2\sin\theta\cos\theta$
2. $\cos(2\theta)=\cos^2\theta-\sin^2\theta$
   $=2\cos^2\theta-1$
   $=1-2\sin^2\theta$
3. $\tan(2\theta)=\dfrac{2\tan\theta}{1-\tan^2\theta}$

Proof

1. $\sin(2\theta)=\sin(\theta+\theta)$ → $2\theta=\theta+\theta$
   $=\sin\theta\cos\theta+\cos\theta\sin\theta$ → Sum identity for sine
   $=2\sin\theta\cos\theta$ → Simplify

2. $\cos(2\theta)=\cos(\theta+\theta)$ → $2\theta=\theta+\theta$
   $=\cos\theta\cos\theta-\sin\theta\sin\theta$ → Sum identity for cosine
   $=\cos^2\theta-\sin^2\theta$ → Simplify

   $\cos(2\theta)=\cos^2\theta-\sin^2\theta$ → Double-Angle identity for cosine
   $=\cos^2\theta-(1-\cos^2\theta)$ → Pythagorean identity
   $=2\cos^2\theta-1$ → Simplify

   $\cos(2\theta)=\cos^2\theta-\sin^2\theta$ → Double-Angle identity for cosine
   $=(1-\sin^2\theta)-\sin^2\theta$ → Pythagorean identity
   $=1-2\sin^2\theta$ → Simplify

3. $\tan(2\theta)=\tan(\theta+\theta)$ → $2\theta=\theta+\theta$
   $=\dfrac{\tan\theta+\tan\theta}{1-\tan\theta\tan\theta}$ → Sum identity for tangent
   $=\dfrac{2\tan\theta}{1-\tan^2\theta}$ → Simplify

Example 1

Let $\sin\theta=\frac{1}{2}$ and $0<\theta<\frac{\pi}{2}$. Find the exact value of $\sin(2\theta)$, $\cos(2\theta)$, and $\tan(2\theta)$.

Solution

In order to use double−angle identity, we first have to find $\cos\theta$ using the Pythagorean identity.
$\sin^2\theta+\cos^2\theta=1$

$\left(\frac{1}{2}\right)^2+\cos^2\theta=1$, $\cos^2\theta=1-\frac{1}{4}=\frac{3}{4}$, $\cos\theta=\pm\frac{\sqrt{3}}{2}$.

Since $0<\theta<\frac{\pi}{2}$, $\cos\theta=\frac{\sqrt{3}}{2}$. And then $\tan\theta=\frac{\sin\theta}{\cos\theta}=\frac{\frac{1}{2}}{\frac{\sqrt{3}}{2}}=\frac{1}{\sqrt{3}}=\frac{\sqrt{3}}{3}$.

Therefore,

$\sin(2\theta)=2\sin\theta\cos\theta$

$=2\cdot\frac{1}{2}\cdot\frac{\sqrt{3}}{2}=\frac{\sqrt{3}}{2}$

$\cos(2\theta)=\cos^2\theta-\sin^2\theta$

$=\left(\frac{\sqrt{3}}{2}\right)^2-\left(\frac{1}{2}\right)^2=\frac{3}{4}-\frac{1}{4}=\frac{1}{2}$

$\tan(2\theta)=\frac{2\tan\theta}{1-\tan^2\theta}$

$=\frac{2\cdot\frac{\sqrt{3}}{3}}{1-\left(\frac{\sqrt{3}}{3}\right)^2}=\frac{\frac{2\sqrt{3}}{3}}{\frac{2}{3}}=\sqrt{3}$

$\sin(2\theta)=\frac{\sqrt{3}}{2}$, $\cos(2\theta)=\frac{1}{2}$, $\tan(2\theta)=\sqrt{3}$

Check Point 1

Solutions_Page 116

Find the exact value of $\sin(2\theta)$, $\cos(2\theta)$, and $\tan(2\theta)$ from the given information.

① $\sin\theta=-\frac{1}{4}$ and θ is in Quadrant III

② $\cot\theta=-\frac{12}{5}$ and $\frac{\pi}{2}<\theta<\pi$

Example 2

Solve the equation $\cos(2x)-\cos x=0$.

Solution

$\cos(2x)-\cos x=0$ → Original equation
$(2\cos^2 x-1)-\cos x=0$ → Double−Angel identity for cosine
$2\cos^2 x-\cos x-1=0$ → Simplify
$(2\cos x+1)(\cos x-1)=0$ → Factor
$\cos x=-\frac{1}{2}$ or $\cos x=1$

(1) For $\cos x=-\frac{1}{2}$ in $[0, 2\pi)$, the solutions are $x=\frac{2\pi}{3}$ and $x=\frac{4\pi}{3}$.
The general solutions are $x=\frac{2\pi}{3}+2\pi n$ $(n\in Z)$ and $x=\frac{4\pi}{3}+2\pi n$ $(n\in Z)$.

(2) For $\cos x=1$ in $[0, 2\pi)$, the solutions are $x=0$.
The general solutions are $x=2\pi n$ $(n\in Z)$.

In the interval $[0, 2\pi)$, $x=\frac{2\pi}{3}$, $x=\frac{4\pi}{3}$ and $x=0$
The general solutions are $x=\frac{2\pi}{3}+2\pi n$, $x=\frac{4\pi}{3}+2\pi n$, and $x=2\pi n$ $(n\in Z)$

Check Point 2

Solutions_Page 117

Find all solutions of the equation in the interval $[0, 2\pi)$ and then find the general solutions of the equation.

① $\sin x=\sin(2x)$

② $\cos(2x)+3\sin x+1=0$

02 Half-Angle Identities

1. $\sin\left(\frac{\theta}{2}\right)=\pm\sqrt{\frac{1-\cos\theta}{2}}$

2. $\cos\left(\frac{\theta}{2}\right)=\pm\sqrt{\frac{1+\cos\theta}{2}}$

3. $\tan\left(\frac{\theta}{2}\right)=\pm\sqrt{\frac{1-\cos\theta}{1+\cos\theta}}$

$=\frac{\sin\theta}{1+\cos\theta}=\frac{1-\cos\theta}{\sin\theta}$

✔ The sign of $\sin\left(\frac{\theta}{2}\right)$, $\cos\left(\frac{\theta}{2}\right)$, and $\tan\left(\frac{\theta}{2}\right)$ depend on the angle $\frac{\theta}{2}$.

Proof

1. $\cos(2\alpha)=1-2\sin^2\alpha$ → Double−Angle identity for cosine

$2\sin^2\alpha=1-\cos(2\alpha)$ → Isolate $\sin^2\alpha$ term

$\sin^2\alpha=\frac{1-\cos(2\alpha)}{2}$ → Divide each side by 2

$\sin\alpha=\pm\sqrt{\frac{1-\cos(2\alpha)}{2}}$ → Take a square root of each side

If $\alpha=\frac{\theta}{2}$, then $\sin\left(\frac{\theta}{2}\right)=\pm\sqrt{\frac{1-\cos\theta}{2}}$

2. $\cos(2\alpha)=2\cos^2\alpha-1$ → Double−Angle identity for cosine

$2\cos^2\alpha=1+\cos(2\alpha)$ → Isolate $\cos^2\alpha$ term

$\cos^2\alpha=\frac{1+\cos(2\alpha)}{2}$ → Divide each side by 2

$\cos\alpha=\pm\sqrt{\frac{1+\cos(2\alpha)}{2}}$ → Take a square root of each side

If $\alpha=\frac{\theta}{2}$, then $\cos\frac{\theta}{2}=\pm\sqrt{\frac{1+\cos\theta}{2}}$

3. $\tan\left(\frac{\theta}{2}\right)=\pm\frac{\sin\left(\frac{\theta}{2}\right)}{\cos\left(\frac{\theta}{2}\right)}=\pm\frac{\sqrt{\frac{1-\cos\theta}{2}}}{\sqrt{\frac{1+\cos\theta}{2}}}=\pm\sqrt{\frac{1-\cos\theta}{1+\cos\theta}}$

$\sqrt{\frac{1-\cos\theta}{1+\cos\theta}}\cdot\sqrt{\frac{1+\cos\theta}{1+\cos\theta}}=\frac{\sin\theta}{1+\cos\theta}$ and $\sqrt{\frac{1-\cos\theta}{1+\cos\theta}}\cdot\sqrt{\frac{1-\cos\theta}{1-\cos\theta}}=\frac{1-\cos\theta}{\sin\theta}$

Example 3

Find the exact value of $\cos 15°$.

Solution

Since 15° lies in Quadrant I, $\cos 15°>0$.

$$\cos 15°=\sqrt{\frac{1+\cos 30°}{2}}=\sqrt{\frac{1+\frac{\sqrt{3}}{2}}{2}}=\sqrt{\frac{\frac{2+\sqrt{3}}{2}}{2}}=\frac{\sqrt{2+\sqrt{3}}}{2}$$

$$\cos 15°=\frac{\sqrt{2+\sqrt{3}}}{2}$$

Check Point 3

Solutions_Page 117

① $\sin\frac{\pi}{8}$ ② $\cos\frac{5\pi}{8}$ ③ $\tan 67.5°$

Example 4

Let $\cos\theta=-\frac{5}{13}$ and θ is in Quadrant II. Find exact value of $\sin\left(\frac{\theta}{2}\right)$, $\cos\left(\frac{\theta}{2}\right)$, and $\tan\left(\frac{\theta}{2}\right)$.

Solution

Since θ is in Quadrant II, $\frac{\pi}{2}<\theta<\pi$. Then, we have
$\frac{1}{2}\left(\frac{\theta}{2}<\theta<\pi\right)$, $\frac{\pi}{4}<\frac{\theta}{2}<\frac{\pi}{2}$ → $\frac{\theta}{2}$ is in Quadrant I.

$$\sin\left(\frac{\theta}{2}\right)=\sqrt{\frac{1-\cos\theta}{2}}=\sqrt{\frac{1-\left(-\frac{5}{13}\right)}{2}}=\sqrt{\frac{\frac{18}{13}}{2}}$$
$$=\sqrt{\frac{9}{13}}=\frac{3\sqrt{13}}{13}$$

$$\cos\left(\frac{\theta}{2}\right)=\sqrt{\frac{1+\cos\theta}{2}}=\sqrt{\frac{1+\left(-\frac{5}{13}\right)}{2}}=\sqrt{\frac{\frac{8}{13}}{2}}$$
$$=\sqrt{\frac{4}{13}}=\frac{2\sqrt{13}}{13}$$

$$\tan\left(\frac{\theta}{2}\right)=\frac{\sin\left(\frac{\theta}{2}\right)}{\cos\left(\frac{\theta}{2}\right)}=\frac{\sin\left(\frac{\theta}{2}\right)}{\cos\left(\frac{\theta}{2}\right)}=\frac{\frac{3\sqrt{13}}{13}}{\frac{2\sqrt{13}}{13}}=\frac{3}{2}$$

$\sin\left(\frac{\theta}{2}\right)=\frac{3\sqrt{13}}{13}$, $\cos\left(\frac{\theta}{2}\right)=\frac{2\sqrt{13}}{13}$, $\tan\left(\frac{\theta}{2}\right)=\frac{3}{2}$

Check Point 4

Solutions_Page 117

Find exact value of $\sin\left(\frac{\theta}{2}\right)$, $\cos\left(\frac{\theta}{2}\right)$, and $\tan\left(\frac{\theta}{2}\right)$ from the given information.

① $\sin\theta=\frac{3}{5}$ and θ is in Quadrant I

② $\sec\theta=2$ and $\frac{3\pi}{2}<\theta<2\pi$

03 Product-to-Sum Identities

1. $\sin\alpha\cos\beta=\frac{1}{2}[\sin(\alpha+\beta)+\sin(\alpha-\beta)]$
2. $\cos\alpha\sin\beta=\frac{1}{2}[\sin(\alpha+\beta)-\sin(\alpha-\beta)]$
3. $\cos\alpha\cos\beta=\frac{1}{2}[\cos(\alpha+\beta)+\cos(\alpha-\beta)]$
4. $\sin\alpha\sin\beta=\frac{1}{2}[\cos(\alpha-\beta)-\cos(\alpha+\beta)]$

Proof

We can prove the product of sine and cosine as the sum of trigonometric functions. To see this, consider the sum and difference identities for the sine function.

$\sin(\alpha+\beta)=\sin\alpha\cos\beta+\cos\alpha\sin\beta$ ··· (1)
$\sin(\alpha-\beta)=\sin\alpha\cos\beta-\cos\alpha\sin\beta$ ··· (2)

$\sin(\alpha+\beta)+\sin(\alpha-\beta)=2\sin\alpha\cos\beta$ → Add (1) and (2)
$\sin\alpha\cos\beta=\frac{1}{2}[\sin(\alpha+\beta)+\sin(\alpha-\beta)]$ → Divide both sides by 2

The other three Product−to−Sum Identities are obtained in a similar manner.

Example 5

Write $\sin(2x)\cos(3x)$ as a sum or difference of trigonometric functions.

Solution

Using the Product−to−Sum identity,

$$\sin(2x)\cos(3x)=\frac{1}{2}[\sin(2x+3x)+\sin(2x-3x)]$$

$$=\frac{1}{2}[\sin(5x)+\sin(-x)]=\frac{1}{2}[\sin(5x)-\sin x].$$

$\sin(2x)\cos(3x)=\frac{1}{2}[\sin(5x)-\sin x]$

Check Point 5

Solutions_Page 118

Write each of the expression as a sum or difference of trigonometric functions.

① $\sin(4x)\sin(3x)$ ② $\cos(2x)\cos(5x)$ ③ $\cos x\sin(3x)$

04 Sum-to-Product Identities

1. $\sin\alpha+\sin\beta=2\sin\left(\frac{\alpha+\beta}{2}\right)\cos\left(\frac{\alpha-\beta}{2}\right)$
2. $\sin\alpha-\sin\beta=2\cos\left(\frac{\alpha+\beta}{2}\right)\sin\left(\frac{\alpha-\beta}{2}\right)$
3. $\cos\alpha+\cos\beta=2\cos\left(\frac{\alpha+\beta}{2}\right)\cos\left(\frac{\alpha-\beta}{2}\right)$
4. $\cos\alpha-\cos\beta=-2\sin\left(\frac{\alpha+\beta}{2}\right)\sin\left(\frac{\alpha-\beta}{2}\right)$

Proof

Sum−to−Product Identities can be easily proved by Product−to−Sum identities.

$$2\sin\left(\frac{\alpha+\beta}{2}\right)\cos\left(\frac{\alpha-\beta}{2}\right)=2\cdot\frac{1}{2}\left[\sin\left(\frac{\alpha+\beta}{2}+\frac{\alpha-\beta}{2}\right)+\sin\left(\frac{\alpha+\beta}{2}-\frac{\alpha-\beta}{2}\right)\right]$$

$$=\sin\left(\frac{\alpha+\beta}{2}+\frac{\alpha-\beta}{2}\right)+\sin\left(\frac{\alpha+\beta}{2}-\frac{\alpha-\beta}{2}\right)$$

$$=\sin\left(\frac{2\alpha}{2}\right)+\sin\left(\frac{2\beta}{2}\right)=\sin\alpha+\sin\beta.$$

Therefore, $\sin\alpha+\sin\beta=2\sin\left(\frac{\alpha+\beta}{2}\right)\cos\left(\frac{\alpha-\beta}{2}\right)$.

The other three Sum−to−Product Identities are obtained in a similar manner.

Example 6

Write $\sin(6x)+\sin(4x)$ as a product of trigonometric functions.

Solution

Using the Sum−to−Product identity,

$$\sin(6x)+\sin(4x)=2\sin\left(\frac{6x+4x}{2}\right)\cos\left(\frac{6x-4x}{2}\right)=2\sin(5x)\cos x.$$

$\sin(6x)+\sin(4x)=2\sin(5x)\cos x$

Check Point 6

Solutions_Page 118

Write each of the expression as a product of trigonometric functions.

① $\sin(6x)-\sin(3x)$ ② $\cos(2x)-\cos(5x)$ ③ $\cos(3x)+\cos(7x)$

Review Exercise

01 Given $\tan\theta = \frac{4}{3}$ and $\pi < \theta < \frac{3\pi}{2}$, find the exact value $\sin(2\theta)$, $\cos(2\theta)$, and $\tan(2\theta)$.

02 Find all solutions of the equation in the interval $[0, 2\pi)$ and then find the general solution of the equation.

(1) $\sin x \cos x - \frac{1}{4} = 0$

(2) $\sin x + 1 - \cos(2x) = 0$

(3) $\sin(2x) = \tan x$

03 Use half−angle identities to find an exact value.

(1) $\sin\left(\frac{\pi}{12}\right)$

(2) $\cos 195°$

(3) $\tan\left(\frac{5\pi}{12}\right)$

04 Given $\cos\theta = \frac{1}{2}$ and $\frac{3\pi}{2} < \theta < 2\pi$, find the exact value of $\sin\left(\frac{\theta}{2}\right)$, $\cos\left(\frac{\theta}{2}\right)$, and $\tan\left(\frac{\theta}{2}\right)$.

05 What is the minimum value of $4\sin x \cos x$?

06 If $0 \le x < \frac{\pi}{2}$ and $\sin x = y$, then what is $\sin(2x)$ in terms of y?

07 Find the exact value of $\cos\left(2\tan^{-1}\left(\frac{3}{4}\right)\right)$.

08 Prove that

$$\cos^4 x = \frac{\cos(4x)}{8} + \frac{\cos(2x)}{2} + \frac{3}{8}.$$

09 Solve the equation $\sin x + \cos x = 1$ in the interval of $[0, 2\pi)$. Check for extraneous solutions.

10 Write $\sin(2\tan^{-1} x)$, where x is any real number, as an algebraic expression in terms of x.

11 Write the product as a sum.

(1) $\cos(3x)\sin(4x)$

(2) $4\sin\left(\frac{x}{2}\right)\sin\left(\frac{x}{3}\right)$

12 Write the sum as a product.

(1) $\cos(4x) + \cos(5x)$

(2) $\sin(3x) + \sin(6x)$

Review Exercise

13 Verify the identities.

(1) $\dfrac{\sin(4x)+\sin(6x)}{\cos(4x)+\cos(6x)}=\tan(5x)$

(2) $\sin x(\sin(3x)+\sin(5x))=\sin(2x)\sin(4x)$

(3) $\dfrac{\cos(2x)-\cos(6x)}{\cos(2x)+\cos(6x)}=\tan(4x)\tan(2x)$

(4) $\dfrac{\cos x+\cos(3x)+\cos(5x)}{\sin x+\sin(3x)+\sin(5x)}=\cot(3x)$

14

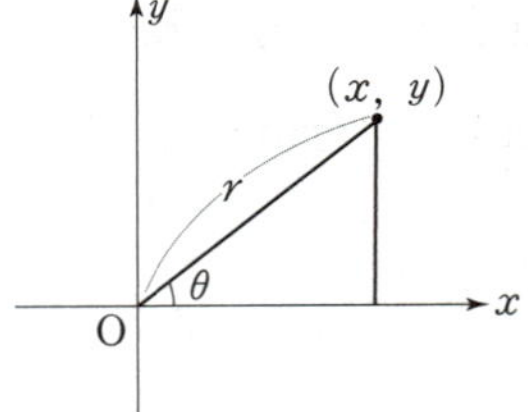

A right triangle is given above. Which of the following expressions is equal to $r^2\sin(2\theta)$?

(A) x
(B) y
(C) $x+y$
(D) $2xy$

15 The function f is given by $f(x)=4\cos^2 x+3$. If the graph of f has an amplitude m and a period p, what is the value of $m+p$?

16 If $\dfrac{\sin(2x)-\cos x}{\cos x}=0$, where $\cos x\neq 0$, then in which quadrant would the angle x lie?

(A) First and second quadrants only
(B) First and third quadrants only
(C) Second and third quadrants only
(D) Second and fourth quadrants only

17 If f is a function such that $f\left(\frac{x}{2}-\frac{\pi}{6}\right)=\sin\left(x-\frac{\pi}{3}\right)$ for all x, then what is $f(x)$?

(A) $\sin(2x)$
(B) $\cos(2x)$
(C) $\sin\left(x-\frac{\pi}{2}\right)$
(D) $\cos\left(x-\frac{\pi}{2}\right)$

18 If $\tan x=m$ for $0<x<\frac{\pi}{2}$, which of the following expressions is equal to $\sin(2x)$ in terms of m?

(A) $\dfrac{1}{\sqrt{1+m^2}}$
(B) $\dfrac{m}{\sqrt{1+m^2}}$
(C) $\dfrac{2}{1+m^2}$
(D) $\dfrac{2m}{1+m^2}$

19

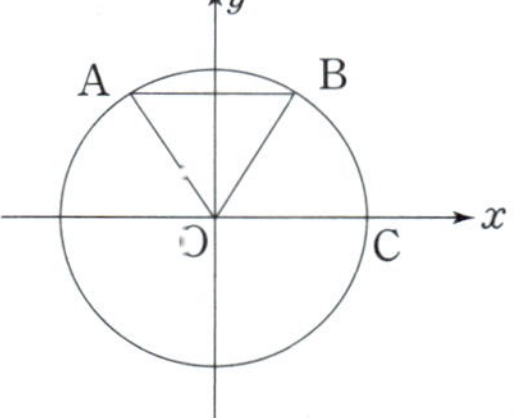

A unit circle is given above. The measure of angle COA is twice the measure of angle COB and the chord AB is parallel to the x-axis. If the coordinates of B is (a, b), which of the following expressions is equal to $\sin\angle AOB$?

(A) a
(B) b
(C) $a+b$
(D) ab

9 Polar Coordinates and Equations

01 Definition of Polar Coordinates

So far, we have been representing graphs of equations as a set of points (x, y) on the rectangular coordinate system. In this section, we will study an alternative method of representing points in a plane, and these points are called the polar coordinates.

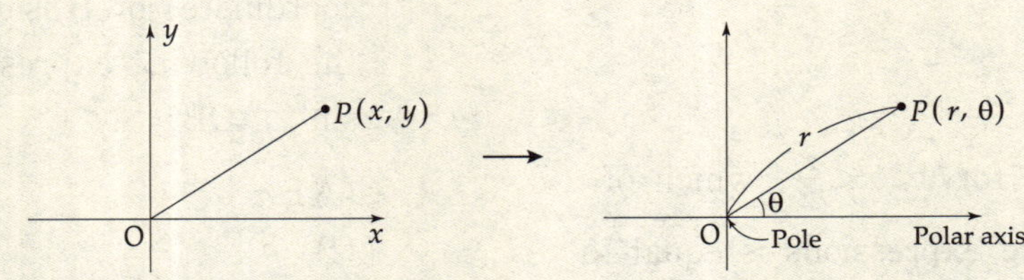

Rectangular Coordinate system　　Polar Coordinate system

r is the directed distance from O to P, and θ is the directed angle as shown above. If r is positive, the point will be in the same quadrant as θ. If r is negative, the point will end up in the quadrant exactly opposite θ.

Example 1

Plot the points with the given polar coordinates $P(r, \theta)$.

① $\left(2, \frac{\pi}{4}\right)$　　② $\left(1, -\frac{\pi}{2}\right)$　　③ $\left(-3, \frac{2\pi}{3}\right)$

Solution

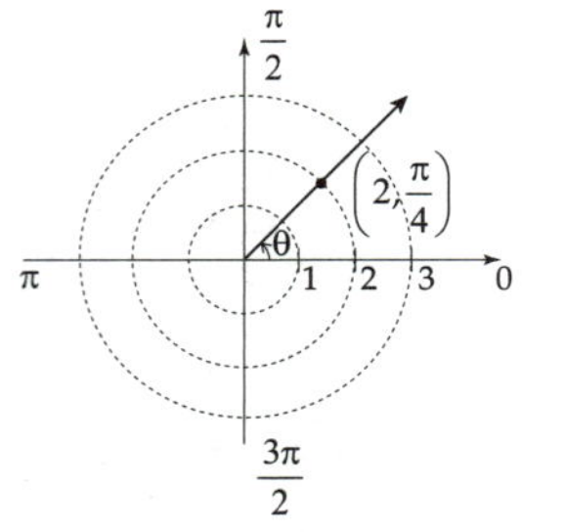

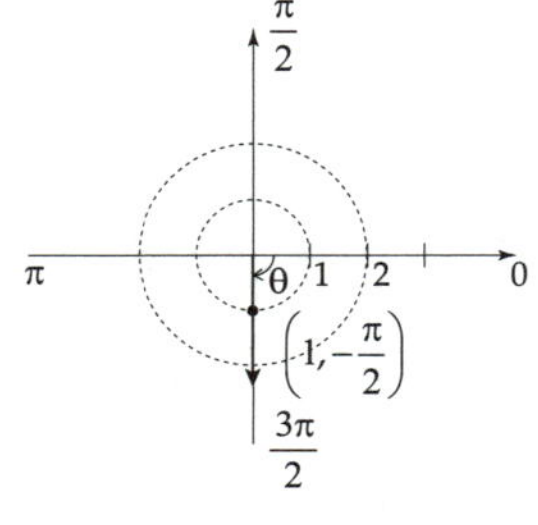

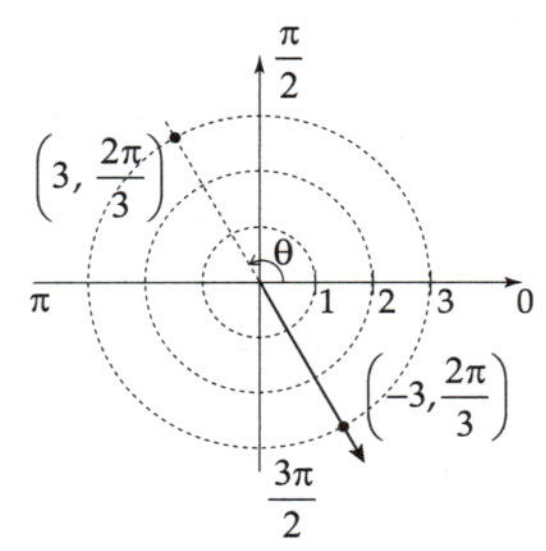

Check Point 1

Solutions_Page 123

Plot the points with the given polar coordinates $P(r,\ \theta)$.

① $\left(2,\ \frac{\pi}{3}\right)$ ② $\left(3,\ \frac{5\pi}{4}\right)$ ③ $\left(-2,\ \frac{5\pi}{3}\right)$ ④ $\left(-1,\ -\frac{2\pi}{3}\right)$

02 Representation of Polar Coordinates

Each rectangular coordinate determines a unique point in the plane. However, the polar coordinates of a point in the plane are not unique. There are infinitely many other ordered pairs that can give the same point. For example,
$\left(2,\ \frac{\pi}{6}\right)=\left(2,\ \frac{13\pi}{6}\right)=\left(-2,\ \frac{7\pi}{6}\right)$ and so on, as shown in Figure below.

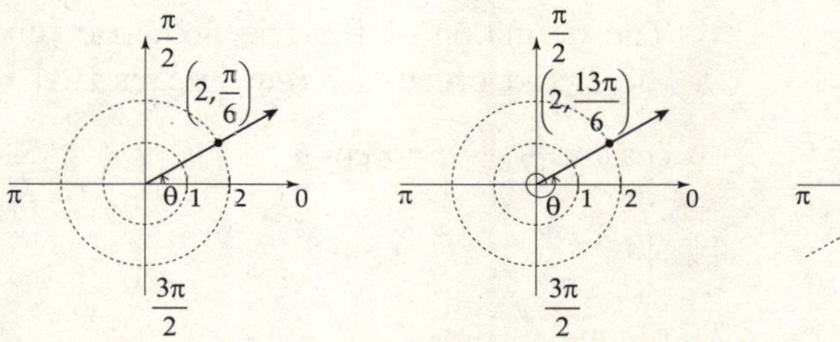

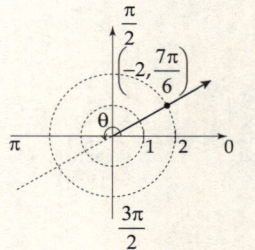

In particular, the point $(r,\ \theta)$ can be represented as
$(r,\ \theta)=(r,\ \theta+2n\pi)=(-r,\ \theta+(2n+1)\pi)$, where n is any integer.

Example 2

Find three different polar coordinates(one positive r and two negative r) that represent the point $\left(4,\ \frac{3\pi}{4}\right)$ in the interval $-2\pi<\theta<2\pi$.

Solution

$\left(4,\ \frac{3\pi}{4}-2\pi\right)=\left(4,\ -\frac{5\pi}{4}\right)$, $\left(-4,\ \frac{3\pi}{4}+\pi\right)=\left(-4,\ \frac{7\pi}{4}\right)$, and $\left(-4,\ \frac{3\pi}{4}-\pi\right)=\left(-4,\ -\frac{\pi}{4}\right)$

$\left(4,\ -\frac{5\pi}{4}\right)$, $\left(-4,\ \frac{7\pi}{4}\right)$, and $\left(-4,\ -\frac{\pi}{4}\right)$

Check Point 2

Solutions_Page 123

For given polar coordinates, find three different polar coordinates (one positive r and two negative r) in the inverval $-2\pi<\theta<2\pi$.

① $\left(2,\ \frac{\pi}{6}\right)$ ② $\left(1,\ -\frac{\pi}{3}\right)$

03 Coordinate Conversion

If we represent both rectangular and polar coordinates in the rectangular coordinate system, the pole is the origin and the polar axis is the positive x−axis, as shown in Figure below.

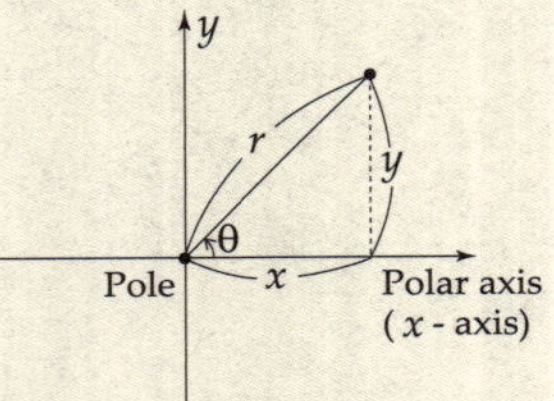

The definition of the trigonometric functions and the Pythagorean theorem implies that

$\cos\theta=\frac{x}{r}\ \rightarrow\ x=r\cos\theta$

$\sin\theta=\frac{y}{r}\ \rightarrow\ y=r\sin\theta$

$\tan\theta=\frac{y}{x}$ and $x^2+y^2=r^2$

Coordinate Conversion

1. Polar → Rectangular	2. Rectangular → Polar
$x=r\cos\theta$ and $y=r\sin\theta$	$\tan\theta=\frac{y}{x}$ and $x^2+y^2=r^2$

Example 3

Find the rectangular coordinate of a point with the polar coordinate $\left(3,\ \frac{7\pi}{6}\right)$.

Solution

For the point $(r,\ \theta)=\left(3,\ \frac{7\pi}{6}\right)$, $x=r\cos\theta=3\cos\left(\frac{7\pi}{6}\right)=-\frac{3\sqrt{3}}{2}$ and $y=r\sin\theta=3\sin\left(\frac{7\pi}{6}\right)=-\frac{3}{2}$.

Thus, the rectangular coordinate is $(x,\ y)=\left(-\frac{3\sqrt{3}}{2},\ -\frac{3}{2}\right)$.

$\left(3,\ \frac{7\pi}{6}\right) \to \left(-\frac{3\sqrt{3}}{2},\ -\frac{3}{2}\right)$

Check Point 3

Solutions_Page 124

Find the rectangular coordinates of the points with the following polar coordinates.

① $\left(2,\ \frac{3\pi}{4}\right)$ ② $\left(4,\ -\frac{\pi}{6}\right)$

Example 4

Find the polar coordinates of the point with the rectangular coordinates.

① $(2,\ 2\sqrt{3})$ ② $(-4,\ 4)$

Solution

①

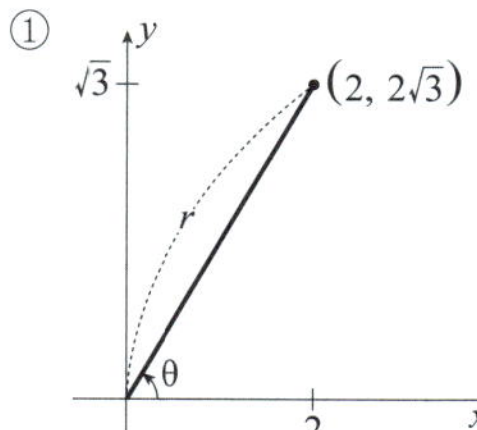

For the point $(x,\ y)=(2,\ 2\sqrt{3})$, $\tan\theta=\frac{2\sqrt{3}}{2}$, $\theta=\tan^{-1}\left(\frac{2\sqrt{3}}{2}\right)=\frac{\pi}{3}$ and $x^2+y^2=r^2$, $r=\sqrt{(2^2+(2\sqrt{3})^2}=4$. Thus, the polar coordinate is $(r,\ \theta)=\left(4,\ \frac{\pi}{3}\right)$

$(2,\ 2\sqrt{3}) \to \left(4,\ \frac{\pi}{3}\right)$

②

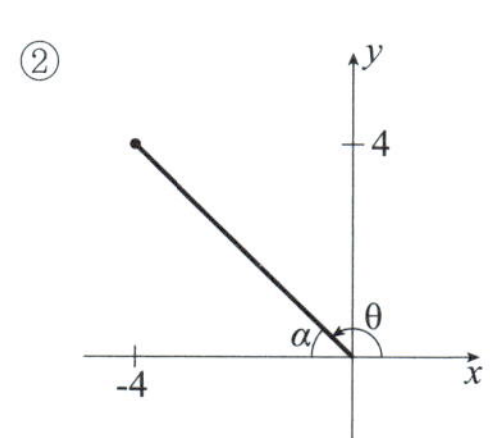

For the point $(x,\ y)=(-4,\ 4)$, $\tan\alpha=\frac{4}{4}=1$, $\alpha=\tan^{-1}(1)=\frac{\pi}{4}$.

Since θ is in Quadrant II, $\theta=\pi-\frac{\pi}{4}=\frac{3\pi}{4}$.

Also, $x^2+y^2=r^2$, $r=\sqrt{(-4)^2+4^2}=4\sqrt{2}$.

Thus, the polar coordinate is $(r,\ \theta)=\left(4\sqrt{2},\ \frac{3\pi}{4}\right)$

$(-4,\ 4) \to \left(4\sqrt{2},\ \frac{3\pi}{4}\right)$

Check Point 4

Solutions_Page 124

Find the polar coordinates of the point with the rectangular coordinates.

① $(1,\ -1)$ ② $(-3,\ -3\sqrt{3})$

04 Equation Conversion

We can also convert a rectangular equation to polar form or vice versa.

1. Rectangular form → Polar form: This is straightforward. Just replace x by $r\cos\theta$ and y by $r\sin\theta$, and then simplify.
2. Polar form → Rectangular form: This often requires more thought. Multiplying both sides of the equation by r or squaring both sides of the equation are the helpful techniques for converting an equation from polar form to rectangular form.

Example 5

Convert the rectangular equation $x^2+y^2=4$ to polar form.

Solution

Since $x^2+y^2=r^2$, $x^2+y^2=4$, $r^2=4$, $r=2$

Alternative Solution

$x^2+y^2=4$, $(r\cos\theta)^2+(r\sin\theta)^2=4$

$r^2\cos^2\theta+r^2\sin^2\theta=4$

$r^2(\cos^2\theta+\sin^2\theta)=4$

$r^2=4$, $r=2$

$x^2+y^2=4 \rightarrow r=2$

Check Point 5

Solutions_Page 124

Convert the rectangular equation to the polar form.

① $x=2$ ② $x-4y+8=0$

Example 6

Convert the polar equation $r=3\cos\theta$ to rectangular form.

Solution

Since $r^2=x^2+y^2$ and $r\cos\theta=x$,

$$r=3\cos\theta$$

$$r^2=3r\cos\theta \quad \rightarrow \text{Multiply both sides by } r$$

$$x^2+y^2=3x,\ x^2+y^2-3x=0$$

$r=3\cos\theta \rightarrow x^2+y^2-3x=0$

Check Point 6

Solutions_Page 124

Convert the polar equation to rectangular form.

① $r=2\sin\theta$

② $r=\dfrac{1}{1+\cos\theta}$

05 Graph Polar Equations by Converting to Rectangular Equations

We will sketch the graph of a polar equation, $r=f(\theta)$. The graph of a polar equation consists of all points that have at least one polar representation $(r,\ \theta)$ whose coordinates satisfy the equation. One method that we can use to graph is to convert the polar equation to rectangular equation.

Example 7-1

Sketch the graph of the polar equation $r=5$.

Solution

Convert the polar equation to a rectangular equation.

$$r=5$$

$$r^2=5^2 \qquad \rightarrow \text{Square both sides}$$

$$x^2+y^2=25 \qquad \rightarrow r^2=x^2+y^2$$

So the graph of $r=5$ is a circle with center at the origin and radius 5.

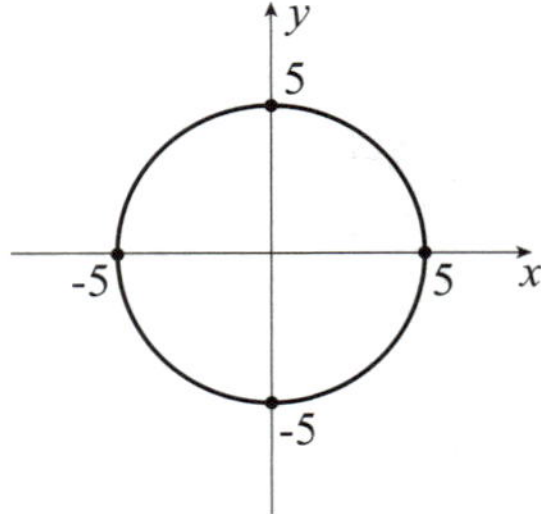

✔ In general, the graph of the equation $r=k$ is a circle of radius $|k|$ centered at the origin.

Example 7–2

Sketch the graph of the polar equation $\theta=\frac{\pi}{6}$.

Solution

Convert the polar equation to a rectangular equation.

$$\theta=\frac{\pi}{6}$$

$$\tan\theta=\tan\frac{\pi}{6} \qquad \rightarrow \text{Take the tangent of both sides}$$

$$\frac{y}{x}=\frac{1}{\sqrt{3}} \qquad \rightarrow \tan\theta=\frac{y}{x}$$

$$y=\frac{1}{\sqrt{3}}x$$

So the graph of $\theta=\frac{\pi}{6}$ is a line passing through the origin with slope $\frac{1}{\sqrt{3}}$.

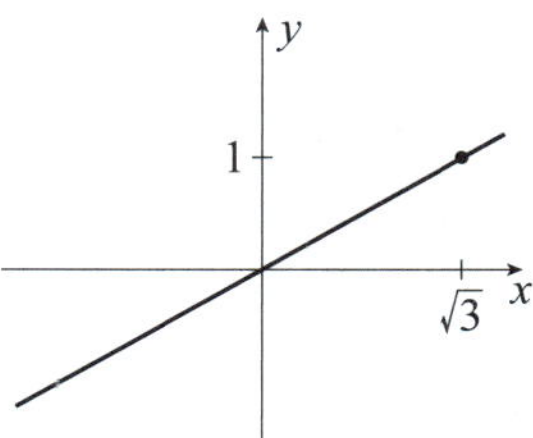

In general, the graph of the equation $\theta = k$ is a line that passes through the origin making an angle of k with the positive x−axis.

Example 7–3

Sketch the graph of the polar equation $r = 4\sec\theta$.

Solution

Convert the polar equation to a rectangular equation.

$$r = 4\sec\theta$$

$$r = \frac{4}{\cos\theta} \qquad \rightarrow \sec\theta = \frac{1}{\cos\theta}$$

$$r\cos\theta = 4 \qquad \rightarrow r\cos\theta = x$$

$$x = 4$$

So the graph of $r = 4\sec\theta$ is a vertical line as shown in Figure below.

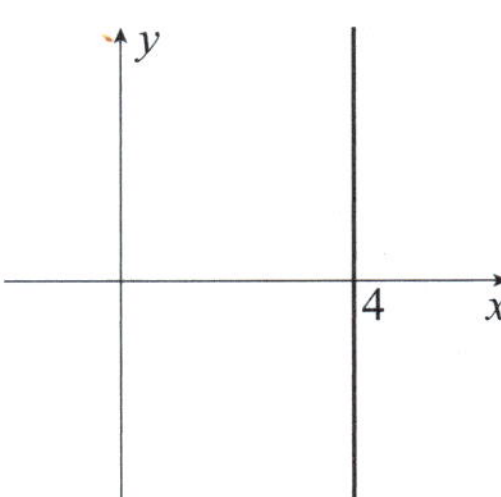

Check Point 7

Solutions_Page 125

Sketch the graph of the polar equation by converting to rectangular equation.

① $r=2$

② $\theta=\frac{\pi}{3}$

③ $r=-\frac{2}{\sin\theta}$

④ $\tan\theta=-1$

06 Graphs Polar Equations by Plotting Points.

We can graph the polar equation by determining the polar coordinates of several points on the curve.

Example 8

Sketch the graph of the polar equation $r=2\cos\theta$.

Solution

Here is a table with values of r for some values of θ.

θ	0	$\frac{\pi}{6}$	$\frac{\pi}{4}$	$\frac{\pi}{3}$	$\frac{\pi}{2}$	$\frac{2\pi}{3}$	$\frac{3\pi}{4}$	$\frac{5\pi}{6}$
r	2	$\sqrt{3}$	$\sqrt{2}$	1	0	-1	$-\sqrt{2}$	$-\sqrt{3}$
θ	π	$\frac{7\pi}{6}$	$\frac{5\pi}{4}$	$\frac{4\pi}{3}$	$\frac{3\pi}{2}$	$\frac{5\pi}{3}$	$\frac{7\pi}{4}$	$\frac{11\pi}{6}$
r	-2	$-\sqrt{3}$	$-\sqrt{2}$	-1	0	1	$\sqrt{2}$	$\sqrt{3}$

If we plot these points and join them to sketch the graph as shown in the Figure below, the graph appears to be a circle with radius of 1.

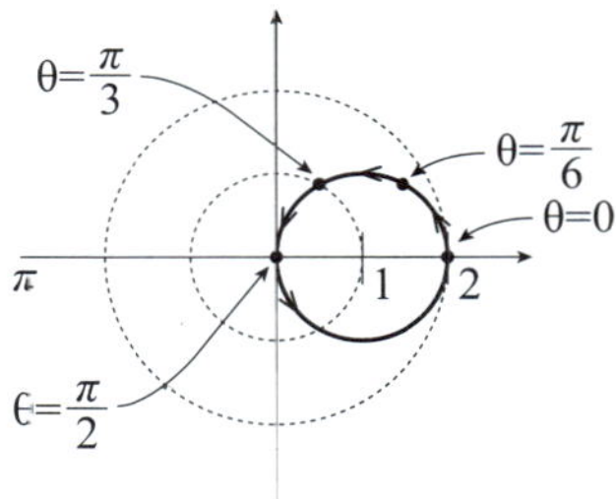

The polar equation $r=2\cos\theta$ in rectangular form is

$r=2\cos\theta$

$r^2=2r\cos\theta$ → Multiply both sides by r

$x^2+y^2=2x$ → $r^2=x^2+y^2$ and $r\cos\theta=x$

$x^2+y^2-2x=0$

$x^2-2x+1-1+y^2=0,\ (x-1)+y^2=1$

We see that the graph of $r=2\cos\theta$ is a circle with center $(1,\ 0)$ and radius of 1.

Check Point 8

Solutions_Page 125

Sketch the graph of the polar equation by plotting points.

① $r=2\sin\theta$ ② $r=2+2\cos\theta$

07 Symmetry

The graph of a polar equation is symmetric to the following if each replacement produces an equivalent polar equation.

Symmetry Test in Polar Graphs

1. About the polar axis: Replace (r, θ) by $(r, -\theta)$ or $(-r, \pi-\theta)$
2. About the line $\theta=\frac{\pi}{2}$: Replace (r, θ) by $(r, \pi-\theta)$ or $(-r, -\theta)$
3. About the pole: Replace (r, θ) by $(-r, \theta)$ or $(r, \pi+\theta)$

If an equivalent equation results, the graph is symmetric.

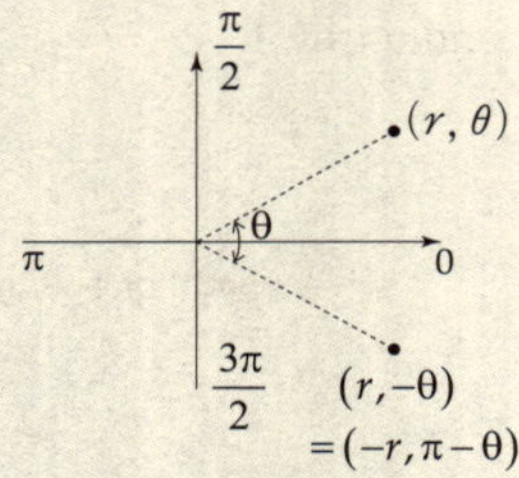

Symmetric about the polar axis.

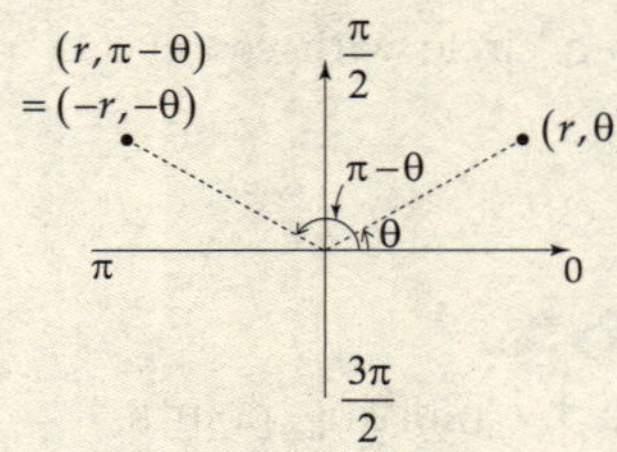

Symmetric about the line $\theta=\frac{\pi}{2}$.

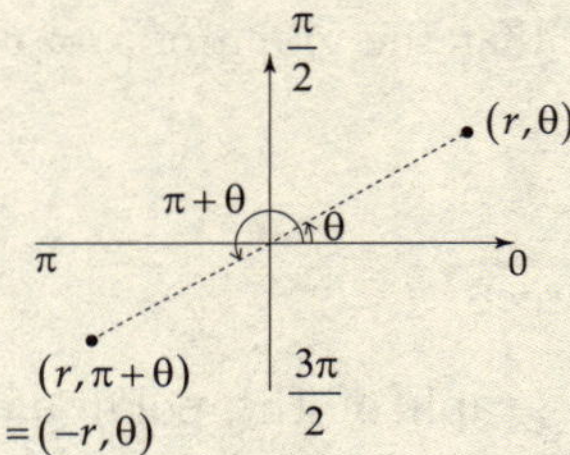

Symmetric about the pole.

Example 9

Show that $r=5\sin(5\theta)$ is symmetric about the line $\theta=\frac{\pi}{2}$.

Solution

We need to replace (r, θ) by $(r, \pi-\theta)$ or $(-r, -\theta)$.

$r=5\sin(5\theta)$ → Original equation

$-r=5\sin(5(-\theta))$ → Replace (r, θ) by $(-r, -\theta)$

$-r=-5\sin(5\theta)$ → $\sin(-\theta)=-\sin\theta$

$r=5\sin(5\theta)$ → Multiply both sides by -1

So, $r=5\sin(5\theta)$ is symmetric about the line $\theta=\frac{\pi}{2}$.

Check Point 9

Solutions_Page 126

① Show that $r=-3\cos(2\theta)$ is symmetric about the polar axis.

② Show that $r=1+4\sin\theta$ is symmetric about the line $\theta=\frac{\pi}{2}$

08 Special Polar Graphs

Below are some basic polar graphs. It includes the names and the graphs of frequently encountered polar graphs.

1. Limacons

(1) $r=a\pm b\cos\theta$ $(a>0,\ b>0)$

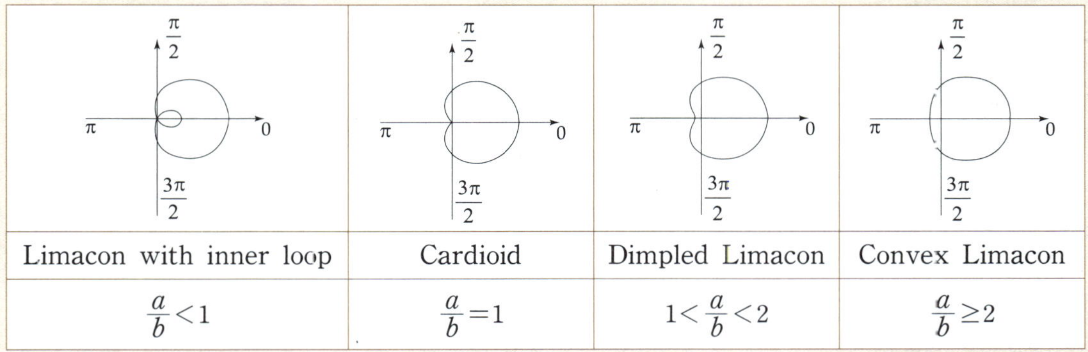

Limacon with inner loop	Cardioid	Dimpled Limacon	Convex Limacon
$\frac{a}{b}<1$	$\frac{a}{b}=1$	$1<\frac{a}{b}<2$	$\frac{a}{b}\geq 2$

(2) $r=a\pm b\sin\theta$ $(a>0,\ b>0)$

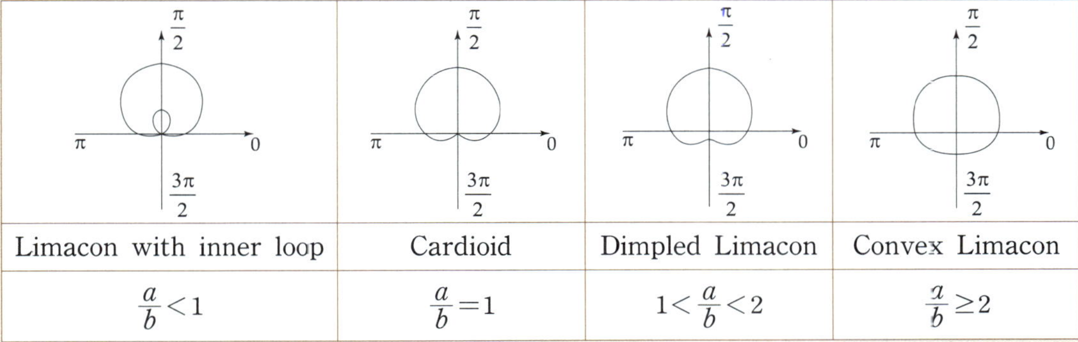

Limacon with inner loop	Cardioid	Dimpled Limacon	Convex Limacon
$\frac{a}{b}<1$	$\frac{a}{b}=1$	$1<\frac{a}{b}<2$	$\frac{a}{b}\geq 2$

✔ Orientation depends on sine or cosine function and the sign of a and b.

Example 10

Sketch the graph of $r=1+2\sin\theta$.

Solution

Since $\frac{1}{2}<1$, the graph is limacon with an inner loop.

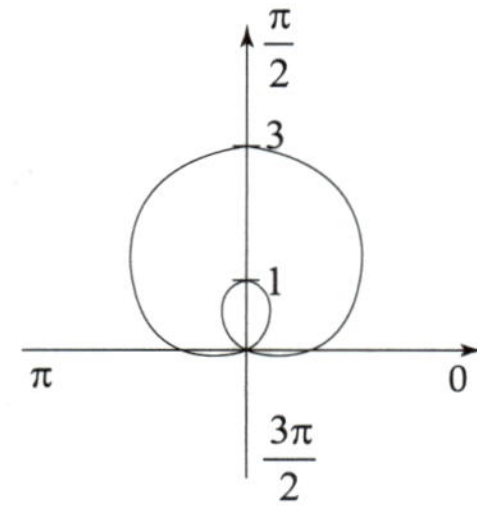

Check Point 10

Solutions_Page 126

Sketch the graph of polar equation.

① $r=2+4\cos\theta$ ② $r=2-2\sin\theta$

2. Rose Curves

The graphs of the polar equations $r=a\cos(n\theta)$ and $r=a\sin(n\theta)$ (n is integer and $n\geq 2$) are rose curves. There are n petals if n is odd, $2n$ petals if n is even.

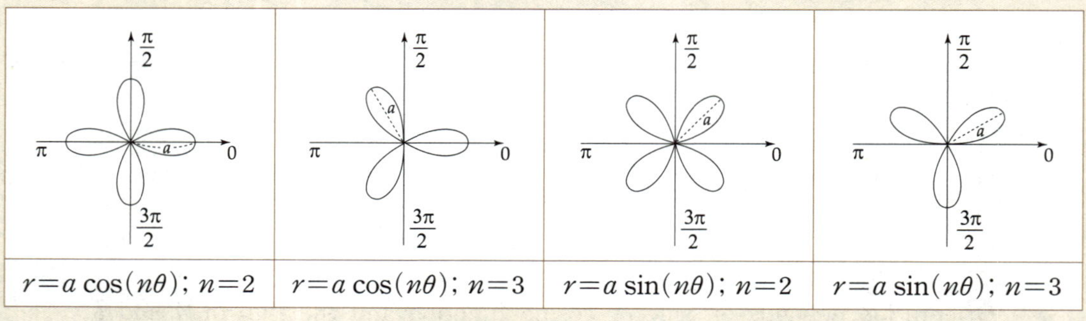

$r=a\cos(n\theta)$; $n=2$	$r=a\cos(n\theta)$; $n=3$	$r=a\sin(n\theta)$; $n=2$	$r=a\sin(n\theta)$; $n=3$

Example 11

Sketch the graph of $r=4\cos(4\theta)$.

Solution

This is a rose curve and since $n=4$, there are $2n=8$ petals.

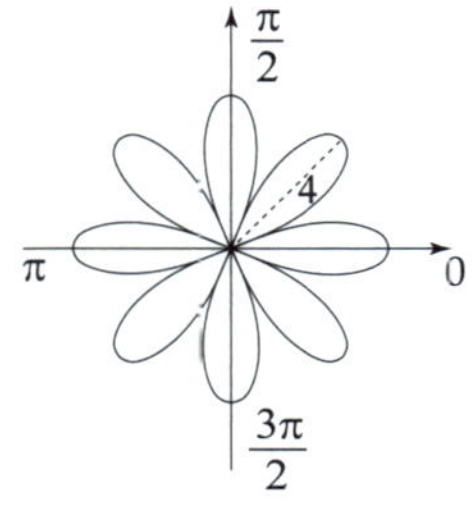

Check Point 11

Solutions_Page 127

Sketch the graph of polar equation.

① $r=3\sin(2\theta)$

② $r=5\cos(3\theta)$

3. Circles and Lemniscates

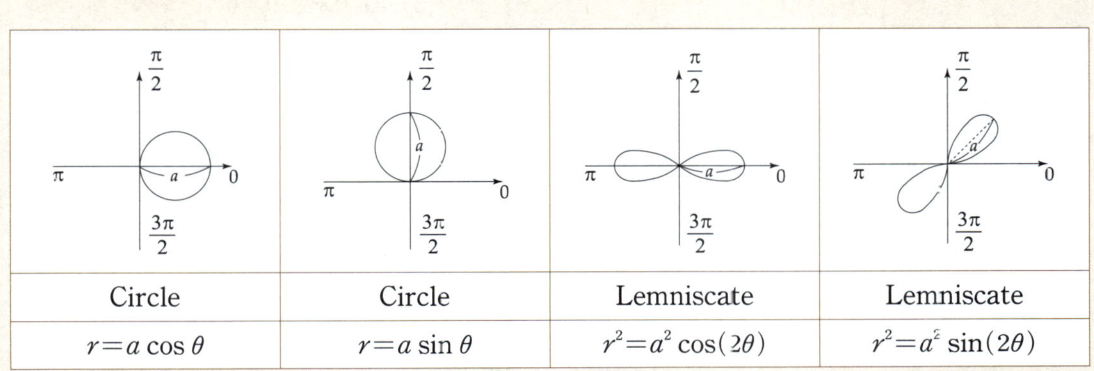

Circle	Circle	Lemniscate	Lemniscate
$r=a\cos\theta$	$r=a\sin\theta$	$r^2=a^2\cos(2\theta)$	$r^2=a^2\sin(2\theta)$

Review Exercise

01 Convert the point to rectangular coordinates.

(1) $\left(4,\ \frac{11\pi}{4}\right)$

(2) $\left(-1,\ -\frac{2\pi}{3}\right)$

02 Convert the point to polar coordinates and then find three additional polar representations of that point in the interval $-2\pi<\theta<2\pi$.

(1) $(1,\ -\sqrt{3})$

(2) $(-4\sqrt{3},\ -4)$

03 Convert the equation to polar form.

(1) $y=5$

(2) $y=-x+1$

(3) $x^2+y^2-4=0$

(4) $x^2+6x+y^2-4y=0$

(5) $2x+3y-9=0$

04 Convert the equation to rectangular form.

(1) $r=3$

(2) $r=6\sin\theta$

(3) $r=-2\sec\theta$

(4) $r=\dfrac{1}{1-\sin\theta}$

(5) $r=\dfrac{1}{1+2\cos\theta}$

Review Exercise

05 Show that $r^2=4\sin(2\theta)$ is symmetric about the pole.

06 Show that $r=2-2\sec\theta$ is symmetric about the polar axis.

07 Sketch the graph of polar equation.

(1) $r=-4$

(2) $\theta=-\dfrac{7\pi}{6}$

(3) $r=-4\sin\theta$

(4) $r=6\csc\theta$

(5) $r=-1+3\sin\theta$

(6) $r=-3-2\cos\theta$

(7) $r=3\cos(2\theta)$

(8) $r=2\sin(5\theta)$

(9) $r^2=4\cos(2\theta)$

(10) $r^2=16\sin(2\theta)$

08 Which of the following expresses the polar coordinates $\left(-4, \frac{\pi}{6}\right)$ in rectangular coordinates?

(A) $(2\sqrt{3}, 2)$
(B) $(2, 2\sqrt{3})$
(C) $(-2\sqrt{3}, -2)$
(D) $(-2, -2\sqrt{3})$

09 Point A has polar coordinates $\left(4, \frac{3\pi}{4}\right)$. All of the following are also polar coordinates of A EXCEPT

(A) $\left(4, \frac{11\pi}{4}\right)$
(B) $\left(4, -\frac{5\pi}{4}\right)$
(C) $\left(-4, -\frac{\pi}{4}\right)$
(D) $\left(-4, \frac{5\pi}{4}\right)$

10 Point A has polar coordinates $\left(-1, \frac{2\pi}{3}\right)$. All of the following are also polar coordinates of A EXCEPT

(A) $\left(-1, -\frac{4\pi}{3}\right)$
(B) $\left(-1, -\frac{\pi}{3}\right)$
(C) $\left(1, \frac{5\pi}{3}\right)$
(D) $\left(1, -\frac{\pi}{3}\right)$

11

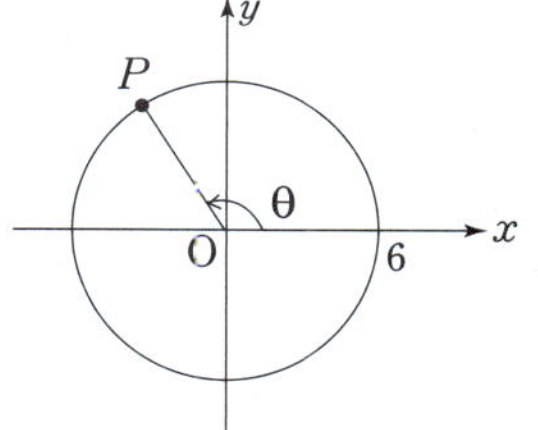

Point P is on the circle as shown in the figure above. If the coordinate of point P is $(-3\sqrt{3}, k)$, what is the degree measure of angle θ?

12 The graph of the polar function $r=f(\theta)$ is given by $r=1-2\cos\theta$ in the polar coordinate system. Which of the following defines $f(\theta)$ for $0\leq\theta<\frac{\pi}{3}$?

(A) The graph is getting close to the origin, because r is positive and decreasing.
(B) The graph is getting close to the origin, because r is negative and increasing.
(C) The graph is getting farther from the origin, because r is positive and increasing.
(D) The graph is getting farther from the origin, because r is negative and decreasing.

Review Exercise

13 The graph of the polar function $r=f(\theta)$ is given by $r=3\sin(2\theta)$ in the polar coordinate system. Which of the following is the graph of the polar function $r=f(\theta)$ in the polar coordinate system for $\frac{\pi}{2}\leq\theta<\pi$?

(A)

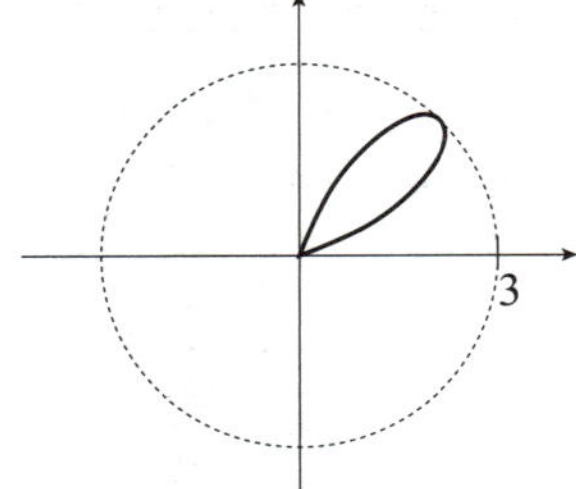

(B)

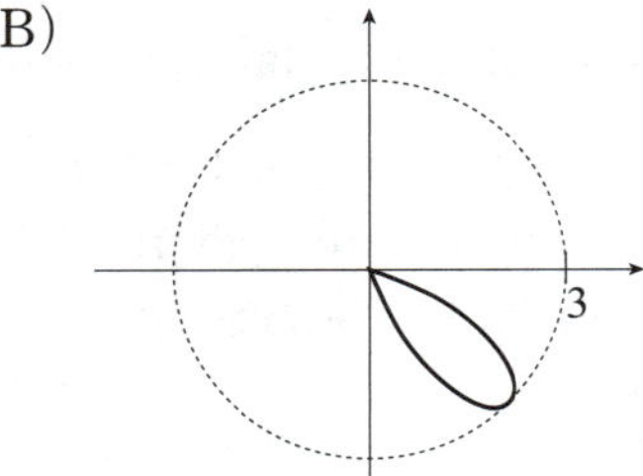

(C)

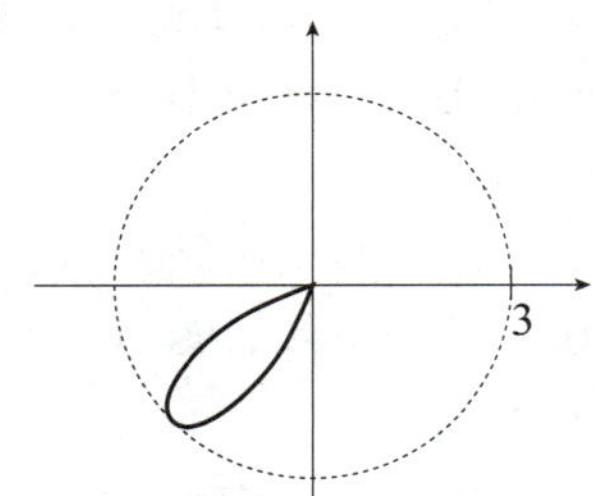

(D)

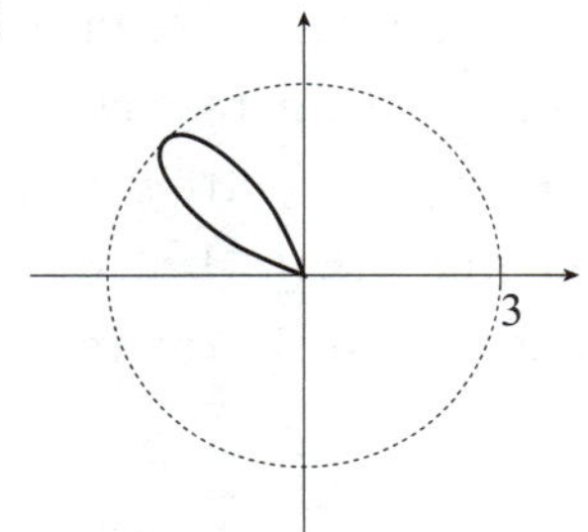

14 The graph of the polar function $r=f(\theta)$ is given by $r=4\cos\theta-4$, where $0\leq\theta\leq\pi$ in the polar coordinate system. Determine the angle θ where the graph of the polar curve is at its maximum distance from the origin.

15 The graph of the polar function $r=f(\theta)$ is in the polar coordinate system. If the distance between point on the graph of polar curve $r=f(\theta)$ and the origin is increasing for $0<\theta\leq\frac{\pi}{2}$ and decreasing for $\frac{\pi}{2}<\theta\leq\pi$, which of the following could define $f(\theta)$?

(A) $f(\theta)=\sin\theta$
(B) $f(\theta)=\cos\theta$
(C) $f(\theta)=1-\sin\theta$
(D) $f(\theta)=1-\cos\theta$

16 The graph of the polar function $r=f(\theta)$ is given by $r=\theta^2-\theta-12$ in the polar coordinate system. Which of the following statements is true for $2<\theta<4$?

(A) The distance between point on the graph of polar curve $r=f(\theta)$ and the origin is increasing because the values of r are positive and increasing.

(B) The distance between point on the graph of polar curve $r=f(\theta)$ and the origin is increasing because the values of r are negative and increasing.

(C) The distance between point on the graph of polar curve $r=f(\theta)$ and the origin is decreasing because the values of r are negative and decreasing.

(D) The distance between point on the graph of polar curve $r=f(\theta)$ and the origin is decreasing because the values of r are negative and increasing.

10 Polar Form of a Complex Numbers

01 The Complex Plane

We already learned the definition of a complex number from Algebra II.
The standard form $z=a+bi$ is sometimes referred to as rectangular form, and just as every real number is associated with a point of the real number line, every complex number is associated with a point of the complex plane. The $x-$axis in this system is referred to as the real axis, and the $y-$axis as the imaginary axis. So real number a is placed along the $x-$axis and imaginary number b along the $y-$axis, thus associating the complex number $a+bi$ with the point $(a,\ b)$. For example, complex number $3+2i$ and $-4-i$ can be plotted shown in Figure below.

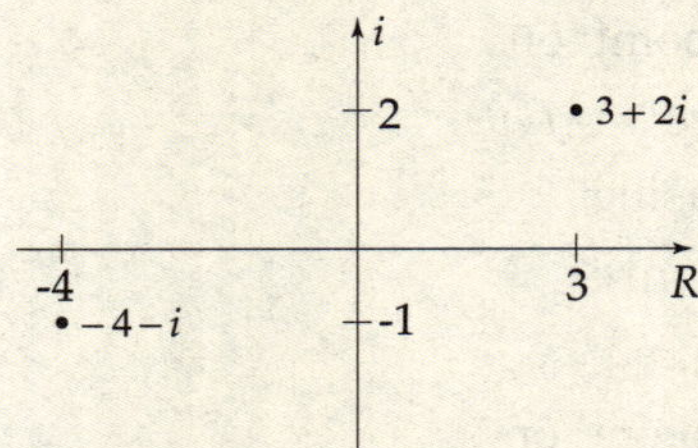

The absolute value, sometimes called as modulus, of the complex number $a+bi$ is defined as the distance between the origin and the point $(a,\ b)$. For example, the absolute value $|3+2i|=\sqrt{3^2+2^2}=\sqrt{13}$ shown in Figure below.

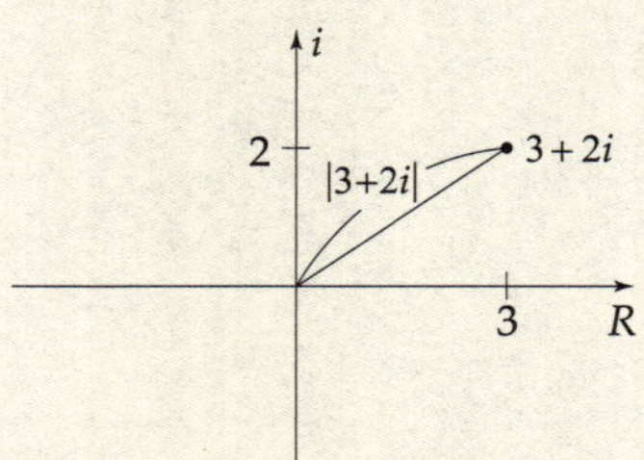

02 Polar Form of a Complex Numbers

In this section, we will study the basic operations of complex numbers in the polar form so that we can work effectively with powers and roots of complex numbers. Let a complex number $z=a+bi$ be on a complex plane with angle θ. Then

$$z=r(\cos\theta+i\sin\theta)$$

The number r is called the modulus of z, and θ is called the argument of z. $z=r(\cos\theta+i\sin\theta)$ is sometimes abbreviated as $z=r\operatorname{cis}\theta$.

Proof

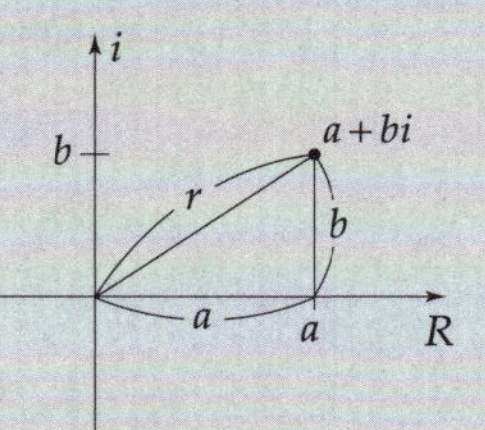

By the definition of trigonometry,

$\cos\theta=\dfrac{a}{r} \rightarrow a=r\cos\theta$ and

$\sin\theta=\dfrac{b}{r} \rightarrow b=r\sin\theta$, where $r=\sqrt{a^2+b^2}$

Consequently, we have

$z=a+bi=r\cos\theta+(r\sin\theta)i=r(\cos\theta+i\sin\theta)$

Example 1

① Write the complex number $z=1+i$ in polar form.

② Write the complex number $z=2\left(\cos\dfrac{2\pi}{3}+i\sin\dfrac{2\pi}{3}\right)$ in standard form.

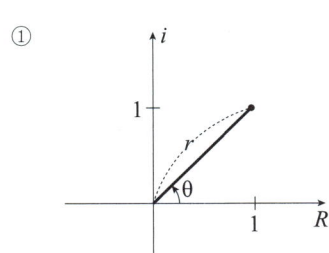

Solution

①

The modulus for z, $r=\sqrt{1^2+1^2}=\sqrt{2}$.

The argument θ lies in Quadrant I, $\tan\theta=1$, $\theta=\tan^{-1}1=\frac{\pi}{4}$.

So, $z=a+bi=r(\cos\theta+i\sin\theta) \rightarrow 1+i=\sqrt{2}\left(\cos\frac{\pi}{4}+i\sin\frac{\pi}{4}\right)$

$1+i=\sqrt{2}\left(\cos\frac{\pi}{4}+i\sin\frac{\pi}{4}\right)$

② We know that $\cos\frac{2\pi}{3}=-\frac{1}{2}$ and $\sin\frac{2\pi}{3}=\frac{\sqrt{3}}{2}$.

So, $z=2\left(\cos\frac{2\pi}{3}+i\sin\frac{2\pi}{3}\right)=2\left(-\frac{1}{2}+\frac{\sqrt{3}}{2}i\right)=-1+\sqrt{3}\,i$.

$2\left(\cos\frac{2\pi}{3}+i\sin\frac{2\pi}{3}\right)=-1+\sqrt{3}\,i$

Check Point 1-1

Solutions_Page 132

Find the polar form of the complex number.

① $2i$ ② $2\sqrt{3}-2i$

Check Point 1-2

Solutions_Page 132

Find the standard from of the complex number.

① $4(\cos 225°+i\sin 225°)$ ② $3\left(\cos\frac{3\pi}{2}+i\sin\frac{3\pi}{2}\right)$

03 Multiplication and Division of Complex Numbers

Multiplying and dividing complex numbers in the polar form are more convenient than in standard form.

Let $z_1=r_1(\cos\theta_1+i\sin\theta_1)$ and $z_2=r_2(\cos\theta_2+i\sin\theta_2)$. Then

1. The Product of Complex Numbers
   $z_1z_2=r_1r_2(\cos(\theta_1+\theta_2)+i\sin(\theta_1+\theta_2))$
2. The Quotient of Complex Numbers
   $\frac{z_1}{z_2}=\frac{r_1}{r_2}(\cos(\theta_1-\theta_2)+i\sin(\theta_1-\theta_2))$

✔ To multiply two complex numbers, we multiply moduli and add arguments, whereas to divide, we divide moduli and subtract arguments.

Proof

Suppose we are given two complex numbers,

$$z_1=r_1(\cos\theta_1+i\sin\theta_1) \text{ and } z_2=r_2(\cos\theta_2+i\sin\theta_2).$$

The product of z_1 and z_2 is given by

$$\begin{aligned} z_1z_2&=r_1(\cos\theta_1+i\sin\theta_1)\cdot r_2(\cos\theta_2+i\sin\theta_2)\\ &=r_1r_2(\cos\theta_1\cdot\cos\theta_2+i\sin\theta_1\cos\theta_2+i\cos\theta_1\sin\theta_2+i^2\sin\theta_1\sin\theta_2)\\ &=r_1r_2(\cos\theta_1\cdot\cos\theta_2-\sin\theta_1\sin\theta_2)+i(\sin\theta_1\cos\theta_2+\cos\theta_1\sin\theta_2)\end{aligned}$$

Applying the sum and difference identity,

$$z_1z_2=r_1r_2\,(\cos(\theta_1+\theta_2)+i\sin(\theta_1+\theta_2)).$$

Now the quotient of z_1 and z_2 is given by

$$\begin{aligned}\frac{z_1}{z_2}&=\frac{r_1(\cos\theta_1+i\sin\theta_1)}{r_2(\cos\theta_2+i\sin\theta_2)}\\ &=\frac{r_1}{r_2}\frac{(\cos\theta_1+i\sin\theta_1)}{(\cos\theta_2+i\sin\theta_2)}\cdot\frac{(\cos\theta_2-i\sin\theta_2)}{(\cos\theta_2-i\sin\theta_2)}\\ &=\frac{r_1}{r_2}\frac{(\cos\theta_1\cos\theta_2-i\cos\theta_1\sin\theta_2+i\sin\theta_1\cos\theta_2-i^2\sin\theta_1\sin\theta_2)}{\cos^2\theta_2-i^2\sin^2\theta_2}\\ &=\frac{r_1}{r_2}\frac{(\cos\theta_1\cos\theta_2+\sin\theta_1\sin\theta_2+i(\sin\theta_1\cos\theta_2-\cos\theta_1\sin\theta_2)}{\cos^2\theta_2+\sin^2\theta_2}\end{aligned}$$

Applying the sum and difference identity for numerator, and the Pythagorean identity for denominator,

$$=\frac{r_1}{r_2}(\cos(\theta_1-\theta_2)+i(\sin\theta_1-\theta_2)).$$

Example 2

Find the product z_1z_2 and the quotient $\frac{z_1}{z_2}$ of the following two complex numbers, $z_1=4\left(\cos\frac{\pi}{6}+i\sin\frac{\pi}{6}\right)$ and $z_2=5\left(\cos\frac{5\pi}{3}+i\sin\frac{5\pi}{3}\right)$.

Solution

$$z_1z_2=4\left(\cos\frac{\pi}{6}+i\sin\frac{\pi}{6}\right)\cdot5\left(\cos\frac{5\pi}{3}+i\sin\frac{5\pi}{3}\right)$$

$$=4\cdot5\left(\cos\left(\frac{\pi}{6}+\frac{5\pi}{3}\right)+i\sin\left(\frac{\pi}{6}+\frac{5\pi}{3}\right)\right)$$ → Multiply moduli and add arguments

$$=20\left(\cos\frac{11\pi}{6}+i\sin\frac{11\pi}{6}\right)$$

$$=20\left(\frac{\sqrt{3}}{2}-\frac{1}{2}i\right)=10\sqrt{3}-10i$$

$$\frac{z_1}{z_2}=\frac{4\left(\cos\frac{\pi}{6}+i\sin\frac{\pi}{6}\right)}{5\left(\cos\frac{5\pi}{3}+i\sin\frac{5\pi}{3}\right)}$$

$$=\frac{4}{5}\left(\cos\left(\frac{\pi}{6}-\frac{5\pi}{3}\right)+i\sin\left(\frac{\pi}{6}-\frac{5\pi}{3}\right)\right)$$ → Divide moduli and subtract arguments

$$=\frac{4}{5}\left(\cos\left(-\frac{3\pi}{2}\right)+i\sin\left(-\frac{3\pi}{2}\right)\right)$$

$$=\frac{4}{5}(0+i)=\frac{4}{5}i$$

$z_1z_2=10\sqrt{3}-10i$, $\frac{z_1}{z_2}=\frac{4}{5}i$

Check Point 2

Solutions_Page 132

Find z_1z_2 and $\frac{z_1}{z_2}$ in standard form.

① $z_1=3(\cos 60°+i\sin 60°)$

$z_2=2(\cos 30°+i\sin 30°)$

② $z_1=6\left(\cos\frac{3\pi}{4}+i\sin\frac{3\pi}{4}\right)$

$z_2=3(\cos\pi+i\sin\pi)$

04 DeMoivre's Theorem (Powers of Complex Numbers)

We can use the product formula to raise a complex number to a power.
Let $z=r(\cos\theta+i\sin\theta)$. Then

$$\begin{aligned} z^2 &= r(\cos\theta+i\sin\theta)\cdot r(\cos\theta+i\sin\theta) \\ &= r^2(\cos(\theta+\theta)+i\sin(\theta+\theta)) \quad \rightarrow \text{Apply multiplication rule} \\ &= r^2(\cos 2\theta+i\sin 2\theta). \end{aligned}$$

Now,
$$\begin{aligned} z^3 &= z^2\cdot z \\ &= r^2(\cos 2\theta+i\sin 2\theta)\cdot r(\cos\theta+i\sin\theta) \\ &= r^3(\cos(2\theta+\theta)+i\sin(2\theta+\theta)) \quad \rightarrow \text{Apply multiplication rule} \\ &= r^2(\cos 3\theta+i\sin 3\theta). \end{aligned}$$

Similarly,
$$\begin{aligned} z^4 &= r^4(\cos 4\theta+i\sin 4\theta) \\ z^5 &= r^5(\cos 5\theta+i\sin 5\theta) \\ &\vdots \\ z^n &= r^n(\cos n\theta+i\sin n\theta). \end{aligned}$$

Above pattern leads to the DeMoivre's Theorem.

DeMoivre's Theorem

> Let $z=r(\cos\theta+i\sin\theta)$ and n be positive integers. Then
> $$z^n=r^n(\cos(n\theta)+i\sin(n\theta)).$$

Example 3

Find $(\sqrt{3}-i)^8$ using the DeMoivre's Theorem

Solution

First convert the complex number to polar form.

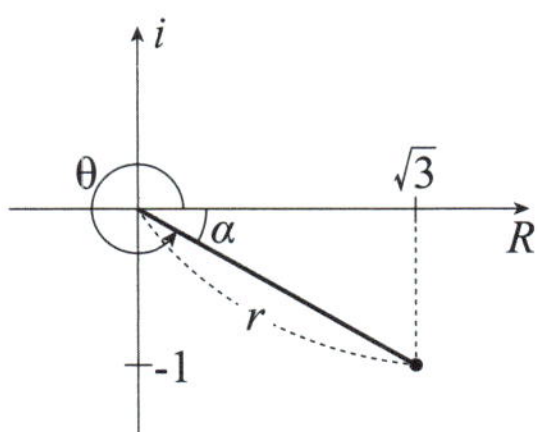

$$r=\sqrt{(\sqrt{3})^2+1^2}=2$$

$$\tan\alpha=\frac{1}{\sqrt{3}} \rightarrow \alpha=\tan^{-1}\frac{1}{\sqrt{3}}=\frac{\pi}{6}$$

Since θ lies in Quadrant IV, $\theta=2\pi-\frac{\pi}{6}=\frac{11\pi}{6}$.

Now by the DeMoivre's Theorem,

$$(\sqrt{3}-i)^8=\left(2\left(\cos\frac{11\pi}{6}+i\sin\frac{11\pi}{6}\right)\right)^8$$
$$=2^8\left(\cos\left(8\cdot\frac{11\pi}{6}\right)+i\sin\left(8\cdot\frac{11\pi}{6}\right)\right)$$
$$=256\left(\cos\frac{44\pi}{3}+i\sin\frac{44\pi}{3}\right)$$
$$=256\left(-\frac{1}{2}+\frac{\sqrt{3}}{2}i\right)=-128+128\sqrt{3}\,i.$$

$(\sqrt{3}-\mathrm{i})^8=-128+128\sqrt{3}\,i$

Check Point 3

Solutions_Page 132

Find the indicated power of the complex number in standard form.

① $\left(2\left(\cos\frac{\pi}{6}+i\ \sin\frac{\pi}{6}\right)\right)^4$ ② $(2-2i)^5$

05 Roots of a Complex Numbers

In the very first chapter of this book, we studied the Fundamental Theorem of Algebra, which states that a polynomial equation of degree n has n solutions, including complex solutions. For example, $x^4=1$ is an equation of degree 4 so that it has four solutions.

$$x^4-1=0$$
$$(x^2-1)(x^2+1)=0$$
$$(x-1)(x+1)(x^2+1)=0$$

The solutions are $x=\pm1$, $x=\pm i$ and each solution is fourth root of 1. Just like the equation, a complex number has exactly n different n^{th} roots. In general, if $c=a+bi$ is an nth root of a complex number z, then we can define $z=c^n=(a+bi)^n$. Now let us derive a formula for an nth root of a complex number using the DeMoivre's theorem. Suppose that $c=s(\cos\alpha+i\sin\alpha)$ is n^{th} root of $z=r(\cos\theta+i\sin\theta)$. Then

$$c^n=z$$

$$(s(\cos\alpha+i\ \sin\alpha))^n=r(\cos\theta+i\sin\theta)$$

$$s^n(\cos n\alpha + i\sin n\alpha) = r(\cos\theta + i\sin\theta).$$

Now, it follows that $s^n = r$, $\cos(n\alpha) = \cos\theta$, and $\sin(n\alpha) = \sin\theta$. First, $s^n = r \rightarrow s = \sqrt[n]{r}$. Also, since both sine and cosine have a period of 2π,

$$n\alpha = \theta + 2\pi k \ (k \in Z)$$

$$\alpha = \frac{\theta + 2\pi k}{n} \ (k \in Z)$$

where $k = 0, 1, 2, \cdots, n-1$.

Here is the summary for finding the nth roots of a complex number.

Finding the nth roots of a complex number

> If n is any positive integer, then the complex number $z = r(\cos\theta + i\sin\theta)$ has n distinct n^{th} roots given by $\sqrt[n]{r}\left(\cos\left(\frac{\theta + 2\pi k}{n}\right) + i\sin\left(\frac{\theta + 2\pi k}{n}\right)\right)$, where $k = 0, 1, 2, \cdots, n-1$.

Example 4

Find the fourth roots of $16(\cos\pi + i\sin\pi)$.

Solution

The fourth roots are given by $\sqrt[4]{16}\left(\cos\left(\frac{\pi + 2\pi k}{4}\right) + i\sin\left(\frac{\pi + 2\pi k}{4}\right)\right)$, where $k = 0, 1, 2$, and 3.

$k=0$; $\sqrt[4]{16}\left(\cos\left(\frac{\pi + 2\pi(0)}{4}\right) + i\sin\left(\frac{\pi + 2\pi(0)}{4}\right)\right) = 2\left(\cos\frac{\pi}{4} + i\sin\frac{\pi}{4}\right) = \sqrt{2} + \sqrt{2}i$

$k=1$; $\sqrt[4]{16}\left(\cos\left(\frac{\pi + 2\pi(1)}{4}\right) + i\sin\left(\frac{\pi + 2\pi(1)}{4}\right)\right) = 2\left(\cos\frac{3\pi}{4} + i\sin\frac{3\pi}{4}\right) = -\sqrt{2} + \sqrt{2}i$

$k=2$; $\sqrt[4]{16}\left(\cos\left(\frac{\pi + 2\pi(2)}{4}\right) + i\sin\left(\frac{\pi + 2\pi(2)}{4}\right)\right) = 2\left(\cos\frac{5\pi}{4} + i\sin\frac{5\pi}{4}\right) = -\sqrt{2} - \sqrt{2}i$

$k=3$; $\sqrt[4]{16}\left(\cos\left(\frac{\pi + 2\pi(3)}{4}\right) + i\sin\left(\frac{\pi + 2\pi(3)}{4}\right)\right) = 2\left(\cos\frac{7\pi}{4} + i\sin\frac{7\pi}{4}\right) = \sqrt{2} - \sqrt{2}i$

$2+\sqrt{2}i, -2+\sqrt{2}i, -2-\sqrt{2}i, 2-\sqrt{2}i$

✔ Notice that $z=16(\cos\pi+i\sin\pi)=16(-1+i(0))=-16$ and
$(2+\sqrt{2}i)^4=(-2+\sqrt{2}i)^4=(-2-\sqrt{2}i)^4=(2-\sqrt{2}i)^4=-16$

Check Point 4

Solutions_Page 133

Find the indicated roots of the complex number in standard form.

① Cube roots of $8\left(\cos\frac{\pi}{2}+i\sin\frac{\pi}{2}\right)$

② Fifth roots of $-32i$

Review Exercise

01 Find the polar form of the complex number.

(1) $-3i$

(2) $-3+3i$

02 Find the standard from of the complex number.

(1) $2(\cos 60° + i\sin 60°)$

(2) $\sqrt{3}\left(\cos\frac{7\pi}{6} + i\sin\frac{7\pi}{6}\right)$

03 Find z_1z_2 and $\frac{z_1}{z_2}$ in standard form.

(1) $z_1 = 2(\cos 120° + i\sin 120°)$
$z_2 = 4(\cos 90° + i\sin 90°)$

(2) $z_1 = 6\left(\cos\frac{4\pi}{3} + i\sin\frac{4\pi}{3}\right)$
$z_2 = 2\left(\cos\frac{13\pi}{6} + i\sin\frac{13\pi}{6}\right)$

04 Find the indicated power of the complex number in standard form.

(1) $\left(\cos\frac{5\pi}{3} + i\sin\frac{5\pi}{3}\right)^3$

(2) $(-1+i)^6$

05 Find the indicated roots of the complex number in standard form.

(1) Square roots of $\left(\cos\frac{5\pi}{4} + i\sin\frac{5\pi}{4}\right)$

(2) Fourth roots of $\frac{\sqrt{3}i - 1}{2}$

Unit Ⅲ Test

01 Rewrite the angle in radian measure.

(1) $-840°$ (2) $28°45'$

02 Rewrite the angle in degree measure.

(1) -2.4π (2) 0.75

03 Find two coterminal angles(one positive and one negative) for the given angle.

(1) $180°$ (2) $\frac{7\pi}{3}$

04 Find the arc length of a circle if the central angle is $\frac{3\pi}{4}$ and the area of the sector is 12π.

05 Find the area of the sector of a circle if the arc length is 4π and central angle is $120°$.

06 A tire with a 9 inch radius is rotating at 25 miles per hour.

(1) What is the linear speed of a tire in miles per minute?

(2) Find the number of revolutions that a tire rotates per minute.
(1 mile=5280 feet)

07 Find the six trigonometric functions of the angle θ.

(1)

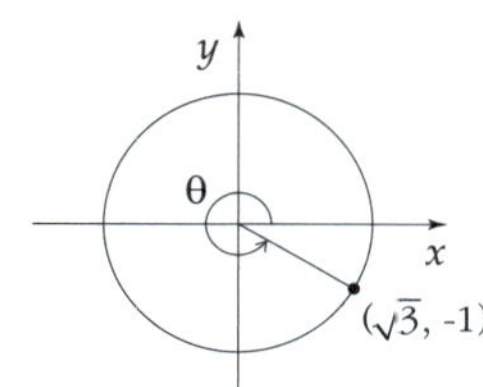

(2)

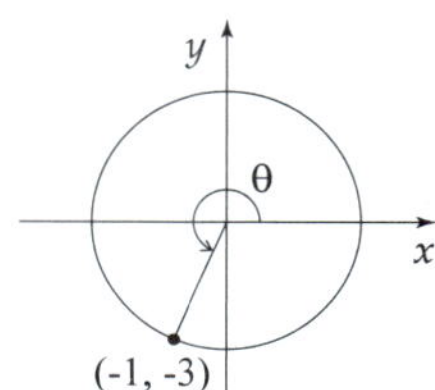

08 Find the six trigonometric functions at each angle.

(1) $\theta=-225°$

(2) $\theta=\frac{11\pi}{6}$

09 Using the given information, find the rest of trigonometric functions of the angle θ.

(1) $\tan\theta=-\frac{2}{5}$, $\cos\theta>0$

(2) $\csc\theta=-\frac{\sqrt{17}}{4}$, $\sec<0$

Unit Ⅲ Test

10 What is the period of the graph of $y=\frac{2}{3}\tan\left(\frac{2x-1}{3}\right)+1$?

11 What is the range of the graph of $y=2\cos\left(\frac{\pi}{3}-2x\right)-2$?

12

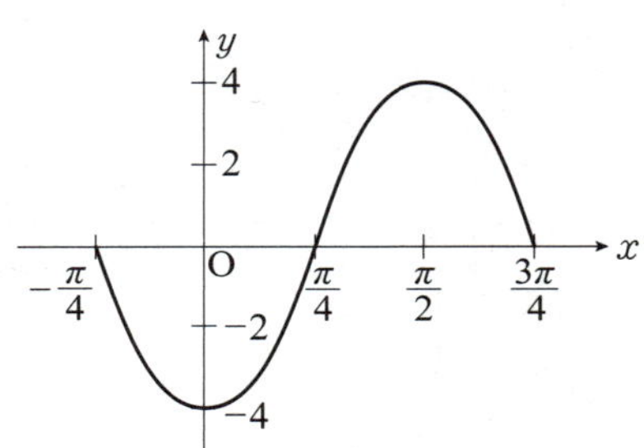

The graph shown above is one period of a function of the form $y=a\sin b(x-c)$, where $a<0$. Find the equation of the function.

13 The function f is given by $f(x)=\sin x$, and the function g is given by $g(x)=\tan x$. Which of the following statements is true about the behavior of the graph of f and g for $\frac{\pi}{2}<x<\pi$?

(A) Both f and g are concave down.
(B) Both f and g are concave up.
(C) f is concave down, but g is concave up.
(D) f is concave up, but g is concave down.

14 The function f is given by $f(x)=\cos(2x)-1$. Which of the following statements is true about the behavior of the graph of f for $\frac{\pi}{4}<x<\frac{3\pi}{4}$?

(A) First, f increase and then decrease, and the graph of f is concave up.
(B) First, f decrease and then increase, and the graph of f is concave up.
(C) First, f increase and then decrease, and the graph of f is concave down.
(D) First, f decrease and then decrease, and the graph of f is concave down.

15 The function f is given by $f(x)=\cos x$ and the function g is given by $g(x)=\sin(x+\pi)$. If $f(x)=g(h(x))$, which of the following could define the function $h(x)$?

(A) $h(x)=x-\frac{\pi}{2}$
(B) $h(x)=x+\pi$
(C) $h(x)=-x-\frac{\pi}{2}$
(D) $h(x)=-x+\frac{\pi}{2}$

Unit III Test

16 Find the value of each expression.

(1) $\cos^{-1}\left(\sin\left(-\frac{5\pi}{4}\right)\right)$ (2) $\cos\left(\arctan\frac{5}{2}\right)$

17 Find the algebraic expression in terms of x equivalent to each expression.

(1) $\tan(\sin^{-1}(3x))$ (2) $\sec(\arcsin(x-1))$

18

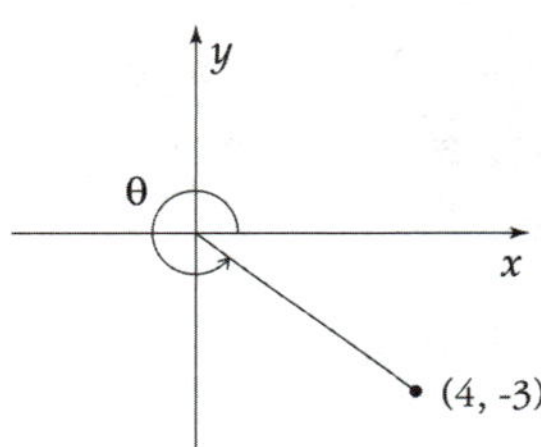

In Figure above, which of the following represents the radian measure of angle θ?

(A) $\tan^{-1}\left(\frac{3}{4}\right)$

(B) $\tan^{-1}\left(-\frac{3}{4}\right)$

(C) $\pi+\tan^{-1}\left(\frac{3}{4}\right)$

(D) $\pi-\tan^{-1}\left(\frac{3}{4}\right)$

(E) $2\pi-\tan^{-1}\left(\frac{3}{4}\right)$

19 If $\cos\theta = \dfrac{3m}{4}$ and $0 \le \theta \le \dfrac{\pi}{2}$, find each of the following in terms of m.

(1) $\csc\theta$

(2) $\sin(\pi-\theta)$

(3) $\sec(\theta+\pi)$

(4) $\tan(2\pi-\theta)$

20

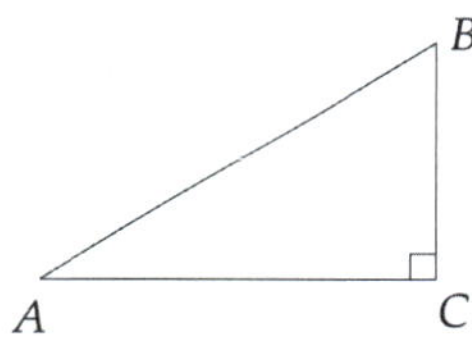

In Figure above, if $\sin A = \dfrac{2}{3}$ and $\overline{BC} = k$, then what is the length of $\overline{AC}$ in terms of k?

21

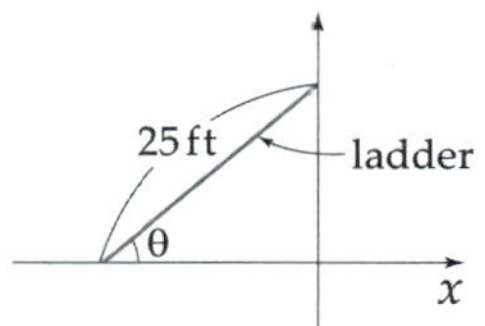

A 25 feet long ladder is placed against a wall as shown in Figure above. If the angle θ between the ladder and the ground changes from 45° to 30°, then what is the distance which the ladder traveled on the ground?

Unit III Test

Solutions_Page 87

22 A passenger in an airplane flying at an altitude of 2,400 feet sees two mountains directly to the east of the plane. If the angles of depression to the top of the mountains are $60°$ and $30°$, respectively, what is the distance between two mountains?

23 A ball on a spring is pulled 12 centimeters below its rest position and then released. The period for the motion is 6 seconds. If D, in centimeters, is the displacement of the ball and t, in seconds, is the time after the ball is released, use $y = a\cos(wt)$ to find an equation that represents the simple harmonic motion of the ball.

24 Using trigonometric identities and the given information, $\csc(-\theta) = \frac{3}{2}$, $\cot\theta > 0$, find the rest of the six trigonometric functions.

25 Simplify the expression.

(1) $(\sin\theta + \cos\theta)(\sin\theta - \cos\theta) + 1$

(2) $\dfrac{\sin\theta - \cos\theta}{\cos\theta + \sin\theta} + \dfrac{1 - \tan\theta}{1 + \tan\theta}$

26 Factor the expression.

(1) $1+\cos^2\theta-\sin\theta$

(2) $\tan^2\theta+\sec^2\theta-\sec\theta$

27 Verify the identity.

(1) $\dfrac{1+\cos\theta}{1-\cos\theta}-\dfrac{1-\cos\theta}{1+\cos\theta}=4\cot\theta\csc\theta$

(2) $\cos^2\theta+1=\dfrac{1+\sec^2\theta}{1+\tan^2\theta}$

28 Let $x=4\sin\theta$, where $0<\theta<\frac{\pi}{2}$. Prove that $\dfrac{x^2}{\sqrt{16-x^2}}=4\sin\theta\tan\theta$

29 Solve the equation in the interval $[0,\ 2\pi)$.

(1) $\tan\left(\dfrac{x}{3}\right)-1=0$

(2) $\cos^2 x-6=\cos x$

(3) $\csc^2 x-4=0$

(4) $\sin x+2\cos^2 x=1$

Unit Ⅲ Test

30 Find the exact value of the expression.

(1) $\cos(-15°)$

(2) $\sin\left(\frac{5\pi}{12}\right)$

(3) $\cos 70°\cos 80° - \sin 70°\sin 80°$

(4) $\dfrac{\tan\left(\frac{\pi}{8}\right) - \tan\left(\frac{3\pi}{8}\right)}{1+\tan\left(\frac{\pi}{8}\right)\tan\left(\frac{3\pi}{8}\right)}$

(5) $\sin\left(\arctan 2 - \arcsin\frac{5}{13}\right)$

(6) $\cos\left(2\sin^{-1}\left(\frac{4}{5}\right)\right)$

31 Find the exact value of the expression if $\sin\alpha = -\frac{5}{13}$ and $\cos\beta = \frac{\sqrt{3}}{2}$.
(both α and β lies in Quadrant IV)

(1) $\sin(\alpha-\beta)$

(2) $\cos(\alpha+\beta)$

(3) $\tan(\alpha-\beta)$

32 Prove the indentity $\sin\left(\frac{\pi}{2}+x\right)+\cos\left(\frac{\pi}{2}+x\right) = \cos x - \sin x$.

33 Solve the equation in the interval $[0, 2\pi)$.

(1) $\sin(2x) - 2\sin x = 0$

(2) $\cos(2x) + 3\sin x = -1$

34 Using the given information, $\csc\theta = -\frac{5}{2}$ and $\pi < \theta < \frac{3\pi}{2}$, find the exact value of $\sin(2\theta)$, $\cos(2\theta)$, and $\tan(2\theta)$.

35 Using the given information, $\tan\theta = 4$ and $\pi < \theta < \frac{3\pi}{2}$, find exact value of $\sin\left(\frac{\theta}{2}\right)$, $\cos\left(\frac{\theta}{2}\right)$, and $\tan\left(\frac{\theta}{2}\right)$.

Unit III Test

Solutions_Page 127

36 Using the sum and difference identities, write the expression $\cos(3x)$ in terms of $\sin x$ and $\cos x$.

37 Solve the equation $\cos(3x)+\cos x=0$ in the interval $[0, 2\pi)$.

38 Write $\sin(2x)\cos(3x)$ as a sum or difference of trigonometric functions.

39 Write $\sin(5x)+\sin(2x)$ as a product of trigonometric functions.

40 Convert the point to polar coordinates and then find two additional polar representations, one with $r>0$, and the other with $r<0$.

(1) $(-2\sqrt{2},\ 2\sqrt{2})$

(2) $(3\sqrt{3},\ -3)$

41 Convert the equation to polar form.

(1) $x^2-2y^2-16=0$

(2) $2x^2-3x+2y^2+2y=0$

42 Convert the equation to rectangular form.

(1) $r=4\cot\theta$

(2) $r=\dfrac{1}{4-6\sin\theta}$

Unit Ⅲ Test

43 Show that $r=-4\sin(3\theta)$ is symmetric about the line $\theta=\frac{\pi}{2}$.

44 Show that $r=1-\cos\theta$ is symmetric about the polar axis.

45 Sketch the graph of polar equation.

(1) $r=-3\cos(3\theta)$

(2) $r=4+4\sin\theta$

46 Find the polar form of the complex number.

(1) $\sqrt{3}-i$

(2) $-2-2\sqrt{3}i$

47 Let $z_1=2\left(\cos\frac{7\pi}{4}+i\sin\frac{7\pi}{4}\right)$ and $z_2=\sqrt{2}\left(\cos\frac{\pi}{2}+i\sin\frac{\pi}{2}\right)$.
Find z_1z_2 and $\frac{z_1}{z_2}$ in standard form.

48 Use DeMoivre's theorem to find $(-3\sqrt{3}-3i)^4$ in standard form.

49 Find the fourth roots of the complex number $16\left(\cos\frac{2\pi}{3}+i\sin\frac{2\pi}{3}\right)$ in standard form.

memo

Unit IV
Functions Involving Parameters, Vectors, and Matrices

1 Parametric Equations

01 Parametric Equations

Parametric equations, or parametric functions, define a curve by expressing the coordinates of points on the curve as functions of a parameter.

1. Parameter(t): The independent variable that defines both x and y coordinates.
2. Parametric Equation: Consists of individual equations for each coordinate, usually expressed as $x=f(t)$ and $y=g(t)$ where t ranges over a defined interval.
3. Parametric Function: Combines the coordinate functions into a single vector−valued function, usually expressed as $f(t)=(x(t), y(t))$ where t ranges over a defined interval.

Parametric equations(functions) offer a powerful way to represent and analyze curves in mathematics, providing a flexible and intuitive approach to understanding the geometry and behavior of curves.

Example 1−1

Given parametric equation, $x=2t-4$ and $y=t^2+1$ where $0\le t\le 4$,

① Sketch the curve of the parametric equation. Indicate its orientation.

② Eliminate the parameter t of the parametric equation.

Solution

① First, we generate the points on the given interval and sketch a graph.

t	x	y
0	-4	1
1	-2	2
2	0	5
3	2	10
4	4	17

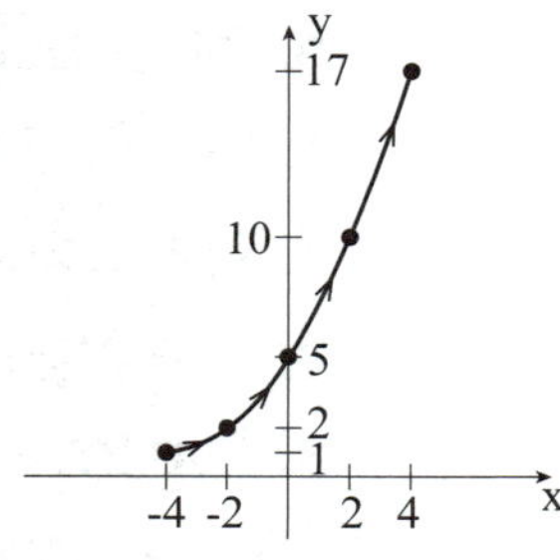

The graph starts at $(-4, 1)$ and goes to $(4, 17)$

② Rewrite the equation $x=2t-4$ for t.

$$x=2t-4,\ x+4=2t,\ \frac{x}{2}+2=t$$

Now, substitute $t=\frac{x}{2}+2$ into the equation y.

$$y=t^2+1,\ y=\left(\frac{x}{2}+2\right)^2+1=\frac{x^2}{4}+2x+5$$

So, by eliminating the third variable t, we can express the parametric equation into a single equation, $y=\frac{x^2}{4}+2x+5$

$y=\frac{x^2}{4}+2x+5$

Example 1-2

$$x=\frac{1}{t} \text{ and } y=\frac{t-1}{t} \text{ where } t\neq 0$$

Sketch the curve represented by the equation above by eliminating the parameter t. Indicate its orientation.

Solution

Solve $x=\frac{1}{t}$ for t,

$$x=\frac{1}{t},\ t=\frac{1}{x}$$

Now, substitute $t=\frac{1}{x}$ into the equation for y.

$$y=\frac{t-1}{t},\ y=\frac{\frac{1}{x}-1}{\frac{1}{x}}=\frac{\frac{1-x}{x}}{\frac{1}{x}}=1-x$$

$y=1-x$

From this equation, we can recognize that the curve is a line. Also, x and y are defined for all t except for $t=0$.

t	x	y
$\frac{1}{4}$	4	-3
$\frac{1}{3}$	3	-2
$\frac{1}{2}$	2	-1
1	1	0

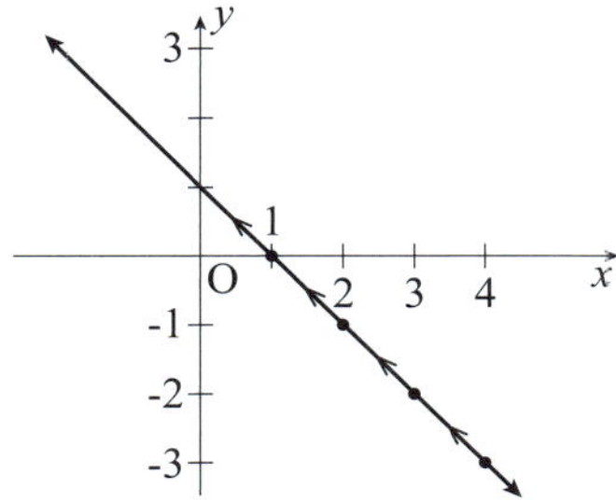

Check Point 1

Solutions_Page 148

Sketch the curve represented by each equation by eliminating the parameter t. Indicate its orientation.

① $x=t-2,\ y=t^3$

② $x=2t+1,\ y=\frac{t}{2}-3$

③ $x=t-1,\ y=\frac{t}{t-1}$ where $t\neq 1$

④ $x=\sqrt{t}+1,\ y=4t-3$ where $t\geq 0$

Example 2

Given parametric equations where $t\geq 0$, find the rectangular equation for each curve. Sketch the curve, indicating its orientation.

① $x=\sin t$ and $y=\cos t$

② $x=\cos t$ and $y=\sin t$

③ $x=-\sin t$ and $y=\cos t$

④ $x=-\cos t$ and $y=\sin t$

Solution

① Using the Pythagorean Identity,

$$\sin^2 t+\cos^2 t=1$$
$$x^2+y^2=1$$

This is the equation of the unit circle centered at the origin.

t	x	y
0	0	1
$\frac{\pi}{2}$	1	0
π	0	-1

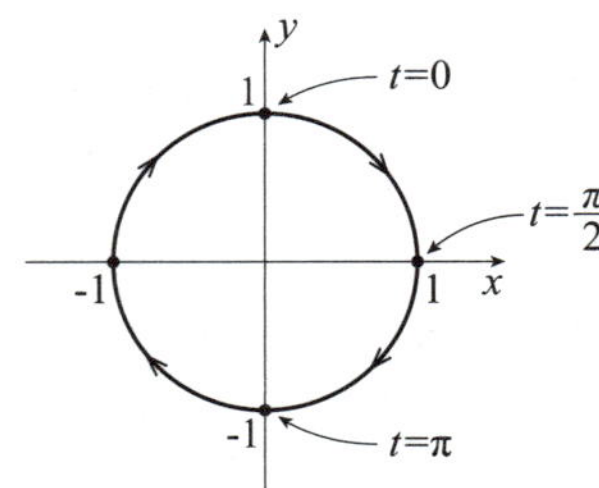

The parametric equations define a unit circle that starts at $(0,\ 1)$ and rotates clockwise.

② Using the Pythagorean Identity,

$$\sin^2 t+\cos^2 t=1$$
$$y^2+x^2=1,\ x^2+y^2=1$$

This is also the equation of the unit circle centered at the origin.

t	x	y
0	1	0
$\frac{\pi}{2}$	0	1
π	-1	0

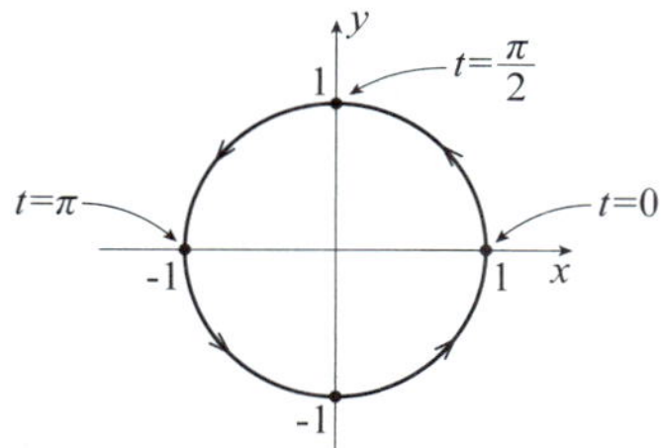

The parametric equations define a unit circle that starts at $(1, 0)$ and rotates counterclockwise.

③ Using the Pythagorean Identity,

$$\sin^2 t+\cos^2 t=1$$
$$(-x)^2+y^2=1,\ x^2+y^2=1$$

t	x	y
0	0	1
$\frac{\pi}{2}$	-1	0
π	0	-1

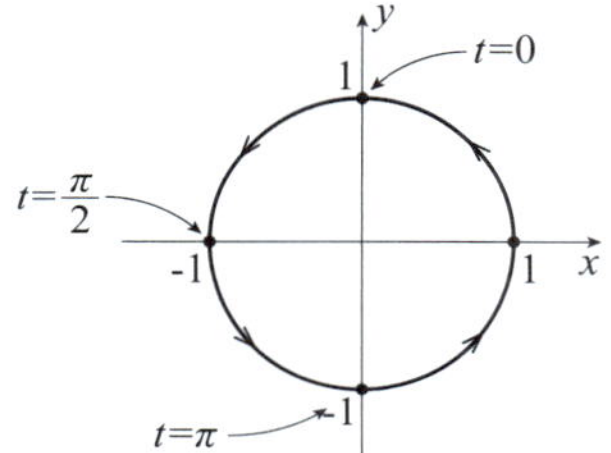

The parametric equations define a unit circle that starts at $(0, 1)$ and rotates counterclockwise.

④ Using the Pythagorean Identity,

$$\sin^2 t+\cos^2 t=1$$
$$y^2+(-x)^2=1,\ x^2+y^2=1$$

t	x	y
0	-1	0
$\frac{\pi}{2}$	0	1
π	1	0

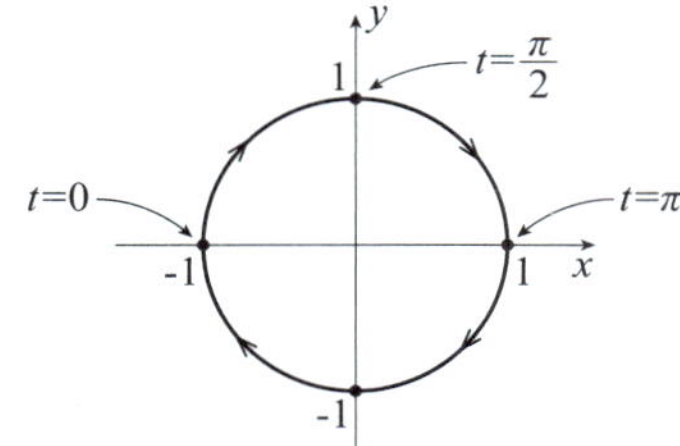

The parametric equations define a unit circle that starts at $(-1, 0)$ and rotates clockwise.

Check Point 2

Solutions_Page 149

Given parametric equations where $t\geq 0$, find the equation in terms of x and y of each curve. Sketch the curve, indicating its orientation.

① $x=3\cos t,\ y=5\sin t$

② $x=-3\sin t,\ y=-5\cos t$

02 Finding Parametric Equations for Curves Defined by Rectangular Equations.

There are multiple ways to interpret a rectangular equation as a set of parametric equations. If we choose an expression to represent x and substitute it into y, then it produces the same graph over the same domain as the rectangular equation. The easiest way of finding parametric equations is to let $x=t$. Then $y=f(t)$ and

$$x=t,\ y=f(t)$$

are parametric equations of the curve.

Example 3

Find parametric equations for $y=(x-1)^2+3$.

Solution

An easiest choice would be to let $x=t$. Then

$$y=(x-1)^2+3,\ y=(t-1)^2+3.$$

So the set of parametric equation is $x=t$, $y=(t-1)^2+3$.
Instead, if we let $x=t+4$, then we have

$$y=(x-1)^2+3,\ y=(t+4-1)^2+3,\ y=(t+3)^2+3.$$

So the set of parametric equation is $x=t+4$, $y=(t+3)^2+3$.

$x=t$, $y=(t-1)^2+3$
$x=t+4$, $y=(t+3)^2+3$

Note If we eliminate the parameter t from both of these parametric equations, each gives us $y=(x-1)^2+3$. In other words, there are an infinite number of ways to choose a set of parametric equations for a curve defined as a rectangular equation.

Check Point 3 Solutions_Page 149

Find two different parametric equations for the rectangular equations.

① $y=-4x-5$ ② $y=\sqrt{2x+1}$

03 Projectile Motion

Projectile motion is a form of motion where an object moves in a parabolic path; the path that the object follows is called its trajectory. It is the motion experienced by an object that is thrown near the Earth's surface and moves along a curved path under the action of gravity only. The effects of air resistance are assumed to be negligible.

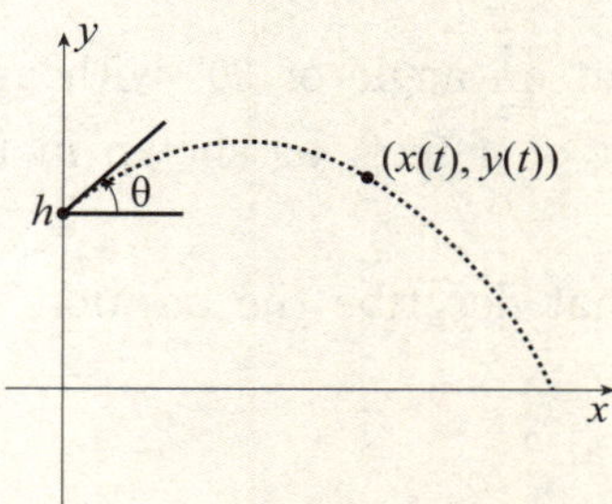

The object's parabolic path in Figure above can be modeled with the parametric equations.

$$\begin{cases} x(t)=(v_0 \cos\theta)t \\ y(t)=-\dfrac{1}{2}gt^2+(v_0 \sin\theta)t+h \end{cases}$$

where h is the initial height of the object, v_0 is the initial velocity of the object, θ is the angle of the initial trajectory with the horizontal, t is the time in seconds, and g is the acceleration due to gravity(approximately 32 ft/sec^2 or 9.8 m/sec^2).

Example 4

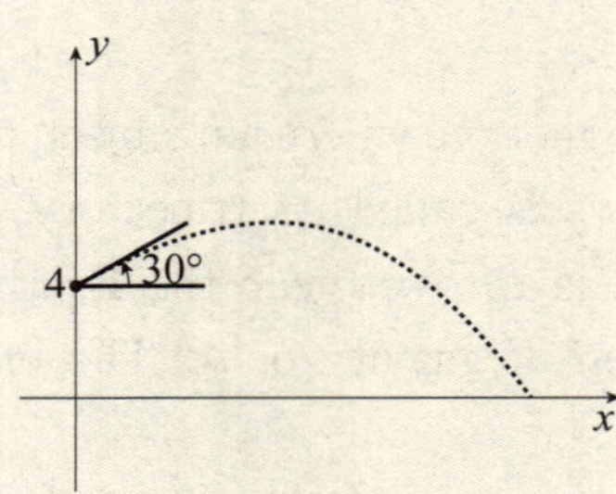

Suppose a batter hits the ball at an angle of 30° with an initial velocity of 120 feet per second and an initial height of 4 feet, as shown in Figure above.

① Find parametric equations that describe the position of the ball as a function of time.
② How long is the ball in the air?
③ When is the ball at its maximum height?
④ Determine the maximum height reached by the ball.
⑤ Determine the horizontal distance that the ball traveled.

Solution

We have $h=4\,ft$, $\theta=30°$, $v_0=120\ ft/\text{sec}$, and $g=32\ ft/\text{sec}^2$.

① $x(t)=(v_0\cos\theta)t$

$$=(120\cos 30°)\cdot t=\left(120\cdot\frac{\sqrt{3}}{2}\right)\cdot t=60\sqrt{3}\,t$$

$$y(t)=-\frac{1}{2}gt^2+(v_0\sin\theta)t+h$$

$$=-\frac{1}{2}(32)t^2+(120\sin 30°)t+4=-16t^2+\left(120\cdot\frac{1}{2}\right)t+4=-16t^2+60t+4$$

$$\begin{cases} x(t)=60\sqrt{3}\,t \\ y(t)=-16t^2+60t+4 \end{cases}$$

② The ball is in the air until it hits the ground. So, to determine the length of time that the ball is in the air, we need to find the time when the height of the ball reaches zero($y=0$).

$$0=-16t^2+60t+4,\quad 0=-4(4t^2-15t-1)$$

$$4t^2-15t-1=0$$

$$t=\frac{15\pm\sqrt{(-15)^2-4(4)(-1)}}{2(4)}=\frac{15\pm\sqrt{241}}{8}\ \rightarrow\ t=-0.066 \text{ or } t=3.816$$

Since $t\geq 0$, the ball is in the air for about 3.816 seconds

③ Note that the height y is a quadratic function of time t. So the maximum height of the ball can be found by determining the vertex of $y=-16t^2+60t+4$. The value of t at the vertex is

$$t=-\frac{b}{2a}=-\frac{60}{2(-16)}=1.875 \text{ sec.}$$

The ball is at its maximum height after 1.875 seconds

④ The maximum height of the ball is $y(1.875)$.

$$y=-16t^2+60t+4$$
$$y(1.875)=-16(1.875)^2+60(1.875)+4=60.25$$

The maximum height of the ball is approximately 60.25 feet

⑤ The ball is in the air for 3.816 seconds. So the horizontal distance that the ball travels is $x(3.816)=60\sqrt{3}\times3.816=396.57$ feet.

The horizontal distance that the ball travels is approximately 396.57 feet

Check Point 4

Solutions_Page 149

Suppose David kicks a soccer ball at an angle of 45° with an initial velocity of 8 meters per second and an initial height of $\frac{1}{2}$ meter.

① Find parametric equations that describe the position of the soccer ball as a function of time.
② How long is the ball in the air?
③ When is the ball at its maximum height?
④ Determine the maximum height reached by the ball.
⑤ Determine the horizontal distance that the ball traveled.

Review Exercise

01 Find the rectangular equation of the curve. Then, sketch the curve indicating its orientation.

(1) $x=t^2-1,\ y=\frac{t}{3}$

(2) $x=\cos t,\ y=\cos^2 t-\cos t-6$

(3) $x=\sin t-1,\ y=2\cos t+2$ where $t\geq 0$

(4) $x=2\cos^2 t,\ y=\sin^2 t$

02 Find parametric equations for each rectangular equation.

(1) $y=\frac{x+1}{x-1}$

(2) $x=y+\sqrt{2}\,y$

03 Find parametric equations for the line with given information.

(1) Slope 2, passing through $(-3,\ 6)$.

(2) Passing through two points $(2,\ 1)$ and $(0,\ -4)$.

04 Find parametric equations for a particle that moves along the ellipse $\frac{x^2}{16}+\frac{y^2}{9}=1$.

(1) The particle starts to move clockwise at $(4, 0)$ and make one complete revolution in 1 second.

(2) The particle starts to move counterclockwise at $(0, 3)$ and make one complete revolution in 2 seconds.

(3) The particle starts to move counterclockwise at $(-4, 0)$ and make one complete revolution in 4 seconds.

(4) The particle starts to move clockwise at $(0, 3)$ and make one complete revolution in 0.5 second.

05 Jason throws a baseball with an initial velocity of 110 feet per second at an angle of $60°$ to the horizontal. The ball leaves Jason's hand at a height of 6 feet.

(1) How long is the ball in the air?

(2) Determine the maximum height reached by the ball.

(3) Determine the horizontal distance that the ball traveled.

06 A ball is fired vertically upward at 240 feet per second at an initial height of 4 feet. How long does it take for the ball to return to the ground?

Review Exercise

07 The parametric function f is given by $f(t)=(x(t),\ y(t))$, where $x(t)=\cos t$ and $y(t)=2\sin t$. Which of the following equations correspond to the given parametric functions?

(A) $x^2+4y^2=1$

(B) $4x^2+y^2=1$

(C) $x^2+\dfrac{y^2}{4}=1$

(D) $\dfrac{x^2}{4}+y^2=1$

08 The parametric function f is given by $f(t)=(x(t),\ y(t))$, where both x and y are positive for all t. Which of the following could be the graph of f?

(A)

(B)

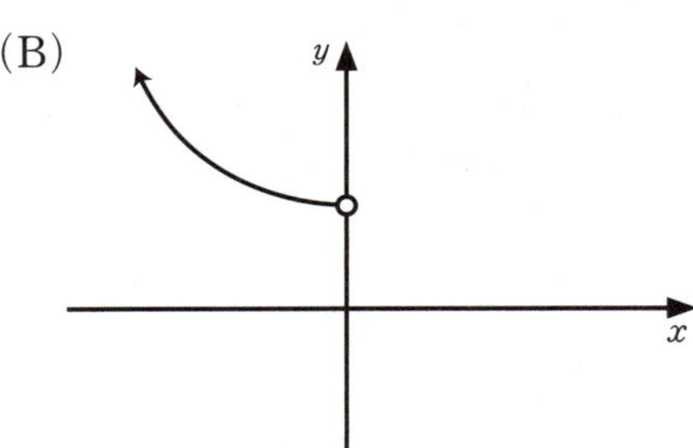

(C)

(D)

09 The parametric function f is given by $f(t)=(x(t),\ y(t))$, where $x(t)=4t+3$ and $y(t)=t^2-2$ for $t\geq 0$.

(1) If the point $A(a,\ a)$ lies on the graph of f, what is the value of a?

(2) Which way is the particle moving as t increases?

(A) The particle is moving to the right and up

(B) The particle is moving to the left and up

(C) The particle is moving to the right and down

(D) The particle is moving to the left and down

10 The parametric function f is given by $f(t)=(x(t),\ y(t))$, where $x(t)=-4t^2+8t-3$ and $y(t)=2t-1$ for $t\geq 0$.

(1) In which quadrant is the particle located at time $t=2$?

(A) Quadrant I

(B) Quadrant II

(C) Quadrant III

(D) Quadrant IV

(2) At what time t is the particle at its farthest point to the right in the $xy-$plane?

(3) What is the $x-$intercept of the particle's trajectory?

(4) Which of the following statements is true for $t>2$?

(A) The particle is moving to the right and down because $x(t)$ is positive and $y(t)$ is negative.

(B) The particle is moving to the right and down because $x(t)$ is increasing and $y(t)$ is decreasing.

(C) The particle is moving to the left and up because $x(t)$ is negative and $y(t)$ is positive.

(D) The particle is moving to the left and up because $x(t)$ is decreasing and $y(t)$ is increasing.

Review Exercise

11 The parametric function f is given by $f(t)=(x(t),\ y(t))$, where $x(t)=2\sin t-1$ and $y(t)=\cos^2 t+2$. Which of the following is the vertex of the graph of f in the xy−plane?

(A) $(-1,\ 3)$
(B) $(3,\ -1)$
(C) $\left(-\frac{1}{4},\ 3\right)$
(D) $\left(3,\ -\frac{1}{4}\right)$

12 The parametric function f is given by $f(t)=(x(t),\ y(t))$, where $x(t)=a+b\sin t$ and $y(t)=c+d\cos t$. If the graph of f is an ellipse centered at $(1,\ -2)$ with the lengths of major and minor axis of 8 and 4, respectively, what is the value of $a+b+c+d$?

memo

2 Conic Sections: Parabola

The conic section is a cross section where a plane intersects with a double−napped right circular cone. The general second−degree equation of any conic sections is given by

$$Ax^2+Cy^2+Dx+Ey+F=0.$$

There are four basic conic sections: circle, parabola, ellipse, and hyperbola. Each of them has its unique geometric properties. Since we already learned about the circle from Geometry, we will learn the other three conic sections in this chapter.

01 Definition of Parabola

A parabola is a set of all points in a plane that are equidistant from a fixed line (directrix) and a fixed point(focus). Refer to the graph below.

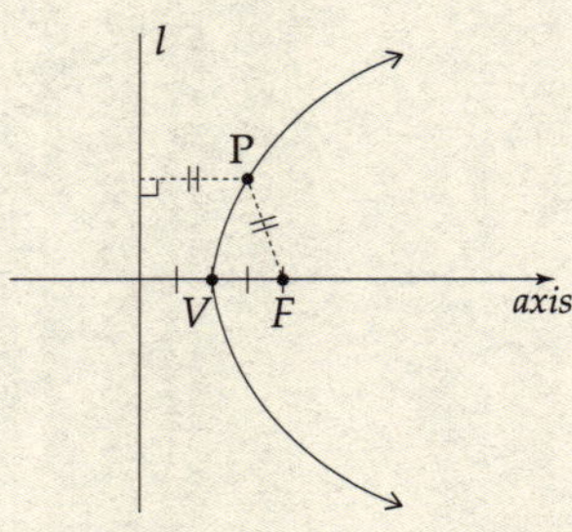

1. Focus: point F.
2. Directrix: line l.
3. Vertex: point V, the mid−point between the focus and the directrix.
4. Axis: passes through the focus and is perpendicular to the directrix.

02 Equation of Parabola in Standard Form

Now let us derive the standard form of the equation of a parabola that opens to the right and has the vertex $(0,\ 0)$.

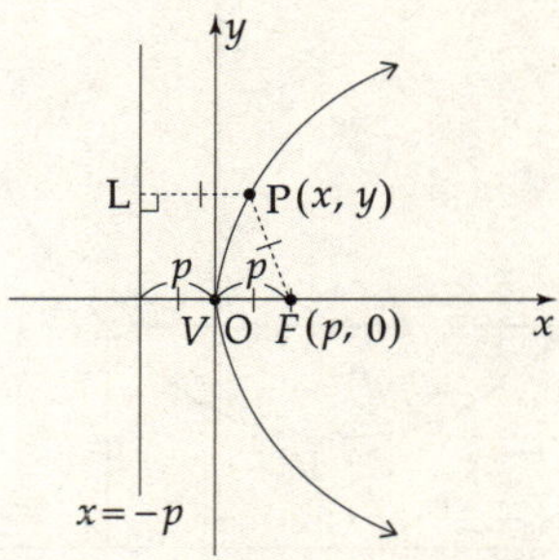

The distance of PF is $\sqrt{(x-p)^2+(y-0)^2}$ and PL is $x+p$.

$$\sqrt{(x-p)^2+(y-0)^2}=x+p \quad \rightarrow \text{Definition of parabola}$$
$$(x-p)^2+y^2=(x+p)^2 \quad \rightarrow \text{Square each side}$$
$$x^2-2xp+p^2+y^2=x^2+2xp+p^2 \quad \rightarrow \text{Expand}$$
$$-2xp+y^2=2xp \quad \rightarrow \text{Simplify}$$
$$y^2=4xp \quad \rightarrow \text{Simplify}$$

The equation $y^2=4px$ is the standard form of a parabola that opens to the right $(p>0)$ or to the left $(p<0)$. When the parabola opens upward $(p>0)$ or downward $(p<0)$, the equation is $x^2=4py$.

03 Focal Diameter

The latus rectum of a parabola is the chord through a focus parallel to the directrix of the parabola as shown in Figure below. The length of the latus rectum is the focal diameter of the parabola.

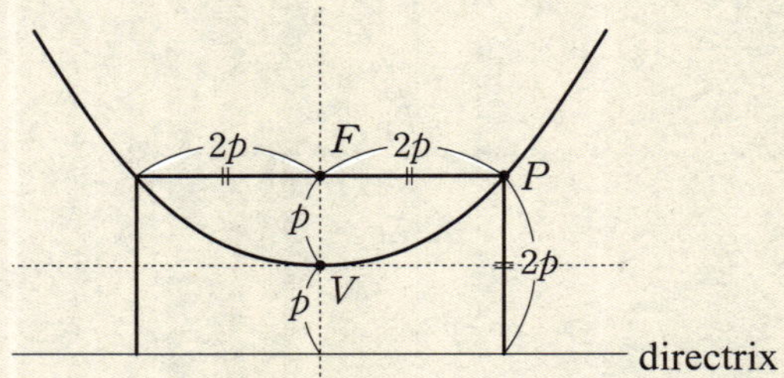

From the figure above, the distance from an endpoint P of the latus rectum to the directrix is $|2p|$. So, by the definition of a parabola, the distance from P to the focus must be $|2p|$ as well. Therefore the focal diameter is $|4p|$.

Here is a summary of the standard equation of parabola.

Equation	$y^2=4px$	$x^2=4py$
Graph	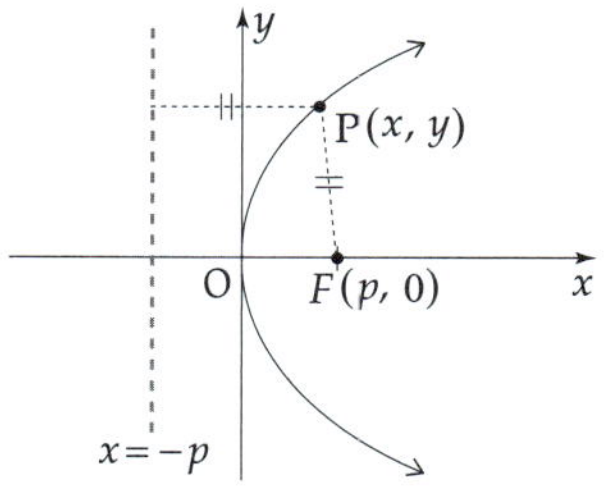 $p>0$ 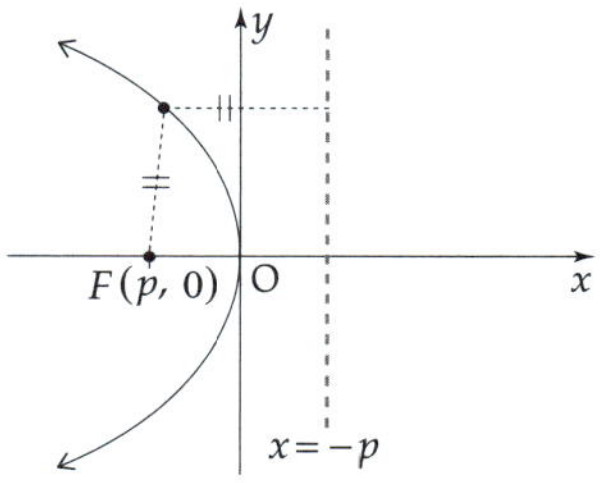 $p<0$	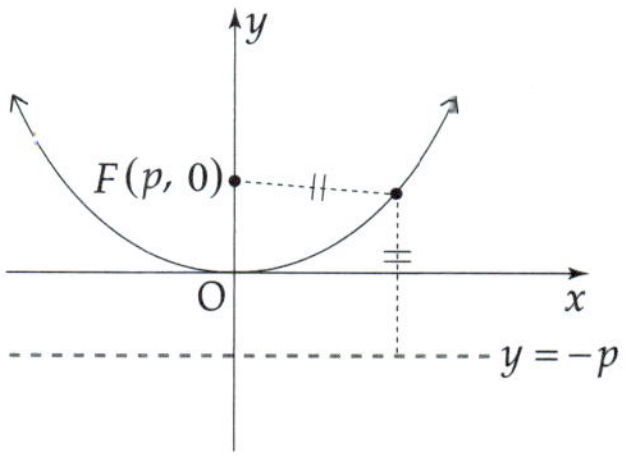 $p>0$ 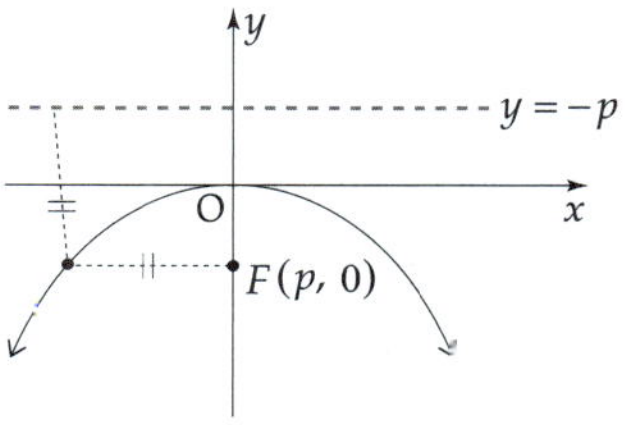 $p<0$
Focus	$F(p,\ 0)$	$F(0,\ p)$
Vertex	$V(0,\ 0)$	$V(0,\ 0)$
Directrix	$x=-p$	$y=-p$
Axis	$y=0$	$x=0$
Focal Diameter	$\lvert 4p\rvert$	$\lvert 4p\rvert$

Example 1

Find the vertex, focus, directrix, and focal diameter of the parabola $x=2y^2$. Then, sketch the graph of the equation.

Solution

The standard equation is $y^2=4px$ → The vertex is $(0, 0)$.

$x=2y^2$, $\frac{1}{2}x=y^2$ → $4p=\frac{1}{2}$, $p=\frac{1}{8}$.

Thus, we have the followings.

Vertex: $(0, 0)$, Focus: $(p, 0)=\left(\frac{1}{8}, 0\right)$, Equation of directrix: $x=-p$ → $x=-\frac{1}{8}$, and Focal diameter: $|4p|=\left|4\cdot\frac{1}{8}\right|=\frac{1}{2}$.

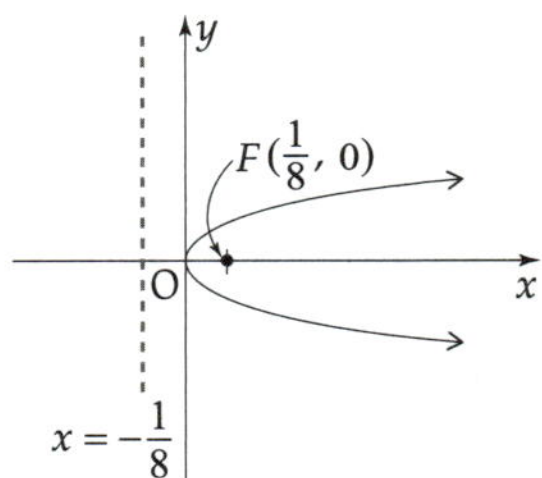

Vertex: $(0, 0)$, Focus: $\left(\frac{1}{8}, 0\right)$, Directrix: $x=-\frac{1}{8}$, Focal diameter: $\frac{1}{2}$

Check Point 1

Solutions_Page 155

Find the vertex, focus, directrix, and focal diameter of the parabola. Then, sketch the graph of the equation.

① $x^2+12y=0$

② $-\frac{1}{4}y^2-6x=0$

04 Translation of Parabola

Equation	$(y-k)^2=4p(x-h)$	$(x-h)^2=4p(y-k)$
	Graph $y^2=4px$ and then shift it h units horizontally and k units vertically.	Graph $x^2=4py$ and then shift it h units horizontally and k units vertically.
Graph	$V(h,k)$, $F(h+p,k)$, $x=-p+h$	$F(h,k+p)$, $V(h,k)$, $y=-p+k$
Focus	$(h+p,\ k)$	$(h,\ k+p)$
Vertex	$(h,\ k)$	$(h,\ k)$
Directrix	$x=-p+h$	$y=-p+k$
Axis	$y=k$	$x=h$

Example 2

Find the standard equation of the parabola with vertex $(2,\ 3)$ and focus $(2,\ 6)$.

Solution

First, sketch the graph of the parabola with given information.

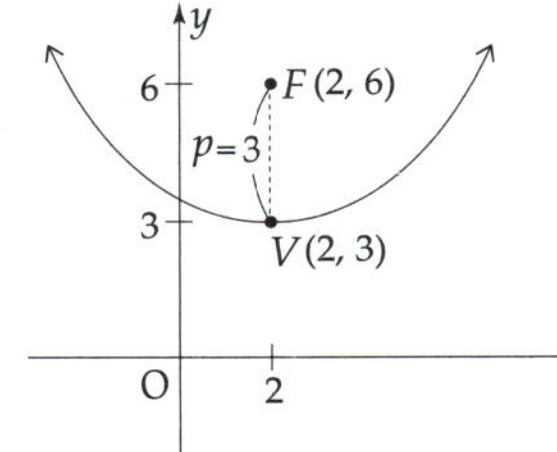

The standard equation is $(x-h)^2=4p(y-k)$. Since the distance between the vertex and focus is 3 and the parabola opens upward, $p=3$. So the equation is
$(x-h)^2=4p(y-k) \rightarrow (x-2)^2=12(y-3)$.

$(x-2)^2=12(y-3)$

Check Point 2

Solutions_Page 155

Find the standard equation of the parabola using given information.

① Vertex: $(0, 0)$; Focus: $(0, -2)$
② Vertex: $(-2, 2)$; Focus: $(-2, 6)$

05 General Equation of Parabola

As we mentioned above, the conic sections are defined with the general second-degree equation $Ax^2+Cy^2+Dx+Ey+F=0$. The equation describes a parabola if and only if $A=0$ or $C=0$, but not both. For example, $2x^2+4x+y-1=0(C=0)$ and $y^2-2x+4y+3=0(A=0)$ are the equations of a parabola.

Example 3

Find the vertex, focus, and directrix of the parabola given by $y^2-4x+2y-7=0$.

Solution

First, find the standard equation of the parabola.

$$
\begin{aligned}
y^2-4x+2y-7=0 \quad &\rightarrow \text{Original equation}\\
y^2+2y=4x+7 \quad &\rightarrow \text{Isolate } y \text{ terms on one side}\\
y^2+2y+1-1=4x+7 \quad &\rightarrow \text{Complete the square on the left side}\\
(y+1)^2=4x+8 \quad &\rightarrow \text{Add 1 to each side}\\
(y+1)^2=4(x+2) \quad &\rightarrow \text{Factor right side}
\end{aligned}
$$

The standard equation is $(y+1)^2=4(x+2)$. Now comparing this equation with $(y-k)^2=4p(x-h)$, we can conclude that $h=-2$, $k=-1$, and $p=1$. Since p is positive, the parabola opens to the right. Thus, we have the followings.

Vertex: $(h,\ k) \rightarrow (-2,\ -1)$, Focus: $(h+p,\ k) \rightarrow (-1,\ -1)$, and
Equation of directrix: $x=-p+h \rightarrow x=-3$.

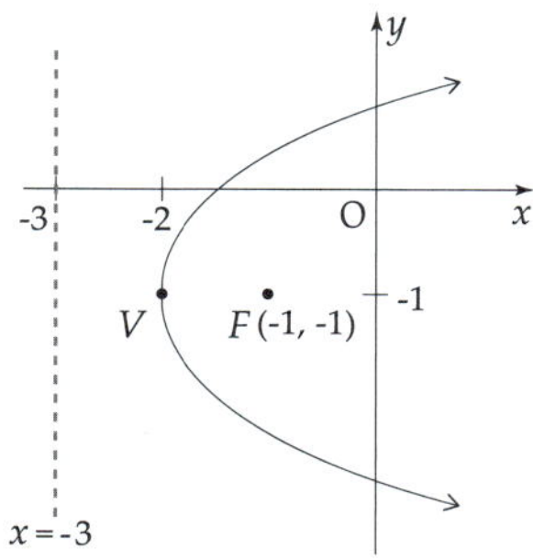

Vertex: $(-2,\ -1)$, Focus: $(-1,\ -1)$, Directrix: $x=-3$

Check Point 3

Solutions_Page 155

Find the vertex, focus, and directrix of the parabola.

① $2x^2+12x+3y=0$ ② $y^2+4y-2x=0$

Review Exercise

01 Find the vertex, focus, directrix, and focal diameter of the parabola.

(1) $x^2-6y+4x-8=0$

(2) $-y^2+4y-x=5$

02 Find the standard equation of the parabola using given information.

(1) Vertex$(-4,\ -2)$; Focus$(1,\ -2)$

(2) Vertex$(4,\ 2)$; Directrix $y=-4$

(3) Focus$(1,\ 0)$; Directrix $x=-3$

(4) Focus$(-2,\ -3)$; Directrix $y=\frac{1}{2}$

03 Find an equation of the parabola whose graph is shown.

(1)

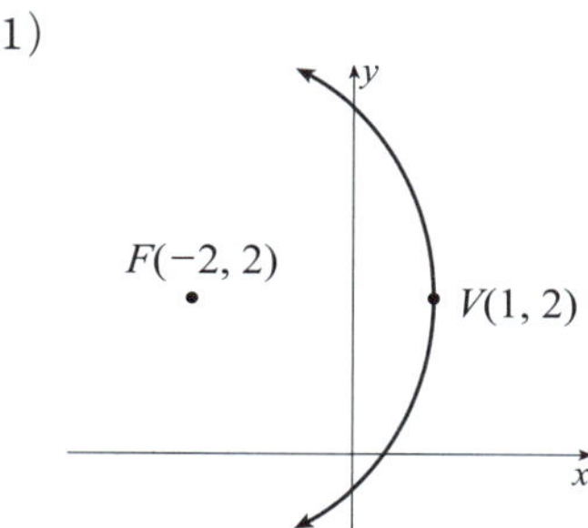

(2)

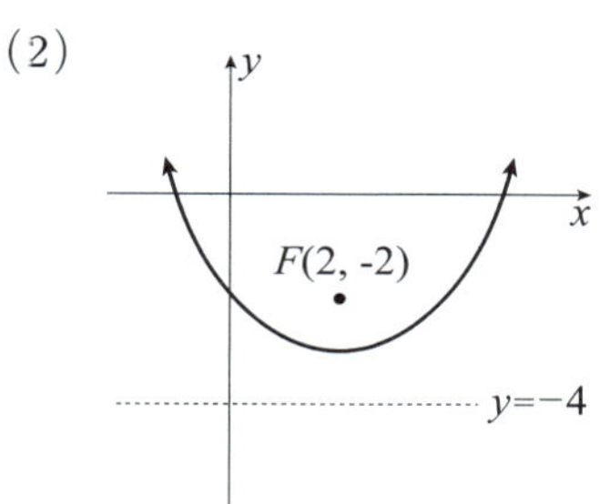

04 Find an equation for the parabola with vertex $(2,\ 1)$ and its directrix is y−axis.

05 Find an equation of a parabola with horizontal directrix and vertex at the origin that passes through the point $P(-4,\ 2)$.

06 The graph of $(y+1)^2=4(x-4)$ has

(A) A vertex at $(-4,\ 1)$
(B) Focus at $(5,\ -1)$
(C) Directrix $y=3$
(D) A parabola opens upward

07 Which of the following equations describes a parabola with focus $(4,\ 0)$ and directrix $x=0$?

(A) $(x-2)^2=4y$

(B) $(x-2)^2=8y$

(C) $y^2=4(x-2)$

(D) $y^2=8(x-2)$

3 Conic Sections: Ellipse

01 Definition of Ellipse

The second type of conic section is an ellipse. An ellipse is a set of all points in a plane where the sum of the distance from two fixed points is constant. There are several terminologies we need to remember. Refer to the following graphs.

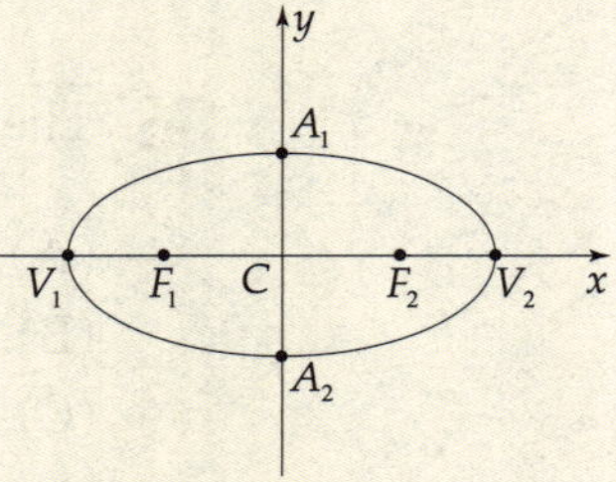

1. Foci (F_1 and F_2): two fixed points.
2. Vertices (V_1 and V_2): the line through the foci intersects at the vertices.
3. Center (C): mid−point of the vertices or foci.
4. Major Axis ($\overline{V_1V_2}$): line segment joining the vertices.
5. Minor Axis ($\overline{A_1A_2}$): line segment perpendicular to the major axis at the center.

02 Equation of Ellipse in Standard Form

Here is how we derive the equation of an ellipse with the vertex (0, 0).

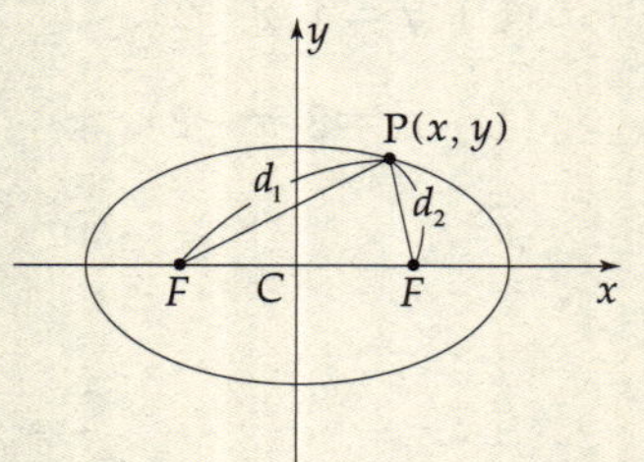

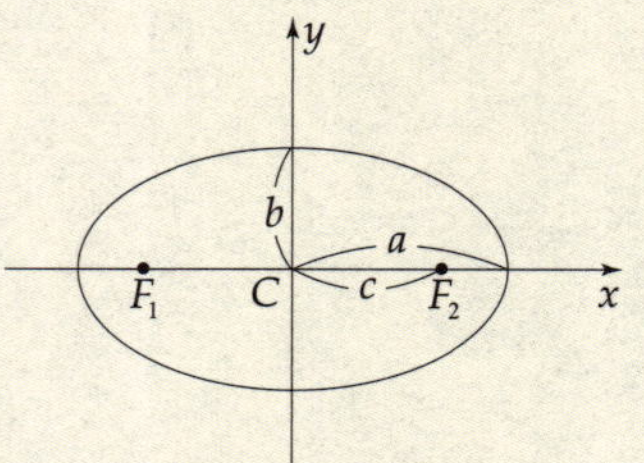

By the definition of ellipse, $d_1+d_2=2a$ and $2\sqrt{(b^2+c^2)}=2a \rightarrow a^2=b^2+c^2$. So,

$$\sqrt{(x+c)^2+y^2}+\sqrt{(x-c)^2+y^2}=2a$$

$$\sqrt{(x-c)^2+y^2}=2a-\sqrt{(x+c)^2+y^2} \quad \rightarrow \text{Isolate radical}$$

$$(x-c)^2+y^2=4a^2-4a\sqrt{(x+c)^2+y^2}+(x+c)^2+y^2 \rightarrow \text{Square both sides}$$

$$a^2+cx=a\sqrt{(x+c)^2+y^2} \quad \rightarrow \text{Simplify}$$

$$(a^2+cx)^2=a^2((x+c)^2+y^2) \quad \rightarrow \text{Square both sides}$$

$$(a^2-c^2)x^2+a^2y^2=a^2(a^2-c^2) \quad \rightarrow \text{Simplify}$$

$$\frac{x^2}{a^2}+\frac{y^2}{a^2-c^2}=1 \quad \rightarrow \text{Divide both sides by } a^2(a^2-c^2)$$

$$\frac{x^2}{a^2}+\frac{y^2}{b^2}=1 \quad \rightarrow a^2-c^2=b^2$$

The standard equation of an ellipse with foci on the $x-$axis is $\frac{x^2}{a^2}+\frac{y^2}{b^2}=1$.

When an ellipse has foci on the $y-$axis, the equation is then $\frac{y^2}{a^2}+\frac{x^2}{b^2}=1$.

Here is a summary of the standard equation of ellipse.

Equation	$\frac{x^2}{a^2}+\frac{y^2}{b^2}=1,\ a>b>0$	$\frac{y^2}{a^2}+\frac{x^2}{b^2}=1,\ a>b>0$
Graph	Foci are on the $x-$axis	Foci are on the $x-$axis
Center	$C(0,\ 0)$	$C(0,\ 0)$
Focus	$F_1(-c,\ 0),\ F_2(c,\ 0)$	$F_1(0,\ -c),\ F_2(0,\ c)$
Vertex	$V_1(-a,\ 0),\ V_2(a,\ 0)$	$V_1(0,\ -a),\ V_2(0,\ a)$
Major Axis	Horizontal axis, $2a$	Vertical axis, $2a$
Minor Axis	Vertical axis, $2b$	Horizontal axis, $2b$

03 Eccentricity of an Ellipse

The eccentricity(e) of an ellipse is the ratio of the distance from the center to the foci(c) and the distance from the center to the vertices(a).

$$e=\frac{c}{a}$$

The eccentricity of an ellipse is a measure of how nearly circular the ellipse. It is strictly greater than zero and less than one. If an ellipse is close to circular, it has an eccentricity close to zero. If an ellipse has an eccentricity close to one, it has high degree of ovalness. Refer to the figure below.

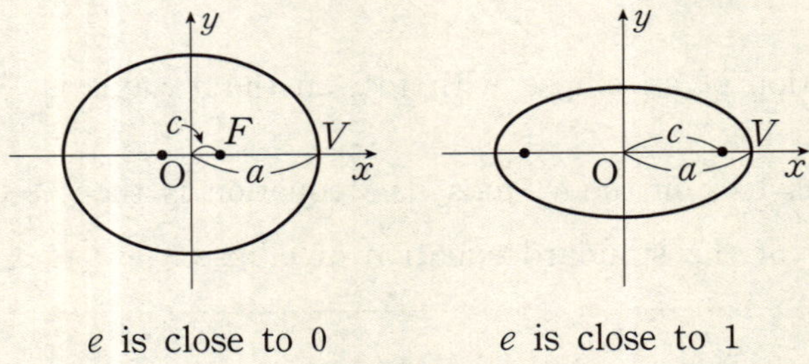

e is close to 0　　　　e is close to 1

Example 1

Find the center, vertices, foci, length of the major and minor axis, and eccentricity of the ellipse $\frac{x^2}{4}+\frac{y^2}{9}=1$. Then, sketch the graph of the equation.

Solution

The standard equation is $\frac{y^2}{a^2}+\frac{x^2}{b^2}=1$ → The center is $(0,\ 0)$.

$$\frac{x^2}{4}+\frac{y^2}{9}=1,\ \frac{y^2}{9}+\frac{x^2}{4}=1$$

$$a^2=9,\ a=3;\ b^2=4,\ b=2$$

$$c=\sqrt{a^2-b^2}=\sqrt{9-4}=\sqrt{5}.$$

Thus, we have the following.

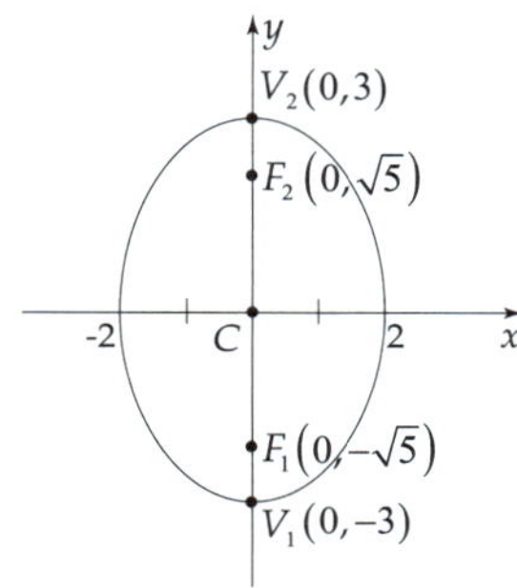

Center: $(0,\ 0)$ Vertices: $(0,\ -a)=(0,\ -3)$ and $(0,\ a)=(0,\ 3)$

Foci: $(0,\ -c)=(0,\ -\sqrt{5})$ and $(0,\ c)=(0,\ \sqrt{5})$

Major Axis: $2a=2\cdot3=6$ Minor Axis: $2b=2\cdot2=4$

Eccentricity: $\frac{c}{a}=\frac{\sqrt{5}}{3}$

Check Point 1

Solutions_Page 159

Find the center, vertices, foci, length of the major and minor axis, and eccentricity of the ellipse. Then sketch the graph

① $\frac{x^2}{4}+\frac{y^2}{16}=1$ ② $3x^2+12y^2=36$

04 Translation of Ellipse

Equation	$\frac{(x-h)^2}{a^2}+\frac{(y-k)^2}{b^2}=1,\ a>b>0$	$\frac{(y-k)^2}{a^2}+\frac{(x-h)^2}{b^2}=1,\ a>b>0$
	Graph $\frac{x^2}{a^2}+\frac{y^2}{b^2}=1$ and then shift it h units horizontally and k units vertically.	Graph $\frac{y^2}{a^2}+\frac{x^2}{b^2}=1$ and then shift it h units horizontally and k units vertically.
Graph		
Center	$C(h,\ k)$	$C(h,\ k)$
Foci	$F_1(-c+h,\ k),\ F_2(c+h,\ k)$	$F_1(h,\ -c+k),\ F_2(h,\ c+k)$
Vertices	$V_1(-a+h,\ k),\ V_2(a+h,\ k)$	$V_1(h,\ -a+k),\ V_2(h,\ a+k)$
Major Axis	Horizontal axis, $2a$	Vertical axis, $2a$
Minor Axis	Vertical axis, $2b$	Horizontal axis, $2b$

✔ Notice that the lengths of major and minor axis do not change.

Example 2-1

Find the standard equation of the ellipse with vertices $(\pm3,\ 0)$and foci $(\pm1,\ 0)$.

Solution

First, sketch the graph of the ellipse with given information.

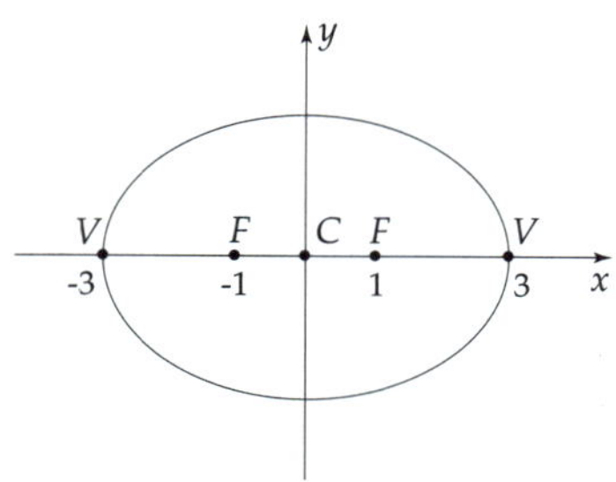

The standard equation is $\frac{x^2}{a^2}+\frac{y^2}{b^2}=1$, where the center is $(0,\ 0)$. From the graph, we know that $a=3$, $c=1$, and $b=\sqrt{a^2-c^2}=\sqrt{9-1}=2\sqrt{2}$. So the equation is

$$\frac{x^2}{3^2}+\frac{y^2}{(2\sqrt{2})^2}=1,\ \frac{x^2}{9}+\frac{y^2}{8}=1$$

$\frac{x^2}{9}+\frac{y^2}{8}=1$

Example 2-2

Find the standard equation of the ellipse with foci $(2,\ 4)$ and $(6,\ 4)$ whose major axis has a length of 6.

Solution

First, sketch the graph of the ellipse with given information.

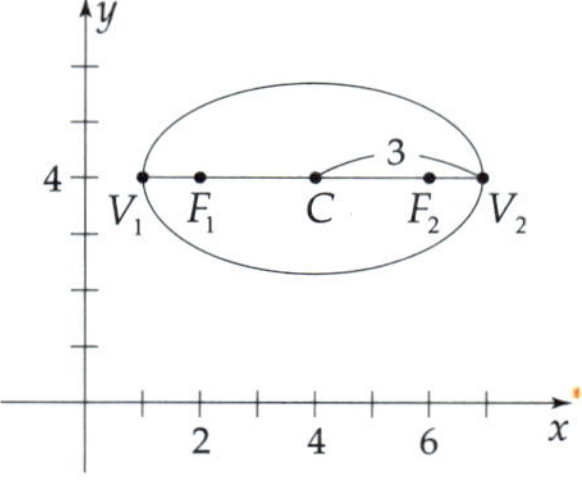

The standard equation is in the form $\frac{(x-h)^2}{a^2}+\frac{(y-k)^2}{b^2}=1$. Since the length of major axis is $2a=6$, $a=3$, and the center is mid-point of two foci $\left(\frac{2+6}{2},\ 4\right)=(4,\ 4)$.

The distance from the center to one of the foci is $c=2$ and $b=\sqrt{a^2-c^2}=\sqrt{3^2-2^2}=\sqrt{5}$.
So the equation is

$$\frac{(x-4)^2}{3^2}+\frac{(y-4)^2}{(\sqrt{5})^2}=1,\ \frac{(x-4)^2}{9}+\frac{(y-4)^2}{5}=1.$$

$\frac{(x-4)^2}{9}+\frac{(y-4)^2}{5}=1$

Check Point 2

Solutions_Page 160

Find the standard form of the equation of an ellipse with the given information.

① Vertices: (0, 6), (0, −6); Foci: (0, 4), (0, −4)

② Foci: (0, 0), (4, 0); Major axis of length: 12

05 General Equation of Ellipse

Given the equation of conic section $Ax^2+Cy^2+Dx+Ey+F=0$, the equation is ellipse if and only if $AC>0$ and $A\neq C$.

For example, $x^2+4y^2-3x+12y+5=0(1\cdot 4>0,\ 1\neq 4)$ is the equation of ellipse.

Example 3

Find the center, vertices, foci, length of the major and minor axis, and eccentricity of the ellipse $x^2+2y^2-4x+4y+2=0$.

Solution

First, find the standard equation of the ellipse.

$$x^2+2y^2-4x+4y+2=0 \quad \rightarrow \text{Original equation}$$

$$(x^2-4x)+2(y^2+2y)=-2 \quad \rightarrow \text{Group terms}$$

$$(x^2-4x+4-4)+2(y^2+2y+1-1)=-2 \quad \rightarrow \text{Complete the square}$$

$$(x-2)^2+2(y+1)^2=4 \quad \rightarrow \text{Simplify}$$

$$\frac{(x-2)^2}{4}+\frac{(y+1)^2}{2}=1 \quad \rightarrow \text{Divide each side by 4}$$

Standard equation is $\frac{(x-2)^2}{4}+\frac{(y+1)^2}{2}=1$. Now, compare this equation with $\frac{(x-h)^2}{a^2}+\frac{(y-k)^2}{b^2}=1$. Since $a>b$, major axis is horizontal and $h=2$, $k=-1$, $a=2$, $b=\sqrt{2}$, $c=\sqrt{a^2-b^2}=\sqrt{4-2}=\sqrt{2}$. Thus, we have the following.

Center: $(h,\ k)=(2,\ -1)$
Foci: $F_1(-c+h,\ k)=(-\sqrt{2}+2,\ -1)$ and $F_2(c+h,\ k)=(\sqrt{2}+2,\ -1)$
Vertices: $V_1(-a+h,\ k)=(0,\ -1)$ and $V_2(a+h,\ k)=(4,\ -1)$
Major axis: $2a=2\cdot2=4$ Minor axis: $2b=2\sqrt{2}$
Eccentricity: $\frac{c}{a}=\frac{\sqrt{2}}{2}$

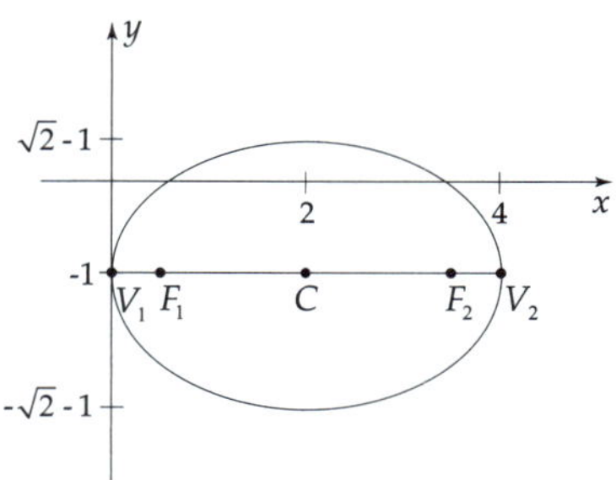

Check Point 3 Solutions_Page 160

Find the center, vertices, foci, length of the major and minor axis, and eccentricity of the ellipse. Then sketch the graph.

① $x^2+4y^2+6x-8y+9=0$
② $9x^2+4y^2+36x-24y+36=0$

Review Exercise

01 What is the length of the major axis of the ellipse whose equation is

$$\frac{(x-2)^2}{9}+\frac{(y-4)^2}{12}=1?$$

02 If $8x^2+4y^2+8y=8$ is equivalent to $\frac{(x-h)^2}{a^2}+\frac{(y-k)^2}{b^2}=1$, which of the following could be values of a and b?

(A) $a=\sqrt{6}$, $b=\sqrt{3}$

(B) $a=2\sqrt{3}$, $b=\frac{\sqrt{6}}{2}$

(C) $a=\frac{\sqrt{6}}{2}$, $b=\sqrt{3}$

(D) $a=\frac{\sqrt{3}}{2}$, $b=\sqrt{6}$

(E) $a=\frac{\sqrt{6}}{2}$, $b=\frac{\sqrt{6}}{2}$

03 Find the center, vertices, foci, length of the major and minor axis, and eccentricity of the ellipse. Then sketch the graph

(1) $4x^2+y^2=20$

(2) $x^2+2y^2+2x-12y+9=0$

04 Find the standard equation of the ellipse using given information.

(1) Vertices: $(-2,\ 0)$, $(-2,\ 6)$
Foci: $(-2,\ 1)$, $(-2,\ 5)$

(2) Center: (6, −5)
Vertex: (6, 7)
Focus: $(6, -5-6\sqrt{3})$

(3) Center: (0, 4); Eccentricity $e=\frac{1}{2}$; Vertices: (−4, 4), (4, 4)

05 In xy−plane, what is the shortest distance between the line $x=8$ and the curve $x^2+4y^2=9$?

06 Find an equation for the ellipse with foci (3, 2), (3, −4), and major axis of length 10.

07 Find an equation for the ellipse with center (6, 0), major axis of length $4\sqrt{5}$, minor axis of $2\sqrt{3}$, and whose foci lie on the x−axis.

08 What is the length of the major axis of the ellipse whose equation is $3x^2+2y^2+6x-12y+9=0$?

4 Conic Sections: Hyperbola

01 Definition of Hyperbola

The third type of conic section is a hyperbola. A hyperbola is a set of all points in a plane where the difference of the distance from two fixed points is constant. There are several terminologies we need to remember. Refer to the following graph.

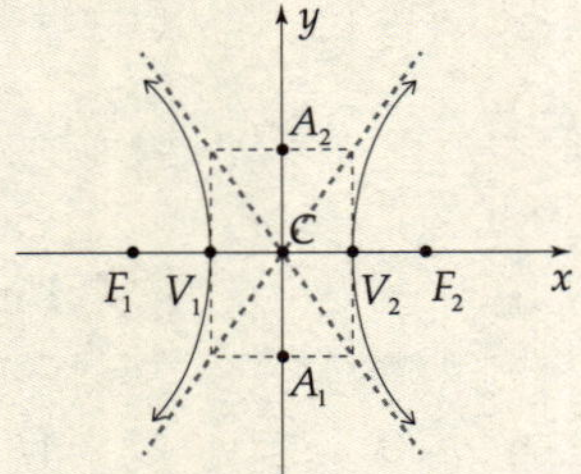

(1) Foci (F_1 and F_2): two fixed points.

(2) Vertices (V_1 and V_2): the line through these foci intersects at the vertices.

(3) Center (C): mid−point of the vertices or foci.

(4) Transverse Axis ($\overline{V_1V_2}$): line segment joining the vertices.

(5) Conjugate Axis ($\overline{A_1A_2}$): line segment perpendicular to the transverse axis at the center.

02 Equation of Hyperbola in Standard Form

Here is how we derive the equation of a hyperbola with the vertex (0, 0).

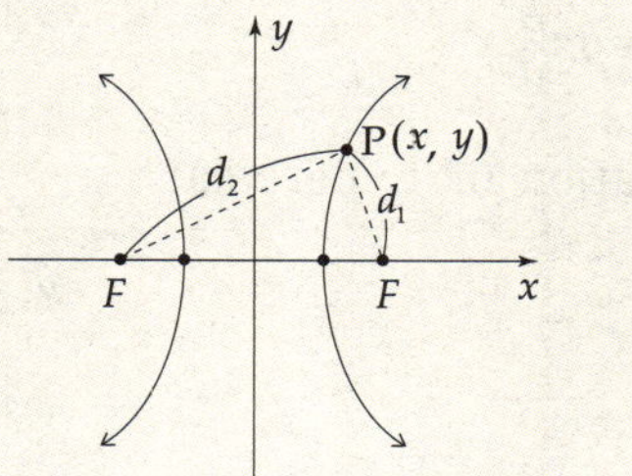

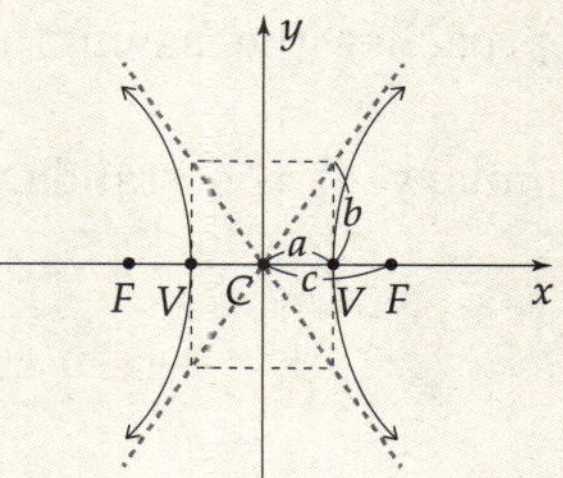

By the definition of hyperbola, $d_2-d_1=2a$ and $c^2=a^2+b^2$. So,

$$\sqrt{(x+c)^2+y^2}-\sqrt{(x-c)^2+y^2}=2a$$

$$\sqrt{(x-c)^2+y^2}=2a+\sqrt{(x+c)^2+y^2} \quad \rightarrow \text{Isolate radical}$$

$$(x-c)^2+y^2=4a^2+4a\sqrt{(x+c)^2+y^2}+(x+c)^2+y^2 \quad \rightarrow \text{Square both sides}$$

$$-a^2-cx=a\sqrt{(x+c)^2+y^2} \quad \rightarrow \text{Simplify}$$

$$(-a^2-cx)^2=a^2((x+c)^2+y^2) \quad \rightarrow \text{Square both sides}$$

$$(c^2-a^2)x^2-a^2y^2=a^2(c^2-a^2) \quad \rightarrow \text{Simplify}$$

$$\frac{x^2}{a^2}-\frac{y^2}{c^2-a^2}=1 \quad \rightarrow \text{Divide both sides by } a^2(c^2-a^2)$$

$$\frac{x^2}{a^2}-\frac{y^2}{b^2}=1 \quad \rightarrow c^2-a^2=b^2$$

The standard equation with foci on the $x-$axis is $\frac{x^2}{a^2}-\frac{y^2}{b^2}=1$, where $c^2=a^2+b^2$.

When a hyperbola has foci on the $y-$axis, the equation is then $\frac{y^2}{a^2}-\frac{x^2}{b^2}=1$.

Now, let us derive the equations of asymptotes. Given $\frac{x^2}{a^2}-\frac{y^2}{b^2}=1$, solve for y.

$$\frac{x^2}{a^2}-\frac{y^2}{b^2}=1, \quad \rightarrow \text{Original equation}$$

$$y^2=\frac{b^2x^2}{a^2}-b^2 \quad \rightarrow \text{Solve for } y^2$$

$$y^2=\frac{b^2x^2}{a^2}\left(1-\frac{a^2}{x^2}\right) \quad \rightarrow \text{Factor right side}$$

$$y=\pm\frac{b}{a}x\sqrt{1-\frac{a^2}{x^2}}$$ → Take square root each side

As x increases or decreases without bound, $\frac{a^2}{x^2}$ approaches zero. So the graph of hyperbola approaches the asymptotes $y=\pm\frac{b}{a}x$.

Here is a summary of the standard equation of hyperbola.

Equation	$\frac{x^2}{a^2}-\frac{y^2}{b^2}=1$	$\frac{y^2}{a^2}-\frac{x^2}{b^2}=1$
Graph	F_1 V_1 C V_2 F_2 x y Foci are on the $x-$axis	y F_2 V_2 C V_1 F_1 x Foci are on the $y-axis$
Center	$C(0,\ 0)$	$C(0,\ 0)$
Foci	$F_1\ (-c,\ 0),\ F_2\ (c,\ 0)$	$F_1\ (0,\ -c),\ F_2\ (0,\ c)$
Vertices	$V_1\ (-a,\ 0),\ V_2\ (a,\ 0)$	$V_1\ (0,\ -a),\ V_2\ (0,\ a)$
Transverse Axis	Horizontal axis, $2a$	Vertical axis, $2a$
Conjugate Axis	Vertical axis, $2b$	Horizontal axis, $2b$
Asymptotes	$y=\pm\frac{b}{a}x$	$y=\pm\frac{a}{b}x$

Example 1

Find the center, vertices, foci, length of the transverse axis, length of the conjugate axis, and the equations of the asymptotes of the hyperbola $\frac{x^2}{9}-\frac{y^2}{16}=1$. Then, sketch the graph of the equation.

Solution

Comparing given equation with $\frac{x^2}{a^2}-\frac{y^2}{b^2}=1$, the center is $(0, 0)$.

$a^2=9$, $a=3$; $b^2=16$, $b=4$, and $c=\sqrt{a^2+b^2}=\sqrt{9+16}=5$. Thus, we have the following.

Center: $(0, 0)$
Vertices: $(-a, 0)=(-3, 0)$ and $(a, 0)=(3, 0)$
Foci: $(-c, 0)=(-5, 0)$ and $(c, 0)=(5, 0)$
Transverse Axis: $2a=2\cdot3=6$
Conjugate Axis: $2b=2\cdot4=8$
Equation of Asymptote: $y=\pm\frac{b}{a}x=\pm\frac{4}{3}x$

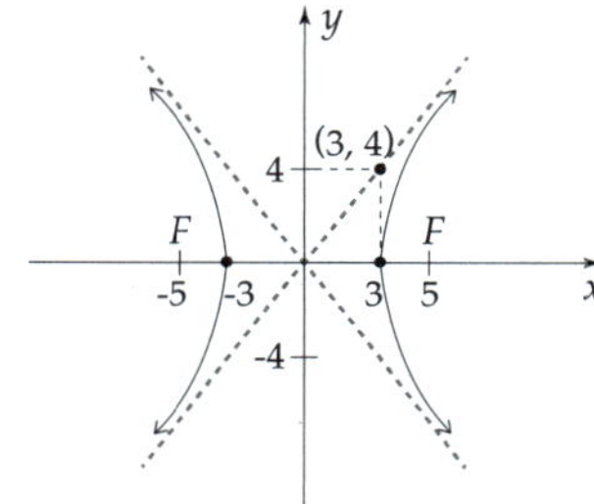

Check Point 1

Solutions_Page 164

Find the center, vertices, foci, length of the transverse axis, length of the conjugate axis, and the equations of the asymptotes. Then, sketch the graph.

① $\frac{x^2}{9}-\frac{y^2}{25}=1$

② $12y^2-24x^2=96$

03 Translation of Hyperbola

Equation	$\dfrac{(x-h)^2}{a^2}-\dfrac{(y-k)^2}{b^2}=1$	$\dfrac{(y-k)^2}{a^2}-\dfrac{(x-h)^2}{b^2}=1$
Graph	Graph $\dfrac{x^2}{a^2}-\dfrac{y^2}{b^2}=1$ and shift it h units horizontally and k units vertically	Graph $\dfrac{y^2}{a^2}-\dfrac{x^2}{b^2}=1$ and shift it h units horizontally and k units vertically
Center	$C(h,\ k)$	$C(h,\ k)$
Foci	$F_1(-c+h,\ k)$, $F_2(c+h,\ k)$	$F_1(h,\ -c+k)$, $F_2(h,\ -c+k)$
Vertices	$V_1(-a+h,\ k)$, $V_2(a+h,\ k)$	$V_1(h,\ -a+k)$, $V_2(h,\ a+k)$
Transverse Axis	Horizontal axis, $2a$	Vertical axis, $2a$
Conjugate Axis	Vertical axis, $2b$	Horizontal axis, $2b$
Asymptotes	$y=\pm\dfrac{b}{a}(x-h)+k$	$y=\pm\dfrac{a}{b}(x-h)+k$

✔ Notice that the lengths of transverse and conjugate axis do not change.

Example 2

Find the standard equation of the hyperbola with foci $(0,\ 3)$, $(6,\ 3)$ and vertices $(2,\ 3)$, $(4,\ 3)$

Solution

First, sketch the graph of the hyperbola with given information.

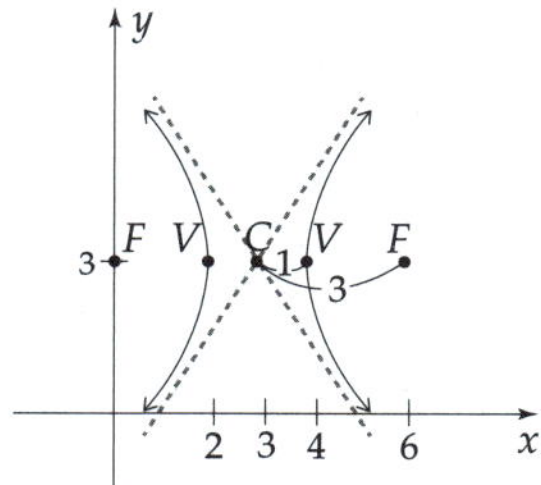

The standard equation is in the form $\frac{(x-k)^2}{a^2}-\frac{(y-h)^2}{b^2}=1$. The center is the mid−point of two foci $\left(\frac{0+6}{2},\ 3\right)=(3,\ 3)$. From the graph, we know that $a=1$, $c=3$, and $b=\sqrt{c^2-a^2}=\sqrt{9-1}=2\sqrt{2}$.

So the equation is $\frac{(x-3)^2}{1^2}-\frac{(y-3)^2}{(2\sqrt{2})^2}=1$, $(x-3)^2-\frac{(y-3)^2}{8}=1$

$(x-3)^2-\frac{(y-3)^2}{8}=1$

Check Point 2

Solutions_Page 164

Find the standard form of the equation of the hyperbola with the given information.

① Vertices: $(0,\ 4)$, $(0,\ -4)$; Foci: $(0,\ 7)$, $(0,\ -7)$

② Vertices: $(-6,\ -2)$, $(6,\ -2)$; Foci: $(-6-\sqrt{3},\ -2)$, $(6+\sqrt{3},\ -2)$

04 General Equation of Hyperbola

Given the equation of conic section $Ax^2+Cy^2+Dx+Ey+F=0$, the equation is hyperbola if and only if $AC<0$.

For example, $x^2-2y^2+4x+8y=0$ $(1\cdot(-2)<0)$ is the equation of hyperbola.

Example 3

Find the center, vertices, foci, and equations of asymptotes of the hyperbola $-x^2+y^2+2x-6y=0$.

Solution

First, find the standard equation of the hyperbola.

$$-x^2+y^2+2x-6y=0 \quad \rightarrow \text{Original equation}$$
$$(y^2-6y)-(x^2-2x)=0 \quad \rightarrow \text{Group terms}$$
$$(y^2-6y+9-9)-(x^2-2x+1-1)=0 \quad \rightarrow \text{Complete the square}$$
$$(y-3)^2-(x-1)^2=8 \quad \rightarrow \text{Simplify}$$
$$\frac{(y-3)^2}{8}-\frac{(x-1)^2}{8}=1 \quad \rightarrow \text{Divide each side by 8}$$

Standard equation is $\frac{(y-3)^2}{8}-\frac{(x-1)^2}{8}=1$ and transverse axis is vertical. Now, comparing this equation with $\frac{(y-k)^2}{8}-\frac{(x-h)^2}{8}=1$, we can conclude that $h=1$, $k=3$, $a=2\sqrt{2}$, $b=2\sqrt{2}$, and $c=\sqrt{a^2+b^2}=\sqrt{8+8}=4$. Thus, we have the following.

Center: $(h, k)=(1, 3)$
Foci: $F_1(h, -c+k)=(1, -1)$ and $F_2(h, c+k)=(1, 7)$
Vertices: $V_1(h, -a+k)=(1, -2\sqrt{2}+3)$ and $V_2(h, a+k)=(1, 2\sqrt{2}+3)$

Equation of Asymptotes: $y=\frac{a}{b}(x-h)+k$, $y=\frac{2\sqrt{2}}{2\sqrt{2}}(x-1)+3$, $y=x+2$

$y=-\frac{a}{b}(x-h)+k$, $y=-\frac{2\sqrt{2}}{2\sqrt{2}}(x-1)+3$, $y=-x+4$

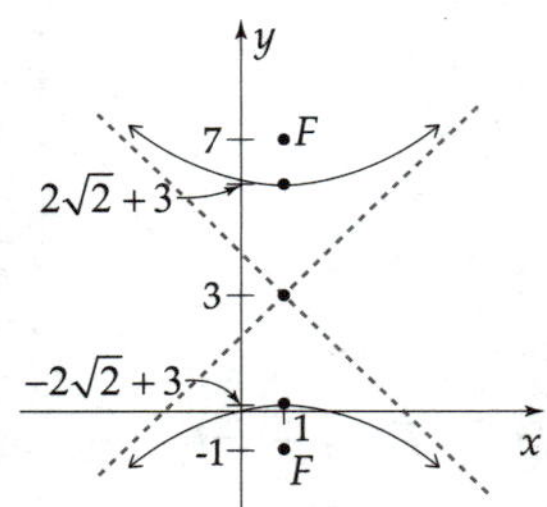

Check Point 3

Solutions_Page 165

Find the center, vertices, foci, and equations of asymptotes of the hyperbola. Then, sketch the graph.

① $x^2-2y^2+12y-26=0$

② $x^2-2y^2-6x-16y-15=0$

Review Exercise

Solutions_Page 165

01 Find the center, vertices, foci, and equations of the asymptotes of the hyperbola. Then, sketch the graph.

(1) $y^2-2x^2=6$

(2) $3x^2-2y^2-6x-8y-17=0$

Find the standard equation of the hyperbola using given information.

02 Vertices: $(\pm 2,\ 0)$; Foci: $(\pm 5,\ 0)$

03 Vertices: $(-1,\ -3)$, $(-7,\ -3)$
Foci: $(0,\ -3)$, $(-8,\ -3)$

04 Foci: $(2,\ -3)$, $(2,\ 5)$;
The length of transverse axis is 2

05 Foci: $(0,\ 2)$, $(6,\ 2)$;
The length of transverse axis: 2

06 Vertices: $(-1,\ -1)$, $(5,\ -1)$
Asymptote: $y=2x-5$, $y=-2x+3$

07 Which of the following points is the center of the hyperbola whose equation is $x^2-y^2+2x-4y=10$?

(A) $(0,\ 0)$
(B) $(-1,\ -2)$
(C) $(-1,\ 2)$
(D) $(1,\ -2)$

08 Which of the following could be the equation of asymptote of the hyperbola whose equation is $\dfrac{(y-2)^2}{4}-\dfrac{x^2}{9}=1$?

(A) $y=-\dfrac{2}{3}x$

(B) $y=-\dfrac{2}{3}x-2$

(C) $y=-\dfrac{3}{2}x-2$

(D) $y=\dfrac{2}{3}x+2$

5 Introduction to Vectors

01 Introduction to Vectors

There are two types of mathematical quantities that we will talk about in this chapter, scalar and vector. A scalar quantity has only its size or magnitude. Examples include height, length, area, volume, and more. Whereas, vector quantity has both magnitude and direction. Examples include force, velocity, acceleration, and more. To represent a vector quantity, we use a directed line segment as shown below.

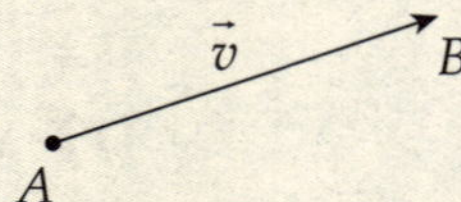

From the figure,

1. Point A is initial point and B is terminal point.
2. A vector is written as $\vec{v}$ or $\overrightarrow{AB}$.
3. The magnitude of vector $\overrightarrow{AB}$ is denoted by $|\overrightarrow{AB}|$ and it is the length of directed line segment.

02 Properties of a Vector, Part 1

1. If a vector has its initial point as the origin, we say that such vector $\vec{v}$ is in standard position.

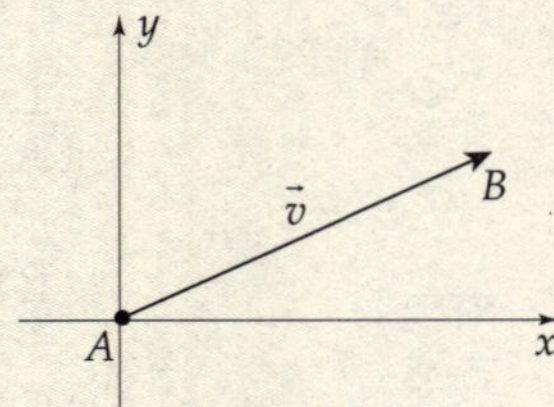

2. The component form of a vector with initial point $A(a_1, a_2)$ and terminal point $B(b_1, b_2)$ is written as $\vec{v}$ or $\overrightarrow{AB}=\langle b_1-a_1,\ b_2-a_2\rangle=\langle v_1,\ v_2\rangle$

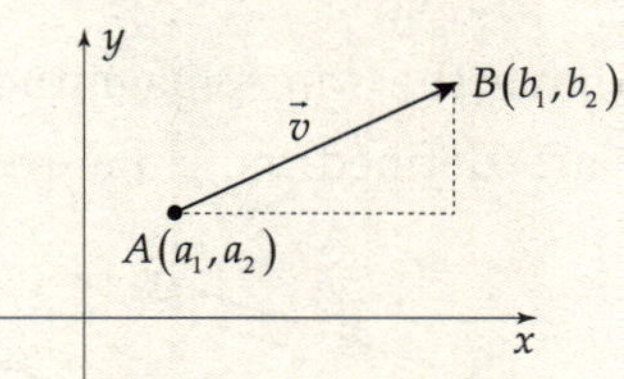

3. The magnitude of a vector $\vec{v}$ is given by $|\vec{v}|=\sqrt{(b_1-a_1)^2+(b_2-a_2)^2}=\sqrt{(v_1^2+v_2^2)}$.

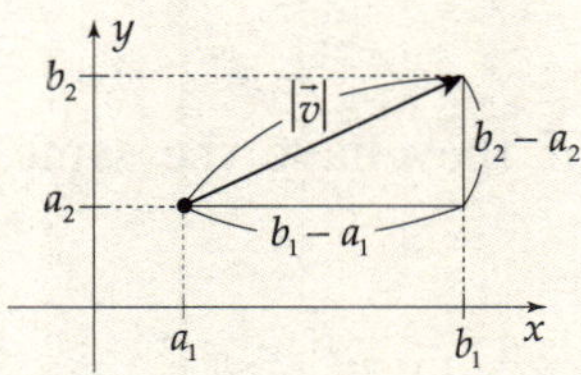

Example 1

Find the component form and magnitude of a vector $\vec{v}$ that has initial point $(2,\ -2)$ and terminal point $(5,\ 2)$.

Solution

The component form $\vec{v}=\langle 5-2,\ 2-(-2)\rangle=\langle 3,\ 4\rangle$

The magnitude $|\vec{v}|=\sqrt{3^2+4^2}=\sqrt{25}=5$

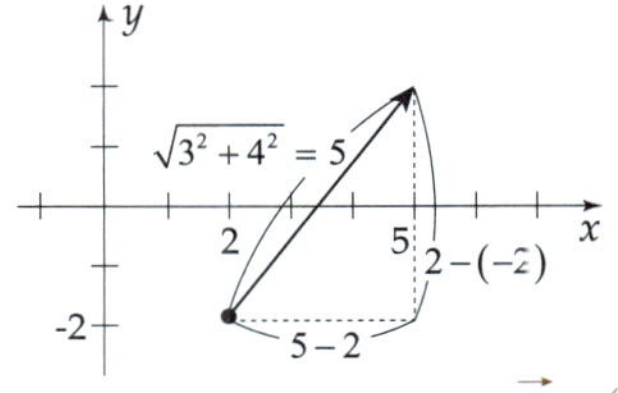

$\vec{v}=\langle 3,\ 4\rangle,\ |\vec{v}|=5$

Check Point 1

Solutions_Page 168

Find the component form and magnitude of a vector that has initial point $A(1,\ 4)$ and terminal point $B(-2,\ 2)$.

03 Properties of a Vector, Part 2

1. If two vectors $\vec{v}$ and $\vec{w}$ have the same magnitude and are pointing in the same direction, then $\vec{v}$ and $\vec{w}$ are defined as same vectors.

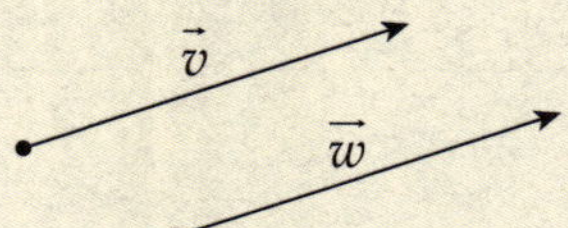

Note ←v_1, v_2→=←w_1, w_2→

2. Two vectors are opposite if they have the same magnitude and opposite direction.

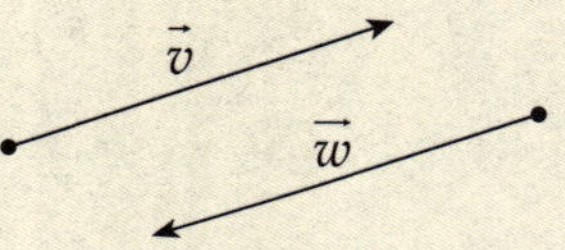

Note ←v_1, v_2→=-←w_1, w_2→ or -←v_1, v_2→=←w_1, w_2→

3. Two vectors are parallel if they have the same or opposite direction.
4. A vector $\vec{v}$ is called the unit vector if its magnitude $|\vec{v}|=1$. It is often written as $\vec{u}$.
5. A vector $\vec{v}$ is the zero vector if its magnitude $|\vec{v}|=0$. It is often written as $\vec{0}$. The component form of the zero vector $\vec{0}=\langle 0,\ 0\rangle$, where it has zero length and no direction.

04 Vector Operations

1. Geometric Vectors

To add two vectors geometrically, place the initial point of one vector at the terminal point of the other. The sum is formed by joining the initial point of the first vector and the terminal point of the second vector. This sum of the vectors is called the resultant vector. Refer to the following method when adding two vectors.

(1) Triangle Method

If $\vec{v}=\overrightarrow{AB}$ and $\vec{w}=\overrightarrow{BC}$, then the sum $\vec{v}+\vec{w}=\overrightarrow{AC}$ as shown in Figure below.

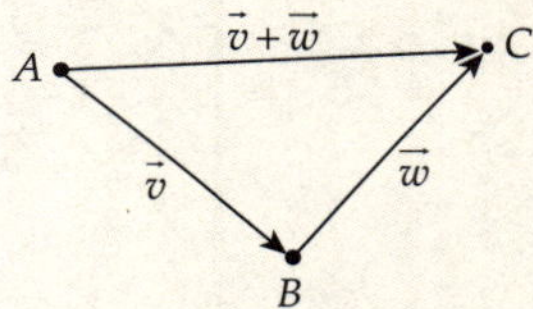

(2) Parallelogram Method

If $\vec{v}=\overrightarrow{AB}$ and $\vec{w}=\overrightarrow{AD}$, then the sum $\vec{v}+\vec{w}=\overrightarrow{AC}$ as shown in Figure below.

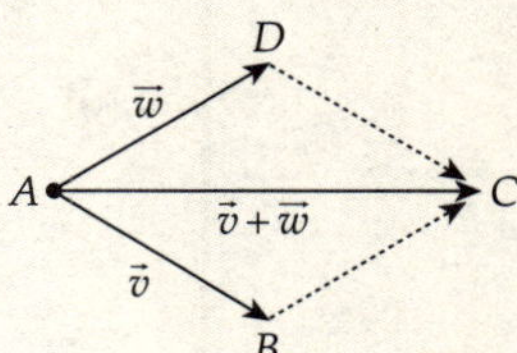

Since $\overrightarrow{AD}=\overrightarrow{BC}$, $\overrightarrow{AB}+\overrightarrow{AD}=\overrightarrow{AB}+\overrightarrow{BC}=\overrightarrow{AC}$.

(3) In the subtraction of two vectors, use the property that $\vec{v}-\vec{w}=\vec{v}+(-\vec{w})$. Refer to the figure below.

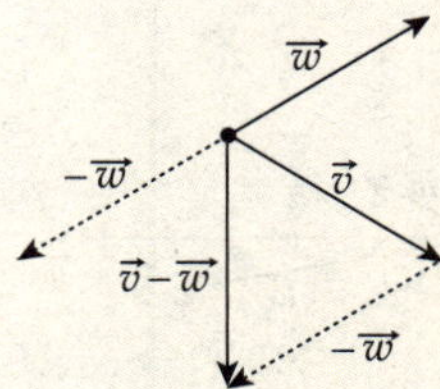

(4) Scalar multiplications are interpreted geometrically as follows.

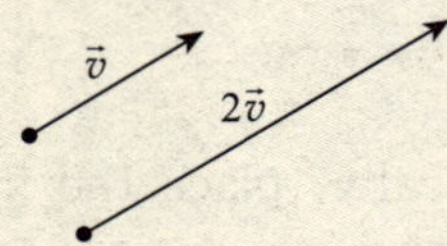

2. Algebraic Vectors

Let $\vec{v}=\langle v_1,\ v_2\rangle$ and $\vec{w}=\langle w_1,\ w_2\rangle$ be vectors and let a be a scalar. Then

(1) $\vec{v}+\vec{w}=\langle v_1+w_1,\ v_2+w_2\rangle$

(2) $\vec{v}-\vec{w}=\langle v_1-w_1,\ v_2-w_2\rangle$

(3) $a\vec{v}=\langle av_1,\ av_2\rangle$

Example 2

Let $\vec{v}=\langle 3,\ -2\rangle$ and $\vec{w}=\langle 2,\ 1\rangle$. Find the component form of the resultant vector and then sketch it.

① $3\vec{w}$　　② $\vec{v}+\vec{w}$　　③ $2\vec{w}-3\vec{v}$

Solution

① $3\vec{w}=3\langle 2,\ 1\rangle=\langle 6,\ 3\rangle$　　$3\vec{w}=\langle 6,\ 3\rangle$

② $\vec{v}+\vec{w}=\langle 3,\ -2\rangle+\langle 2,\ 1\rangle=\langle 3+2,\ -2+1\rangle=\langle 5,-1\rangle$　　$\vec{v}+\vec{w}=\langle 5,\ -1\rangle$

③ $2\vec{w}-3\vec{v}=2\langle 2,\ 1\rangle-3\langle 3,\ -2\rangle=\langle 4,\ 2\rangle-\langle 9,\ -6\rangle=\langle -5,\ 8\rangle$　　$2\vec{w}-3\vec{v}=\langle -5,\ 8\rangle$

①
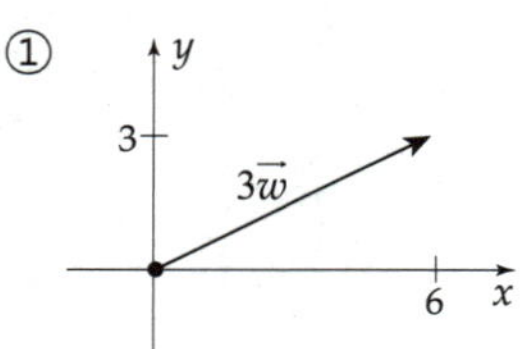

②
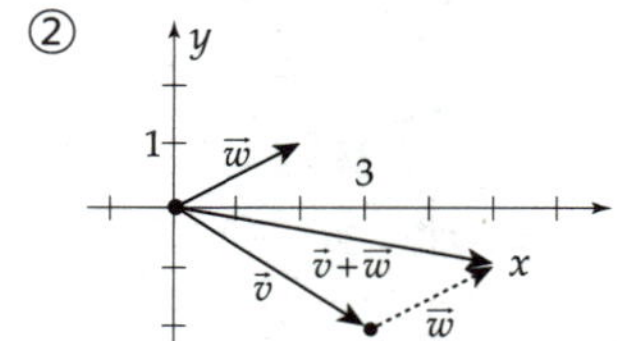

③
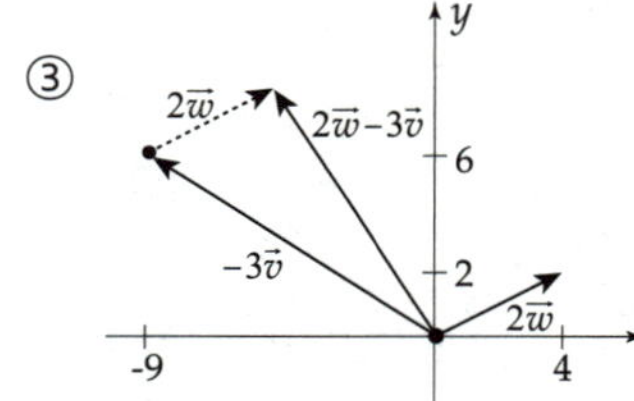

Check Point 2

Solutions_Page 168

Let $\vec{v}=\langle 2,\ 3\rangle$, $\vec{w}=\langle -2,\ 1\rangle$, and $\vec{x}=\langle 4,\ 0\rangle$.

Find the component form of the resultant vector and then sketch it.

① $\vec{v}-\vec{w}$

② $3\vec{v}-2\vec{x}$

05 Properties of Vector Operations

The following properties of vector addition and multiplication by a scalar are true.

1. Vector Addition
   (1) $\vec{v}+\vec{w}=\vec{w}+\vec{v}$
   (2) $(\vec{v}+\vec{w})+\vec{u}=\vec{w}+(\vec{v}+\vec{u})$
   (3) $\vec{v}+\vec{0}=\vec{0}+\vec{v}=\vec{v}$
   (4) $\vec{v}+(-\vec{v})=\vec{0}$

2. Vector Multiplied by a Scalar, a and b
   (1) $a(b\vec{v})=ab(\vec{v})$
   (2) $(a+b)\vec{v}=a\vec{v}+b\vec{v}$
   (3) $a(\vec{v}+\vec{w})=a\vec{v}+a\vec{w}$
   (4) $1\cdot\vec{v}=\vec{v}$ and $0\cdot\vec{v}=0$

3. Length of a vector
   (1) $|a\vec{v}|=|a|\,|\vec{v}|$

06 Unit Vectors

1. Definition of Unit Vector

   A unit vector $\vec{u}$ of a nonzero vector $\vec{v}$ is

$$\vec{u}=\frac{\vec{v}}{|\vec{v}|}=\frac{1}{|\vec{v}|}\vec{v},$$

   where the vector $\vec{u}$ is called the unit vector in the direction of $\vec{v}$.

2. Standard Unit Vector

   There are two standard unit vectors, $i=\langle 1,\ 0\rangle$ and $j=\langle 0,\ 1\rangle$, in a plane.

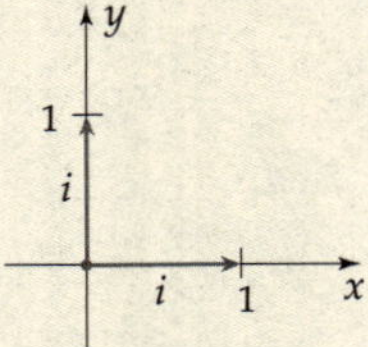

Any vector $\vec{v}$ can be written as an expression in terms of the standard unit vectors.

$$\begin{aligned}\vec{v}&=\langle v_1,\ v_2\rangle=\langle v_1,\ 0\rangle+\langle 0,\ v_2\rangle\\&=v_1\langle 1,\ 0\rangle+v_2\langle 0,\ 1\rangle=v_1 i+v_2 j.\end{aligned}$$

The scalars v_1 and v_2 are each called the horizontal and vertical components of the vector $\vec{v}$. The vector sum $v_1 i+v_2 j$ is called a linear combination of the vectors i and j. For example, the vector $\vec{v}=\langle 5,\ 12\rangle$ can be written as $\langle 5,\ 12\rangle=5i+12j$ or vice versa.

Example 3

Find a unit vector in the direction of $\vec{v}=\langle 3,\ 4\rangle$ and verify that it has a magnitude of 1.

Solution

The unit vector $\vec{u}$ in the direction of $\vec{v}$ is

$$\vec{u}=\frac{\vec{v}}{|\vec{v}|}=\frac{\langle 3,\ 4\rangle}{\sqrt{3^2+4^2}}=\frac{\langle 3,\ 4\rangle}{5}=\left\langle \frac{3}{5},\ \frac{4}{5}\right\rangle$$

Its magnitude is

$$\sqrt{\left(\frac{3}{5}\right)^2+\left(\frac{4}{5}\right)^2}=\sqrt{\frac{9}{25}+\frac{16}{25}}=\sqrt{\frac{25}{25}}=1$$

$\vec{u}=\left\langle \frac{3}{5},\ \frac{4}{5}\right\rangle$, $\sqrt{\left(\frac{3}{5}\right)^2+\left(\frac{4}{5}\right)^2}=1$

Check Point 3

Solutions_Page 168

Find a unit vector in the direction of the given vector.

① $\vec{v}=\langle -6,\ 8\rangle$ ② $\vec{w}=5i-12j$

07 Direction Angles

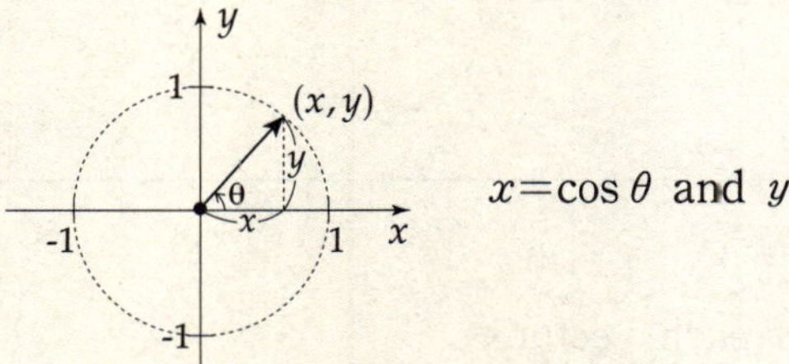

$x=\cos\theta$ and $y=\sin\theta$

Assume the unit vector $\vec{u}$ is in standard position at angle θ from the positive x-axis as shown in Figure above. Then,

$$\vec{u}=\langle x,\ y\rangle=\langle\cos\theta,\ \sin\theta\rangle=\cos\theta i+\sin\theta j$$

Because $\vec{u}=\frac{\vec{v}}{|\vec{v}|}$, $\vec{v}=|\vec{v}|\cdot\vec{u}=|\vec{v}|\langle\cos\theta,\ \sin\theta\rangle=|\vec{v}|\cos\theta i+|\vec{v}|\sin\theta j$.

Direction angle θ for the vector $\vec{u}$ is defined as

$$\tan\theta=\frac{y}{x}\ \rightarrow\ \theta=\left|\tan^{-1}\left(\frac{y}{x}\right)\right|$$

Note that angle θ is a reference angle if it is in Quadrant II, III, or IV.

Example 4

Find the component form of the vector $\vec{v}$ with direction angle $30°$ and magnitude 8.

Solution

$$\vec{v}=|\vec{v}|\langle\cos\theta,\ \sin\theta\rangle=8\langle\cos 30°,\ \sin 30°\rangle=8\left\langle\frac{\sqrt{3}}{2},\ \frac{1}{2}\right\rangle=\langle 4\sqrt{3},\ 4\rangle \text{ or } \vec{v}=4\sqrt{3}\,i+4j$$

$\vec{v}=\langle 4\sqrt{3},\ 4\rangle$ or $\vec{v}=4\sqrt{3}\,i+4j$

Check Point 4

Solutions_Page 168

Find the component form of the vector.

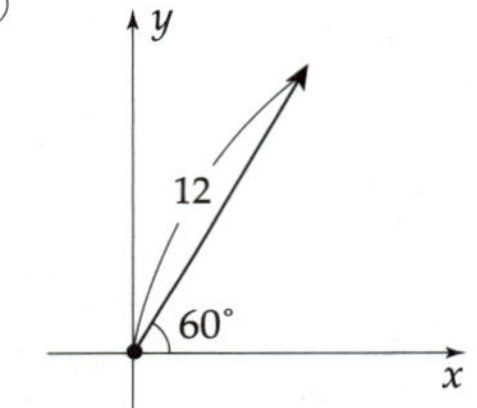

②

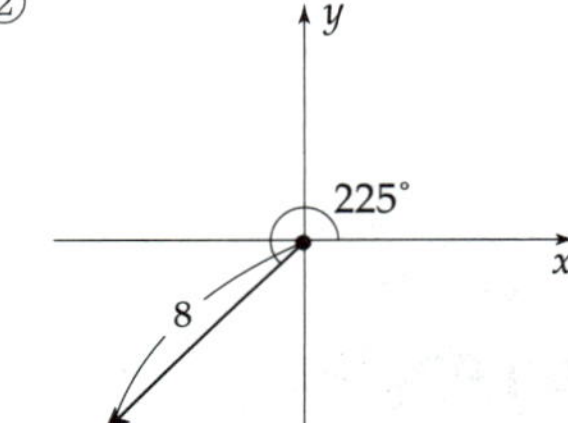

Example 5

Find the direction angle of each vector.

① $\vec{v}=\langle 5,\ 2\rangle$ ② $\vec{w}=\langle -2,\ 3\rangle$

Solution

① $\vec{v}=\langle 5,\ 2\rangle$

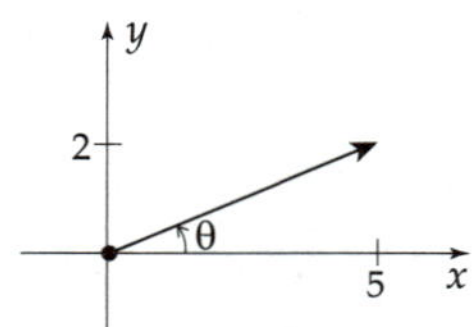

$\tan\theta=\frac{2}{5}$, $\theta=\tan^{-1}\left(\frac{2}{5}\right)=21.801°$

$\theta=\tan^{-1}\left(\frac{2}{5}\right)=21.801°$

So the direction angle is $\theta=21.801°$.

$\theta=21.801°$

② $\overrightarrow{w}=\langle -2,\ 3\rangle$

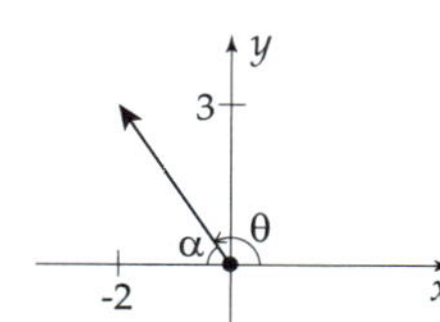

$\tan\alpha=\dfrac{3}{2}$, $\alpha=\tan^{-1}\left(\dfrac{3}{2}\right)=56.310°$.

So the direction angle is $\theta=180°-56.310°=123.690°$.

$\theta=123.690°$

Check Point 5

Solutions_Page 168

Find the direction angle of the vector.

① $\overrightarrow{v}=\langle 5,\ -3\rangle$

② $\overrightarrow{w}=-i-4j$

Review Exercise

01 What is the magnitude of the vector $\vec{v}$ with initial point $(-2,\ 2)$ and terminal point $(0,\ -1)$?

02 Let $\vec{v}=\langle 3,\ -1\rangle$, $\vec{w}=\langle 5,\ 3\rangle$, and $\vec{x}=\langle -2,\ -3\rangle$. Find the component form and sketch the resultant vector.

(1) $\vec{w}-\vec{x}$ (2) $2\vec{v}+3\vec{x}$

03

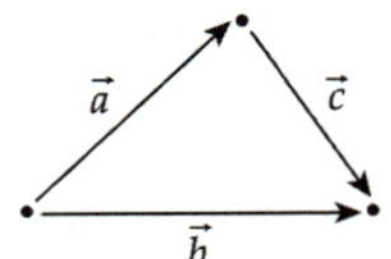

Which of the following denotes the vector operation shown above?

(A) $\vec{a}+\vec{b}=\vec{c}$ (B) $\vec{a}-\vec{b}=\vec{c}$
(C) $\vec{b}+\vec{c}=\vec{a}$ (D) $\vec{a}+\vec{c}=\vec{b}$
(E) $\vec{c}-\vec{a}=\vec{b}$

04 If the magnitude of vectors $\vec{v}$ and $\vec{w}$ are 4 and 8, respectively, then which of the following could NOT be the magnitude of vector $\vec{v}-\vec{w}$?

(A) 4 (B) 7
(C) 9 (D) 12
(E) 13

05 Find a unit vector in the direction of the given vector.

(1) $\vec{v}=\langle -3,\ 4\rangle$

(2) $\vec{x}=-4i-5j$

06 Find the component form of the vector.

(1)

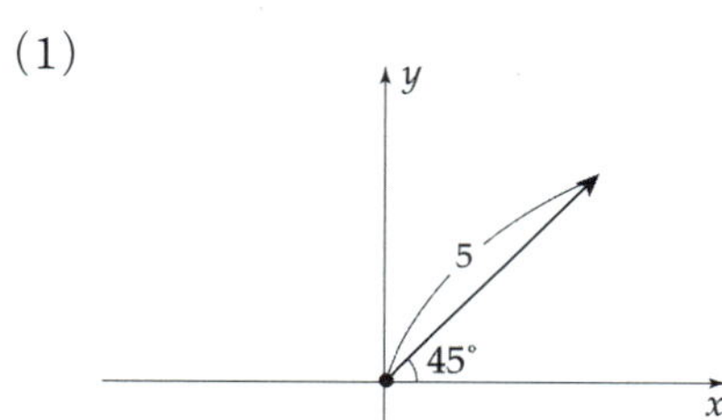

(2)

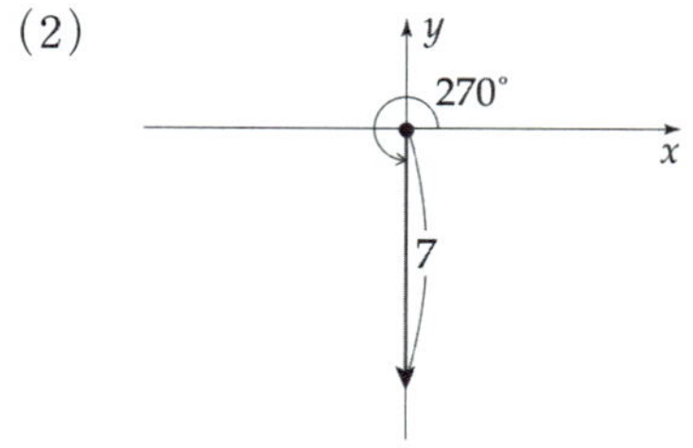

07 Find the direction angle of the vector.

(1) $\vec{v}=\langle 4,\ -7\rangle$

(2) $\vec{w}=-5i+4j$

08

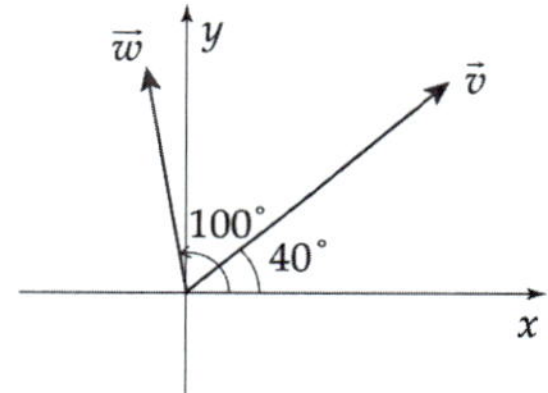

In Figure above, if $|\vec{v}|=6$ and $|\vec{w}|=2$, then what is the value of $|\vec{v}-\vec{w}|$?

6 Dot Product of the Vectors

01 Dot Product of Two Vectors

In this section, we will learn another vector operation, the dot product. The dot product of two vectors results in a scalar, not a vector. Here is the definition of the dot product. Let $\vec{v}=\langle v_1, v_2\rangle$ and $\vec{w}=\langle w_1, w_2\rangle$. Then, their dot product, denoted as $\vec{v}\cdot\vec{w}$, is defined by

$$\vec{v}\cdot\vec{w}=v_1w_1+v_2w_2$$

02 Properties of the Dot Product

The following properties of dot product of vectors are true. Let $\vec{v}=\langle v_1, v_2\rangle$, $\vec{w}=\langle w_1, w_2\rangle$, and $x=\langle x_1, x_2\rangle$ be vectors and let a be a scalar.

1. $\vec{v}\cdot\vec{w}=\vec{w}\cdot\vec{v}$
2. $\vec{v}\cdot\vec{v}=|\vec{v}|^2$
3. $0\cdot\vec{v}=0$
4. $\vec{v}\cdot(\vec{w}+\vec{x})=\vec{v}\cdot\vec{w}+\vec{v}\cdot\vec{x}$
5. $a(\vec{v}\cdot\vec{w})=(a\vec{v})\cdot\vec{w}=\vec{v}\cdot(a\vec{w})$

Proof

1. $\vec{v}\cdot\vec{w}=v_1w_{1+}v_2w_2=w_1v_1+w_2v_2=\vec{w}\cdot\vec{v}$
2. $\vec{v}\cdot\vec{v}=v_1{}^2+v_2{}^2=(\sqrt{v_1{}^2+v_2{}^2})^2=|\vec{v}|^2$
3. $0\cdot\vec{v}=0\cdot v_1+0\cdot v_2=0$
4. $\vec{v}\cdot(\vec{w}+\vec{x})=\vec{v}\cdot\langle w_1+x_1,\ w_2+x_2\rangle$
$$=v_1(w_1+x_1)+v_2(w_2+x_2)$$
$$=(v_1w_1+v_1x_1)+(v_2w_2+v_2x_2)$$
$$=(v_1w_1+v_2w_2)+(v_1x_1+v_2x_2)=\vec{v}\cdot\vec{w}+\vec{v}\cdot\vec{x}$$
5. $a(\vec{v}\cdot\vec{w})=a(v_1w_1+v_2w_2)$
$$=(av_1)w_1+(av_2)w_2$$
$$=\langle av_1,\ av_2\rangle\cdot\langle w_1,\ w_2\rangle=(a\vec{v})\cdot\vec{w}$$

Example 1

Find the dot product of $\vec{v}$ and $\vec{w}$.

① $\vec{v}=\langle 2, 5\rangle$, $\vec{w}=\langle 4, 1\rangle$

② $\vec{v}=\langle -3, 1\rangle$, $\vec{w}=\langle 5, 0\rangle$

Solution

① $\vec{v}\cdot\vec{w}=\langle 2, 5\rangle\cdot\langle 4, 1\rangle=(2)(4)+(5)(1)=13.$ $\vec{v}\cdot\vec{w}=13$

② $\vec{v}\cdot\vec{w}=\langle -3, 1\rangle\cdot\langle 5, 0\rangle=(-3)(5)+(1)(0)=-15.$ $\vec{v}\cdot\vec{w}=-15$

Check Point 1

Solutions_Page 170

Find the dot product of $\vec{v}$ and $\vec{w}$.

① $\vec{v}=\left\langle -2, \frac{5}{2}\right\rangle$, $\vec{w}=\langle 5, 4\rangle$

② $\vec{v}=3i-4j$, $\vec{w}=-2i-j$

03 The Angle Between Two Vectors

Let $\vec{v}$ and $\vec{w}$ be two nonzero vectors in standard position as shown in Figure below. The angle between $\vec{v}$ and $\vec{w}$, θ, can be found using the dot product. Remember θ is always $0<\theta<180°$.

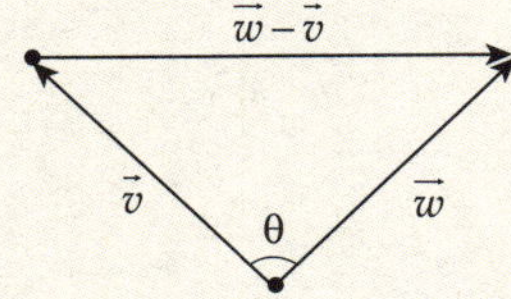

Proof

Consider a triangle determined by vectors $\vec{v}$, $\vec{w}$, and $\vec{w}-\vec{v}$. By the Law of Cosine,

$$|\vec{w}-\vec{v}|^2=|\vec{v}|^2+|\vec{w}|^2-2|\vec{v}||\vec{w}|\cos\theta$$
$$(\vec{w}-\vec{v})\cdot(\vec{w}-\vec{v})=|\vec{v}|^2+|\mathrm{w}|^2-2|\vec{v}||\vec{w}|\cos\theta$$
$$\vec{w}\cdot\vec{w}-\vec{w}\cdot\vec{v}-\vec{v}\cdot\vec{w}+\vec{v}\cdot\vec{v}=|\vec{v}|^2+|\mathrm{w}|^2-2|\vec{v}||\vec{w}|\cos\theta$$
$$|\vec{w}|^2-2\vec{v}\cdot\vec{w}+|\vec{v}|^2=|\vec{v}|^2+|\mathrm{w}|^2-2|\vec{v}||\vec{w}|\cos\theta$$
$$-2\vec{v}\cdot\vec{w}=-2|\vec{v}||\vec{w}|\cos\theta$$
$$\cos\theta=\frac{\vec{v}\cdot\vec{w}}{|\vec{v}||\vec{w}|},\ \theta=\cos^{-1}\left(\frac{\vec{v}\cdot\vec{w}}{|\vec{v}||\vec{w}|}\right)$$

Example 2

Find the angle between two vectors, $\vec{v}=\langle 3,\ 4\rangle$ and $\vec{w}=\langle -2,\ 5\rangle$.

Solution

$$\cos\theta=\frac{\vec{v}\cdot\vec{w}}{|\vec{v}||\vec{w}|}=\frac{\langle 3,\ 4\rangle\cdot\langle -2,\ 5\rangle}{\sqrt{3^2+4^2}\sqrt{(-2)^2+5^2}}=\frac{-6+20}{\sqrt{25}\sqrt{29}}=\frac{14}{5\sqrt{29}}$$

$$\theta=\cos^{-1}\left(\frac{14}{5\sqrt{29}}\right)\approx 58.671°.$$

$\theta=58.671°$

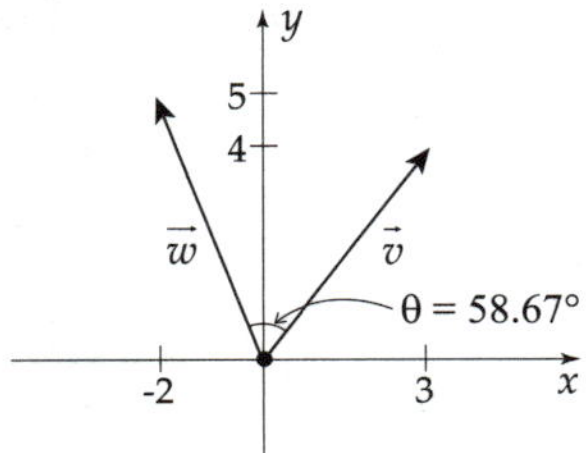

Check Point 2 Solutions_Page 170

Find the angle θ between two vectors.

① $\vec{v}=\langle 2,\ 5\rangle$, $\vec{w}=\langle 4,\ -1\rangle$

② $\vec{v}=\langle -4,\ -2\rangle$, $\vec{w}=\langle 3,\ -2\rangle$

04 Orthogonal Vectors

$\cos\theta = \dfrac{\vec{v}\cdot\vec{w}}{|\vec{v}||\vec{w}|}$ can be expressed as $\vec{v}\cdot\vec{w} = |\vec{v}||\vec{w}|\cos\theta$. Vectors $\vec{v}$ and $\vec{w}$ are orthogonal(meaning perpendicular) if and only if $\vec{v}\cdot\vec{w}=0$. This is because two vectors are orthogonal when $\theta=90°$ and this makes $\vec{v}\cdot\vec{w} = |\vec{v}||\vec{w}|\cos 90° = 0$.

Example 3

State whether two vectors are orthogonal.

① $\vec{v}=\langle 3,\ 2\rangle$, $\vec{w}=\langle -4,\ 6\rangle$

② $\vec{v}=\langle -2,\ 1\rangle$, $\vec{w}=\langle 3,\ 5\rangle$

Solution

① Two vectors $\vec{v}=\langle 3,\ 2\rangle$ and $\vec{w}=\langle -4,\ 6\rangle$ are orthogonal because $\vec{v}\cdot\vec{w}=(3)(-4)+(2)(6)=0$.

② Two vectors $\vec{v}=\langle -2,\ 1\rangle$ and $\vec{w}=\langle 3,\ 5\rangle$ are NOT orthogonal because $\vec{v}\cdot\vec{w}=(-2)(3)+(1)(5)\neq 0$.

Check Point 3

Solutions_Page 171

State whether two vectors are orthogonal.

① $\vec{v}=\langle -2,\ -4\rangle$, $\vec{w}=\left\langle -\dfrac{1}{4},\ \dfrac{2}{3}\right\rangle$

② $\vec{v}=5j$, $\vec{w}=-4i$

05 Projecting One Vector onto Another

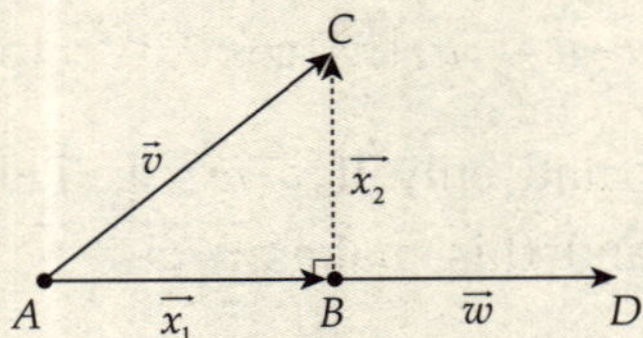

Let $\vec{v}=(\overrightarrow{AC})$ and $\vec{w}=(\overrightarrow{AD})$ be nonzero vectors such that $\vec{v}=\vec{x_1}+\vec{x_2}$, where $\vec{x_1}$ and $\vec{x_2}$ are orthogonal and $\vec{x_1}$ is parallel to $\vec{w}$, as shown in Figure above.
The vector $\vec{x_1}$ is the projection of $\vec{v}$ onto $\vec{w}$ and is denoted by $\vec{x_1}=\text{proj}_w\, v$.
Now let's derive the formula.

$\vec{v}=\vec{x_1}+\vec{x_2}=a\vec{w}+\vec{x_2}$, where a is a constant.
$\vec{v}\cdot\vec{w}=(a\vec{w}+\vec{x_2})\cdot\vec{w}$ → Multiply both sides by $\vec{w}$
$\vec{v}\cdot\vec{w}=a\vec{w}\cdot\vec{w}+(\vec{x_2})\cdot\vec{w}$
$\vec{v}\cdot\vec{w}=a|\vec{w}|^2+0$ → $(\vec{x_2})\cdot\vec{w}=0$ because $\vec{x_2}$ and $\vec{w}$ are orthogonal vectors

Now, we have $\vec{v}\cdot\vec{w}=a|\vec{w}|^2$, $a=\dfrac{\vec{v}\cdot\vec{w}}{|\vec{w}|^2}$. Therefore,

$$\vec{x_1}=\text{proj}_w\, v=a\vec{w}=\frac{\vec{v}\cdot\vec{w}}{|\vec{w}|^2}\vec{w} \Rightarrow \text{proj}_w\, v=\frac{\vec{v}\cdot\vec{w}}{|\vec{w}|^2}\vec{w}$$

If $\vec{x_1}$ is identified, $\vec{x_2}$ can be easily identified as
$\vec{v}=\vec{x_1}+\vec{x_2}$, $\vec{x_2}=\vec{v}-\vec{x_1}$

Example 4

Find the vector projection of $\vec{v}=\langle 4,\ 2\rangle$ onto $\vec{w}=\langle 5,\ -2\rangle$. Then write $\vec{v}$ as the sum of two orthogonal vectors.

Solution

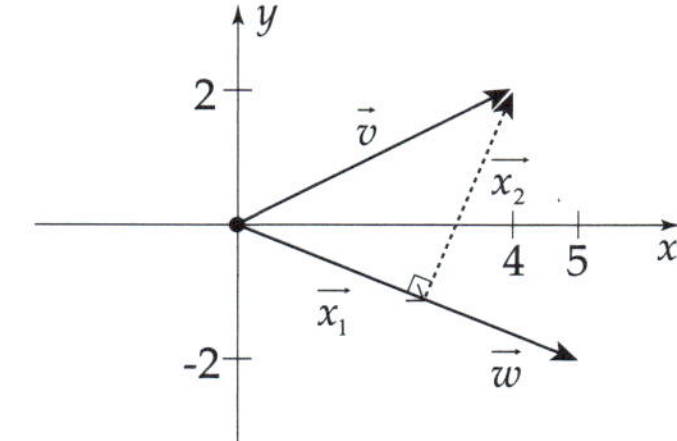

Let $\vec{v}=\vec{x_1}+\vec{x_2}$, where $\vec{x_1}=\text{proj}_w\ v$ and $\vec{x_2}=\vec{v}-\vec{x_1}$. Then,

$$\vec{x_1}=\text{proj}_w\ \vec{v}=\frac{\vec{v}\cdot\vec{w}}{|\vec{w}|^2}\vec{w}=\frac{\langle 4,\ 2\rangle\cdot\langle 5,\ -2\rangle}{(\sqrt{5^2+(-2)^2})^2}\langle 5,\ -2\rangle$$

$$=\frac{16}{29}\langle 5,\ -2\rangle=\left\langle\frac{80}{29},\ -\frac{32}{29}\right\rangle.$$

$$\vec{x_2}=\vec{v}-(\vec{x_1})=\langle 4,\ 2\rangle-\left\langle\frac{80}{29},\ -\frac{32}{29}\right\rangle=\left\langle\frac{36}{29},\ \frac{90}{29}\right\rangle.$$

So $\vec{v}=\vec{x_1}+\vec{x_2}=\left\langle\frac{80}{29},\ -\frac{32}{29}\right\rangle+\left\langle\frac{36}{29},\ \frac{90}{29}\right\rangle$

$$\vec{v}=\vec{x_1}+\vec{x_2}=\left\langle\frac{80}{29},\ -\frac{32}{29}\right\rangle+\left\langle\frac{36}{29},\ \frac{90}{29}\right\rangle$$

Check Point 4

Solutions_Page 171

Find the vector projection of $\vec{v}$ onto $\vec{w}$. Then write $\vec{v}$ as a sum of two orthogonal vectors.

① $\vec{v}=\langle 4,\ 1\rangle,\ \vec{w}=\langle 3,\ -4\rangle$

② $\vec{v}=\langle -6,\ 2\rangle,\ \vec{w}=\langle -4,\ 5\rangle$

Review Exercise

01 Find the dot product of $\vec{v}$ and $\vec{w}$, and state whether the vectors are orthogonal.

(1) $\vec{v}=\langle 3,\ 4\rangle$, $\vec{w}=\langle -1,\ 2\rangle$

(2) $\vec{v}=-2i-3j$, $\vec{w}=6i-4j$

02 Given $\vec{v}=\langle 2,\ 1\rangle$, $\vec{w}=\langle -1,\ 4\rangle$, and $\vec{x}=\langle 2,\ -3\rangle$, find the expression.

(1) $2\vec{v}\cdot\vec{w}$

(2) $\vec{x}\cdot\vec{x}$

(3) $(\vec{v}\cdot 3\vec{w})\vec{x}$

(4) $(\vec{v}\cdot\vec{w})-(\vec{v}\cdot\vec{x})$

03 Find the angle θ between the vectors.

(1) $\vec{v}=\langle 1,\ 3\rangle$, $\vec{w}=\langle 3,\ -2\rangle$

(2) $\vec{v}=4i-5j$, $\vec{w}=7i$

04 Find the vector projection of $\vec{v}$ onto $\vec{w}$. Then write $\vec{v}$ as a sum of two orthogonal vectors.

(1) $\vec{v}=\langle 5,\ 3\rangle$, $\vec{w}=\langle 3,\ -3\rangle$

(2) $\vec{v}=-4i+4j$, $\vec{w}=i+2j$

7 Application of Vectors

Vectors can be used to model any quantity possessing both magnitude and direction. In this section, we will study several types of vectors that apply to the real world.

01 Velocity

The velocity of a moving object is described by a vector because velocity has both magnitude and direction. The magnitude of velocity is speed. In this application problem, there is an angle called bearing. A bearing is an angle measured in degrees clockwise from north to east. Bearings are often used for navigation.

Example 1

An airplane is flying on a bearing of 53° at 460 miles per hour. Find the component form of the vector that represents the velocity of an airplane.

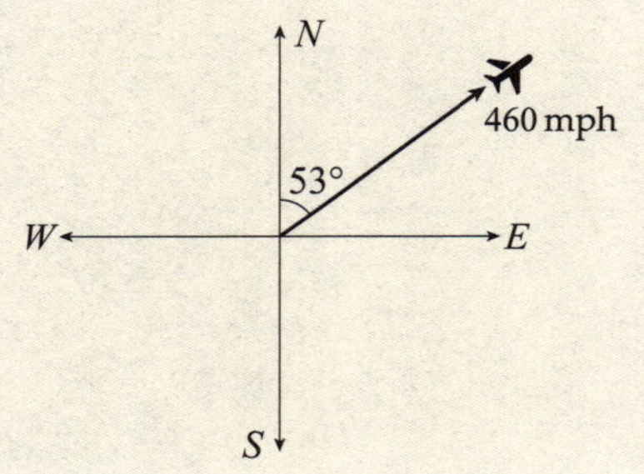

Solution

If we let $\vec{v}$ be the velocity of the airplane, $\vec{v}$ has a magnitude of 460 and direction angle of $\theta=90°-53°=37°$.

$$\vec{v}=|\vec{v}|\langle\cos\theta,\ \sin\theta\ \rangle=460\langle\cos 37°,\ \sin 37°\rangle$$
$$=\langle 460\cos 37°,\ 460\sin 37°\rangle\approx\ \langle 367.372, 276.835\rangle$$

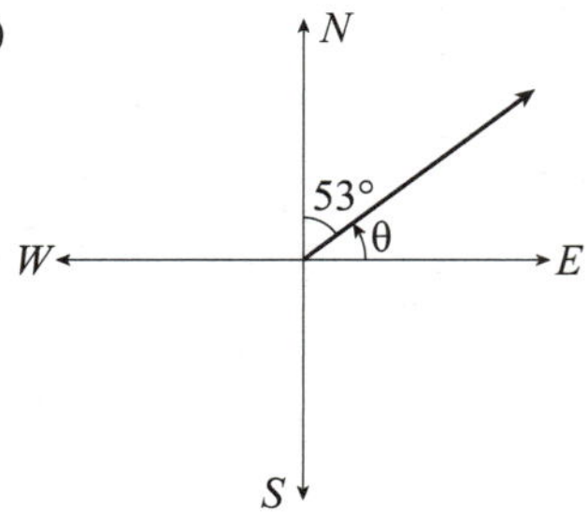

Check Point 1

Solutions_Page 172

An airplane is flying on a bearing of 135° at 380 miles per hour. Determine the component form of the velocity of the airplane.

Example 2

An airplane took off from Los Angeles International Airport and is flying at a speed of 630 miles per hour with a bearing of 300°. During the flight, the airplane encounters a wind with a velocity of 55 miles per hour in the direction of $S30°W$. What are the actual speed and direction of the airplane?

Solution

Let the velocity of the airplane and wind be $\vec{a}$ and $\vec{w}$.

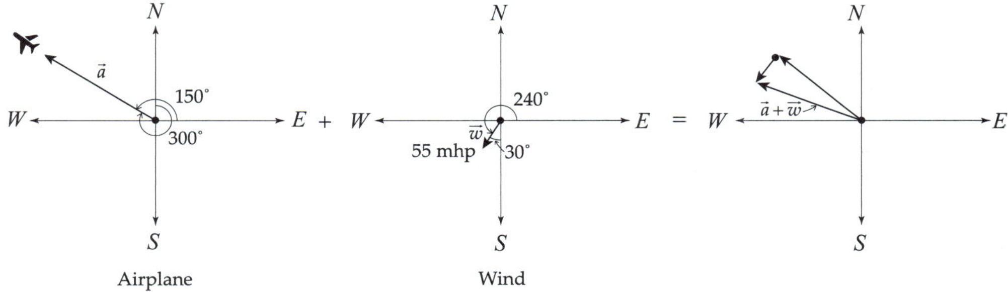

The velocity of the airplane is

$$\vec{a}=|\vec{a}|\langle\cos\theta°,\ \sin\theta°\rangle$$
$$=630\langle\cos 150°,\ \sin 150°\rangle$$
$$=\langle -315\sqrt{3},\ 315\rangle$$

The velocity of the wind is

$$\vec{w}=|\vec{w}|\langle\cos\theta°,\ \sin\theta°\rangle$$
$$=55\langle\cos 240°,\ \sin 240°\rangle$$
$$=\left\langle -\frac{55}{2},\ -\frac{55\sqrt{3}}{2}\right\rangle$$

So the velocity of the airplane with the wind is

$$\vec{v}=\vec{a}+\vec{w}=\langle -315\sqrt{3},\ 315\rangle+\left\langle -\frac{55}{2},\ -\frac{55\sqrt{3}}{2}\right\rangle\approx\langle -573.096,\ 267.369\rangle$$

Now the speed of the airplane with wind is

$$|\vec{v}|=\sqrt{(-573.096)^2+(267.369)^2}\approx 632.396\ \text{mph}$$

Finally, let us find the direction angle θ.

$$\tan\alpha=\frac{267.369}{573.096}$$

$$\alpha=\tan^{-1}\left(\frac{267.369}{573.096}\right)\approx 25.011^\circ.$$

which implies that $\theta=180^\circ-25.011^\circ=154.989^\circ$.
So the airplane is flying at 632.396 mph in the direction of 154.989°.

632.396 miles per hour in the direction of 154.989°

Check Point 2

Solutions_Page 172

An airplane is traveling to New York at 540 mph with a bearing of 230°. At certain point, the airplane encounters a wind blowing at 38 mph in the direction of $S55^\circ W$. Find the actual speed and direction of the airplane.

02 Force

Force is another quantity that can be represented by a vector. When all the forces that act upon an object are balanced, then the object is said to be in a state of equilibrium, and their resultant equals zero.

Example 3

A 100 lb box is at the top of a ramp that is inclined 30° to the horizontal, as shown in the figure. Determine the magnitude of the force needed to prevent the box from sliding down the ramp(A force is applied parallel to the ramp and assume that friction is not a factor).

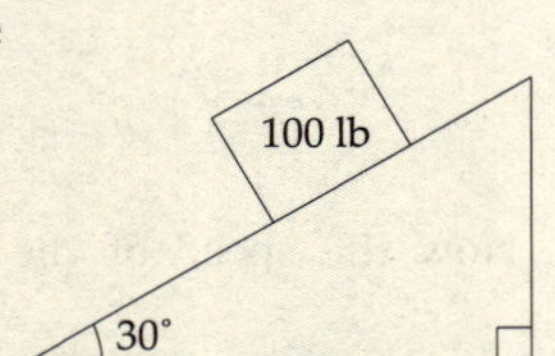

Solution

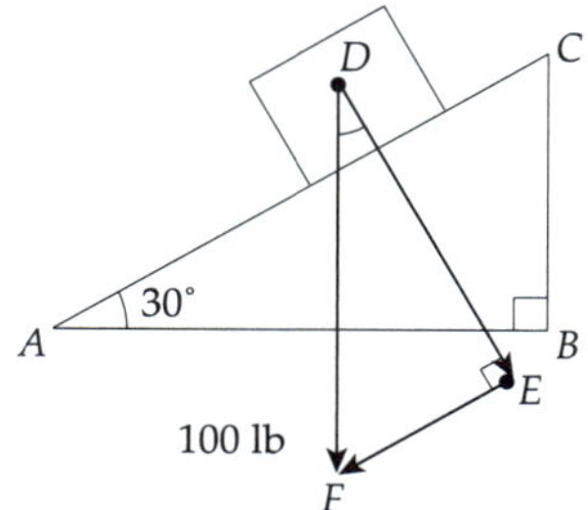

Note that △ABC and △DEF are similar. Now, we need to find $\overrightarrow{EF}$.

$$\overrightarrow{EF}=\overrightarrow{DF}\sin 30°=100\sin 30°=50 \text{ lb}.$$

The magnitude of force needed to prevent the box from sliding is 50 lb.

50 lb

Check Point 3

Solutions_Page 173

A 75 lb box is at the top of a ramp that is inclined at 45° to the horizontal. Determine the magnitude of the force needed to prevent the box from sliding down the ramp(A force is applied parallel to the ramp and assume that friction is not a factor).

Example 4

A large steel ball with 450 lb is supported by two wires, as shown in the figure. Find the magnitude of the tension in each wire.

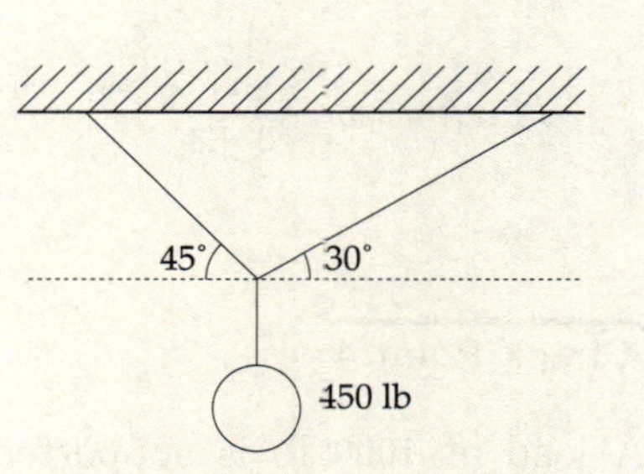

Solution

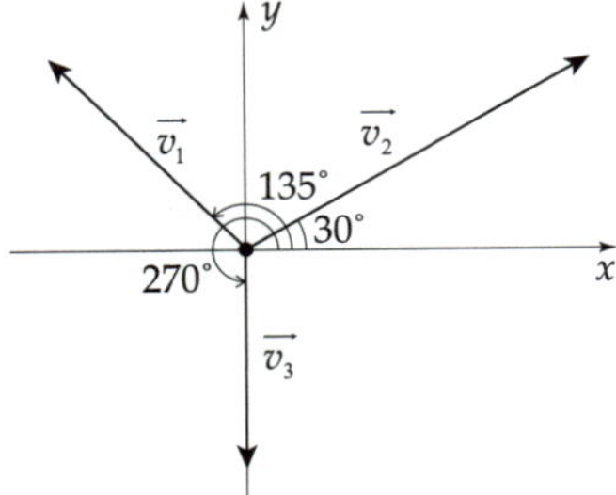

Since the ball is not accelerating, it is in a state of equilibrium. So their resultant $\vec{v_1}+\vec{v_2}+\vec{v_3}=0$.

$$\vec{v_1}=|\vec{v_1}|\langle\cos 135°,\ \sin 135°\rangle=|\vec{v_1}|\left\langle-\frac{\sqrt{2}}{2},\ \frac{\sqrt{2}}{2}\right\rangle$$

$$\vec{v_2}=|\vec{v_2}|\langle\cos 30°,\ \sin 30°\rangle=|\vec{v_2}|\left\langle\frac{\sqrt{3}}{2},\ \frac{1}{2}\right\rangle$$

$$\vec{v_3}=450\langle\cos 270°,\ \sin 270°\rangle=450\langle 0,\ -1\rangle=\langle 0,\ -450\rangle.$$

Now we set the sum of the components equal to 0 and solve for $|\vec{v_1}|$ and $|\vec{v_2}|$.

$$-\frac{\sqrt{2}}{2}|\vec{v_1}|+\frac{\sqrt{3}}{2}|\vec{v_2}|=0 \quad\rightarrow\quad -\sqrt{2}|\vec{v_1}|+\sqrt{3}|\vec{v_2}|=0 \quad\rightarrow\ (1)$$

$$\frac{\sqrt{2}}{2}|\vec{v_1}|+\frac{1}{2}|\vec{v_2}|-450=0 \quad\rightarrow\quad \sqrt{2}|\vec{v_1}|+|\vec{v_2}|=900 \quad\rightarrow\ (2)$$

Solve the system of equations above to eliminate $|\vec{v_1}|$ by adding (1) and (2) :

$$\sqrt{3}|\vec{v_2}|+|\vec{v_2}|=900,\ \ |\vec{v_2}|(\sqrt{3}+1)=900,\ \ |\vec{v_2}|=\frac{900}{\sqrt{3}+1}$$

Finally, substitute $|\vec{v_2}|$ into equation (2) to find $|\vec{v_1}|$.

$$\sqrt{2}\,|\vec{v_1}|+\frac{900}{\sqrt{3}+1}=900$$

$$\sqrt{2}\,|\vec{v_1}|=900-\frac{900}{\sqrt{3}+1},\ \ |\vec{v_1}|=\frac{1}{\sqrt{2}}\left(900-\frac{900}{\sqrt{3}+1}\right)$$

$|\vec{v_1}|=\frac{900}{\sqrt{3}+1}$ and $|\vec{v_2}|=\frac{1}{\sqrt{2}}\left(900-\frac{900}{\sqrt{3}+1}\right)$

Check Point 4

Solutions_Page 173

A load of 1000 lb is supported by two wires, as shown in the figure. Find the magnitude of tension in each wire.

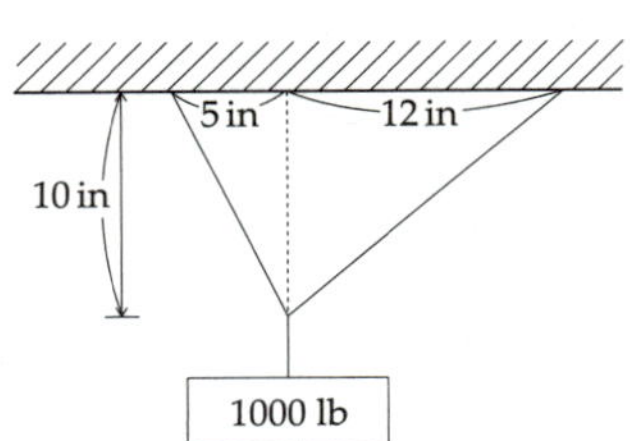

03 Work

Work done on an object is defined as a constant force $\overrightarrow{F}$ displacing an object by an amount $\overrightarrow{d}$, and it is given by $W=\overrightarrow{F}\cdot\overrightarrow{d}$.

Example 5

David pulls a rope attached to a box by exerting a force of 55 lb, as shown in the figure. Find the work done in moving the box 8 feet(The weight of the rope is not a factor).

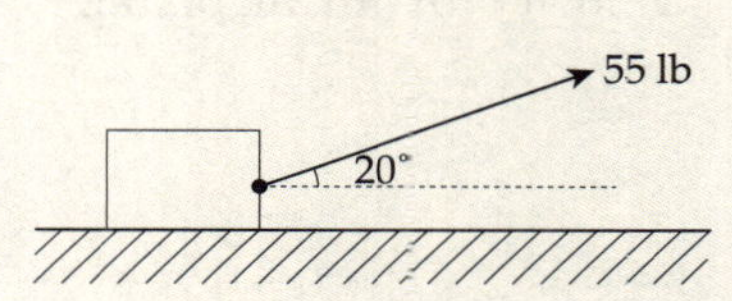

Solution

The horizontal force acting on the box is $\overrightarrow{F}=|\overrightarrow{F}|\cos\theta$.

So the work done is $W=\overrightarrow{F}\cdot\overrightarrow{d}=|\overrightarrow{F}|\cos\theta\cdot\overrightarrow{d}=55\cos 20°\cdot 8 \approx 413.465\ ft-lb$.

$W=413.465\ ft-lb$

Check Point 5

Solutions_Page 173

Find the work done lifting a 1200 lb box 7 feet off the floor.

Review Exercise

01

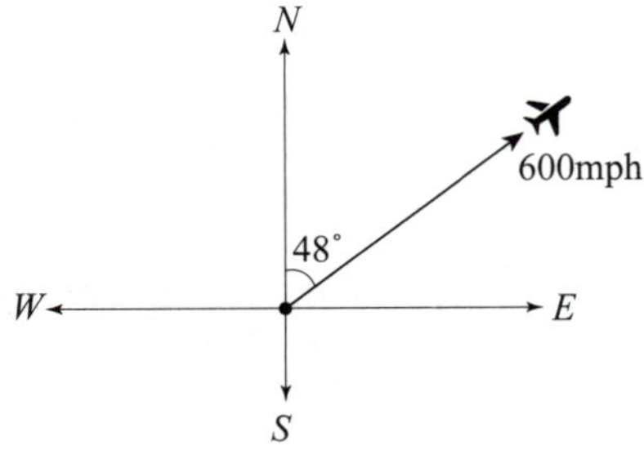

An airplane is flying on a bearing of 48°at 600 miles per hour, as shown in Figure above. Find the component form of the vector represents the velocity of an airplane.

02

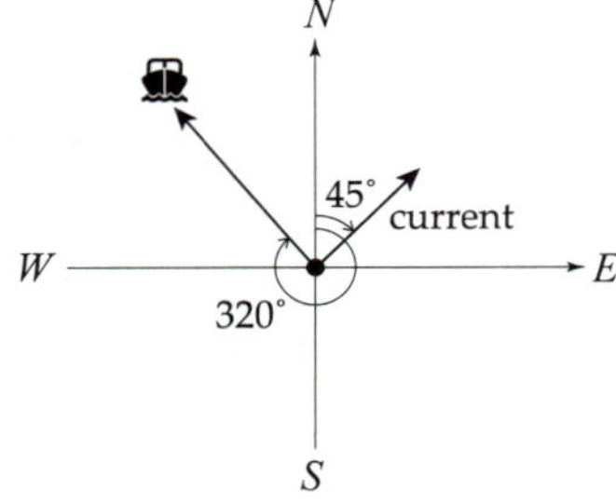

A ship is heading on a bearing of 320° at 45 miles per hour. If the current flow with a velocity of 5 miles per hour in the direction of $N45°E$, as shown in Figure above. What are the actual speed and direction of the ship?

03

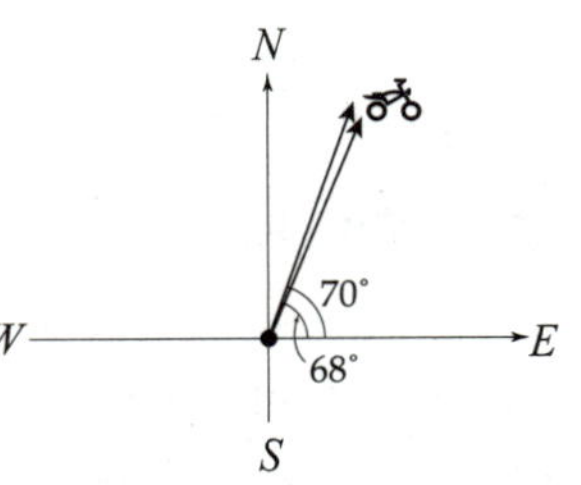

A motorcycle is traveling in the direction of 70° with a speed of 85 miles per hour. Because of the wind, its groundspeed decreases to 82 miles per hour and direction becomes 68°, as shown in Figure above. Find the speed and direction of the wind.

04 A force of 80 Newton is applied in the direction of $N60°E$. Determine the horizontal and vertical component of the force.

05

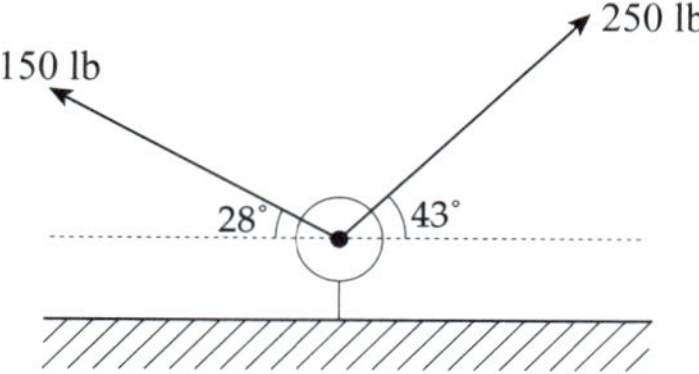

Forces with magnitudes 150 lb and 250 lb act on a hook, as shown in Figure above. Find the direction and magnitude of the resultant force.

06

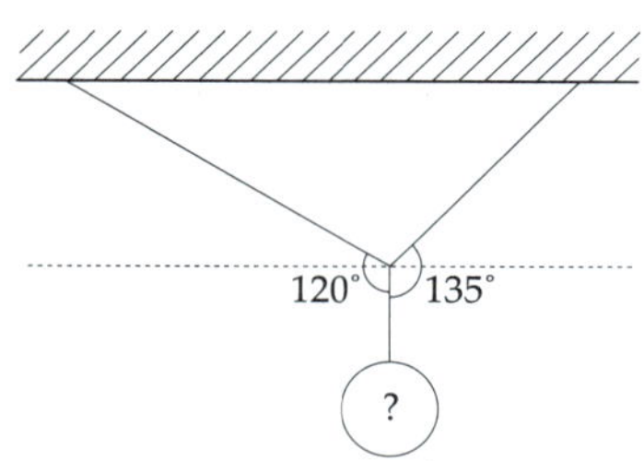

Paul wants to hang a ball from the ceiling by two cables, as shown in the figure. If the longer cable has a tension of 200 lb, what is the heaviest ball that can be supported by the cables?

07

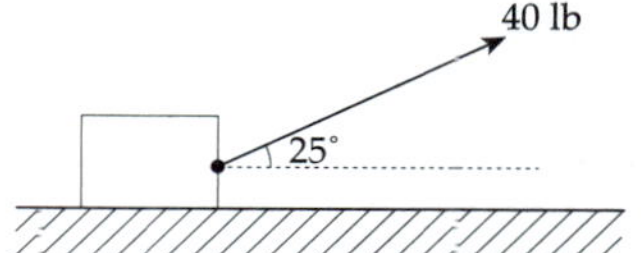

A wagon is pulled by exerting a force of 40 lb on a handle, as shown in Figure above. Determine the work done in pulling the wagon 65 feet horizontally.

8 The Algebra of Matrices

01 Definition of Matrix

A matrix is a rectangular array of numbers. Matrices, the plural of matrix, are powerful tool to solve systems of linear equations and manipulate large data sets. Here is the definition of the matrix. Let m and n be positive integers. An $m \times n$ matrix (read "m by n matrix") is a rectangular array made up of m row and n columns of real numbers.

$$A=\begin{bmatrix} a_{11} & a_{12} & \cdots & a_{1n} \\ a_{21} & a_{21} & \cdots & a_{2n} \\ \vdots & \vdots & & \vdots \\ a_{m1} & a_{m2} & \cdots & a_{mn} \end{bmatrix}$$

A matrix is usually denoted by a capital letter, and each member or entry, a_{ij}, of the matrix is referred to by two subscripts. For example, the entry in row 3 and column 2 is denoted by a_{32}. A matrix having m row and n columns is said to be order mxn and a matrix consisting of only one row or column is called a row matrix and column matrix, respectively. If $m=n$, then a matrix is called a square matrix. For a square matrix, the entries a_{11}, a_{22}, a_{33} $\cdots$ are called the main diagonals entries. We define two matrices are equal matrices if they have the same order and their corresponding entries are equal.

Example 1

① The matrix $\begin{bmatrix} 1 & 0 \\ 2 & 4 \\ -4 & 3 \end{bmatrix}$ has order 3×2.

② The matrix $[2\ \ -1\ \ 0]$ has order 1×3 and it is a row matrix.

③ The matrix $\begin{bmatrix} 1 & 0 & -1 \\ -2 & 3 & 0 \\ 0 & 4 & -3 \end{bmatrix}$ has order 3×3 and it is a square matrix.

1, 3 and -3 are main diagonal entries.

Example 1–1

① $\begin{bmatrix} 2 & 3 \\ 1 & 5 \end{bmatrix}+\begin{bmatrix} 4 & -2 \\ 0 & 3 \end{bmatrix}$　② $\begin{bmatrix} 2 & 3 \\ 1 & 5 \end{bmatrix}-\begin{bmatrix} 4 & -2 \\ 0 & 3 \end{bmatrix}$

Solution

① $\begin{bmatrix} 2 & 3 \\ 1 & 5 \end{bmatrix}+\begin{bmatrix} 4 & -2 \\ 0 & 3 \end{bmatrix}=\begin{bmatrix} 2+4 & 3+(-2) \\ 1+0 & 5+3 \end{bmatrix}=\begin{bmatrix} 6 & 1 \\ 1 & 8 \end{bmatrix}$

$\begin{bmatrix} 6 & 1 \\ 1 & 8 \end{bmatrix}$

② $\begin{bmatrix} 2 & 3 \\ 1 & 5 \end{bmatrix}-\begin{bmatrix} 4 & -2 \\ 0 & 3 \end{bmatrix}=\begin{bmatrix} 2-4 & 3-(-2) \\ 1-0 & 5-3 \end{bmatrix}=\begin{bmatrix} -2 & 5 \\ 1 & 2 \end{bmatrix}$

$\begin{bmatrix} -2 & 5 \\ 1 & 2 \end{bmatrix}$

Example 1–2

Given the matrix $A=\begin{bmatrix} 1 & 3 \\ 2 & -1 \end{bmatrix}$, find $2A$.

Solution

$2A=2\begin{bmatrix} 1 & 3 \\ 2 & -1 \end{bmatrix}=\begin{bmatrix} 1\times2 & 3\times2 \\ 2\times2 & -1\times2 \end{bmatrix}=\begin{bmatrix} 2 & 6 \\ 4 & -2 \end{bmatrix}$

$2A=\begin{bmatrix} 2 & 6 \\ 4 & -2 \end{bmatrix}$

Check Point 1

Solutions_Page 175

Given matrices $A=\begin{bmatrix} 1 & -2 \\ 3 & 2 \end{bmatrix}$, $B=\begin{bmatrix} 0 & 4 \\ -4 & 1 \end{bmatrix}$, and $C=\begin{bmatrix} 3 & 5 \\ -2 & 3 \\ 1 & -4 \end{bmatrix}$, find

① $3A$　② $A+B$　③ $A-C$　④ $2B-A$

02 Addition and Subtraction of Matrices

We simply add or subtract two matrices of the same order by adding or subtracting their corresponding entries.

Let $A=[a_{ij}]$ and $B=[b_{ij}]$ be matrices of order $m\times n$. Then

1. $A+B=[a_{ij}+b_{ij}]$
2. $A-B=[a_{ij}-b_{ij}]$

The Sum or difference of two matrices of different orders is undefined.

03 Scalar Multiplication

The product of a matrix A and a scalar k is defined as follows.

Let $A=[a_{ij}]$ be an $m\times n$ matrix and k be a scalar. Then

$$kA=[ka_{ij}]$$

The $m\times n$ matrix $kA=[ka_{ij}]$ is a scalar multiple of A.

04 Zero Matrix

The $m \times n$ matrix consisting entirely of zeros is called the zero matrix and denoted as O. There are two properties involving zero matrix we need to remember.

Let $A=[a_{ij}]$ and $B=-A=[-a_{ij}]$ be any $m \times n$ matrices. Then

1. $A+O=A$ → O is the additive identity for set of all $m \times n$ matrices.
2. $A+B=O$ → The matrix B is called additive inverse of A.

05 Multiplications of Matrices

The definition of matrix multiplication indicates a row-by-column multiplication, and the product AB is only defined when the number of columns of matrix A equals the number of rows of matrix B. The product is obtained by adding the products of the entries of a row of A by the corresponding entries of a column B.

Let A be an $m \times n$ matrix and B be an $n \times l$ matrix.
Then the product AB is an $m \times l$ matrix.

1. m, n, $m \times n$ × n, l, $n \times l$ = m, l, $m \times l$

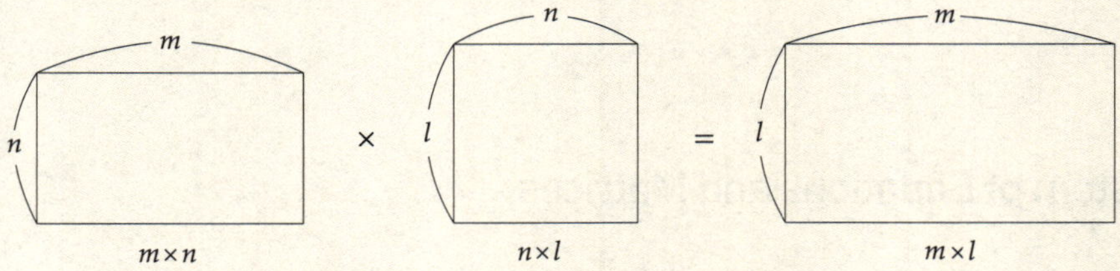

   where $c_{ij}=a_{i1}b_{1j}+a_{i2}b_{2j}+\cdots+a_{ir}b_{rj}$

2. $\underbrace{A}_{m \times n} \times \underbrace{B}_{n \times l} = \underbrace{AB}_{m \times l}$

Example 2

Let $A=\begin{bmatrix} 2 & 1 \\ 3 & -3 \end{bmatrix}$ and $B=\begin{bmatrix} 2 & -2 & 3 \\ -1 & 4 & 0 \end{bmatrix}$, Find AB.

Solution

First, note that A is a 2×2 matrix and B is a 2×3 matrix, so the product AB is defined and is a 2×3 matrix.

$$\underbrace{A}_{2\times 2} \times \underbrace{B}_{2\times 3} = \underbrace{AB}_{2\times 3}$$

To find the entries of the product, multiply each row of A by each column of B.

$$\begin{aligned} AB&=\begin{bmatrix} 2 & 1 \\ 3 & -3 \end{bmatrix}=\begin{bmatrix} 2 & -2 & 3 \\ -1 & 4 & 0 \end{bmatrix} \\ &=\begin{bmatrix} (2)(2)+(1)(-1) & (2)(-2)+(1)(4) & (2)(3)+(1)(0) \\ (3)(2)+(-3)(-1) & (3)(-2)+(-3)(4) & (3)(3)+(-3)(0) \end{bmatrix} \\ &=\begin{bmatrix} 3 & 0 & 6 \\ 9 & -18 & 9 \end{bmatrix} \end{aligned}$$

$$AB=\begin{bmatrix} 3 & 0 & 6 \\ 9 & -18 & 9 \end{bmatrix}$$

Check Point 2

Solutions_Page 175

Given matrices $A=\begin{bmatrix} 3 & 1 \\ 2 & -1 \end{bmatrix}$, $B=\begin{bmatrix} 2 & -1 & 4 \\ -3 & 0 & 5 \end{bmatrix}$, and $C=\begin{bmatrix} 4 & 0 \\ 3 & -1 \\ -2 & 3 \end{bmatrix}$, find

① AB　② BC　③ AC　④ CA

06 System of Equations and Matrices

In Algebra II, we learned how to solve the linear systems using the method of elimination and substitution. Now, we will apply new method called Gaussian elimination to solve the system. Matrices can be used to record the coefficients as we go through the steps of the Gaussian elimination process. I will explain the method of Gaussian elimination precisely through an example.

Example 3

Solve the system $\begin{cases} 2x+y-2z=6 \\ x-y+z=-2 \\ 3x-y+4z=-3 \end{cases}$ using Gaussian elimination.

Solution

$\begin{bmatrix} 2 & 1 & -2 & 6 \\ 1 & -1 & 1 & -2 \\ 3 & -1 & 4 & -3 \end{bmatrix}$ → The matrix derived from coefficients of the system, including constant terms, is called augmented matrix.

$\begin{bmatrix} 2 & 1 & -2 \\ 1 & -1 & 1 \\ 3 & -1 & 4 \end{bmatrix}$ → The matrix derived from only coefficients of the system is called coefficients matrix.

$\begin{bmatrix} 1 & a_{12} & a_{13} & a_{14} \\ 0 & 1 & a_{23} & a_{24} \\ 0 & 0 & 1 & a_{34} \end{bmatrix}$ → This form is called Row−Echelon form.

Our goal is to transform the augmented matrix to Row−Echelon form using row operations. Let's begin with augmented matrix.

$$\begin{bmatrix} 2 & 1 & -2 & 6 \\ 1 & -1 & 1 & -2 \\ 3 & -1 & 4 & -3 \end{bmatrix}$$ → Write augmented matrix.

$$\begin{matrix} R_2 \\ R_1 \\ \ \end{matrix} \begin{bmatrix} 1 & -1 & 1 & -2 \\ 2 & 1 & -2 & 6 \\ 3 & -1 & 4 & -3 \end{bmatrix}$$ → Interchange R_1 and R_2 so that $a_{11}=1$.

$$\begin{matrix} \ \\ 2R_1-R_2 \rightarrow \\ 3R_1-R_2 \rightarrow \end{matrix} \begin{bmatrix} 1 & -1 & 1 & 2 \\ 0 & -3 & 4 & -10 \\ 0 & -2 & -1 & -3 \end{bmatrix}$$ → Perform operations on R_2 and R_3 so that $a_{21}=0$ and $a_{31}=0$.

$$-\left(\frac{1}{3}\right)R_2 \rightarrow \begin{bmatrix} 1 & -1 & 1 & -2 \\ 0 & 1 & -\frac{4}{3} & \frac{10}{3} \\ 0 & -2 & -1 & -3 \end{bmatrix}$$ → Multiply R_2 by $-\frac{1}{3}$ so that $a_{22}=1$.

$$2R_2+R_3 \rightarrow \begin{bmatrix} 1 & -1 & 1 & -2 \\ 0 & 1 & -\frac{4}{3} & \frac{10}{3} \\ 0 & 0 & -\frac{11}{3} & \frac{11}{3} \end{bmatrix}$$ → Perform operations on R_3 so that $a_{32}=0$.

$$-\left(\frac{3}{11}\right)R_3 \rightarrow \begin{bmatrix} 1 & -1 & 1 & -2 \\ 0 & 1 & -\frac{4}{3} & \frac{10}{3} \\ 0 & 0 & 1 & -1 \end{bmatrix}$$ → Multiply R_3 by $-\frac{3}{11}$ so that $a_{33}=1$.

Now, the matrix is in the row-echelon form, and the corresponding system is

$$\begin{cases} x-y+z=-2 \\ y-\frac{4}{3}z=\frac{10}{3} \\ z=-1 \end{cases}$$

Using substitution, $y-\frac{4}{3}(-1)=\frac{10}{3}$, $y=2$ and $x-(2)+(-1)=-2$, $x=1$.

The solution is $x=1$, $y=2$, and $z=-1$

Check Point 3

Solutions_Page 176

Solve the system using Gaussian elimination.

① $\begin{cases} x-2y+3z=6 \\ 2x+4y-5z=-7 \\ 3x+4z=7 \end{cases}$

② $\begin{cases} x-4y+3z=6 \\ 2x-2y+5z=-6 \end{cases}$

Review Exercise

Solutions_Page 177

If posible, find (a) $\frac{1}{2}B$, (b) $A+B$, and (c) $2B-3A$.

01 $A=\begin{bmatrix} 1 & 4 \\ 3 & -2 \end{bmatrix}$, $B=\begin{bmatrix} 6 & 8 \\ -4 & -1 \end{bmatrix}$

02 $A=\begin{bmatrix} \frac{3}{2} \\ 4 \\ -\frac{1}{2} \end{bmatrix}$, $B=\begin{bmatrix} -2 \\ 1 \\ \frac{5}{2} \end{bmatrix}$

03 $A=\begin{bmatrix} -2 & 0 & 4 \\ 0 & -3 & -1 \\ 2 & \frac{1}{3} & -\frac{3}{4} \end{bmatrix}$, $B=\begin{bmatrix} 4 & -5 \\ 1 & 4 \\ -3 & -\frac{1}{2} \end{bmatrix}$

04 $A=\begin{bmatrix} \frac{1}{3} & 1 & -2 \\ 3 & 0 & 2 \\ -5 & 4 & -\frac{5}{3} \end{bmatrix}$, $B=\begin{bmatrix} 4 & -2 & 0 \\ -1 & 4 & 6 \\ 3 & -2 & 12 \end{bmatrix}$

If posible, find (a) AB, (b) BA, and (c) B^2

05 $A=\begin{bmatrix} -2 & 0 \\ 3 & 4 \end{bmatrix}$, $B=\begin{bmatrix} 4 & 2 \\ -1 & -3 \end{bmatrix}$

06 $A=\begin{bmatrix} 1 & 4 & \frac{2}{3} \end{bmatrix}$, $B=\begin{bmatrix} 2 \\ 5 \\ -3 \end{bmatrix}$

07 $A=\begin{bmatrix} 3 & 2 \\ -2 & 0 \\ 4 & 1 \end{bmatrix}$, $B=\begin{bmatrix} 3 & \frac{1}{2} \\ -2 & \frac{1}{4} \end{bmatrix}$

08 $A=\begin{bmatrix} 1 & 0 & 2 \\ \frac{1}{2} & 4 & 6 \end{bmatrix}$, $B=\begin{bmatrix} 0 & 3 & 5 \\ 3 & -2 & 0 \\ -4 & 1 & -1 \end{bmatrix}$

Review Exercise

Solve the system using Gaussian elimination.

09 $\begin{cases} x+4y-3z=0 \\ -x-2y-2z=-4 \\ -2x+6y+7z=8 \end{cases}$

10 $\begin{cases} x-2y-z=-4 \\ 2x+3y+z=9 \\ 4x-4y+3z=-1 \end{cases}$

11 $\begin{cases} 3x-2y-z=-5 \\ 2x+3y+z=7 \\ 4x-4y+3z=-5 \end{cases}$

12 $\begin{cases} 2z+y-z=3 \\ x-2y+z=2 \\ 2x-4y+2z=-1 \end{cases}$

13 $\begin{cases} 2x+4y-2z=3 \\ 3x-2y-4z=1 \end{cases}$

14 $\begin{cases} x-3y-\frac{1}{2}z=-1 \\ \frac{1}{3}x+z=-3 \end{cases}$

15 $\begin{bmatrix} 1 & -2 & 3 \\ 2 & x & 4 \end{bmatrix}+\begin{bmatrix} -4 & 1 & 0 \\ -1 & -3 & 5 \end{bmatrix}$

$=\begin{bmatrix} -3 & -1 & 3 \\ 1 & y & 9 \end{bmatrix}$

If $x=-2$, then what is the value of y?

(A) -8
(B) -5
(C) 0
(D) 3

16 Suppose A, B, and C are matrices and $AB=C$. If matrix A has dimensions 3×4 matrix C has dimensions 3×2, what are the dimensions of B?

(A) 3×2
(B) 3×3
(C) 4×3
(D) 4×2

17 If matrix A has dimensions 3×2 and matrix B has dimensions 3×3, which of the following statements must be true?

I. The product AB does not exist.
II. The product AB exists and has dimensions 3×2.
III. The product BA exists and has dimensions 3×2.

(A) II and III only
(B) I and II only
(C) I and III only
(D) I, II, and III

9 The Inverse of Matrices

01 Identity Matrix

The $n \times n$ matrix with 1's on the main diagonal and 0's elsewhere is called the identity matrix of order n and is denoted by

$$I_n = \begin{bmatrix} 1 & 0 & 0 & \cdots & 0 \\ 0 & 1 & 0 & \cdots & 0 \\ 0 & 0 & 1 & \cdots & 0 \\ \vdots & \vdots & \vdots & & \vdots \\ 0 & 0 & 0 & \cdots & 1 \end{bmatrix}$$

Note that identity matrix must be square matrix.

For example, $I_2 = \begin{bmatrix} 1 & 0 \\ 0 & 1 \end{bmatrix}$, $I_3 = \begin{bmatrix} 1 & 0 & 0 \\ 0 & 1 & 0 \\ 0 & 0 & 1 \end{bmatrix}$, and $I_4 = \begin{bmatrix} 1 & 0 & 0 & 0 \\ 0 & 1 & 0 & 0 \\ 0 & 0 & 1 & 0 \\ 0 & 0 & 0 & 1 \end{bmatrix}$.

For any $n \times n$ square matrix A, $AI_n = I_nA = A$.

For example, $\begin{bmatrix} 1 & -2 \\ 3 & 4 \end{bmatrix}\begin{bmatrix} 1 & 0 \\ 0 & 1 \end{bmatrix} = \begin{bmatrix} 1 & -2 \\ 3 & 4 \end{bmatrix}$ $(AI = A)$

and $\begin{bmatrix} 1 & 0 \\ 0 & 1 \end{bmatrix}\begin{bmatrix} 1 & -2 \\ 3 & 4 \end{bmatrix} = \begin{bmatrix} 1 & -2 \\ 3 & 4 \end{bmatrix}$ $(IA = A)$.

02 The Inverse of a Matrix

In Algebra, if a is a nonzero real number, then its inverse is $a^{-1}=\frac{1}{a}$.

The number a^{-1} is called the multiplicative inverse of a because $a\cdot a^{-1}=a\cdot\frac{1}{a}=1$.

The definition of the multiplicative inverse of a matrix is similar.

Definition of Inverse of a Matrix

Let A and B be $n\times n$ square matrices such that $AB=BA=I_n$.
Then B is the inverse of A and we write $B=A^{-1}$.
Thus, $AB=BA=I_n \leftrightarrow AA^{-1}=A^{-1}A=I_n$.
The symbol A^{-1} is read "A inverse".

Example 1

Verify that $A=\begin{bmatrix}7 & 3\\ 2 & 1\end{bmatrix}$ and $B=\begin{bmatrix}-1 & -3\\ 2 & 6\end{bmatrix}$ are inverse matrices.

Solution

$$AB=\begin{bmatrix}7 & 3\\ 2 & 1\end{bmatrix}\begin{bmatrix}1 & -3\\ -2 & 7\end{bmatrix}=\begin{bmatrix}7-6 & -21+21\\ 2-2 & -6+7\end{bmatrix}=\begin{bmatrix}1 & 0\\ 0 & 1\end{bmatrix}=I_2$$

$$BA=\begin{bmatrix}1 & -3\\ -2 & 7\end{bmatrix}\begin{bmatrix}7 & 3\\ 2 & 1\end{bmatrix}=\begin{bmatrix}7-6 & 3-3\\ -14+14 & -6+7\end{bmatrix}=\begin{bmatrix}1 & 0\\ 0 & 1\end{bmatrix}=I_2$$

Since we have $AB=BA=I_2$, we can conclude $B=A^{-1}$ and $A=B^{-1}$.

$\begin{bmatrix}7 & 3\\ 2 & 1\end{bmatrix}$ and $\begin{bmatrix}-1 & -3\\ 2 & 6\end{bmatrix}$ are inverse matrices.

Not every square matrix has an inverse. If a square matrix A has an inverse, then A is called invertible or nonsingular, otherwise, A is called singular.

Check Point 1

Solutions_Page 181

Verify that the matrices are inverse of each other.

① $A=\begin{bmatrix} -2 & -1 \\ 6 & 4 \end{bmatrix}$, $B=\begin{bmatrix} -2 & -\frac{1}{2} \\ 3 & 1 \end{bmatrix}$ ② $A=\begin{bmatrix} 3 & 2 & 2 \\ 4 & 3 & 5 \\ 0 & 0 & 2 \end{bmatrix}$, $B=\begin{bmatrix} 3 & -2 & 2 \\ -4 & 3 & -\frac{7}{2} \\ 0 & 0 & 2 \end{bmatrix}$

03 Finding the Inverse Matrices

1. Inverse of 2×2 Matrices

   For a 2×2 matrix, there are three ways to find its inversesystem of linear equations, Gauss−Jordan elimination, and a formula.

2. Inverse of 3×3 Matrices

   For a 3×3 matrix, we use Gauss−Jordan elimination to find its inverse.

Example 2

Find the inverse of the matrix $A=\begin{bmatrix} 1 & 2 \\ -2 & -3 \end{bmatrix}$.

Solution

Method 1: Using system of linear equations

$$\begin{bmatrix} 1 & 2 \\ -2 & -3 \end{bmatrix}\begin{bmatrix} a_{11} & a_{12} \\ a_{21} & a_{22} \end{bmatrix}=\begin{bmatrix} 1 & 0 \\ 0 & 1 \end{bmatrix} \rightarrow AA^{-1}=I$$

We have two sets of systems, $\begin{cases} a_{11}+2a_{21}=1 \\ -2a_{11}-3a_{21}=0 \end{cases}$ and $\begin{cases} a_{12}+2a_{22}=0 \\ -2a_{12}-3a_{22}=1 \end{cases}$.

Now, we solve the two systems to determine $a_{11}=-3$, $a_{21}=2$, $a_{12}=-2$, and $a_{22}=1$

So the inverse of A is $A^{-1}=\begin{bmatrix} -3 & -2 \\ 2 & 1 \end{bmatrix}$.

Method 2: Using Gauss−Jordan elimination

$$\begin{bmatrix} 1 & 2 \\ -2 & -3 \end{bmatrix}\begin{bmatrix} 1 & 0 \\ 0 & 1 \end{bmatrix} \to [A|I]$$

$$2R_1+R_2 \to \begin{bmatrix} 1 & 2 \\ 0 & 1 \end{bmatrix}\begin{bmatrix} 1 & 0 \\ 2 & 1 \end{bmatrix}$$

$$-2R_1+R_2 \to \begin{bmatrix} 1 & 0 \\ 0 & 1 \end{bmatrix}\begin{bmatrix} -3 & -2 \\ 2 & 1 \end{bmatrix} \to [I|A^{-1}]$$

Through Gauss−Jordan elimination, we obtain $[I|A^{-1}]$ from $[A|I]$.

$$\overset{A}{\begin{bmatrix} 1 & 2 \\ -2 & -3 \end{bmatrix}}\overset{I}{\begin{bmatrix} 1 & 0 \\ 0 & 1 \end{bmatrix}} \Rightarrow \overset{I}{\begin{bmatrix} 1 & 0 \\ 0 & 1 \end{bmatrix}}\overset{A^{-1}}{\begin{bmatrix} -3 & -2 \\ 2 & 1 \end{bmatrix}}$$

This procedure works for any square matrix that has an inverse.

Method 3: Using the formula

There is a formula to find the inverse of a 2×2 matrix, and this method only works for 2×2 matrices.

If A is a 2×2 matrix given by $A=\begin{bmatrix} a & c \\ b & d \end{bmatrix}$,

$$A^{-1}=\frac{1}{ad-bc}\begin{bmatrix} d & -c \\ -b & a \end{bmatrix}, \text{ where } ad-bc\neq0$$

If $ad-bc=0$, the inverse A^{-1} does not exist.

Now, let us find the inverse of $A=\begin{bmatrix} 1 & 2 \\ -2 & -3 \end{bmatrix}$, using the formula.

$$A^{-1}=\frac{1}{(1)(-3)-(-2)(2)}\begin{bmatrix} -3 & -2 \\ 2 & 1 \end{bmatrix}=\begin{bmatrix} -3 & -2 \\ 2 & 1 \end{bmatrix}$$

For a 3×3 matrix, always use the method of Gauss−Jordan elimination to find the inverse matrix.

$$A^{-1}=\begin{bmatrix} -3 & -2 \\ 2 & 1 \end{bmatrix}$$

Check Point 2

Solutions_Page 182

Find the inverse of the matrix.

① $A=\begin{bmatrix} 3 & 4 \\ -1 & 2 \end{bmatrix}$

② $A=\begin{bmatrix} 2 & 2 & 1 \\ -2 & -1 & 1 \\ -1 & -3 & -3 \end{bmatrix}$

Review Exercise

Verify that the matrices are inverses of each other.

01 $A=\begin{bmatrix}1 & 0\\3 & 2\end{bmatrix}$, $B=\begin{bmatrix}1 & 0\\-\frac{3}{2} & \frac{1}{2}\end{bmatrix}$

02 $A=\begin{bmatrix}-5 & 4\\2 & -2\end{bmatrix}$, $B=\begin{bmatrix}-1 & -2\\-1 & -\frac{5}{2}\end{bmatrix}$

03 $A=\begin{bmatrix}4 & 1 & 2\\2 & 0 & 1\\-1 & -2 & 0\end{bmatrix}$, $B=\begin{bmatrix}-2 & 4 & -1\\1 & -2 & 0\\4 & -7 & 2\end{bmatrix}$

04 $A=\begin{bmatrix}1 & -4 & 0\\1 & 2 & 0\\1 & 2 & 1\end{bmatrix}$, $B=\begin{bmatrix}\frac{1}{3} & \frac{2}{3} & 0\\-\frac{1}{6} & \frac{1}{6} & 0\\0 & -1 & 1\end{bmatrix}$

Find the inverse, if exists, of the matrix.

05 $\begin{bmatrix}-2 & 3\\-1 & 2\end{bmatrix}$

06 $\begin{bmatrix}-2 & 4\\1 & 1\end{bmatrix}$

Find the inverse, if exists, of the matrix.

07 $\begin{bmatrix} 1 & 0 & 1 \\ 3 & 2 & -1 \\ 0 & -1 & 4 \end{bmatrix}$

Solve the system using corresponding matrix equation.

08 $\begin{cases} -2x+4y=2 \\ x+y=2 \end{cases}$

09 $\begin{cases} -3x-2y=1 \\ -x+4y=-9 \end{cases}$

10 $\begin{cases} x+z=2 \\ 3x+2y-z=-2 \\ -y+4z=10 \end{cases}$

11 $\begin{cases} 2x+2y+z=-2 \\ -2x-y+z=5 \\ -x-3y-3z=-2 \end{cases}$

Review Exercise

12 $x-2y+3z=6$
$2x+4y-5z=-7$
$3x+4z=7$

Which of the following expressions represents the system of equations given above?

(A) $\begin{bmatrix} x \\ y \\ z \end{bmatrix}=\begin{bmatrix} 6 \\ -7 \\ 7 \end{bmatrix}\begin{bmatrix} 1 & -2 & 3 \\ 2 & 4 & -5 \\ 3 & 0 & 4 \end{bmatrix}$

(B) $\begin{bmatrix} x \\ y \\ z \end{bmatrix}=\begin{bmatrix} 6 \\ -7 \\ 7 \end{bmatrix}\begin{bmatrix} 1 & -2 & 3 \\ 2 & 4 & -5 \\ 3 & 0 & 4 \end{bmatrix}^{-1}$

(C) $\begin{bmatrix} x \\ y \\ z \end{bmatrix}=\begin{bmatrix} 1 & -2 & 3 \\ 2 & 4 & -5 \\ 3 & 0 & 4 \end{bmatrix}\begin{bmatrix} 6 \\ -7 \\ 7 \end{bmatrix}$

(D) $\begin{bmatrix} x \\ y \\ z \end{bmatrix}=\begin{bmatrix} 1 & -2 & 3 \\ 2 & 4 & -5 \\ 3 & 0 & 4 \end{bmatrix}^{-1}\begin{bmatrix} 6 \\ -7 \\ 7 \end{bmatrix}$

13 
At H−Mart, two students, A and B, purchased the following items for the new school year:

	A	B
Pen	5	8
Mechanical Pencil	12	6
Notebook	4	5

Each pen costs \$1.5, each mechanical pencil costs \$2.5, and each notebook costs \$3. Which of the following matrices represents the total cost, in dollars, of the items purchased by each student?

(A) $\begin{bmatrix} 5 & 8 \\ 12 & 6 \\ 4 & 5 \end{bmatrix}\begin{bmatrix} 1.5 \\ 2.5 \\ 3 \end{bmatrix}$

(B) $\begin{bmatrix} 5 & 8 \\ 12 & 6 \\ 4 & 5 \end{bmatrix}\begin{bmatrix} 1.5 & 2.5 & 3 \end{bmatrix}$

(C) $\begin{bmatrix} 5 & 12 & 4 \\ 8 & 6 & 5 \end{bmatrix}\begin{bmatrix} 1.5 \\ 2.5 \\ 3 \end{bmatrix}$

(D) $\begin{bmatrix} 5 & 12 & 4 \\ 8 & 6 & 5 \end{bmatrix}\begin{bmatrix} 1.5 & 2.5 & 3 \end{bmatrix}$

memo

10 Determinants and Cramer's Rule

Determinant is a real number that is associated with every square matrix. In this section, we will discuss how to find determinant of a square matrix and learn how this is applied to Cramer's rule.

01 2×2 Determinants

Let $A=\begin{bmatrix} a_{11} & a_{12} \\ a_{21} & a_{22} \end{bmatrix}$. Then the determinant of A, denoted by $|A|$, is given by

$$|A|=\begin{vmatrix} a_{11} & a_{12} \\ a_{21} & a_{22} \end{vmatrix}=a_{11}a_{22}-a_{12}a_{21}$$

1. The determinant is the difference of the products of the two diagonals of the matrix.
2. Note that $|A|$ does not denote absolute value A.

Example 1

Find the determinant of the matrix $A=\begin{bmatrix} 3 & -4 \\ 2 & 1 \end{bmatrix}$ and $B=\begin{bmatrix} -3 & 6 \\ 2 & -4 \end{bmatrix}$.

Solution

$|A|=\begin{vmatrix} 3 & -4 \\ 2 & 1 \end{vmatrix}=(3)(1)-(-4)(2)=11$

$|B|=\begin{vmatrix} -3 & 6 \\ 2 & -4 \end{vmatrix}=(-3)(-4)-(6)(2)=0$

$|A|=11,\ |B|=0$

Check Point 1

Solutions_Page 185

Find the determinant of the matrix.

① $\begin{bmatrix} 5 & 4 \\ -3 & -2 \end{bmatrix}$ ② $\begin{bmatrix} -2 & 3 \\ -1 & 2 \end{bmatrix}$

02 Minors and Cofactors

For any $n \times n$ matrix where $n > 1$, the following are defined.

1. The **minor** M_{ij} of entry a_{ij} is the determinant of the $(n-1)\times(n-1)$ obtained by deleting i^{th} row and j^{th} column of the matrix.

2. The cofactor C_{ij} of entry a_{ij} is defined as $C_{ij}=(-1)^{i+j}M_{ij}$.

   Sign pattern for cofactors are given by $\begin{bmatrix} + & - & + & - & \cdots \\ - & + & - & + & \cdots \\ + & - & + & - & \cdots \\ - & + & - & + & \cdots \\ \vdots & \vdots & \vdots & \vdots & \end{bmatrix}$

Notice that the spot has negative signs if $i+j=odd$ and positive signs if $i+j=even$.

Example 2

Find M_{12} and C_{12} of the matrix $\begin{bmatrix} 3 & 2 & 5 \\ -2 & 4 & 2 \\ 1 & 1 & -4 \end{bmatrix}$.

Solution

To find M_{12}, first delete 1st row and 2nd column of $\begin{bmatrix} 3 & 2 & 5 \\ -2 & 4 & 2 \\ 1 & 1 & -4 \end{bmatrix}$.

Now $M_{12}=\begin{vmatrix} -2 & 2 \\ 1 & -4 \end{vmatrix}=(-2)(-4)-(1)(2)=6$ and $C_{12}=(-1)^{1+2}M_{12}=(-1)^3 6=-6$.

$M_{12}=6$, $C_{12}=-6$

Check Point 2

Solutions_Page 185

Find the given cofactors of the matrix.

① $\begin{bmatrix} -2 & 1 \\ 6 & 3 \end{bmatrix}$; C_{11}

② $\begin{bmatrix} 2 & 3 & 0 \\ 3 & 5 & -2 \\ -1 & -2 & 4 \end{bmatrix}$; C_{23}

03 3×3 Determinants

The determinant of a 3×3 or higher order matrix is the sum of the entries in any row (or column) of given matrix multiplied by their respective cofactors. Here is several ways to find the determinant of a 3×3 matrix.

Let the matrix $A=\begin{bmatrix} a_{11} & a_{12} & a_{13} \\ a_{21} & a_{22} & a_{23} \\ a_{31} & a_{32} & a_{33} \end{bmatrix}$.

For example, if we find the cofactors of the entries in the *first row*, then we have

$$|A|=\begin{bmatrix} a_{11} & a_{12} & a_{13} \\ a_{21} & a_{22} & a_{23} \\ a_{31} & a_{32} & a_{33} \end{bmatrix}=a_{11}C_{11}+a_{12}C_{12}+a_{13}C_{13}.$$

Now find the cofactors of the entries in the *first column*, then the determinant is

$$|A|=\begin{bmatrix} a_{11} & a_{12} & a_{13} \\ a_{21} & a_{22} & a_{23} \\ a_{31} & a_{32} & a_{33} \end{bmatrix}=a_{11}C_{11}+a_{21}C_{21}+a_{31}C_{31}$$

and so on.

Example 3

Find the determinant of $\begin{bmatrix} 3 & 2 & 5 \\ -2 & 4 & 2 \\ 1 & 1 & -4 \end{bmatrix}$ by expanding along the following row or column.

① First row ② Seocnd column

Solution

① First row: $\begin{vmatrix} 3 & 2 & 5 \\ -2 & 4 & 2 \\ 1 & 1 & -4 \end{vmatrix} = a_{11}C_{11} + a_{12}C_{12} + a_{13}C_{13}$

$$= 3\cdot(-1)^{1+1}\begin{vmatrix} 4 & 2 \\ 1 & -4 \end{vmatrix} + 2\cdot(-1)^{1+2}\begin{vmatrix} -2 & 2 \\ 1 & -4 \end{vmatrix} + 5\cdot(-1)^{1+3}\begin{vmatrix} -2 & 4 \\ 1 & 1 \end{vmatrix}$$

$$= 3(-16-2) - 2(8-2) + 5(-2-4) = -96$$

② Second column: $\begin{vmatrix} 3 & 2 & 5 \\ -2 & 4 & 2 \\ 1 & 1 & -4 \end{vmatrix} = a_{12}C_{12} + a_{22}C_{22} + a_{32}C_{32}$

$$= 2\cdot(-1)^{1+2}\begin{vmatrix} -2 & 2 \\ 1 & -4 \end{vmatrix} + 4\cdot(-1)^{2+2}\begin{vmatrix} 3 & 5 \\ 1 & -4 \end{vmatrix} + 1\cdot(-1)^{3+3}\begin{vmatrix} 3 & 5 \\ -2 & 2 \end{vmatrix}$$

$$= -2(8-2) + 4(-12-5) - (6+10) = -96$$

As you can see, we can find the determinant by expanding along any row or column.

$$\begin{vmatrix} 3 & 2 & 5 \\ -2 & 4 & 2 \\ 1 & 1 & -4 \end{vmatrix} = -96$$

Check Point 3

Solutions_Page 185

Find the deter,omamt of the matrix.

① $\begin{bmatrix} 2 & -2 & 3 \\ -1 & 3 & 6 \\ -1 & 1 & 2 \end{bmatrix}$ ② $\begin{bmatrix} 6 & 1 & 5 \\ 2 & -4 & 0 \\ -3 & -2 & 0 \end{bmatrix}$

04 Cramer's Rule

Cramer's Rule is determined by determinants and it is used to solve a system of equations. Let us derive the rule. For the system $\begin{cases} a_{11}x+a_{12}y=b_1 \\ a_{21}x+a_{22}y=b_2 \end{cases}$, the solution is found by the following steps.

$$(a_{11}x+a_{12}y=b_1)\times a_{21}=a_{11}a_{21}x+a_{12}a_{21}y=a_{21}b_1 \quad (1)$$
$$(a_{21}x+a_{22}y=b_2)\times a_{11}=a_{11}a_{21}x+a_{11}a_{22}y=a_{11}b_2 \quad (2)$$

(2)−(1) gives $a_{11}a_{22}y-a_{12}a_{21}y=a_{11}b_2-a_{21}b_1$

$$y(a_{11}a_{22}-a_{12}a_{21})=a_{11}b_2-a_{21}b_1$$

$$y=\frac{a_{11}b_2-a_{21}b_1}{a_{11}a_{22}-a_{21}a_{12}}$$

In a similar manner, $x=\dfrac{b_1a_{22}-a_{22}b_2}{a_{11}a_{22}-a_{21}a_{12}}$

Notice that both denominators of x and y are determinant(denoted by D) of coefficient matrix of the system. The numerators of x and y are determinants (denoted by D_x and D_y) formed by using the column of constants as replacements for the coefficients of x and y. Here is a summary of Cramer's Rule

Cramer's Rule

(1) For the system $\begin{cases} a_{11}x+a_{12}y=b_1 \\ a_{21}x+a_{22}y=b_2 \end{cases}$, $x=\dfrac{D_x}{D}$ and $y=\dfrac{D_y}{D}$

where $D=\begin{vmatrix} a_{11} & a_{12} \\ a_{21} & a_{22} \end{vmatrix}$, $D_x=\begin{vmatrix} b_1 & a_{12} \\ b_2 & a_{22} \end{vmatrix}$, and $D_y=\begin{vmatrix} a_{11} & b_1 \\ a_{21} & b_2 \end{vmatrix}$

(2) For the system $\begin{cases} a_{11}x+a_{12}y+a_{13}z=b_1 \\ a_{21}x+a_{22}y+a_{23}z=b_2 \\ a_{31}x+a_{32}y+a_{33}z=b_3 \end{cases}$, $x=\dfrac{D_x}{D}$, $y=\dfrac{D_y}{D}$, and $z=\dfrac{D_z}{D}$

where $D=\begin{vmatrix} a_{11} & a_{12} & a_{13} \\ b_{21} & a_{22} & a_{23} \\ b_{31} & a_{32} & a_{33} \end{vmatrix}$, $D_x=\begin{vmatrix} b_1 & a_{12} & a_{13} \\ b_2 & a_{22} & a_{23} \\ b_3 & a_{32} & a_{33} \end{vmatrix}$, $D_y=\begin{vmatrix} a_{11} & b_1 & a_{13} \\ a_{21} & b_2 & a_{23} \\ a_{31} & b_3 & a_{33} \end{vmatrix}$, and $D_z=\begin{vmatrix} a_{11} & a_{12} & b_1 \\ a_{21} & a_{22} & b_2 \\ a_{31} & a_{32} & b_3 \end{vmatrix}$

Know that we can only apply Cramer's Rule when $D \neq 0$.

For example, the solution for y of the given system is

$$\begin{cases} a_{11}x+a_{12}y+a_{13}z=b_1 \\ a_{21}x+a_{22}y+a_{23}z=b_2 \\ a_{31}x+a_{32}y+a_{33}z=b_3 \end{cases} \rightarrow y=\frac{D_y}{D}=\frac{\begin{vmatrix} a_{11} & b_1 & a_{13} \\ a_{21} & b_2 & a_{23} \\ a_{31} & b_3 & a_{33} \end{vmatrix}}{\begin{vmatrix} a_{11} & a_{12} & a_{13} \\ a_{21} & a_{22} & a_{23} \\ a_{31} & a_{32} & a_{33} \end{vmatrix}}$$

Example 4

Use Cramer's Rule to solve the system $\begin{cases} 3x-2y=4 \\ -x+4y=2 \end{cases}$.

Solution

First, find the determinant D, D_x, and D_y.

$$D=\begin{vmatrix} 3 & -2 \\ -1 & 4 \end{vmatrix}=12-2=10,\ D_x=\begin{vmatrix} 4 & -2 \\ 2 & 4 \end{vmatrix}=16+4=20, \text{ and } D_y=\begin{vmatrix} 3 & 4 \\ -1 & 2 \end{vmatrix}=6+4=10$$

Since the dterminant is not zero, we now can apply Cramer's Rule.

$$x=\frac{D_x}{D}=\frac{20}{10}=2 \text{ and } y=\frac{D_y}{D}=\frac{10}{10}=1$$

So the solution is $x=2$ and $y=1$.

$x=2$ and $y=1$

Check Point 4

Solutions_Page 186

Use Cramers Rule to solve the system.

① $\begin{cases} -2x+3y=-3 \\ -x+2y=-1 \end{cases}$

② $\begin{cases} x+z=4 \\ 3x+2y-z=4 \\ -y+4z=6 \end{cases}$

Review Exercise

Solutions_Page 186

Find the given cofactors of the matrix.

01 $\begin{bmatrix} -2 & 0 \\ 3 & 4 \end{bmatrix}$; C_{11}

02 $\begin{bmatrix} 6 & 8 \\ -4 & -1 \end{bmatrix}$; C_{12}

03 $\begin{bmatrix} -2 & 4 \\ 1 & 1 \end{bmatrix}$; C_{22}

04 $\begin{bmatrix} 0 & 3 & 5 \\ 3 & -2 & 0 \\ -4 & 1 & -1 \end{bmatrix}$; C_{21}

05 $\begin{bmatrix} 3 & 2 & 2 \\ 4 & 3 & 5 \\ 0 & 0 & 2 \end{bmatrix}$; C_{32}

06 $\begin{bmatrix} -2 & 0 & 4 \\ 0 & -3 & -1 \\ \frac{3}{2} & \frac{1}{3} & -\frac{3}{4} \end{bmatrix}$; C_{13}

Find the determinant of the matrix.

07 $\begin{bmatrix} 4 & -2 \\ -2 & 1 \end{bmatrix}$

08 $\begin{bmatrix} -3 & -2 \\ -1 & 4 \end{bmatrix}$

09 $\begin{bmatrix} 1 & 0 & 1 \\ 3 & 2 & -1 \\ 0 & -1 & 4 \end{bmatrix}$

Review Exercise

Find the determinant, if exists, of the matrix.

10 $\begin{bmatrix} 3 & 0 & 1 \\ 0 & 2 & 0 \\ 2 & 4 & 1 \end{bmatrix}$

11 $\begin{bmatrix} 2 & 2 & 1 \\ -2 & -1 & 1 \\ -1 & -3 & -3 \end{bmatrix}$

Use Cramer's rule to solve the system.

12 $\begin{cases} 4x+2y=12 \\ -2x+y=-6 \end{cases}$

13 $\begin{cases} 2x+2y+z=0 \\ -2x-y+z=-5 \\ -x-3y-3z=7 \end{cases}$

memo

Unit IV Test

01 Find the rectangular equation for the curve by eliminating the parameter t.

(1) $x=2t^2+5,\ y=3t-2$

(2) $x=4\sin t-3,\ y=2\cos^2 t+1$

02 Find parametric equations for the line that passes through two point $(-1,\ 5)$ and $(1,\ 1)$.

03 Find parametric equations for a particle that moves along the circle $(x-2)^2+y^2=4$.

(1) The particle starts to move clockwise at the origin and make one complete revolution in 6 seconds.

(2) The particle starts to move counterclockwise at $(2,\ 2)$ and make one complete revolution in 2 seconds.

Solutions_Page 188

04 A soccer ball is kicked 2 feet above the ground with an initial velocity 40 feet per second at an angle of $30°$ to the horizontal.

(1) How long is the ball in the air?

(2) When is the ball at its maximum height?

(3) Determine the maximum height reached by the ball.

(4) Determine the horizontal distance that the ball traveled.

05 Find the vertex, focus, directrix, and focal diameter of the parabola. Then sketch the graph.

(1) $4x^2+\frac{1}{2}y=0$

(2) $x^2+2y-6x=1$

Unit IV Test

06 Write the standard form of the equation of the parabola with the given information.

(1) Vertex $(0,\ 0)$; Focus $(0,\ 5)$

(2) Vertex $(5,\ 1)$; Directrix $x=-\frac{3}{4}$

(3) Focus $(-2,\ 0)$; Directrix $x=4$

07 Find the center, vertices, foci, eccentricity, length of the major axis, and the length of the minor axis of given ellipse. Then sketch the graph.

(1) $25(x-2)^2+y^2=25$

(2) $-2x^2-16x-\frac{1}{2}y^2+y=0$

08 Find the standard form of the equation of an ellipse with the given information.

(1) Vertices: $(7,\ 9)$, $(-1,\ 9)$; Foci: $(2,\ 9)$, $(4,\ 9)$

(2) Vertices: $(3,\ 2)$, $(3,\ -6)$; The length of minor axis: $4\sqrt{3}$

09 Find the center, vertices, foci, length of the transverse axis, length of the conjugate axis, and the equations of the asymptotes. Then, sketch the graph.

(1) $3x^2-4y^2-30x+8y+35=0$

(2) $-2x^2+3y^2+4x-60y+268=0$

10 Find the standard form of the equation of the hyperbola with the given information.

(1) Foci: (4, 3), (4, 11); The length of transverse axis: 4

(2) Vertices: (0, 2), (6, 2); Asymptotes: $y=\frac{2}{3}x$, $y=4-\frac{2}{3}x$

11 If $x=2\sin t$ and $y=\cos t-1$, which of the following expressions is true?

(A) $x^2+(y+1)^2=4$
(B) $(x+1)^2+y^2=4$
(C) $\frac{x^2}{4}+(y+1)^2=1$
(D) $(x+1)^2+\frac{y^2}{4}=1$

Unit IV Test

12 Which of the following best describes the graph of $x^2-y^2+2x-4y=0$?

(A) Circle
(B) Parabola
(C) Ellipse
(D) Hyperbola

13 Let $A=(-1,\ 3)$, $B=(2,\ 5)$, and $C=(4,\ -2)$. Find the component form and magnitude of the vector.

(1) $\overrightarrow{AB}$

(2) $\overrightarrow{AB}+\overrightarrow{CB}$

(3) $\overrightarrow{BC}-2\overrightarrow{BA}$

14 Let $\vec{v}=\langle 3,\ -1\rangle$, $\vec{w}=\langle 5,\ 3\rangle$, and $\vec{x}=\langle -2, -3\rangle$. Find the component form and sketch the resultant of the vector.

(1) $\vec{v}+\vec{w}$

(2) $\vec{x}+2\vec{w}-\vec{v}$

15

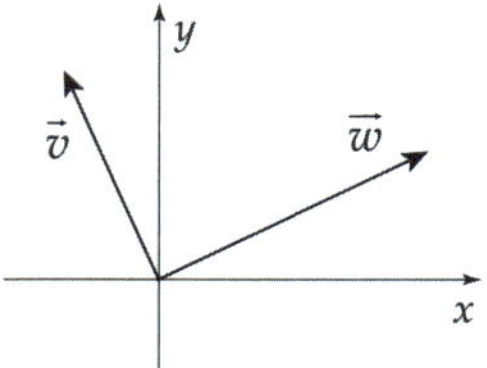

Given two vectors $\vec{v}$ and $\vec{w}$, as shown in Figure above, draw the resultant vector that represents $\vec{v}+\vec{w}$.

16 If the magnitude of vectors $\vec{a}$ and $\vec{b}$ are 7 and 11, respectively, then which of the following could NOT be the magnitude of vector $2\vec{b}+3\vec{a}$?

(A) 1 (B) 8 (C) 43 (D) 50

17 Find a unit vector in the direction of the given vector.

(1) $\vec{v}=\langle 2, 5\rangle$

(2) $\vec{w}=i-j$

Unit IV Test

18 Find the component form of the vector.

(1)

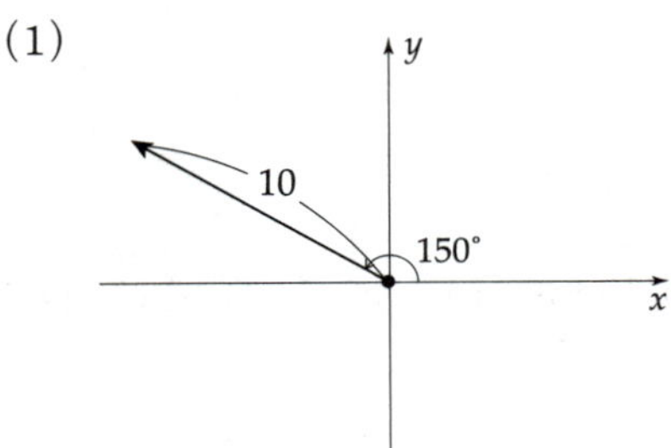

(2)

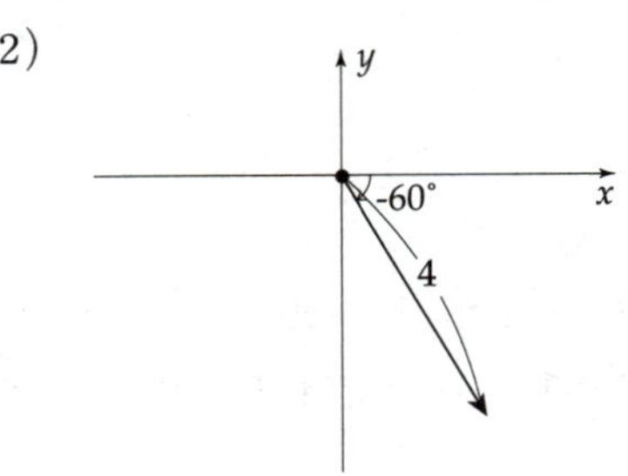

19 Find the direction angle of the vector.

(1) $\vec{v}=\langle 2,\ 1\rangle$

(2) $\vec{x}=3i-j$

20 Find the dot product of $\vec{v}$ and $\vec{w}$, and state whether the vectors are orthogonal.

(1) $\vec{v}=\langle -2,\ -4\rangle$, $\vec{w}=\left\langle -\frac{1}{4},\ \frac{2}{3}\right\rangle$

(2) $\vec{v}=-\frac{4}{3}i+6j$, $\vec{w}=9i+\frac{3}{4}j$

21 Given $\vec{v}=\langle 4,\ -3\rangle$, $\vec{w}=\langle -3,\ 1\rangle$, and $\vec{x}=-2i+4j$, find the expression.

(1) $\vec{v}\cdot\vec{v}$

(2) $(\vec{x}\cdot\vec{w})\vec{v}$

(3) $(\vec{w}\cdot\vec{x})+(\vec{w}\cdot\vec{v})$

22 Find the angle θ between two vectors.

(1) $\vec{v}=\langle -4,\ 2\rangle$, $\vec{w}=\langle -3,\ -4\rangle$

(2) $\vec{v}=2i+2j$, $\vec{w}=-5i-3j$

23 Find the vector projection of $\vec{v}$ onto $\vec{w}$. Then write $\vec{v}$ as a sum of two orthogonal vectors.

(1) $\vec{v}=\langle -7,\ 2\rangle$, $\vec{w}=\langle -4,\ -5\rangle$

(2) $\vec{v}=-i-7j$, $\vec{w}=-5i-2j$

Unit IV Test

24 An airplane is heading at a speed of 500 miles per hour with a bearing of 45°. If the airplane experiences a 30 miles per hour crosswind flowing due east, find the actual speed and the direction of the airplane.

25 Given that the forces $\vec{F_1}=\langle -2,\ 2\sqrt{3}\rangle$ and $\vec{F_2}=\langle -1,\ -5\sqrt{3}\rangle$ are acting on a point A, find the direction and magnitude of the force required in order for the forces to be in equilibrium.

26 Daniel is pulling a sled horizontally by exerting 40 lb on the rope that's tied to its front end. If the rope makes an angle of 30° with horizontal, what is the work done in moving the sled 100 feet?

27 Given the matrices $A=\begin{bmatrix} 2 & 4 \\ 1 & 3 \end{bmatrix}$ and $B=\begin{bmatrix} 5 & 1 \\ 2 & 6 \end{bmatrix}$,

(1) Calculate the product AB.

(2) Verify if the product AB is equal to the product BA.

28 Consider the matrix $C=\begin{bmatrix} 3 & 7 \\ 2 & 5 \end{bmatrix}$

(1) Find the determinant of matrix C.

(2) If the determinant is non−zero, calculate the inverse of matrix C

29 If matrix A has dimensions $m \times k$ and matrix B has dimensions $k \times l$, where m, k, and l are distinct positive integers, which of the following statements must be true?

(A) The sum $A+B$ exists and has dimensions $m \times l$
(B) The difference $A-B$ exists and has dimensions $m \times l$
(C) The product AB exists and has dimensions $m \times l$
(D) The product BA exists and has dimensions $m \times l$

Unit IV Test

30

	John	Eugene
Blueberry	6	5
Butterfinger	8	10
Caramel Delight	4	7

The table above shows the number of each donut that John and Eugene buy for their family members. Each Blueberry costs 60 cents, each Butterfinger costs 85 cents, and each Caramel Delight costs 1 dollar. Which of the following matrix represents the total costs, in cents, of items for John and Eugene?

(A) $\begin{bmatrix} \text{Eugene} \\ \text{John} \end{bmatrix} = \begin{bmatrix} 60 \\ 85 \\ 100 \end{bmatrix} \begin{bmatrix} 6 & 5 \\ 8 & 10 \\ 4 & 7 \end{bmatrix}$

(B) $[\text{John} \quad \text{Eugene}] = [60 \quad 85 \quad 100] \begin{bmatrix} 6 & 5 \\ 8 & 10 \\ 4 & 7 \end{bmatrix}$

(C) $[\text{John} \quad \text{Eugene}] = [60 \quad 85 \quad 100] \begin{bmatrix} 6 & 8 & 4 \\ 5 & 10 & 7 \end{bmatrix}$

(D) $\begin{bmatrix} \text{Eugene} \\ \text{John} \end{bmatrix} = \begin{bmatrix} 6 & 8 & 4 \\ 5 & 10 & 7 \end{bmatrix} \begin{bmatrix} 60 \\ 85 \\ 100 \end{bmatrix}$

31

Student Name	Number of Items Sold			Total Amount
	Cookies	Brownies	Chips	
Annie	24	16	15	\$93
Jenny	18	22	12	\$87
Betty	20	18	16	\$95

Annie, Jenny, and Betty are selling hand–made cookies, brownies, and chips for school fundraiser. The table above shows the number of each item sold and the total amount collected by each of three students. Using the matrices, what is the cost of each brownie?

(A) \$1
(B) \$1.5
(C) \$2
(D) \$2.5

memo

AP PRE CALCULUS

REVIEW AND WORKBOOK

JOSEPH PAK

JM EDU

AP PRECALCULUS

REVIEW AND WORKBOOK

SOLUTIONS MANUAL

JMEDU

JOSEPH PAK

Solutions Manual

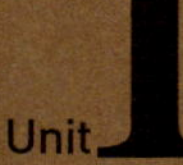

Unit I Polynomial and Rational Functions

1. Relations and Functions

Check Point 1

$f(x)=2x^3-5x^2+1$
$f(-2)=2(-2)^3-5(-2)^2+1$
$=-16-20+1=-35$
$f(-2)=-35$

Check Point 2

The domain is the set of all $x-$coordinates in the given points. So, the domain is: $\{-1, 0, 2, 3\}$. The range is the set of all $y-$coordinates in the given points. Since 3 is repeated, we only list it once in the range. So, the range is: $\{3, 4\}$.

Domain: $\{-1, 0, 2, 3\}$
Range: $\{3, 4\}$

Check Point 3

First, set the denominator equal to zero and solve for x.

$$2x^3+x^2-6x=x(2x^2+x-6)$$
$$=x(2x-3)(x+2)$$

The denominator is zero at $x=0$, $x=\frac{3}{2}$, and $x=-2$. Therefore, the domain of the function g is all real numbers except $x=0$, $x=\frac{3}{2}$, and $x=-2$. In interval notation, the domain is $(-\infty, -2)\cup(-2, 0)\cup\left(0, \frac{3}{2}\right)\cup\left(\frac{3}{2}, \infty\right)$.

Check Point 4

The function is defined when $3x+1\geq 0$, $x\geq -\frac{1}{3}$. Therefore, the domain of the function g is all real numbers x such that $x\geq -\frac{1}{3}$. In interval notation, the domain is $\left[-\frac{1}{3}, \infty\right)$.

Review Exercises

01

$f(x)=2x-1$
$f(1)+2f(2)=2\cdot1-1+2(2\cdot2-1)$
$=1+6=7$

02

$f(x)=\dfrac{a}{x-1}+x-1$

$f(2)=2f(-1)$

$\dfrac{a}{2-1}+2-1=2\left(\dfrac{a}{-1-1}+(-1)-1\right)$

$a+1=-a-4$

$2a=-5,\ a=-\frac{5}{2}$

03

$f(x)=3-2x^2$

$3-2x^2=0$

$$2x^2=3,\ x^2=\frac{3}{2},\ x=\pm\frac{\sqrt{6}}{2}$$

Since $x<0$, the value of x is $-\frac{\sqrt{6}}{2}$.

04

I. $f(2)=2^2-4=0$

II. $f(2)=2^2+2-6=0$

III. $f(2)=\frac{2-2}{2^2-4}=\frac{0}{0}=$undefined

Therefore, the correct answer is (C).

05

$f(x)=ax^2+bx+c$

$f(0)=a(0)^2+b(0)+c=-1,\ c=-1$

$f(-1)=a(-1)^2+b(-1)+c$

$\quad =a-b-1=3,\ a-b=4$

06

$f(x)=2+\sqrt{\frac{x}{2}-4}$

Since $\frac{x}{2}-4\geq 0$, we can be assured that $\sqrt{\frac{x}{2}-4}\geq 0$. Therefore, $f(x)=2+\sqrt{\frac{x}{2}-4}\geq 2$.

Among the 4 answer choices, option (D) 0 cannot be the value of $f(x)$.

07

$f(x)=\frac{1}{\sqrt{x^2-4}}$

The denominator $\sqrt{x^2-4}$ must not be zero and $x^2-4>0$.

$$x^2-4>0$$
$$(x+2)(x-2)>0$$

Therefore, the domain of the function is $x<-2$ or $x>2$. The answer is (D).

08

$f(x)=\frac{\sqrt{2x+1}}{x^2+x}$

The denominator x^2+x must not be zero.

$x^2+x=x(x+1)\neq 0$

$\quad x\neq 0$ or $x\neq -1$

The function is defined when $2x+1\geq 0$,

$\Rightarrow x\geq -\frac{1}{2}$.

Therefore, combining the above two domains gives $-\frac{1}{2}\leq x<0$ or $x>0$.

The answer is (D).

09

The correct answer is (B) $f(x)=|x+2|$ because $|x+2|$ is defined for all x.

10

The heights of the rectangles from the left are $y(0)$, $y(2)$, and $y(4)$, respectively. Therefore, the sum of the areas of the three inscribed rectangles is as follows:

$A=2\cdot y(0)+2\cdot y(2)+2\cdot y(2)$

$\quad =2(0^2+2)+2(2^2+2)+2(4^2+2)$

$\quad =52$

2. Rates of Change

Check Point 1

The average rate of change of f over $-1 \leq x \leq 2$ is

$$\frac{\Delta y}{\Delta x}=\frac{f(2)-f(-1)}{2-(-1)}=\frac{0-7}{3}=-\frac{7}{3}$$

Check Point 2

Let $(x_1,\ y_1)=(-4,-1)$ and $(x_2,\ y_2)=(2,\ 35)$. The rate of change(slope) of the line is

$$\frac{\Delta y}{\Delta x}=\frac{35-(-1)}{2-(-4)}==\frac{36}{6}=6$$

Check Point 3

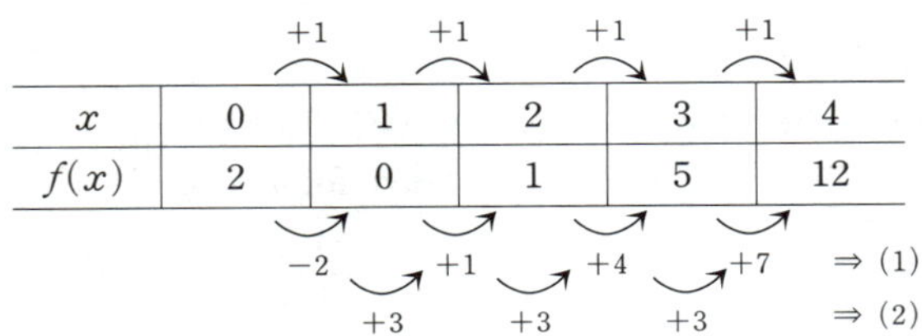

x	0	1	2	3	4
$f(x)$	2	0	1	5	12

(1): The rate of change is not constant.
(2): The rate of change is increasing constantly.
Therefore, the function f is quadratic, and its graph of parabola would be concave up.

Review Exercises

01

From $x=0$ to $x=1$, the rate of change is -1.
From $x=1$ to $x=2$, the rate of change is 1.
From $x=2$ to $x=3$, the rate of change is 3.
From $x=3$ to $x=4$, the rate of change is 5.
The rate of change is increasing in the interval $0 \leq x \leq 4$. Therefore, the correct answer is (C).

02

Since the rate of change is increasing in the interval $0<x<2$, the graph of f is concave up in this interval. Therefore, the answer is (A).

03

The graph of f is concave up in the interval $x<3$. Consequently, the rate of change is increasing in this interval. Therefore, the correct answer is (A) $-2<x<3$.

04

In the interval $1<x<5$, the graph of f is strictly increasing. Therefore, it can be concluded that the rate of change is positive in this interval. The answer is (C).

05

If the rate of change of f is negative, the graph of f is decreasing. If the rate of change of f is increasing, the graph of f is concave up. Therefore, combining both characteristics, we can conclude that the graph of f is decreasing and concave up. The answer is (C).

06

From $x=-1$ to $x=1$, the rate of change is -1.
From $x=1$ to $x=2$, the rate of change is 2.
From $x=2$ to $x=4$, the rate of change is -2.
From $x=4$ to $x=6$, the rate of change is 3.5.
The rate of change is greatest for $4<x<6$. Thus, the correct answer is (D).

07

In the graph of f, the rate of change is negative for $x<1$, $2<x<4$, and $x>6$ because the graph of f is decreasing in these intervals. Therefore, the correct answer is (B).

08

For each interval:
$0\le x\le 1$: Rate of change$=-8$
→ The function decreases by $(1-0)(8)=8$.
$1\le x\le 4$: Rate of change$=-3$
→ The function decreases by $(4-1)(3)=9$.
$4\le x\le 6$: Rate of change$=5$
→ The function increases by $(6-4)(5)=10$.
$6\le x\le 10$: Rate of change$=10$
→ The function increases by $(10-6)(10)=40$.
Therefore, the answer is (B).

09

Since the function f is quadratic with a positive leading coefficient, its graph is a concave up parabola. Therefore, the graph of f exhibits an increasing rate of change for all x. The answer is (C).

10

$$\begin{aligned} g(x) &= -2x^2-8x+5 \\ &= -2(x^2+4x+4-4)+5 \\ &= -2(x+2)^2+13 \end{aligned}$$

The graph of g has a vertex at $x=-2$ and is concave down due to its negative leading coefficient. Therefore, for $x>-2$, the graph of g has a negative rate of change, and for $x<-2$, the graph of g has a positive rate of change. The answer is (B).

11

Given that the rate of change of f is positive for $x<4$ and negative for $x>4$, it means that the function is increasing before $x=4$ and decreasing after $x=4$. This behavior indicates a local maximum at $x=4$. Therefore, the answer is (A).

12

Given that the rate of change of f is increasing for $x<4$ and decreasing for $x>4$, this indicates that the graph of f changes concavity at $x=4$. Specifically, the graph is concave up where the rate of change is increasing and concave down where the rate of change is decreasing. Therefore, the correct answer is (D).

3. Polynomial Functions of Higher Degree

Check Point 1

① $g(x)=5+2x^2-3x^4 \rightarrow g(x)=-3x^4+2x^2+5$

A polynomial function with degree 4 (Quartic function).

Leading coefficient: -3

Constant term: 5

② $h(x)=x+5x^2+6x^3-1$

$\rightarrow h(x)=6x^3+5x^2+x-1$

A polynomial function with degree 3 (Cubic function).

Leading coefficient: 6

Constant term: -1

Check Point 2

① $f(x)=4x^3-x$

Degree: 3(odd)

Leading coefficient: 4(positive)

It increases as $x \rightarrow \infty$

but decreases as $x \rightarrow -\infty$

② $f(x)=-x^4+2x^2-4x-3$

Degree: 4(even)

Leading coefficient: -1(negative)

It decreases as $x \rightarrow \infty$

and decreases as $x \rightarrow -\infty$

Check Point 3

① $f(x)=x^3+x^2-12x$

$x(x^2+x-12)=0$

$x(x-3)(x+4)=0$

The zeros are -4, 0, and 3

② $f(x)=3x^3-x^2+6x-2$

$x^2(3x-1)+2(3x-1)=0$

$(3x-1)(x^2+2)=0$

The zeros are $\frac{1}{3}$ and $\pm\sqrt{2}i$

Check Point 4

① $g(x)=4x^4-16x^2$

$4x^2(x^2-4)=0$

$4x^2(x-2)(x+2)=0$

The zeros are 0 and ± 2

② $h(x)=2x^3-4x^2+2x$

$2x(x^2-2x+1)=0$

$2x(x-1)^2=0$

The zeros are 0 and 1

Check Point 5

① $f(x)=(x-1)(x+1)^2(x-2) \rightarrow n=4,\ a_n=1$

It increases as $x \rightarrow \infty$; increases as $x \rightarrow -\infty$

Zeros: -1(multiplicity 2), 1, and 2

Additional Point:

$f(0)=(0-1)(0+1)^2(0-2)=2$

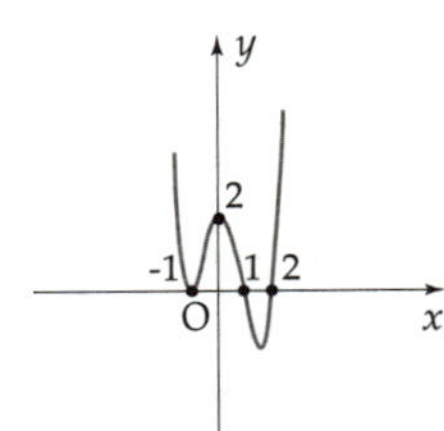

② $g(x)=-x^5-x^4 \rightarrow n=5,\ a_n=-1$

$=-x^4(x+1)$

It decreases as $x \rightarrow \infty$;

increases as $x \rightarrow -\infty$

Zeros: -1 and 0(multiplicity 4)

Additional Point: $g(1)=-(1)^4(1+1)=-2$

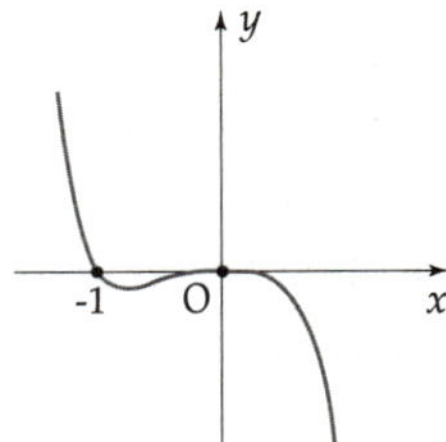

Review Exercises

01

(1) $f(x)=-3x^4+x^2+x-4 \rightarrow n=4,\ a_n=-3$

Degree is even and leading coefficient is negative. So the graph decreases as $x\rightarrow\infty$ and also decreases as $x\rightarrow-\infty$.

(2) $f(x)=4x^3-2x^2-5x+1 \rightarrow n=3,\ a_n=4$

Degree is odd and leading coefficient is positive. So the graph increases as $x\rightarrow\infty$ but decreases as $x\rightarrow-\infty$.

(3) $g(x)=-x^5-2x^4+\dfrac{x^2}{4} \rightarrow n=5,\ a_n=-1$

Degree is odd and leading coefficient is negative. So the graph decreases as $x\rightarrow\infty$ but increases as $x\rightarrow-\infty$.

02

$h(x)=-4+2x-6x^2+\dfrac{2x^4}{3}$

$h(x)=\dfrac{2x^4}{3}-6x^2+2x-4 \rightarrow n=4,\ a_n=\dfrac{2}{3}$

Since the degree of $h(x)$ is even and leading coefficient is positive, the graph increases as $x\rightarrow\infty$ and also increases as $x\rightarrow-\infty$. So I and II are correct. The answer is (A).

03

Since the graph increases as $x\rightarrow\infty$ but decreases as $x\rightarrow-\infty$, the leading coefficient $a>0$. Also, $d>0$ because the graph has positive y-intercept. So the answer is (A).

04

(1) $f(x)=x^3-9x$

$x^3-9x=0$

$x(x^2-9)=0$

$x(x-3)(x+3)=0$

$x=0,\ x=3$, and $x=-3$

(2) $f(x)=-2x^4+10x^3-8x^2$

$-2x^4+10x^3-8x^2=0$

$-2x^2(x^2-5x+4)=0$

$-2x^2(x-1)(x-4)=0$

$x=0,\ x=1$, and $x=4$

(3) $g(x)=x^3-4x^2-x+4$

$x^3-4x^2-x+4=0$

$x^2(x-4)-(x-4)=0$

$(x-4)(x^2-1)=0$

$(x-4)(x-1)(x+1)=0$

$x=4,\ x=1$, and $x=-1$

(4) $h(x)=x^4-5x^2+4$

$x^4-5x^2+4=0$

$(x^2)^2-5(x^2)+4=0$

$(x^2-1)(x^2-4)=0$

$(x-1)(x+1)(x-2)(x+2)=0$

$x=1,\ x=-1,\ x=2$ and $x=-2$

05

(1) $f(x)=(x-1)(x+2)(x-3)$

End Behavior: Since the degree is 3(odd) and leading coefficient is 1(positive), the graph increases as $x\rightarrow\infty$ but decreases as $x\rightarrow-\infty$.

Zeros: $x=1,\ x=-2$, and $x=3$

Additional Points: $f(0)=6$ and $f(2)=-4$

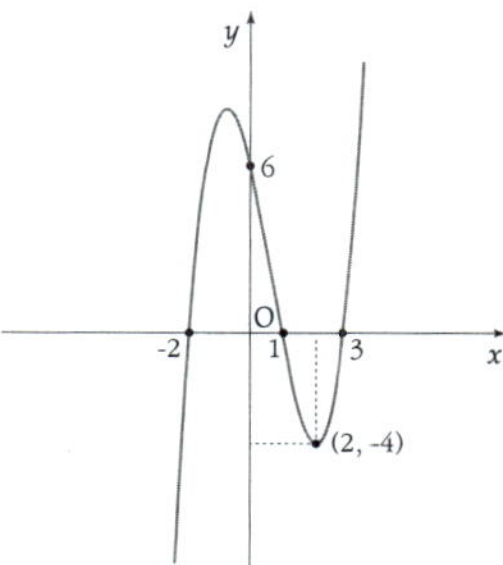

(2) $f(x)=-2x^4+8x^2$

End Behavior: Since the degree is 4(even) and leading coefficient is -2(negative), the graph decreases as $x\rightarrow\infty$ and also decreases as $x\rightarrow-\infty$.

Zeros: $-2x^4+8x^2=0$

$-2x^2(x^2-4)=0$

$-2x^2(x-2)(x+2)=0$

$x=0$(Multiplicity 2), $x=2$, and $x=-2$

Additional Points: $f(-1)=6$ and $f(1)=6$

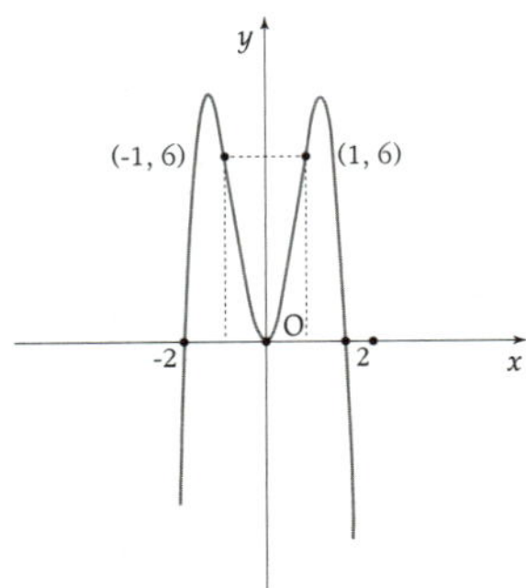

(3) $h(x)=-2x^5-x^4+6x^3$

End Behavior: Since the degree is 5(odd) and leading coefficient is -2(negative), the graph decreases as $x \to \infty$ but increases as $x \to -\infty$.

Zeros: $-2x^5-x^4+6x^3=0$

$-x^3(2x^2+x-6)=0$

$-x^3(2x-3)(x+2)=0$

$x=0$(Multiplicity 3), $x=\frac{3}{2}$, and $x=-2$

Additional Points: $f(-1)=-5$ and $f(1)=3$

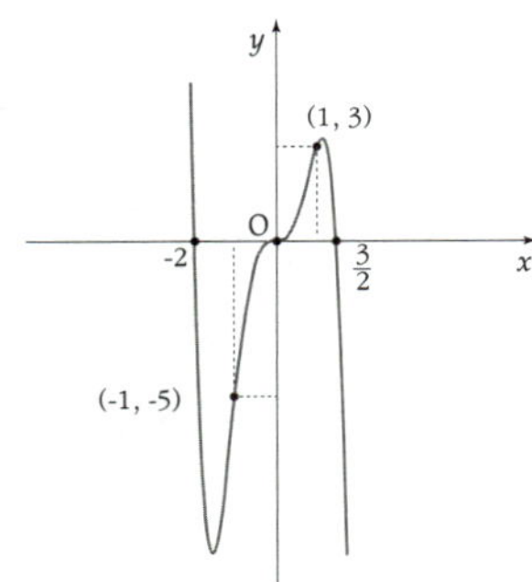

(4) $f(x)=-x^3(x+2)(x-3)$

End Behavior: Since the degree is 5(odd) and leading coefficient is -1(negative), the graph decreases as $x \to \infty$ but increases as $x \to -\infty$.

Zeros: $x=-2$, $x=0$(Multiplicity 3), $x=3$

Additional Points: $f(1)=6$

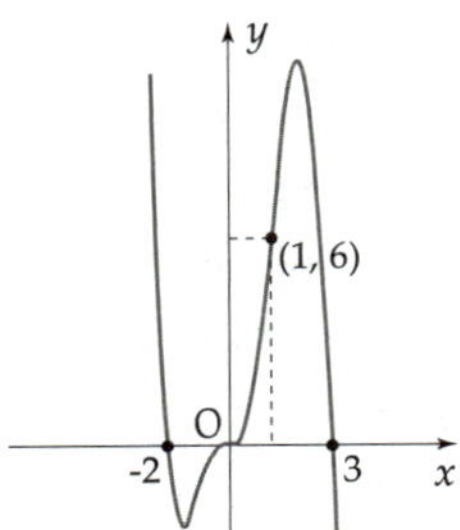

(5) $h(x)=x^3-5x^2-2x+10$

End Behavior: Since the degree is 3(odd) and leading coefficient is 1(positive), the graph increases as $x \to \infty$ and decreases as $x \to -\infty$.

Zeros: $x^3-5x^2-2x+10=0$

$x^2(x-5)-2(x-5)=0$

$(x-5)(x^2-2)=0$

$x=5$ and $x=\pm\sqrt{2}$

Additional Points: $f(0)=10$

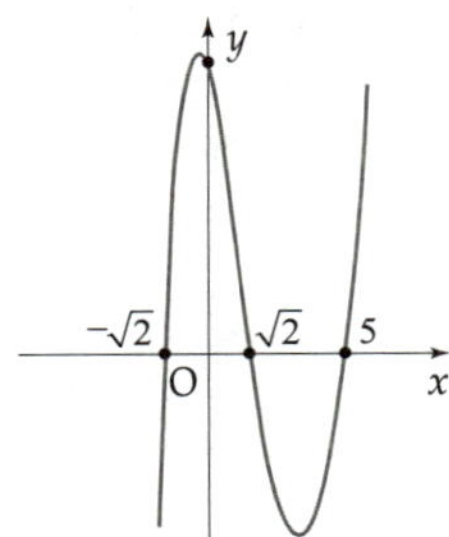

06

Since there are 2 turning points, smallest possible degree of the polynomial above has to be 3.

07

Degree: $(2x+1)^3$ has degree 3 and $(3x-1)$ has degree 1. Therefore, the total degree is $3+1=4$.
Leading Coefficient: The leading term of $(2x+1)^3$ is $8x^3$ and the leading term of $(3x-1)$ is $3x$. Thus, the leading coefficient is $8\cdot3=24$.
The correct answer is (B).

08

(1) If a is positive, the quadratic function opens upwards, and the graph has a global minimum but no global maximum.
(2) If a is negative, the quadratic function opens downwards, and the graph has a global maximum but no global minimum.

Therefore, the correct answer is (B).

09

The graph of f has two zeros: one at $x=-2$(where it touches the $x-$axis) and another at $x=3$(where it passes through the $x-$axis). Additionally, since the graph of f decreases without bound as x decreases without bound, and increases without bound as x increases without bound, the leading term of the function f must have a positive leading coefficient and the highest degree must be odd. Therefore, the correct answer is (B).

10

Given $g(x)=\frac{f(x)}{x}$ and $g(x)$ is a polynomial of degree 4:
Degree$(g(x))$=Degree$(f(x))-1$
Therefore, the correct answer is (C) f is a polynomial of degree 5.

11

(1) The degree of the polynomial must be even, as only even-degree polynomials can have the same behavior (both going to ∞).
(2) The leading coefficient must be positive to ensure the polynomial grows towards positive infinity in both directions.

Therefore, the correct answer is (A).

12

For a polynomial with an odd degree and a negative leading coefficient:
(1) As x approaches $-\infty$, the polynomial $g(x)$ will approach ∞.
(2) As x approaches ∞, the polynomial $g(x)$ will approach $-\infty$.

Therefore, the correct answer is (C).

13

If $\lim_{x\to\infty} h(x)=-\infty$ and $\lim_{x\to\infty} h(x)=\infty$, we need to find function $h(x)$ with an odd degree and a negative leading coefficient. Therefore, the correct answer is (D).

14

$$\begin{aligned} g(x) &= x^3-4x^2+4x \\ &= x(x^2-4x+4) \\ &= x(x-2)^2 \end{aligned}$$

The graph of g is roughly drawn as follows.

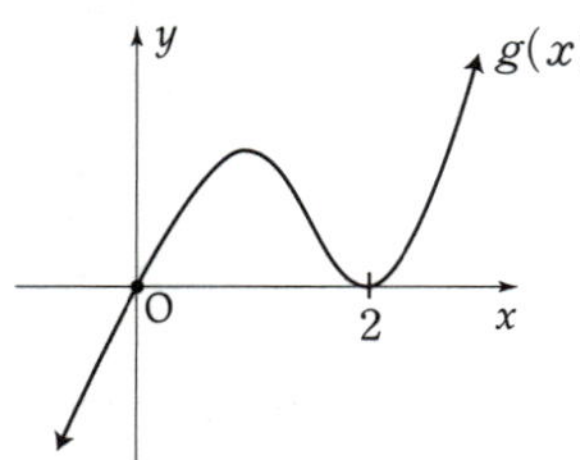

Therefore, the correct statement is (C) g has a local maximum between $x=0$ and $x=2$.

4. Division of Polynomials

Check Point 1

①

$$\begin{array}{r} x^2-8x+19 \\ x+2\,\overline{\big)\,x^3-6x^2+\ 3x-\ 4} \\ \underline{x^3+2x^2\qquad\qquad} \\ -8x^2+\ 3x-\ 4 \\ \underline{-8x^2-16x\qquad} \\ 19x-\ 4 \\ \underline{19x+38} \\ -42 \end{array}$$

$$\frac{x^3-6x^2+3x-4}{x+2}=x^2-8x+19-\frac{42}{x+2}$$

②

$$\begin{array}{r} x^2-2 \\ x^2+2\,\overline{\big)\,x^4\qquad\ -5} \\ \underline{x^4+2x^2\qquad} \\ -2x^2-5 \\ \underline{-2x^2-4} \\ -1 \end{array}$$

$$\frac{x^4-5}{x^2+2}=x^2-2-\frac{1}{x^2+2}$$

Check Point 2

① $\dfrac{x^2-4x+1}{x-3}$ →

$$\begin{array}{r|rrr} 3 & 1 & -4 & 1 \\ & & 3 & -3 \\ \hline & 1 & -1 & \boxed{-2} \end{array}$$

$$\frac{x^2-4x+1}{x-3}=x-1-\frac{2}{x-3}$$

② $\dfrac{x^3+4x^2-9x+2}{x+3}$ →

$$\begin{array}{r|rrrr} -3 & 1 & 4 & -9 & 2 \\ & & -3 & -3 & 36 \\ \hline & 1 & 1 & -12 & \boxed{38} \end{array}$$

$$\frac{x^3+4x^2-9x+2}{x+3}=x^2+x-12+\frac{38}{x+3}$$

Check Point 3

Let $f(x)=6x^3-11x^2-2x-1$.

Then, $f\left(\frac{1}{2}\right)=R$ and

$f\left(\frac{1}{2}\right)=6\left(\frac{1}{2}\right)^3-11\left(\frac{1}{2}\right)^2-2\left(\frac{1}{2}\right)-1=-4.$

So the remainder is -4.

Check Point 4

① Let $f(x)=x^3-21x+20$. Since $f(-5)=(-5)^3-21(-5)+20=0$, $x+5$ is a factor $x^3-21x+20$.

② Let $f(x)=2x^3-15x^2+24x+b$. Then, $f(2)=2(2)^3-15(2)^2+24(2)+b=0$

$16-60+48+b=0 \rightarrow b=-4$

Review Exercises

01

(1)

$$\begin{array}{r} 3x+2 \\ 2x^2-1\,\big)\overline{\,6x^3+4x^2-7x-1} \\ \underline{6x^3\qquad\quad -3x\quad\;\;} \\ 4x^2-4x-1 \\ \underline{4x^2\qquad\;\; -2} \\ -4x+1 \end{array}$$

$$\frac{6x^2+4x^2-7x-1}{2x^2-1}=3x+2-\frac{4x-1}{2x^2-1}$$

(2)

$$\begin{array}{r} x+3 \\ x^2-2x-1\,\big)\overline{\,x^3+\;x^2-\;x+1} \\ \underline{x^3-2x^2-\;x\quad\;\;} \\ 3x^2\qquad +1 \\ \underline{3x^2-6x-3} \\ 6x+4 \end{array}$$

$$\frac{x^3+x^2-x+1}{x^2-2x-1}=x+3+\frac{6x+4}{x^2-2x-1}$$

(3)

$$\begin{array}{r} 6x^2+3x-1 \\ 2x^2+3\,\big)\overline{\,12x^4+6x^3+16x^2+12x-7} \\ \underline{12x^4\qquad\quad +18x^2\qquad\qquad} \\ 6x^3-\;2x^2+12x-7 \\ \underline{6x^3\qquad\quad +\;9x\quad\;\;} \\ -\;2x^2+\;3x-7 \\ \underline{-\;2x^2\qquad\quad -3} \\ 3x-4 \end{array}$$

$$\frac{12x^4+6x^3+16x^2+12x-7}{2x^2+3}$$

$$=6x^2+3x-1+\frac{3x-4}{2x^2+3}$$

(4)

$$\begin{array}{r} x^2 \\ x^3-2\,\big)\overline{\,x^5\qquad\quad -1} \\ \underline{x^5-2x^2\qquad} \\ 2x^2-1 \end{array}$$

$$(x^5-1)\div(x^3-2)=x^2+\frac{2x^2-1}{x^3-2}$$

02

(1) $\dfrac{x^3-4x^2-2x+9}{x-4} \rightarrow$

$$\begin{array}{r|rrrr} 4 & 1 & -4 & -2 & 9 \\ & & 4 & 0 & -8 \\ \hline & 1 & 0 & -2 & \boxed{1} \end{array}$$

$$\frac{x^3-4x^2-2x+9}{x-4}=x^2-2+\frac{1}{x-4}$$

(2) $\dfrac{x^5-2x^3-1}{x-2} \rightarrow$

$$\begin{array}{r|rrrrrr} 2 & 1 & 0 & -2 & 0 & 0 & -1 \\ & & 2 & 4 & 4 & 8 & 16 \\ \hline & 1 & 2 & 2 & 4 & 8 & \boxed{15} \end{array}$$

$$\frac{x^5-2x^3-1}{x-2}=x^4+2x^3+2x^2+4x+8+\frac{15}{x-2}$$

(3) $\dfrac{3x^3+5x^2-\frac{1}{2}x+4}{x+1} \rightarrow$

$$\begin{array}{r|rrrr} -1 & 3 & 5 & -\frac{1}{2} & 4 \\ & & -3 & -2 & \frac{5}{2} \\ \hline & 3 & 2 & -\frac{5}{2} & \boxed{\frac{13}{2}} \end{array}$$

$$\frac{3x^3+5x^2-\frac{1}{2}x+4}{x+1}=3x^2+2x-\frac{5}{2}+\frac{13}{2(x+1)}$$

(4) $(2x^2-5x+1)\div(2x-1) \rightarrow$

$$\begin{array}{r|rrr} \frac{1}{2} & 2 & -5 & 1 \\ & & 1 & -2 \\ \hline & 2 & -4 & \boxed{-1} \end{array}$$

This is actually the division,

$$\frac{2x^2-5x+1}{x-\frac{1}{2}}=2x-4-\frac{1}{x-\frac{1}{2}}.$$ Therefore,

$$\frac{2x^2-5x+1}{2x-1}=\frac{1}{2}\left(\frac{2x^2-5x+1}{x-\frac{1}{2}}\right)$$

$$=\frac{1}{2}\left(2x-4-\frac{1}{x-\frac{1}{2}}\right)$$

$$=x-2-\frac{1}{2x-1}$$

03

Using the remainder theorem, we have

$\frac{f(x)}{(x-2)} \rightarrow f(2)=R$

$f(2)=(2)^3-4(2)^2+5(2)-1=1$

So the remainder is 1.

04

Since $x+2$ is a factor of $x^4-2x^3+bx^2+4$, we have the following.

$(-2)^4-2(-2)^3+b(-2)^2+4=0$

$16+16+4b+4=0,\ b=-9$

05

(1) Let $f(x)=2x^3-x^2-5x-2$.

Since $f(2)=2(2)^3-(2)^2-5(2)-2=0$,

$x-2$ is a factor of $f(x)$.

Now using synthetic division

	2	−1	−5	−2
2		4	6	2
	2	3	1	0

, we have

$$\frac{2x^3-x^2-5x-2}{x-2}=2x^2+3x+1$$ and

$2x^2+3x+1=(2x+1)(x+1)$.

So the factors are $(x-2)$, $(2x+1)$, and $(x+1)$.

(2) Let $f(x)=x^4+x^3-11x^2-9x+18$.

$f(1)=(1)^4+(1)^3-11(1)^2-9(1)+18=0$

$\rightarrow x-1$ is a factor of $f(x)$.

$f(-3)=(-3)^4+(-3)^3-11(-3)^2-9(-3)+18=0$

$\rightarrow x+3$ is also a factor of $f(x)$.

Now using synthetic division twice,

	1	1	−11	−9	18
1		1	2	−9	−18
	1	2	−9	−18	0
−3		−3	3	18	
	1	−1	−6	0	

$\rightarrow x^4+x^3-11x^2-9x+18$

$=(x-1)(\underline{x^3+2x^2-9x-18})$

$(\underline{x^3+2x^2-9x-18})=(x+3)(\underline{x^2-x-6})$

$(\underline{x^2-x-6})=(x-3)(x+2)$

So the factors are $(x-1)$, $(x+3)$, $(x-3)$, and $(x+2)$.

06

Using the remainder theorem,

$p(-1)$

$=3(-1)^{150}+5(-1)^{100}-4(-1)^{75}-7(-1)^{25}-10$

$=3+5+4+7-10=9$.

The remainder is 9.

07

Let $f(x)=x^3+ax^2+bx+3$. Then, using the remainder theorem,

$f(1)=(1)^3+a(1)^2+b(1)+3=2$ and

$f(-1)=(-1)^3+a(-1)^2+b(-1)+3=8$.

Now we have the system

$\begin{cases}1+a+b+3=2\\-1+a-b+3=8\end{cases} \rightarrow \begin{cases}a+b=-2\\a-b=6\end{cases}$.

Solving the system, we have

$a=2$ and $b=-4$. So $a+b=2+(-4)=-2$.

08

Since $2x^3+kx^2-5x-2$ is divisible by $x+1$, we can find the value of b using factor theorem.

$2(-1)^3+k(-1)^2-5(-1)-2=0$

$-2+k+5-2=0,\ k=-1.$

We can now use the synthetic division to find the rest of the factors.

$$\frac{2x^3-x^2-5x-2}{x+1} \rightarrow \begin{array}{r|rrrr} -1 & 2 & -1 & -5 & -2 \\ & & -2 & 3 & 2 \\ \hline & 2 & -3 & -2 & \boxed{0} \end{array}$$

$$\frac{2x^3-x^2-5x-2}{x+1}=2x^2-3x-2$$

$$\begin{aligned}2x^3-x^2-5x-2&=(2x^2-3x-2)(x+1)\\&=(x-2)(2x+1)(x+1)\end{aligned}$$

Since $(x-2)(x+1)=x^2-x-2$, the polynomial is also divisible by x^2-x-2. So the answer is (A).

5. Real Zeros of Polynomial Functions

Check Point 1

① $f(x)=x^3-3x^2-4x+12$

p: factors of 12; q: factors of 1

The possible rational zeros:

$$\pm\frac{p}{q}=\pm\frac{1,\ 2,\ 3,\ 4,\ 6,\ 12}{1}$$

$$=\pm1,\ \pm2,\ \pm3,\ \pm4,\ \pm6,\ \pm12$$

$f(2)=(2)^3-3(2)^2-4(2)+12=0$

So $x-2$ is a factor of $f(x)$. We can now use the synthetic division to find the rest of the factors.

$$\begin{array}{r|rrrr} 2 & 1 & -3 & -4 & 12 \\ & & 2 & -2 & -12 \\ \hline & 1 & -1 & -6 & \boxed{0} \end{array}$$

$$\begin{aligned}\rightarrow x^3-3x^2-4x+12&=(x-2)(x^2-x-6)\\&=(x-2)(x-3)(x+2)\end{aligned}$$

Therefore, $f(x)=(x-2)(x-3)(x+2)$ and the rational zeros are $x=2$, $x=3$, and $x=-2$.

Alternate Solution:

Factor $x^3-3x^2-4x+12$ by grouping.

$$\begin{aligned}x^3-3x^2-4x+12&=x^2(x-3)-4(x-3)\\&=(x-3)(x^2-4)\\&=(x-3)(x-2)(x+2)\end{aligned}$$

So $f(x)=(x-2)(x-3)(x+2)$ and the rational zeros are $x=2$, $x=3$, and $x=-2$.

② $f(x)=2x^3-7x^2+2x+3$

p: factors of 3; q: factors of 2

The possible rational zeros:

$$\pm\frac{p}{q}=\pm\frac{1,3}{1,2}=\pm1,\ \pm3,\ \pm\frac{1}{2},\ \pm\frac{3}{2}$$

$f(1)=2(1)^3-7(1)^2+2(1)+3=0$

So $x-1$ is a factor of $f(x)$. We can now use the synthetic division to find the rest of the factors.

$$\begin{array}{r|rrrr} & 2 & -7 & 2 & 3 \\ 1 & & 2 & -5 & -3 \\ \hline & 2 & -5 & -3 & \boxed{0} \end{array}$$

$\rightarrow 2x^3-7x^2+2x+3=(x-1)(2x^2-5x-3)$
$=(x-1)(x-3)(2x+1)$

Therefore $f(x)=(x-1)(x-3)(2x+1)$ and the rational zeros are $x=1$, $x=3$, and $x=-\frac{1}{2}$.

Check Point 2

$f(x)=x^3+2x^2-2x-12$ has three complex zeros.

p: factors of 12; q: factors of 1

The possible rational zeros:

$$\pm\frac{p}{q}=\pm\frac{1,\ 2,\ 3,\ 4,\ 6,\ 12}{1}$$
$$=\pm1,\ \pm2,\ \pm3,\ \pm4,\ \pm6,\ \pm12$$

$f(2)=(2)^3+2(2)^2-2(2)-12=0$

So $x-2$ is a factor of $f(x)$. We can now use the synthetic division to find the rest of the factors.

$$\begin{array}{r|rrrr} & 1 & 2 & -2 & -12 \\ 2 & & 2 & 8 & 12 \\ \hline & 1 & 4 & 6 & \boxed{0} \end{array}$$

$\rightarrow x^3+2x^2-2x-12=(x-2)(x^2+4x+6)$

Using the quadratic formula, we can determine the zeros of x^2+4x+6.

$$x=\frac{-4\pm\sqrt{4^2-4(1)(6)}}{2(1)}=-2\pm\sqrt{2}i.$$

So the zeros are $x=2$ and $x=-2\pm\sqrt{2}i$

Check Point 3

① $f(x)=(x+1)(x-2)(x-3)=x^3-4x^2+x+6.$

② From the zeros $2i$ and $-2i$,

$x^2-(2i+(-2i))x+(2i\cdot(-2i))$
$=x^2-4i^2=x^2+4.$

So $f(x)=(x+1)(x^2+4)=x^3+x^2+4x+4.$

Check Point 4

$f(x)=x^4+2x^3+x+2 \rightarrow$ No sign change.

$f(-x)=(-x)^4+2(-x)^3+(-x)+2$
$=\underbrace{x^4-2x^3}_{+\text{ to }-}\underbrace{-x+2}_{-\text{ to }+}$

$\rightarrow$ Two sign changes.

The number of possible zero combinations:

Positive	Negative	Imaginary
0	2	2
0	0	4

p: factors of 2; q: factors of 1

The possible rational zeros:

$\pm\frac{p}{q}=\pm\frac{1,\ 2}{1}=\pm1,\ \pm2.$

Since there is no positive zero, we look for a zero from negative numbers.

$f(-1)=(-1)^4+2(-1)^3+(-1)+2=0.$

$f(-2)=(-2)^4+2(-2)^3+(-2)+2=0$

So $x+1$ and $x+2$ are factors of $f(x)$.

We can now use the synthetic division to find the rest of the factors.

$$\begin{array}{r|rrrrr} & 1 & 2 & 0 & 1 & 2 \\ -1 & & -1 & -1 & 1 & -2 \\ \hline & 1 & 1 & -1 & 2 & \boxed{0} \\ -2 & & -2 & 2 & -2 & \\ \hline & 1 & -1 & 1 & \boxed{0} & \end{array}$$

$\rightarrow x^4+2x^3+x+2=(x+1)(x^3+x^2-x+2)$
$=(x+1)(x+2)(x^2-x+1)$

Using the quadratic formula, we can determine the zeros of x^2-x+1.

$$x=\frac{-(-1)\pm\sqrt{(-1)^2-4(1)(1)}}{2(1)}$$

$$=\frac{1\pm\sqrt{3}i}{2}$$

Therefore, the zeros are $x=-1$, $x=-2$ and $x=\frac{1}{2}\pm\frac{\sqrt{3}i}{2}$.

Check Point 5

① $2x^2-3x<2$

$2x^2-3x-2<0$

$(2x+1)(x-2)<0$

The zeros are $x=-\frac{1}{2}$ and $x=2$.

Choose a test point from each interval; $x=-1$, $x=0$, and $x=3$.

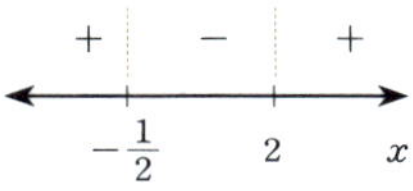

The solution set is $\left(-\frac{1}{2},\ 2\right)$.

$\left(-\frac{1}{2},\ 2\right)$

② $x^3-x^2-2x\geq 0$

$x(x^2-x-2)\geq 0$

$x(x+1)(x-2)\geq 0$

The zeros are $x=-1$, $x=0$, and $x=2$.

Choose a test point from each interval; $x=-2$, $x=-0.5$, $x=1$, and $x=3$.

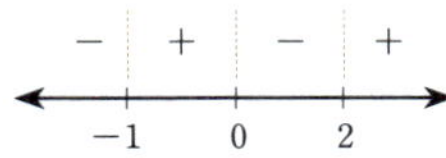

The solution set is $[-1,\ 0]\cup[2,\ \infty)$.

$[-1,\ 0]\cup[2,\ \infty)$

Review Exercises

01

(1) $g(x)=x^4-x^3-2x-4$

p: factors of 4; q: factors of 1

The possible rational zeros:

$\pm\frac{p}{q}=\pm\frac{1,\ 2,\ 4}{1}=\pm1,\ \pm2,\ \pm4.$

$g(-1)=(-1)^4-(-1)^3-2(-1)-4=0$

$g(2)=(2)^4-(2)^3-2(2)-4=0$

So $x+1$ and $x-2$ are factors of $g(x)$. We can now use the synthetic division to find the rest of the factors.

	1	−1	0	−2	−4
−1		−1	2	−2	4
	1	−2	2	−4	0
2		2	0	4	
	1	0	2	0	

→ x^4-x^3-2x-4

$=(x+1)(x^3-2x^2+2x-4)$

$=(x+1)(x-2)(x^2+2)$

Therefore, $g(x)=(x+1)(x-2)(x^2+2)$ and the rational zeros are $x=-1$ and $x=2$.

(2) $f(x)=x^3-10x^2+31x-30$

p: factors of 30; q: factors of 1

The possible rational zeros:

$\pm\frac{p}{q}=\pm\frac{1,\ 2,\ 3,\ 5,\ 6,\ 10,\ 15,\ 30}{1}$

$=\pm1,\ \pm2,\ \pm3,\ \pm5,\ \pm6,\ \pm10,\ \pm15,\ \pm30$

$f(2)=(2)^3-10(2)^2+31(2)-30=0$

So $x-2$ is a factor of $f(x)$. We can now use the synthetic division to find the rest of the factors.

	1	−10	31	−30
2		2	−16	30
	1	−8	15	0

→ $x^3-10x^2+31x-30$

$=(x-2)(x^2-8x+15)$

$=(x-2)(x-3)(x-5)$

Therefore, $f(x)=(x-2)(x-3)(x-5)$ and the rational zeros are $x=2$, $x=3$, and $x=5$.

(3) $g(x)=3x^3+x^2-22x-24$

p: factors of 24; q: factors of 3

The possible rational zeros

$$\pm\frac{p}{q}=\pm\frac{1,\ 2,\ 3,\ 4,\ 6,\ 8,\ 12,\ 24}{1,\ 3}$$

$$=\pm1,\ \pm2,\ \pm3,\ \pm4,\ \pm6,\ \pm8,\ \pm12,\ \pm24,\ \pm\frac{1}{3},\ \pm\frac{2}{3},\ \pm\frac{4}{3},\ \pm\frac{8}{3}$$

$g(-2)=3(-2)^3+(-2)^2-22(-2)-24=0$

So $x+2$ is a factor of $g(x)$. We can now use the synthetic division to find the rest of the factors.

-2	3	1	-22	-24
		-6	10	24
	3	-5	-12	0

$\rightarrow 3x^3+x^2-22x-24$

$=(x+2)(3x^2-5x-12)$

$=(x+2)(x-3)(3x+4)$

Therefore, $g(x)=(x+2)(x-3)(3x+4)$ and the rational zeros are $x=-2$, $x=-\frac{4}{3}$, and $x=3$.

(4) $h(x)=6x^4-17x^3+10x^2+7x-6$

p: factors of 6; q: factors of 6

The possible rational zeros:

$$\pm\frac{p}{q}=\pm\frac{1,\ 2,\ 3,\ 6}{1,\ 2,\ 3,\ 6}$$

$$=\pm1,\ \pm2,\ \pm3,\ \pm6,\ \pm\frac{1}{2},\ \pm\frac{3}{2},\ \pm\frac{1}{3},\ \pm\frac{2}{3},\ \pm\frac{1}{6}.$$

$h(1)=6(1)^4-17(1)^3+10(1)^2+7(1)-6=0$

So $x-1$ is a factor of $h(x)$. We can now use the synthetic division.

1	6	-17	10	7	-6
		6	-11	-1	6
	6	-11	-1	6	0

$\rightarrow 6x^4-17x^3+10x^2+7x-6$

$=(x-1)(\underbrace{6x^3-11x^2-x+6}_{k(x)})$

$k(1)=6(1)^3-11(1)^2-(1)+6=0$

So $x-1$ is also a factor of $h(x)$.

1	6	-11	-1	6
		6	-5	-6
	6	-5	-6	0

$\rightarrow (x-1)(x-1)(6x^2-5x-6)$

$=(x-1)^2(2x-3)(3x+2)$

Therefore, $h(x)=(x-1)^2(2x-3)(3x+2)$ and the rational zeros are $x=1$, $x=\frac{3}{2}$, and $x=-\frac{2}{3}$.

02

$f(x)=x^4+3x^3+2x^2-3x-3$ has four complex zeros.

p: factors of 3; q: factors of 1

The possible rational zeros:

$$\pm\frac{p}{q}=\pm\frac{1,\ 3}{1}=\pm1,\ \pm3.$$

$f(1)=(1)^4+3(1)^3+2(1)^2-3(1)-3=0$

$f(-1)=(-1)^4+3(-1)^3+2(-1)^2-3(-1)-3=0$

So $x-1$ and $x+1$ are factors of $f(x)$. We can now use the synthetic division to find the rest of the factors.

1	1	3	2	-3	-3
		1	4	6	3
-1	1	4	6	3	0
		-1	-3	-3	
	1	3	3	0	

$\rightarrow x^4+3x^3+2x^2-3x-3$

$=(x-1)(x^3+4x^2+6x+3)$

$=(x-1)(x+1)(x^2+3x+3)$

Using the quadratic formula, we can determine the zeros of x^2+3x+3.

$$x=\frac{-3\pm\sqrt{3^2-4(1)(3)}}{2(1)}=\frac{-3\pm\sqrt{3}i}{2}$$

Therefore, the zeros are $x=\pm1$ and $x=-\frac{3}{2}\pm\frac{\sqrt{3}i}{2}$.

03

(1) Complex conjugate of i is $-i$.

$(x-i)(x+i)=x^2-i^2=x^2+1$

or

$x^2-(i+(-i))x+(i\cdot(-i))=x^2-i^2=x^2+1$

So x^2+1 is a factor of $f(x)$. We can now use the long division to find the rest of the factor.

$$\begin{array}{r|l} & 2x-1 \\ x^2+1 & 2x^3-x^2+2x-1 \\ & 2x^3 \quad\; +2x \\ \hline & -x^2 \qquad -1 \\ & -x^2 \qquad -1 \\ \hline & 0 \end{array}$$

$\rightarrow 2x^3-x^2+2x-1$

$=(x^2+1)(2x-1)$

Therefore, the zeros are $x=\frac{1}{2}$ and $x=\pm i$.

(2) Complex conjugate of $1-2i$ is $1+2i$.

$(x-(1-2i))(x-(1+2i))$

$=((x-1)+2i)((x-1)-2i)$

$=(x-1)^2-4i^2=x^2-2x+5$

or

$x^2-((1-2i)+(1+2i))x+((1-2i)\cdot(1+2i))$

$=x^2-2x+5$

So x^2-2x+5 is a factor of $f(x)$. We can now use the long division to find the rest of the factor.

$$\begin{array}{r|l} & x-3 \\ x^2-2x+5 & x^3-5x^2+11x-15 \\ & x^3-2x^2+5x \\ \hline & -3x^2+6x-15 \\ & -3x^2+6x-15 \\ \hline & 0 \end{array}$$

$\rightarrow x^3-5x^2+11x-15$

$=(x^2-2x+5)(x-3)$

Therefore, the zeros are $x=3$ and $x=1\pm 2i$.

04

(1) Zeros: 1, -2, $3+2i$

Complex conjugate of $3+2i$ is $3-2i$.

The expression with two zeros, $3\pm 2i$, can be written as

$x^2-\{(3+2i)+(3-2i)\}x+(3+2i)\cdot(3-2i)$

$=x^2-6x+(9-4i^2)=x^2-6x+13$.

So $f(x)=(x-1)(x+2)(x^2-6x+13)$

$=x^4-5x^3+5x^2+25x-26$.

(2) Zeros: 2(multiplicity2), $-1-3i$

Complex conjugate of $-1-3i$ is $-1+3i$.

The expression with two zeros, $-1\pm 3i$, can be written as

$x^2-((-1-3i)+(-1+3i))x$

$+(-1-3i)\cdot(-1+3i)$

$=x^2+2x+(1-9i^2)=x^2+2x+10$.

So $f(x)=(x-2)^2(x^2+2x+10)$

$=x^4-2x^3+6x^2-32x+40$.

05

Since the third-degree polynomial function has zeros -2, 1, and 3, we can write the function with the leading coefficient a

$f(x)=a(x+2)(x-1)(x-3)$

$=a(x^3-2x^2-5x+6)$

Since the coefficient of x^2 is -5,

$-2a=-5$, $a=\frac{5}{2}$.

$f(x)=\frac{5}{2}(x^3-2x^2-5x+6)$

$=\frac{5}{2}x^3-5x^2-\frac{25}{2}x+15$

06

$f(x)=2x^5-3x^4-7x^3+8x^2-11x+12$

$\rightarrow$ Four sign changes

$f(-x)=2(-x)^5-3(-x)^4-7(-x)^3+8(-x)^2$

$-11(-x)+12$

$=-2x^5-3x^4+7x^3+8x^2+11x+12$

$\rightarrow$ One sign changes

The number of possible zero combinations:

Positive	Negative	Imaginary
4	1	0
2	1	2
0	1	4

07

$f(x)=x^3+2x^2+3x+6$ → No sign change

$f(-x)=(-x)^3+2(-x)^2+3(-x)+6$

$=-x^3+2x^2-3x+6$

→ Three sign changes

The number of possible zero combinations:

Positive	Negative	Imaginary
0	3	0
0	1	2

p: factors of 6; q: factors of 1

The possible rational zero:

$\pm\frac{p}{q}=\pm\frac{1,\ 2,\ 3,\ 6}{1}=\pm1,\ \pm2,\ \pm3,\ \pm6.$

Since there is no positive zero, we look for a zero from negative numbers.

$f(-2)=(-2)^3+2(-2)^2+3(-2)+6=0$

So $x+2$ is a factor of $f(x)$. We can now use the synthetic division to find the rest of the factors.

$$\begin{array}{r|rrrr} & 1 & 2 & 3 & 6 \\ -2 & & -2 & 0 & -6 \\ \hline & 1 & 0 & 3 & \boxed{0} \end{array}$$

→ $x^3+2x^2+3x+6=(x+2)(x^2+3)$

Therefore, the zeros are $x=-2$ and $x=\pm\sqrt{3}i$.

08

First of all, if you look at the answer choices, you can see that the coefficient of f is 1. Since f is a polynomial function with degree 3 and $f(-2)=0$ and $f(1)=0$, we have $f(x)=(x+2)(x-1)(x-k)$, where k is a real number. Now we can determine the value of k using one of the values on the table. We will substitute $f(0)=4$ → $(0,\ 4)$.

$4=(0+2)(0-1)(0-k)$

$4=2k,\ k=2$

So the function $f(x)=(x-2)(x-1)(x+2)$.

The answer is (C).

09

(1) $(x+5)(2x-3)(4-x)\le0$

The zeros are $x=-5$, $x=\frac{3}{2}$, and $x=4$.

Choose a test point from each interval; $x=-6$, $x=0$, $x=2$, and $x=5$.

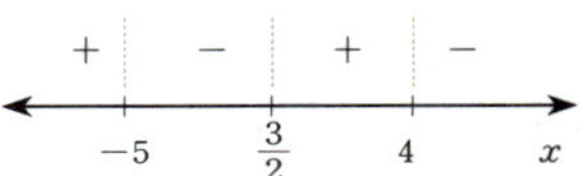

The solution set is $\left[-5,\ \frac{3}{2}\right]\cup[4,\ \infty)$.

(2) $6x^2+2>3-x$

$6x^2+x-1>0$

$(2x+1)(3x-1)>0$

The zeros are $x=-\frac{1}{2}$ and $x=\frac{1}{3}$.

Choose a test point from each interval; $x=-1$, $x=0$, and $x=1$.

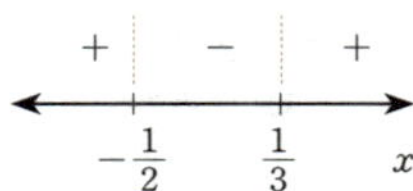

The solution set is $\left(-\infty,\ -\frac{1}{2}\right)\cup\left(\frac{1}{3},\ \infty\right)$.

(3) $4x^3+9x\le12x^2$

$4x^3-12x^2+9x\le0$

$x(4x^2-12x+9)\le0$

$x(2x-3)^2\le0$

The zeros are $x=0$, and $x=\frac{3}{2}$.

Choose a test point from each interval; $x=-1$, $x=1$, and $x=2$.

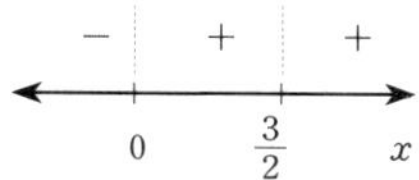

The solution set is $(-\infty, 0]$ and $x=\frac{3}{2}$.

(4)
$$\begin{aligned} x^3-4x^2-4x+16&\geq 0 \\ x^2(x-4)-4(x-4)&\geq 0 \\ (x-4)(x^2-4)&\geq 0 \\ (x-4)(x-2)(x+2)&\geq 0 \end{aligned}$$

The zeros are $x=-2$, $x=2$, and $x=4$. Choose a test point from each interval; $x=-3$, $x=0$, $x=3$, and $x=5$.

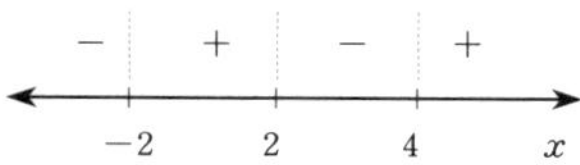

The solution set is $[-2, 2]\cup[4, \infty)$.

10

(A) There is no information provided about $x=-2$ being a zero.

(B) Since h is a polynomial of degree 5, it must have exactly 5 zeros. We already know two of them are real. The remaining three zeros could be real or complex. However, we cannot conclude that h must have at least 2 complex zeros.

(C) This is not necessarily true either. The remaining three zeros could be complex or a mix of real and complex zeros. There is no requirement that the remaining zeros must all be real.

(D) h can be written as $h(x)=(x-2)(x-4)\cdot f(x)$, where $f(x)$ is a polynomial of degree 3.

Therefore, the correct answer is (D).

11

Since g is a polynomial with real coefficients, the complex zeros must come in conjugate pairs. Therefore, if $(x+i)$ is a factor, $(x-i)$ must also be a factor. So the least possible degree of g is the sum of the degrees of linear factors: $(x-2)$, $(x+5)$, $(x+i)$, and $(x-i)$. Therefore, the least possible degree of g is 4.

12

$$\begin{aligned} h(x)=x^3-4x^2-4x+16&<0 \\ x^2(x-4)-4(x-4)&<0 \\ (x-4)(x^2-4)&<0 \\ (x-4)(x-2)(x+2)&<0 \end{aligned}$$

The zeros are $x=-2$, $x=2$, and $x=4$. Choose a test point from each interval; $x=-3$, $x=0$, $x=3$, and $x=5$.

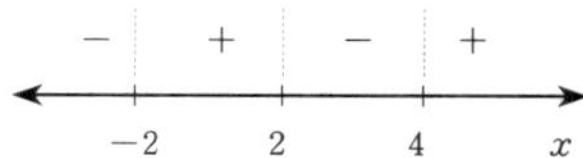

The solution set is $(-\infty, -2)\cup(2, 4)$.

6. Rational Functions

Check Point 1

$f(x)=\frac{3}{x}$

Vertical Asymptote: $x=0$

Horizontal Asymptote: $y=0$

Additional Point(s):

$f(1)=\frac{3}{1}=3 \rightarrow (1,3)$

$f(-1)=\frac{3}{(-1)}=-3 \rightarrow (-1,-3)$

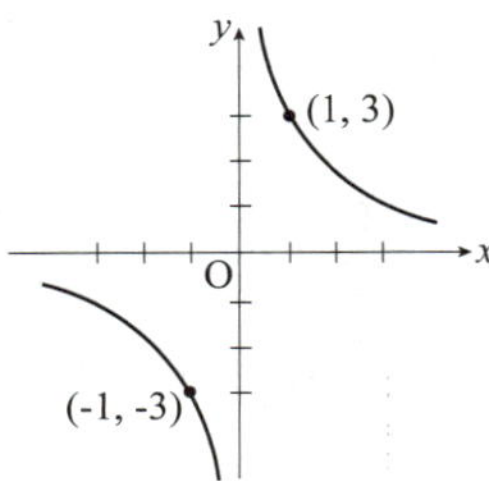

Domain: $(-\infty,\ 0)\cup(0,\ \infty)$

Range: $(-\infty,\ 0)\cup(0,\ \infty)$

Check Point 2

① $f(x)=\frac{2}{x+3} \rightarrow$ Graph $f(x)=\frac{2}{x}$ first and then shift it 3 units to the left.

Vertical Asymptote: $x+3=0,\ x=-3$

Horizontal Asymptote: $y=0$

y−intercept: $f(0)=\frac{2}{(0)+3}=\frac{2}{3} \rightarrow y=\frac{2}{3}$

Additional Point(s):

$f(-4)=\frac{2}{-4+3}=-2 \rightarrow (-4,\ -2)$

$f(-2)=\frac{2}{-2+3}=2 \rightarrow (-2,\ 2)$

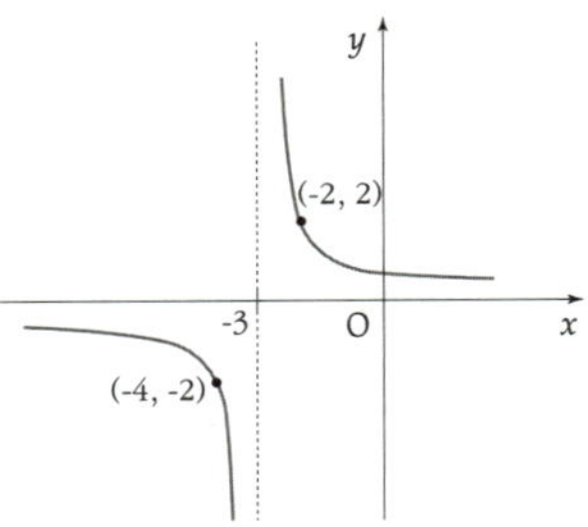

Domain: $(-\infty,\ -3)\cup(-3,\ \infty)$

Range: $(-\infty,\ 0)\cup(0,\ \infty)$

② $g(x)=3+\frac{4}{x-2} \rightarrow$ Graph $f(x)=\frac{4}{x}$ first and then shift it 2 units to the right and 3 units up.

Vertical Asymptote: $x-2=0,\ x=2$

Horizontal Asymptote: $y=3$

y−intercept: $g(0)=3+\frac{4}{0-3}=\frac{5}{3} \rightarrow y=\frac{5}{3}$

x−intercept:

$0=3+\frac{4}{x-3},\ \frac{4}{x-3}=-3$

$x-3=-\frac{4}{3},\ x=\frac{5}{3}$

Additional Point(s):

$g(1)=3+\frac{4}{1-2}=-1 \rightarrow (1,\ -1)$

$g(3)=3+\frac{4}{3-2}=7 \rightarrow (3,\ 7)$

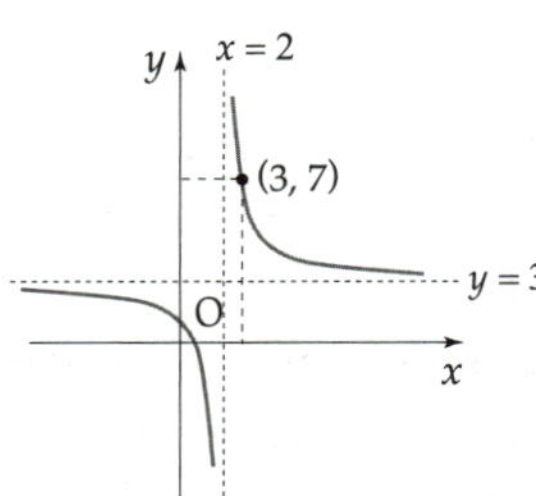

Domain: $(-\infty,\ 2)\cup(2,\ \infty)$

Range: $(-\infty,\ 3)\cup(3,\ \infty)$

Check Point 3

Let n and m be the degree of numerator and denominator, respectively.

① $g(x)=\dfrac{1}{2x-3}$

Vertical Asymptote: $2x-3=0,\ x=\dfrac{3}{2}$

Horizontal Asymptote: $n=0$ and $m=1$ $\rightarrow y=0$

y−intercept:

$g(0)=\dfrac{1}{2(0)-3}=-\dfrac{1}{3}\ \rightarrow y=-\dfrac{1}{3}$

Additional Point(s):

$g(1)=\dfrac{1}{2(1)-3}=-1\rightarrow(1,\ -1)$

$g(2)=\dfrac{1}{2(2)-3}=1\rightarrow(2,\ 1)$

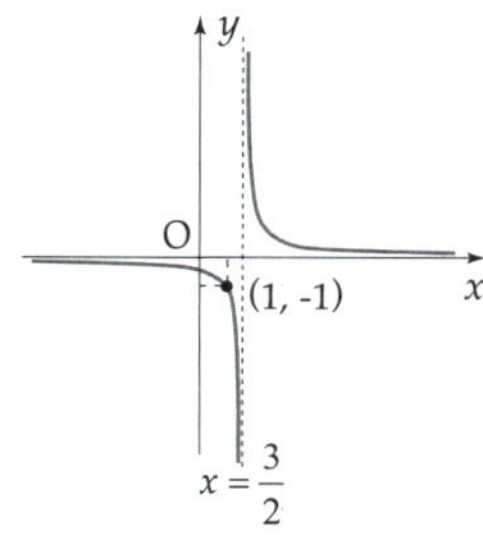

Domain: $\left(-\infty,\ \dfrac{3}{2}\right)\cup\left(\dfrac{3}{2},\ \infty\right)$

Range: $(-\infty,\ 0)\cup(0,\ \infty)$

② $h(x)=\dfrac{3x-2}{1-2x}$

Vertical Asymptote: $1-2x=0,\ x=\dfrac{1}{2}$

Horizontal Asymptote:

$n=1$ and $m=1\rightarrow y=-\dfrac{3}{2}$

y−intercept:

$h(0)=\dfrac{3(0)-2}{1-2(0)}=\dfrac{-2}{1}=-2\rightarrow y=-2$

x−intercept:

$0=\dfrac{3x-2}{1-2x},\ 3x-2=0,\ x=\dfrac{2}{3}$

Additional Point(s):

$h(1)=\dfrac{3(1)-2}{1-2(1)}=\dfrac{1}{-1}=-1\rightarrow(1,\ -1)$

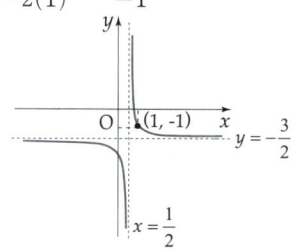

Domain: $\left(-\infty,\ \dfrac{1}{2}\right)\cup\left(\dfrac{1}{2},\infty\right)$

Range: $\left(-\infty,\ -\dfrac{3}{2}\right)\cup\left(-\dfrac{3}{2},\ \infty\right)$

Check Point 4

$$\begin{array}{r}x-1\\ x+1\overline{)x^2\qquad+1}\\ \underline{x^2+x}\\ -x+1\\ \underline{-x-1}\\ 2\end{array}$$

$\rightarrow\dfrac{x^2+1}{x+1}=x-1+\dfrac{2}{x+1}$

Slant Asymptote: $y=x-1$

Vertical Asymptote: $x+1=0,\ x=-1$

y−intercept: $f(0)=\dfrac{(0)^2+1}{(0)+1}\rightarrow(0,\ 1)$

Additonal Point(s):

$f(1)=\dfrac{(1)^2+1}{(1)+1}=1\rightarrow(1,\ 1)$

$f(-2)=\dfrac{(-2)^2+1}{(-2)+1}=-5\rightarrow(-2,-5)$

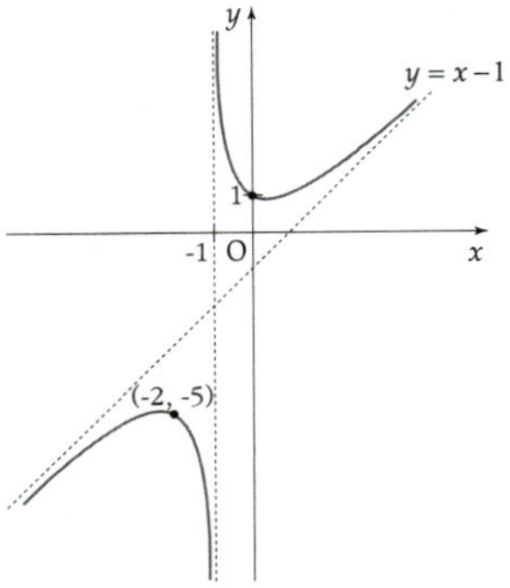

Domain: $(-\infty, -1)\cup(-1, \infty)$

Check Point 5

① $\dfrac{2x-3}{2+x}\le 0$

The zeros is $x=\dfrac{3}{2}$ and it is undefined at $x=-2$.

Choose a test point from each interval; $x=-3$, $x=0$, and $x=2$.

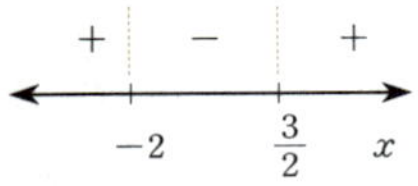

The solution set is $\left(-2, \dfrac{3}{2}\right]$.

②
$$\frac{2}{x-2}>\frac{1}{x+1}$$
$$\frac{2}{x-2}-\frac{1}{x+1}>0$$
$$\frac{2(x+1)-(x-2)}{(x-2)(x+1)}>0$$
$$\frac{x+4}{(x-2)(x+1)}>0$$

The zeros is $x=-4$ and it is undefined at $x=-1$ and $x=2$. Choose a test point from each interval; $x=-5$, $x=-3$, $x=0$ and $x=3$.

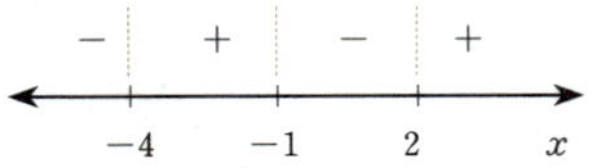

The solution set is $(-4, -1)\cup(2, \infty)$.

$(-4, -1)\cup(2, \infty)$

Review Exercises

01

(1) $f(x)=-\dfrac{1}{2x}-2$ → Graph $f(x)=-\dfrac{1}{2x}$ first and then shift it 2 units down.

Vertical Asymptote: $x=0$

Horizontal Asymptote: $y=-2$

x−intercept: $0=-\dfrac{1}{2x}-2$, $x=-\dfrac{1}{4}$

Additional Point(s):

$f(1)=-\dfrac{1}{2(1)}-2=-\dfrac{5}{2}$ → $\left(1, -\dfrac{5}{2}\right)$

$f(-1)=-\dfrac{1}{2(-1)}-2=-\dfrac{3}{2}$ → $\left(-1, -\dfrac{3}{2}\right)$

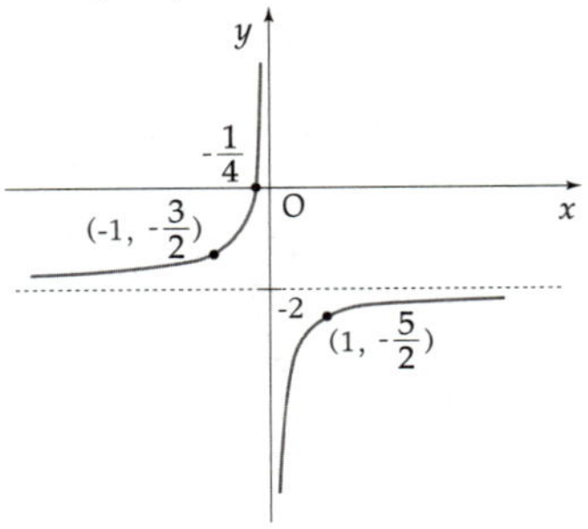

Domain: $(-\infty, 0)\cup(0, \infty)$

Range: $(-\infty, -2)\cup(-2, \infty)$

(2) $h(x)=-\dfrac{3}{2x-3}+1$ → Graph $h(x)=-\dfrac{3}{2x}$ first and then shift it $\dfrac{3}{2}$ units to the right and 1 unit up.

Vertical Asymptote: $2x-3=0$, $x=\dfrac{3}{2}$

Horizontal Asymptote: $y=1$

x−intercept: $0=-\dfrac{3}{2x-3}+1$ → $x=3$

y−intercept: $h(0)=-\dfrac{3}{2(0)-3}+1=2$ → $y=2$

Additional Point(s):

$h(2)=-\dfrac{3}{2(2)-3}+1=-2$ → $(2, -2)$

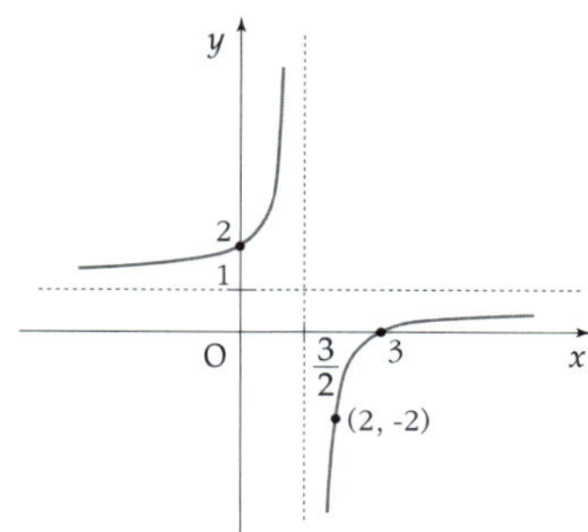

Domain: $\left(-\infty, \frac{3}{2}\right) \cup \left(\frac{3}{2}, \infty\right)$

Range: $(-\infty, 1) \cup (1, \infty)$

02

Let n and m be the degree of numerator and denominator, respectively.

(1) $f(x)=\dfrac{x-1}{3x+2}$

Vertical Asymptote: $3x+2=0$, $x=-\dfrac{2}{3}$

Horizontal Asymptote:

$n=1$ and $m=1 \rightarrow y=\dfrac{1}{3}$

$x-$intercept: $0=\dfrac{x-1}{3x+2}$, $x=1$

$y-$intercept: $f(0)=\dfrac{(0)-1}{3(0)+2}=-\dfrac{1}{2}$

$\rightarrow y=-\dfrac{1}{2}$

Additional Point(s):

$f(-1)=\dfrac{(-1)-1}{3(-1)+2}=2 \rightarrow (-1, 2)$

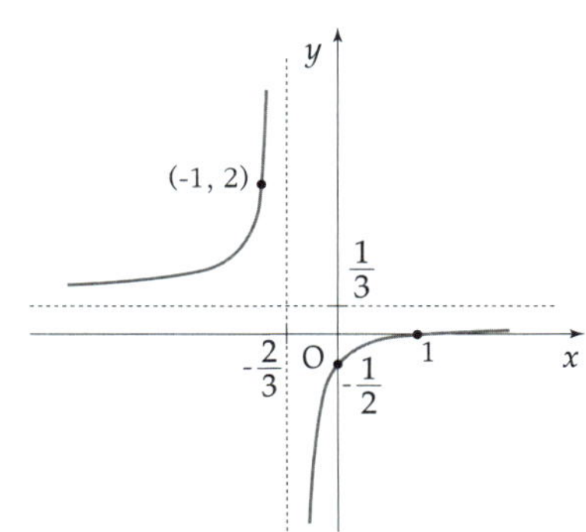

Domain: $\left(-\infty, -\frac{2}{3}\right) \cup \left(-\frac{2}{3}, \infty\right)$

Range: $\left(-\infty, \frac{1}{3}\right) \cup \left(\frac{1}{3}, \infty\right)$

(2) $g(x)=\dfrac{1}{x^2-4} \rightarrow g(x)=\dfrac{1}{(x-2)(x+2)}$

Vertical Asymptote: $x^2-4=0$, $x=\pm 2$

Horizontal Asymptote:

$n=0$ and $m=2 \rightarrow y=0$

$y-$intercept:

$g(0)=\dfrac{1}{(0)^2-4}=-\dfrac{1}{4} \rightarrow y=-\dfrac{1}{4}$

Additional Point(s):

$g(-3)=\dfrac{1}{(-3)^2-4}=\dfrac{1}{5} \rightarrow \left(-3, \frac{1}{5}\right)$

$g(-1)=\dfrac{1}{(-1)^2-4}=-\dfrac{1}{3} \rightarrow \left(-1, -\frac{1}{3}\right)$

$g(1)=\dfrac{1}{(1)^2-4}=-\dfrac{1}{3} \rightarrow \left(1, -\frac{1}{3}\right)$

$g(3)=\dfrac{1}{(3)^2-4}=\dfrac{1}{5} \rightarrow \left(3, \frac{1}{5}\right)$

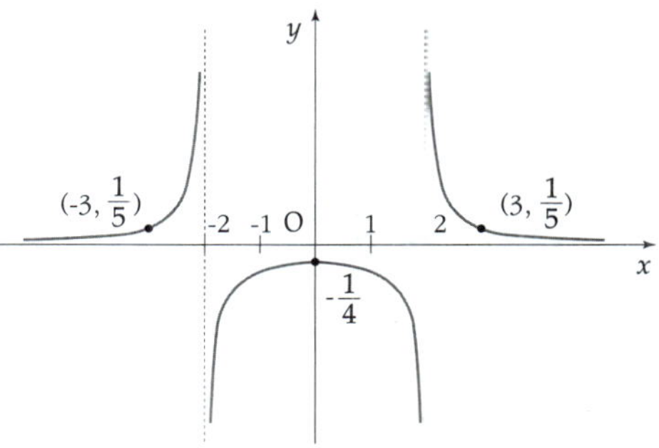

Domain: $(-\infty, -2) \cup (-2, 2) \cup (2, \infty)$

Range: $\left(-\infty, -\frac{1}{4}\right] \cup (0, \infty)$

(3) $h(x)=\dfrac{3+x-2x^2}{x^2+3x+2}=-\dfrac{(2x-3)(x+1)}{(x+2)(x+1)}$

$\rightarrow h(x)=-\dfrac{2x-3}{x+2}$

Vertical Asymptote: $x+2=0$, $x=-2$

Horizontal Asymptote:

$n=2$ and $m=2 \rightarrow y=\dfrac{-2}{1}=-2$

Hole: $x+1=0$, $x=-1 \rightarrow (-1, 5)$

x−intercept: $0=-\dfrac{2x-3}{x+2}$, $2x-3=0$, $x=\dfrac{3}{2}$

y−intercept: $h(0)=-\dfrac{2(0)-3}{(0)+2}=\dfrac{3}{2} \rightarrow y=\dfrac{3}{2}$

Additional Point(s):

$h(-4)=-\dfrac{2(-4)-3}{(-4)+2}=-\dfrac{11}{2} \rightarrow \left(-4,\ -\dfrac{11}{2}\right)$

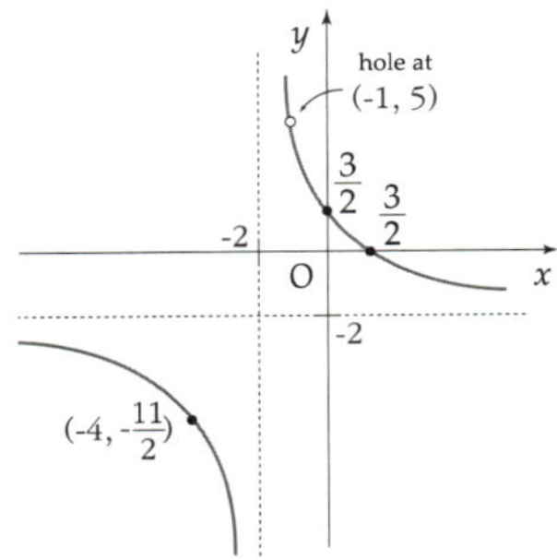

Domain: $(-\infty,\ -2)\cup(-2,\ -1)\cup(-1,\ \infty)$

Range: $(-\infty,\ -2)\cup(-2,\ 5)\cup(5,\ \infty)$

(4) $f(x)=\dfrac{2}{x^2+1}$

Horizontal Asymptote:

$n=0$ and $m=2 \rightarrow y=0$

y−intercept: $f(0)=\dfrac{2}{(0)^2+1}=2 \rightarrow y=2$

Additional Point(s):

$f(-1)=\dfrac{2}{(-1)^2+1}=1 \rightarrow (-1,\ 1)$

$f(1)=\dfrac{2}{(1)^2+1}=1 \rightarrow (1,\ 1)$

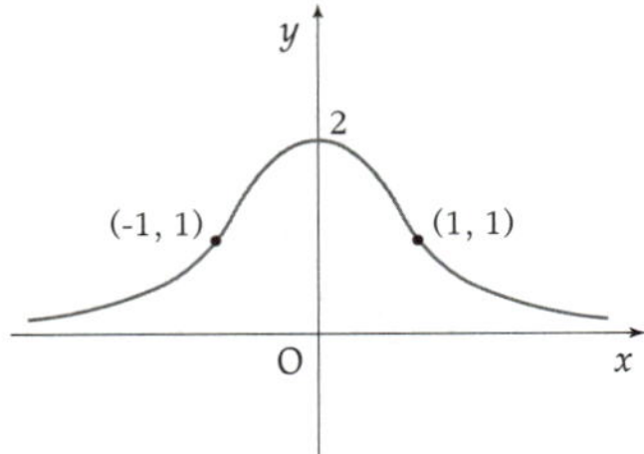

Domain: $(-\infty,\ \infty)$

Range: $(0,\ 2]$

This is a special type of rational function. Notice that the function reaches the maximum value when the value of denominator is the least.

03

(1)

$$\begin{array}{r} x-2 \\ x-2\overline{)x^2-4x+3} \\ \underline{x^2-2x} \\ -2x+3 \\ \underline{-2x+4} \\ -1 \end{array}$$

$\rightarrow \dfrac{x^2-4x+3}{x-2}=x-2-\dfrac{1}{x-2}$

Slant Asymptote: $y=x-2$

Vertical Asymptote: $x-2=0$, $x=2$

x−intercept: $0=\dfrac{x^2-4x+3}{x-2}=\dfrac{(x-1)(x-3)}{x-2}$

$\rightarrow x=1,\ x=3.$

y−intercept:

$f(0)=\dfrac{(0)^2-4(0)+3}{(0)-2)}=-\dfrac{3}{2} \rightarrow y=-\dfrac{3}{2}$

Additional Point(s)

$f(1)=\dfrac{(1)^2-4(1)+3}{(1)-2)}=0 \rightarrow (1,\ 0)$

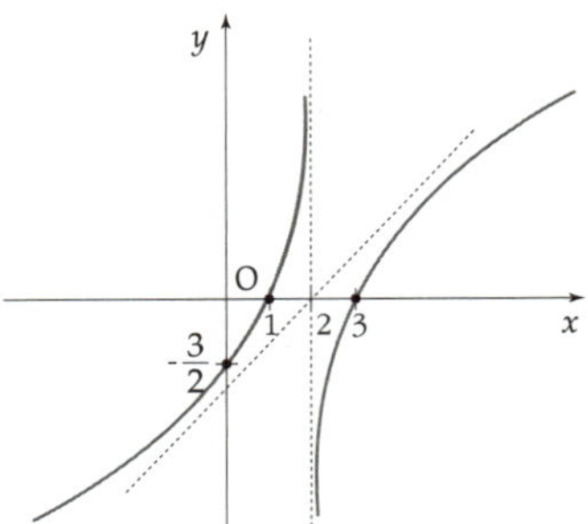

Domain: $(-\infty,\ 2)\cup(2,\ \infty)$

(2) $f(x)=\dfrac{2x^3-3x^2-2x}{2x^2+3x+1}$

$=\frac{x(x-2)(2x+1)}{(x+1)(2x+1)}$

$=\frac{x^2-2x}{x+1}$

$$\begin{array}{r} x-3 \\ x+1\overline{)x^2-2x} \\ \underline{x^2+\ x} \\ -3x \\ \underline{-3x-3} \\ 3 \end{array}$$

$\rightarrow \frac{x^2-4x+3}{x-2}=x-3+\frac{3}{x+1}$

Slant Asymptote: $y=x-3$

Vertical Asymptote: $x+1=0,\ x=-1$

Hole: $2x+1=0,\ x=-\frac{1}{2}$

x–intercept: $0=\frac{x^2-2x}{x+1}=\frac{x(x-2)}{x+1}$

$x=0,\ x=2$

y–intercept: $f(0)=\frac{(0)^2-2(0)}{(0)+1}=0 \rightarrow y=0$

Additional Point(s):

$f(-2)=\frac{(-2)^2-2(-2)}{(-2)+1}=-8 \rightarrow (-2,\ 8)$

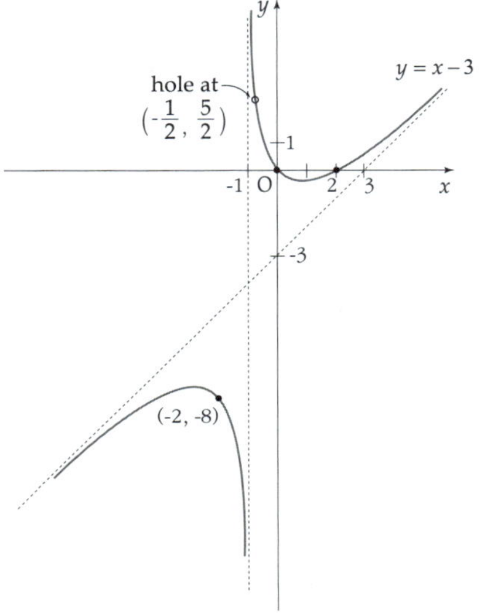

Domain: $(-\infty,\ -1)\cup\left(-1,\ -\frac{1}{2}\right)\cup\left(-\frac{1}{2},\infty\right)$

04

$y=\frac{x^2-x-6}{2x^2-8}=\frac{(x-3)(x+2)}{2(x^2-4)}$

$=\frac{(x-3)(x+2)}{2(x-2)(x+2)}=\frac{x-3}{2(x-2)}$

Vertical Asymptote: $x-2=0,\ x=2$

Horizontal Asymptote:

$n=2$ and $m=2 \rightarrow y=\frac{1}{2}=0.5$

Hole: $x+2=0,\ x=-2$

So I and III are correct. The answer is (C).

05

In order not to have a vertical asymptote, the denominator and the numerator must have the same factor.

$r(x)=\frac{5x+k}{x-3}=\frac{5\left(x+\frac{k}{5}\right)}{x-3}$

$\rightarrow \frac{k}{5}=-3,\ k=-15$

06

(A) $f(x)=\frac{x-3}{x-1}$

Zero: $x-3=0,\ x=3$

Vertical Asymptote: $x-1=0,\ x=1$

Horizontal Asymptote:

$n=1$ and $m=1 \rightarrow y=\frac{1}{1}=1$

(B) $f(x)=\frac{x-3}{x^2-1}=\frac{x-3}{(x-1)(x+1)}$

Zero: $x-3=0,\ x=3$

Vertical Asymptote:

$x-1=0,\ x=1;\ x+1=0,\ x=-1$

Horizontal Asymptote:

$n=1$ and $m=2 \rightarrow y=0$

(C) $f(x)=\frac{x^2-4x+3}{x-1}=\frac{(x-1)(x-3)}{x-1}=x-3$

Zero: $x-3=0$, $x=3$

Neither vertical nor horizontal asymptote exist.

Hole: $x-1=0$, $x=1$

(D) $f(x)=\dfrac{x^2-4x+3}{x^2-1}=\dfrac{(x-1)(x-3)}{(x-1)(x+1)}=\dfrac{x-3}{x+1}$

Zero: $x-3=0$, $x=3$

Vertical Asymptote: $x+1=0$, $x=-1$

Horizontal Asymptote:

$n=2$ and $m=2 \rightarrow y=\dfrac{1}{1}=1$

Hole: $x-1=0$, $x=1$

Only (D) satisfies the conditions. So the answer is (D).

07

To graph of $g(x)=\dfrac{1}{2x+1}-3$, we graph $y=\dfrac{1}{2x}$ and then shift $\dfrac{1}{2}$ unit to the left and 3 units down. Therefore, the graph of g has a horizontal asymptote $y=-3$, which means that the range of g is $(-\infty, -3)\cup(-3, \infty)$.

08

(1) $\dfrac{1}{x}-2<0$, $\dfrac{1-2x}{x}<0$

The zero is $x=\dfrac{1}{2}$, and it is undefined at $x=0$. Choose a test point from each interval; $x=-1$, $x=0.1$, and $x=1$.

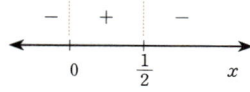

The solution set is $(-\infty, 0)\cup\left(\dfrac{1}{2}, \infty\right)$.

(2) $\dfrac{2-x}{x+1}\leq 0$

The zero is $x=2$, and it is undefined at $x=-1$. Choose a test point from each interval; $x=-2$, $x=0$, and $x=3$.

The solution set is $(-\infty, -1)\cup[2, \infty)$.

(3) $\dfrac{3}{x-3}>\dfrac{4}{x+1}$, $\dfrac{3}{x-3}-\dfrac{4}{x+1}>0$

$$\frac{3(x+1)-4(x-3)}{(x-3)(x+1)}>0$$

$$\frac{-x+15}{(x-3)(x+1)}>0$$

The zero is $x=15$, and it is undefined at $x=-1$ and $x=3$. Choose a test point from each interval; $x=-2$, $x=0$, $x=4$, and $x=16$.

The solution set is $(-\infty, -1)\cup(3, 15)$.

(4) $\dfrac{x^3-x}{x^2-x-12}\geq 0$, $\dfrac{x(x^2-1)}{(x-4)(x+3)}\geq 0$

$$\frac{x(x-1)(x+1)}{(x-4)(x+3)}\geq 0$$

The zeros are $x=-1$, $x=0$, and $x=1$, and it is undefined at $x=-3$ and $x=4$. Choose a test point from each interval;

$x=-4$, $x=-2$, $x=-0.5$, $x=0.5$, $x=2$ and $x=5$.

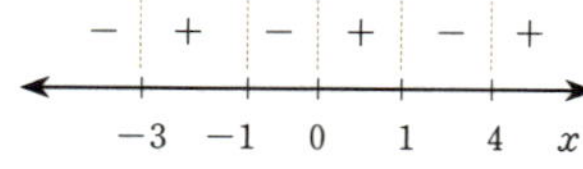

The solution set is $(-3, -1]\cup[0, 1]\cup(4, \infty)$.

09

For a rational function $f(x)=\frac{p(x)}{q(x)}$ to have a slant asymptote, the degree of the numerator $p(x)$ must be exactly one more than the degree of the denominator $q(x)$. Additionally, the leading coefficient of the polynomial $p(x)$ divided by the leading coefficient of the polynomial $q(x)$ will give the slope of the slant asymptote. Therefore, the degree of $q(x)$ must be $4-1=3$ and the leading coefficient of $q(x)$ must be 1. Thus, the correct answer is (C).

10

The degrees of the numerator and the denominator are both 3. Thus, the horizontal asymptote is $y=\frac{4}{2}=2$.

This means that as $x \to \infty$ or $x \to -\infty$, $f(x)$ approaches 2. Therefore, the correct statement is (C).

11

When the degree of the numerator (polynomial $p(x)$) is greater than the degree of the denominator(polynomial $q(x)$), the rational function does not have a horizontal asymptote. Instead, the function will approach ∞ or $-\infty$ as $x \to \infty$. The specific behavior depends on the leading coefficients and the signs. Since we are not given the specific sign of leading coefficients, we cannot determine whether the function will approach ∞ or $-\infty$. Thus, the correct answer is (D).

12

The degree of the denominator is 3. For the function to have a horizontal asymptote, the degrees of the numerator and denominator must be the same. Therefore, we must have $b=2$. Additionally, For the horizontal asymptote to be $y=3$, the ratio of the leading coefficients of the numerator and the denominator must be 3:

$$\frac{a}{2}=3,\ a=6$$

Therefore, the value of $a+b$ is 8.

13

$$f(x)=\frac{x^2-9}{x^2-1}<0,\ \frac{(x+3)(x-3)}{(x+1)(x-1)}<0$$

The zeros are $x=-3$ and $x=3$, and it is undefined at $x=-1$ and $x=1$. Choose a test point from each interval; $x=-4$, $x=-2$, $x=0$, $x=2$, and $x=4$.

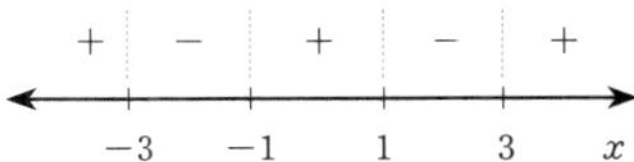

The solution set is $-3<x<-1$ or $1<x<3$. Thus, the answer is (A).

7. Transformation of Functions

Review Exercises

01

To transform $y=f(x)$ by shifting it 2 units to the left and 3 units up:

(1) Horizontal shift left by 2 units:
$f(x) \to f(x+2)$

(2) Vertical shift up by 3 units:
$f(x+2) \to f(x+2)+3$

So, the correct transformation is (D) $y=f(x+2)+3$.

02

To find the new point after shifting the graph of $y=f(x)$ which passes through $(-2, 4)$:

(1) Shift 2 units to the right:
$(-2+2, 4)=(0, 4)$

(2) Shift 1 unit down: $(0, 4-1)=(0, 3)$

So, the new point is (B) $(0, 3)$.

03

Given f passes through $(-1, 1)$ and g passes through $(1, -1)$,

(1) Horizontal shift from -1 to 1:
Shift $f(x)$ 2 units to the right: $f(x-2)$.

(2) Vertical shift from 1 to -1:
Shift $f(x)$ 2 units down: $f(x-2)-2$.

So the correct answer is (C).

04

The given property $h(x)=h(x-1)$ implies that the function is periodic with a period of 1. This means the function repeats its values every 1 unit. For graph (A), this is a constant function, which repeats its value for every x. Hence, $h(x)=h(x-1)$ holds true. So the correct answer is (A).

05

To determine the translation for $f(x)=x^2$ to become $f(x)=x^2+4x+m$:

(1) Complete the square:
$x^2+4x+m=(x+2)^2-4+m$

(2) Interpret the translation:
$(x+2)^2$: 2 units to the left
$-4+m$: $m-4$ units up since $m>4$

Therefore, the correct answer is (B).

06

(1) Vertically stretched by a factor of 3:
$y=\sqrt{x} \to y=3\sqrt{x}$

(2) Reflected in the $y-$axis:
$y=3\sqrt{x} \to y=3\sqrt{-x}$

(3) Translated 2 units down:
$y=3\sqrt{-x} \to y=3\sqrt{-x}-2$

Combining all the transformations, the resulting function is: $g(x)=3\sqrt{-x}-2$

So, the answer is (D).

07

(1) Vertically stretched by a factor of 4:
$y=4f(x)$

(2) Reflected in the $y-$axis:
$y=4f(-x)$

(3) Translated 3 units down:
$y=4f(-x)-3 \to g(x)=4f(-x)-3$

$$g(-2)=4f(-(-2))-3$$
$$=4f(2)-3$$
$$=4\cdot4-3=13$$

Therefore, $g(-2)=13$.

08

(1) Horizontal Translation:

$2x+1=0,\ x=-\frac{1}{2}$

This is a horizontal translation 0.5 units to the left.

(2) Horizontal Dilation: $2x+1$

The factor inside f is $2x$, which represents a horizontal compression by a factor of $\frac{1}{2}$.

(3) Vertical Dilation: The factor outside f is 2, which represents a vertical stretch by a factor of 2.

Based on the transformations described, the correct interpretation matches option (C).

Unit I Test

01

$f(x)=-2x^3+5x^2-4x+1$

The degree of the function f is 3(odd) and its leading coefficient -2(negative). So the function decreases as $x\to\infty$ but increases as $x\to-\infty$. So the answer is (B).

02

$f(x)=-x^4+5x^3+x$

End behavior: Since the leading term is $-x^4$, as $x\to\pm\infty$, $f(x)\to-\infty$.

It eventually decreases as x moves towards both positive and negative infinity.

Therefore, statements III and IV are true.

The answer is (D).

03

Positive rate of change for $x<4$: This means f is increasing for $x<4$.

Negative rate of change for $x>4$: This means f is increasing for $x>4$.

If f is increasing up to $x=4$ and then decreasing after $x=4$, f has a local maximum at $x=4$. Therefore, the correct answer is (A).

04

Rate of change is increasing for $x<4$: This means f is concave up for $x<4$.

Rate of change is decreasing for $x>4$: This means f is concave down for $x>4$.

Therefore, the correct answer is (D).

05

The degree n and the leading coefficient a_n

determine the direction of the graph as $x \to \infty$ and $x \to -\infty$. $\lim_{x\to\infty} f(x)=\infty$ implies $a_n>0$. $\lim_{x\to-\infty} f(x)=-\infty$ implies n is odd, since an odd power of x results in opposite signs for positive and negative x.
Therefore, the answer is (C).

06

(1) $f(x)=(x-1)(x+1)^2(x-2)$

$0=(x-1)(x+1)^2(x-2)$

$x=1$, $x=-1$(multiplicity 2) and $x=2$

The degree of f is 4(even) and its leading coefficient is 1(positive). So, f increases as $x \to \infty$ and also increases as $x \to -\infty$.

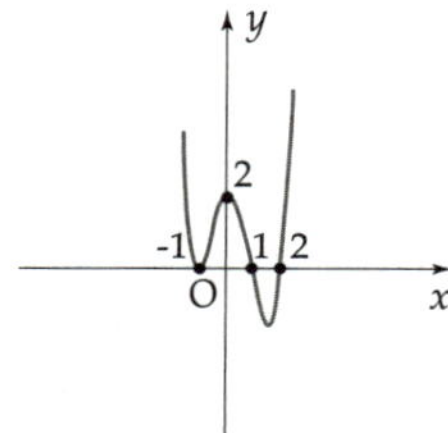

(2) $g(x)=2x^3-3x^2-8x+12$

$0=2x^3-3x^2-8x+12$

$x^2(2x-3)-4(2x-3)=0$

$(x^2-4)(2x-3)=0$

$(x+2)(x-2)(2x-3)=0$, $x=\pm 2$ and $x=\frac{3}{2}$

The degree of g is 3(odd) and its leading coefficient is 2(positive). So, g increases as $x \to \infty$ but decreases as $x \to -\infty$.

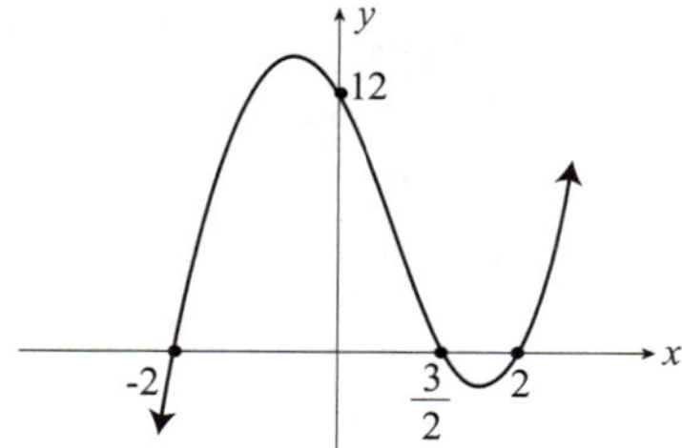

07

$$
\begin{array}{r}
4x^2+5x+4 \\
2x-1\overline{)8x^3+6x^2+3x-4} \\
\underline{8x^3-4x^2} \\
10x^2+3x-4 \\
\underline{10x^2-5x} \\
8x-4 \\
\underline{8x-4} \\
0
\end{array}
$$

$\to \dfrac{8x^3+6x^2+3x-4}{2x-1}=4x^2+5x+4$

08

	1	0	0	0	0	−5
−3		−3	9	−27	81	−243
	1	−3	9	−27	81	−248

$\to \dfrac{x^5-5}{x+3}=x^4-3x^3+9x^2-27x+81-\dfrac{248}{x+3}$

09

Using the remainder theorem,

$g(1)=4(1)^{2017}-3(1)^{2010}+2(1)-1$

$=4-3+2-1=2$

The remainder is 2.

10

Let $f(x)=x^4+ax^2-x+b$.

Using the remainder theorem,

$f(-2)=(-2)^4+a(-2)^2-(-2)+b=16$

$16+4a+2+b=16$, $4a+b=-2 \to (1)$

$f(-3)=(-3)^4+a(-3)^2-(-3)+b=4$

$81+9a+3+b=77$, $9a+b=-7 \to (2)$

Solving the system of equations of (1) and (2),

$\begin{matrix} 4a+b=-2 \\ 9a+b=-7 \end{matrix} \to a=-1$ and $b=2$

Therefore, $a+b=-1+2=1$.

11

Let $f(x)=bx^4-15x^3+27x^2-10x$. Using the factor theorem,

$f(2)=b(2)^4-15(2)^3+27(2)^2-10(2)=0$

$16b-120+108-20=0$, $16b=32$, $b=2$

12

Using the synthetic division,

	6	−7	−37	8	12
3		18	33	−12	−12
	6	11	−4	−4	0
−2		−12	2	4	
	6	−1	−2	0	

→ $6x^4-7x^3-37x^2+8x+12$

$=(x-3)(x+2)(6x^2-x-2)$

$=(x-3)(x+2)(2x+1)(3x-2)$

The remaining linear factors are $2x+1$ and $3x-2$.

13

If a polynomial $p(x)=2x^3+ax^2-5x-2$ is divisible by $x+1$, then $x+1$ is a factor of $p(x)$. Using the factor theorem,

$2(-1)^3+a(-1)^2-5(-1)-2=0$

$-2+a+5-2=0$, $a=-1$

So the polynomial is $p(x)=2x^3-x^2-5x-2$.

If we divide $p(x)$ by $x+1$, the quotient is $2x^2-3x-2$ and

$2x^2-3x-2=(2x+1)(x-2)$

Therefore,

$p(x)=(x+1)(2x+1)(x-2)$

Since $(x+1)(x-2)=x^2-x-2$, $p(x)$ is also divisible by x^2-x-2. So, the answer is (A).

14

(1) $g(x)=4x^3-7x^2+x-6$

p: factors of 6; q: factors of 4

The possible rational zeros:

$\pm\frac{p}{q}=\pm\frac{1,\ 2,\ 3,\ 6}{1,\ 2,\ 4}=\pm1,\ \pm2,\ \pm3,\ \pm6,\ \pm\frac{1}{2},$
$\pm\frac{3}{2}, \pm\frac{1}{4}, \pm\frac{3}{4}$

$g(2)=4(2)^3-7(2)^2+(2)-6=0$.

So $x-2$ is a factor of $g(x)$. Now, use the synthetic division to find the rest of the factors.

	4	−7	1	−6
2		8	2	6
	4	1	3	0

→ $4x^3-7x^2+x-6=(x-2)(4x^2+x+3)$

The zeros of $4x^2+x+3$ are

$x=\frac{-1\pm\sqrt{1^2-4(4)(3)}}{2(4)}=\frac{-1\pm\sqrt{47}i}{8}$.

Therefore, the zeros of g are $x=2$ and $x=\frac{-1\pm\sqrt{47}i}{8}$.

(2) $g(x)=x^4+x^3-x^2-4x-12$

p: factors of 12; q: factors of 1

The possible rational zeros:

$\pm\frac{p}{q}=\pm\frac{1,\ 2,\ 3,\ 4,\ 6,\ 12}{1}$

$=\pm1,\ \pm2,\ \pm3,\ \pm4,\ \pm6,\ \pm12$

$g(2)=(2)^4+(2)^3-(2)^2-4(2)-12=0$

$g(-2)=(-2)^4+(-2)^3-(-2)^2-4(-2)-12$
$=0$

So $x-2$ and $x+2$ are factors of $g(x)$. Now, use the synthetic division to find the rest of the factors.

	1	1	−1	−4	−12
2		2	6	10	12
	1	3	5	6	0
−2		−2	−2	−6	
	1	1	3	0	

→ $x^4+x^3-x^2-4x-12$

$=(x-2)(x+2)(x^2+x+3)$

The zeros of x^2+x+3 are

$$x=\frac{-1\pm\sqrt{1^2-4(1)(3)}}{2(1)}=\frac{-1\pm\sqrt{11}i}{2}.$$

Therefore, the zeros of g are $x=\pm2$ and

$$x=\frac{-1\pm\sqrt{11}i}{2}.$$

15

$$f(x)=2x^3+4x^2-18x-36$$
$$0=2x^2(x+2)-18(x+2)$$
$$0=2(x+2)(x^2-9)$$
$$0=2(x+2)(x-3)(x+3);\ x=-2,\ x=\pm3$$

Since the polynomial function f has three zeros, it intersects the x−axis at three points. Therefore, the answer is (D).

16

If $2+i$ is a zero of f, then $2-i$ is another zero of f(complex conjugate). From two zeros $2\pm i$, we have

$$x^2-((2+\mathrm{i})+(2-\mathrm{i}))x+(2+\mathrm{i})(2-\mathrm{i})$$
$$=x^2-4x+(4-i^2)=x^2-4x+5$$

So x^2-4x+5 is a factor of $f(x)$. We can now use the long division to find the rest of the factor.

$$\begin{array}{r} x-2 \\ x^2-4x+5\overline{)x^3-6x^2+13x-10} \\ \underline{x^3-4x^2+5x} \\ -2x^2+8x-10 \\ \underline{-2x^2+8x-10} \\ 0 \end{array}$$

$$\rightarrow x^3-6x^2+13x-10=(x^2-4x+5)(x-2)$$

Therefore, the remaining zeros is $x=2$.

17

If $-1+i$ is a zero of f, then $-1-i$ is another zero of f(complex conjugate).

From two zeros $-1\pm i$, we have

$$x^2-((-1+i)+(-1-i))x+(-1+i)(-1-i)$$
$$=x^2+2x+(1-i^2)=x^2+2x+2$$

So, the function f is

$$f(x)=3(x-1)(x^2+2x+2)=3x^3+3x^2-6$$

18

$$x^2-3x-10<0$$
$$(x-5)(x+2)<0$$

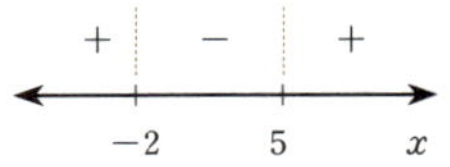

The polynomial $x^2-3x-10$ is less than 0 in the interval $(-2, 5)$ and the interval $(-2, 5)$ includes the integers: -1, 0, 1, 2, 3, and 4. So, there are 6 integers in this interval.

19

Let n and m be the degree of numerator and denominator, respectively.

(A) $f(x)=\dfrac{2x-1}{2x+4}$

Zero: $2x-1=0,\ x=\frac{1}{2}$

Vertical Asymptote: $2x+4=0,\ x=-2$

Horizontal Asymptote:

$n=1$ and $m=1 \rightarrow y=\frac{2}{2}=1$

(B) $f(x)=\dfrac{2x+2}{x^2-1}=\dfrac{2(x+1)}{(x-1)(x+1)}=\dfrac{2}{x-1}$

No zero exists.

Vertical Asymptote: $x-1=0,\ x=1$

Horizontal Asymptote:

$n=1$ and $m=2 \rightarrow y=0$

Hole: $x+1=0,\ x=-1$

(C) $f(x)=\dfrac{2x^2-2}{x^2+x-2}=\dfrac{2(x-1)(x+1)}{(x-1)(x+2)}=\dfrac{2x+2}{x+2}$

Zero: $2x+2=0,\ x=-1$

Vertical Asymptote: $x+2=0,\ x=-2$

Horizontal Asymptote:

$n=2$ and $m=2 \rightarrow y=\frac{2}{1}=2$

(D) $f(x)=\frac{2x^2-4}{x^2+3x+2}=\frac{2(x^2-2)}{(x+1)(x+2)}$

Zero: $2x^2-4=0,\ x^2=2,\ x=\pm\sqrt{2}$

Vertical Asymptote:

$x+1=0,\ x=-1;\ x+2=0,\ x=-2$

Horizontal Asymptote:

$n=2$ and $m=2 \rightarrow y=\frac{2}{1}=2$

Only (C) satisfies the conditions. So the answer is (C).

20

$$h(x)=\frac{(x-1)(x+2)f(x)}{(x-1)^2(x+2)^2}$$
$$=\frac{(x-1)(x+2)(3x^2-4)}{(x-1)^2(x+2)^2}$$

The factors $(x-1)$ and $(x+2)$ in the numerator and denominator can be cancelled:

$$h(x)=\frac{(3x^2-4)}{(x-1)(x+2)}$$

The degree of the numerator is equal to the degree of the denominator. Therefore, the graph of h has a horizontal asymptote at $y=3$. The answer is (B).

21

$$f(x)=\frac{2x^2-32}{x^2-7x+12}$$
$$=\frac{2(x^2-16)}{(x-3)(x-4)}$$
$$=\frac{2(x+4)\cancel{(x-4)}}{(x-3)\cancel{(x-4)}}=\frac{2(x+4)}{x-3}$$

Vertical asymptote: $x=3$

Horizontal asymptote: Since the degrees of the numerator and the denominator are the same, $y=\frac{2}{1}=2$

Therefore, the correct answer is (B).

22

Let n and m be the degree of numerator and denominator, respectively.

$$f(x)=\frac{2x^2+1}{x^3-x^2-x}=\frac{2x^2+1}{x(x^2-x-1)}$$

Vertical Asymptote:

$$x=0;\ x^2-x-1=0,\ x=\frac{1\pm\sqrt{5}}{2}$$

Horizontal Asymptote:

$n=2$ and $m=3 \rightarrow y=0$

There are a total of 4 asymptotes (3 vertical asymptotes and 1 horizontal asymptote). The answer is (D).

23

Let n and m be the degree of numerator and denominator, respectively.

$$y=\frac{x^2-x-2}{x^2+4x+3}=\frac{(x-2)(x+1)}{(x+3)(x+1)}=\frac{x-2}{x+3}$$

Vertical Asymptote: $x+3=0,\ x=-3$

Horizontal Asymptote:

$n=2$ and $m=2 \rightarrow y=\frac{1}{1}=1$

Hole: $x+1=0,\ x=-1 \rightarrow \left(-1,\ -\frac{3}{2}\right)$

x-intercept: $0=\frac{x-2}{x+3},\ x=2$

y-intercept: $y(0)=\frac{0-2}{0+3}=-\frac{2}{3},\ y=-\frac{2}{3}$

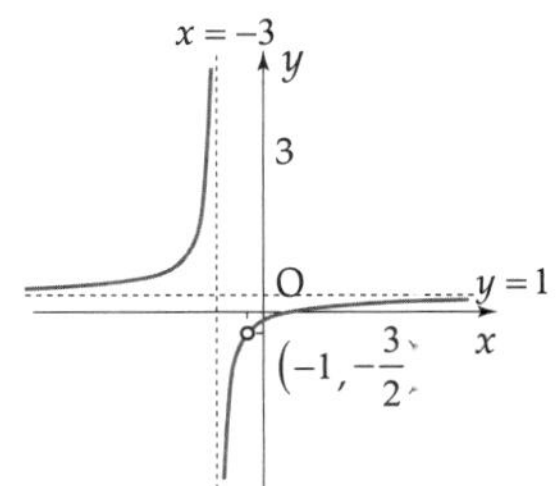

Domain: $(-\infty, -3)\cup(-3, -1)\cup(-1, \infty)$

Range: $\left(-\infty, -\frac{3}{2}\right)\cup\left(-\frac{3}{2}, 1\right)\cup(1, \infty)$

24

$$y=\frac{3x^3+2x^2-3x-2}{2x^2+x-3}=\frac{x^2(3x+2)-(3x+2)}{(x-1)(2x+3)}$$
$$=\frac{(x^2-1)(3x+2)}{(x-1)(2x+3)}=\frac{(x-1)(x+1)(3x+2)}{(x-1)(2x+3)}$$
$$=\frac{3x^2+5x+2}{2x+3}$$

Using the long division,

$$\begin{array}{r|l} & \frac{3}{2}x+\frac{1}{4} \\ 2x+3 & 3x^2+5x+2 \\ & 3x^3+\frac{9}{2}x \\ \hline & \frac{1}{2}x+2 \\ & \frac{1}{2}x+\frac{3}{4} \\ \hline & \frac{5}{4} \end{array}$$

$$\rightarrow \frac{3}{2}x+\frac{1}{4}+\frac{5}{4(2x+3)}$$

Slant Asymptote: $y=\frac{3}{2}x+\frac{1}{4}$

Vertical Asymptote: $2x+3=0$, $x=-\frac{3}{2}$

25

$$f(x)=\frac{x^2-4}{x-2}=\frac{(x-2)(x+2)}{x-2}=x+2$$

As x approaches 2, $f(x)$ approaches $2+2=4$. Therefore, the correct answer is (C).

26

To determine which of the given expressions approaches 4 as x increases without bound, we need to analyze the behavior of each expression as $x \rightarrow \infty$. For the answer choice (B), we have

$$\frac{4x+4}{x+1}=\frac{4(x+1)}{x+1}=4$$

So, this expression is exactly 4 for all $x\neq-1$. Therefore, (B) approach 4 as x increases without bound.

27

$$f(x)=\frac{x^2-16}{x-2}=\frac{(x-4)(x+4)}{x-2}\geq 0$$

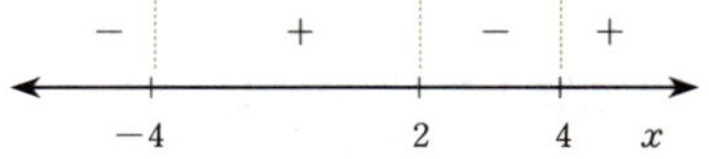

$f(x)$ is greater than or equal to 0 in the interval $-4\leq x<2$ or $x\geq 4$. Therefore, the correct answer is (C).

28

Translating the function 2 units to the right and 3 units down:

$$g(x)=f(x-2)-3$$
$$=[(x-2)^3+1]-3$$
$$=(x-2)^3-2$$

Now evaluate $g(1)$.

$$g(1)=(1-2)^3-2=-3$$

Therefore, the correct answer is (D).

memo

Unit II

Exponential and Logarithmic Functions

1. Arithmetic and Geometric Sequence

Check Point 1

① $a_n=n^2-n+3,\ a_1=1^2-1+3=3$

$a_2=2^2-2+3=5,\ a_3=3^2-3+3=9$

$a_{(n+1)}=(n+1)^2-(n+1)+3$

$=n^2+2n+1-n-1+3=n^2+n+3$

② $a_n=\dfrac{n^3}{(2n-1)^2},\ a_1=\dfrac{1^3}{(2(1)-1)^2}=\dfrac{1}{1^2}=1$

$a_2=\dfrac{2^3}{(2(2)-1)^2}=\dfrac{8}{3^2}=\dfrac{8}{9}$

$a_3=\dfrac{3^3}{(2(3)-1)^2}=\dfrac{27}{5^2}=\dfrac{27}{25}$

$a_{(n+1)}=\dfrac{(n+1)^3}{(2(n+1)-1)^2}=\dfrac{(n+1)^3}{(2n+1)^2}$

Check Point 2

① 2, 5, 8, 11, $\cdots \rightarrow a_1=2$ and $d=3$

$a_n=a_1+(n-1)d$

$a_n=2+(n-1)(3),\ a_n=3n-1$

$a_{10}=3(10)-1=29$

② 4, 1, −2, −5, $\cdots \rightarrow a_1=4$ and $d=-3$

$a_n=a_1+(n-1)d$

$a_n=4+(n-1)(-3),\ a_n=-3n+7$

$a_{10}=-3(10)+7=-23$

Check Point 3

① $a_{12}=38,\ d=4$

$a_n=a_1+(n-1)d$

$38=a_1+(12-1)(4),\ a_1=-6$

$a_n=-6+(n-1)(4)=4n-10,\ a_n=4n-10$

② $a_{12}=10,\ a_4=-38$

$$a_n=a_1+(n-1)d \rightarrow \begin{array}{r} 10=a_1+(12-1)d \\ -\ \ -38=a_1+(4-1)d \\ \hline 48=8d \rightarrow d=6 \end{array}$$

$10=a_1+(12-1)(6),\ a_1=-56$

$a_n=a_1+(n-1)d=-56+(n-1)\cdot 6=6n-62$

$a_n=6n-62$

Alternative solution:

$a_n=a_k+(n-k)d$

$a_{12}=a_4+(12-4)d,\ 10=-38+8d,\ d=6$

$a_n=a_1+(n-1)d,\ a_4=a_1+(4-1)d$

$-38=a_1+3\cdot 6,\ a_1=-56$

$a_n=a_1+(n-1)d=-56+(n-1)\cdot 6=6n-62$

$a_n=6n-62$

Check Point 4

① 3, 9, 27, 81,$\cdots$ $a_1=3$ and $r=3$

$a_n=a_1r^{n-1},\ a_n=3\cdot 3^{n-1}$

$a_{10}=3\cdot 3^{10-1}=3^{10},\ a_{10}=3^{10}$

② −5, 10, −20, 40,$\cdots$ $a_1=-5$ and $r=-2$

$a_n=a_1r^{n-1}$

$a_n=(-5)\cdot(-2)^{n-1}=(-1\cdot 5)\cdot(-1\cdot 2)^{n-1}$

$=(-1)\cdot 5\cdot(-1)^{n-1}\cdot 2^{n-1}=(-1)^n\cdot 5\cdot 2^{n-1}$

$a_n=(-1)^n\cdot 5\cdot 2^{n-1}$

$a_{10}=(-1)^{10}\cdot 5\cdot 2^{10-1}=5\cdot 2^9,\ a_{10}=5\cdot 2^9$

Check Point 5

① $a_2=3,\ r=-2$

$a_n=a_1r^{n-1},\ 3=a_1(-2)^{2-1},\ a_1=-\dfrac{3}{2}$

$a_n=\left(-\dfrac{3}{2}\right)\cdot(-2)^{n-1}$

② $a_3=10,\ a_6=1250$

$a_n=a_1r^{n-1}$

$\begin{cases} a_6=a_1r^{6-1} \\ a_3=a_1r^{3-1} \end{cases} \rightarrow \begin{cases} 1250=a_1r^5 \\ 10=a_1r^2 \end{cases}$

$\dfrac{a_1r^5}{a_1r^2}=\dfrac{1250}{10}$, $r^3=125$, $r=5$

$a_3=a_1r^{3-1}$, $10=a_1\cdot 5^2$, $a_1=\dfrac{10}{25}=\dfrac{2}{5}$

$a_n=a_1r^{n-1}=\dfrac{2}{5}\cdot 5^{n-1}$, $a_n=\dfrac{2}{5}\cdot 5^{n-1}$

Alternative solution:

$a_n=a_kr^{n-k}$, $a_6=a_3r^{6-3}$

$1250=10\cdot r^3$, $r^3=125$, $r=5$

$a_n=a_1r^{n-1}$

$a_3=a_1r^{3-1}$, $10=a_1\cdot 5^2$, $a_1=\dfrac{2}{5}$

$a_n=a_1r^{n-1}=\dfrac{2}{5}\cdot 5^{n-1}$, $a_n=\dfrac{2}{5}\cdot 5^{n-1}$

Check Point 6

① $a_1=6$, $a_2=-2$, $a_n=a_{n-1}-a_{n-2}$

$a_3=a_2-a_1=-2-6=-8$

$a_4=a_3-a_2=-8-(-2)=-6$

$a_5=a_4-a_3=-6-(-8)=2$

So the first 5 terms are 6, −2, −8, −6, 2

② $a_1=6$, $a_2=4$, $a_n=\dfrac{a_{n-1}-n}{2}+\dfrac{3a_{n-2}}{4}$

$a_3=\dfrac{a_2-3}{2}+\dfrac{3a_1}{4}=\dfrac{4-3}{2}+\dfrac{3(6)}{4}=\dfrac{1}{2}+\dfrac{9}{2}=5$

$a_4=\dfrac{a_3-4}{2}+\dfrac{3a_2}{4}=\dfrac{5-4}{2}+\dfrac{3(4)}{4}=\dfrac{1}{2}+3=\dfrac{7}{2}$

$a_5=\dfrac{a_4-5}{2}+\dfrac{3a_3}{4}=\dfrac{\frac{7}{2}-5}{2}+\dfrac{3(5)}{4}=-\dfrac{3}{4}+\dfrac{15}{4}=3$

So the first 5 terms are 6, 4, 5, $\dfrac{7}{2}$, 3

Review Exercises

01

15, 9, 3, −3, ⋯ is an arithmetic sequence with $a_1=15$ and $d=-6$.

$a_n=a_1+(n-1)d$

$a_n=15+(n-1)(-6)=-6n+21$

$a_{10}=-6(10)+21=-39$

02

$a_4=24$, $a_8=8$

$a_n=a_1+(n-1)d \rightarrow \begin{cases} 24=a_1+(4-1)d \\ 8=a_1+(8-1)d \end{cases}$

$$\begin{array}{rl} & 24=a_1+3d \\ - & 8=a_1+7d \\ \hline & 16=-4d \rightarrow d=-4 \end{array}$$

$a_n=a_1+(n-1)d$, $a_8=a_1+(8-1)(-4)$

$8=a_1-28$, $a_1=36$

Alternative solution:

$a_n=a_k+(n-k)d$, $a_8=a_4+(8-4)d$

$8=24+4d$, $d=-4$

$a_n=a_1+(n-1)d$, $a_8=a_1+(8-1)(-4)$

$8=a_1-28$, $a_1=36$

03

200, 100, 50, 25, ⋯ is a geometric sequence with $a_1=200$ and $r=\dfrac{1}{2}$.

$a_n=a_1r^{n-1}$. $a_n=200\left(\dfrac{1}{2}\right)^{n-1}$

$a_8=200\left(\dfrac{1}{2}\right)^{8-1}=200\times\dfrac{1}{2^7}=\dfrac{25}{16}$, $a_8=\dfrac{25}{16}$

04

$a_3=5$, $a_6=625$

$a_n=a_1r^{n-1} \rightarrow \begin{cases} a_6=a_1r^{6-1} \\ a_3=a_1r^{3-1} \end{cases}$

$\begin{cases} 625=a_1r^5 \\ 5=a_1r^2 \end{cases} \rightarrow \dfrac{a_1r^5}{a_1r^2}=\dfrac{625}{5}$, $r^3=125$, $r=5$

$a_n=a_1r^{n-1}$

$a_3=a_1r^{3-1}$. $5=a_1(5)^2$, $a_1=\dfrac{1}{5}$

Alternative solution:

$a_n=a_kr^{n-k}$, $a_6=a_3r^{6-3}$

$625=5\cdot r^3$, $r^3=125$, $r=5$

$a_n=a_1r^{n-1}$, $a_3=a_1r^{3-1}$

$5=a_1(5)^2$, $a_1=\dfrac{1}{5}$

05

The sequence is defined recursively.

$a_1=10,\ a_n=a_{n-1}-4n-1$

$a_2=a_1-4(2)-1=10-8-1=1$

$a_3=a_2-4(3)-1=1-12-1=-12$

$a_4=a_3-4(4)-1=-12-16-1=-29$

06

When 2 is added to each of the terms, the resulting numbers form a geometric sequence with ratio $r=3$.

$\{-1,\ 1,\ 7,\ 25\}$

$\{-1+2,\ 1+2,\ 7+2,\ 25+2\}=\{1,\ 3,\ 9,\ 27\}$

$r=\dfrac{a_n}{a_{n-1}},\ r=\dfrac{27}{9}=\dfrac{9}{3}=\dfrac{3}{1}=3$

So the answer is (C).

07

$a_1=2,\ a_5=14,\ a_n=a_1+(n-1)d$

$a_5=a_1+(5-1)d,\ 14=2+4d,\ d=3$

So we have an arithmetic sequence 2, 5, 8, 11, $\cdots$. Since we are looking for the first term of the sequence to exceed 600,

$$a_n=a_1+(n-1)d>600$$
$$2+(n-1)\cdot 3>600$$
$$3n-1>600$$

The minimum value of n satisfying the above inequality is 201. Therefore,

$a_{201}=2+(201-1)\cdot 3=602.$

The value of the first term to exceed 600 is 602.

08

Since 2 additional squares are added for each new row, this is an arithmetic sequence with

$a_1=1$ and $d=2$. In 100th row, we have

$$a_n=a_1+(n-1)d$$
$$a_{100}=1+(100-1)\cdot 2=199$$

There are 199 squares.

09

The sequence is defined recursively and $a_1=2$.

$n=1$(a_1 is even); $a_2=a_1+3=2+3=5$

$n=2$(a_2 is odd); $a_3=2a_2-2=2\cdot 5-2=8$

$n=3$(a_3 is even); $a_4=a_3+3=8+3=11$

$n=4$(a_4 is odd); $a_5=2a_4-2=2\cdot 11-2=20$

The sum of the first five terms is

$a_1+a_2+a_3+a_4+a_5=2+5+8+11+20=46$

10

Every time the ball bounces, the height of the ball rebounded is $\dfrac{2}{3}$ times the previous height. If we let the height of the ball after the first bounce be $a_1=243\times\dfrac{2}{3}=162$, this is a geometric sequence with $a_1=162$ and $r=\dfrac{2}{3}$. Then the height of the ball after fifth bounce(a_5) is

$a_n=a_1r^{n-1},\ a_5=162\cdot\left(\dfrac{2}{3}\right)^4=32\ ft.$

The height of the ball is 32 ft.

11

A geometric sequence has a common ratio r:

$$r=\frac{27}{81}=\frac{9}{27}=\frac{3}{9}=\frac{1}{3}$$

Since r is constant, it is a geometric sequence with $r=\frac{1}{3}$. Thus, the correct answer is (C).

12

An arithmetic sequence has a common difference d:

$$d=3-(-3)=6$$
$$d=9-3=6$$
$$d=15-9=6$$

Since d is constant, it is an arithmetic sequence with a common difference of 6. The answer is (A).

13

Using the formula for the nth term of an arithmetic sequence

$$a_8=a_4+4d$$
$$4d=a_8-a_4=16,\ d=4$$

Now find the value of $a_{21}-a_{15}$.

$$a_{21}=a_{15}+6d$$
$$a_{21}-a_{15}=6d=6(4)=24$$

Thus, the value of $a_{21}-a_{15}$ is 24.

14

Using the formula for the nth term of a geometric sequence

$$g_8=g_4\cdot r^4$$
$$r^4=g_8\div g_4=16,\ r=2$$

Now find the value of $g_{21}\div g_{15}$.

$$g_{21}=g_{15}\cdot r^6$$
$$g_{21}\div g_{15}=r^6=2^6=64$$

Thus, the value of $g_{21}\div g_{15}=64$.

15

(1) Arithmetic Sequence

$$a_7=a_4+3d$$
$$1=8+3d,\ d=-\frac{7}{3}$$

If the sequence is arithmetic,

$$a_4=a_1+3d$$
$$8=a_1+3\left(-\frac{7}{3}\right),\ a_1=15 \text{ and}$$
$$a_8=a_7+d=1+\left(-\frac{7}{3}\right)=-\frac{4}{3}$$

None of the given options match this.

(2) Geometric Sequence

$$g_7=g_4\cdot r^3$$
$$1=8r^3,\ r=\frac{1}{2}$$

If the sequence is geometric,

$$g_4=g_1\cdot r^3$$
$$8=g_1\cdot\left(\frac{1}{2}\right)^3,\ g_1=64 \text{ and}$$
$$g_6=g_4\cdot r^2=8\cdot\left(\frac{1}{2}\right)^2=2$$

Therefore, the correct answer is (D).

2. Exponential Functions

Check Point 1

① $(a^4)^2\times(a^2)^{-3}\times a^5\div a^3$

$=a^8\times a^{-6}\times a^5\div a^3=a^{8+(-6)+5-3}=a^4$

② $(xy^2z^2)^2\div x^3y\times(x^3z)^3\times y^5z^3$

$=x^2y^4z^4\div x^3y\times x^9z^3\times y^5z^3$

$=x^{2-3+9}y^{4-1+5}z^{4+3+3}=x^8y^8z^{10}$

③ $\dfrac{(8ab)^3}{a^4}\times\dfrac{b^2}{16a^4}\div\dfrac{(4b)^3}{32}$

$=\dfrac{(2^3ab)^3}{a^4}\times\dfrac{b^2}{2^4a^4}\div\dfrac{(2^2b)^3}{2^5}$

$=\dfrac{2^9a^3b^3}{a^4}\times\dfrac{b^2}{2^4a^4}\times\dfrac{2^5}{2^6b^3}$

$=\dfrac{2^9b^3}{a}\times\dfrac{b^2}{2^4a^4}\times\dfrac{1}{2b^3}$

$=\dfrac{2^9b^5}{2^5a^5b^3}=\dfrac{2^4b^2}{a^5}$

④ $\dfrac{3a^4}{b}\div(9ab)^2\times\sqrt{81a^3b^4}$

$=\dfrac{3a^4}{b}\times\dfrac{1}{(3^2ab)^2}\times(3^4a^3b^4)^{\frac{1}{2}}$

$=\dfrac{3a^4}{b}\times\dfrac{1}{3^4a^2b^2}\times3^2a^{\frac{3}{2}}b^2$

$=\dfrac{3^3a^{\frac{11}{2}}b^2}{3^4a^2b^3}=\dfrac{a^{\frac{7}{2}}}{3b}=\dfrac{a^3\sqrt{a}}{3b}$

Check Point 2

① $f(x)=4^x$

x	$f(x)=4^x$
-1	$4^{-1}=\frac{1}{4}$
0	$4^0=1$
1	$4^1=4$
2	$4^2=16$

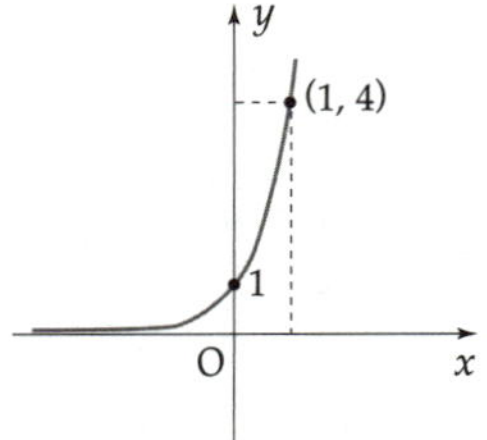

Domain: $(-\infty,\ \infty)$
Range: $(0,\ \infty)$
Horizontal Asymptote: $y=0$

② $f(x)=\left(\frac{1}{4}\right)^x$

x	$f(x)=\left(\frac{1}{4}\right)^x$
-1	$\left(\frac{1}{4}\right)^{-1}=4$
0	$\left(\frac{1}{4}\right)^0=1$
1	$\left(\frac{1}{4}\right)^1=\frac{1}{4}$
2	$\left(\frac{1}{4}\right)^2=\frac{1}{16}$

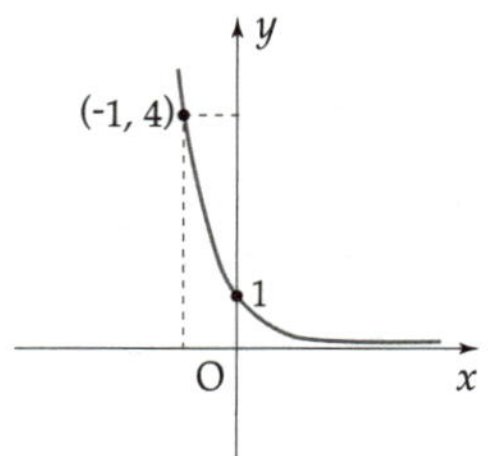

Domain: $(-\infty, \infty)$
Range: $(0, \infty)$
Horizontal Asymptote: $y=0$

Check Point 3

① $f(x)=2^x+3$

Graph $y=2^x$ first and then shift it 3 units up.

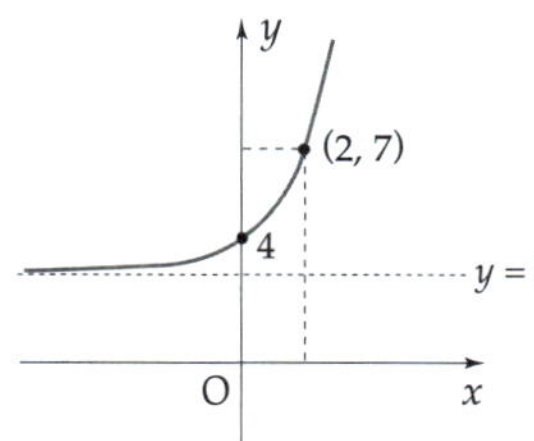

Domain: $(-\infty, \infty)$
Range: $(3, \infty)$
Horizontal Asymptote: $y=3$

② $g(x)=2^{x-1}+4$

Graph $y=2^x$ first and then shift it 1 unit to the right and 4 units up.

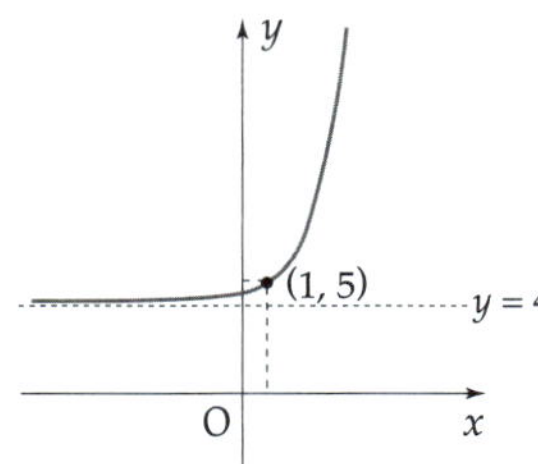

Domain: $(-\infty, \infty)$
Range: $(4, \infty)$
Horizontal Asymptote: $y=4$

Check Point 4

To graph $y=-2^x+3$, reflect the graph of $f(x)=2^x$ about the x-axis, and then shift it 3 units up.

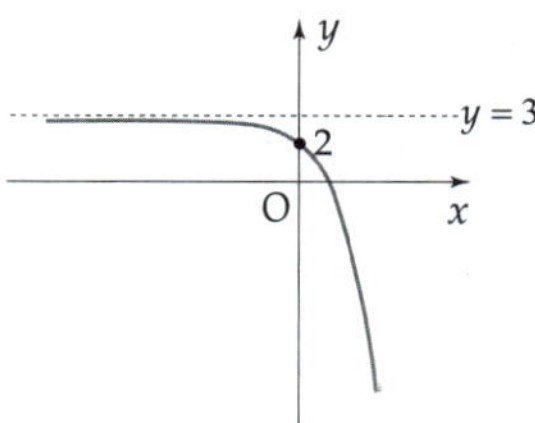

Domain: $(-\infty, \infty)$
Range: $(-\infty, 3)$
Horizontal Asymptote: $y=3$

Check Point 5

$$f(x)=3\cdot\left(\frac{1}{4}\right)^x$$

(1) As x approaches positive infinity, $\left(\frac{1}{4}\right)^x$ approaches 0.

Therefore, $\lim_{x\to\infty}f(x)=\lim_{x\to\infty}3\cdot\left(\frac{1}{4}\right)^x=0$.

(2) As x approaches negative infinity, $\left(\frac{1}{4}\right)^x$ grows exponentially.

Therefore, $\lim_{x\to-\infty}f(x)=\lim_{x\to-\infty}3\cdot\left(\frac{1}{4}\right)^x=\infty$.

Review Exercises

01

(1) $(x^2)^3\times(xy^2)^4\times x^3y$
$=x^6\times x^4y^8\times x^3y$
$=x^{6+4+3}y^{8+1}=x^{13}y^9$

(2) $(ab^3)^4\div(b^6)^{\frac{1}{2}}\times a^4b\div(a^2b)^2$
$=a^4b^{12}\div b^3\times a^4b\div a^4b^2$
$=a^{4+4-4}b^{12-3+1-2}=a^4b^8$

(3) $(2x)^4\times(8x^2y)^2\div\left(\frac{xy^4}{16}\right)^{-3}$

$=(2x)^4\times(2^3x^2y)^2\div(2^{-4}xy^4)^{-3}$

$=2^4x^4\times2^6x^4y^2\div2^{12}x^{-3}y^{-12}$

$=2^{4+6-12}x^{4+4-(-3)}y^{2-(-12)}$

$=2^{-2}x^{11}y^{14}=\frac{x^{11}y^{14}}{4}$

(4) $xy^3\div\sqrt{81x^{-2}y^4}\times\sqrt{(9y^3)^3}$

$=xy^3\div(3^4x^{-2}y^4)^{\frac{1}{2}}\times(3^2y^3)^{\frac{3}{2}}$

$=xy^3\div3^2x^{-1}y^2\times3^3y^{\frac{9}{2}}$

$=3^{-2+3}x^{1-(-1)}y^{3-2+\frac{9}{2}}=3x^2y^{\frac{11}{2}}$

02

(1) $f(x)=3^x$

x	$f(x)=3^x$
-1	$3^{-1}=\frac{1}{3}$
0	$3^0=1$
1	$3^1=3$
2	$3^2=9$

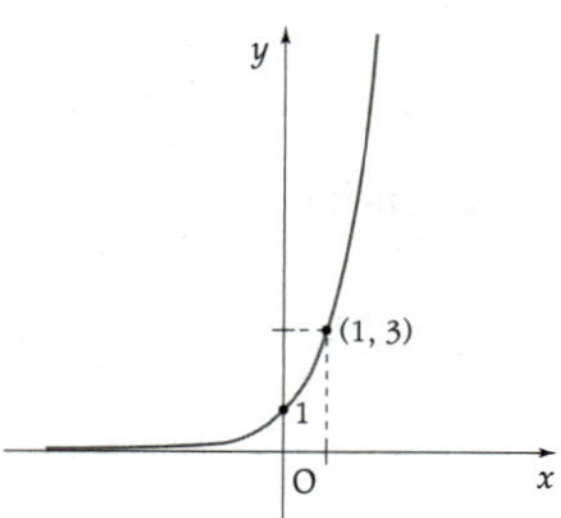

Domain: $(-\infty,\ \infty)$
Range: $(0,\ \infty)$
Horizontal Asymptote: $y=0$

(2) $f(x)=-\left(\frac{4}{3}\right)^x$

x	$f(x)=-\left(\frac{4}{3}\right)^x$
-1	$-\left(\frac{4}{3}\right)^{-1}=-\frac{3}{4}$
0	$-\left(\frac{4}{3}\right)^0=-1$
1	$-\left(\frac{4}{3}\right)^1=-\frac{4}{3}$
2	$-\left(\frac{4}{3}\right)^2=-\frac{16}{9}$

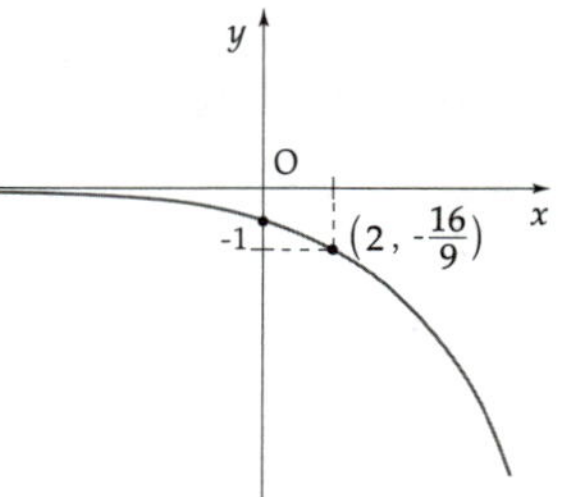

Domain: $(-\infty,\ \infty)$
Range: $(-\infty,\ 0)$
Horizontal Asymptote: $y=0$

(3) $y=-4^{-x}$

x	$f(x)=-4^{-x}$
-1	$-4^{-(-1)}=-4$
0	$-4^{-(0)}=-1$
1	$-4^{-(-1)}=-\frac{1}{4}$
2	$-4^{-(2)}=-\frac{1}{16}$

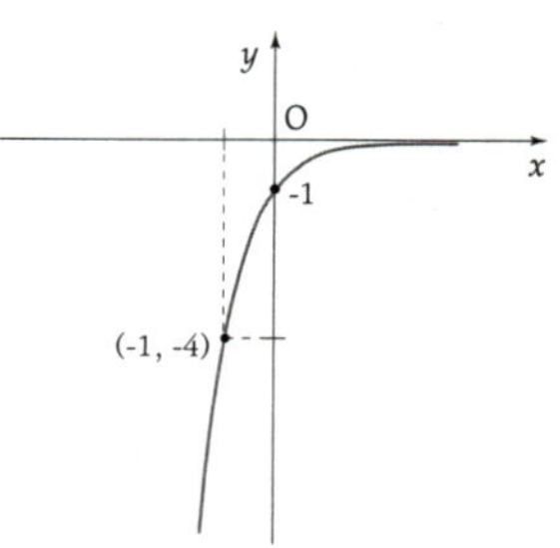

Domain: $(-\infty,\ \infty)$
Range: $(-\infty,\ 0)$
Horizontal Asymptote: $y=0$

03

(1) $f(x)=3^{x-2}$

Graph $y=3^x$ first and then shift it 2 units to the right.

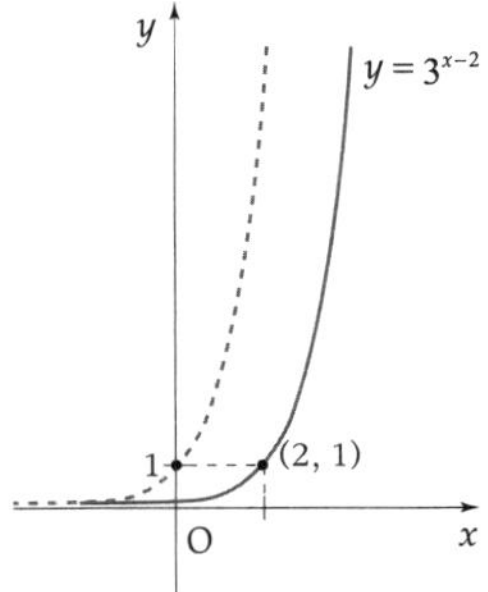

Domain: $(-\infty,\ \infty)$

Range: $(0,\ \infty)$

Horizontal Asymptote: $y=0$

(2) $g(x)=3^x-2$

Graph $y=3^x$ first and then shift it 2 units down.

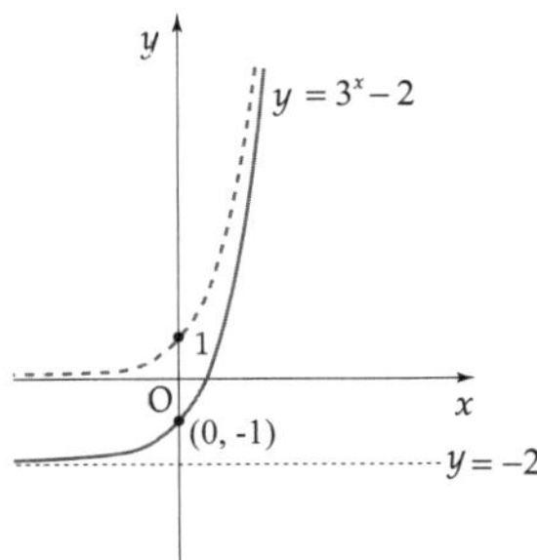

Domain: $(-\infty,\ \infty)$

Range: $(-2,\ \infty)$

Horizontal Asymptote: $y=-2$

(3) $y=3^{x+2}+\dfrac{3}{2}$

Graph $y=3^x$ first and then shift it 2 units to the left and $\dfrac{3}{2}$ units up.

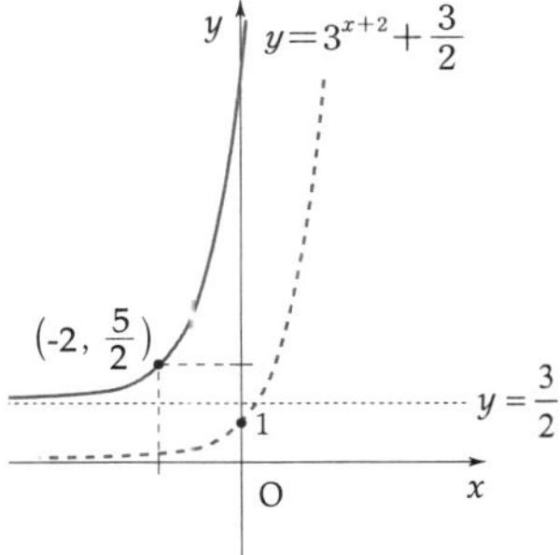

Domain: $(-\infty,\ \infty)$

Range: $\left(\dfrac{3}{2},\ \infty\right)$

Horizontal Asymptote: $y=\dfrac{3}{2}$

04

(1) $f(x)=-3^{x+1}-2$

To graph $f(x)=-3^{x+1}-2$, reflect the graph of $y=3^x$ about the $x-axis$, and then shift it 1 unit to the left and 2 units down.

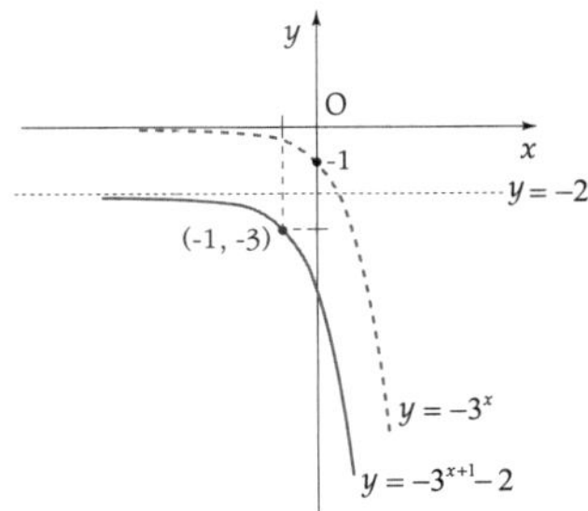

Domain $(-\infty,\ \infty)$

Range: $(-\infty,\ -2)$

Horizontal Asymptote: $y=-2$

(2) $g(x)=2^{-x}+1$

To graph $g(x)=2^{-x}+1$, reflect the graph of $y=2^x$ about the $y-axis$, and then shift it 1 unit up.

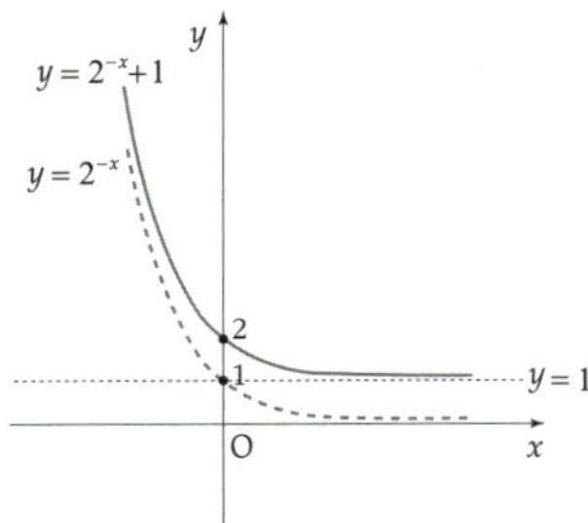

Domain: $(-\infty,\ \infty)$
Range: $(1,\ \infty)$
Horizontal Asymptote: $y=1$

(3) $y=-\left(\frac{1}{2}\right)^{-x-3}+1 \rightarrow y=-\left(\frac{1}{2}\right)^{-(x+3)}+1$

To graph $y=-\left(\frac{1}{2}\right)^{-(x+3)}+1$, reflect the graph of $y=\left(\frac{1}{2}\right)^{x}$ about the origin, and then shift it 3 units to the left and 1 unit up.

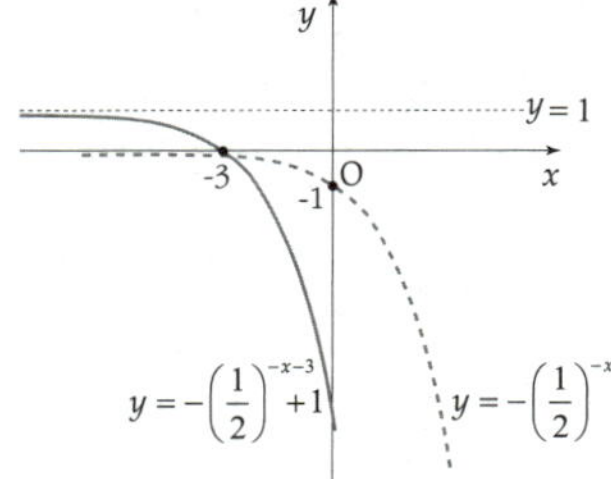

Domain: $(-\infty,\ \infty)$
Range: $(-\infty,\ 1)$
Horizontal Asymptote: $y=1$

05

(1) $2^{3a+1}=32,\ 2^{3a+1}=2^5$

$3a+1=5,\ a=\frac{4}{3}$

(2) $3^{a+4}=27^{3-2a},\ 3^{a+4}=(3^3)^{3-2a}$

$3^{a+4}=3^{9-6a},\ a+4=9-6a$

$7a=5,\ a=\frac{5}{7}$

(3) $5^{-2}=\frac{5^{\frac{1}{x}}\times 25^{\frac{2}{x}}}{25^{-\frac{3}{x}}},\ 5^{-2}=\frac{5^{\frac{1}{x}}\times (5^2)^{\frac{2}{x}}}{(5^2)^{-\frac{3}{x}}}$

$5^{-2}=\frac{5^{\frac{1}{x}}\times 5^{\frac{4}{x}}}{5^{-\frac{6}{x}}},\ 5^{-2}=5^{\frac{1}{x}+\frac{4}{x}-\left(-\frac{6}{x}\right)}$

$5^{-2}=5^{\frac{11}{x}},\ -2=\frac{11}{x},\ x=-\frac{11}{2}$

(4) $\frac{2^{b+3}}{32^{\frac{b}{5}}}=\frac{4^{2b+3}}{8^{-b}},\ \frac{2^{b+3}}{(2^5)^{\frac{b}{5}}}=\frac{(2^2)^{2b+3}}{(2^3)^{-b}}$

$\frac{2^{b+3}}{2^b}=\frac{2^{4b+6}}{2^{-3b}},\ 2^{b+3-b}=2^{4b+6-(-3b)}$

$2^3=2^{7b+6},\ 3=7b+6,\ b=-\frac{3}{7}$

06

$4^x+4^x+4^x+4^x=4^{2x+3}$
$4\cdot 4^x=4^{2x+3},\ 4^{x+1}=4^{2x+3}$
$x+1=2x+3,\ x=-2.$

07

$f(x)=m^x \rightarrow f(a+b)=m^{a+b}$
(A) $f(a)+f(b)=m^a+m^b$
(B) $f(a)f(b)=m^a m^b=m^{a+b}$
(C) $f(ab)=m^{ab}=(m^a)^b$ or $(m^b)^a$
(D) $f(m^a)+f(m^b)=m^{ma}+m^{mb}$
So the answer is (B).

08

Since the point (2, 4) passes through the function $y=a^{x-1}+2$, we have $4=a^{2-1}+2,\ a=2$. Now substitute $\left(m,\ \frac{9}{4}\right)$ into $y=2^{x-1}+2$ to find m.

$\frac{9}{4}=2^{m-1}+2,\ \frac{1}{4}=2^{m-1}$
$2^{-2}=2^{m-1} \rightarrow -2=m-1,\ m=-1.$

09

$f(x)=8\cdot16^{2x+1}$

Using properties of exponents, we can rewrite $8\cdot16^{2x+1}$ as:

$$8\cdot16^{2x+1}=2^3(2^4)^{2x+1}$$
$$=2^3\cdot2^{8x+4}=2^{8x+7}$$

Therefore, the correct answer is (A).

10

Using properties of exponents, we can rewrite $81\cdot\left(\frac{1}{9}\right)^{x-1}$ as:

$$81\cdot\left(\frac{1}{9}\right)^{x-1}=3^4(3^{-2})^{x-1}$$
$$=3^4\cdot3^{-2x+2}=3^{-2x+6}$$

Therefore, the value of k in $g(x)=3^k$ is:

$k=-2x+6$

11

The population $P(t)$ at time t is modeled by $P(t)=200(1.02)^t$. So the population after 10 years is

$$P(10)=200(1.02)^{10}=243.798$$

Therefore, the population after 10 years is approximately 244.

12

To solve question 12, determine the exponential function $C(t)$ for the chemical amount over time given:

(1) Calculate r using the amount from day 0 to day 1: $r=\frac{160}{200}=0.8$

So the function is $C(t)=200(0.8)^t$. Now verify the function.

$$C(2)=200(0.8)^2=128$$
$$C(3)=200(0.8)^3=102.4$$

Therefore, the exponential function that models the amount of the chemical is (D).

13

(1) $h(x)=4^x$

$$g(x)=\frac{h(x)}{16}=\frac{4^x}{4^2}=4^{x-2}$$

The expression 4^{x-2} represents a horizontal translation of the graph of $h(x)=4^x$ to the right by 2 units. Therefore, the correct statement is (A).

(2) $h(x)=4^x=2^{2x}$

$$f(x)=2^{2x-2}=2^{2(x-1)}$$

The expression $2^{2(x-1)}$ represents a horizontal translation of the graph of $h(x)=2^{2x}$ to the right by 1 unit. Therefore, the correct statement is (B).

14

A 1.5% increase per unit x means $g(x)$ follows:

$$g(x)=g_0(1+0.015)^x=g_0(1.015)^x$$

where g_0 is the initial value. Since the function increases by 1.5% per unit increase in x, the base of the exponential function should be 1.015. Therefore, the correct answer is (C).

15

A linear decrease means the population decreases by a fixed amount each year.

(A) Linear increase

(B) Linear decrease

(C) Exponential increase

(D) Exponential decrease

The only option that correctly describes a linear decrease is (B).

16

$y=2-x$ decreases linearly.

$y=0.5^x-0.25$ decreases exponentially.

For $x=0$: $y=2-0=2$ and

$y=0.5^0-0.25=0.75$.

The linear function is greater than the exponential function $x=0$.

For $x=2$: $y=2-2=0$ and $y=0.5^2-0.25=0$.

Both functions have the same value at $x=2$. Thus, the exponential function is less than the linear function in the interval $0<x<2$. The correct statement is (D).

17

The function $f(x)=4\cdot5^x$ is an exponential function with a base greater than 1.

As $x\to\infty$, 5^x grows without bound.

$$\lim_{x\to\infty}f(x)=\lim_{x\to\infty}4\cdot5^x=\infty$$

As $x\to-\infty$, 5^x approaches 0.

$$\lim_{x\to-\infty}f(x)=\lim_{x\to-\infty}4\cdot5^x=0$$

Thus, the correct statement is (A).

18

The base of the exponential function $g(x)=2\cdot0.5^x$ is 0.5, which is between 0 and 1. This indicates exponential decay.

As $x\to\infty$, 0.5^x approaches 0.

$$\lim_{x\to\infty}g(x)=\lim_{x\to\infty}2\cdot0.5^x=0$$

As $x\to-\infty$, 0.5^x grows without bound.

$$\lim_{x\to-\infty}g(x)=\lim_{x\to-\infty}2\cdot0.5^x=\infty$$

Therefore, the horizontal asymptote of the function $g(x)=2\cdot0.5^x$ is $y=0$.

3. Composition of Functions and Inverse Functions

Check Point 1

① $f\circ g=f(g(x))=f(2x)$

$=\frac{1}{2}(2x)^2-2=2x^2-2$

② $g\circ f=g(f(x))=g\left(\frac{1}{2}x^2-2\right)$

$=2\left(\frac{1}{2}x^2-2\right)=x^2-4$

③ $(f\circ g)(2)=f(g(2))=f(2(2))$

$=f(4)=\frac{1}{2}(4)^2-2=6$

④ $(g\circ g\circ f)(-1)=g(g(f(-1)))$

$=g\left(g\left(\frac{1}{2}(-1)^2-2\right)\right)=g\left(g\left(-\frac{3}{2}\right)\right)$

$=g\left(2\left(-\frac{3}{2}\right)\right)=g(-3)=2(-3)=-6$

Check Point 2

Domain of $f(x)=\frac{2}{x}$: All real numbers except for $x=0$

Domain of $g(x)=2x+5$: All real numbers

① $f\circ g=f(g(x))=f(2x+5)=\frac{2}{2x+5}$

Domain of $f\circ g\Rightarrow y=\frac{2}{2x+5}$:

All real numbers except for $x=-\frac{5}{2}$

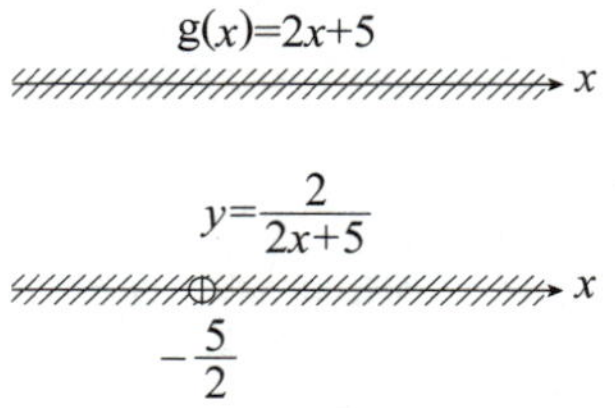

Domain of $f\circ g$: All real numbers except for $x=-\frac{5}{2}$

② $g\circ f=g\left(\frac{2}{x}\right)=2\left(\frac{2}{x}\right)+5=\frac{4}{x}+5$

Domain of $g \circ f \Rightarrow y=\frac{4}{x}+5$:

All real numbers except for $x=0$

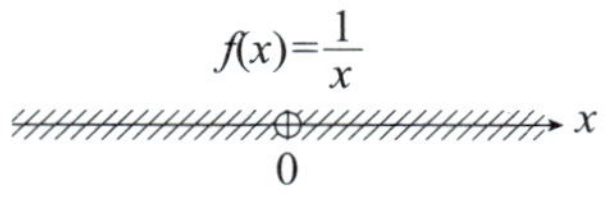

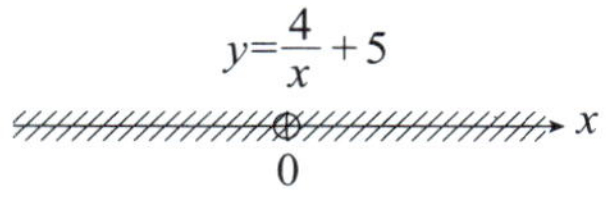

Domain of $g \circ f$: All real numbers except for $x=0$

③ $f \circ f=f\left(\frac{2}{x}\right)=\frac{2}{\left(\frac{2}{x}\right)}=x$

Domain of $f \circ f \Rightarrow y=x$: All real numbers

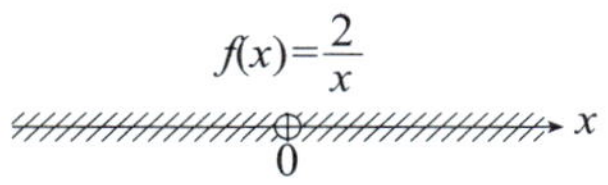

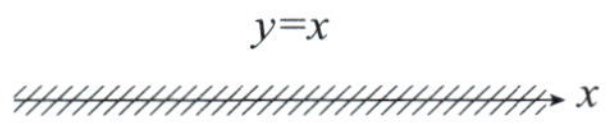

Domain of $f \circ f$: All real numbers except for $x=0$

Check Point 3

① $g(5)=2\sqrt{5-1}+1=2(2)+1=5$

② $5=2\sqrt{x-1}+1,\ 4=2\sqrt{x-1}$

$\sqrt{x-1}=2,\ x-1=4$

$x=5,\ g^{-1}(5)=5$

③ $a=2\sqrt{x-1}+1,\ a-1=2\sqrt{x-1}$

$\frac{a-1}{2}=\sqrt{x-1},\ x-1=\frac{(a-1)^2}{4}$

$x=\frac{(a-1)^2}{4}+1$

$g^{-1}(a)=\frac{(a-1)^2}{4}+1$ where $a \geq 1$

Check Point 4

① $f(3)=c$

② $f^{-1}(b)=4$

③ $f^{-1}(d)=1$

④ $(f^{-1})^{-1}(4)=f(4)=b$

⑤ $(f^{-1} \circ f)(4)=4$

⑥ $(f \circ f^{-1})(a)=a$

Check Point 5

If g is inverse of f, $(f \circ g)(x)=x$ and $(g \circ f)(x)=x$.

$(f \circ g)(x)=f(g(x))=f\left(\frac{1-2x}{4}\right)$

$=-2\left(\frac{1-2x}{4}\right)+\frac{1}{2}$

$=\frac{-1+2x}{2}+\frac{1}{2}=x$

$(g \circ f)(x)=g(f(x))=g\left(-2x+\frac{1}{2}\right)$

$=\frac{1-2\left(-2x+\frac{1}{2}\right)}{4}$

$=\frac{1+4x-1}{4}=x$

Check Point 6

① $f(x)=\sqrt{x-3}+1,\ y=\sqrt{x-3}+1$

$x=\sqrt{y-3}+1, x-1=\sqrt{y-3}$

$(x-1)^2=(\sqrt{y-3})^2,\ (x-1)^2=y-3$

$(x-1)^2-3=y$

$f^{-1}(x)=(x-1)^2+3$, where $x \geq 1$

f^{-1} is a function because f is a one-to-one.

② $f(x)=\sqrt[3]{x}+1,\ y=\sqrt[3]{x}+1$

$x=\sqrt[3]{y}+1,\ x-1=\sqrt[3]{y}$

$(x-1)^3=y$

$f^{-1}(x)=(x-1)^3$

f^{-1} is a function because f is a one-to-one.

Check Point 7

① $f(x)=-4x-3$, $y=-4x-3$

$x=-4y-3$, $x+3=-4y$

$y=-\dfrac{x+3}{4}$

$f^{-1}(x)=-\dfrac{x+3}{4}$

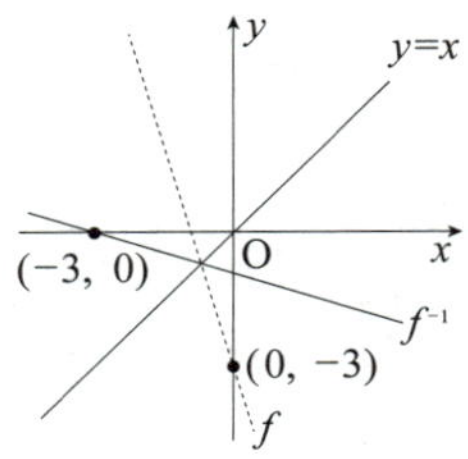

② $f(x)=\dfrac{2-3x}{3}$, $y=\dfrac{2-3x}{3}$

$x=\dfrac{2-3y}{3}$, $3x=2-3y$

$3y=2-3x$, $y=\dfrac{2-3x}{3}$

$f^{-1}(x)=\dfrac{2-3x}{3}$

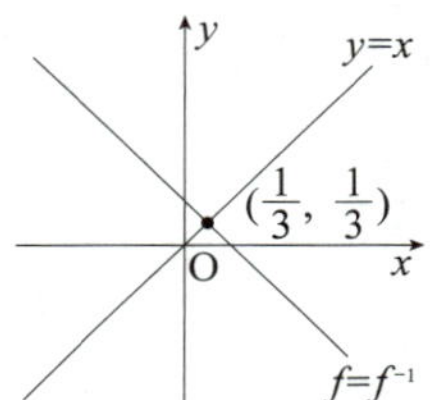

③ $f(x)=x^2-3$, $x\geq 0$

$y=x^2-3$

$x=y^2-3$, $x+3=y^2$

$y=\sqrt{x+3}$

$f^{-1}(x)=\sqrt{x+3}$, $x\geq -3$

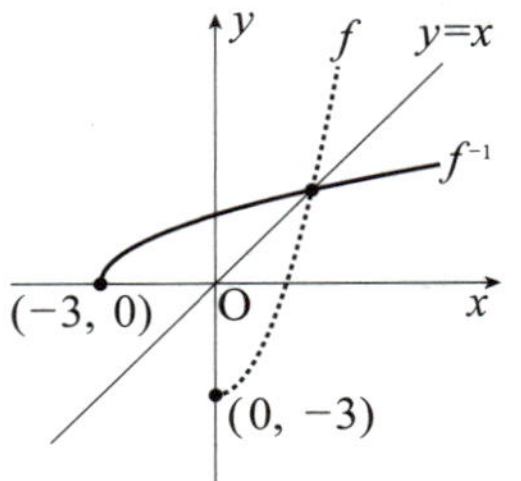

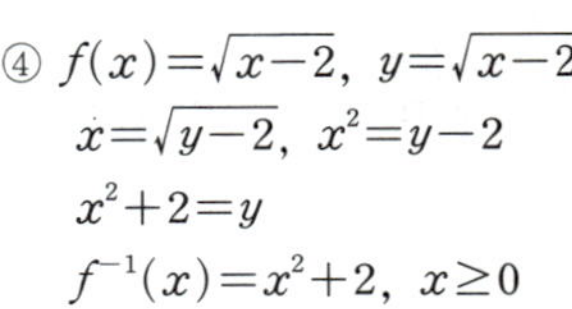

④ $f(x)=\sqrt{x-2}$, $y=\sqrt{x-2}$

$x=\sqrt{y-2}$, $x^2=y-2$

$x^2+2=y$

$f^{-1}(x)=x^2+2$, $x\geq 0$

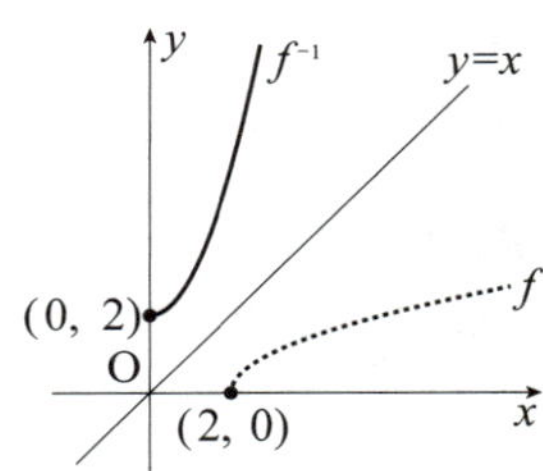

Review Exercises

01

(1) $(f\circ g)(-4)=f(g(-4))=f\left(\dfrac{1}{(-4)-1}\right)$

$=2\left(-\dfrac{1}{5}\right)-1=-\dfrac{7}{5}$

(2) $(g\circ h)\left(\dfrac{2}{3}\right)=g\left(h\left(\dfrac{2}{3}\right)\right)=g\left(\sqrt{3\left(\dfrac{2}{3}\right)+2}\right)$

$=g(2)=\dfrac{1}{2-1}=1$

(3) $g\circ f=g(f(x))=g(2x-1)$

$=\dfrac{1}{(2x-1)-1}=\dfrac{1}{2x-2}$

Domain of f: All real numbers

Domain of $g\circ f \Rightarrow y=\dfrac{1}{2x-2}$:

All real numbers except for $x=1$

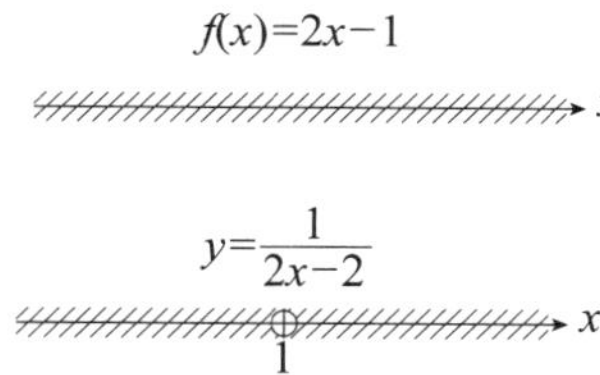

Domain of $g\circ f$: All real numbers except for $x=1$

(4) $g\circ h=g(h(x))=g(\sqrt{3x+2})$

$$=\frac{1}{\sqrt{3x+2}-1}$$

Domain of h: $\left\{x \mid x\geq -\frac{2}{3}\right\}$

Domain of $g\circ h \Rightarrow y=\frac{1}{\sqrt{3x+2}-1}$:

$\sqrt{3x+2}-1\neq 0,\ \sqrt{3x+2}\neq 1$

$3x+2\neq 1,\ x\neq -\frac{1}{3}$

All real numbers except for $x=-\frac{1}{3}$

Domain of $g\circ h$: $\left\{x \mid x\geq -\frac{2}{3},\text{ but } x\neq -\frac{1}{3}\right\}$

02

(1) $(f\circ g)(2)=f(g(2))=f(-2(2)+5)$

$$=f(1)=4(1)-a=4-a$$

Since $(f\circ g)(2)=4$,

$$4-a=4,\ a=0$$

(2) $(g\circ g)(b)=g(g(b))$

$$=g(-2b+5)$$
$$=-2(-2b+5)+5$$
$$=4b-5$$

Since $(g\circ g)(b)=-11$,

$$4b-5=-11,\ b=-\frac{6}{4}=-\frac{3}{2}$$

03

From $f(1-4x)=\frac{3x-2}{4}$, let $1-4x=u$.

Then, $-4x=u-1,\ x=\frac{1-u}{4}$.

Rewriting f as a function of u, we have

$$f(u)=\frac{3\left(\frac{1-u}{4}\right)-2}{4}=\frac{\frac{3-3u}{4}-2}{4}$$

$$=\frac{\frac{-3u-5}{4}}{4}=-\frac{3u+5}{16}$$

(1) By substituting x for u,

$$f(x)=-\frac{3x+5}{16}$$

(2) By substituting $4a-1$ for u,

$$f(4a-1)=-\frac{3(4a-1)+5}{16}=-\frac{12a+2}{16}$$

$$=-\frac{6a+1}{8}$$

04

From $f\left(\frac{3x+1}{2}\right)=2x+5$, let $\frac{3x+1}{2}=u$.

Then, $3x+1=2u,\ x=\frac{2u-1}{3}$.

Rewriting f as a function of u, we have

$$f(u)=2\left(\frac{2u-1}{3}\right)+5=\frac{4u-2}{3}+5$$

$$=\frac{4u+13}{3}$$

Therefore,

$$f(2)+f(5)=\frac{4(2)+13}{3}+\frac{4(5)+13}{3}$$

$$=\frac{21}{3}+\frac{33}{3}=7+11=18$$

05

$f\cdot g=f(g(x))=f(kx+1)$

$$=3(kx+2)-2=3kx+4$$

$g\cdot f=g(f(x))=f(3x-2)$

$$=k(3x-2)+2=3kx-2k+2$$

Since $f \circ g = g \circ f$,

$$3kx+4=3kx-2k+2$$
$$4=-2k+2,\ k=-1$$

06

(1) Since $f \circ h = f(h(x)) = g$,

$-3h(x)+4=4x-1$

$-3h(x)=4x-5,\ h(x)=-\frac{4}{3}x+\frac{5}{3}$

(2) Since $h \circ g = h(g(x)) = f$,

$h(4x-1)=-3x+4.$

If we let $4x-1=u$, then $x=\frac{u+1}{4}$ and

we have $h(u)=-3\left(\frac{u+1}{4}\right)+4.$

If we rewire this function as a function of x,

$$h(x)=-3\left(\frac{x+1}{4}\right)+4$$

07

(1) $(f \circ g)(0)=f(g(0))=f(-1)=0$

(2) $(g \circ f)(2)=g(f(2))=g(-2)=-1$

08

(1) $3=\frac{1+x}{x-2},\ 3(x-2)=1+x$

$3x-6=1+x,\ 2x=7$

$x=\frac{7}{2},\ f^{-1}(3)=\frac{7}{2}$

(2) $k=\frac{1+x}{x-2},\ k(x-2)=1+x$

$kx-2k=1+x,\ kx-x=1+2k$

$x(k-1)=1+2k,\ x=\frac{1+2k}{k-1}$

$f^{-1}(k)=\frac{1+2k}{k-1}$

09

If g is inverse of f, $(f \circ g)(x)=x$ and $(g \circ f)(x)=x$.

(1) $f(x)=2x-1,\ g(x)=\frac{x+1}{2}$

$$(f \circ g)(x)=f(g(x))=f\left(\frac{x+1}{2}\right)$$
$$=2\left(\frac{x+1}{2}\right)-1$$
$$=x+1-1=x$$
$$(g \circ f)(x)=g(f(x))=g(2x-1)$$
$$=\frac{(2x-1)+1}{2}=\frac{2x}{2}=x$$

(2) $f(x)=\sqrt{x-4},\ g(x)=x^2+4$ where $x\geq 0$

$$(f \circ g)(x)=f(g(x))=f(x^2+4)$$
$$=\sqrt{(x^2+4)-4}=\sqrt{x^2}=x$$
$$(g \circ f)(x)=g(f(x))=g(\sqrt{x-4})$$
$$=(\sqrt{x-4})^2+4=x-4+4=x$$

10

(1) $f(x)=4-x^2,\ x\geq 0$

$y=4-x^2,\ x=4-y^2$

$x-4=-y^2,\ 4-x=y^2$

$y=\sqrt{4-x},\ f^{-1}(x)=\sqrt{4-x}$

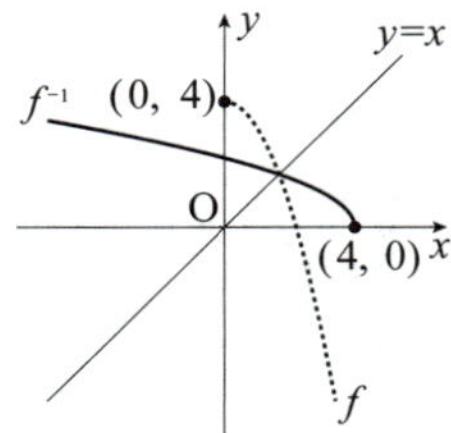

(2) $f(x)=\frac{2}{x},\ y=\frac{2}{x}$

$x=\frac{2}{y},\ y=\frac{2}{x},\ f^{-1}(x)=\frac{2}{x}$

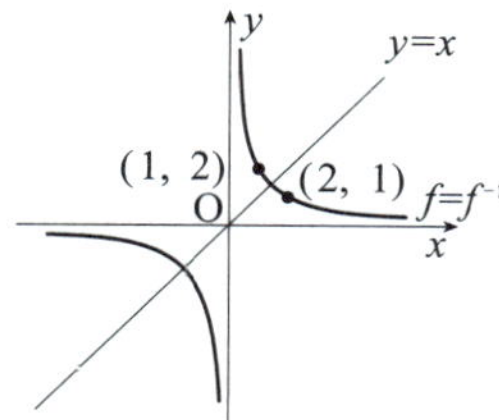

11

If $f^{-1}(a)=4$, then $a=f(4)$.
$a=f(4)=5(4)+2=22$

12

If $f^{-1}(2)=1$, then $2=f(1)$.
$f(1)=3\sqrt{b(1)-2}+1=2$
$3\sqrt{b-2}=1$, $\sqrt{b-2}=\frac{1}{3}$
$b-2=\frac{1}{9}$, $b=\frac{19}{9}$

13

Since the graph of f^{-1} passes through two points $(2, -3)$ and $(10, 1)$,

$f^{-1}(2)=-3 \qquad f^{-1}(10)=1$
$2=f(-3) \qquad 10=f(1)$
$2=-3a+b \qquad 10=a+b$

Solving the system, we have
$a=2$ and $b=8$.
Therefore, $a+b=2+8=10$

14

We need to find the inverse function $W(C)$ for the given concentration function $C(W)=\frac{100}{W+2}$, and understand its representation.

$$C=\frac{100}{W+2}$$

$$W+2=\frac{100}{C}$$

$$W=\frac{100}{C}-2$$

The inverse function $W(C)$ represents the amount of water needed to achieve a certain concentration C of tea syrup. Thus, the correct answer is (A).

4. Logarithmic Functions

Check Point 1

① $\log_2 64=6$
The base is 2 and the exponent is 6.
So $2^6=64$.

② $\log_5\left(\frac{1}{25}\right)=-2$
The base is 5 and the exponent is -2.
So $5^{-2}=\frac{1}{25}$.

③ $2^3=8$
The base is 2 and the exponent is 3.
So $\log_2 8=3$.

④ $9^0=1$
The base is 9 and the exponent is 0.
So $\log_9 1=0$.

Check Point 2

① $\log_3 9=x$
$3^x=9$, $3^x=3^2$, $x=2$

② $2\log_{\frac{1}{2}} 32=x$, $\log_{\frac{1}{2}} 32=\frac{x}{2}$
$\left(\frac{1}{2}\right)^{\frac{x}{2}}=32$, $(2^{-1})^{\frac{x}{2}}=2^5$
$2^{-\frac{x}{2}}=2^5$, $-\frac{x}{2}=5$, $x=-10$

③ $\log_{\sqrt{2}} 4=x$, $(\sqrt{2})^x=4$

$\left(2^{\frac{1}{2}}\right)^x=2^2,\ 2^{\frac{x}{2}}=2^2$

$\frac{x}{2}=2,\ x=4$

Check Point 3

① $f(x)=\log_5 x$

x	$f(x)=\log_5 x$
$\frac{1}{25}$	$\log_5\left(\frac{1}{25}\right)=-2$
$\frac{1}{5}$	$\log_5\left(\frac{1}{5}\right)=-1$
1	$\log_5 1=0$
5	$\log_5 5=1$
25	$\log_5 25=2$

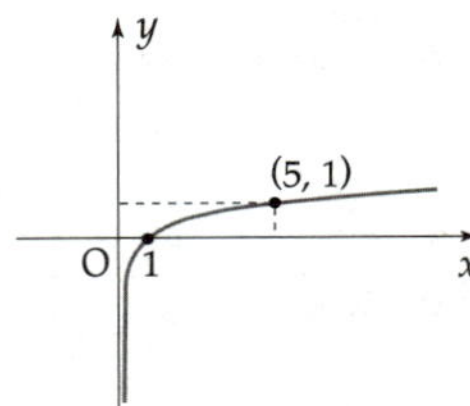

Domain: $(0,\ \infty)$
Range: $(-\infty,\ \infty)$
Vertical Asymptote: $x=0$

② $f(x)=\log_{\frac{1}{4}} x$

x	$f(x)=\log_{\frac{1}{4}} x$
$\frac{1}{16}$	$\log_{\frac{1}{4}}\left(\frac{1}{16}\right)=2$
$\frac{1}{4}$	$\log_{\frac{1}{4}}\left(\frac{1}{4}\right)=1$
1	$\log_{\frac{1}{4}} 1=0$
4	$\log_{\frac{1}{4}} 4=-1$
16	$\log_{\frac{1}{4}} 16=-2$

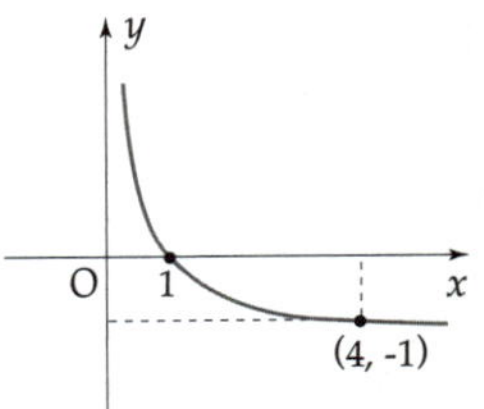

Domain: $(0,\ \infty)$
Range: $(-\infty,\ \infty)$
Vertical Asymptote: $x=0$

Check Point 4

① $f(x)=\log_2 x+1$

Graph $y=\log_2 x$ first and then shift it 1 unit up.

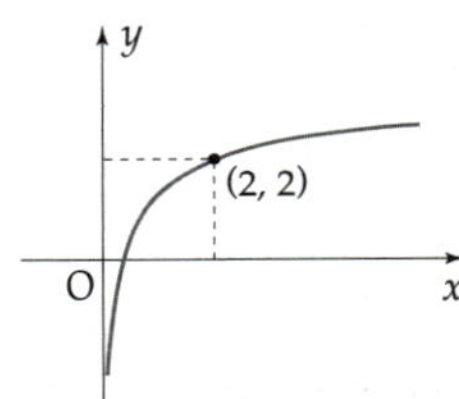

Domain: $(0,\infty)$
Range: $(-\infty,\infty)$
Vertical Asymptote: $x=0$

② $f(x)=\log_4(x+1)$

Graph $y=\log_4 x$ first and then shift it 1 unit to the left.

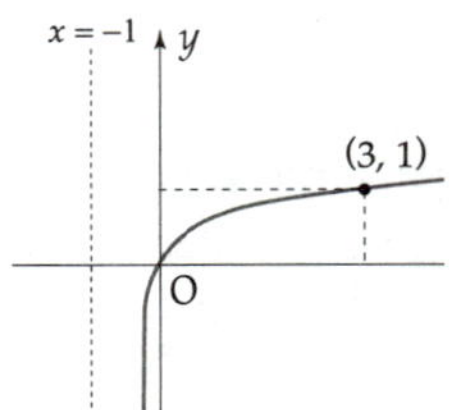

Domain: $(-1,\ \infty)$
Range: $(-\infty,\ \infty)$

Vertical Asymptote: $x=-1$

Check Point 5

To graph $f(x)=-\log_2(x+4)$, reflect the graph of $y=\log_2 x$ about the $x-$axis, and then shift it 4 units to the left.

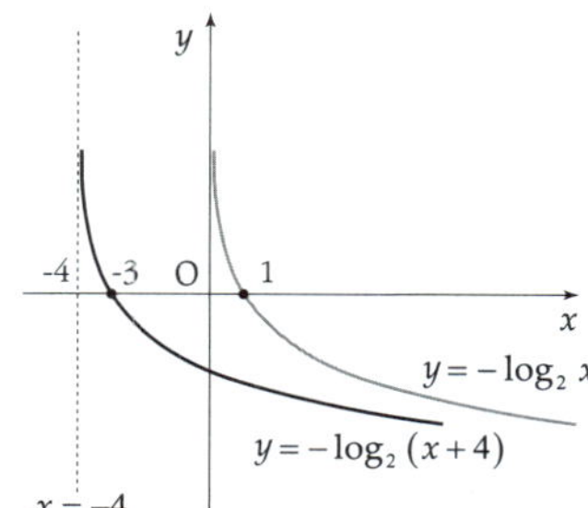

Domain: $(-4, \infty)$

Range: $(-\infty, \infty)$

Vertical Asymptote: $x=-4$

Check Point 6

(1) As x approaches infinity, $-\log_2 x$ decreases without bound. Therefore,

$$\lim_{x\to\infty} f(x)=\lim(-\log_2 x)=-\infty$$

(2) As x approaches zero from the right, $-\log_2 x$ increases without bound. Therefore,

$$\lim_{x\to 0^+} f(x)=\lim_{x\to 0^+}(-\log_2 x)=\infty$$

Review Exercises

01

(1) $\log_2 32=5$

The base is 2 and the exponent is 5. So $2^5=32$.

(2) $\log_{11} 1=0$

The base is 11 and the exponent is 0. So $11^0=1$.

(3) $\log_{25} 5=\frac{1}{2}$

The base is 25 and the exponent is $\frac{1}{2}$.

So $25^{\frac{1}{2}}=5$.

(4) $\log_6\left(\frac{1}{216}\right)=-3$

The base is 6 and the exponent is -3.

So $6^{-3}=\frac{1}{216}$.

(5) $\log_{\frac{2}{3}}\left(\frac{8}{27}\right)=3$

The base is $\frac{2}{3}$ and the exponent is 3.

So $\left(\frac{2}{3}\right)^3=\frac{8}{27}$.

(6) $\log_{\frac{1}{2}} 16=-4$

The base is $\frac{1}{2}$ and the exponent is -4.

So $\left(\frac{1}{2}\right)^{-4}=16$.

02

(1) $7^2=49$

The base is 7 and the exponent is 2. So $\log_7 49=2$.

(2) $16^0=1$

The base is 16 and the exponent is 0. So $\log_{16} 1=0$.

(3) $25^{\frac{3}{2}}=125$

The base is 25 and the exponent is $\frac{3}{2}$.

So $\log_{25} 125=\frac{3}{2}$.

(4) $3^{-4}=\frac{1}{81}$

The base is 3 and the exponent is -4.

So $\log_3\left(\frac{1}{81}\right)=-4$.

03

(1) $\log_4 64=x$

$4^x=64,\ 4^x=4^3,\ x=3$

(2) $\log_{64} 4=x$

$64^x=4,\ 4^{3x}=4^1,\ 3x=1,\ x=\frac{1}{3}$

(3) $\frac{2}{3}\log_4 x=-2,\ \log_4 x=-3$

$x=4^{-3}=\frac{1}{4^3}=\frac{1}{64}$

(4) $\frac{1}{10}\log_{\frac{1}{3}} x=-\frac{3}{5},\ \log_{\frac{1}{3}} x=-6$

$x=\left(\frac{1}{3}\right)^{-6}=(3^{-1})^{-6}=3^6=729$

(5) $\log_2(\log_4 x)=-1$

$\log_4 x=2^{-1},\ \log_4 x=\frac{1}{2},\ x=4^{\frac{1}{2}}=2$

(6) $x=\log_{\frac{1}{5}} 25-2=-2-2=-4$

04

(1) $y=\log_3 x$

x	$y=\log_3 x$
$\frac{1}{3}$	$\log_3\left(\frac{1}{3}\right)=-1$
1	$\log_3 1=0$
3	$\log_3 3=1$
9	$\log_3 9=2$

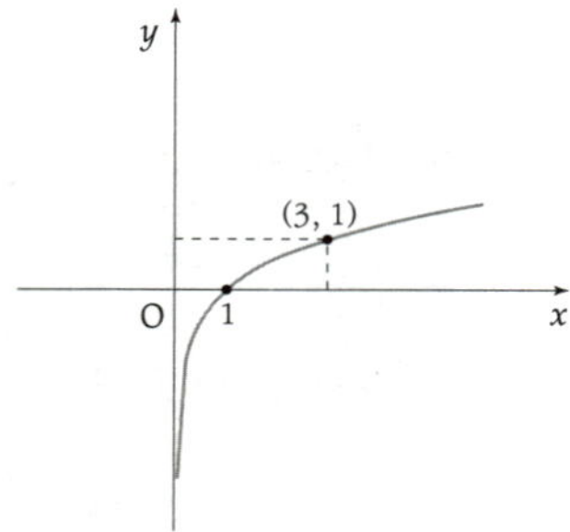

Domain: $(0,\ \infty)$

Range: $(-\infty,\ \infty)$

Vertical Asymptote: $x=0$

(2) $y=\log_{\frac{1}{2}} x$

x	$y=\log_{\frac{1}{2}} x$
8	$\log_{\frac{1}{2}} 8=-3$
4	$\log_{\frac{1}{2}} 4=-2$
2	$\log_{\frac{1}{2}} 2=-1$
1	$\log_{\frac{1}{2}} 1=0$
$\frac{1}{2}$	$\log_{\frac{1}{2}}\left(\frac{1}{2}\right)=1$

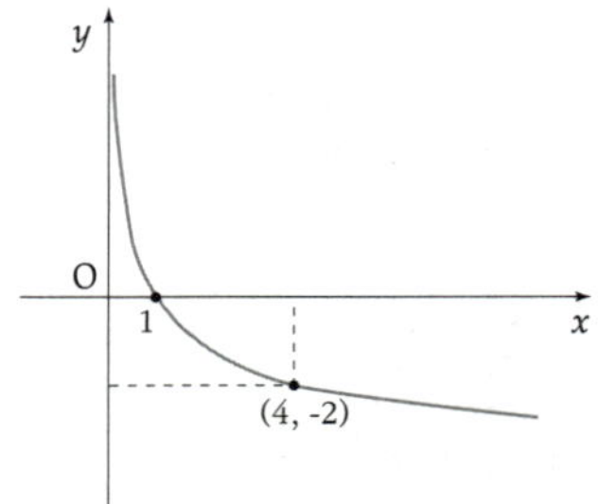

Domain: $(0,\ \infty)$

Range: $(-\infty,\ \infty)$

Vertical Asymptote: $x=0$

(3) $y=\log_4(-x)$

x	$y=\log_4(-x)$
$-\frac{1}{4}$	$\log_4\left(\frac{1}{4}\right)=-1$
-1	$\log_4 (1)=0$
-4	$\log_4 (4)=1$
-16	$\log_4 (16)=2$

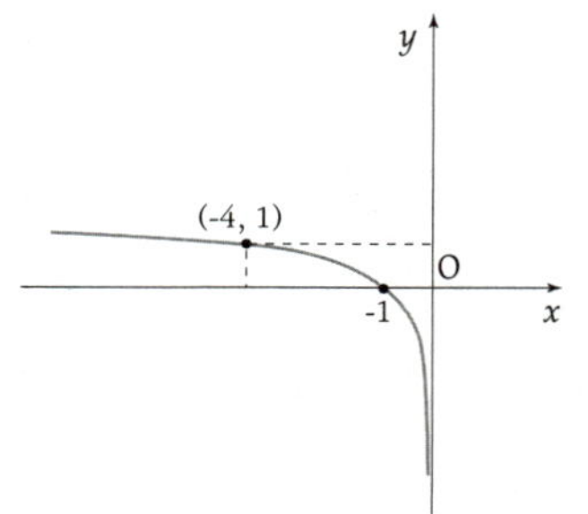

Domain: $(-\infty,\ 0)$
Range: $(-\infty,\ \infty)$
Vertical Asymptote: $x=0$

05

(1) $f(x)=\log_2(x+3)$

Graph $y=\log_2 x$ first and then shift it 3 units to the left.

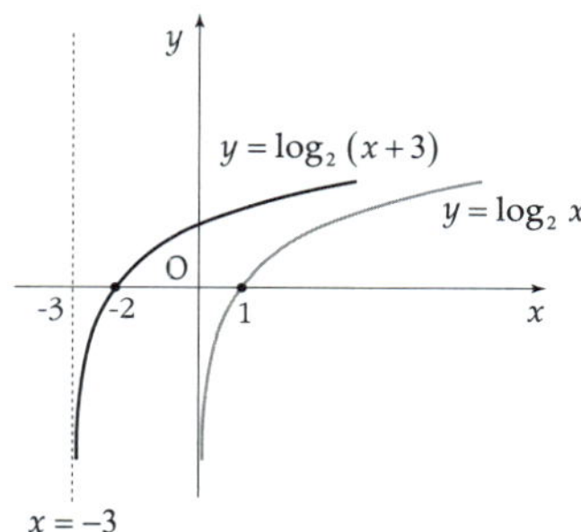

Domain: $(-3,\ \infty)$
Range: $(-\infty,\ \infty)$
Vertical Asymptote: $x=-3$

(2) $g(x)=\log_3 x-2$

Graph $y=\log_3 x$ first and then shift it 2 units down.

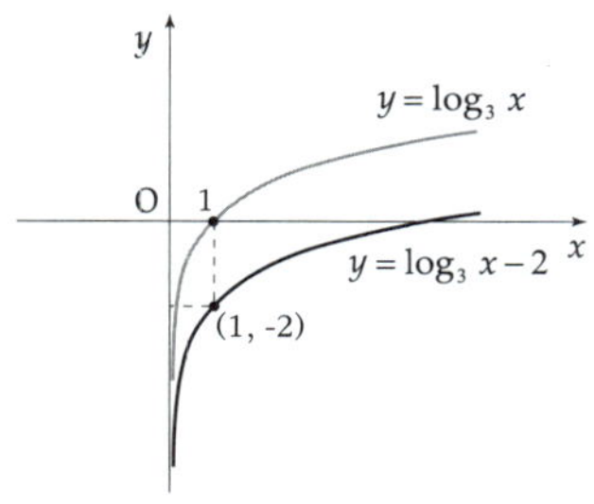

Domain: $(0,\ \infty)$
Range: $(-\infty,\ \infty)$
Vertical Asymptote: $x=0$

(3) $y=\log_4(x-1)+4$

Graph $y=\log_4 x$ first and then shift it 1 unit to the right and 4 units up.

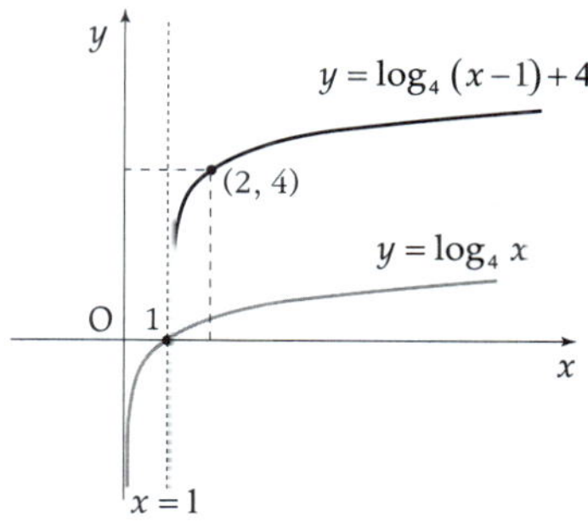

Domain: $(1,\ \infty)$
Range: $(-\infty,\ \infty)$
Vertical Asymptote: $x=1$

06

(1) $g(x)=\log_3(-x)-2$

To graph $g(x)=\log_3(-x)-2$, reflect the graph of $y=\log_3 x$, about the y−axis, and then shift it 2 units down.

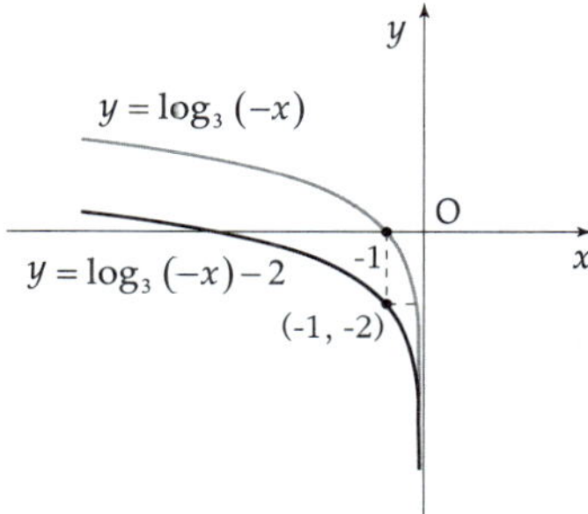

Domain: $(-\infty,\ 0)$
Range: $(-\infty,\ \infty)$
Vertical Asymptote: $x=0$

(2) $y=-\log_{\frac{2}{3}}(x-3)+5$

To graph $y=-\log_{\frac{2}{3}}(x-3)+5$, reflect the graph of $y=\log_{\frac{2}{3}} x$, about the x−axis, and then shift it 3 units to the right and 5 units up.

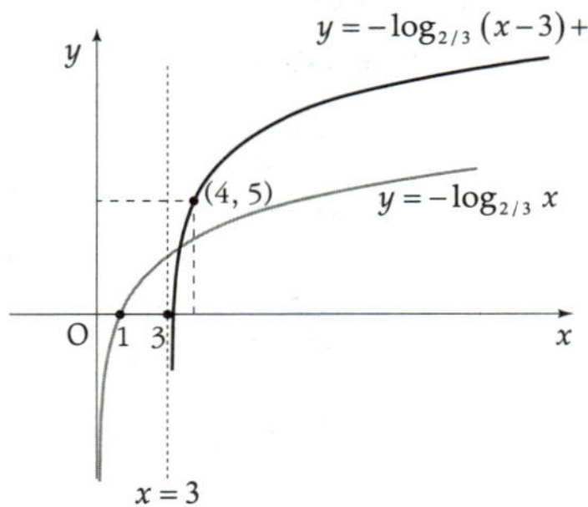

Domain: $(3, \infty)$

Range: $(-\infty, \infty)$

Vertical Asymptote: $x=3$

07

$\log_b 4=-\frac{2}{3} \rightarrow b^{-\frac{2}{3}}=4$

$\left(b^{-\frac{2}{3}}\right)^{-\frac{3}{2}}=(4)^{-\frac{3}{2}},\ b=\frac{1}{4^{\frac{3}{2}}}$

$b=\frac{1}{(2^2)^{\frac{3}{2}}},\ b=\frac{1}{2^3},\ b=\frac{1}{8}$

08

Let $\log_{2\sqrt{2}}\left(\frac{1}{64}\right)=x$.

$(2\sqrt{2})^x=\frac{1}{64},\ \left(2\cdot 2^{\frac{1}{2}}\right)^x=\frac{1}{2^6}$

$\left(2^{\frac{3}{2}}\right)^x=2^{-6},\ 2^{\frac{3x}{2}}=2^{-6}$

$\frac{3x}{2}=-6,\ x=-4.$

Therefore, $\log_{2\sqrt{2}}\left(\frac{1}{64}\right)=-4$.

09

$y=2\log_3(3x-1)-1,\ y+1=2\log_3(3x-1)$

$\frac{y+1}{2}=\log_3(3x-1),\ 3x-1=3^{\frac{y+1}{2}}$

$3x=3^{\frac{y+1}{2}}+1,\ x=\frac{3^{\frac{y+1}{2}}+1}{3}$

10

Calculate $\log_2 y$ for each y value

$\log_2 2=1,\ \log_2 4=2,\ \log_2 8=3$

Thus, the correct answer is (C).

11

(A) $3\log_3 6$. Since $\log_3 6\neq 1,\ 3\log_3 6\neq 3$.

(B) $-\frac{1}{4}\log_4\left(\frac{1}{64}\right)$

$=-\frac{1}{4}\log_4(4^{-3})$

$=-\frac{1}{4}(-3)\log_4 4=\frac{3}{4}\cdot 1=\frac{3}{4}$

(C) $\frac{1}{2}\log_4 128$

$=\frac{1}{2}\log_4 4^3\cdot 2$

$=\frac{1}{2}(\log_4 4^3+\log_4 2)$

$=\frac{1}{2}(3\log_4 4+\log_4 2)$

$=\frac{1}{2}\left(3\cdot 1+\frac{1}{2}\right)=\frac{7}{4}$

(D) $-\frac{3}{2}\log_5\frac{1}{25}$

$=-\frac{3}{2}\log_5(5^{-2})$

$=-\frac{3}{2}(-2)\log_5 5=3\cdot 1=3$

Therefore, the correct answer is (D).

12

$a=\frac{\log_4 5}{2}$

$2a=\log_4 5 \rightarrow 4^{2a}=5$

The correct answer is (C).

13

(A) This table shows a linear function, as y increases by 5 for each unit increase in x.

(B) This table shows an exponential function, as y doubles for each unit increase in x.

(C) In this table, x increases multiplicatively by a factor of 2, while y increases additively by 1. This is consistent with a logarithmic function.

(D) This table shows a linear function, as y increases by $\frac{1}{6}$ for each unit increase in x.

Thus, the correct answer is (C).

14

$h(x)=2^{3x}-2$

$x=2^{3y}-2$

$x+2=2^{3y}$

$3y=\log_2(x+2)$

$y=\frac{1}{3}\log_2(x+2)$

$\rightarrow h^{-1}(x)=\frac{1}{3}\log_2(x+2)$

Thus, the correct answer is (A).

15

$f(x)=\log_3(\log_2 x)$

$x=\log_3(\log_2 y)$

$\log_2 y=3^x$

$y=2^{3^x} \rightarrow f^{-1}(x)=2^{3^x}$

Thus, the expression for the inverse function $f^{-1}(x)$ is 2^{3^x}.

16

The graph of $f(x)=-\frac{1}{2}\log_3 x$ decreases without bound as x increases without bound. As x approaches zero from the right, the graph of f increases without bound. Additionally, the graph of f is concave up, indicating that the rate of f increases without bound. Therefore, the correct statement is (B).

17

For $x=1$: $x=5^1=5=A$ and $y=\log_5 1=0=B$

For $x=5$: $x=5^5=3125=C$ and

$y=\log_5 5=1=D$

Therefore, the value of $A+B+C+D$ is $5+0+3125+1=3131$.

18

$f(x)=4^x$

$x=4^y \rightarrow y=\log_4 x$

$f^{-1}(x)=\log_4 x$

For (B), if $x=64$, $f^{-1}(64)=\log_4 64=3$ and if $x=1024$, $f^{-1}(1024)=\log_4 1024=5$.

Additionally, the logarithmic function $\log_4 x$ is defined only for positive x. So the values in Option (C) and (D) do not fall within the domain of the logarithmic function $\log_4 x$. Therefore, the correct table of values for the inverse function is (B).

19

The function 4^x is an exponential function with the range $(0, \infty)$. Subtracting 12 shifts the entire graph downward by 12 units. Therefore, the new range of $f(x)=4^x-12$ is $(-12, \infty)$. The domain of the inverse function is the range of the original function. Hence, the domain of $f^{-1}(x)$ is $(-12, \infty)$.

20

The logarithmic function fits the description. For a logarithmic function (D) $g(x)=\log_3 x$, if x becomes $3x$, then

$$\begin{aligned} g(3x) &= \log_3(3x) \\ &= \log_3 3+\log_3 x=1+\log_3 x \\ &= 1+g(x) \end{aligned}$$

This matches the given condition: "each time the output value increases by 1, the corresponding input value triples." So the answer is (D).

21

$$f(x)=a\log_b(2x-c)$$

The expression $2x-c$ must be positive.

$$2x-c>0,\ x>\frac{c}{2}$$

The domain of $f(x)$ is the set of all x values greater than $\frac{c}{2} \Rightarrow \left(\frac{c}{2},\ \infty\right)$.

The answer is (B).

22

Logarithmic function $\log_4 x$ is increasing and concave down. This means that as x increases, the graph of f also increases and is concave down. Since f is concave down, the rate of increase is decreasing. Therefore, the correct answer is (B).

23

As x approaches -1 from the right, $x+1$ approaches 0 from the positive side and then $\log_5(x+1)$ approaches $-\infty$. Therefore, $\lim_{x\to-1^+} f(x)=\lim_{x\to-1^+}(2\log_5(x+1)-2)=-\infty$.
As x approaches ∞, $x+1$ approaches ∞. So $\log_5(x+1)$ also approaches ∞. Therefore,
$\lim_{x\to\infty} f(x)=\lim_{x\to\infty}(2\log_5(x+1)-2)=\infty$. Thus, the correct answer is (D).

5. Properties of Logarithms

Check Point 1

① $\log_4 4+\log_9 1=1+0=1$

② $\log_2 8+\log_4 2=\log_2 2^3+\log_4 4^{\frac{1}{2}}$

$=3\log_2 2+\frac{1}{2}\log_4 4=3+\frac{1}{2}=\frac{7}{2}$

③ $\log_5\sqrt{25}-\frac{1}{2}\log_3 27=\log_5 5-\frac{1}{2}\log_3 3^3$

$=1-\frac{1}{2}\cdot 3\log_3 3$

$=1-\frac{3}{2}=-\frac{1}{2}$

Check Point 2

① $\log_3\left(\frac{x}{9}\right)=\log_3 x-\log_3 3^2=\log_3 x-2$

② $\ln\left(\frac{ab^4}{\sqrt{c}}\right)=\ln a+\ln b^4-\ln c^{\frac{1}{2}}$

$=\ln a+4\ln b-\frac{1}{2}\ln c$

③ $\log_4\sqrt[4]{256x^3}=\log_4(4^4x^3)^{\frac{1}{4}}=\log_4 4x^{\frac{3}{4}}$

$=\log_4 4+\log_4 x^{\frac{3}{4}}=1+\frac{3}{4}\log_4 x$

Check Point 3

① $\log_2 3-\log_2 x=\log_2\left(\frac{3}{x}\right)$

② $2\log_5 2+4\log_5 x=\log_5 2^2+\log_5 x^4$

$=\log_5(4x^4)$

③ $5\log 2-\frac{1}{2}\log a-\frac{5}{2}\log b$

$=\log 2^5-\log a^{\frac{1}{2}}-\log b^{\frac{5}{2}}$

$=\log\left(\frac{32}{\sqrt{a}\cdot\sqrt{b^5}}\right)=\log\left(\frac{32}{\sqrt{ab^5}}\right)$

④ $\ln a-\frac{1}{2}(3\ln b+4)=\ln a-\frac{3}{2}\ln b-2$

$=\ln a-\ln b^{\frac{3}{2}}-\ln e^2$

$=\ln\left(\frac{a}{\sqrt{b^3}\cdot e^2}\right)=\ln\left(\frac{a}{e^2\cdot\sqrt{b^3}}\right)$

Review Exercises

01

(1) $\frac{1}{2}\log_3\left(\frac{1}{3}\right)+2\log_5 25=\frac{1}{2}\log_3 3^{-1}+2\log_5 5^2$

$=-\frac{1}{2}\log_3 3+4\log_5 5$

$=-\frac{1}{2}+4=\frac{7}{2}$

(2) $\log\left(\frac{1}{1000}\right)-\log\left(\frac{1}{10}\right)+2\log\left(\frac{1}{100}\right)$

$=\log 10^{-3}-\log 10^{-1}+2\log 10^{-2}$

$=-3\log 10-(-1)\log 10+2(-2)\log 10$

$=-3+1-4=-6$

(3) $\log_3\sqrt{27}+\frac{1}{2}\log_3 3-\log_3\sqrt[3]{9}$

$=\log_3 3^{\frac{3}{2}}+\frac{1}{2}-\log_3 3^{\frac{2}{3}}$

$=\frac{3}{2}\log_3 3+\frac{1}{2}-\frac{2}{3}\log_3 3$

$=\frac{3}{2}+\frac{1}{2}-\frac{2}{3}=\frac{4}{3}$

(4) $2\ln e^3+\ln 25+2\ln 2$

$=6\ln e+\ln 5^2+2\ln 2$

$=6\ln e+2\ln 5+2\ln 2$

$=6+2\ln(5\cdot 2)=6+2\ln 10$

(5) Exponent:

$\log_2 4-\frac{1}{2}\log_2 64=\log_2 2^2-\frac{1}{2}\log_2 2^6$

$=2\log_2 2-3\log_2 2$

$=2-3=-1$

Therefore, $2^{-1}=\frac{1}{2}$.

(6) Exponent:

$\log_5 60-\log_5 3-1$

$=\log_5 60-\log_5 3-\log_5 5$

$=\log_5\left(\frac{60}{3\cdot 5}\right)=\log_5 4$

Therefore, $5^{\log_5 4}=4$.

02

> When using calculator, you can use either common log or natural log.

(1) $\log_2 5=\dfrac{\log 5}{\log 2}\approx 2.3219$

Or, $\log_2 5=\dfrac{\ln 5}{\ln 2}\approx 2.3219$

(2) $\log_{\frac{1}{2}}\left(\dfrac{7}{9}\right)=\dfrac{\log\left(\frac{7}{9}\right)}{\log\left(\frac{1}{2}\right)}\approx 0.3626$

Or, $\log_{\frac{1}{2}}\left(\dfrac{7}{9}\right)=\dfrac{\ln\left(\frac{7}{9}\right)}{\ln\left(\frac{1}{2}\right)}\approx 0.3626$

03

(1) $\log_2(16x^2y)=\log_2 16+\log_2 x^2+\log_2 y$
$=4+2\log_2 x+\log_2 y$

(2) $\log_4\left(\dfrac{y^2}{16x}\right)=\log_4 y^2-\log_4 16-\log_4 x$
$=2\log_4 y-2-\log_4 x$

(3) $\log_a\sqrt{\dfrac{ab^2}{4}}=\log_a\left(\dfrac{ab^2}{4}\right)^{\frac{1}{2}}$
$=\dfrac{1}{2}(\log_a a+\log_a b^2-\log_a 2^2)$
$=\dfrac{1}{2}(1+2\log_a b-2\log_a 2)$
$=\dfrac{1}{2}+\log_a b-\log_a 2$

(4) $\ln\left(\dfrac{\sqrt[3]{ab^5}}{2}\right)=\ln\left(\dfrac{(ab^5)^{\frac{1}{3}}}{2}\right)$
$=\ln(ab^5)^{\frac{1}{3}}-\ln 2$
$=\dfrac{1}{3}(\ln a+\ln b^5)-\ln 2$
$=\dfrac{1}{3}(\ln a+5\ln b)-\ln 2$
$=\dfrac{1}{3}\ln a+\dfrac{5}{3}\ln b-\ln 2$

04

(1) $2(\log_4 x-\log_4 z)=2\log_4\left(\dfrac{x}{z}\right)=\log_4\left(\dfrac{x}{z}\right)^2$

(2) $3\log_2 x+\dfrac{3}{2}\log_2 y+3$
$=\log_2 x^3+\log_2 y^{\frac{3}{2}}+\log_2 2^3$
$=\log_2 x^3+\log_2\sqrt{y^3}+\log_2 8$
$=\log_2(8x^3y\sqrt{y})$

(3) $\dfrac{1}{2}(\log_a(x^2-x-2)-\log_a(x-2)-2\log_a x)$
$=\dfrac{1}{2}(\log_a(x^2-x-2)-\log_a(x-2)-\log_a x^2)$
$=\dfrac{1}{2}\log_a\left(\dfrac{x^2-x-2}{(x-2)x^2}\right)=\dfrac{1}{2}\log_a\left(\dfrac{(x-2)(x+1)}{(x-2)x^2}\right)$
$=\dfrac{1}{2}\log_a\left(\dfrac{x+1}{x^2}\right)=\log_a\left(\dfrac{x+1}{x^2}\right)^{\frac{1}{2}}=\log_a\left(\dfrac{\sqrt{x+1}}{x}\right)$

05

(1) $\log_a 90=\log_a 2\cdot 3^2\cdot 5$
$=\log_a 2+\log_a 3^2+\log_a 5$
$=\log_a 2+2\log_a 3+\log_a 5$
$=0.64+2(1.12)+1.64=4.52$

(2) $\log_a\left(\dfrac{12}{25}\right)=\log_a 12-\log 25$
$=\log_a 2^2\cdot 3-\log_a 5^2$
$=\log_a 2^2+\log_a 3-2\log_a 5$
$=2\log_a 2+\log_a 3-2\log_a 5$
$=2(0.64)+1.12-2(1.64)=-0.88$

(3) $\log_a\sqrt{108}=\log_a(2^2\cdot 3^3)^{\frac{1}{2}}=\dfrac{1}{2}\log_a(2^2\cdot 3^3)$
$=\dfrac{1}{2}(\log_a 2^2+\log_a 3^3)$
$=\dfrac{1}{2}(2\log_a 2+3\log_a 3)$
$=\dfrac{1}{2}(2(0.64)+3(1.12))=2.32$

06

First, $\log_b\sqrt{a}=c$, $\log_b a^{\frac{1}{2}}=c$
$\dfrac{1}{2}\log_b a=c$, $\log_b a=2c$.

Therefore,
$2\log_b a^3=2\cdot 3\log_b a$

$$=6\log_b a$$
$$=6(2c)=12c$$

07

Let $x=\log_5(\log_2 k)$.
Then $\log_7(x)=0$ and $x=7^0=1$.
So, $\log_5(\log_2 k)=1$. Again, let $y=\log_2 k$.
Then, $\log_5(y)=1$ and $y=5^1=5$.
Therefore, $\log_2 k=5$ and $k=2^5=32$.

08

First, we have $108=2^2\cdot 3^3$ and $25=5^2$. So

$$\log_k\left(\frac{108}{25}\right)=\log_k\left(\frac{2^2\cdot 3^3}{5^2}\right)$$
$$=\log_k 2^2+\log_k 3^3-\log_k 5^2$$
$$=2\log_k 2+3\log_k 3-2\log_k 5$$
$$=2a+3b-2c$$

09

Using the change of base formula, we can express $\log_4 m^5$ as follows:

$$\log_4 m^5=\frac{\log_2 m^5}{\log_2 4}=\frac{\log_2 m^5}{2}$$

Therefore, $\dfrac{\log_2 m^5}{\log_4 m^5}=\dfrac{\log_2 m^5}{\frac{\log_2 m^5}{2}}=\dfrac{1}{\frac{1}{2}}=2.$

10

Use the properties of logarithms to find the value of this expression.

$$9^{\log_3 5}=(3^2)^{\log_3 5}=3^{2\log_3 5}$$
$$=3^{\log_3 5^2}=3^{\log_3 25}=25$$

11

Use the properties of logarithms, particularly the change of base formula.

$$\log_4 6\times\log_6 8\times\log_8 10\times\log_{10}16$$
$$=\frac{\cancel{\log 6}}{\log 4}\times\frac{\cancel{\log 8}}{\cancel{\log 6}}\times\frac{\cancel{\log 10}}{\cancel{\log 8}}\times\frac{\log 16}{\cancel{\log 10}}$$
$$=\frac{\log 16}{\log 4}=\log_4 16=2$$

12

Using the property of logarithms,

$$f(x)=\ln x$$
$$3f(a)-0.5f(b)=3\ln a-0.5\ln b$$
$$=\ln a^3-\ln\sqrt{b}=\ln\frac{a^3}{\sqrt{b}}$$

Therefore, the correct answer is (A).

13

Using the property of logarithms,

$$f(x)=\log_4 x$$
$$f(x^2)+f\left(\frac{x}{16}\right)=\log_4 x^2+\log_4\frac{x}{16}$$
$$=2\log_4 x+\log_4 x-\log_4 16$$
$$=3\log_4 x-2$$

Therefore, the correct answer is (D).

14

Using the property of logarithms,

$$\ln a-\frac{1}{2}\ln b=2\left(\ln m-\frac{1}{2}\ln n\right)+3\ln k$$
$$\ln a-\ln\sqrt{b}=2\ln m-\ln n+3\ln k$$
$$\ln a-\ln\sqrt{b}=\ln m^2-\ln n+\ln k^3$$
$$\ln\frac{a}{\sqrt{b}}=\ln\frac{m^2k^3}{n}\ \rightarrow\ \frac{a}{\sqrt{b}}=\frac{m^2k^3}{n}$$
$$a=\frac{m^2k^3\sqrt{b}}{n}$$

Therefore, the correct answer is (A).

15

$$f(g(x))=f\left(\frac{x}{10}\right)=\log\left(\frac{x}{10}\right)^4$$
$$=4\log\left(\frac{x}{10}\right)=4(\log x-\log 10)$$
$$=4(\log x-1)=4\log x-4$$

Therefore, the correct answer is (C).

16

$$\log_3\left(\frac{27^{2m}}{81^n}\right)=\log_3 27^{2m}-\log_3 81^n$$
$$=2m\log_3 27-n\log_3 81$$
$$=2m\cdot 3-n\cdot 4$$
$$=6m-4n \Leftrightarrow am+bn$$

Given that $\log_3\left(\frac{27^{2m}}{81^n}\right)$ is equivalent to the expression $am+bn$, we can deduce that $6m-4n$ is equal to $am+bn$. Therefore, $a=6$ and $b=-4$. Thus, $a+b=6+(-4)=2$.

17

$$g(x)=2\log_5(x^2)=4\log_5 x$$

The function $g(x)$ is obtained by multiplying the function $f(x)$ by 4. This indicates a vertical dilation by a factor of 4. So the correct answer is (B).

18

$$f(x)=\log_2 x \text{ and } g(x)=\log_2(2x)$$

The function $g(x)$ is obtained by multiplying the function x by 2. This indicates a horizontal dilation by a factor of $\frac{1}{2}$. Also, since

$$g(x)=\log_2(2x)=\log_2 2+\log_2 x$$
$$=1+\log_2 x,$$

$g(x)$ is the result of translating $f(x)$ 1 unit up. Therefore, statements II and III are true, and the answer is (D).

19

$$f(x)=2\log_4(4x-1)-1$$
$$x=2\log_4(4y-1)-1$$
$$\frac{x+1}{2}=\log_4(4y-1)$$
$$4y-1=4^{\frac{x+1}{2}}$$
$$4y=4^{\frac{x+1}{2}}+1$$
$$y=\frac{4^{\frac{x+1}{2}}+1}{4}=4^{\frac{x+1}{2}-1}+\frac{1}{4}=4^{\frac{x-1}{2}}+\frac{1}{4}$$

Therefore, $f^{-1}(x)=4^{\frac{x-1}{2}}+\frac{1}{4}$.

20

$$g(x)=2\ln x+\frac{1}{2}\ln x=\frac{5}{2}\ln x$$
$$x=\frac{5}{2}\ln y$$
$$\frac{2x}{5}=\ln y,\ y=e^{\frac{2x}{5}}$$

Therefore, $g^{-1}(x)=e^{\frac{2x}{5}}$. The answer is (C).

21

$y=4\cdot 3^{x+1}$

Apply the logarithm to both sides:

$$\log y=\log 4\cdot 3^{x+1}$$
$$=\log 4+\log 3^{x+1}$$
$$=\log 4+(x+1)\log 3$$
$$=\log 4+\log 3+\log 3\cdot x$$
$$=\log 12+\log 3\cdot x$$

Since $\log y=ax+b$, we have

$a=\log 12$ and $b=\log 3$

Therefore,

$$\log k=a+b$$
$$=\log 12+\log 3=\log 36$$

$k=36$

6. Exponential and Logarithmic Equations

Check Point 1

① $5^{x-4}=125$

$5^{x-4}=5^3$

$x-4=3,\ x=7$

② $64^{2x+1}=\frac{1}{256}$ Undefined Undefined

$(2^6)^{2x+1}=2^{-8},\ 2^{12x+6}=2^{-8}$

$12x+6=-8,\ x=-\frac{7}{6}$

③ $4^x-2=10,\ 4^x=12$

Take the log with base 4 on each side.

$\log_4 4^x=\log_4 12$

$x\log_4 4=\log_4 12$

$x=\log_4 12$

④ $e^{0.1x}-7=-4,\ e^{0.1x}=3$

$\ln e^{0.1x}=\ln 3,\ 0.1x\ln e=\ln 3,$

$0.1x=\ln 3,\ x=10\ln 3$

Check Point 2

① $4+\log_2(x+1)=6$

$\log_2(x+1)=2$

$x+1=2^2,\ x=3$

Check the Solution

$4+\log_2(3+1)=4+\log_2 4$

$=4+2=6$

Solution checks!

② $\log_2(x+1)-\log_2(x-2)=1$

$\log_2\left(\frac{x+1}{x-2}\right)=1$

$\frac{x+1}{x-2}=2,\ x+1=2(x-2)$

$x+1=2x-4,\ x=5$

Check the Solution

$\log_2(5+1)-\log_2(5-2)$

$=\log_2(6)-\log_2(3)$

$=\log_2\left(\frac{6}{3}\right)=\log_2 2=1$

Solution checks!

③ $\log_4(2x+1)=\log_4 5+\log_4(-x-4)$

$\log_4(2x+1)=\log_4(5(-x-4))$

$\log_4(2x+1)=\log_4(-5x-20)$

$2x+1=-5x-20,\ x=-3$

Check the Solution

$\log_4(2(-3)+1)=\log_4 5+\log_4(-(-3)-4)$

$\log_4(-5)\neq\log_4 5+\log_4(-1)$

$x=-3$ is extraneous solution. Therefore, the equation above has NO solution.

④ $\ln\sqrt{x-4}-3=1,\ \ln x(x-4)^{\frac{1}{2}}=4$

$\frac{1}{2}\ln(x-4)=4,\ \ln(x-4)=8$

$x-4=e^8,\ x=4+e^8$

Check the Solution

$\ln\sqrt{4+e^8-4}-3$

$=\ln\sqrt{e^8}-3=\ln e^4-3$

$=4\ln e-3=4-3=1$

Solution checks!

Review Exercises

01

(1) $2^{2x-3}-32=0,\ 2^{2x-3}=32$

$2^{2x-3}=2^5,\ 2x-3=5,\ x=4$

(2) $3^{x+1}-9\sqrt{27}=0,\ 3^{x+1}=9\sqrt{27}$

$3^{x+1}=3^2\cdot 3^{\frac{3}{2}},\ 3^{x+1}=3^{\frac{7}{2}}$

$x+1=\frac{7}{2},\ x=\frac{5}{2}$

(3) $e^{3x-1}-8=2,\ e^{3x-1}=10$

$\ln e^{3x-1}=\ln 10$

$(3x-1)\ln e=\ln 10$

$3x-1=\ln 10,\ x=\frac{\ln 10+1}{3}$

(4) $\left(\frac{1}{4}\right)^{1-4x}=4\sqrt[4]{4},\ (2^{-2})^{1-4x}=2^2(2^2)^{\frac{1}{4}}$

$2^{-2+8x}=2^{2+\frac{1}{2}},\ -2+8x=\frac{5}{2},\ x=\frac{9}{16}$

(5) $2^{x^2-4x}=\left(\frac{1}{2}\right)^{x+2},\ 2^{x^2-4x}=(2^{-1})^{x+2}$

$2^{x^2-4x}=2^{-x-2}$, $x^2-4x=-x-2$

$x^2-3x+2=0$, $(x-1)(x-2)=0$

$x=1$ or $x=2$

(6) $\left(\frac{2}{3}\right)^{x^2+3x}=\left(\frac{3}{2}\right)^{2x+6}$, $\left(\frac{2}{3}\right)^{x^2+3x}=\left(\left(\frac{2}{3}\right)^{-1}\right)^{2x+6}$

$\left(\frac{2}{3}\right)^{x^2+3x}=\left(\frac{2}{3}\right)^{-(2x+6)}$, $x^2+3x=-(2x+6)$

$x^2+5x+6=0$, $(x+3)(x+2)=0$

$x=-3$ or $x=-2$

02

(1) $\log_4(4x-2)=\log_4(x+7)$

$4x-2=x+7$

$3x=9$, $x=3$

Check the Solution

$\log_4(4(3)-2)=\log_4(3+7)$

$\log_4 10=\log_4 10$

Solution checks!

(2) $\ln(3x-5)=2$

$3x-5=e^2$

$3x=e^2+5$, $x=\frac{e^2+5}{3}$

Check the Solution

$\ln\left(3\left(\frac{e^2+5}{3}\right)-5\right)$

$=\ln(e^2+5-5)=\ln e^2$

$=2\ln e=2$

Solution checks!

(3) $\log(x^2-3x)=1$

$x^2-3x=10^1$

$x^2-3x-10=0$

$(x-5)(x+2)=0$

$x=5$ or $x=-2$

Check the Solution

$\log(5^2-3(5))=\log(10)=1$

solution checks!

Check the Solution

$\log((-2)^2-3(-2))=\log(10)=1$

Solution checks!

(4) $\log_3(2x-1)+\log_3(x-2)=2$

$\log_3(2x-1)(x-2)=2$

$(2x-1)(x-2)=3^2$

$2x^2-5x+2=9$

$2x^2-5x-7=0$

$(x+1)(2x-7)=0$

$x=-1$ or $x=\frac{7}{2}$

Check the Solution: $x=-1$

$\log_3(2(-1)-1)+\log_3((-1)-2)$

$=\underbrace{\log_3(-3)}_{\text{Undefined}}+\underbrace{\log_3(-3)}_{\text{Undefined}}\neq 2$

$x=-1$ is extraneous solution.

Check the Solution: $x=\frac{7}{2}$

$\log_3\left(2\left(\frac{7}{2}\right)-1\right)+\log_3\left(\left(\frac{7}{2}\right)-2\right)$

$=\log_3(6)+\log_3\left(\frac{3}{2}\right)$

$=\log_3\left(6\cdot\frac{3}{2}\right)=\log_3(9)=2$

Solution checks!

03

Take a natural logarithm on each side and then solve for m.

$\ln 2^{m-1}=\ln n$

$(m-1)\ln 2=\ln n$

$m-1=\frac{\ln n}{\ln 2}$, $m=\frac{\ln n}{\ln 2}+1$

The answer is (C)

04

Take the logarithm with any base on each side of $1.24^a=4.25^b$ and then solve for $\frac{a}{b}$.

$\log 1.24^a=\log 4.25^b$

$a\log 1.24=b\log 4.25$

$\frac{a}{b}=\frac{\log 4.25}{\log 1.24}$

05

$4^{2x+3}-2=4,\ 4^{2x+3}=6$

Take a logarithm with base 4 on each side and then solve for x.

$\log_4 4^{2x+3}=\log_4 6$

$(2x+3)\log_4 4=\log_4 6$

$2x+3=\log_4 6,\ x=\dfrac{\log_4 6-3}{2}$

06

Using the definition of logarithm,

$\log_4(\log_3(\log_2 k))=\dfrac{1}{2}$

$\log_3(\log_2 k)=4^{\frac{1}{2}},\ \log_3(\log_2 k)=2$

$\log_2 k=3^2,\ \log_2 k=9$

$k=2^9=512$

07

Let $a\cdot 3^b=15 \to (1)$ and $a\cdot 27^b=60 \to (2)$.

Dividing (2) by (1) gives

$\dfrac{a\cdot 27^b}{a\cdot 3^b}=\dfrac{60}{15},\ \dfrac{27^b}{3^b}=4,\ \left(\dfrac{27}{3}\right)^b=4$

$9^b=4,\ b=\log_9 4$

08

Let $3^x=A$.

Then $9^x=(3^2)^x=(3^x)^2=A^2$.

$9^x-3^x-6=0$

$A^2-A-6=0$

$(A-3)(A+2)=0,\ A=3$ or $A=-2$

$A=3 \to 3^x=3,\ x=1$

$A=-2 \to 3^x=-2$, No solution

So, the solution is $x=1$.

09

(1) $3^{2x+1}-3^{2x}=18$

$3\cdot 3^{2x}-3^{2x}=18$

$2\cdot 3^{2x}=18$

$3^{2x}=9,\ 3^{2x}=3^2$

$2x=2,\ x=1$

(2) $\log_3 x+\log_3(x-2)-1=0$

$\log_3 x(x-2)=1$

$x(x-2)=3$

$x^2-2x-3=0$

$(x-3)(x+1)=0,\ x=3$ or $x=-1$

Check the solution:

$x=3$: $\log_3 3+\log_3(3-2)-1=0$

$1+0-1=0$

Solution checks.

$x=1$: $\log_3(-1)+\log_3(-1-2)-1\neq 0$

$x=1$ is an extraneous solution.

Therefore, the solution is $x=3$.

10

(1) $4^{x+1}>8^x,\ (2^2)^{x+1}>(2^3)^x$

$2^{2x+2}>2^{3x}$

$2x+2>3x,\ 2>x$

(2) Check the domain of the original logarithmic function:

$x^2-3x>0$

$x(x-3)>0,\ x<0$ or $x>3$

Now solve the inequality:

$\log_2(x^2-3x)<2$

$x^2-3x<2^2$

$x^2-3x-4<0$

$(x-4)(x+1)<0,\ -1<x<4$

Therefore, the solution to the inequality is: $-1<x<0$ or $3<x<4$.

(3)

$5^{2x-1}\leq 125^{x-2},\ 5^{2x-1}\leq (5^3)^{x-2}$

$$5^{2x-1} \le 5^{3x-6}$$
$$2x-1 \le 3x-6,\ 5 \le x$$

11

$y=\log_5(5x+6)$: Domain is $5x+6>0$, $x>-\frac{6}{5}$
$y=2\log_5 x$: Domain is $x>0$
Set the equations equal to each other and then solve:

$$\log_5(5x+6)=2\log_5 x$$
$$\log_5(5x+6)=\log_5 x^2$$
$$5x+6=x^2$$
$$x^2-5x-6=0$$
$$(x-6)(x+1)=0,\ x=6 \text{ or } x=-1$$

Since $x=-1$ is not within the domain of $y=2\log_5 x$, there is only one intersection at $x=6$. The answer is (B).

12

$y=\ln x$: Domain is $x>0$.
$y=\ln(x+2)+\ln(x+6)$: Both $x+2$ and $x+6$ must be greater than 0, so the domain is $x>-2$. Set the equations equal to each other and then solve:

$$\ln x=\ln(x+2)+\ln(x+6)$$
$$\ln x=\ln(x+2)(x+6)$$
$$x=x^2+8x+12$$
$$x^2+7x+12=0$$
$$(x+4)(x+3)=0,\ x=-4 \text{ or } x=-3$$

Since neither $x=-4$ nor $x=-3$ fall within the domain of $y=\ln x$, there are no points of intersection. Therefore, the correct answer is (D).

13

$f(x)=\log(x-3)+\log(x+2)$: Both $x-3$ and $x+2$ must be greater than 0, so the domain is $x>3$.
Now solve the inequality:

$$f(x)=\log(x-3)+\log(x+2)<\log 14$$
$$\log(x-3)(x+2)<\log 14$$
$$(x-3)(x+2)<14$$
$$x^2-x-20<0$$
$$(x-5)(x+4)<0,\ -4<x<5$$

Therefore, the solution to the inequality is $3<x<5$. The correct answer is (C).

14

$f(x)=\ln(3x+14)-\ln(x^2+5x-10)$
Both $3x+14$ and $x^2+5x-10$ must be greater than 0, so the domain of f, using the calculator, is $x>1.531$. Now solve the inequality:

$$f(x)=\ln(3x+14)-\ln(x^2+5x-10)<0$$
$$\ln\frac{3x+14}{x^2+5x-10}<0,\ \frac{3x+14}{x^2+5x-10}<1$$
$$3x+14<x^2+5x-10$$
$$0<x^2+2x-24$$
$$0<(x+6)(x-4),\ x<-6 \text{ or } x>4$$

Therefore, the solution to the inequality is $x>4$. The correct answer is (B).

7. Application of Exponentials and Logarithms

For convenience, all answers in this section were solved with ln.

Check Point 1

① $A=P(1+r)^t$

$A=10,000(1+0.06)^{20}$

$=\$32,071.36$

② $A=P\left(1+\frac{r}{n}\right)^{nt}$

$A=10,000\left(1+\frac{0.06}{4}\right)^{(4)(20)}$

$=\$32,906.63$

③ $A=P\left(1+\frac{r}{n}\right)^{nt}$

$A=10,000\left(1+\frac{0.06}{12}\right)^{(12)(20)}$

$=\$33,102.05$

④ $A=Pe^{rt}$

$A=10,000e^{(0.06)(20)}=\$33,201.17$

Check Point 2

① $A=Pe^{rt}$

$2\times1,000=1,000e^{(0.05)t}$

$2=e^{(0.05)t}$, $\ln2=\ln e^{(0.05)t}$

$\ln 2=0.05t$, $t=\frac{\ln 2}{0.05}\approx13.86$

It takes about 13.86 years

② $A=P\left(1+\frac{r}{n}\right)^{nt}$

$10,000=7,500\left(1+\frac{0.06}{2}\right)^{(2)t}$

$\frac{4}{3}=\left(1+\frac{0.06}{2}\right)^{2t}$, $\frac{4}{3}=1.03^{2t}$

$\ln\left(\frac{4}{3}\right)=\ln 1.03^{2t}$, $\ln\left(\frac{4}{3}\right)=2t\cdot\ln 1.03$

$t=\frac{1}{2\ln 1.03}\cdot\ln\left(\frac{4}{3}\right)=4.87$

It takes about 4.87 years

Check Point 3

Since the number of bacteria increases 9% per hour, we need to determine the number of bacteria after 24 hours(1 day).

$P=250$, $r=0.09$, and $t=24$.

$A=Pe^{rt}=250e^{(0.09)(24)}\approx 2167.78$

Approximately 2168 bacteria

Check Point 4

$P=5$ and $A=\frac{5}{2}$ when $t=1600$.

$A=Pe^{rt}$

$\frac{5}{2}=5e^{r(1600)}$, $\frac{1}{2}=e^{r(1600)}$

$\ln\left(\frac{1}{2}\right)=\ln e^{r(1600)}$, $\ln\left(\frac{1}{2}\right)=1600r\ln e$

$r=\frac{1}{1600}\ln\left(\frac{1}{2}\right)$

So the equation is $A=5e^{\frac{1}{1600}\ln\left(\frac{1}{2}\right)\cdot t}$.

Now, substitute 1 for A.

$1=5e^{\frac{1}{1600}\ln\left(\frac{1}{2}\right)\cdot t}$, $\frac{1}{5}=e^{\frac{1}{1600}\ln\left(\frac{1}{2}\right)\cdot t}$

$\ln\left(\frac{1}{5}\right)=\ln e^{\frac{1}{1600}\ln\left(\frac{1}{2}\right)\cdot t}$, $\frac{1}{1600}\ln\left(\frac{1}{2}\right)\cdot t=\ln\left(\frac{1}{5}\right)$

$t=\frac{1600\ln\left(\frac{1}{5}\right)}{\ln\left(\frac{1}{2}\right)}\approx 3715.08$

Approximately 3715 years

Review Exercises

01

$A=P\left(1+\frac{r}{n}\right)^{nt}$

$3,000=2,000\left(1+\frac{0.055}{2}\right)^{2t}$

$\frac{3}{2}=1.0275^{2t},\ \ln\left(\frac{3}{2}\right)=\ln 1.0275^{2t}$

$\ln\left(\frac{3}{2}\right)=2t\cdot\ln 1.0275,\ t=\frac{\ln\left(\frac{3}{2}\right)}{2\ln 1.0275}\approx 7.473$

Approximately 7.473 years

02

$A=Pe^{rt}$

$3\times 8,000=8,000e^{r(20)},\ 3=e^{20r}$

$\ln 3=\ln e^{20r},\ \ln 3=20r\cdot\ln e$

$r=\frac{\ln 3}{20}\approx 0.0549\rightarrow 5.49\%$

Approximately 5.49%

03

25% increase in P: $P+\frac{25}{10}P=1.25P$

$A=P\left(1+\frac{r}{n}\right)^{nt}$

$1.25P=P\left(1+\frac{0.035}{4}\right)^{4t}$

$1.25=1.00875^{4t},\ \ln 1.25=\ln 1.00875^{4t}$

$\ln 1.25=4t\ln 1.00875,\ \frac{\ln 1.25}{\ln 1.00875}=4t$

$t=\frac{\ln 1.25}{4\ln 1.00875}\approx 6.403$

Approximately 6.403 years

04

$A=Pe^{rt}$

$600=500e^{(0.04)t},\ \frac{6}{5}=e^{0.04t}$

$\ln\left(\frac{6}{5}\right)=\ln e^{0.04t},\ \ln\left(\frac{6}{5}\right)=0.04t\ln e$

$t=\frac{\ln\left(\frac{6}{5}\right)}{0.04}\approx 4.558$

Approximately 4.558 years

05

$A=P(1+r)^t$

$A=20(1+0.4)^8=295.158\approx 295$

Approximately 295 bacteria

06

$A=P(1+r)^t$

$\frac{1}{2}\cdot 28,000=28,000(1+r)^5$

$\frac{1}{2}=(1+r)^5,\ \left(\frac{1}{2}\right)^{\frac{1}{5}}=((1+r)^5)^{\frac{1}{5}}$

$\left(\frac{1}{2}\right)^{\frac{1}{5}}=1+r,\ r=\left(\frac{1}{2}\right)^{\frac{1}{5}}-1=-0.12945$

$\rightarrow r=-12.945\%$

Annual percent decrease is about 12.945%

07

20% increase in P: $P+\frac{20}{100}P=1.20P$

$A=Pe^{rt}$

$1.2P=Pe^{r(5)},\ 1.2=e^{5r}$

$\ln 1.2=\ln e^{5r},\ \ln 1.2=5r\ln e$

$r=\frac{\ln 1.2}{5}\approx 0.036$

(A) $A=5,000e^{(0.036)(10)}=7166.65$

Approximately, 7167 people

(B) $2\times 5,000=5,000e^{(0.036)t}$

$2=e^{(0.036)t},\ \ln 2=\ln e^{(0.036)t}$

$\ln 2=0.036t \ln e,\ t=\dfrac{\ln 2}{0.036}\approx 19.25$

Approximately 19.25 years

08

$A=Pe^{rt}$

At 10 A.M., $P=125{,}000$ and $t=0$.

At 2 P.M., $A=850{,}000$ and $t=4$.

$850{,}000=125{,}000e^{r(4)},\ \dfrac{34}{5}=e^{4r}$

$\ln\left(\dfrac{34}{5}\right)=\ln e^{4r},\ \ln\left(\dfrac{34}{5}\right)=4r\ln e$

$r=\dfrac{1}{4}\ln\left(\dfrac{34}{5}\right)\approx 0.479$

So the equation is $A=125{,}000e^{0.479t}$.

At 8 P.M., $A=125{,}000e^{0.479(10)}\approx 1.504\times 10^7$.

Approximately 1.504×10^7 bacteria

09

$A=Pe^{rt}$

$2=10e^{r(1200)},\ \dfrac{1}{5}=e^{1200r}$

$\ln\left(\dfrac{1}{5}\right)=\ln e^{1200r},\ \ln\left(\dfrac{1}{5}\right)=1200r\ln e$

$r=\dfrac{1}{1200}\ln\left(\dfrac{1}{5}\right)$

So the equation is $A=10e^{\frac{1}{1200}\ln\left(\frac{1}{5}\right)t}$.

$5=10e^{\frac{1}{1200}\ln\left(\frac{1}{5}\right)t},\ \dfrac{1}{2}=e^{\frac{1}{1200}\ln\left(\frac{1}{5}\right)t}$

$\ln\left(\dfrac{1}{2}\right)=\ln e^{\frac{1}{1200}\ln\left(\frac{1}{5}\right)t},$

$\ln\left(\dfrac{1}{2}\right)=\dfrac{1}{1200}\ln\left(\dfrac{1}{5}\right)t\ln e$

$t=\dfrac{1200\ln\left(\frac{1}{2}\right)}{\ln\left(\frac{1}{5}\right)}\approx 516.812$

Half-Life is approximately 517 years

10

$A=Pe^{rt}$

$\dfrac{P}{2}=Pe^{r(5730)},\ \dfrac{1}{2}=e^{5730r}$

$\ln\left(\dfrac{1}{2}\right)=\ln e^{5730r},\ \ln\left(\dfrac{1}{2}\right)=5730r\ln e$

$r=\dfrac{1}{5730}\ln\left(\dfrac{1}{2}\right)$

So the equation is $A=Pe^{\frac{1}{5730}\ln\left(\frac{1}{2}\right)\cdot t}$.

$0.4P=Pe^{\frac{1}{5730}\ln\left(\frac{1}{2}\right)\cdot t},\ 0.4=e^{\frac{1}{5730}\ln\left(\frac{1}{2}\right)\cdot t}$

$\ln 0.4=\ln e^{\frac{1}{5730}\ln\left(\frac{1}{2}\right)\cdot t}$

$\ln 0.4=\dfrac{1}{5730}\ln\left(\dfrac{1}{2}\right)\cdot t\ln e$

$t=\dfrac{5730\ln 0.4}{\ln\left(\frac{1}{2}\right)}\approx 7574.65$

The bone is approximately 7575 years old

11

$A=P(1+r)^t$

$1000<10(1+0.6)^t$

$100<1.6^t\ \ \ln 100<\ln 1.6^t$

$\ln 100<t\ln 1.6,\ \dfrac{\ln 100}{\ln 1.6}<t$

$\dfrac{\ln 100}{\ln 1.6}<t,\ 9.79<t$

The number of bacteria increases by 60% per hour, So after about 10 hours, the number of bacteria first exceeds 1000.

After 10 hours

8. Competing Function Model Validation

Check Point 1

Using the calculator, the equation of the best−fit using quadratic regression is $y=-1.661x^2+9.189x+3.75$. Now predict the height of the projectile at 5.5 seconds:

$$y=-1.661(5.5)^2+9.189(5.5)+3.75=4.044$$

So, the predicted height is 4.044 meters.

Review Exercises

01

(1) Using the calculator, the equation of the best−fit using exponential regression is

$$y=100.014(1.800)^x.$$

(2) The population of the bacteria culture at 5 hours is

$$y(5)=100.014(1.800)^5=1889.83\fallingdotseq 1890$$

02

(1) Using the calculator, the equation of the best−fit line using linear regression is

$$y=-0.005x+40.6$$

(2) The mileage of a car that weighs 3200 pounds is

$$y=-0.005(3200)+40.6=24.6 \text{ mpg}.$$

03

Since the residual is positive(1500), it means that the observed salary is higher than the predicted salary by \$1,500 for someone with 9 years of experience. Thus, the point A indicates that the observed salary for 9 years of experience is \$1,500 higher than the predicted salary. Therefore, the correct answer is (A).

04

For a linear regression model to be appropriate, the residuals should be randomly scattered without any pattern. Since the given residual plot shows a curved pattern, the linear regression model is not appropriate for the data. Therefore, the correct answer is (B).

05

For a linear regression model to be appropriate, the residuals should be randomly scattered without any pattern. Since the given residual plot shows no pattern, the linear regression model is appropriate, and the exponential model is NOT suitable for the data. Therefore, the correct answer is (D).

9. Semi-log Plots

Check Point 1

x	y	$\log y$
0	3300	3.519
1	550	2.740
2	91.67	1.962
3	15.28	1.184
4	2.55	0.407

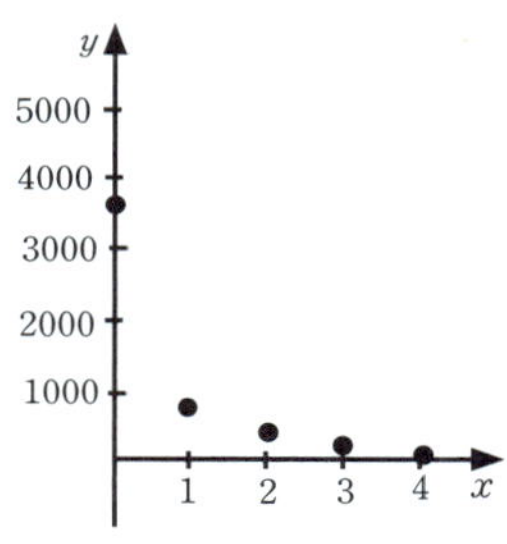

$x-y$ plane

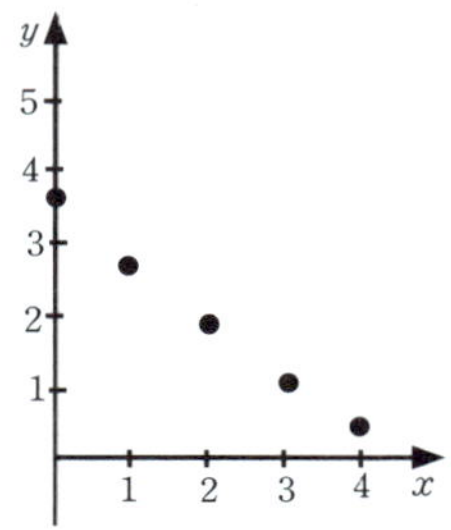

$x-\log y$ plane

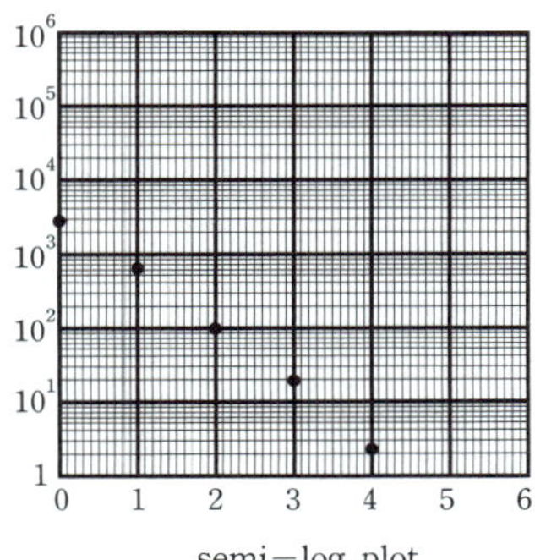

semi−log plot

Review Exercises

01

(A) $f(x)=2x$

$\log(f(x))=\log(2x)=\log 2+\log x$

This is not linear in x.

(B) $f(x)=x^2$

$\log(f(x))=\log(x^2)=2\log x$

This is not linear in x.

(C) $f(x)=2^x$

$\log(f(x))=\log(2^x)=x\log 2=\log 2\cdot x$

This is a linear function of x with slope $\log 2$.

(D) $f(x)=\log_2 x$

$\log(f(x))=\log(\log_2 x)$

This is not linear in x.

Therefore, the correct answer is (C).

02

The table that best matches the points shown in the semi−log plot above is (C).

03

The equation of the line that passes through the points (1, 6) and (16, 51) is $y=3x+3$. Since the the y−axis is $\log_2 y$, we have

$$\log_2 y=3x+3$$

$$y=2^{3x+3}=2^{3x}\cdot 2^3=8\cdot 2^{3x}$$

Therefore, the correct answer is (C).

04

I. $x-\log y$ plane: Represents a straight line for an exponential function.

II. Semi−log plot: Also represents a straight line for an exponential function.

Therefore, both I and II correctly represent

the graph of an exponential function. The correct answer is (C).

05

$$g(x)=5\cdot 4^x$$
$$\ln(g(x))=\ln(5\cdot 4^x)=\ln 5+\ln 4^x$$
$$=\ln 5+x\cdot\ln 4=\ln 4\cdot x+\ln 5$$
$$\Rightarrow a=\ln 4,\ b=\ln 5$$

Therefore, the value of $a+b$ is

$$a+b=\ln 4+\ln 5=\ln 20$$

The correct answer is (B).

06

The values $\log y$ suggests a linear increase by 4 units for every 2 units increase in x. This confirms a linear relationship:

$$\log y=2x+2$$
$$y=10^{2x+2}$$

Therefore, the function h is exponential when both the values of x and $\log y$ are linear. The answer is (A).

07

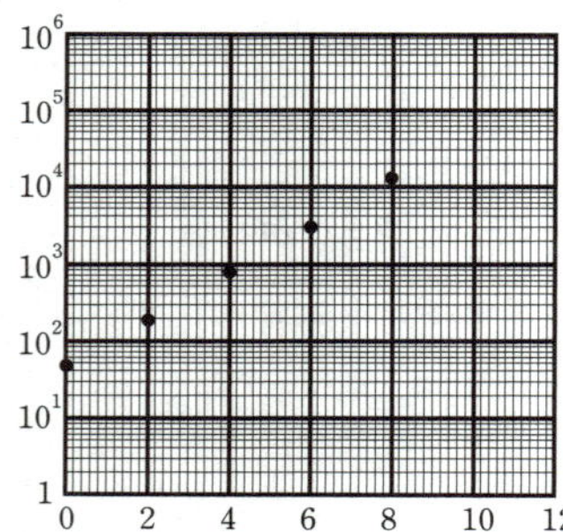

The exponential model for the population growth can be written as $y=a\cdot b^x$. The initial population is $50(a=50)$, and it increases four times every two years. Therefore, we have $y=50\cdot 4^{\frac{x}{2}}$.

Unit II Test

01

$$f(x)=\left(\frac{1}{3}\right)^x-2=(3^{-1})^x-2=3^{-x}-2$$

To graph $f(x)=3^{-x}-2$, reflect the graph of $y=3^x$ about the $y-$axis, and then shift 2 units down.

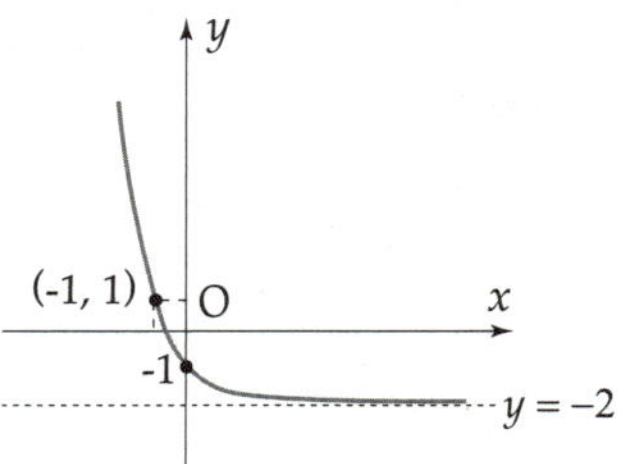

Domain: $(-\infty, \infty)$
Range: $(-2, \infty)$
Horizontal Asymptote: $y=-2$

02

If the graph of $y=4^x$ is reflected about the $x-$axis, we have $y=-4^x$ and then if we shift this graph 2 units to the right, we have $y=-4^{x-2}$.

03

(1) $\log_5 25=2$

The base is 5 and the exponent is 2. So $5^2=25$.

(2) $\log_{\frac{1}{3}} 27=-3$

The base is $\frac{1}{3}$ and the exponent is -3. So $\left(\frac{1}{3}\right)^{-3}=27$.

04

(1) $4^{-3}=\frac{1}{64}$

The base is 4 and the exponent is -3.

So $\log_4\frac{1}{64}=-3$.

(2) $\left(\frac{1}{25}\right)^{\frac{1}{2}}=\frac{1}{5}$

The base is $\frac{1}{25}$ and the exponent is $\frac{1}{2}$.

So $\log_{\frac{1}{25}}\frac{1}{5}=\frac{1}{2}$.

05

(1) $\frac{1}{2}\log_3 x=-1,\ \log_3 x=-2$

$3^{-2}=x,\ x=\frac{1}{9}$

(2) $\log_x 27=\frac{3}{2},\ x^{\frac{3}{2}}=27$

$x^{\frac{3}{2}}=3^3,\ x^{\frac{3}{2}}=9^{\frac{3}{2}},\ x=9$

06

To graph $g(x)=-\log_2(x)-4$, reflect the graph of $y=\log_2 x$ about the x−axis, and then shift it 4 units down.

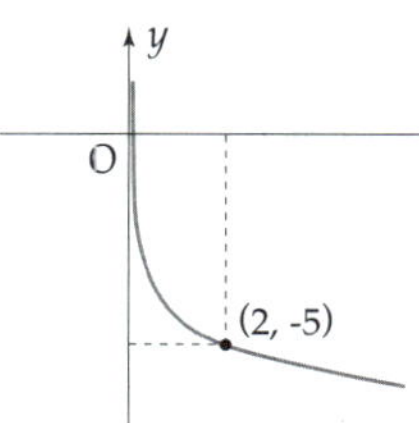

Domain: $(0,\ \infty)$

Range: $(-\infty,\ \infty)$

Vertical Asymptote: $x=0$

07

If the graph of $y=\ln x$ is reflected in the y−axis, we have $y=\ln(-x)$ and then if we shift this graph 1 unit to the left and 2 units up, we have

$y=\ln(-(x+1))+2,\ y=\ln(-x-1)+2.$

08

(1) $y=\frac{1}{2}\log_2(x+4),\ 2y=\log_2(x+4)$

$2^{2y}=x+4,\ x=2^{2y}-4$

(2) $y=2+\frac{3}{2}\log_{\frac{1}{2}}(2-x),\ y-2=\frac{3}{2}\log_{\frac{1}{2}}(2-x)$

$\frac{2}{3}(y-2)=\log_{\frac{1}{2}}(2-x),\ \left(\frac{1}{2}\right)^{\frac{2}{3}(y-2)}=2-x$

$x=2-\left(\frac{1}{2}\right)^{\frac{2}{3}(y-2)}$

09

(1) $\frac{1}{2}\log_6 9-2\log_6 6+\log_6 2$

$=\log_6 9^{\frac{1}{2}}-2\cdot 1+\log_6 2$

$=\log_6 3-2+\log_6 2$

$=\log_6(3\cdot 2)-2=\log_6 6-2=1-2=-1$

(2) $\ln e^{-2}+\ln\left(\frac{1}{e^4}\right)+4\ln 1$

$=-2\ln e+(\ln 1-\ln e^4)+4\cdot 0$

$=-2\cdot 1+(0-4\ln e)+0$

$=-2-4\cdot 1=-6$

(3) $2^{\log_2 6+2\log_2 4-\log_2 5}=2^{\log_2 6+\log_2 4^2-\log_2 5}$

$=2^{\log_2\left(\frac{6.16}{5}\right)}=2^{\log_2\left(\frac{96}{5}\right)}=\frac{96}{5}$

(4) $e^{-\frac{1}{2}\ln 3+\ln 12}=e^{\ln 3^{-\frac{1}{2}}+\ln 12}=e^{\ln\left(\frac{1}{\sqrt{3}}\right)+\ln 12}$

$=e^{\ln\frac{1}{\sqrt{3}}\cdot 12}=e^{\ln\frac{12}{\sqrt{3}}}=4\sqrt{3}$

10

(A) $\log 1000=\log 10^3=3\log 10=3\cdot 1=3$

(B) $-\log_2\left(\frac{1}{8}\right)=-(\log_2 1-\log_2 8)$

$=-(0-\log_2 2^3)=3\log_2 2=3$

(C) $\log_5 15\neq 3$

(D) $-\log_4\left(\frac{1}{64}\right)=-(\log_4 1-\log_4 64)$

$=-(0-\log_4 4^3)=3\log_4 4=3$

So the answer is (C).

11

(1) $\log(2\sqrt{x}y^5)=\log 2+\log\sqrt{x}+\log y^5$

$=\log 2+\log x^{\frac{1}{2}}+\log y^5$

$=\log 2+\frac{1}{2}\log x+5\log y$

(2) $\ln\left(\frac{ab^3}{\sqrt{c}}\right)^3=3\ln\left(\frac{ab^3}{\sqrt{c}}\right)$

$=3(\ln a+\ln b^3-\ln\sqrt{c})$

$=3\left(\ln a+\ln b^3-\ln c^{\frac{1}{2}}\right)$

$=3\left(\ln a+3\ln b-\frac{1}{2}\ln c\right)$

$=3\ln a+9\ln b-\frac{3}{2}\ln c$

12

(1) $\log_3 5+2\log_3 x-\frac{1}{3}\log_3 y$

$=\log_3 5+\log_3 x^2-\log_3 y^{\frac{1}{3}}$

$=\log_3 5+\log_3 x^2-\log_3 \sqrt[3]{y}=\log_3\left(\frac{5x^2}{\sqrt[3]{y}}\right)$

(2) $\frac{2}{3}(\ln(4a^2-1)-\ln(2a+1)+2\ln a)$

$=\frac{2}{3}(\ln(2a-1)(2a+1)-\ln(2a+1)+\ln a^2\ )$

$=\frac{2}{3}\ln\left(\frac{(2a-1)(2a+1)\cdot a^2}{(2a+1)}\right)$

$=\frac{2}{3}\ln(a^2(2a-1))$

$=\ln(a^2(2a-1))^{\frac{2}{3}}=\ln\sqrt[3]{a^4(2a-1)^2}$

13

(1) $\log_a\left(\frac{1}{75}\right)^2=\log_a 75^{-2}=-2\log_a 75$

$=-2\log_a(3\cdot 5^2)=-2(\log_a 3+\log_a 5^2)$

$=-2(\log_a 3+2\log_a 5)=-2(y+2z)$

$=-2y-4z$

(2) $\log_a \sqrt[3]{180}=\log_a(180)^{\frac{1}{3}}=\frac{1}{3}\log_a(2^2\cdot 3^2\cdot 5)$

$=\frac{1}{3}(\log_a 2^2+\log_a 3^2+\log_a 5)$

$=\frac{1}{3}(2\log_a 2+2\log_a 3+\log_a 5)$

$=\frac{1}{3}(2x+2y+z)=\frac{2}{3}x+\frac{2}{3}y+\frac{1}{3}z$

14

(1) $-5^{5x-4}+10=4$, $5^{5x-4}=6$,

$\log_5 5^{5x-4}=\log_5 6$, $(5x-4)\log_5 5=\log_5 6$,

$5x-4=\log_5 6$, $x=\frac{\log_5 6+4}{5}$

(2) $e^{10-4x}-9=15$, $e^{10-4x}=24$

$\ln e^{10-4x}=\ln 24$, $(10-4x)\ln e=\ln 24$

$10-4x=\ln 24$, $x=\frac{10-\ln 24}{4}$

(3) $\log_3(4x-1)=\log_3(2x+1)-\frac{1}{2}\log_3 9$

$\log_3(4x-1)=\log_3(2x+1)-\log_3 3$

$\log_3(4x-1)=\log_3\left(\frac{2x+1}{3}\right)$

$4x-1=\frac{2x+1}{3}$, $12x-3=2x+1$

$10x=4$, $x=\frac{2}{5}$

(4) $-\log_4(x-1)+\log_4 x=\frac{1}{2}$

$\log_4\left(\frac{x}{x-1}\right)=\frac{1}{2}$

$\frac{x}{x-1}=4^{\frac{1}{2}}$, $\frac{x}{x-1}=2$

$x=2x-2$, $x=2$

15

Take a natural logarithm on each side.

$4^a=6^b$, $\ln 4^a=\ln 6^b$

$a\ln 4=b\ln 6$, $\frac{a}{b}=\frac{\ln 6}{\ln 4}$

We can also use a log with base 4 or 6.

$4^a=6^b$, $\log_4 4^a=\log_4 6^b$

$a\log_4 4=b\log_4 6$, $\frac{a}{b}=\log_4 6$

or

$4^a=6^b$, $\log_6 4^a=\log_6 6^b$

$a\log_6 4=b\log_6 6$, $\frac{a}{b}=\frac{1}{\log_6 4}$

16

Let $2^x=A$. Then $4^x=(2^2)^x=(2^x)^2=A^2$.

$6\cdot 4^x+2^x-15=0$

$6A^2+A-15=0$

$(3A+5)(2A-3)=0$, $A=-\frac{5}{3}$ or $A=\frac{3}{2}$

$A=-\frac{5}{3}\rightarrow 2^x=-\frac{5}{3}$, No solution

$A=\frac{3}{2}\rightarrow 2^x=\frac{3}{2}$, $x=\log_2\left(\frac{3}{2}\right)$

So, the solution is $x=\log_2\left(\frac{3}{2}\right)$

17

$16^{k-1}=5$, $(2^4)^{k-1}=5$, $2^{4k-4}=5$

$\frac{2^{4k}}{2^4}=5$, $2^{4k}=80$

Now, use $2^{4k}=80$ to find the value 4^{2k+1}.

$4^{2k+1}=(2^2)^{2k+1}=2^{4k+2}$

$=2^{4k}\cdot 2^2=80\cdot 4=320$

18

$A=P\left(1+\frac{r}{n}\right)^{nt}$

$1{,}000=500\left(1+\frac{0.12}{12}\right)^{12t}$

$2=1.01^{12t}$, $\ln 2=\ln 1.01^{12t}$

$\ln 2=12t\cdot\ln 1.01$, $t=\frac{\ln 2}{12\ln 1.01}\approx 5.805$

19

$A=P(1+r)^t$

$A=18{,}000(1+(-0.15))^4$

$A=18{,}000(0.85)^4=9{,}396.11$

20

$A=P(1+r)^t$

$2P=P(1+r)^{15}$, $2=(1+r)^{15}$

$2^{\frac{1}{15}}=\left((1+r)^{15}\right)^{\frac{1}{15}}$, $2^{\frac{1}{15}}=1+r$

$r=2^{\frac{1}{15}}-1=0.0473\rightarrow r=4.73\%$

21

$a_3=-2$, $a_{11}=-\frac{1}{6}$

$a_n=a_k+(n-k)d$

$a_{11}=a_3+(11-3)d$, $-\frac{1}{6}=-2+8d$, $d=\frac{11}{48}$

$a_n=a_1+(n-1)d$

$a_3=a_1+(3-1)d$, $-2=a_1+2\cdot\frac{11}{48}$, $a_1=-\frac{59}{24}$

22

$a_3=\frac{1}{32}$, $a_8=-1$

$a_n=a_k r^{n-k}$

$a_8=a_3 r^{8-3}$, $-1=\frac{1}{32}\cdot r^5$, $r=-2$

$a_n=a_1 r^{n-1}$

$a_3=a_1 r^{3-1}$, $\frac{1}{32}=a_1\cdot(-2)^2$, $a_1=\frac{1}{128}$

23

Let the machinery's value be $V(t)$. Since annual depreciation is 12%, we have

$V(t)=50{,}000\cdot(1-0.12)^t$

To determine the time when the machinery's value is $25,000:

$$25{,}000=50{,}000\cdot(1-0.12)^t$$
$$0.5=0.88^t$$
$$\ln 0.5=\ln 0.88^t,\ \ln 0.5=t\cdot\ln 0.88$$
$$t=\frac{\ln 0.5}{\ln 0.88}=5.42$$

The machinery's value will be $25,000 between 5 and 6 years after its initial purchase. Therefore, the answer is (C).

24

The initial population is 200 and the daily growth rate is 7%. So the population $P(t)$ after t days is:

$$P(t)=200\cdot(1+0.07)^t=200(1.07)^t$$

Therefore, the answer is (C).

25

An arithmetic sequence can be seen as a discrete version of a linear function, while a geometric sequence can be viewed as a discrete version of an exponential function. Therefore, the graph of P and Q that satisfies the given conditions is as follows(a_0 is the first term):

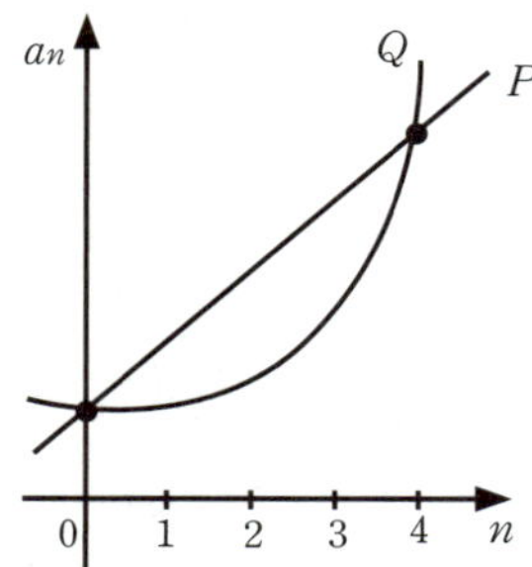

The third term(a_2) of the arithmetic sequence is greater than the third term of the geometric sequence. The answer is (B).

26

$$2^n+2^{n+1}=k$$
$$2^n+2^n\cdot 2=k$$
$$3\cdot 2^n=k,\ 2^n=\frac{k}{3}$$

The expression for $2^{n-1}+2^{n+2}$ in terms of k is

$$2^{n-1}+2^{n+2}=\frac{2^n}{2}+2^n\cdot 2^2$$
$$=\left(\frac{1}{2}+2^2\right)2^n$$
$$=\frac{9}{2}\cdot 2^n=\frac{9}{2}\cdot\frac{k}{3}=\frac{3k}{2}$$

The correct answer is (B)

27

Exponential functions $a\cdot b^x$ where $a=12$ and $b=\frac{1}{3}$ decreases as x increases.

As x approaches infinity, $\left(\frac{1}{3}\right)^x$ approaches 0:

$$\lim_{x\to\infty} g(x)=\lim_{x\to\infty} 12\cdot\left(\frac{1}{3}\right)^t=12\cdot 0=0$$

Therefore, the correct is (B).

28

(1) $(f\circ g)(2)=f(g(2))=f(4(2)-1)$

$$=f(7)=\frac{2}{7-2}=\frac{2}{5}$$

(2) $(g\circ h)(0)=g(h(0))=g(\sqrt{2(0)+1}+3)$

$$=g(4)=4(4)-1=15$$

29

$$f(x)=g(h(x)),\ 3x+1=\frac{h(x)-3}{2}$$
$$6x+2=h(x)-3,\ h(x)=6x+5$$

The correct answer is (B).

30

$g(x)=2x^2+1,\ g(a)=2a^2+1$

$f(g(a))=f(2a^2+1)$

$=\log_2(2a^2+1-2)=\log_2(2a^2-1)=0$

$2a^2-1=2^0$

$2a^2=2,\ a^2=1,\ a=\pm1$

The correct answer is (B).

31

(1) $(f\circ g)(0)=f(g(0))=f(-1)=2$

(2) $(g\circ f)(-1)=g(f(-1))=g(2)=2$

32

Find the inverse of g.

$g(x)=x+3k-1,\ y=x+3k-1$

$x=y+3k-1,\ y=x-3k+1$

$g^{-1}(x)=x-3k+1$

Since $g=g^{-1}$, we have

$x+3k-1=x-3k+1$

$6k=2,\ k=\frac{1}{3}$

33

Find the inverse of f.

$f(x)=\frac{ax+b}{x-c},\ y=\frac{ax+b}{x-c}$

$x=\frac{ay+b}{y-c},\ x(y-c)=ay+b$

$xy-cx=ay+b,\ xy-ay=cx+b$

$y(x-a)=cx+b,\ y=\frac{cx+b}{x-a}$

$f^{-1}(x)=\frac{cx+b}{x-a}$

$\Rightarrow a=3,\ b=1,\ c=5$

Therefore, $a+b+c=3+1+5=9$

34

Since the graph of h^{-1} passes through two points $(-4, 6)$ and $(8, 3)$,

$f^{-1}(-4)=6,\qquad f^{-1}(8)=3$

$-4=f(6),\qquad 8=f(3)$

$-4=6a+b,\qquad 8=3a+b$

Solving the system, we have

$a=-4$ and $b=20$.

Therefore, $a+b=-4+20=16$.

35

$1-4^{2y}=x,\ 4^{2y}=1-x$

$\log_4 4^{2y}=\log_4(1-x)$

$2y=\log_4(1-x)$

$y=\frac{1}{2}\log_4(1-x),\ y=\log_4\sqrt{1-x}$

The correct answer is (C).

36

(A) $\ln e^2=2\ln e=2$

(B) $\log_3 9=\log_3 3^2=2\log_3 3=2$

(C) $-\log_{0.5} 4=-\log_{0.5} 2^2$

$=-\log_{0.5}\left(\frac{1}{2}\right)^{-2}$

$=2\log_{0.5}\left(\frac{1}{2}\right)=2$

(D) $\log_4 8\neq2$

The correct answer is (D).

37

The range of the inverse function of f is equal to the domain of f. The domain of f is

$x-4>0,\ x>4$

Therefore, the domain of f is $x>4$.

In interval notation, this is $(4, \infty)$.

38

For $f(x)=\log_2 x$, output $f(x)$ increases by 1 whenever the input x doubles. Therefore, the correct answer is (D).

39

The function $f(x)=2\cdot 3^{x-1}$ is an exponential function with a base $b=3$ (where $3>1$), and it increases at an increasing rate over the given domain, as shown below.

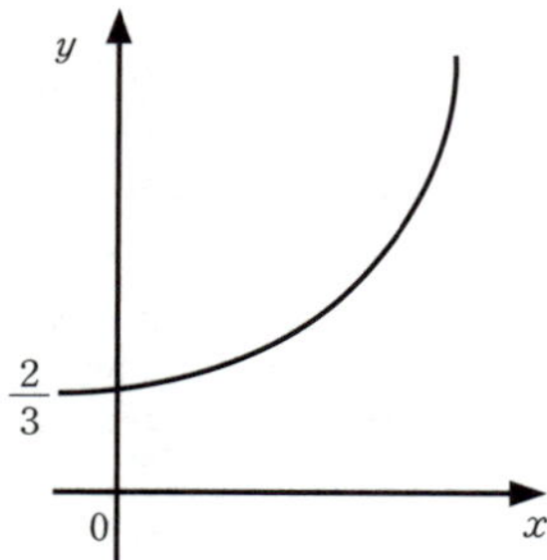

Therefore, the correct answer is (A).

40

(1) Behavior as $x\to 0^+$: $2^x \to 1$
and $\log_2 x \to -\infty$

(2) Behavior as $x\to\infty$: $2^x \to \infty$
and $\log_2 x\to\infty$

Therefore,

$\lim_{x\to 0^+} f(x)=\lim_{x\to 0^+}(2^x+\log_2 x)=1+(-\infty)=-\infty$

and

$\lim_{x\to\infty} f(x)=\lim_{x\to\infty}(2^x+\log_2 x)=\infty+\infty=\infty$

The correct answer is (D).

41

$$f(x)=1-\log_4(4x-8)$$
$$x=1-\log_4(4y-8)$$
$$\log_4(4y-8)=1-x$$
$$4y-8=4^{1-x}$$
$$4y=4^{1-x}+8,\ y=\frac{4^{1-x}}{4}+2=4^{-x}+2$$

The correct answer is (D).

42

$$f(x)=\log_2 x$$
$$\begin{aligned} f(4x)+f\left(\frac{x^2}{8}\right)&=\log_2(4x)+\log_2\left(\frac{x^2}{8}\right)\\ &=\log_2 4+\log_2 x+\log_2 x^2-\log_2 8\\ &=2+\log_2 x+2\log_2 x-3\\ &=3\log_2 x-1\end{aligned}$$

The correct answer is (A).

43

Using a graphing calculator, we obtained the equation of the line of best fit:

$$y=-11.714x+1661.429$$

The predicted electricity consumption for a month with an average temperature of 75°F is:

$$y=-11.714(75)+1661.429=782.879$$

Approximately 783 kWh.

44

A residual plot with no pattern indicates that a linear model is appropriate, whereas a residual plot with a pattern suggests that a linear model is not appropriate.

Therefore, the correct answer is (C).

45

An exponential function will appear linear in a semi−log plot. For (A),

$$\log f(x)=\log 2^{x+3}$$
$$=(x+3)\log 2=\log 2\cdot x+3\log 2$$

The y−intercept is $3\log 2=\log 2^3=\log 8$.
Therefore, the correct answer is (A).

46

$$A(t)=24-15\cdot 2^{-\frac{1}{15}t}$$

(A) $A(15)=24-15\cdot 2^{-\frac{1}{15}\cdot 15}$
$=24-15\cdot 2^{-1}=16.5$

(B) $A(0)=24-15\cdot 2^{-\frac{1}{15}\cdot 0}=24-15\cdot 1=9$

(C) As t increases without bound, $2^{-\frac{1}{15}t}$ approaches 0. So, over a long period, the thermometer's reading will approach 24°C.

(D) The thermometer's reading increases as t increases.

Therefore, the correct answer is (C).

memo

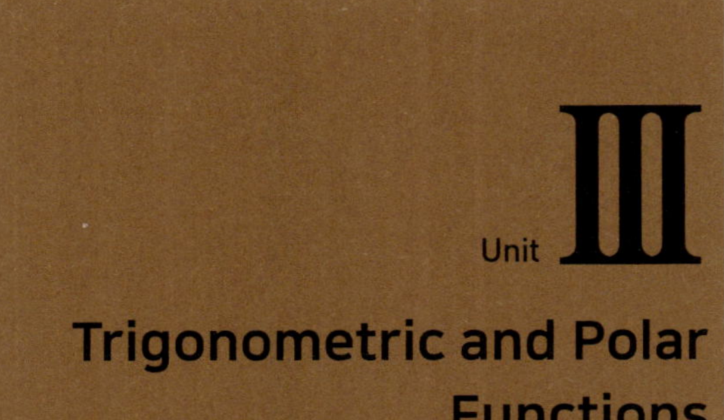

1. Angles and Their Measures

Check Point 1-1

① $38.755° = 38° + (0.755 \times 60)'$
$= 38° + 45.3'$
$= 38° + 45' + (0.3 \times 60)''$
$= 38°45'18''$

② $-58.12° = -58° - (0.12 \times 60)'$
$= -58° - 7.2'$
$= -58° - 7' - (0.2 \times 60)''$
$= -58°7'12''$

Check Point 1-2

① $27°35'42'' = \left(27 + \frac{35}{60} + \frac{42}{3600}\right)°$
$= 27.595°$

② $-34'26'' = -\left(\frac{34}{60} + \frac{26}{3600}\right)°$
$= 0.574°$

Check Point 2-1

① $150° \times \frac{\pi}{180°} = \frac{5\pi}{6}$

② $315° \times \frac{\pi}{180°} = \frac{7\pi}{4}$

Check Point 2-2

① $\frac{13\pi}{6} \times \frac{180°}{\pi} = 390°$

② $\frac{7\pi}{11} \times \frac{180°}{\pi} = \left(\frac{1260}{11}\right)°$

Check Point 3

① Positive : $270° + 360° = 630°$
Negative : $270° - 360° = -90°$

② Positive : $-47° + 360° = 313°$
Negative : $-47° - 360° = -407°$

③ Positive : $\frac{5\pi}{7} + 2\pi = \frac{19\pi}{7}$
Negative : $\frac{5\pi}{7} - 2\pi = -\frac{9\pi}{7}$

④ Positive : $-5 + 2\pi$
Negative : $-5 - 2\pi$

Check Point 4

① Arc Length : $l = r\theta = (6)\left(\frac{3\pi}{5}\right) = \frac{18\pi}{5}$

Area : $A = \frac{1}{2}r^2\theta = \frac{1}{2}(6)^2\left(\frac{3\pi}{5}\right) = \frac{54\pi}{5}$

② $80° \times \frac{\pi}{180°} = \frac{4\pi}{9}$

Arc Length : $l = r\theta = \left(\frac{9}{2}\right)\left(\frac{4\pi}{9}\right) = 2\pi$

Area : $A = \frac{1}{2}r^2\theta = \frac{1}{2}\left(\frac{9}{2}\right)^2\left(\frac{4\pi}{9}\right) = \frac{9\pi}{2}$

Check Point 5

① Since the angle rotated in 1 revolution is 2π radians, the angular speed in radians per second is

$$w = \frac{20\ \cancel{\text{rev}}}{1\ \cancel{\text{min}}} \times \frac{2\pi\ \text{rad}}{1\ \cancel{\text{rev}}} \times \frac{1\ \cancel{\text{min}}}{60\ \text{sec}} = \frac{2\pi}{3}\ \text{rad/sec.}$$

② Since the circumference of the wheel is $2\pi(5) = 10\pi$ cm, the linear speed in cm per second is

$$v=\frac{20\ \text{rev}}{1\ \text{min}}\times\frac{10\pi\ \text{cm}}{1\ \text{rev}}\times\frac{1\ \text{min}}{60\ \text{sec}}=\frac{10\pi}{3}\ \text{cm/sec}.$$

Review Exercises

01

(1) $21.26°=21°+(0.26\times60)'$
$=21°+15.6'$
$=21°+15'+(0.6\times60)''$
$=21°+15'+36''$

(2) $135.465°=135°+(0.465\times60)'$
$=135°+27.9'$
$=135°+27'+(0.9\times60)''$
$=135°+27'+54''$

02

(1) $37°51'16''=37°+\left(51'\times\frac{1°}{60'}\right)+\left(16''\times\frac{1°}{3600''}\right)$
$=37.854°$

(2) $265°25'45''=265°+\left(25'\times\frac{1°}{60'}\right)+\left(45''\times\frac{1°}{3600''}\right)$
$=265.429°$

03

(1) $\frac{11\pi}{4}=\frac{11\pi}{4}\times\frac{180°}{\pi}=495°$

(2) $-\frac{15\pi}{6}=-\frac{5\pi}{2}=-\frac{5\pi}{2}\times\frac{180°}{\pi}=-450°$

(3) $495°=495°\times\frac{\pi}{180°}=\frac{11\pi}{4}$

(4) $-300°=-300°\times\frac{\pi}{180°}=-\frac{5\pi}{3}$

04

(1) Positive : $\frac{5\pi}{6}+2\pi=\frac{17\pi}{6}$; $\frac{5\pi}{6}+(2\pi\times2)=\frac{29\pi}{6}$

Negative : $\frac{5\pi}{6}-2\pi=-\frac{7\pi}{6}$

(2) Positive :

$-\frac{9\pi}{4}+(2\pi\times2)=\frac{7\pi}{4}$; $-\frac{9\pi}{4}+(2\pi\times3)=\frac{15\pi}{4}$

Negative : $-\frac{9\pi}{4}+2\pi=-\frac{\pi}{4}$

(3) Positive : $495°-360°=135°$; $495°+360°=855°$

Negative : $495°-(360°\times2)=-225°$

(4) Positive :

$-300°+360°=60°$; $-300°+(360°\times2)=420°$

Negative $-300°-360=-660°$

05

(1) Arc length $l=r\theta$.

$2=4\cdot\theta$

$\theta=\frac{1}{2}\ rad$

(2) Arc length $l=r\theta$.

$9\pi=r\cdot\frac{2\pi}{3}$, $r=\frac{27}{2}$

06

(1) Area of a sector :
$A=\frac{1}{2}r^2\theta=\frac{1}{2}(3)^2\left(\frac{\pi}{4}\right)=\frac{9\pi}{8}$

(2) $225°\times\frac{\pi}{180°}=\frac{5\pi}{4}$ and

$l=r\theta$, $15\pi=r\cdot\frac{5\pi}{4}$, $r=12$

Area of a sector :

$A=\frac{1}{2}rl=\frac{1}{2}(12)(15\pi)=90\pi$

07

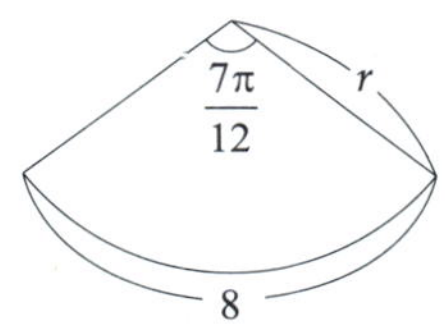

$l=r\theta$
$8=r\left(\frac{7\pi}{12}\right)$, $r=\frac{96}{7\pi}$ inches

08

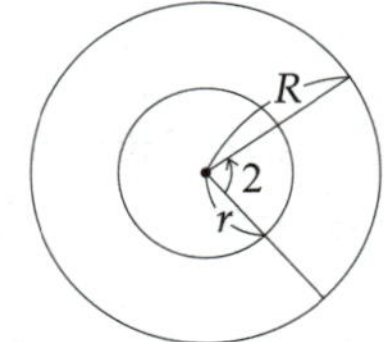

Since the radius of the larger circle is twice the radius of the smaller circle $R=2r$.

Larger Sector : $A_L=\frac{1}{2}R^2\theta=\frac{1}{2}(2r)^2(2)=4r^2$

Smaller Sector : $A_S=\frac{1}{2}r^2\theta=\frac{1}{2}r^2(2)=r^2$

So the ratio of the area of larger sector to the smaller sector is

$\frac{A_L}{A_S}=\frac{4r^2}{r^2}=4$ or $A_L : A_S=4 : 1$

09

The arc length is $l=8\pi$ and the area of sector is $A=26\pi$.

$A=\frac{1}{2}rl$

$26\pi=\frac{1}{2}r(8\pi)$, $r=\frac{13}{2}$

$l=r\theta$

$8\pi=\left(\frac{13}{2}\right)\theta$, $\theta=\frac{16\pi}{13}$

10

(1) First, convert the unit from $\frac{\text{mi}}{\text{hr}}$ to $\frac{\text{ft}}{\text{mi}}$

$\frac{40\ \cancel{\text{mi}}}{\cancel{\text{hr}}}\times\frac{5280\ \text{ft}}{1\ \cancel{\text{mi}}}\times\frac{1\ \cancel{\text{hr}}}{60\ \text{min}}=3520\ \text{ft/min}$

Since the circumference of the tire is $2\pi(2)=4\pi$ ft, the number of rev/min is

$\frac{3520\ \cancel{\text{ft}}}{\text{min}}\times\frac{1\ \text{rev}}{4\pi\ \cancel{\text{ft}}}=280.113\ \text{rev/min}$

(2) Since the tire rotates 280.113 revolutions per minute, the angular speed of the tire is

$w=\frac{280.113\ \cancel{\text{rev}}}{\text{min}}\times\frac{2\pi\ \text{rad}}{1\ \cancel{\text{rev}}}=1760\ \text{rad/min}$

2. Trigonometric Functions of Angles

Check Point 1

① $\sin\theta=y=\frac{15}{17}$ $\quad\csc\theta=\frac{1}{\sin\theta}=\frac{17}{15}$

$\cos\theta=x=\frac{8}{17}$ $\quad\sec\theta=\frac{1}{\cos\theta}=\frac{17}{8}$

$\tan\theta=\frac{y}{x}=\frac{\frac{15}{17}}{\frac{8}{17}}=\frac{15}{8}$ $\quad\cot\theta=\frac{1}{\tan\theta}=\frac{8}{15}$

② $\sin\theta=y=\frac{4}{5}$ $\quad\csc\theta=\frac{1}{\sin\theta}=\frac{5}{4}$

$\cos\theta=x=-\frac{3}{5}$ $\quad\sec\theta=\frac{1}{\cos\theta}=-\frac{5}{3}$

$\tan\theta=\frac{y}{x}=\frac{\frac{4}{5}}{-\frac{3}{5}}=-\frac{4}{3}$ $\quad\cot\theta=\frac{1}{\tan\theta}=-\frac{3}{4}$

Check Point 2

①

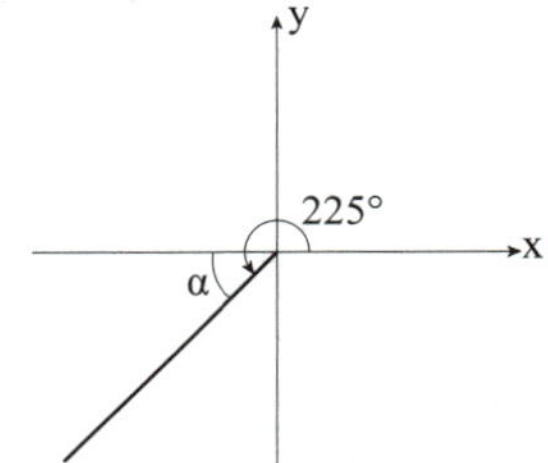

The reference angle is $\alpha=225°-180°=45°$

②

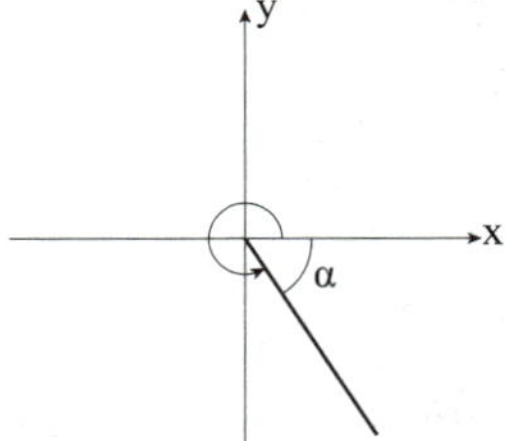

The reference angle is $\alpha=2\pi-\frac{5\pi}{3}=\frac{\pi}{3}$

Check Point 3

①

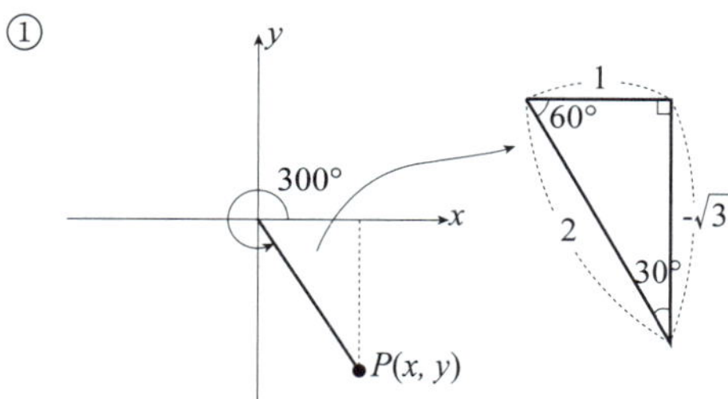

The reference angle is $360°-300°=60°$.

$\sin 300°=-\dfrac{\sqrt{3}}{2}$

$\csc 300°=\dfrac{1}{\sin 300°}=-\dfrac{2}{\sqrt{3}}=-\dfrac{2\sqrt{3}}{3}$

$\cos 300°=\dfrac{1}{2}$ $\quad$ $\sec 300°=\dfrac{1}{\cos 300°}=2$

$\tan 300°=-\dfrac{\sqrt{3}}{1}=-\sqrt{3}$

$\cot 300°=\dfrac{1}{\tan 300°}=-\dfrac{1}{\sqrt{3}}=-\dfrac{\sqrt{3}}{3}$

②

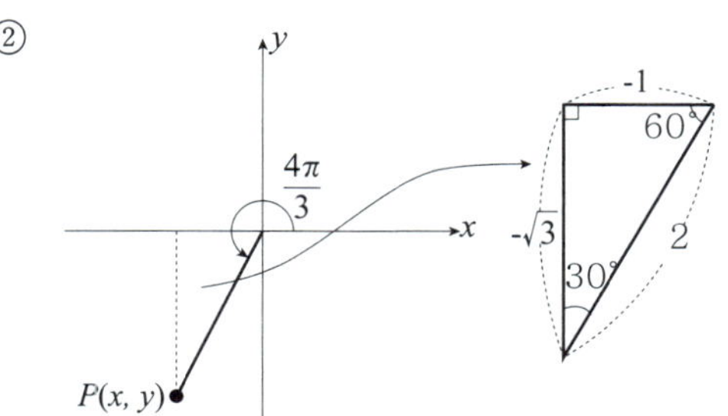

The reference angle is $\dfrac{4\pi}{3}-\pi=\dfrac{\pi}{3}=60°$.

$\sin \dfrac{4\pi}{3}=-\dfrac{\sqrt{3}}{2}$

$\csc \dfrac{4\pi}{3}=\dfrac{1}{\sin \dfrac{4\pi}{3}}=-\dfrac{2}{\sqrt{3}}=-\dfrac{2\sqrt{3}}{3}$

$\cos \dfrac{4\pi}{3}=-\dfrac{1}{2}$

$\sec \dfrac{4\pi}{3}=\dfrac{1}{\cos \dfrac{4\pi}{3}}=-2$

$\tan \dfrac{4\pi}{3}=\dfrac{-\sqrt{3}}{-1}=\sqrt{3}$

$\cot \dfrac{4\pi}{3}=\dfrac{1}{\tan \dfrac{4\pi}{3}}=\dfrac{1}{\sqrt{3}}=\dfrac{\sqrt{3}}{3}$

③

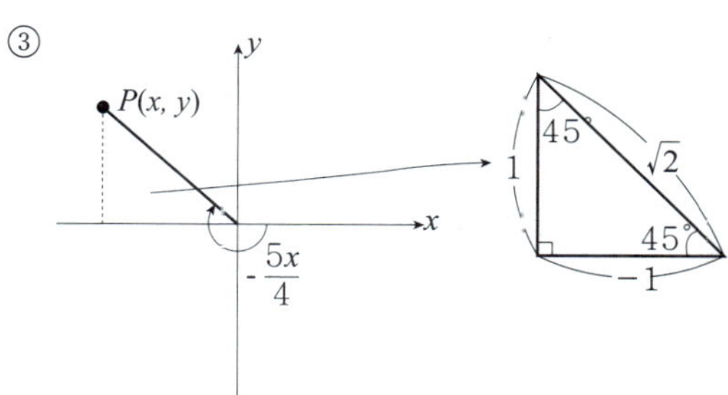

The reference angle is $\dfrac{5\pi}{4}-\pi=\dfrac{\pi}{4}=45°$.

$\sin\left(-\dfrac{5\pi}{4}\right)=\dfrac{1}{\sqrt{2}}=\dfrac{\sqrt{2}}{2}$

$\csc\left(-\dfrac{5\pi}{4}\right)=\dfrac{1}{\sin\left(-\dfrac{5\pi}{4}\right)}=\sqrt{2}$

$\cos\left(-\dfrac{5\pi}{4}\right)=-\dfrac{1}{\sqrt{2}}=-\dfrac{\sqrt{2}}{2}$

$\sec\left(-\dfrac{5\pi}{4}\right)=\dfrac{1}{\cos\left(-\dfrac{5\pi}{4}\right)}=-\sqrt{2}$

$\tan\left(-\dfrac{5\pi}{4}\right)=\dfrac{1}{-1}=-1$

$\cot\left(-\dfrac{5\pi}{4}\right)=\dfrac{1}{\tan\left(-\dfrac{5\pi}{4}\right)}=-1$

Check Point 4

① $\cos\theta=\dfrac{4}{5}$, $\cot\theta=\dfrac{4}{3}$

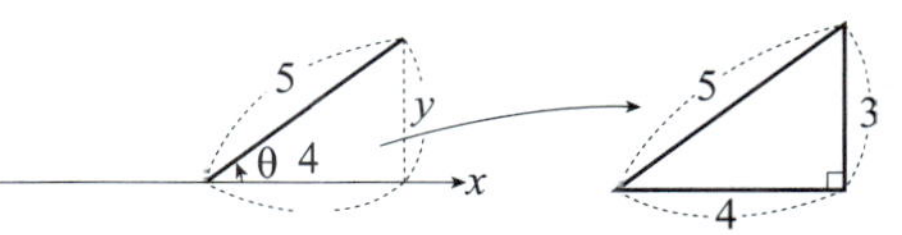

Since both $\cos\theta>0$ and $\cot\theta>0$, θ lies in Quadrant I as shown in Figure above.

$x^2+y^2=r^2$, $4^2+y^2=5^2$

$y^2=9$, $y=3$

$\sin\theta=\dfrac{3}{5}$ $\qquad$ $\csc\theta=\dfrac{5}{3}$

$\tan\theta=\dfrac{3}{4}$ $\qquad$ $\sec\theta=\dfrac{5}{4}$

② $\csc\theta=\dfrac{7}{5}$, $\cot\theta<0$

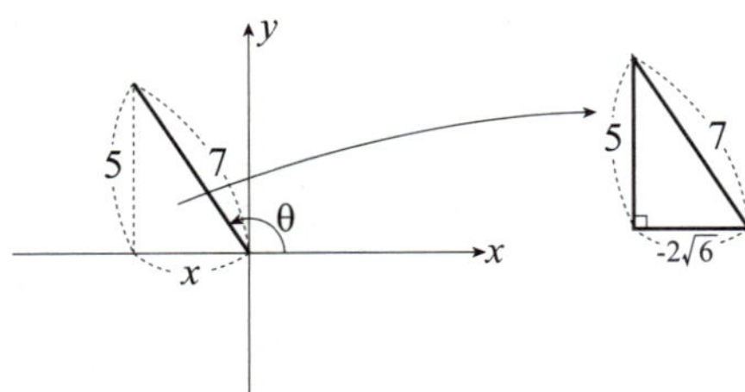

Since $\csc\theta>0$ and $\cot\theta<0$, θ lies in Quadrant II as shown in Figure above.

$x^2+y^2=r^2$, $x^2+5^2=7^2$

$x^2=24$, $x=-\sqrt{24}=-2\sqrt{6}$

$\sin\theta=\dfrac{5}{7}$

$\cos\theta=-\dfrac{2\sqrt{6}}{7}$ $\qquad$ $\sec\theta=-\dfrac{7}{2\sqrt{6}}=-\dfrac{7\sqrt{6}}{12}$

$\tan\theta=-\dfrac{5}{2\sqrt{6}}=-\dfrac{5\sqrt{6}}{12}$

$\cot\theta=-\dfrac{2\sqrt{6}}{5}$

Review Exercises

01

(1)

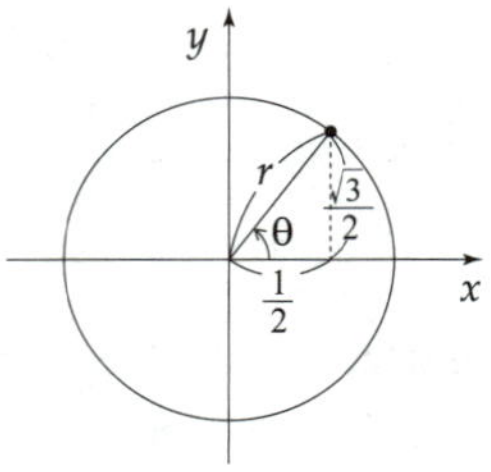

$x^2+y^2=r^2$, $\left(\dfrac{1}{2}\right)^2+\left(\dfrac{\sqrt{3}}{2}\right)^2=r^2$

$\dfrac{1}{4}+\dfrac{3}{4}=r^2$, $r=1$ → Unit Circle

$\sin\theta=y=\dfrac{\sqrt{3}}{2}$ $\qquad$ $\csc\theta=\dfrac{2}{\sqrt{3}}=\dfrac{2\sqrt{3}}{3}$

$\cos\theta=x=\dfrac{1}{2}$ $\qquad$ $\sec\theta=2$

$\tan\theta=\dfrac{y}{x}=\dfrac{\frac{\sqrt{3}}{2}}{\frac{1}{2}}=\sqrt{3}$

$\cot\theta=\dfrac{1}{\sqrt{3}}=\dfrac{\sqrt{3}}{3}$

(2)

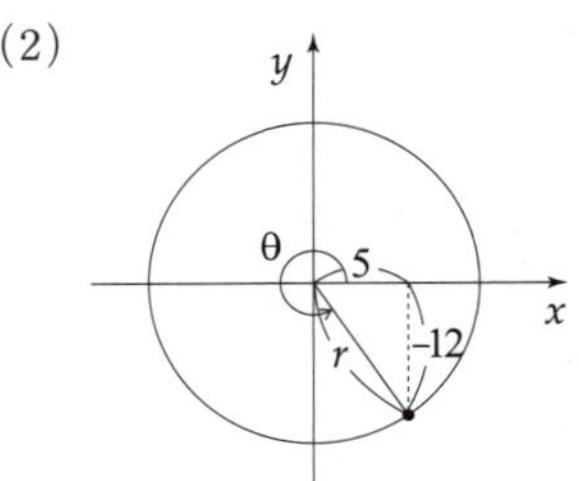

$x^2+y^2=r^2$, $5^2+(-12)^2=r^2$

$25+144=r^2$, $r=13$ → Not a Unit Circle

$\sin\theta=-\dfrac{12}{13}$ $\qquad$ $\csc\theta=-\dfrac{13}{12}$

$\cos\theta=\dfrac{5}{13}$ $\qquad$ $\sec\theta=\dfrac{13}{5}$

$\tan\theta=-\dfrac{12}{5}$ $\qquad$ $\cot\theta=-\dfrac{5}{12}$

02

(1)

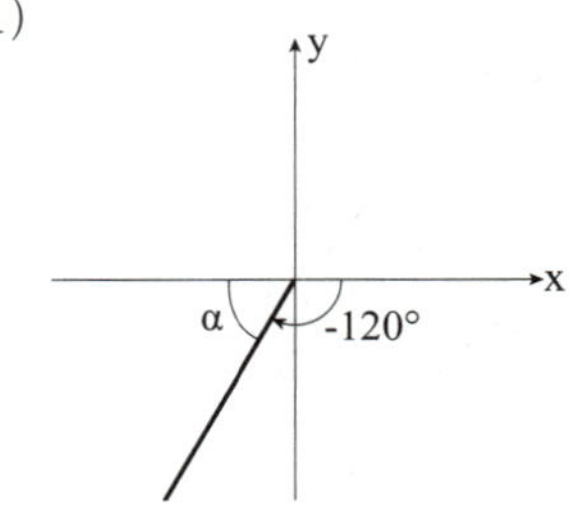

The reference angle is $\alpha=180°-120°=60°$

(2)

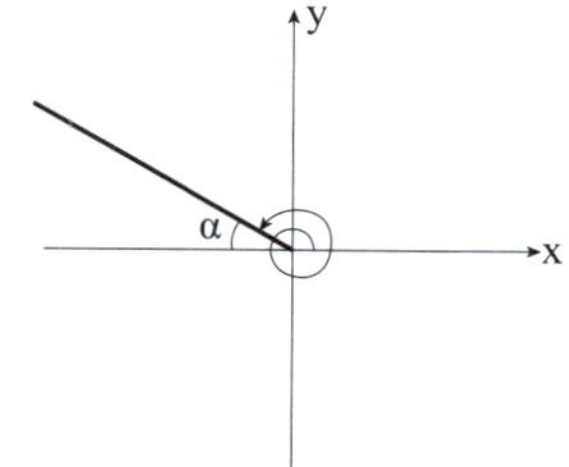

$$\frac{17\pi}{6} = \frac{17\pi}{6} - 2\pi = \frac{5\pi}{6}$$

The reference angle is $\alpha = \pi - \frac{5\pi}{6} = \frac{\pi}{6}$

03

(1)

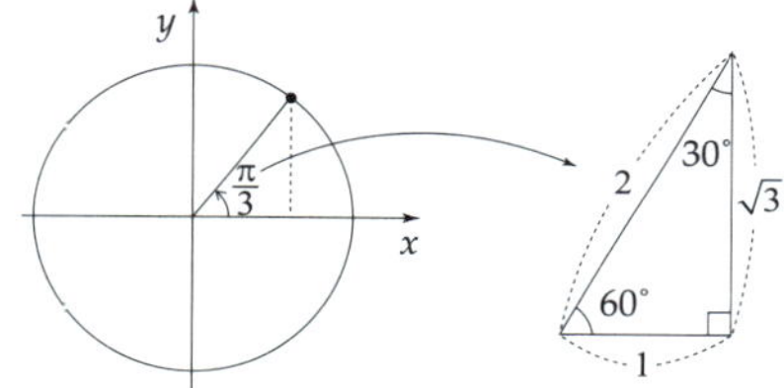

$\sin\frac{\pi}{3} = \frac{\sqrt{3}}{2}$ $\csc\frac{\pi}{3} = \frac{2}{\sqrt{3}} = \frac{2\sqrt{3}}{3}$

$\cos\frac{\pi}{3} = \frac{1}{2}$ $\sec\frac{\pi}{3} = 2$

$\tan\frac{\pi}{3} = \frac{\sqrt{3}}{1} = \sqrt{3}$ $\cot\frac{\pi}{3} = \frac{1}{\sqrt{3}} = \frac{\sqrt{3}}{3}$

(2)

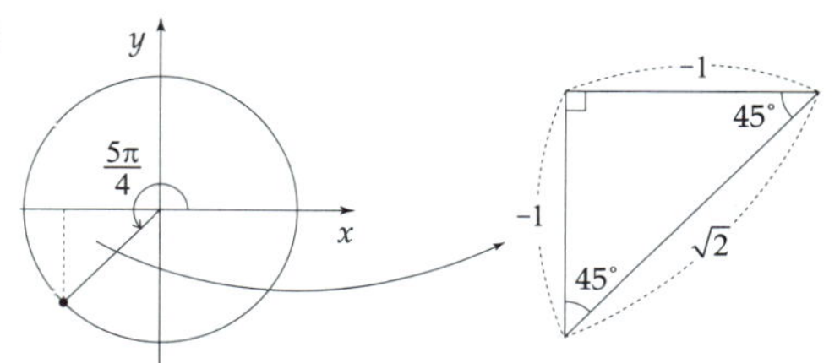

The reference angle

$\alpha = \frac{5\pi}{4} - \pi = \frac{\pi}{4}$ or $\alpha = 45°$.

$\sin\frac{5\pi}{4} = -\frac{1}{\sqrt{2}} = -\frac{\sqrt{2}}{2}$ $\csc\frac{5\pi}{4} = -\sqrt{2}$

$\cos\frac{5\pi}{4} = -\frac{1}{\sqrt{2}} = -\frac{\sqrt{2}}{2}$ $\sec\frac{5\pi}{4} = -\sqrt{2}$

$\tan\frac{5\pi}{4} = \frac{-1}{-1} = 1$ $\cot\frac{5\pi}{4} = 1$

(3)

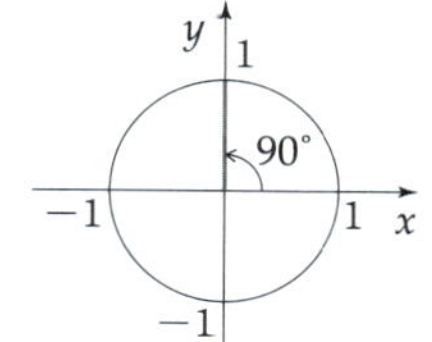

Using the unit circle in Figure above,

$\sin 90° = y = 1$ $\csc 90° = 1$

$\cos 90° = x = 0$ $\sec 90° = \frac{1}{0} = \text{undef}$

$\tan 90° = \frac{y}{x} = \frac{1}{0} = \text{undef}$

$\cot 90° = \frac{0}{1} = 0$

(4)

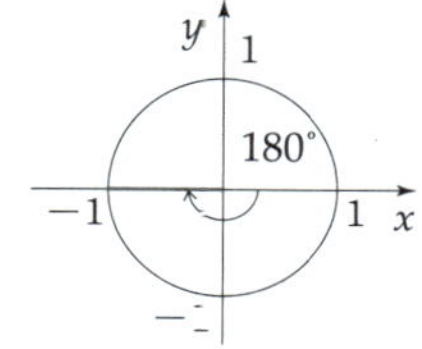

Using the unit circle in Figure above,

$\sin(-180°) = y = 0$ $\csc(-180°) = \frac{1}{0} = \text{undef}$

$\cos(-180°) = x = -1$ $\sec(-180°) = -1$

$\tan(-180°) = \frac{y}{x} = \frac{0}{-1} = 0$

$\cot(-180°) = \frac{-1}{0} = \text{undef}$

04

(1) $\sin\theta = \frac{1}{2}$, $\tan\theta = \frac{1}{\sqrt{3}}$

Since $\sin\theta > 0$ and $\tan\theta > 0$, θ lies in Quadrant I.

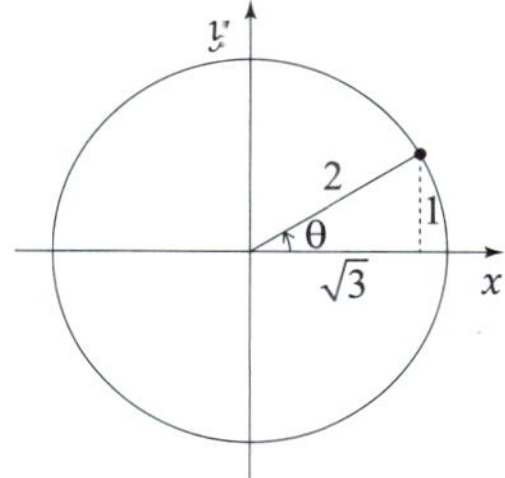

$\csc\theta = 2$ $\cot\theta = \sqrt{3}$

$\cos\theta=\frac{\sqrt{3}}{2}$ $\sec\theta=\frac{2}{\sqrt{3}}=\frac{2\sqrt{3}}{3}$

(2) $\cos\theta=\frac{2}{3}$, $\tan<0$

Since $\cos\theta>0$ and $\tan\theta<0$, θ lies in Quadrant IV.

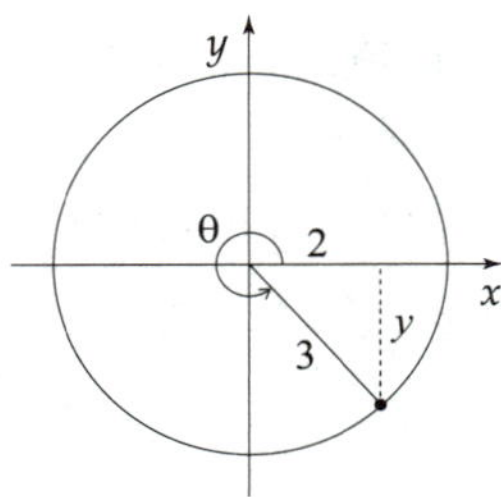

$x^2+y^2=r^2$, $2^2+y^2=3^2$

$y^2=5$, $y=-\sqrt{5}$

$\sin\theta=-\frac{\sqrt{5}}{3}$ $\csc\theta=-\frac{3}{\sqrt{5}}=-\frac{3\sqrt{5}}{5}$

$\sec\theta=\frac{3}{2}$

$\tan\theta=-\frac{\sqrt{5}}{2}$ $\cot\theta=-\frac{2}{\sqrt{5}}=-\frac{2\sqrt{5}}{5}$

(3) $\sec\theta=-3$, $\sin\theta<0$

Since $\sec\theta<0$ and $\sin\theta<0$, θ lies in Quadrant III.

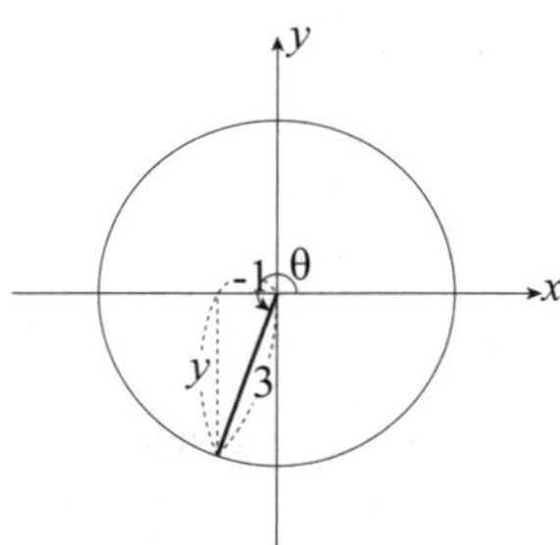

$x^2+y^2=r^2$, $(-1)^2+y^2=3^2$

$y^2=8$, $y=-2\sqrt{2}$

$\sin\theta=-\frac{2\sqrt{2}}{3}$ $\csc\theta=-\frac{3}{2\sqrt{2}}=-\frac{3\sqrt{2}}{4}$

$\cos\theta=-\frac{1}{3}$

$\tan\theta=\frac{-2\sqrt{2}}{-1}=2\sqrt{2}$ $\cot\theta=\frac{1}{2\sqrt{2}}=\frac{\sqrt{2}}{4}$

(4) $\cot\theta=-\frac{2}{\sqrt{5}}$, $\sec\theta>0$

Since $\cot\theta<0$ and $\sec\theta>0$, θ lies in Quadrant IV.

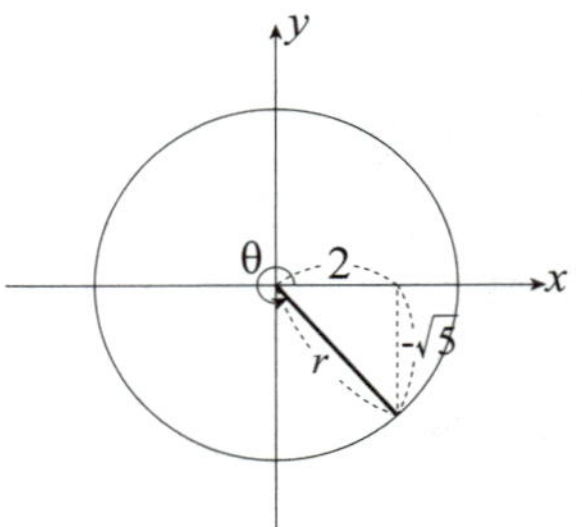

$x^2+y^2=r^2$, $(2)^2+(-\sqrt{5})^2=r^2$

$r^2=9$, $r=3$

$\sin\theta=-\frac{\sqrt{5}}{3}$ $\csc\theta=-\frac{3}{\sqrt{5}}=-\frac{3\sqrt{5}}{5}$

$\tan\theta=-\frac{\sqrt{5}}{2}$

$\cos\theta=\frac{2}{3}$ $\sec\theta=\frac{3}{2}$

05

(1) $\cot\theta<0$ and $\sec\theta\tan\theta<0$

	I	II	III	IV
$\cot\theta$	+	−	+	−
$\sec\theta$	+	−	−	+
$\tan\theta$	+	−	+	−
$\sec\theta\tan\theta$	+	+	−	−

Since both $\cot\theta<0$ and $\sec\theta\ \tan\theta<0$, θ lies in Quadrant IV.

(2) $\sin\theta\cos\theta>0$ and $\cos\theta\tan\theta<0$

	I	II	III	IV
$\sin\theta$	+	+	−	−
$\cos\theta$	+	−	−	+
$\sin\theta\ \cos\theta$	+	−	+	−
$\tan\theta$	+	−	+	−
$\cos\theta\tan\theta$	+	+	−	−

Since $\sin\theta\cos\theta>0$ but $\cos\theta\tan\theta<0$, θ lies in Quadrant III.

06

Let $\overline{BC}=a$. By the Pythagorean theorem,

$4^2+a^2=k^2$

$a^2=k^2-16$, $a=\sqrt{k^2-16}$

Since $\sin x=\frac{1}{2}$, we have

$\frac{a}{k}=\frac{1}{2}$, $\frac{\sqrt{k^2-16}}{k}=\frac{1}{2}$

$2\sqrt{k^2-16}=k$, $4(k^2-16)=k^2$

$4k^2-64=k^2$, $3k^2=64$

$k^2=\frac{64}{3}$, $k=\frac{8}{\sqrt{3}}=\frac{8\sqrt{3}}{3}$

Alternative Solution

Since $\sin x=\frac{1}{2}$, the ratio of $\overline{BC}:\overline{AC}:\overline{AB}$ is equal to $1:\sqrt{3}:2$. So, we have

$\frac{\sqrt{3}}{2}=\frac{4}{k}$, $\sqrt{3}k=8$

$k=\frac{8}{\sqrt{3}}=\frac{8\sqrt{3}}{3}$

07

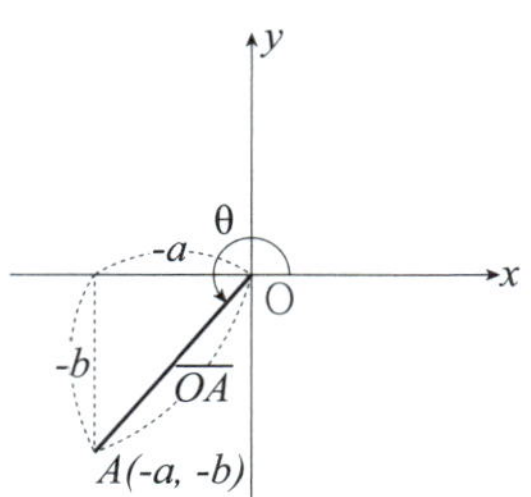

By the Pythagorean theorem,

$(-a)^2+(-b)^2=\overline{OA}^2$, $\overline{OA}=\sqrt{a^2+b^2}$

$\sin\theta=-\frac{b}{\sqrt{a^2+b^2}}$ $\quad\csc\theta=-\frac{\sqrt{a^2+b^2}}{b}$

$\cos\theta=-\frac{a}{\sqrt{a^2+b^2}}$ $\quad\sec\theta=-\frac{\sqrt{a^2+b^2}}{a}$

$\tan\theta=\frac{-b}{-a}=\frac{b}{a}$ $\quad\cot\theta=\frac{a}{b}$

08

If $\cos\theta=m$ and $0<\theta<\frac{\pi}{2}$, we have the following triangle :

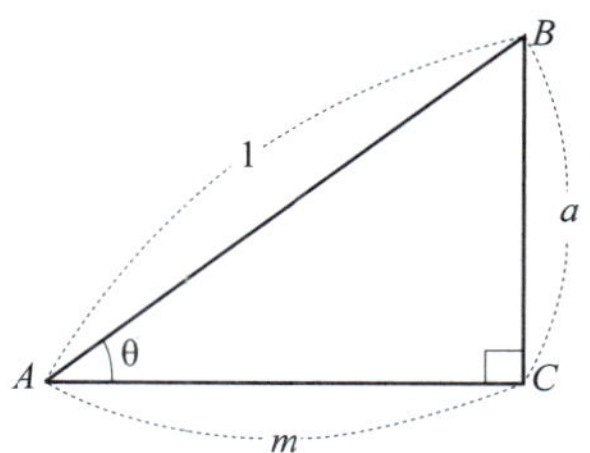

By the Pythagorean theorem,

$a^2+m^2=1^2$

$a^2=1^2-m^2$, $a=\sqrt{1-m^2}$

Therefore,

$$\tan\theta+\csc\theta=\frac{\sqrt{1-m^2}}{m}+\frac{1}{\sqrt{1-m^2}}$$

$$=\frac{(1-m^2)+m}{m\sqrt{1-m^2}}=\frac{-m^2+m+1}{m\sqrt{1-m^2}}$$

09

(1) If $\sin x=k$ and $0<x<\frac{\pi}{2}$, we could have the following triangle :

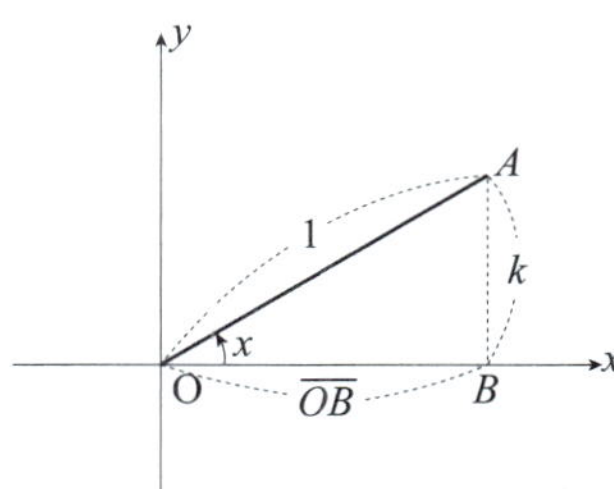

By the Pythagorean theorem,

$\overline{OB}^2+k^2=1^2$

$\overline{OB}^2=1^2-k^2$, $\overline{OB}=\sqrt{1-k^2}$

Therefore, $\cos x=\frac{\sqrt{1-k^2}}{1}=\sqrt{1-k^2}$.

(2) If the angle is $\pi-x$, we have the following triangle :

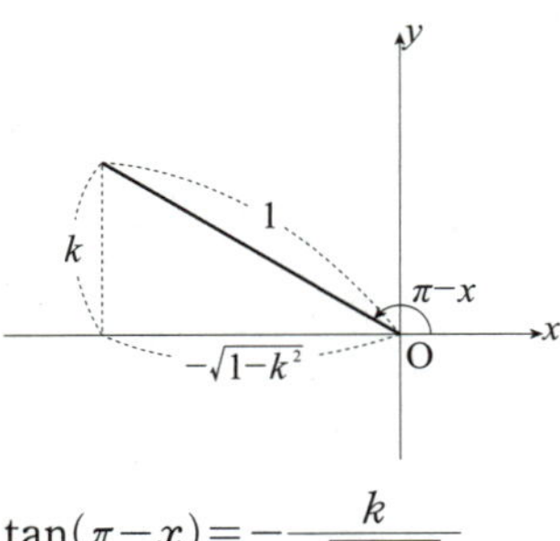

$\tan(\pi-x)=-\dfrac{k}{\sqrt{1-k^2}}$

(3) If the angle is $x+\pi$, we have the following triangle :

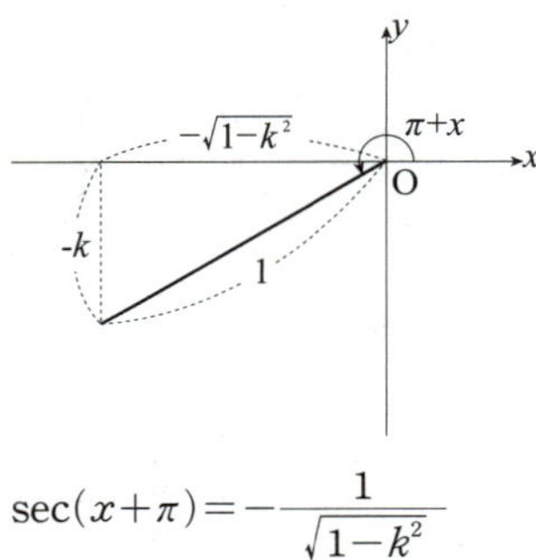

$\sec(x+\pi)=-\dfrac{1}{\sqrt{1-k^2}}$

(4) If the angle is $2\pi-x$, we have the following triangle :

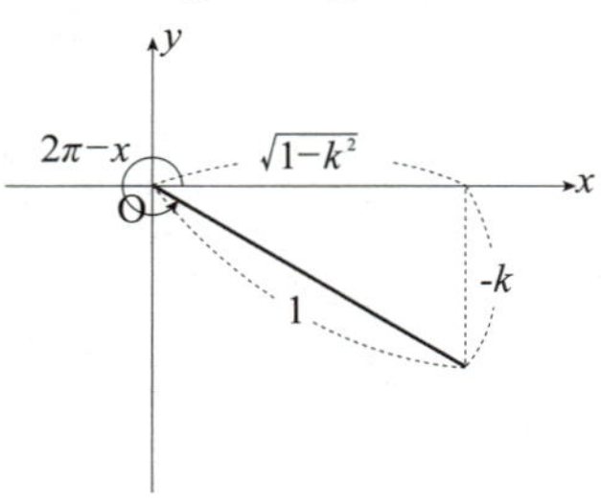

$\csc(2\pi-x)=-\dfrac{1}{k}$

10

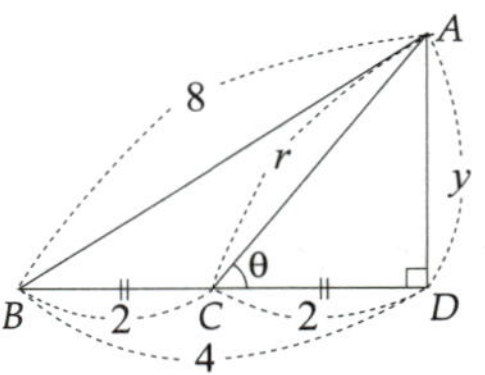

Applying the Pythagorean theorem at triangle ABD, we have

$y^2+4^2=8^2$, $y^2=48$, $y=4\sqrt{3}$

This time, applying the Pythagorean theorem at triangle ACD, we have

$r^2=y^2+2^2$, $r^2=48+4=52$, $r=2\sqrt{13}$

Now, $\sin\theta=\dfrac{y}{r}=\dfrac{4\sqrt{3}}{2\sqrt{13}}=\dfrac{2\sqrt{3}}{\sqrt{13}}=\dfrac{2\sqrt{39}}{13}$.

11

(1) The radius r(OB) of the circle is $r=\sqrt{(-3)^2+4^2}=5$. Therefore, the coordinates of B give us $\cos\theta=\dfrac{-3}{5}$ and $\sin\theta=\dfrac{4}{5}$. So

$$\sin\theta+\cos\theta=\frac{4}{5}+\left(-\frac{3}{5}\right)=\frac{1}{5}$$

(2) The slope of OB is given by $\dfrac{4-0}{-3-0}=-\dfrac{4}{3}$.

(3) Convert revolutions per minute to centimeters per second.

$$\frac{4\,\cancel{\text{rev}}}{\cancel{\text{min}}}\times\frac{2\pi(5)\text{cm}}{1\,\cancel{\text{rev}}}\times\frac{1\,\cancel{\text{min}}}{60\text{ sec}}=\frac{2\pi}{3}\text{ cm/sec}$$

12

The radius r of the circle is $r=\sqrt{(-4\sqrt{3})^2+4^2}=8$.

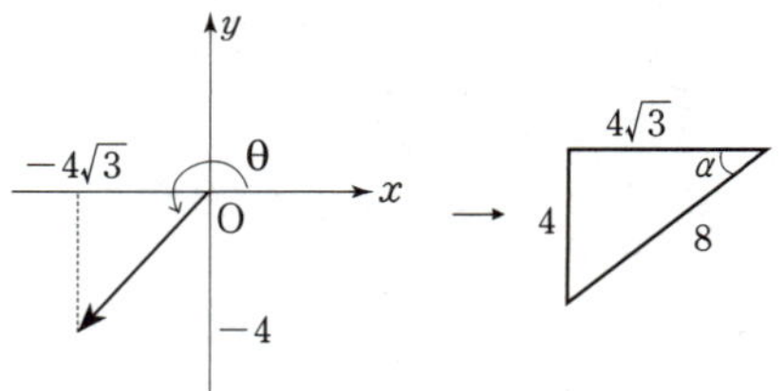

$\theta=\pi+\alpha=\pi+\frac{\pi}{6}=\frac{7\pi}{6}$.

Therefore, $r\theta=8\cdot\frac{7\pi}{6}=\frac{28\pi}{3}$.

13

If we let $\angle BOC=x$, then $\angle AOC=2x$. Since $\angle AOB=90°$,

$\angle BOC+\angle AOC=3x=90°$, $x=30°$

Therefore, angle $\theta=180°+60°=240°$.

(1) Since $\theta=240°$, the coordinate C is $\left(\cos240°, \sin240°\right)=\left(-\frac{1}{2}, -\frac{\sqrt{3}}{2}\right)$.

(2) Slope m of the terminal side OC:

$$m=\frac{\sin 240°}{\cos 240°}=\frac{-\frac{\sqrt{3}}{2}}{-\frac{1}{2}}=\sqrt{3}$$

(3) $\sin\angle AOC\times\cos\angle BOC=\sin60°\times\cos30°$

$$=\frac{\sqrt{3}}{2}\times\frac{\sqrt{3}}{2}=\frac{3}{4}$$

14

(1) Since AOB is an equilateral triangle, AB is equal to the radius of the circle OB. Therefore, $AB=4$.

(2)

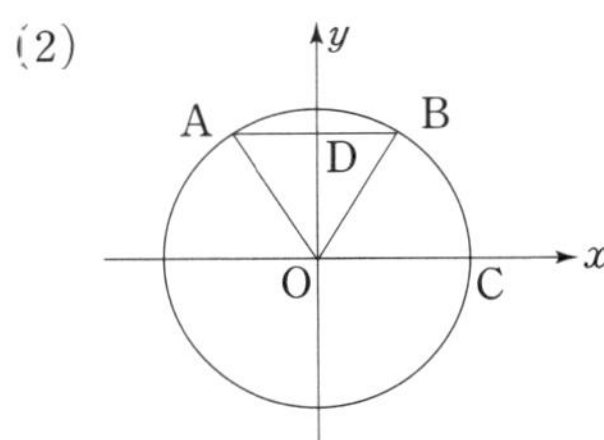

Since AB is parallel to the x−axis, triangle AOD and BOD are congruent so that the measure of angle AOD and BOD are each 30 degrees. Therefore,

$$\sin\angle COB-\sin\angle COA=\sin60°-\sin120°=\frac{\sqrt{3}}{2}-\frac{\sqrt{3}}{2}=0$$

15

The angle α is in the first quadrant.

$\cos\alpha=-\cos\beta \Rightarrow \cos\beta<0$

$\sin\alpha=\sin\beta \Rightarrow \sin\beta>0$

For $\cos\beta$ to be negative and $\sin\beta$ to be positive, β must be in the second quadrant. Therefore,

$\beta=\pi-\alpha$, $\alpha=\pi-\beta$

The correct answer is (C).

16

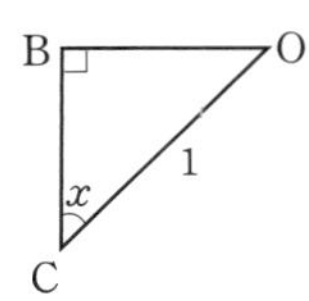

In triangle BOC above,

$$\sin x=\frac{OB}{1}=OB$$

Therefore, $AB=1-OB=1-\sin x$.

The correct answer is (C).

17

Using Pythagorean theorem, $3^2+BC^2=a^2$.

Since $\sin A=h$, we have $\frac{BC}{a}=h$, $a=\frac{BC}{h}$.

Now substitute $\frac{BC}{h}$ for a in the equation $3^2+BC^2=a^2$.

$$3^2+BC^2=\left(\frac{BC}{h}\right)^2$$

$$9h^2+h^2BC^2=BC^2$$

$$BC^2-h^2BC^2=9h^2,\ BC^2(1-h^2)=9h^2$$

$$BC^2=\frac{9h^2}{1-h^2},\ BC=\frac{3h}{\sqrt{1-h^2}}$$

Therefore, the correct answer is (A).

3. Graphs of Trigonometric Functions

Check Point 1

① $y=\frac{1}{2}\sin x$

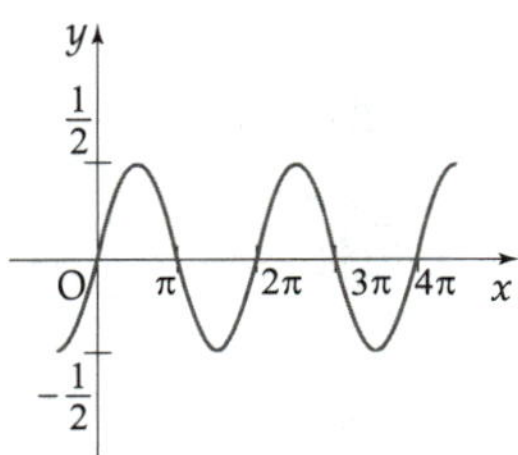

Domain : $(-\infty,\ \infty)$ Range : $\left\{y \middle| -\frac{1}{2}\le y\le \frac{1}{2}\right\}$

Amplitude : $\frac{1}{2}$ Period : 2π

② $y=\cos(3x)$

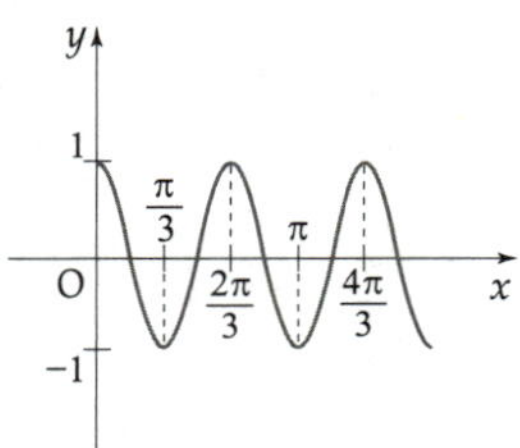

Domain : $(-\infty,\ \infty)$ Range : $\{y|-1\le y\le 1\}$

Amplitude : 1 Period : $\frac{2\pi}{3}$

③ $y=-3\cos\left(\frac{x}{2}\right)$

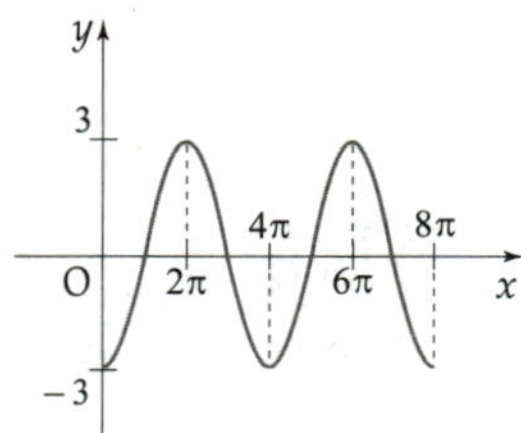

Domain : $(-\infty,\ \infty)$ Range : $\{y|-3\le y\le 3\}$

Amplitude : 3 Period : $\frac{\pi}{\frac{1}{2}}=4\pi$

Check Point 2

① $y=-2\cos(4x)-1$

First, graph $y=-2\cos(4x)$ and then shift it 1 unit down.

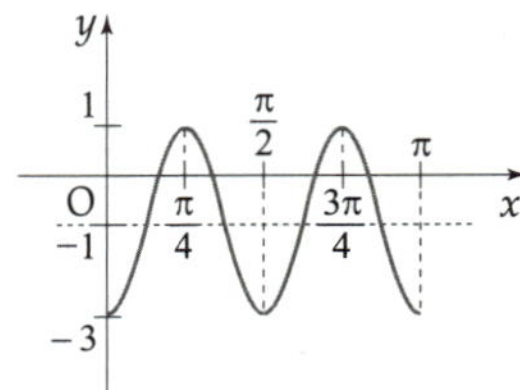

Domain : $(-\infty,\ \infty)$ Range : $\{y|-3\le y\le 1\}$

Amplitude : 2 Period : $\frac{2\pi}{4}=\frac{\pi}{2}$

② $y=\frac{3}{2}\sin 2\left(x+\frac{\pi}{2}\right)$

First, graph $y=\frac{3}{2}\sin(2x)$ and then shift it $\frac{\pi}{2}$ units to the left.

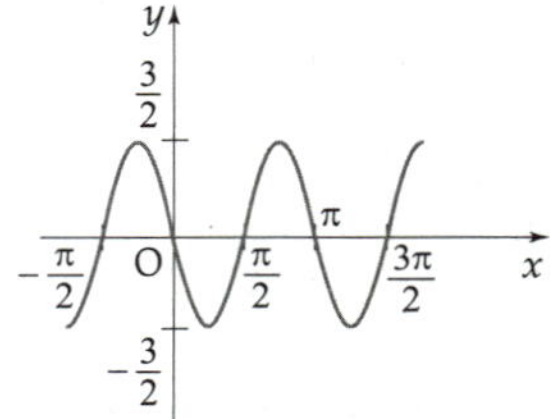

Domain : $(-\infty,\ \infty)$ Range : $\left\{y \middle| -\frac{3}{2}\le y\le \frac{3}{2}\right\}$

Amplitude : $\frac{3}{2}$ Period : $\frac{2\pi}{2}=\pi$

Check Point 3

① $y=3\tan\left(\frac{x}{3}\right)$

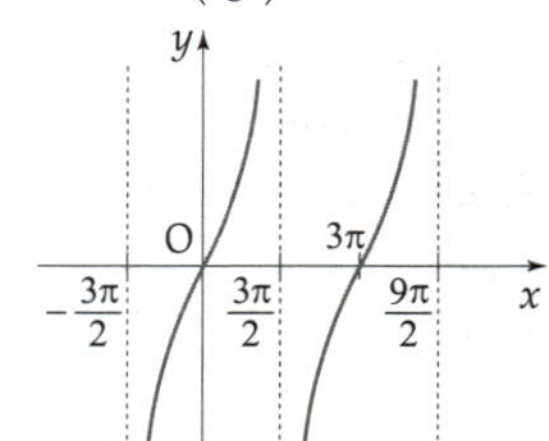

Domain : All real numbers except

$x=\frac{3\pi}{2}+3n\pi \ (n\in Z)$

Range : $(-\infty, \infty)$ Period : $\frac{\pi}{\frac{1}{3}}=3\pi$

Asymptote : $x=\left(\frac{\pi}{2}+n\pi\right)\cdot 3$

$=\frac{3\pi}{2}+3n\pi \ (n\in Z)$

② $y=-\tan\left(2x-\frac{\pi}{2}\right)+1=-\tan 2\left(x-\frac{\pi}{4}\right)+1$

First, graph $y=-\tan(2x)$ and then shift it $\frac{\pi}{4}$ units to the right and 1 unit up.

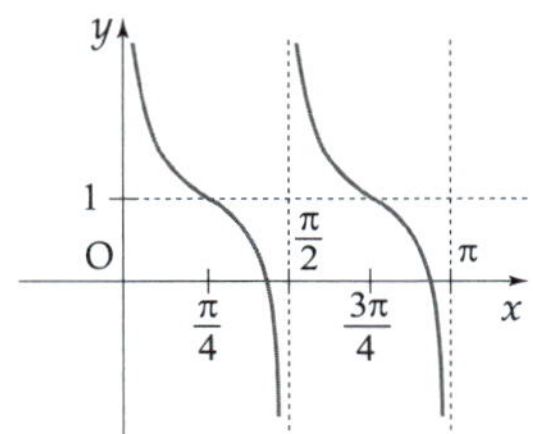

Domain : All real numbers except

$x=\frac{n\pi}{2} \ (n\in Z)$

Range : $(-\infty, \infty)$ Period : $\frac{\pi}{2}$

Asymptote : $x=\left(\frac{\pi}{2}+n\pi\right)\cdot\frac{1}{2}+\frac{\pi}{4}=\frac{n\pi}{2} \ (n\in Z)$

Check Point 4

① $y=\sec(\pi x)$

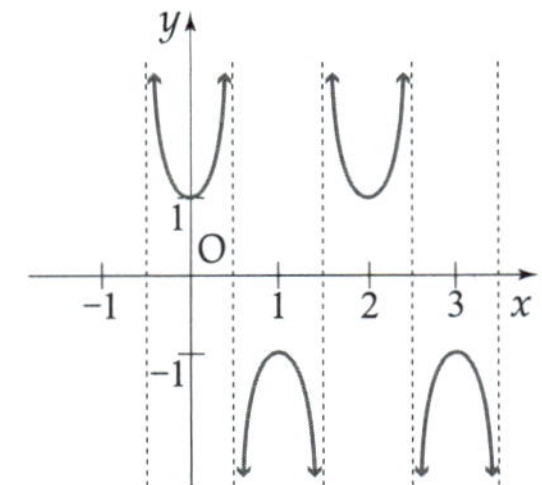

Domain : All real numbers except

$x=\frac{1}{2}+n(n\in Z)$

Range : $(-\infty, -1]\cup[1, \infty)$

Period : $\frac{2\pi}{\pi}=2$

Asymptote : $x=\frac{1}{2}+n \ (n\in Z)$

② $y=-2\cot\left(\frac{\pi x}{2}\right)-1$

First, graph $y=-2\cot\left(\frac{\pi x}{2}\right)$ and then shift it 1 unit down

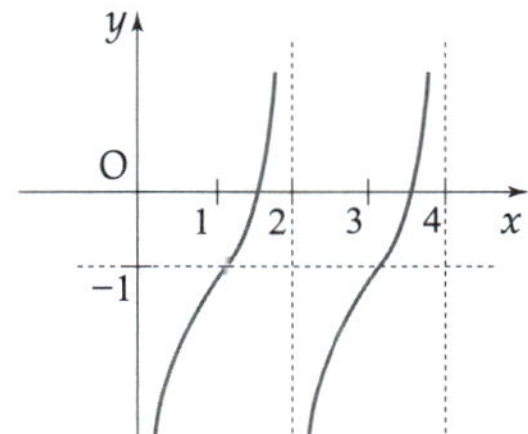

Domain : All real numbers except

$x=2n \ (n\in Z)$

Range : $(-\infty, \infty)$ Period : $\frac{\pi}{\frac{\pi}{2}}=2$

Asymptote : $x=\frac{n\pi}{\frac{\pi}{2}}=2n \ (n\in Z)$

③ $y=-\csc(2x-\pi)=-\csc 2\left(x-\frac{\pi}{2}\right)$

First, graph $y=-2\csc(2x)$ and then shift it $\frac{\pi}{2}$ units to the right

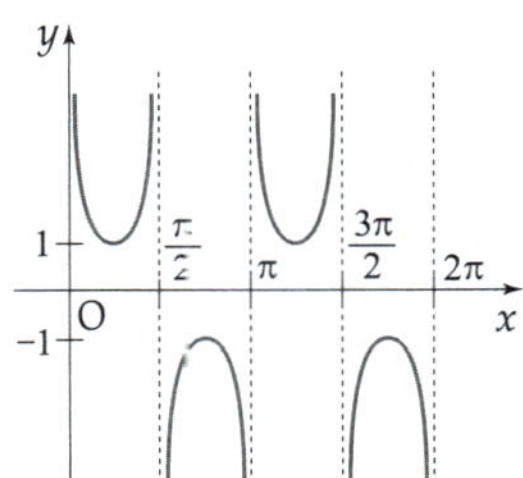

Domain : All real numbers except

$x=\frac{\pi n}{2} \ (n\in Z)$

Range : $(-\infty, -1]\cup[1, \infty)$

Period : $\frac{2\pi}{2}=\pi$

Asymptote : $x=\frac{\pi n}{2} \ (n\in Z)$

Solutions Manual

Review Exercises

01

In the form of the function $y=a\sin b(x-h)+k$, the amplitude is always $|a|$. So the amplitude of the function f is $|-2|=2$.

02

In the form of the function $y=a\sin b(x-h)+k$, the period is always $\frac{2\pi}{b}$. So the period of the function f is $\frac{2\pi}{2}=\pi$.

03

For the function $f(x)=\frac{1}{\pi}\cos\left(\frac{x}{\pi}\right)$, the amplitude is $\left|\frac{1}{\pi}\right|=\frac{1}{\pi}$ and the period is $\frac{2\pi}{\frac{1}{\pi}}=2\pi^2$.

04

The function $y=-\frac{1}{2}\sin(x-2)$ has an amplitude of $\left|-\frac{1}{2}\right|=\frac{1}{2}$. So the range of $y=-\frac{1}{2}\sin(x-2)$ is $-\frac{1}{2}\le y\le\frac{1}{2}$.

Since the graph of $f(x)=1-\frac{1}{2}\sin(x-2)$ is shifted 1 unit up from $y=-\frac{1}{2}\sin(x-2)$, the range of $f(x)$ is

$-\frac{1}{2}+1\le f(x)\le\frac{1}{2}+1$, $\frac{1}{2}\le f(x)\le\frac{3}{2}$

05

P is located at the end of one period of the graph. The period of the function $g(x)=-2\cos(4x)-1$ is $\frac{2\pi}{4}=\frac{\pi}{2}$. So the x−coordinate of P is $\frac{\pi}{2}$. Now, the y−coordinate of P is

$$g\left(\frac{\pi}{2}\right)=-2\cos\left(4\cdot\frac{\pi}{2}\right)-1$$
$$=-2\cos(2\pi)-1=-2\cdot1-1=-3$$

The coordinate of the point P is $\left(\frac{\pi}{2}, -3\right)$.

06

Notice that $-1\le\cos 2x\le1$. So the function $f(x)=1-\cos(2x)$ has a maximum value when $\cos(2x)=-1$. Therefore, $2x=\pi$, $x=\frac{\pi}{2}$. (C) is the answer.

07

If $y=2\cos x$ is shifted $\frac{\pi}{4}$ units to the left and 4 units up, we have the equation $y=2\cos\left(x+\frac{\pi}{4}\right)+4$. So the answer is (B).

08

We can easily find the answer by comparing the graphs of sine and cosine.

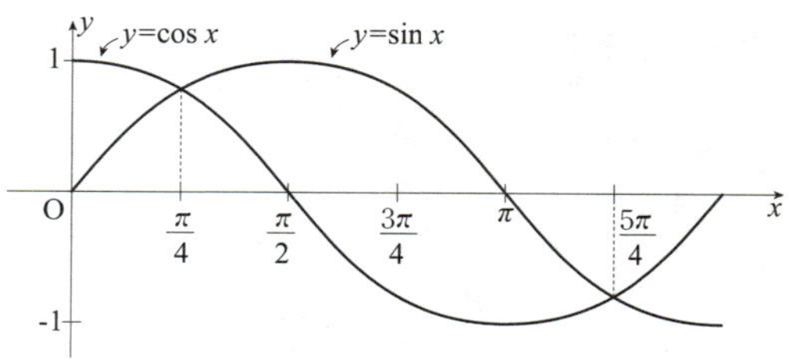

In the domain of $0<x<\frac{5\pi}{4}$, $\sin x<\cos x$ when $0<x<\frac{\pi}{4}$. So the answer is (A).

09

(A) and (B) : the graph of sine and cosine decreases on the interval $\left(\frac{\pi}{2}, \pi\right)$.
(C) : The graph of tangent always increases where the function is defined.
(D) : The graph of cotangent always decreases where the function is defined.
So the answer is (C).

10

The equation of asymptote :
$x=\frac{\pi}{4}+n\pi,\ n\in Z$

The period : $\frac{9\pi}{4}-\frac{\pi}{4}=2\pi$

The graph is a reciprocal of $y=2\sin x$ where shifted $\frac{\pi}{4}$ units to the right.
So the graph of the Figure is
$y=2\csc\left(x-\frac{\pi}{4}\right)$. The answer is (A).

11

The amplitude : 1
The period : $\pi-0=\pi$
Since the graph starts at -1, the function is $y=-\cos(2x)$. So $a+b=-1+2=1$.

12

The graph of $y=2\sin(2x)$ has an amplitude of 2 and a period of π as shown below.

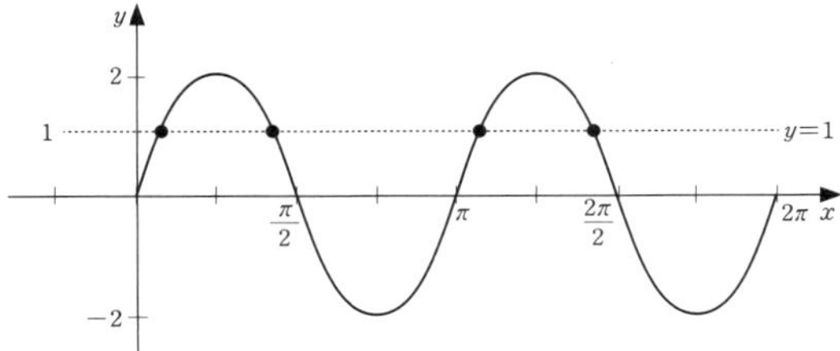

Therefore, there are 4 values of x on $0<x<2\pi$ for which $y=1$. The correct answer is (C).

13

In the second quadrant, the sine function is positive and decreasing. Since y is greater than x and both angles are in the second quadrant, $\sin y$ will be less than $\sin x$ because the sine function decreases in this range. Therefore, the correct answer is (C).

14

In the third quadrant, the tangent function is positive and increasing. Since y is greater than x and both angles are in the third quadrant, $\tan y$ will be greater than $\tan x$ because the tangent function increases in this range. Therefore, the correct answer is (A).

15

The value of the function $\cos x$ represents the vertical displacement from the $x-$axis. Therefore, the correct answer is (D).

16

The cosine function $\cos\left(2x-\frac{\pi}{2}\right)$ reaches its maximum value of 1 when $2x-\frac{\pi}{2}=0$.

$2x-\frac{\pi}{2}=0 \Rightarrow 2x=\frac{\pi}{2},\ x=\frac{\pi}{4}$

Therefore, the maximum value of $f(x)$ occurs at $x=\frac{\pi}{4}$.

The correct answer is (B).

17

The graph of $y=\sin\left(\frac{x}{2}\right)$ has a period of 4π as shown below.

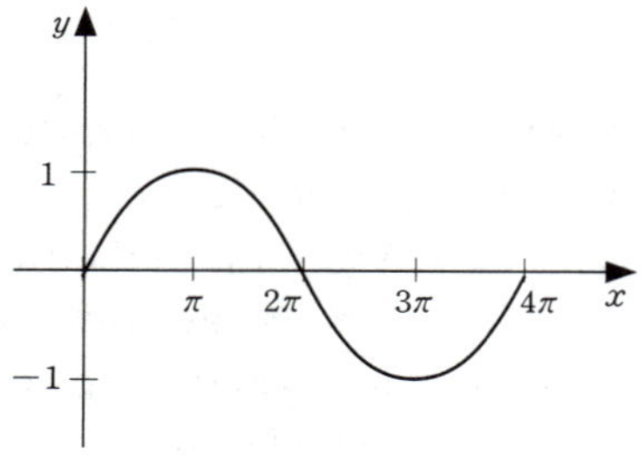

Therefore, the interval where $\sin\left(\frac{x}{2}\right)$ is increasing and concave up is $3\pi<x<4\pi$.
The answer is (D).

18

The frequency f is the reciprocal of the period T. Since the period of the graph is $\frac{1}{4}$, the frequency f is:

$$f=\frac{1}{T}=\frac{1}{\frac{1}{4}}=4$$

19

The sine function can be represented as a cosine function with a phase shift. Specifically,

$\sin x=\cos\left(x-\frac{\pi}{2}\right)$ or $\cos x=\sin\left(x+\frac{\pi}{2}\right)$.

This relationship shows that the sine function is equivalent to the cosine function shifted to the right by $\frac{\pi}{2}$ or that the cosine function is equivalent to the sine function shifted to the left by $\frac{\pi}{2}$.

Therefore, the correct answer is (B).

20

The tangent function $\tan x$ is an odd function, meaning $\tan(-x)=-\tan x$. The absolute value function $|\tan x|$ is even because $|\tan(-x)|=|-\tan x|=|\tan x|$.
Therefore, the correct answer is (B).

21

The maximum value is 12 and the minimum value is 4.

Amplitude $a=\frac{12-4}{2}=4$

Vertical shift $c=\frac{12+4}{2}=8$

The period 8 corresponds to $\frac{2\pi}{b}=8,\ b=\frac{\pi}{4}$.

Therefore, the function f is $f(x)=4\cos\left(\frac{\pi}{4}x\right)+8$ and the value of abc is

$abc=(4)\left(\frac{\pi}{4}\right)(8)=8\pi$

22

The vertical asymptotes occur where the angle of the tangent function equals $\frac{\pi}{2}+\pi n$ for integer n:

$$2x-\pi=\frac{\pi}{2}+\pi n$$

$$2x=\frac{3\pi}{2}+\pi n,\ x=\frac{3\pi}{4}+\frac{\pi n}{2}=\frac{\pi}{4}+\frac{\pi n}{2}$$

Therefore, the correct answer is (B).

23

The period 2π corresponds to

$$\frac{\pi}{b}=2\pi,\quad b=\frac{1}{2}.$$

Vertical shift $c=1$. Therefore, the function f is $f(x)=\tan\left(\frac{1}{2}x\right)+1$ and the value of $b+c$ is $b+c=\frac{1}{2}+1=\frac{3}{2}$.

24

$\csc x$ has vertical asymptotes where $\sin x=0$ and $\sin x=0$ at $x=\pi n$, where n is an integer. Therefore, the correct answer is (D).

25

The cotangent function $\cot(2x-\pi)$ has vertical asymptotes where

$$2x-\pi=\pi n$$

$$2x=\pi+\pi n,\ x=\frac{\pi+\pi n}{2}=\frac{\pi n}{2}$$

Therefore, the correct answer is (C).

26

The sine function $\sin x$ ranges from -1 to 1.

When $\sin x=-1$, $f(x)=2-\frac{3}{2}(-1)=3.5$

When $\sin x=1$, $f(x)=2-\frac{3}{2}(1)=0.5$

Therefore, the range of the function f is $0.5\leq y\leq 3.5$. The answer is (D).

27

The secant function $\sec x$ has a range of $(-\infty,\ -1]\cup[1,\ \infty)$.

Therefore, $1+2\sec(x+\pi)$ ranges

$1+2(-\infty,\ -1]\cup[1,\ \infty)=[-\infty,\ -1]\cup[3,\ \infty)$.

The correct answer is (B).

4. Inverse Trigonometric Functions

Check Point 1

① If $\arccos\frac{1}{2}=y$,

then $\frac{1}{2}=\cos y$ in the range of $[0, \pi]$.

Since $\cos\frac{\pi}{3}=\frac{1}{2}$, $\arccos\frac{1}{2}=\frac{\pi}{3}$.

② If $\sin^{-1}\left(-\frac{1}{2}\right)=y$,

then $-\frac{1}{2}=\sin y$ in the range of $\left[-\frac{\pi}{2}, \frac{\pi}{2}\right]$.

Since $\sin\left(-\frac{\pi}{6}\right)=-\frac{1}{2}$, $\sin^{-1}\left(-\frac{1}{2}\right)=-\frac{\pi}{6}$.

③ If $\cos^{-1}\frac{\sqrt{2}}{2}=y$,

then $\frac{\sqrt{2}}{2}=\cos y$ in the range of $[0, \pi]$.

Since $\cos\frac{\pi}{4}=\frac{\sqrt{2}}{2}$, $\cos^{-1}\frac{\sqrt{2}}{2}=\frac{\pi}{4}$.

④ If $\sin^{-1}(-1)=y$,

then $-1=\sin y$ in the range of $\left[-\frac{\pi}{2}, \frac{\pi}{2}\right]$.

Since $\sin\left(-\frac{\pi}{2}\right)=-1$, $\sin^{-1}(-1)=-\frac{\pi}{2}$.

Check Point 2

① If $\tan^{-1}(-1)=y$,

then $-1=\tan y$ in the range of $\left(-\frac{\pi}{2}, \frac{\pi}{2}\right)$.

Since $\tan\left(-\frac{\pi}{4}\right)=-1$, $\tan^{-1}(-1)=-\frac{\pi}{4}$.

② If $\arctan\left(-\frac{1}{\sqrt{3}}\right)=y$,

then $-\frac{1}{\sqrt{3}}=\tan y$ in the range of $\left(-\frac{\pi}{2}, \frac{\pi}{2}\right)$.

Since $\tan\left(-\frac{\pi}{6}\right)=-\frac{1}{\sqrt{3}}$,

$\arctan\left(-\frac{1}{\sqrt{3}}\right)=-\frac{\pi}{6}$.

Check Point 3

① First, $\cos\frac{\pi}{4}=\frac{\sqrt{2}}{2}$. If $\arcsin\frac{\sqrt{2}}{2}=y$,

then $\sin y=\frac{\sqrt{2}}{2}$ in the range of $\left[-\frac{\pi}{2}, \frac{\pi}{2}\right]$.

Since $\sin\frac{\pi}{4}=\frac{\sqrt{2}}{2}$, $\frac{\pi}{4}=\arcsin\frac{\sqrt{2}}{2}$.

Thus, $\arcsin\left(\cos\frac{\pi}{4}\right)=\arcsin\frac{\sqrt{2}}{2}=\frac{\pi}{4}$.

② First, $\cos\frac{11\pi}{6}=\frac{\sqrt{3}}{2}$. If $\cos^{-1}\left(\frac{\sqrt{3}}{2}\right)=y$,

then $\cos y=\frac{\sqrt{3}}{2}$ in the range of $[0, \pi]$.

Since $\cos\frac{\pi}{6}=\frac{\sqrt{3}}{2}$, $\frac{\pi}{6}=\cos^{-1}\frac{\sqrt{3}}{2}$.

Thus, $\cos^{-1}\left(\cos\frac{11\pi}{6}\right)=\cos^{-1}\frac{\sqrt{3}}{2}=\frac{\pi}{6}$.

③ If $\arctan\sqrt{3}=y$, then $\tan y=\sqrt{3}$ in the range of $\left(-\frac{\pi}{2}, \frac{\pi}{2}\right)$.

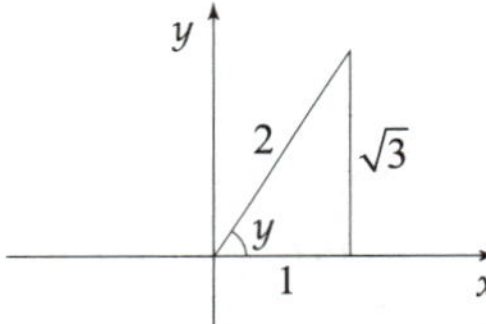

Thus, $\sin(\arctan\sqrt{3})=\sin y=\frac{\sqrt{3}}{2}$.

④ If $\sin^{-1}\left(-\frac{1}{5}\right)=y$, then $\sin y=-\frac{1}{5}$

in the range of $\left[-\frac{\pi}{2}, \frac{\pi}{2}\right]$.

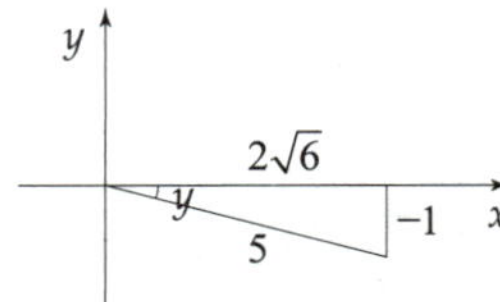

Thus, $\tan\left(\sin^{-1}\left(-\frac{1}{5}\right)\right)=\tan y=\frac{-1}{2\sqrt{6}}=-\frac{\sqrt{6}}{12}$.

⑤ If $\cos^{-1}\frac{1}{\sqrt{3}}=y$, then $\cos y=\frac{1}{\sqrt{3}}$ in the range of $[0, \pi]$.

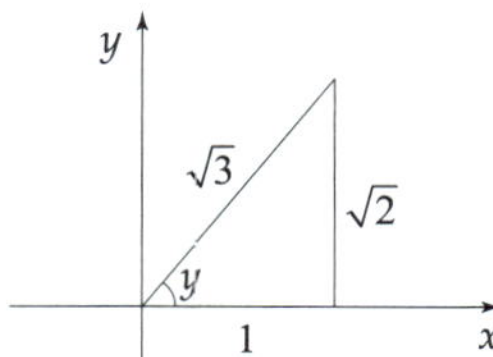

Thus, $\sin\left(\cos^{-1}\frac{1}{\sqrt{3}}\right)=\sin y=\frac{\sqrt{2}}{\sqrt{3}}=\frac{\sqrt{6}}{3}$.

Review Exercises

01

(1) If $\sin^{-1}\frac{\sqrt{3}}{2}=y$, then $\frac{\sqrt{3}}{2}=\sin y$ in the range of $\left[-\frac{\pi}{2}, \frac{\pi}{2}\right]$.

Since $\sin\frac{\pi}{3}=\frac{\sqrt{3}}{2}$, $\sin^{-1}\frac{\sqrt{3}}{2}=\frac{\pi}{3}$.

(2) If $\arctan(-\sqrt{3})=y$, then $-\sqrt{3}=\tan y$ in the range of $\left(-\frac{\pi}{2}, \frac{\pi}{2}\right)$.

Since $\tan\left(-\frac{\pi}{3}\right)=-\sqrt{3}$, $\arctan(-\sqrt{3})=-\frac{\pi}{3}$.

(3) If $\cos^{-1}1=y$, then $1=\cos y$ in the range of $[0, \pi]$.

Since $\cos 0=1$, $\cos^{-1}1=0$.

(4) It is impossible to evaluate $\arcsin(-4)$ because -4 is not in the domain of $y=\arcsin x$.

So $\arcsin(-4)$ is undefined.

02

(1) $\tan\theta=\frac{x}{5}$, $\theta=\tan^{-1}\frac{x}{5}$

(2) $\cos\theta=\frac{4}{x+1}$, $\theta=\cos^{-1}\frac{4}{x+1}$

03

(1) First $\sin\frac{5\pi}{3}=-\frac{\sqrt{3}}{2}$.

If we let $\arcsin\left(-\frac{\sqrt{3}}{2}\right)=y$, then $-\frac{\sqrt{3}}{2}=\sin y$ in the range of $\left[-\frac{\pi}{2}, \frac{\pi}{2}\right]$.

Since $\sin\left(-\frac{\pi}{3}\right)=-\frac{\sqrt{3}}{2}$, $-\frac{\pi}{3}=\arcsin\left(-\frac{\sqrt{3}}{2}\right)$.

Thus, $\arcsin\left(\sin\frac{5\pi}{3}\right)=\arcsin\left(-\frac{\sqrt{3}}{2}\right)=-\frac{\pi}{3}$.

(2) If $\cos^{-1}\frac{5}{13}=y$, then $\frac{5}{13}=\cos y$ in the range of $[0, \pi]$.

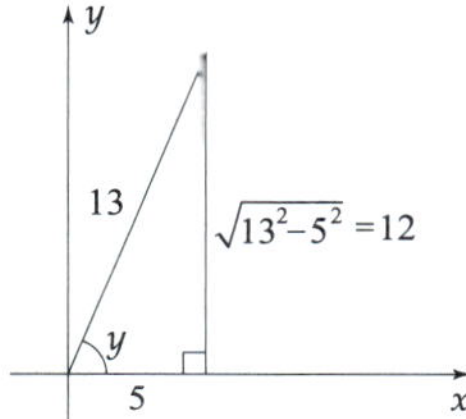

Thus, $\sin\left(\cos^{-1}\frac{5}{13}\right)=\sin y=\frac{12}{13}$.

(3) First $\sin(3\pi)=0$.

If we let $\cos^{-1}0=y$, then $0=\cos y$ in the range of $[0, \pi]$.

Since $\cos\frac{\pi}{2}=0$, $\frac{\pi}{2}=\cos^{-1}0$.

Thus, $\cos^{-1}(\sin(3\pi))=\cos^{-1}0=\frac{\pi}{2}$.

(4) If $\tan^{-1}(-2)=y$, then $-2=\tan y$ in the range of $\left(-\frac{\pi}{2}, \frac{\pi}{2}\right)$.

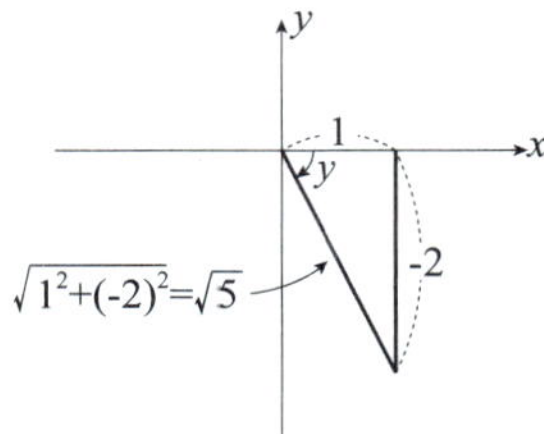

Thus, $\sin(\tan^{-1}(-2))=\sin y=-\frac{2}{\sqrt{5}}=-\frac{2\sqrt{5}}{5}$.

04

(1) If $\sin^{-1}x=y$, then $x=\sin y$.

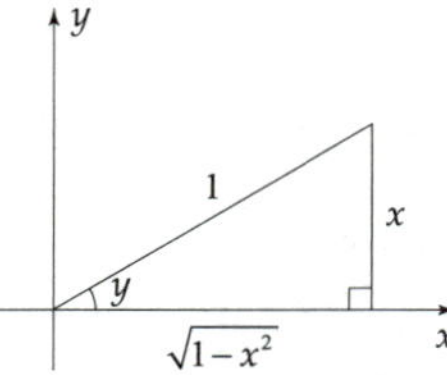

Thus, $\sec(\sin^{-1}x)=\sec y=\dfrac{1}{\sqrt{1-x^2}}$.

(2) If $\tan^{-1}\dfrac{1}{x}=y$, then $\tan y=\dfrac{1}{x}$.

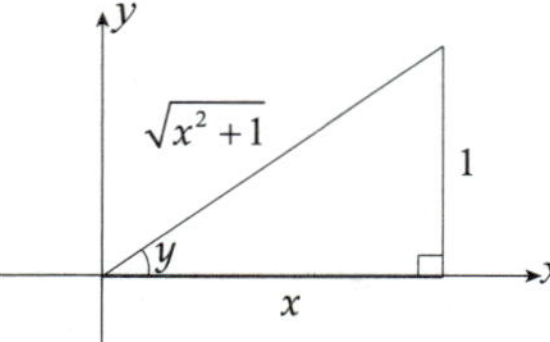

Thus, $\cos\left(\tan^{-1}\dfrac{1}{x}\right)=\cos y=\dfrac{x}{\sqrt{x^2+1}}$.

05

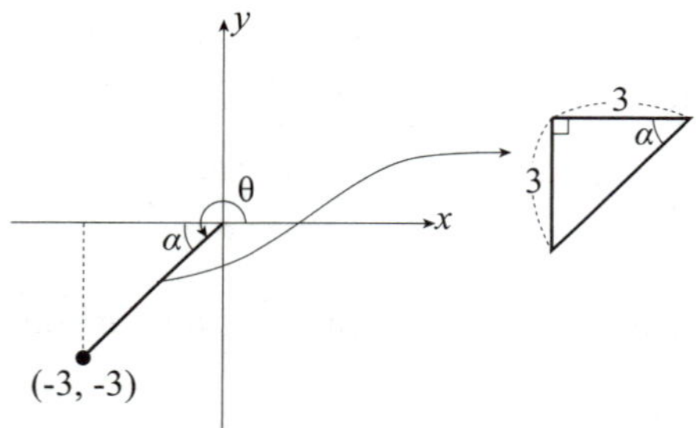

$\tan\alpha=\dfrac{3}{3}=1,\ \alpha=\tan^{-1}1=\dfrac{\pi}{4}$

$\theta=\pi+\alpha=\pi+\dfrac{\pi}{4}=\dfrac{5\pi}{4}$.

06

Since $\tan x=\dfrac{2}{5}$ and $\pi\le x<\dfrac{3\pi}{2}$, the angle x must be in third quadrant and the point $P(-5,\ -2)$ is one of the possible coordinate with angle x as shown in Figure.

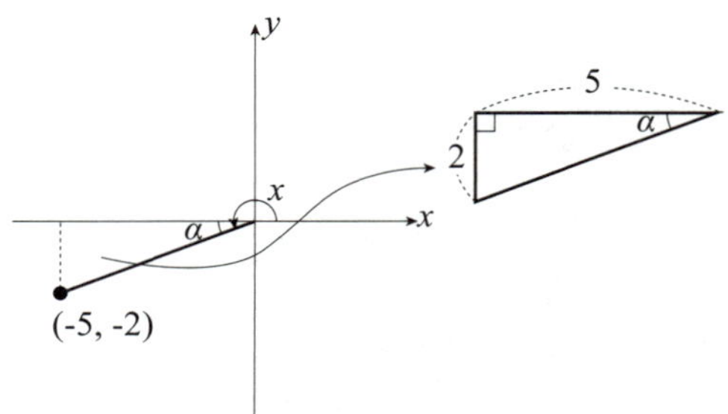

$\tan\alpha=\dfrac{2}{5},\ \alpha=\tan^{-1}\left(\dfrac{2}{5}\right)$

$x=\pi+\alpha=\pi+\tan^{-1}\left(\dfrac{2}{5}\right)$

Therefore,

$\cos x=\cos\left(\pi+\tan^{-1}\left(\dfrac{2}{5}\right)\right)=-0.928$.

07

The sine function $2\sin(2x)$ has a range of $[-2,\ 2]$. The range of $f(x)$ becomes the domain of $f^{-1}(x)$. Therefore, the domain of the inverse function $f^{-1}(x)$ is $[-2,\ 2]$.

08

The cosine function $\dfrac{1}{2}\cos(2\pi x)$ has a range of $\left[-\dfrac{1}{2},\ \dfrac{1}{2}\right]$. The range of $f(x)$ becomes the domain of $f^{-1}(x)$. Therefore, the domain of the inverse function $f^{-1}(x)$ is $\left[-\dfrac{1}{2},\ \dfrac{1}{2}\right]$.

09

The length of the largest interval over which the inverse function can be defined corresponds to one complete increasing or decreasing section of the function. Therefore, the length of the largest interval of $x-$values over which the inverse function of f can be defined is 4, either from 0 to 4 or from 4 to 8.

10

$y=2\sin(\pi x) \Rightarrow x=2\sin(\pi y)$

$\frac{x}{2}=\sin(\pi y)$

$\pi y=\arcsin\left(\frac{x}{2}\right),\ y=\frac{1}{\pi}\arcsin\left(\frac{x}{2}\right)$

Therefore, the correct answer is (B).

11

Using Pythagorean theorem,

$BC=\sqrt{4^2-k^2}=\sqrt{16-k^2}$

Now, using the definition of sine:

$$\sin\theta=\frac{\sqrt{16-k^2}}{4}$$

$$\theta=\sin^{-1}\frac{\sqrt{16-k^2}}{4}$$

$$h(k)=\sin^{-1}\frac{\sqrt{16-k^2}}{4}$$

Therefore, the correct answer is (A).

12

Using Pythagorean theorem,

$x=\sqrt{(1-a)^2-1^2}=\sqrt{a^2-2a}=\sqrt{a(a-2)}$

Now, using the definition of cosine:

$$\cos\theta=\frac{x}{1-a}=\frac{\sqrt{a(a-2)}}{1-a}$$

$$\theta=\cos^{-1}\frac{\sqrt{a(a-2)}}{1-a}$$

Therefore, the correct answer is (C).

5. Real-Life Problems with Trigonometry

Check Point 1

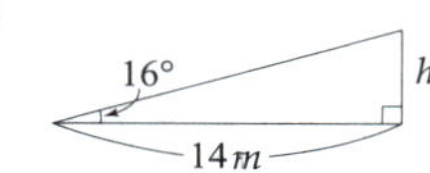

h : the height of the post

$\tan 16°=\frac{h}{14},\ h=14\tan 16° \approx 4.014$

Approximately 4.014 meters

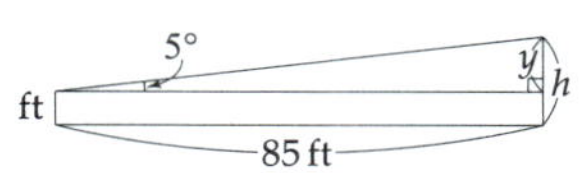

h : the height of the tree and $h=y+5$

$\tan 5°=\frac{y}{85},\ y=85\tan 5°$

So $h=85\tan 5°+5 \approx 12.437$.

Approximately 12.437 feet

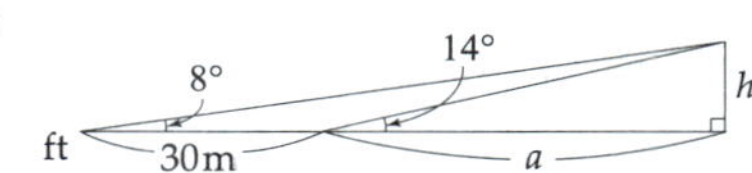

h : the height of the building

$\tan 14°=\frac{h}{a},\ a=\frac{h}{\tan 14°}$

$\tan 8°=\frac{h}{a+30},\ a+30=\frac{h}{\tan 8°},\ a=\frac{h}{\tan 8°}-30$

So we have $\frac{h}{\tan 14°}=\frac{h}{\tan 8°}-30$.

$$\frac{h}{\tan 8°}-\frac{h}{\tan 14°}=30$$

$$h\left(\frac{1}{\tan 8°}-\frac{1}{\tan 14°}\right)=30$$

$$h=30\div\left(\frac{1}{\tan 8°}-\frac{1}{\tan 14°}\right)\approx 9.663$$

Approximately 9.663 meters

④ 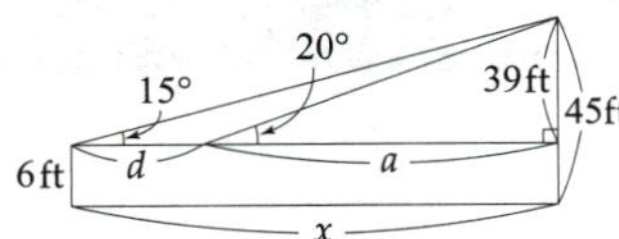

d : the distance the person traveled

$\tan 15° = \frac{39}{x}$, $x = \frac{39}{\tan 15°}$

$\tan 20° = \frac{39}{a}$, $a = \frac{39}{\tan 20°}$

$d = x - a$

$= \frac{39}{\tan 15°} - \frac{39}{\tan 20°} \approx 38.398.$

Approximately 38.398 feet

Check Point 2

① From the function $f(x) = 3\cos(3\pi t)$,

Amplitude : $|a| = |3| = 3$ inches

Period : $p = \frac{2\pi}{w} = \frac{2\pi}{3\pi} = \frac{2}{3}$ second

Frequency :

$f = \frac{1}{p} = \frac{3}{2}$ cycles per second(Hz)

② 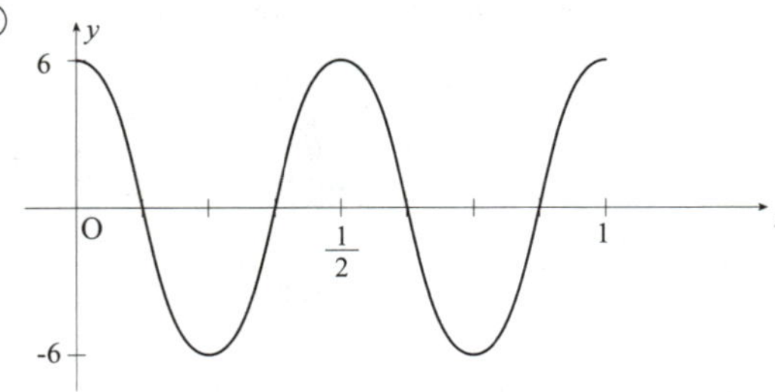

(A) Since the displacement at $t=0$ is a maximum, it would be better to use $y = a\cos(wt)$ to describe the motion. Knowing that the amplitude is 6 and the period is 0.5, we have

$a = 6$ and $p = \frac{2\pi}{w} = 0.5$, $w = 4\pi$.

Therefore, putting it together, we get $y = 6\cos(4\pi t)$.

(B) The displacement of the mass after 1.2 seconds is $y(1.2) = 6\cos(4\pi(1.2)) \approx -4.854$.

Review Exercises

01

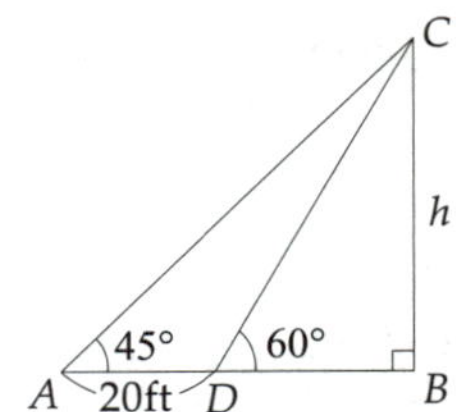

h : the height of the building

First, the triangle BCD is $30°-60°-90°$ right triangle. So $\overline{BD} = \frac{h}{\sqrt{3}}$. Also, the triangle ABC is isosceles right triangle. So $\overline{AB} = \overline{BC}$. Therefore,

$20 + \frac{h}{\sqrt{3}} = h$, $h\left(1 - \frac{1}{\sqrt{3}}\right) = 20$

$h = 20 \div \left(1 - \frac{1}{\sqrt{3}}\right) \approx 47.321$

Approximately 47.321 ft

02

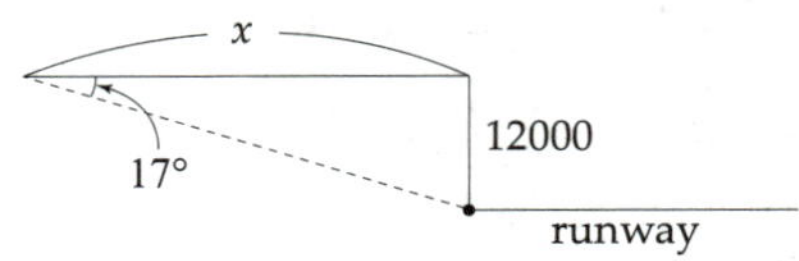

x : the horizontal distance from runway

$\tan 17° = \frac{12,000}{x}$

$x = \frac{12,000}{x} \approx 39,250.2$

Approximately 39,250.2 feet

03

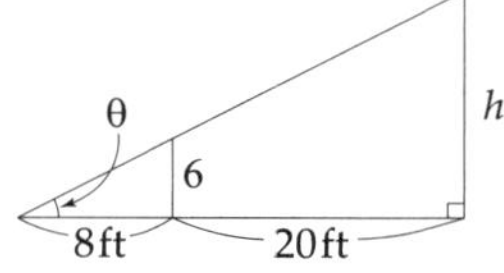

h : the height of the post

Using the similarity of the triangle,

$\frac{h}{6}=\frac{8+20}{8}$, $8h=168$, $h=21$

Approximately 21 feet

04

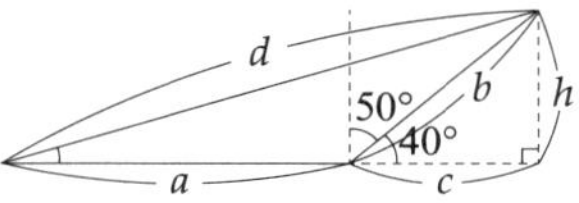

d : the directed distance Steven traveled

$a=80\times4=320$, $b=80\times2=160$

$\sin 40°=\frac{h}{b}$, $h=160\sin 40°\approx102.846$

By the Pythagorean theorem,

$c^2+h^2=b^2$, $c=\sqrt{160^2-102.846^2}\approx122.567$

$(a+c)^2+h^2=d^2$,

$d=\sqrt{(320+122.567)^2+102.846^2}\approx454.36$

Approximately 454.36 miles

05

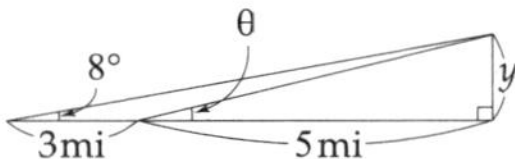

θ : angle of elevation to the top of the mountain

$\tan 8°=\frac{y}{3+5}$, $y=8\tan 8°$

$\tan\theta=\frac{y}{5}=\frac{8\tan 8°}{5}$

$\theta=\tan^{-1}\left(\frac{8\tan 8°}{5}\right)\approx12.673°$

Approximately 12.673°

06

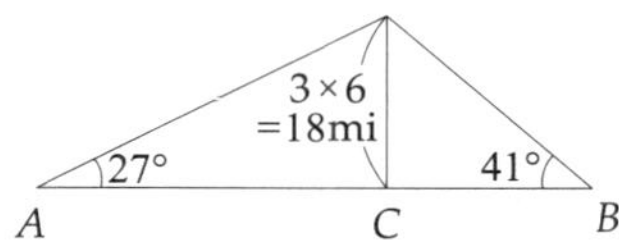

$\tan 27°=\frac{18}{\overline{AC}}$, $\overline{AC}=\frac{18}{\tan 27°}$

$\tan 41°=\frac{18}{\overline{CB}}$, $\overline{CB}=\frac{18}{\tan 41°}$

$\overline{AB}=\overline{AC}+\overline{CB}=\frac{18}{\tan 27°}+\frac{18}{\tan 41°}\approx56.034$

Approximately 56.034 miles

07

$\frac{8\ rev}{60\ \sec}=\frac{1\ rev}{x\ \sec}\rightarrow x=\frac{15}{2}$ sec

$y=k+a\cos(w(t-h))$

Amplitude : $a=6$

Period : $\frac{2\pi}{w}=\frac{15}{2}\rightarrow w=\frac{4\pi}{15}$

Horizontal shift : $h=2$

Veritacal shift : $k=4$

Therefore, $y=4+6\cos\left(\frac{4\pi}{15}(t-2)\right)$

08

Since the displacement at $t=0$ is $y=0$, it would be better to use $y=a\sin(wt)$ to describe the motion. Knowing that the amplitude is 3 and the period is $\frac{1}{3}$, we have

$a=3$ and $p=\frac{2\pi}{w}=\frac{1}{3}$, $w=6\pi$.

Therefore, putting it together, we get

$y=3\sin(6\pi t)$.

09

Since the amplitude of

$y=-0.4\cos\left(\frac{2\pi}{5}t\right)+20$ is $a=|-0.4|=0.4$,

the maximum displacement is

0.4+20=20.4 meters. Also, since the period is $p=\frac{2\pi}{\frac{2\pi}{5}}=5$, the frequency is $f=\frac{1}{p}=\frac{1}{5}$.

10

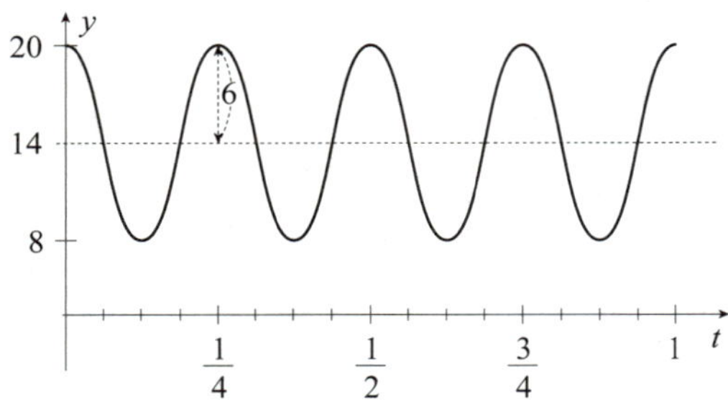

(1) The amplitude is $a=\frac{20-8}{2}=6$.

(2) Since the mass oscillates 4 cycles per second, the period of this motion is $p=\frac{1}{f}=\frac{1}{4}$.

(3) We can use $y=a\cos(wt)+d$ to describe the motion.
we have $a=6$, $p=\frac{2\pi}{w}=\frac{1}{4} \rightarrow w=8\pi$, and $d=14$. Therefore, putting it together, we get $y=6\cos(8\pi t)+14$.

(4) The distance between maximum and minimum displacement is $20-8=12$ cm. Since the mass travels $2\times 12=24$ cm in $\frac{1}{4}$ sec (one period), the total distance the mass travels in 2 seconds is

$$\frac{24\text{ cm}}{\frac{1}{4}\text{ sec}}=\frac{x\text{ cm}}{2\text{ sec}}$$

$\frac{x}{4}=48$, $x=192$ cm

11

Amplitude $A=\frac{\text{Peak}-\text{Lowest}}{2}=\frac{90-60}{2}=15$.

The correct answer is (A).

12

The midline h is the average of the highest and lowest water levels

$$A=\frac{\text{Highest}+\text{Lowest}}{2}=\frac{10+2}{2}=6$$

The value for h is 6.

13

Amplitude

$A=\frac{\text{Highest}-\text{Lowest}}{2}=\frac{90-60}{2}=15$.

Midline $M=\frac{\text{Highest}+\text{Lowest}}{2}=\frac{90+60}{2}=75$.

The general form of the sinusoidal function is

$f(t)=a\sin(b(t-c))+d$.

Given the 24−hour period, $\frac{2\pi}{b}=24$, $b=\frac{\pi}{12}$.

So the function could be

$f(t)=15\sin\left(\frac{\pi}{12}(t-2)\right)+75$.

The correct answer is (A).

14

The period of the function g is $\frac{2\pi}{\frac{2\pi}{365}}=365$.

So the function g completes one full cycle every 365 days. The cosine function g increases over the interval 0 to 182.5 days and concave down in the interval $92<t<182$. Therefore, the correct answer is (B).

15

Amplitude: Radius=25m(half the diameter).
Vertical shift: Midline=25m(radius)+5m (lowest point)=30m.
Given the 4 minute period, $\frac{2\pi}{b}=4$, $b=\frac{\pi}{2}$.
The rider starts at the lowest point, so the function is a cosine function starting at its minimum. So the correct answer is (B).

16

Maximum temperature: 22°C at 12 hours.
Minimum temperature: 10°C at 0 and 24 hours.

Midline: $\frac{22+10}{2}=16$°C.

Amplitude A$=\frac{22-10}{2}=6$°C.

Given the 24−hour period, $\frac{2\pi}{b}=24$, $b=\frac{\pi}{12}$.

So the function can be either

$$T(t)=-6\cos\left(\frac{\pi}{12}t\right)+16 \text{ or}$$

$$T(t)=6\sin\left(\frac{\pi}{12}(t-6)\right)+16.$$

The correct answer is (C).

17

Amplitude $A=6$cm.

Given the 6−second period, $\frac{2\pi}{b}=6$, $b=\frac{\pi}{3}$.

So the function is $D=-6\cos\left(\frac{\pi}{3}t\right)$.

The correct answer is (D)

6. Fundamental Trigonometric Identities

Check Point 1

① $\cos\theta=\frac{1}{\sqrt{2}}$, $\tan\theta<0$

Since $\cos\theta>0$ and $\tan\theta<0$, θ lies in Quadrant IV. From $\sin^2\theta+\cos^2\theta=1$, we have

$$\sin^2\theta=1-\cos^2\theta=1-\left(\frac{1}{\sqrt{2}}\right)^2=\frac{1}{2},$$

$$\sin\theta=-\frac{1}{\sqrt{2}}$$

$$\csc\theta=\frac{1}{\sin\theta}=-\sqrt{2},\ \sec\theta=\frac{1}{\cos\theta}=\sqrt{2}$$

$$\tan\theta=\frac{\sin\theta}{\cos\theta}=\frac{-\frac{1}{\sqrt{2}}}{\frac{1}{\sqrt{2}}}=-1,\ \cot\theta=\frac{1}{\tan\theta}=-1$$

$\sin\theta=-\frac{\sqrt{2}}{2}$, $\cos\theta=\frac{\sqrt{2}}{2}$, $\tan\theta=-1$
$\csc\theta=-\sqrt{2}$, $\sec\theta=\sqrt{2}$, $\cot\theta=-1$

② $\sin\theta=\frac{1}{2}$, $\cos\theta<0$

Since $\sin\theta>0$ and $\cos\theta<0$, θ lies in Quadrant II. From $\sin^2\theta+\cos^2\theta=1$, we have

$$\cos^2\theta=1-\sin^2\theta=1-\left(\frac{1}{2}\right)^2=\frac{3}{4},\ \cos\theta=-\frac{\sqrt{3}}{2}$$

$$\csc\theta=\frac{1}{\sin\theta}=2,\ \sec\theta=\frac{1}{\cos\theta}=-\frac{2}{\sqrt{3}}=-\frac{2\sqrt{3}}{3}$$

$$\tan\theta=\frac{\sin\theta}{\cos\theta}=\frac{\frac{1}{2}}{-\frac{\sqrt{3}}{2}}=\frac{1}{\sqrt{3}}=-\frac{\sqrt{3}}{3}$$

$$\cot\theta=\frac{1}{\tan\theta}=-\sqrt{3}$$

$\sin\theta=\frac{1}{2}$, $\cos\theta=-\frac{\sqrt{3}}{2}$, $\tan\theta=-\frac{\sqrt{3}}{3}$
$\csc\theta=2$, $\sec\theta=-\frac{2\sqrt{3}}{3}$, $\cot\theta=-\sqrt{3}$

③ $\tan\theta=-2$, $\cos\theta>0$

Since $\tan\theta<0$ and $\cos\theta>0$, θ lies in Quadrant IV. From $1+\tan^2\theta=\sec^2\theta$, we have

$1+(-2)^2=\sec^2\theta$, $5=\sec^2\theta$, $\sec\theta=\sqrt{5}$

$\cos\theta=\dfrac{1}{\sec\theta}=\dfrac{1}{\sqrt{5}}=\dfrac{\sqrt{5}}{5}$

$\tan\theta=\dfrac{\sin\theta}{\cos\theta}$,

$\sin\theta=\tan\theta\cdot\cos\theta=-2\cdot\dfrac{\sqrt{5}}{5}=-\dfrac{2\sqrt{5}}{5}$

$\csc\theta=\dfrac{1}{\sin\theta}=-\dfrac{\sqrt{5}}{2}$, $\cot\theta=\dfrac{1}{\tan\theta}=-\dfrac{1}{2}$

$\sin\theta=-\dfrac{2\sqrt{5}}{5}$, $\cos\theta=\dfrac{\sqrt{5}}{5}$, $\tan\theta=-2$

$\csc\theta=-\dfrac{\sqrt{5}}{2}$, $\sec\theta=\sqrt{5}$, $\cot\theta=-\dfrac{1}{2}$

④ $\sec\theta=4$, $\sin\theta>0$

Since $\sec\theta>0$ and $\sin\theta>0$, θ lies in Quadrant I. From $1+\tan^2\theta=\sec^2\theta$, we have

$1+\tan^2\theta=4^2$, $\tan^2\theta=15$, $\tan\theta=\sqrt{15}$

$\cos\theta=\dfrac{1}{\sec\theta}=\dfrac{1}{4}$, $\cot\theta=\dfrac{1}{\tan\theta}=\dfrac{1}{\sqrt{15}}=\dfrac{\sqrt{15}}{15}$

$\tan\theta=\dfrac{\sin\theta}{\cos\theta}$, $\sin\theta=\tan\theta\cdot\cos\theta=\sqrt{15}\cdot\dfrac{1}{4}=\dfrac{\sqrt{15}}{4}$

$\csc\theta=\dfrac{1}{\sin\theta}=\dfrac{4}{\sqrt{15}}=\dfrac{4\sqrt{15}}{15}$

$\sin\theta=\dfrac{\sqrt{15}}{4}$, $\cos\theta=\dfrac{1}{4}$, $\tan\theta=\sqrt{15}$

$\csc\theta=\dfrac{4\sqrt{15}}{15}$, $\sec\theta=4$, $\cot\theta=\dfrac{\sqrt{15}}{15}$

Check Point 2

① $\tan\left(-\dfrac{\pi}{6}\right)=-\tan\dfrac{\pi}{6}=-\dfrac{1}{\sqrt{3}}=-\dfrac{\sqrt{3}}{3}$

② $\sec\left(-\dfrac{5\pi}{3}\right)=\sec\dfrac{5\pi}{3}=2$

Check Point 3

① $\cos\dfrac{\pi}{3}=\sin\left(\dfrac{\pi}{2}-\dfrac{\pi}{3}\right)=\sin\dfrac{\pi}{6}=\dfrac{1}{2}$

② $\csc\dfrac{\pi}{6}=\sec\left(\dfrac{\pi}{2}-\dfrac{\pi}{6}\right)=\sec\dfrac{\pi}{3}=2$

Check Point 4

① $\sin\left(\dfrac{\pi}{2}-\theta\right)\sec\theta=\cos\theta\cdot\dfrac{1}{\cos\theta}=1$

② $\dfrac{1-\cos^2\theta}{\cos^2\theta-1}=\dfrac{1-\cos^2\theta}{-(1-\cos^2\theta)}=-1$

③ $\dfrac{\sin^2\theta}{1-\cos\theta}-\cos\theta=\dfrac{\sin^2\theta}{1-\cos\theta}-\dfrac{\cos\theta\,(1-\cos\theta)}{1-\cos\theta}$

$=\dfrac{\sin^2\theta-\cos\theta\,(1-\cos\theta)}{1-\cos\theta}$

$=\dfrac{\sin^2\theta-\cos\theta+\cos^2\theta}{1-\cos\theta}$ → $\sin^2\theta+\cos^2\theta=1$

$=\dfrac{1-\cos\theta}{1-\cos\theta}=1$

④ $\sin\theta\sec\theta+\cos\theta\csc\theta=\dfrac{\sin\theta}{\cos\theta}+\dfrac{\cos\theta}{\sin\theta}$

$=\dfrac{\sin^2\theta}{\cos\theta\sin\theta}+\dfrac{\cos^2\theta}{\cos\theta\sin\theta}$ → $\sin^2\theta+\cos^2\theta=1$

$=\dfrac{1}{\cos\theta\sin\theta}=\sec\theta\csc\theta$

Check Point 5

① Let $\cos x = A$.

$\cos^2 x - \cos x - 2 = A^2 - A - 2$

$= (A+1)(A-2) = (\cos x + 1)(\cos x - 2)$

② Let $\tan\theta = A$.

$\tan^3\theta - 4\tan\theta = A^3 - 4A$

$= A(A^2-4) = A(A-2)(A+2)$

$= \tan\theta(\tan\theta - 2)(\tan\theta + 2)$

③ $\cos^2\theta\sec^2\theta - \cos^2\theta = \cos^2\theta(\sec^2\theta - 1)$

$= \cos^2\theta(1+\tan^2\theta - 1)$

$= \cos^2\theta\tan^2\theta = \cos^2\theta \cdot \dfrac{\sin^2\theta}{\cos^2\theta} = \sin^2\theta$

④ Let $\cot\theta = A$.

$2\cot^4\theta - 4\cot^2\theta + 2 = 2A^4 + 4A^2 + 2$

$= 2(A^4 - 2A^2 + 1) = 2(A^2+1)^2$

$= 2(\cot^2\theta + 1)^2$

$= 2(\csc^2\theta)^2 = 2\csc^4\theta$

Check Point 6

① $\sec\theta - \cos\theta = \sin\theta\tan\theta$

Work on left side to reach right side.

$$\sec\theta - \cos\theta = \frac{1}{\cos\theta} - \frac{\cos^2\theta}{\cos\theta}$$
$$= \frac{1-\cos^2\theta}{\cos\theta} = \frac{\sin^2\theta}{\cos\theta}$$
$$= \sin\theta\frac{\sin\theta}{\cos\theta} = \sin\theta\tan\theta$$

② $\sin^2\theta - \cos^2\theta = 1 - 2\cos^2\theta$

Work on left side to reach right side.

$\sin^2\theta - \cos^2\theta = (1-\cos^2\theta) - \cos^2\theta$

$= 1 - 2\cos^2\theta$

③ $\tan\theta + \cot\theta = \sec\theta\csc\theta$

Work on left side to reach right side.

$$\tan\theta + \cot\theta = \frac{\sin\theta}{\cos\theta} + \frac{\cos\theta}{\sin\theta}$$
$$= \frac{\sin^2\theta + \cos^2\theta}{\cos\theta\sin\theta}$$
$$= \frac{1}{\cos\theta\sin\theta} = \sec\theta\csc\theta$$

④ $-\cot^2\theta = (1+\csc\theta)(1+\csc(-\theta))$

Work on right side to reach left side.

$(1+\csc\theta)(1+\csc(-\theta))$

$= (1+\csc\theta)(1-\csc\theta) = 1 - \csc^2\theta$

$= 1 - (1+\cot^2\theta) = -\cot^2\theta$

⑤ $\sin\theta(1+\cot^2\theta) = \csc\theta$

Work on left side to reach right side.

$\sin\theta(1+\cot^2\theta) = \sin\theta(\csc^2\theta)$

$= \sin\theta \cdot \dfrac{1}{\sin^2\theta} = \dfrac{1}{\sin\theta} = \csc\theta$

⑥ $\cot\theta = \dfrac{\sin\left(\frac{\pi}{2} - \theta\right)}{\sin\theta}$

Work on right side to reach left side.

$$\frac{\sin\left(\frac{\pi}{2}-\theta\right)}{\sin\theta} = \frac{\cos\theta}{\sin\theta} = \cot\theta$$

Review Exercises

01

$\sec\theta = -\dfrac{5}{2}$, $\cos\theta = \dfrac{1}{\sec\theta} = -\dfrac{2}{5}$

Since $\sec\theta < 0$ and $\sin\theta > 0$, θ lies in Quadrant II. From $\sin^2\theta + \cos^2\theta = 1$, we have

$\sin^2\theta = 1 - \cos^2\theta = 1 - \left(-\dfrac{2}{5}\right)^2 = \dfrac{21}{25}$, $\sin\theta = \dfrac{\sqrt{21}}{5}$

$\csc\theta = \dfrac{1}{\sin\theta} = \dfrac{5}{\sqrt{21}} = \dfrac{5\sqrt{21}}{21}$

$$\tan\theta = \frac{\sin\theta}{\cos\theta} = \frac{\frac{\sqrt{21}}{5}}{-\frac{2}{5}} = -\frac{\sqrt{21}}{2}$$

$\cot\theta = \dfrac{1}{\tan\theta} = -\dfrac{2}{\sqrt{21}} = -\dfrac{2\sqrt{21}}{21}$

$\sin\theta = \dfrac{\sqrt{21}}{5}$, $\cos\theta = -\dfrac{2}{5}$, $\tan\theta = -\dfrac{\sqrt{21}}{2}$

$\csc\theta = \dfrac{5\sqrt{21}}{21}$, $\sec\theta = -\dfrac{5}{2}$, $\cot\theta = -\dfrac{2\sqrt{21}}{21}$

02

(1) Using the identity $\cot\theta=\dfrac{1}{\tan\theta}$,

$$\frac{\cot\theta+1}{\tan\theta+1}=\frac{\frac{1}{\tan\theta}+\frac{\tan\theta}{\tan\theta}}{\tan\theta+1}=\frac{\frac{1+\tan\theta}{\tan\theta}}{\tan\theta+1}$$

$$=\frac{1+\tan\theta}{\tan\theta(\tan\theta+1)}=\frac{1}{\tan\theta}=\cot\theta$$

(2) Using the identity $\sin(-\theta)=-\sin\theta$ and $\cos(-\theta)=\cos\theta$,

$$\frac{\sin(-\theta)}{1+\cos(-\theta)}-\frac{\sin(-\theta)}{1-\cos(-\theta)}$$

$$=\frac{-\sin\theta}{1+\cos\theta}+\frac{\sin\theta}{1-\cos\theta}$$

$$=\frac{-\sin\theta(1-\cos\theta)+\sin\theta(1+\cos\theta)}{(1+\cos\theta)(1-\cos\theta)}$$

$$=\frac{-\sin\theta+\sin\theta\cos\theta+\sin\theta+\sin\theta\cos\theta}{(1+\cos\theta)(1-\cos\theta)}$$

$$=\frac{2\sin\theta\cos\theta}{1-\cos^2\theta}\rightarrow 1-\cos^2\theta=\sin^2\theta$$

$$=\frac{2\sin\theta\cos\theta}{\sin^2\theta}=\frac{2\cos\theta}{\sin\theta}=2\cot\theta$$

(3) $\dfrac{1}{\cos^2\theta}-\sin\theta\sec\theta\tan\theta$

$$=\frac{1}{\cos^2\theta}-\sin\theta\frac{1}{\cos\theta}\frac{\sin\theta}{\cos\theta}$$

$$=\frac{1-\sin^2\theta}{\cos^2\theta}=\frac{\cos^2\theta}{\cos^2\theta}=1$$

(4) $\dfrac{\cos\theta-1}{\sin\theta}+\dfrac{\sin\theta}{\cos\theta-1}=\dfrac{(\cos\theta-1)^2+\sin^2\theta}{\sin\theta(\cos\theta-1)}$

$$=\frac{\cos^2\theta-2\cos\theta+1+\sin^2\theta}{\sin\theta(\cos\theta-1)}$$

$$=\frac{-2\cos\theta+2}{\sin\theta(\cos\theta-1)}=-\frac{2(\cos\theta-1)}{\sin\theta(\cos\theta-1)}$$

$$=-2\csc\theta$$

03

Using the identity $\tan(-x)=-\tan x$ and $\sec(-x)=\sec x$,

$\tan x-\tan(-x)+\sec x-\sec(-x)$

$=\tan x+\tan x+\sec x-\sec x$

$=2\tan x$

So the answer is (A).

04

Since $\sin^2\theta+\cos^2\theta=1$, $\cos^2\theta=1-\sin^2\theta$.

$1+\cos^2\theta-\sin\theta=1+(1-\sin^2\theta)-\sin\theta$

$=-(\sin^2\theta+\sin\theta-2)$

Let $\sin\theta=A$.

$-(\sin^2\theta+\sin\theta-2)=-(A^2+A-2)$

$=-(A+2)(A-1)=-(\sin\theta+2)(\sin\theta-1)$

$1+\cos^2\theta-\sin\theta=-(\sin\theta+2)(\sin\theta-1)$

05

Using the identity $\sin(-\theta)=-\sin\theta$ and $\cos(-\theta)=\cos\theta$,

$e^{\frac{\sin\theta}{\cos\theta}}\cdot e^{\frac{\sin(-x)}{\cos(-x)}}=e^{\frac{\sin\theta}{\cos\theta}}\cdot e^{\frac{-\sin\theta}{\cos\theta}}$

$=e^{\tan x}\cdot e^{-\tan x}=e^{\tan x-\tan x}=e^0=1$

06

(A) $\cos(2x)\sec(2x)=\cos(2x)\dfrac{1}{\cos(2x)}=1$

(B) $\sqrt{\sin^2 x+\cos x^2}=\sqrt{1}=1$

(C) $\dfrac{1}{\cos^2 x}-\dfrac{\sin^2 x}{\cos^2 x}=\dfrac{1-\sin^2 x}{\cos^2 x}=\dfrac{\cos^2 x}{\cos^2 x}=1$

(D) $\sin\left(\dfrac{\pi}{2}-x\right)-\cos x=\cos x-\cos x=0$

(E) $\dfrac{\sec x}{\cos x}-\dfrac{\tan x}{\cot x}=\sec x\cdot\dfrac{1}{\cos x}-\tan x\cdot\dfrac{1}{\cot x}$

$=\sec x\cdot\sec x-\tan x\cdot\tan x$

$=\sec^2 x-\tan^2 x=1$

Therefore, the answer is (D).

07

By definition of unit circle, $\overline{AC}=\sin\theta$ and $\overline{OC}=\cos\theta$. So, $\overline{BC}=1-\cos\theta$.

Using the Pythagorean theorem,

$$\overline{AB}=\sqrt{(\overline{AC})^2+(\overline{BC})^2}=\sqrt{\sin^2\theta+(1-\cos\theta)^2}$$
$$=\sqrt{\sin^2\theta+1-2\cos\theta+\cos^2\theta}$$
$$=\sqrt{(\sin^2\theta+\cos^2\theta)+1-2\cos\theta}$$
$$=\sqrt{1+1-2\cos\theta}=\sqrt{2-2\cos\theta}$$

The answer is (A).

08

(1) $\sin\theta+\cos\theta=\dfrac{\tan\theta+1}{\sec\theta}$

Work on right side to reach left side.

$$\frac{\tan\theta+1}{\sec\theta}=\frac{\frac{\sin\theta}{\cos\theta}+\frac{\cos\theta}{\cos\theta}}{\frac{1}{\cos\theta}}$$
$$=\frac{\frac{\sin\theta+\cos\theta}{\cos\theta}}{\frac{1}{\cos\theta}}=\sin\theta+\cos\theta$$

(2) $\dfrac{1}{\sec\theta-\tan\theta}=\sec\theta+\tan\theta$

Work on left side to reach right side.

$$\frac{1}{\sec\theta-\tan\theta}=\frac{1}{\sec\theta-\tan\theta}\cdot\frac{\sec\theta+\tan\theta}{\sec\theta+\tan\theta}$$
$$=\frac{\sec\theta+\tan\theta}{\sec^2\theta-\tan^2\theta}$$
$$=\frac{\sec\theta+\tan\theta}{1}=\sec\theta+\tan\theta$$

(3) $-\dfrac{\sin\theta}{1+\cos\theta}=\dfrac{\cos\theta-1}{\sin\theta}$

Work on left side to reach right side.

$$-\frac{\sin\theta}{1+\cos\theta}=-\frac{\sin\theta}{1+\cos\theta}\cdot\frac{1-\cos\theta}{1-\cos\theta}$$
$$=-\frac{\sin\theta(1-\cos\theta)}{1-\cos^2\theta}$$
$$=-\frac{\sin\theta(1-\cos\theta)}{\sin^2\theta}$$
$$=\frac{\cos\theta-1}{\sin\theta}$$

(4) $2\cot\theta=\dfrac{\sin\theta}{1-\cos\theta}-\dfrac{\sin\theta}{1+\cos\theta}$

Work on right side to reach left side.

$$\frac{\sin\theta}{1-\cos\theta}-\frac{\sin\theta}{1+\cos\theta}$$
$$=\frac{\sin\theta(1+\cos\theta)-\sin\theta(1-\cos\theta)}{(1-\cos\theta)(1+\cos\theta)}$$
$$=\frac{\sin\theta+\sin\theta\cos\theta-\sin\theta+\sin\theta\cos\theta}{1-\cos^2\theta}$$
$$=\frac{2\sin\theta\cos\theta}{1-\cos^2\theta}$$
$$=\frac{2\sin\theta\cos\theta}{\sin^2\theta}$$
$$=\frac{2\cos\theta}{\sin\theta}=2\cot\theta$$

(5) $\dfrac{\sin\theta}{1-\cos\theta}=\dfrac{1}{\csc\theta-\cot\theta}$

Work with each side separately.

Left side :

$$\frac{\sin\theta}{1-\cos\theta}=\frac{\sin\theta}{1-\cos\theta}\cdot\frac{1+\cos\theta}{1+\cos\theta}$$
$$=\frac{\sin\theta(1+\cos\theta)}{1-\cos^2\theta}$$
$$=\frac{\sin\theta(1+\cos\theta)}{\sin^2\theta}$$
$$=\frac{1+\cos\theta}{\sin\theta}=\frac{1}{\sin\theta}+\frac{\cos\theta}{\sin\theta}$$
$$=\csc\theta+\cot\theta$$

Right side :

$$\frac{1}{\csc\theta-\cot\theta}=\frac{1}{\csc\theta-\cot\theta}\cdot\frac{\csc\theta+\cot\theta}{\csc\theta+\cot\theta}$$
$$=\frac{\csc\theta+\cot\theta}{\csc^2\theta-\cot^2\theta}$$
$$=\frac{\csc\theta+\cot\theta}{1}$$
$$=\csc\theta+\cot\theta$$

So the identity is verified.

(6) $\sin\theta\cos\theta=\dfrac{1}{\tan\theta+\cot\theta}$

Work on right side to reach left side.

$$\frac{1}{\tan\theta+\cot\theta}=\frac{1}{\frac{\sin\theta}{\cos\theta}+\frac{\cos\theta}{\sin\theta}}=\frac{1}{\frac{\sin^2\theta+\cos^2\theta}{\cos\theta\sin\theta}}$$
$$=\frac{1}{\frac{1}{\cos\theta\sin\theta}}=\sin\theta\cos\theta$$

(7) $\sin\theta(\cos^4\theta-2\cos^2\theta+1)=\sin^5\theta$

Work on left side to reach right side.

$\sin\theta(\cos^4\theta-2\cos^2\theta+1)=\sin\theta(\cos^2-1)^2$

$=\sin\theta(-\sin^2\theta)^2=\sin\theta\cdot\sin^4\theta=\sin^5\theta$

(8) $\sec^5\theta\tan^3\theta$

$=\sec^6\theta(\sec\theta\tan\theta)-\sec^4\theta(\sec\theta\tan\theta)$

Work on right side to reach left side.

$\sec^6\theta(\sec\theta\tan\theta)-\sec^4\theta(\sec\theta\tan\theta)$

$=\sec^7\theta\tan\theta-\sec^5\theta\tan\theta$

$=\sec^5\theta\tan\theta(\sec^2\theta-1)\rightarrow\sec^2\theta-1=\tan^2\theta$

$=\sec^5\theta\tan\theta\cdot\tan^2\theta=\sec^5\theta\tan^3\theta$

(9) $\dfrac{\cot\theta-\tan\theta}{\cot\theta+\tan\theta}=\cos^2\theta-\sin^2\theta$

Work on left side to reach right side.

$$\frac{\cot\theta-\tan\theta}{\cot\theta+\tan\theta}=\frac{\frac{\cos\theta}{\sin\theta}-\frac{\sin\theta}{\cos\theta}}{\frac{\cos\theta}{\sin\theta}+\frac{\sin\theta}{\cos\theta}}=\frac{\frac{\cos^2\theta-\sin^2\theta}{\sin\theta\cos\theta}}{\frac{\cos^2\theta+\sin^2\theta}{\sin\theta\cos\theta}}$$
$$=\frac{\cos^2\theta-\sin^2\theta}{\cos^2\theta+\sin^2\theta}=\cos^2\theta-\sin^2\theta$$

(10) $3\csc^2\theta-3\csc^2\theta\cos^2\theta-\cos^2\theta-\sin^2\theta=2$

Work on left side to reach right side.

$3\csc^2\theta-3\csc^2\theta\cos^2\theta-\cos^2\theta-\sin^2\theta$

$=3\csc^2\theta(1-\cos^2\theta)-(\cos^2\theta+\sin^2\theta)$

$=3\dfrac{1}{\sin^2\theta}(\sin^2\theta)-1=3-1=2$

09

Use the identity: $\sin^2\left(\frac{1}{x}\right)+\cos^2\left(\frac{1}{x}\right)=1$ for $x=m,\ n,\ k$. Therefore,

$\cos^2\left(\frac{1}{m}\right)+\cos^2\left(\frac{1}{n}\right)+\cos^2\left(\frac{1}{k}\right)=3-2.47=0.53$

10

Simplify the denominator: $\cos^2x-1=-\sin^2x$

$-\dfrac{\sin x}{\cos^2x-1}=-\dfrac{\sin x}{-\sin^2x}=\dfrac{1}{\sin x}=\csc x$

The correct answer is (D).

11

Use the identity: $\tan^2x+1=\sec^2x$

Since $\sec x=\dfrac{1}{\cos x}=\dfrac{5}{4}$,

$\tan^2x+1=\sec^2x=\left(\dfrac{5}{4}\right)^2=\dfrac{25}{16}$.

12

I. $\sec(2x)\csc(2x)=\dfrac{1}{\cos(2x)}\cdot\dfrac{1}{\sin(2x)}\neq1$

II. Use the identity: $\tan^2x+1=\sec^2x$

$\sec^2x-\left(\dfrac{\sin x}{\cos x}\right)^2=\sec^2x-\tan^2x=1$

III. Use the Double−Angle identity:

$\cos(2x)=1-2\sin^2x$

$2\sin^2x+\cos(2x)=2\sin^2x+1-2\sin^2x=1$

Therefore, expression II and III are correct. The answer is (D).

13

$\tan x=\dfrac{1}{a},\ \dfrac{\sin x}{\cos x}=\dfrac{1}{a},\ a=\dfrac{\cos x}{\sin x}$

$\sin x=\dfrac{1}{b},\ b=\dfrac{1}{\sin x}$

Therefore,

$a+b=\frac{\cos x}{\sin x}+\frac{1}{\sin x}=\frac{1+\cos x}{\sin x}$

The correct answer is (D).

14

Simplify each part:

$\sin(-x)=-\sin x,\ \cos(-x)=\cos x$

Therefore,

$2^{\sin x\ \cos x}\cdot 2^{\sin(-x)\cos(-x)}=2^{\sin x\ \cos x}\cdot 2^{-\sin x\ \cos x}$

$=2^{\sin x\ \cos x}\cdot\frac{1}{2^{\sin x\ \cos x}}=1$

The correct answer is (A).

7. Trigonometric Equations and Identities, Part I

Check Point 1

① $\sqrt{2}\sin x+1=0$

$\sin x=-\frac{1}{\sqrt{2}} \rightarrow x=\frac{5\pi}{4}$ and $x=\frac{7\pi}{4}$

The solutions are $x=\frac{5\pi}{4}$ and $x=\frac{7\pi}{4}$

General Solution :

$x=\frac{5\pi}{4}+2\pi n(n\in Z),\ x=\frac{7\pi}{4}+2\pi n(n\in Z)$

② $\sqrt{3}\sec x+2=0$

$\sec x=-\frac{2}{\sqrt{3}} \rightarrow x=\frac{5\pi}{6}$ and $x=\frac{7\pi}{6}$

The solutions are $x=\frac{5\pi}{6}$ and $x=\frac{7\pi}{6}$

General Solution :

$x=\frac{5\pi}{6}+2\pi n(n\in Z),\ x=\frac{7\pi}{6}+2\pi n(n\in Z)$

③ $\sin^2 x=\sin x$

$\sin^2 x-\sin x=0,\ \sin x(\sin x-1)=0$

$\sin x=0$ or $\sin x=1$

$\sin x=0 \rightarrow x=0$ and $x=\pi$

$\sin x=1 \rightarrow x=\frac{\pi}{2}$

The solutions are $x=0,\ x=\frac{\pi}{2}$ and $x=\pi$

General Solution :

$x=\pi n(n\in Z),\ x=\frac{\pi}{2}+2\pi n(n\in Z)$

④ $\tan x-2\tan x\cos x=0$

$\tan x(1-2\cos x)=0$

$\tan x=0$ or $\cos x=\frac{1}{2}$

$\tan x=0 \rightarrow x=0$ and $x=\pi$

$\cos x=\frac{1}{2} \rightarrow x=\frac{\pi}{3}$ and $x=\frac{5\pi}{3}$

The solutions are $x=0,\ x=\frac{\pi}{3},\ x=\pi$ and $x=\frac{5\pi}{3}$

General Solution :

$x=\pi n(n\in Z),\ x=\frac{\pi}{3}+2\pi n(n\in Z)$

$x=\frac{5\pi}{3}+2\pi n(n\in Z)$

Check Point 2

① $\sin(2x)=1$

$2x=\frac{\pi}{2},\ 2x=\frac{5\pi}{2} \rightarrow x=\frac{\pi}{4},\ x=\frac{5\pi}{4}$

The solutions are $x=\frac{\pi}{4}$ and $x=\frac{5\pi}{4}$

General Solution :

$2x=\frac{\pi}{2}+2\pi n(n\in Z) \rightarrow x=\frac{\pi}{4}+\pi n(n\in Z)$

② $\sin x(2\cos(2x)+1)=0$

$\sin x=0$ or $2\cos(2x)+1=0$

$\sin x=0 \rightarrow x=0$ and $x=\pi$

$2\cos(2x)+1=0,\ \cos(2x)=-\frac{1}{2}$

$2x=\frac{2\pi}{3},\ 2x=\frac{4\pi}{3},\ 2x=\frac{8\pi}{3}$, and $2x=\frac{10\pi}{3}$

$\rightarrow x=\frac{\pi}{3},\ x=\frac{2\pi}{3},\ x=\frac{4\pi}{3}$, and $x=\frac{5\pi}{3}$

The solutions are $x=0,\ x=\frac{\pi}{3},\ x=\frac{2\pi}{3}$,
$x=\pi,\ x=\frac{4\pi}{3}$, and $x=\frac{5\pi}{3}$

General Solution :

$x=\pi n(n\in Z)$

$2x=\frac{2\pi}{3}+2\pi n(n\in Z) \rightarrow x=\frac{\pi}{3}+\pi n(n\in Z)$

$2x=\frac{4\pi}{3}+2\pi n(n\in Z) \rightarrow x=\frac{2\pi}{3}+\pi n(n\in Z)$

Check Point 3

① $1+\sin x-2\cos^2 x=0$

$1+\sin x-2(1-\sin^2 x)=0$

$2\sin^2 x+\sin x-1=0$

$(2\sin x-1)(\sin x+1)=0$

$2\sin x-1=0$ or $\sin x+1=0$

$\sin x=\frac{1}{2}$ or $\sin x=-1$

$\sin x=\frac{1}{2} \rightarrow x=\frac{\pi}{6}$ and $x=\frac{5\pi}{6}$

$\sin x=-1 \rightarrow x=\frac{3\pi}{2}$

The solutions are $x=\frac{\pi}{6},\ x=\frac{5\pi}{6}$ and $x=\frac{3\pi}{2}$

General Solution :

$x=\frac{\pi}{6}+2\pi n(n\in Z),\ x=\frac{5\pi}{6}+2\pi n(n\in Z)$

$x=\frac{3\pi}{2}+2\pi n(n\in Z)$

② $\tan^2 x=3-2\sec^2 x$

$\tan^2 x=3-2(1+\tan^2 x)$

$\tan^2 x=3-2-2\tan^2 x,\ 3\tan^2 x=1$

$\tan^2 x=\frac{1}{3},\ \tan x=\pm\frac{1}{\sqrt{3}}$

$\tan x=\frac{1}{\sqrt{3}} \rightarrow x=\frac{\pi}{6}$ and $x=\frac{7\pi}{6}$

$\tan x=-\frac{1}{\sqrt{3}} \rightarrow x=\frac{5\pi}{6}$ and $x=\frac{11\pi}{6}$

The solutions are $x=\frac{\pi}{6},\ x=\frac{5\pi}{6},\ x=\frac{7\pi}{6}$
and $x=\frac{11\pi}{6}$

General Solution :

$x=\frac{\pi}{6}+\pi n(n\in Z),\ x=\frac{5\pi}{6}+\pi n(n\in Z)$

Check Point 4

① $\sin 105°=\sin(60°+45°)$

$=\sin 60°\cos 45°+\cos 60°\sin 45°$

$=\frac{\sqrt{3}}{2}\frac{\sqrt{2}}{2}+\frac{1}{2}\frac{\sqrt{2}}{2}=\frac{\sqrt{6}+\sqrt{2}}{4}$

② $\cos\frac{7\pi}{12}=\cos\left(\frac{\pi}{4}+\frac{\pi}{3}\right)$

$=\cos\frac{\pi}{4}\cos\frac{\pi}{3}-\sin\frac{\pi}{4}\sin\frac{\pi}{3}$

$=\frac{\sqrt{2}}{2}\frac{1}{2}-\frac{\sqrt{2}}{2}\frac{\sqrt{3}}{2}=\frac{\sqrt{2}-\sqrt{6}}{4}$

③ $\sin 100°\cos 35°+\cos 100°\sin 35°$

$=\sin(100+35)°=\sin 135°=\frac{\sqrt{2}}{2}$

④ $\cos\frac{\pi}{12}\cos\frac{\pi}{4}+\sin\frac{\pi}{12}\sin\frac{\pi}{4}$

$=\cos\left(\frac{\pi}{12}-\frac{\pi}{4}\right)=\cos\left(-\frac{\pi}{6}\right)=\frac{\sqrt{3}}{2}$

⑤ $\tan\frac{11\pi}{12}=\tan\left(\frac{2\pi}{3}+\frac{\pi}{4}\right)$

$$=\frac{\tan\frac{2\pi}{3}+\tan\frac{\pi}{4}}{1-\tan\frac{2\pi}{3}\tan\frac{\pi}{4}}$$

$$=\frac{-\sqrt{3}+1}{1-(-\sqrt{3}\cdot 1)}$$

$$=\frac{1-\sqrt{3}}{1+\sqrt{3}}=\sqrt{3}-2$$

⑥ $$\frac{\tan\frac{\pi}{8}-\tan\frac{3\pi}{8}}{1+\tan\frac{\pi}{8}\tan\frac{3\pi}{8}}=\tan\left(\frac{\pi}{8}-\frac{3\pi}{8}\right)$$

$$=\tan\left(-\frac{\pi}{4}\right)=-1$$

Check Point 5

$\sin\left(x+\frac{\pi}{4}\right)+\sin\left(x-\frac{\pi}{4}\right)=1$

$\sin x\cos\frac{\pi}{4}+\cos x\sin\frac{\pi}{4}+\sin x\cos\frac{\pi}{4}$

$-\cos x\sin\frac{\pi}{4}=1$

$2\sin x\cos\frac{\pi}{4}=1$

$2\sin x\left(\frac{\sqrt{2}}{2}\right)=1$

$\sin x=\frac{1}{\sqrt{2}}\rightarrow x=\frac{\pi}{4}$ and $x=\frac{3\pi}{4}$

The solutions are $x=\frac{\pi}{4}$ and $x=\frac{3\pi}{4}$

General Solution :

$x=\frac{\pi}{4}+2\pi n(n\in Z)$, $x=\frac{3\pi}{4}+2\pi n(n\in Z)$

Review Exercises

01

(1) $2\cos^2 x+\cos x=0$

$\cos x(2\cos x+1)=0$

$\cos x=0\rightarrow x=\frac{\pi}{2}$ and $x=\frac{3\pi}{2}$

$\cos x=-\frac{1}{2}\rightarrow x=\frac{2\pi}{3}$ and $x=\frac{4\pi}{3}$

The solutions are $x=\frac{\pi}{2}$, $x=\frac{2\pi}{3}$, $x=\frac{4\pi}{3}$

and $x=\frac{3\pi}{2}$

General Solution :

$x=\frac{\pi}{2}+\pi n(n\in Z)$

$x=\frac{2\pi}{3}+2\pi n(n\in Z)$, $x=\frac{4\pi}{3}+2\pi n(n\in Z)$

(2) $4\sin^2 x-1=0$, $4\sin^2 x=1$

$\sin^2 x=\frac{1}{4}$, $\sin x=\pm\frac{1}{2}$

$\sin x=\frac{1}{2}\rightarrow x=\frac{\pi}{6}$ and $x=\frac{5\pi}{6}$

$\sin x=-\frac{1}{2}\rightarrow x=\frac{7\pi}{6}$ and $x=\frac{11\pi}{6}$

The solutions are $x=\frac{\pi}{6}$, $x=\frac{5\pi}{6}$, $x=\frac{7\pi}{6}$

and $x=\frac{11\pi}{6}$

General Solution :

$x=\frac{\pi}{6}+\pi n(n\in Z)$, $x=\frac{5\pi}{6}+\pi n(n\in Z)$

(3) $3\tan(3x)+\sqrt{3}=0$

$3\tan(3x)=-\sqrt{3}$, $\tan(3x)=-\frac{\sqrt{3}}{3}$

$3x=\frac{5\pi}{6}$, $3x=\frac{11\pi}{6}$, $3x=\frac{17\pi}{6}$, $3x=\frac{23\pi}{6}$,

$3x=\frac{29\pi}{6}$, and $\frac{35\pi}{6}$

$\rightarrow x=\frac{5\pi}{18}$, $x=\frac{11\pi}{18}$, $x=\frac{17\pi}{18}$, $x=\frac{23\pi}{18}$,

$x=\frac{29\pi}{18}$, and $\frac{35\pi}{18}$

The solutions are $x=\frac{5\pi}{18}$, $x=\frac{11\pi}{18}$,

$x=\frac{17\pi}{18}$, $x=\frac{23\pi}{18}$, $x=\frac{29\pi}{18}$, and $\frac{35\pi}{18}$

General Solution :

$3x=\frac{5\pi}{6}-\pi n(n\in Z)\rightarrow x=\frac{5\pi}{18}+\frac{\pi n}{3}(n\in Z)$

(4) $\tan^2 x-2\tan x-3=0$

$(\tan x-3)(\tan x+1)=0$

$\tan x=3\rightarrow x\approx 1.249$ and $x\approx 4.391$

$\tan x=-1\rightarrow x=\frac{3\pi}{4}$ and $x=\frac{7\pi}{4}$

The solutions are $x=1.249$, $x=\frac{3\pi}{4}$,

$x=4.391$ and $x=\frac{7\pi}{4}$

General Solution :

$x\approx 1.249+\pi n(n\in Z)$, $x=\frac{3\pi}{4}+\pi n(n\in Z)$

(5) $\sec x \tan x - 4\sin x = 0$

$\frac{1}{\cos x} \cdot \frac{\sin x}{\cos x} - 4\sin x = 0$

$\sin x\left(\frac{1}{\cos^2 x} - 4\right) = 0$

$\sin x(\sec^2 x - 4) = 0$

$\sin x(\sec x - 2)(\sec x + 2) = 0$

$\sin x = 0 \rightarrow x = 0$ and $x = \pi$

$\sec x = 2$, $\cos x = \frac{1}{2} \rightarrow x = \frac{\pi}{3}$ and $x = \frac{5\pi}{3}$

$\sec x = -2$, $\cos x = -\frac{1}{2} \rightarrow x = \frac{2\pi}{3}$ and $x = \frac{4\pi}{3}$

The solutions are $x=0$, $x=\frac{\pi}{3}$, $x=\frac{2\pi}{3}$,

$x=\pi$, $x=\frac{4\pi}{3}$, $x=\frac{5\pi}{3}$

General Solution :

$x=\pi n(n\in Z)$, $x=\frac{\pi}{3}+\pi n(n\in Z)$

$x=\frac{2\pi}{3}+\pi n(n\in Z)$

(6) $2\sin^2(3x)+\sin(3x)-1=0$

$(2\sin(3x)-1)(\sin(3x)+1)=0$

$\sin(3x)=\frac{1}{2}$

$3x=\frac{\pi}{6}$, $3x=\frac{5\pi}{6}$, $3x=\frac{13\pi}{6}$, $3x=\frac{17\pi}{6}$,

$3x=\frac{25\pi}{6}$, and $3x=\frac{29\pi}{6}$

$\rightarrow x=\frac{\pi}{18}$, $x=\frac{5\pi}{18}$, $x=\frac{13\pi}{18}$, $x=\frac{17\pi}{18}$,

$x=\frac{25\pi}{18}$, and $x=\frac{29\pi}{18}$

$\sin(3x)=-1$

$3x=\frac{3\pi}{2}$, $3x=\frac{7\pi}{2}$, and $3x=\frac{11\pi}{2}$

$\rightarrow x=\frac{\pi}{2}$, $x=\frac{7\pi}{6}$, and $x=\frac{11\pi}{6}$

The solutions are $x=\frac{\pi}{18}$, $x=\frac{5\pi}{18}$, $x=\frac{\pi}{2}$,

$x=\frac{13\pi}{18}$, $x=\frac{17\pi}{18}$, $x=\frac{7\pi}{6}$, $\frac{25\pi}{18}$,

$x=\frac{29\pi}{18}$ and $x=\frac{11\pi}{6}$

General Solution :

$3x=\frac{\pi}{6}+2\pi n(n\in Z) \rightarrow x=\frac{\pi}{18}+\frac{2\pi n}{3}$ $(n\in Z)$,

$3x=\frac{5\pi}{6}+2\pi n(n\in Z) \rightarrow x=\frac{5\pi}{18}+\frac{2\pi n}{3}$ $(n\in Z)$,

$3x=\frac{3\pi}{2}+2\pi n(n\in Z) \rightarrow x=\frac{\pi}{2}+\frac{2\pi n}{3}$ $(n\in Z)$

(7) $\tan^3 x=3\tan x$, $\tan^3 x-3\tan x=0$

$\tan x(\tan^2 x-3)=0$

$\tan x=0 \rightarrow x=0$ and $x=\pi$

$\tan^2 x=3$, $\tan x=\pm\sqrt{3}$

$\tan x=\sqrt{3} \rightarrow x=\frac{\pi}{3}$ and $x=\frac{4\pi}{3}$

$\tan x=-\sqrt{3} \rightarrow x=\frac{2\pi}{3}$ and $x=\frac{5\pi}{3}$

The solutions are $x=0$, $x=\frac{\pi}{3}$, $x=\frac{2\pi}{3}$,

$x=\pi$, $x=\frac{4\pi}{3}$ and $x=\frac{5\pi}{3}$

General Solution :

$x=\pi n(n\in Z)$, $x=\frac{\pi}{3}+\pi n(n\in Z)$,

$x=\frac{2\pi}{3}+\pi n(n\in Z)$

(8) $3\tan^4 x-10\tan^2 x+3=0$. Let $\tan^2 x=A$.

$3A^2-10A+3=0$

$(3A-1)(A-3)=0$

$(3\tan^2 x-1)(\tan^2 x-3)=0$

$\tan^2 x=\frac{1}{3}$, $\tan x=\pm\frac{1}{\sqrt{3}}$

$\tan x=\frac{1}{\sqrt{3}} \rightarrow x=\frac{\pi}{6}$ and $x=\frac{7\pi}{6}$

$\tan x=-\frac{1}{\sqrt{3}} \rightarrow x=\frac{5\pi}{6}$ and $x=\frac{11\pi}{6}$

$\tan^2 x=3$, $\tan x=\pm\sqrt{3}$

$\tan x=\sqrt{3} \rightarrow x=\frac{\pi}{3}$ and $x=\frac{4\pi}{3}$

$\tan x=-\sqrt{3} \rightarrow x=\frac{2\pi}{3}$ and $x=\frac{5\pi}{3}$

The solutions are $x=\frac{\pi}{6}$, $x=\frac{\pi}{3}$, $x=\frac{2\pi}{3}$,

$x=\frac{5\pi}{6}$, $x=\frac{7\pi}{6}$, $x=\frac{4\pi}{3}$, $x=\frac{5\pi}{3}$

and $x=\frac{11\pi}{6}$

General Solution :

$x=\frac{\pi}{6}+\pi n(n\in Z)$, $x=\frac{5\pi}{6}+\pi n(n\in Z)$,

$x=\frac{\pi}{3}+\pi n(n\in Z)$, $x=\frac{2\pi}{3}+\pi n(n\in Z)$

02

(1) $\sin\frac{\pi}{12}=\sin\left(\frac{\pi}{4}-\frac{\pi}{6}\right)$

$=\sin\frac{\pi}{4}\cos\frac{\pi}{6}-\cos\frac{\pi}{4}\sin\frac{\pi}{6}$

$=\frac{\sqrt{2}}{2}\cdot\frac{\sqrt{3}}{2}+\frac{\sqrt{2}}{2}\cdot\frac{1}{2}=\frac{\sqrt{6}-\sqrt{2}}{4}$

(2) $\tan\frac{11\pi}{12}=\tan\left(\frac{2\pi}{3}+\frac{\pi}{4}\right)$

$=\frac{\tan\frac{2\pi}{3}+\tan\frac{\pi}{4}}{1-\tan\frac{2\pi}{3}\tan\frac{\pi}{4}}$

$=\frac{-\sqrt{3}+1}{1-(-\sqrt{3})\cdot 1}$

$=\frac{1-\sqrt{3}}{1+\sqrt{3}}=\sqrt{3}-2$

(3) $\cos 51°\cos 6°+\sin 51°\sin 6°$

$=\cos(51°-6°)=\cos 45°=\frac{\sqrt{2}}{2}$

(4) $\sin\frac{\pi}{4}\cos\frac{\pi}{12}+\cos\frac{\pi}{4}\sin\frac{\pi}{12}$

$=\sin\left(\frac{\pi}{4}+\frac{\pi}{12}\right)=\sin\frac{\pi}{3}=\frac{\sqrt{3}}{2}$

03

$\sin^2\alpha+\cos^2\alpha=1,\ \left(\frac{3}{5}\right)^2+\cos^2\alpha=1$

$\cos^2\alpha=1-\frac{9}{25}=\frac{16}{25},\ \cos\alpha=\pm\frac{4}{5}$

Since θ is Quadrant II, $\cos\alpha=-\frac{4}{5}$

$\sin^2\beta+\cos^2\beta=1,\ \sin^2\beta+\left(-\frac{1}{2}\right)^2=1$

$\sin^2\beta=1-\frac{1}{4}=\frac{3}{4},\ \sin\beta=\pm\frac{\sqrt{3}}{2}$

Since θ is Quadrant II, $\sin\beta=\frac{\sqrt{3}}{2}$

(1) $\sin(\alpha+\beta)=\sin\alpha\cos\beta+\cos\alpha\sin\beta$

$=\frac{3}{5}\cdot\left(-\frac{1}{2}\right)+\left(-\frac{4}{5}\right)\cdot\frac{\sqrt{3}}{2}$

$=-\frac{3}{10}-\frac{4\sqrt{3}}{10}=-\frac{3+4\sqrt{3}}{10}$

(2) $\cos(\alpha+\beta)=\cos\alpha\cos\beta-\sin\alpha\sin\beta$

$=\left(-\frac{4}{5}\right)\cdot\left(-\frac{1}{2}\right)-\frac{3}{5}\cdot\frac{\sqrt{3}}{2}$

$=\frac{2}{5}-\frac{3\sqrt{3}}{10}=\frac{4-3\sqrt{3}}{10}$

(3) $\tan\alpha=\frac{\sin\alpha}{\cos\alpha}=\frac{\frac{3}{5}}{-\frac{4}{5}}=-\frac{3}{4}$

$\tan\beta=\frac{\sin\beta}{\cos\beta}=\frac{\frac{\sqrt{3}}{2}}{-\frac{1}{2}}=-\sqrt{3}$

$\tan(\alpha+\beta)=\frac{\tan\alpha+\tan\beta}{1-\tan\alpha\tan\beta}$

$=\frac{-\frac{3}{4}+(-\sqrt{3})}{1-\left(-\frac{3}{4}\right)\cdot(-\sqrt{3})}$

$=\frac{\frac{-3-4\sqrt{3}}{4}}{\frac{4-3\sqrt{3}}{4}}=\frac{3+4\sqrt{3}}{3\sqrt{3}-4}$

$=\frac{25\sqrt{3}+48}{11}$

04

(1) $\sin(X+Y)=\sin X\cos Y+\cos X\sin Y$

$=\frac{x}{z}\cdot\frac{x}{z}+\frac{y}{z}\cdot\frac{y}{z}=\frac{x^2+y^2}{z^2}=\frac{z^2}{z^2}=1$

(2) $\cos(X+Y)=\cos X\cos Y-\sin X\sin Y$

$=\frac{y}{z}\cdot\frac{x}{z}-\frac{x}{z}\cdot\frac{y}{z}=0$

05

$\tan\left(\frac{\pi}{2}+x\right)=-\cot x$

Work on left side to reach right side.

$\tan\left(\frac{\pi}{2}+x\right)=\frac{\sin\left(\frac{\pi}{2}+x\right)}{\cos\left(\frac{\pi}{2}+x\right)}$

$=\frac{\sin\frac{\pi}{2}\cos x+\cos\frac{\pi}{2}\sin x}{\cos\frac{\pi}{2}\cos x-\sin\frac{\pi}{2}\sin x}$

$=\frac{1\cdot\cos x+0\cdot\sin x}{0\cdot\cos x-1\cdot\sin x}=\frac{\cos x}{-\sin x}$

$=-\cot x$

06

$$\cos\left(x-\frac{\pi}{4}\right)+\cos\left(x+\frac{\pi}{4}\right)=\sqrt{2}\cos x$$

Work on left side to reach right side.

$$\cos\left(x-\frac{\pi}{4}\right)+\cos\left(x+\frac{\pi}{4}\right)$$
$$=\cos x\cos\frac{\pi}{4}+\sin x\sin\frac{\pi}{4}+\cos x\cos\frac{\pi}{4}-\sin x\sin\frac{\pi}{4}$$
$$=2\cos x\cos\frac{\pi}{4}=2\cos x\cdot\frac{\sqrt{2}}{2}=\sqrt{2}\cos x$$

07

$\sin(2x)\cos x-\cos x\sin x=0$

$\cos x(\sin(2x)-\sin x)=0$

$\cos x(\sin(x+x)-\sin x)=0$

$\cos x(\sin x\cos x+\cos x\sin x-\sin x)=0$

$\cos x(2\sin x\cos x-\sin x)=0$

$\cos x[\sin x(2\cos x-1)]=0$

$\cos x\sin x(2\cos x-1)=0$

$\cos x=0\ \rightarrow\ x=\frac{\pi}{2}$ and $x=\frac{3\pi}{2}$

$\sin x=0\ \rightarrow\ x=0$ and $x=\pi$

$\cos x=\frac{1}{2}\ \rightarrow\ x=\frac{\pi}{3}$ and $x=\frac{5\pi}{3}$

The solutions are $x=0$, $x=\frac{\pi}{3}$, $x=\frac{\pi}{2}$, $x=\pi$, $x=\frac{3\pi}{2}$ and $x=\frac{5\pi}{3}$

08

(1) Let $\alpha=\sin^{-1}\left(\frac{2}{3}\right)$ and $\beta=\tan^{-1}\left(\frac{1}{2}\right)$.

Then we have $\sin\alpha=\frac{2}{3}$ and $\tan\beta=\frac{1}{2}$.

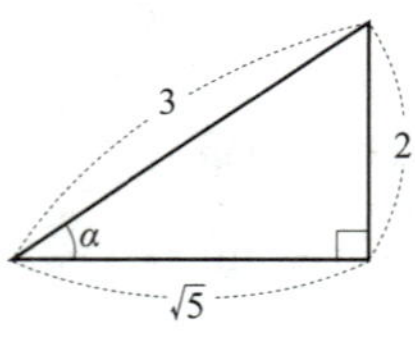

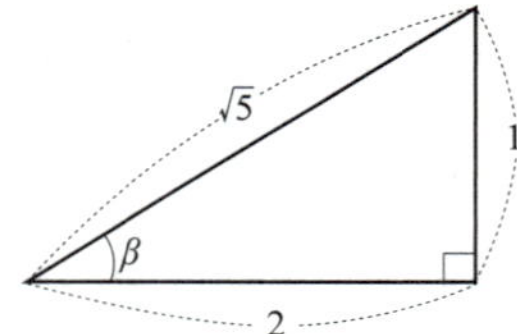

$$\cos\left(\sin^{-1}\left(\frac{2}{3}\right)-\tan^{-1}\left(\frac{1}{2}\right)\right)$$
$$=\cos(\alpha-\beta)$$
$$=\cos\alpha\cos\beta+\sin\alpha\sin\beta$$
$$=\frac{\sqrt{5}}{3}\cdot\frac{2}{\sqrt{5}}+\frac{2}{3}\cdot\frac{1}{\sqrt{5}}=\frac{2\sqrt{5}+2}{3\sqrt{5}}=\frac{10+2\sqrt{5}}{15}$$

(2) Let $\alpha=\arctan(-2)$.

Then we have $\tan\alpha=-2$.

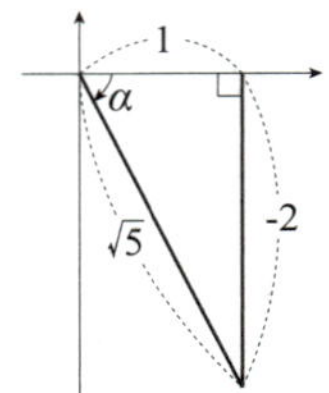

$$\sin(2\arctan(-2))=\sin(2\alpha)=\sin(\alpha+\alpha)$$
$$=\sin\alpha\cos\alpha+\cos\alpha\sin\alpha$$
$$=2\sin\alpha\cos\alpha$$
$$=2\left(-\frac{2}{\sqrt{5}}\right)\left(\frac{1}{\sqrt{5}}\right)=-\frac{4}{5}$$

09

Let $\alpha=\sin^{-1}a$ and $\beta=\tan^{-1}b$. Then we can sketch triangles with angles α and β such that $\sin\alpha=a$ and $\tan\beta=b$, as shown in Figure below.

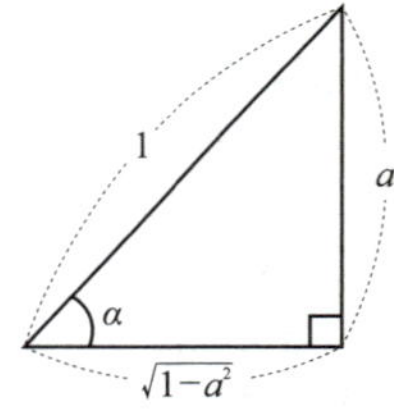

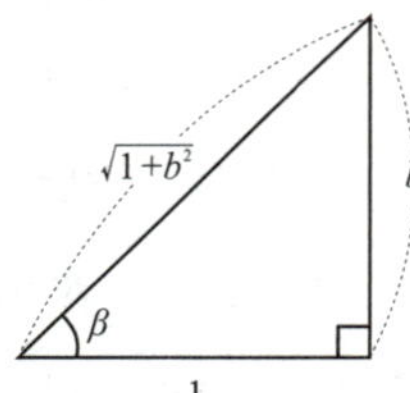

Now, using the sum and difference identity,

$$\cos(\sin^{-1}a+\tan^{-1}b)$$
$$=\cos(\alpha+\beta)$$
$$=\cos\alpha\cos\beta-\sin\alpha\sin\beta$$
$$=\frac{\sqrt{1-a^2}}{1}\cdot\frac{1}{\sqrt{1+b^2}}-\frac{a}{1}\cdot\frac{b}{\sqrt{1+b^2}}$$
$$=\frac{\sqrt{1-a^2}-ab}{\sqrt{1+b^2}}$$

10

$\sin(3x)$
$=\sin(2x+x)$
$=\sin 2x\cos x+\cos 2x\sin x$
$=\sin(x+x)\cos x+\cos(x+x)\sin x$
$=(\sin x\cos x+\cos x\sin x)\cos x$
$\quad+(\cos x\cos x-\sin x\sin x)\sin x$
$=\sin x\cos^2 x+\cos^2 x\sin x+\sin x\cos^2 x-\sin^3 x$
$=2\sin x\cos^2 x+\sin x\cos^2 x-\sin^3 x$

11

Set the functions equal:
$2\sin x+1=-2,\ \sin x=-\frac{3}{2}$
The sine function has a range of $[-1, 1]$. Since $\sin x=-\frac{3}{2}$ is outside this range, there are no solutions. The correct answer is (A).

12

$3\sin x-2\cos^2 x=0$
$3\sin x-2(1-\sin^2 x)=0$
$2\sin^2 x+3\sin x-2=0$
$(2\sin x-1)(\sin x+2)=0$
$\sin x=\frac{1}{2},\ x=\frac{\pi}{6}$
$\sin x=-2$(not valid as $-1\le\sin x\le 1$)
Therefore, the correct answer is (B).

13

Set the functions equal:
$3-\tan^2 x=2\sec^2 x$
$3-\tan^2 x=2(\tan^2 x+1)$
$3\tan^2 x=1,\ \tan^2 x=\frac{1}{3}$
$\tan x=\pm\frac{1}{\sqrt{3}},\ x=\frac{\pi}{6}$ and $x=\frac{5\pi}{6}$

14

$2\tan x-8=0,\ \tan x=4$
Recall that the tangent function has a period of π. Find the general solution for x:
$x=\arctan 4+\pi n$, where n is any integer
Therefore, the correct answer is (D).

15

$\cos A=\cos\frac{7\pi}{12}=\cos\left(\frac{\pi}{3}+\frac{\pi}{4}\right)=\frac{a}{4}$
Using the identity:
$\cos\left(\frac{\pi}{3}+\frac{\pi}{4}\right)=\cos\frac{\pi}{3}\cos\frac{\pi}{4}-\sin\frac{\pi}{3}\sin\frac{\pi}{4}$
$=\frac{1}{2}\cdot\frac{\sqrt{2}}{2}-\frac{\sqrt{3}}{2}\cdot\frac{\sqrt{2}}{2}=\frac{\sqrt{2}-\sqrt{6}}{4}$
Therefore,
$\frac{\sqrt{2}-\sqrt{6}}{4}=\frac{a}{4},\ a=\sqrt{2}-\sqrt{6}$

16

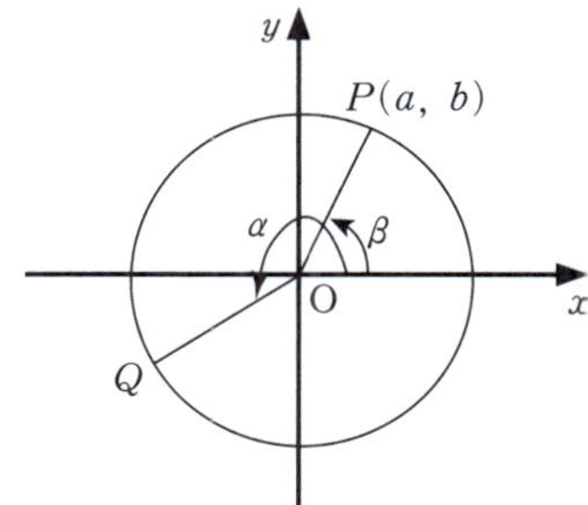

$\sin\angle POQ=\sin(\alpha-\beta)$
$=\sin\alpha\cos\beta-\cos\alpha\sin\beta$
$=-\frac{1}{\sqrt{2}}\cdot a-\left(-\frac{1}{\sqrt{2}}\right)\cdot b$
$=-\frac{a}{\sqrt{2}}+\frac{b}{\sqrt{2}}=\frac{b-a}{\sqrt{2}}$

17

Using the identity:

$$\tan\left(-\frac{\pi}{4}\right)=\cos\left(x-\frac{\pi}{2}\right)$$

$$-1=\cos x\cos\frac{\pi}{2}+\sin x\sin\frac{\pi}{2}$$

$$-1=\cos x\cdot 0+\sin x\cdot 1$$

$$\sin x=-1,\ x=\frac{3\pi}{2}$$

8. Trigonometric Equations and Identities, Part II

Check Point 1

① From $\sin^2\theta+\cos^2\theta=1$,

$$\cos^2\theta=1-\sin^2\theta=1-\left(-\frac{1}{4}\right)^2=\frac{15}{16},$$

$$\cos\theta=\pm\frac{\sqrt{15}}{4}.$$

Since θ is in Quadrant III, $\cos\theta=-\frac{\sqrt{15}}{4}$

$$\tan\theta=\frac{\sin\theta}{\cos\theta}=\frac{-\frac{1}{4}}{-\frac{\sqrt{15}}{4}}=\frac{1}{\sqrt{15}}=\frac{\sqrt{15}}{15}$$

$$\sin(2\theta)=2\sin\theta\cos\theta=2\left(-\frac{1}{4}\right)\left(-\frac{\sqrt{15}}{4}\right)=\frac{\sqrt{15}}{8}$$

$$\cos(2\theta)=1-2\sin^2\theta=1-2\left(-\frac{1}{4}\right)^2=\frac{7}{8}$$

$$\tan(2\theta)=\frac{2\tan\theta}{1-\tan^2\theta}=\frac{2\left(\frac{1}{\sqrt{15}}\right)}{1-\left(\frac{1}{\sqrt{15}}\right)^2}=\frac{\sqrt{15}}{7}$$

$\sin(2\theta)=\frac{\sqrt{15}}{8}$, $\cos(2\theta)=\frac{7}{8}$, $\tan(2\theta)=\frac{\sqrt{15}}{7}$

② Since $\frac{\pi}{2}<\theta<\pi$, θ is in Quadrant II.

$\tan\theta=\frac{1}{\cot\theta}=-\frac{5}{12}$. From $1+\tan^2\theta=\sec^2\theta$,

$$\sec^2\theta=1+\tan^2\theta=1+\left(-\frac{5}{12}\right)^2=\frac{169}{144},$$

$$\sec\theta=\pm\frac{13}{12}$$

Since θ is in Quadrant II, $\sec\theta=-\frac{13}{12}$.

$$\cos\theta=\frac{1}{\sec\theta}=-\frac{12}{13}$$

$$\tan\theta=\frac{\sin\theta}{\cos\theta},$$

$$\sin\theta=\tan\theta\cos\theta=\left(-\frac{5}{12}\right)\left(-\frac{12}{13}\right)=\frac{5}{13}$$

$$\sin(2\theta)=2\sin\theta\cos\theta=2\left(\frac{5}{13}\right)\left(-\frac{12}{13}\right)=-\frac{120}{169}$$

$$\cos(2\theta)=1-2\sin^2\theta=1-2\left(\frac{5}{13}\right)^2=\frac{119}{169}$$

$$\tan(2\theta)=\frac{2\tan\theta}{1-\tan^2\theta}=\frac{2\left(-\frac{5}{12}\right)}{1-\left(-\frac{5}{12}\right)^2}=-\frac{120}{119}$$

$\sin(2\theta)=-\frac{120}{169}$, $\cos(2\theta)=\frac{119}{169}$, $\tan(2\theta)=-\frac{120}{119}$

Check Point 2

① $\sin x=\sin(2x)$

$\sin(2x)-\sin x=0$

$2\sin x\cos x-\sin x=0$

$\sin x(2\cos x-1)=0$

$\sin x=0 \rightarrow x=0$ and $x=\pi$

$\cos x=\frac{1}{2} \rightarrow x=\frac{\pi}{3}$ and $x=\frac{5\pi}{3}$

General Solution :

$x=\pi n(n\in Z)$, $x=\frac{\pi}{3}+2\pi n(n\in Z)$

$x=\frac{5\pi}{3}+2\pi n(n\in Z)$

② $\cos(2x)+3\sin x+1=0$

$(1-2\sin^2 x)+3\sin x+1=0$

$-2\sin^2 x+3\sin x+2=0$

$2\sin^2 x-3\sin x-2=0$

$(2\sin x+1)(\sin x-2)=0$

$\sin x=-\frac{1}{2} \rightarrow x=\frac{7\pi}{6}$ and $x=\frac{11\pi}{6}$

$\sin x=2 \rightarrow$ No solution exists

General Solution :

$x=\frac{7\pi}{6}+2\pi n(n\in Z)$, $x=\frac{11\pi}{6}+2\pi n(n\in Z)$

Check Point 3

① Since $\frac{\pi}{8}$ lies in Quadrant I, $\sin\frac{\pi}{8}>0$.

$$\sin\left(\frac{\pi}{8}\right)=\sqrt{\frac{1-\cos\frac{\pi}{4}}{2}}=\sqrt{\frac{1-\frac{\sqrt{2}}{2}}{2}}=\frac{\sqrt{2-\sqrt{2}}}{2}$$

② Since $\frac{5\pi}{8}$ lies in Quadrant II, $\cos\frac{5\pi}{8}<0$.

$$\cos\left(\frac{5\pi}{8}\right)=-\sqrt{\frac{1+\cos\frac{5\pi}{4}}{2}}=-\sqrt{\frac{1-\frac{\sqrt{2}}{2}}{2}}$$
$$=-\frac{\sqrt{2-\sqrt{2}}}{2}$$

③ Since 67.5° lies in Quadrant I, $\tan 67.5°>0$.

$$\tan 67.5°=\frac{1-\cos 135°}{\sin 135°}=\frac{1-\left(-\frac{\sqrt{2}}{2}\right)}{\frac{\sqrt{2}}{2}}$$
$$=\frac{2+\sqrt{2}}{\sqrt{2}}=\frac{2\sqrt{2}+2}{2}=\sqrt{2}+1$$

Check Point 4

① Since θ is in Quadrant I, $\frac{\theta}{2}$ is also in Quadrant I.

From $\sin^2\theta+\cos^2\theta=1$,

$\cos^2\theta=1-\sin^2\theta=1-\left(\frac{3}{5}\right)^2=\frac{16}{25}$, $\cos\theta=\frac{4}{5}$

$$\sin\left(\frac{\theta}{2}\right)=\sqrt{\frac{1+\cos\theta}{2}}=\sqrt{\frac{1-\left(\frac{4}{5}\right)}{2}}=\sqrt{\frac{\frac{1}{5}}{2}}=\frac{\sqrt{10}}{10}$$

$$\cos\left(\frac{\theta}{2}\right)=\sqrt{\frac{1+\cos\theta}{2}}=\sqrt{\frac{1+\left(\frac{4}{5}\right)}{2}}=\sqrt{\frac{\frac{9}{5}}{2}}=\frac{3\sqrt{10}}{10}$$

$$\tan\left(\frac{\theta}{2}\right)=\frac{\sin\left(\frac{\theta}{2}\right)}{\cos\left(\frac{\theta}{2}\right)}=\frac{\frac{\sqrt{10}}{10}}{\frac{3\sqrt{10}}{10}}=\sqrt{\frac{1}{9}}=\frac{1}{3}$$

$\sin\left(\frac{\theta}{2}\right)=\frac{\sqrt{10}}{10}$, $\cos\left(\frac{\theta}{2}\right)=\frac{3\sqrt{10}}{10}$, $\tan\left(\frac{\theta}{2}\right)=\frac{1}{3}$

② Since $\frac{3\pi}{2}<\theta<2\pi$, $\frac{3\pi}{4}<\frac{\theta}{2}<\pi$.

$\rightarrow \frac{\theta}{2}$ is in Quadrant II

$\cos\theta=\frac{1}{\sec\theta}=\frac{1}{2}$

$$\sin\left(\frac{\theta}{2}\right)=\sqrt{\frac{1-\cos\theta}{2}}=\sqrt{\frac{1-\left(\frac{1}{2}\right)}{2}}=\sqrt{\frac{\frac{1}{2}}{2}}=\frac{1}{2}$$

$$\cos\left(\frac{\theta}{2}\right)=-\sqrt{\frac{1+\cos\theta}{2}}=-\sqrt{\frac{1+\left(\frac{1}{2}\right)}{2}}=-\sqrt{\frac{\frac{3}{2}}{2}}$$

$$=-\frac{\sqrt{3}}{2}$$

$$\tan\left(\frac{\theta}{2}\right)=-\frac{\sin\left(\frac{\theta}{2}\right)}{\cos\left(\frac{\theta}{2}\right)}=\frac{\frac{1}{2}}{\frac{-\sqrt{3}}{2}}=-\frac{\sqrt{3}}{3}$$

$\sin\left(\frac{\theta}{2}\right)=\frac{1}{2}$, $\cos\left(\frac{\theta}{2}\right)=-\frac{\sqrt{3}}{2}$, $\tan\left(\frac{\theta}{2}\right)=-\frac{\sqrt{3}}{3}$

Check Point 5

① $\sin(4x)\sin(3x)$

$$=\frac{1}{2}[\cos(4x-3x)-\cos(4x+3x)]$$

$$=\frac{1}{2}[\cos x-\cos(7x)]$$

② $\cos(2x)\cos(5x)$

$$=\frac{1}{2}[\cos(2x+5x)+\cos(2x-5x)]$$

$$=\frac{1}{2}[\cos(7x)+\cos(-3x)]$$

$$=\frac{1}{2}[\cos(7x)+\cos(3x)]$$

③ $\cos x\sin(3x)$

$$=\frac{1}{2}[\sin(x+3x)-\sin(x-3x)]$$

$$=\frac{1}{2}[\sin(4x)-\sin(-2x)]$$

$$=\frac{1}{2}[\sin(4x)+\sin(2x)]$$

Check Point 6

① $\sin(6x)-\sin(3x)$

$$=2\cos\left(\frac{6x+3x}{2}\right)\sin\left(\frac{6x-3x}{2}\right)$$

$$=2\cos\left(\frac{9x}{2}\right)\sin\left(\frac{3x}{2}\right)$$

② $\cos(2x)-\cos(5x)$

$$=-2\sin\left(\frac{2x+5x}{2}\right)\sin\left(\frac{2x-5x}{2}\right)$$

$$=-2\sin\left(\frac{7x}{2}\right)\sin\left(-\frac{3x}{2}\right)$$

$$=2\sin\left(\frac{7x}{2}\right)\sin\left(\frac{3x}{2}\right)$$

③ $\cos(3x)+\cos(7x)$

$$=2\cos\left(\frac{3x+7x}{2}\right)\cos\left(\frac{3x-7x}{2}\right)$$

$$=2\cos(5x)\cos(-2x)=2\cos(5x)\cos(2x)$$

Review Exercises

01

Since $\pi<\theta<\frac{3\pi}{2}$, θ is in Quadrant III.

$\sec^2\theta=1+\tan^2\theta=1+\left(\frac{4}{3}\right)^2=\frac{25}{9}$, $\sec\theta=-\frac{5}{3}$

$\cos\theta=\frac{1}{\sec\theta}=-\frac{3}{5}$

$\tan\theta=\frac{\sin\theta}{\cos\theta}$, $\sin\theta=\tan\theta\cos\theta=\frac{4}{3}\left(-\frac{3}{5}\right)=-\frac{4}{5}$

$\sin(2\theta)=2\sin\theta\cos\theta=2\left(-\frac{4}{5}\right)\left(-\frac{3}{5}\right)=\frac{24}{25}$

$\cos(2\theta)=\cos^2\theta-\sin^2\theta$

$$=\left(-\frac{3}{5}\right)^2-\left(-\frac{4}{5}\right)^2=\frac{9}{25}-\frac{16}{25}=-\frac{7}{25}$$

$$\tan(2\theta)=\frac{2\tan\theta}{1-\tan^2\theta}=\frac{2\left(\frac{4}{3}\right)}{1-\left(\frac{4}{3}\right)^2}=\frac{\frac{8}{3}}{-\frac{7}{9}}=-\frac{24}{7}$$

$\sin(2\theta)=\frac{24}{25}$, $\cos(2\theta)=-\frac{7}{25}$, $\tan(2\theta)=-\frac{24}{7}$

02

(1) $\sin x\cos x-\frac{1}{4}=0$, $\sin x\cos x=\frac{1}{4}$

$2\sin x\cos x=\frac{1}{2}$, $\sin(2x)=\frac{1}{2}$

$2x=\frac{\pi}{6}$, $2x=\frac{5\pi}{6}$, $2x=\frac{13\pi}{6}$, and $2x=\frac{17\pi}{6}$

$\rightarrow$ $x=\frac{\pi}{12}$, $x=\frac{5\pi}{12}$, $x=\frac{13\pi}{12}$, and $x=\frac{17\pi}{12}$

The solutions are $x=\frac{\pi}{12}$, $x=\frac{5\pi}{12}$, $x=\frac{13\pi}{12}$, and $x=\frac{17\pi}{12}$

General Solution :

$2x=\frac{\pi}{6}+2\pi n(n\in Z)\rightarrow x=\frac{\pi}{12}+\pi n(n\in Z)$

$2x=\frac{5\pi}{6}+2\pi n(n\in Z)\rightarrow x=\frac{5\pi}{12}+\pi n(n\in Z)$

(2) $\sin x+1-\cos(2x)=0$

$\sin x+1-(1-2\sin^2 x)=0$

$2\sin^2 x+\sin x=0$, $\sin x(2\sin x+1)=0$

$\sin x=0$ or $\sin x=-\frac{1}{2}$

$\sin x=0 \rightarrow x=0$ and $x=\pi$

$\sin x=-\frac{1}{2} \rightarrow x=\frac{7\pi}{6}$ and $x=\frac{11\pi}{6}$

The solutions are $x=0$, $x=\pi$, $x=\frac{7\pi}{6}$ and $x=\frac{11\pi}{6}$

General Solution :

$x=\pi n(n\in Z)$, $x=\frac{7\pi}{6}+2\pi n(n\in Z)$, $x=\frac{11\pi}{6}+2\pi n(n\in Z)$

(3) $\sin(2x)=\tan x$

$2\sin x\cos x-\tan x=0$

$\left(2\sin x\cos x-\frac{\sin x}{\cos x}=0\right)\cdot\cos x$

$2\sin x\cos^2 x-\sin x=0$

$\sin x(2\cos^2 x-1)=0$

$\sin x=0$ or $\cos x=\pm\frac{1}{\sqrt{2}}$

$\sin x=0 \rightarrow x=0$ and $x=\pi$

$\cos x=\frac{1}{\sqrt{2}} \rightarrow x=\frac{\pi}{4}$ and $x=\frac{7\pi}{4}$

$\cos x=-\frac{1}{\sqrt{2}} \rightarrow x=\frac{3\pi}{4}$ and $x=\frac{5\pi}{4}$

The solutions are $x=0$, $x=\frac{\pi}{4}$, $x=\frac{3\pi}{4}$, $x=\pi$, $x=\frac{5\pi}{4}$ and $x=\frac{7\pi}{4}$

General Solution :

$x=\pi n(n\in Z)$, $x=\frac{\pi}{4}+\frac{\pi n}{2}(n\in Z)$

03

(1) Since $\frac{\pi}{12}$ lies in Quadrant I, $\sin\left(\frac{\pi}{12}\right)>0$.

$$\sin\left(\frac{\pi}{12}\right)=\sqrt{\frac{1-\cos\frac{\pi}{6}}{2}}=\sqrt{\frac{1-\frac{\sqrt{3}}{2}}{2}}=\frac{\sqrt{2-\sqrt{3}}}{2}$$

(2) Since 195° lies in Quadrant III, $\cos 195°<0$.

$$\cos 195°=-\sqrt{\frac{1+\cos 390°}{2}}=-\sqrt{\frac{1+\frac{\sqrt{3}}{2}}{2}}$$

$$=-\frac{\sqrt{2+\sqrt{3}}}{2}$$

(3) Since $\frac{5\pi}{12}$ lies in Quadrant I, $\tan\left(\frac{5\pi}{12}\right)>0$

$$\tan\left(\frac{5\pi}{12}\right)=\frac{1-\cos\frac{5\pi}{6}}{\sin\left(\frac{5\pi}{6}\right)}=\frac{1-\left(-\frac{\sqrt{3}}{2}\right)}{\frac{1}{2}}$$

$$=\frac{\frac{2+\sqrt{3}}{2}}{\frac{1}{2}}=2+\sqrt{3}$$

04

If $\frac{3\pi}{2}<\theta<2\pi$, then $\frac{3\pi}{4}<\frac{\theta}{2}<\pi$.

So θ is in Quadrant II.

$$\sin\left(\frac{\theta}{2}\right)=\sqrt{\frac{1-\cos\theta}{2}}=\sqrt{\frac{1-\frac{1}{2}}{2}}=\sqrt{\frac{\frac{1}{2}}{2}}=\frac{1}{2}$$

$$\cos\left(\frac{\theta}{2}\right)=-\sqrt{\frac{1+\cos\theta}{2}}=-\sqrt{\frac{1+\frac{1}{2}}{2}}$$

$$=-\sqrt{\frac{\frac{3}{2}}{2}}=-\frac{\sqrt{3}}{2}$$

$$\tan\left(\frac{\theta}{2}\right)=\frac{\sin\frac{\theta}{2}}{\cos\frac{\theta}{2}}=\frac{\frac{1}{2}}{-\frac{\sqrt{3}}{2}}=-\frac{1}{\sqrt{3}}=-\frac{\sqrt{3}}{3}$$

$\sin\left(\frac{\theta}{2}\right)=\frac{1}{2}$, $\cos\left(\frac{\theta}{2}\right)=-\frac{\sqrt{3}}{2}$, $\tan\left(\frac{\theta}{2}\right)=-\frac{\sqrt{3}}{3}$

05

From double angle identity,

$2\sin x\cos x=\sin(2x)$.

So we have

$4\sin x\cos x$

$=2\cdot 2\sin x\cos x=2\sin(2x)$.

Recall that

$-1\le\sin(2x)\le 1$, $-2\le 2\sin(2x)\le 2$.

Since the minimum value of $\sin(2x)$ is -1, the minimum of $2\sin(2x)$ is -2.

06

If $\sin x=y$ and $0\le x<\frac{\pi}{2}$, then we have the following Figure below.

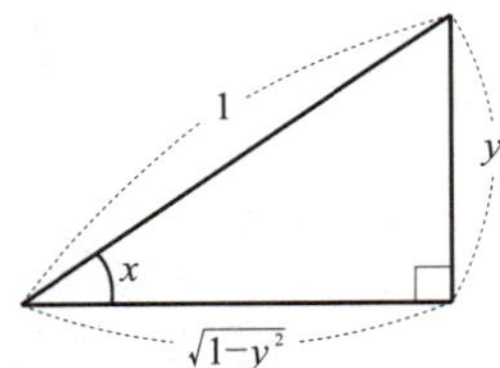

$\cos x=\frac{\sqrt{1-y^2}}{1}=\sqrt{1-y^2}$

$\sin(2x)=2\sin x\cos x=2y\sqrt{1-y^2}$

07

Let $\alpha=\tan^{-1}\left(\frac{3}{4}\right)$. Then $\tan\alpha=\frac{3}{4}$ and we have the following Figure below.

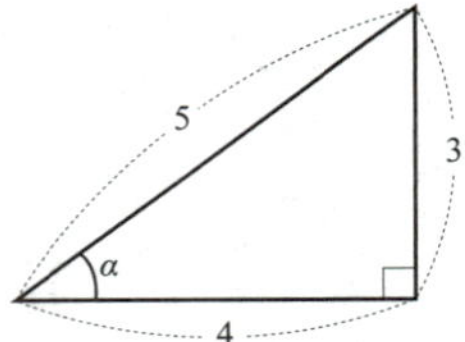

$\cos\left(2\tan^{-1}\left(\frac{3}{4}\right)\right)=\cos(2\alpha)=2\cos^2\alpha-1$

$=2\left(\frac{4}{5}\right)^2-1=\frac{32}{25}-\frac{25}{25}=\frac{7}{25}$

08

Notice that the expression on the right side is the sum of the first power of cosine. To reduce the power, we can use the following property :

$\cos(2x)=2\cos^2 x-1$, $\cos^2 x=\frac{1+\cos(2x)}{2}$

$\cos^4 x=(\cos^2 x)^2$

$=\left(\frac{1+\cos(2x)}{2}\right)^2$

$=\frac{1}{4}(1+2\cos(2x)+\cos^2(2x))$

$=\frac{1}{4}\left(1+2\cos(2x)+\frac{1+\cos(4x)}{2}\right)$

$=\frac{1}{4}\left(1+2\cos(2x)+\frac{1}{2}+\frac{\cos(4x)}{2}\right)$

$=\frac{1}{4}\left(\frac{\cos(4x)}{2}+2\cos(2x)+\frac{3}{2}\right)$

$=\frac{\cos(4x)}{8}+\frac{\cos(2x)}{2}+\frac{3}{8}$

09

$\sin x+\cos x=1$

$(\sin x+\cos x)^2=1^2$ → Square both sides

$\sin^2 x+2\sin x\cos x+\cos^2 x=1$

$1+\sin(2x)=1$

$\sin(2x)=0$

$2x=0$, $2x=\pi$, $2x=2\pi$, and $2x=3\pi$

→ $x=0$, $x=\frac{\pi}{2}$, $x=\pi$ and $x=\frac{3\pi}{2}$

Check the solution :

$x=0$; $\sin 0+\cos 0=0+1=1$

$x=\frac{\pi}{2}$; $\sin\left(\frac{\pi}{2}\right)+\cos\left(\frac{\pi}{2}\right)=1+0=1$

$x=\pi$; $\sin\pi+\cos\pi=0+(-1)=-1\neq 1$

$x=\frac{3\pi}{2}$; $\sin\left(\frac{3\pi}{2}\right)+\cos\left(\frac{3\pi}{2}\right)=-1+0=-1\neq 1$

So the solutions are $x=0$ and $x=\frac{\pi}{2}$.

10

$\sin(2\tan^{-1}x)$ → If we let $\theta=\tan^{-1}x$, then $\tan\theta=x$ and we have the following Figure below.

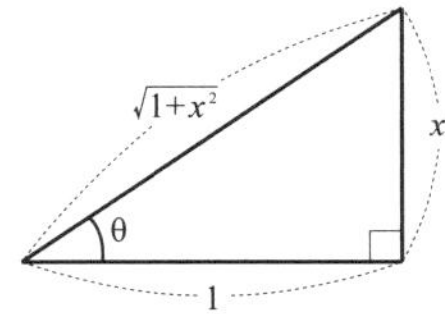

$\sin(2\tan^{-1}x)=\sin(2\theta)=2\sin\theta\cos\theta$

$=2\cdot\dfrac{x}{\sqrt{1+x^2}}\cdot\dfrac{1}{\sqrt{1+x^2}}=\dfrac{2x}{1+x^2}$

11

(1) $\cos(3x)\sin(4x)$

$=\frac{1}{2}[\sin(3x+4x)-\sin(3x-4x)]$

$=\frac{1}{2}[\sin(7x)-\sin(-x)]$

$=\frac{1}{2}[\sin(7x)+\sin x]$

(2) $4\sin\left(\frac{x}{2}\right)\sin\left(\frac{x}{3}\right)$

$=4\cdot\frac{1}{2}\left[\cos\left(\frac{x}{2}-\frac{x}{3}\right)-\cos\left(\frac{x}{2}+\frac{x}{3}\right)\right]$

$=2\left[\cos\left(\frac{x}{6}\right)-\cos\left(\frac{5x}{6}\right)\right]$

12

(1) $\cos(4x)+\cos(5x)$

$=2\cos\left(\frac{4x+5x}{2}\right)\cos\left(\frac{4x-5x}{2}\right)$

$=2\cos\left(\frac{9x}{2}\right)\cos\left(\frac{-x}{2}\right)=2\cos\left(\frac{9x}{2}\right)\cos\left(\frac{x}{2}\right)$

(2) $\sin(3x)+\sin(6x)$

$=2\sin\left(\frac{3x+6x}{2}\right)\cos\left(\frac{3x-6x}{2}\right)$

$=2\sin\left(\frac{9x}{2}\right)\cos\left(\frac{-3x}{2}\right)=2\sin\left(\frac{9x}{2}\right)\cos\left(\frac{3x}{2}\right)$

13

(1) $\dfrac{\sin(4x)+\sin(6x)}{\cos(4x)+\cos(6x)}=\tan(5x)$

Work on left side to reach right side.

$\dfrac{\sin(4x)+\sin(6x)}{\cos(4x)+\cos(6x)}$

$=\dfrac{2\sin\left(\frac{4x+6x}{2}\right)\cos\left(\frac{4x-6x}{2}\right)}{2\cos\left(\frac{4x+6x}{2}\right)\cos\left(\frac{4x-6x}{2}\right)}$

$=\dfrac{\sin(5x)\cos(-x)}{\cos(5x)\cos(-x)}=\dfrac{\sin(5x)}{\cos(5x)}=\tan(5x)$

(2) $\sin x(\sin(3x)+\sin(5x))=\sin(2x)\sin(4x)$

Work on left side to reach right side.

$\sin x(\sin(3x)+\sin(5x))$

$=\sin x\left(2\sin\left(\frac{3x+5x}{2}\right)\cos\left(\frac{3x-5x}{2}\right)\right)$

$=\sin x(2\sin(4x)\cos(-x))$

$=\sin x\cdot 2\sin(4x)\cos x$

$=2\sin x\cos x\sin(4x)$

$=\sin(2x)\sin(4x)$

(3) $\dfrac{\cos(2x)-\cos(6x)}{\cos(2x)+\cos(6x)}=\tan(4x)\tan(2x)$

Work on left side to reach right side.

$\dfrac{\cos(2x)-\cos(6x)}{\cos(2x)+\cos(6x)}$

$=\dfrac{-2\sin\left(\frac{2x+6x}{2}\right)\sin\left(\frac{2x-6x}{2}\right)}{2\cos\left(\frac{2x+6x}{2}\right)\cos\left(\frac{2x-6x}{2}\right)}$

$=\dfrac{-\sin(4x)\sin(-2x)}{\cos(4x)\cos(-2x)}=\dfrac{\sin(4x)\sin(2x)}{\cos(4x)\cos(2x)}$

$=\tan(4x)\tan(2x)$

(4) $\dfrac{\cos x+\cos(3x)+\cos(5x)}{\sin x+\sin(3x)+\sin(5x)}=\cot(3x)$

Work on left side to reach right side.

$\dfrac{\cos x+\cos(3x)+\cos(5x)}{\sin x+\sin(3x)+\sin(5x)}$

$=\dfrac{(\cos x+\cos(5x))+\cos(3x)}{(\sin x+\sin(5x))+\sin(3x)}$

$$=\frac{\left(2\cos\left(\frac{x+5x}{2}\right)\cos\left(\frac{x-5x}{2}\right)\right)+\cos(3x)}{\left(2\sin\left(\frac{x+5x}{2}\right)\cos\left(\frac{x-5x}{2}\right)\right)+\sin(3x)}$$

$$=\frac{2\cos(3x)\cos(-2x)+\cos(3x)}{2\sin(3x)\cos(-2x)+\sin(3x)}$$

$$=\frac{2\cos(3x)+\cos(3x)}{2\sin(3x)+\sin(3x)}$$

$$=\frac{3\cos(3x)}{3\sin(3x)}=\cot(3x)$$

14

In the figure, $\sin\theta=\frac{y}{r}$ and $\cos\theta=\frac{x}{r}$. Using the identity:

$$r^2\sin(2\theta)=r^2\cdot 2\sin\theta\cos\theta$$
$$=2r^2\cdot\frac{y}{r}\cdot\frac{x}{r}=2xy$$

Therefore, the answer is (D).

15

Use the identity: $\cos(2x)=2\cos^2x-1$

$$f(x)=4\cos^2x+3$$
$$=2(2\cos^2x-1)+5=2\cos(2x)+5$$

Amplitude: $m=2$

Period: $p=\frac{2\pi}{2}=\pi$

Therefore, the value of $m+p=2+\pi$.

16

Using the identity:

$$\frac{\sin(2x)-\cos x}{\cos x}=\frac{2\sin x\cos x-(\cos x)}{\cos x}$$
$$=\frac{\cos x(2\sin x-1)}{\cos x}$$
$$=2\sin x-1=0$$
$$\sin x=\frac{1}{2}$$

The value of sine is positive in the first and second quadrants. Therefore, the correct answer is (A).

17

$f\left(\frac{x}{2}-\frac{\pi}{6}\right)=\sin\left(x-\frac{\pi}{3}\right)$ ⇒ Let $\frac{x}{2}-\frac{\pi}{6}=a$.

Then $\frac{x}{2}=a+\frac{\pi}{6}$, $x=2a+\frac{\pi}{3}$.

So we have

$f(a)=\sin\left(2a+\frac{\pi}{3}-\frac{\pi}{3}\right)=\sin(2a)$ and

if we substitute x for a, $f(x)=\sin(2x)$.

Therefore, the correct answer is (A).

18

If $\tan x=m$ for $0<x<\frac{\pi}{2}$, we have following figure below.

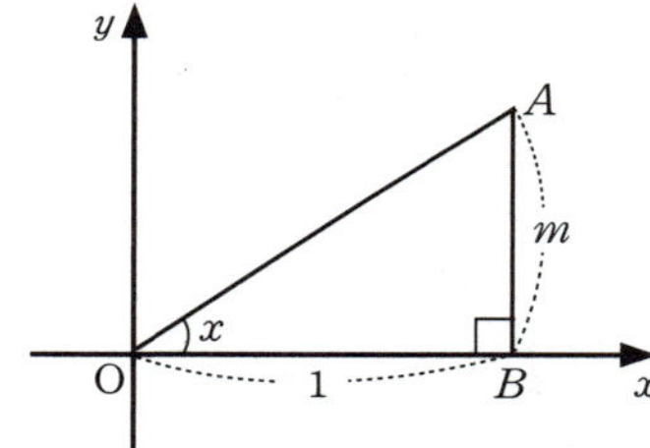

Using Pythagorean theorem, $OA=\sqrt{1+m^2}$.

Using the identity,

$$\sin(2x)=2\sin x\cos x$$
$$=2\cdot\frac{m}{\sqrt{1+m^2}}\cdot\frac{1}{\sqrt{1+m^2}}=\frac{2m}{1+m^2}$$

Therefore, the answer is (D).

19

Since $\angle COA=2\angle COB$, $\angle AOB=\angle COB$. The coordinates of B is (a, b).

Therefore, $\sin\angle AOB=\sin\angle COB=b$. The correct answer is (B).

9. Polar Coordinates and Equations

Check Point 1

① $\left(2,\ \frac{\pi}{3}\right)$

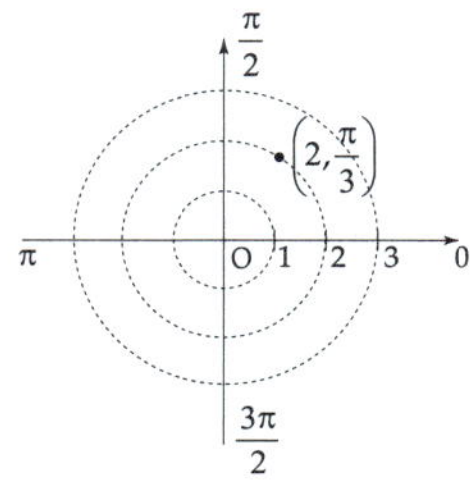

② $\left(3,\ \frac{5\pi}{4}\right)$

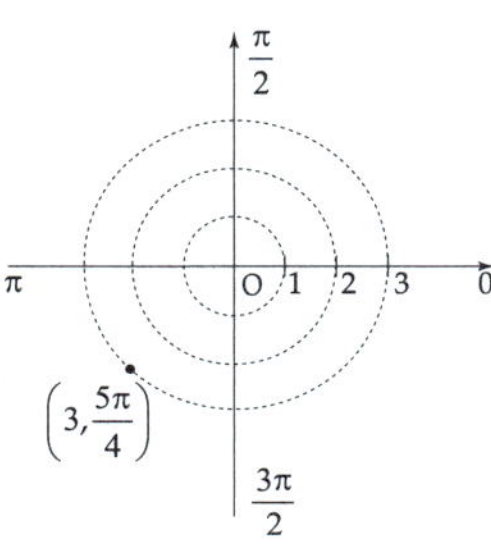

③ $\left(-2,\ \frac{5\pi}{3}\right)$

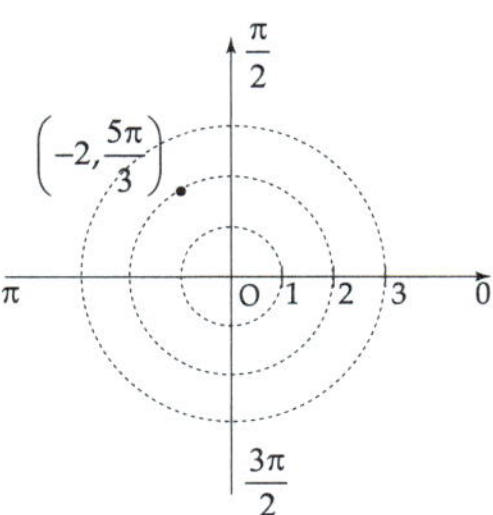

④ $\left(-1,\ -\frac{2\pi}{3}\right)$

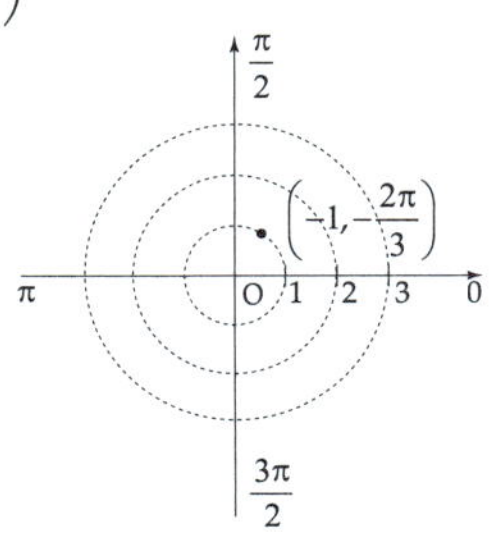

Check Point 2

① $\left(2,\ \frac{\pi}{6}-2\pi\right)=\left(2,\ -\frac{11\pi}{6}\right)$,

$\left(-2,\ \frac{\pi}{6}+\pi\right)=\left(-2,\ \frac{7\pi}{6}\right)$,

$\left(-2,\ \frac{\pi}{6}-\pi\right)=\left(-2,\ -\frac{5\pi}{6}\right)$

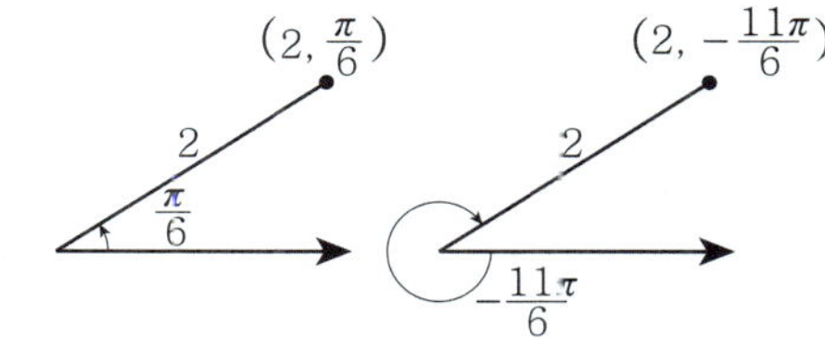

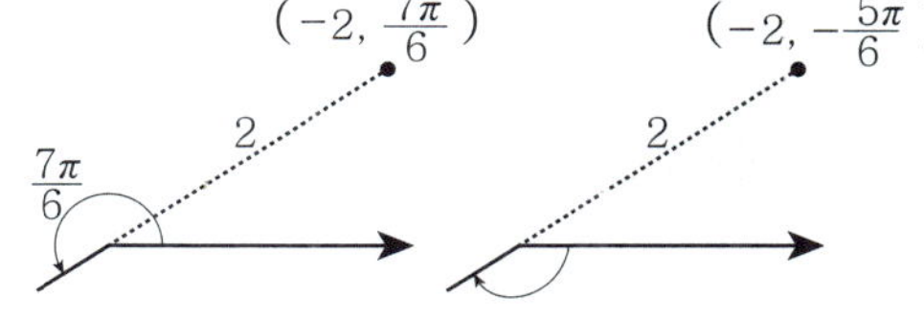

$\left(2,\ -\frac{11\pi}{6}\right)$, $\left(-2,\ \frac{7\pi}{6}\right)$, and $\left(-2,\ -\frac{5\pi}{6}\right)$

② $\left(1,\ -\frac{\pi}{3}+2\pi\right)=\left(1,\ \frac{5\pi}{3}\right)$,

$\left(-1,\ -\frac{\pi}{3}+\pi\right)=\left(-1,\ \frac{2\pi}{3}\right)$,

$\left(-1,\ -\frac{\pi}{3}-\pi\right)=\left(-1,\ -\frac{4\pi}{3}\right)$

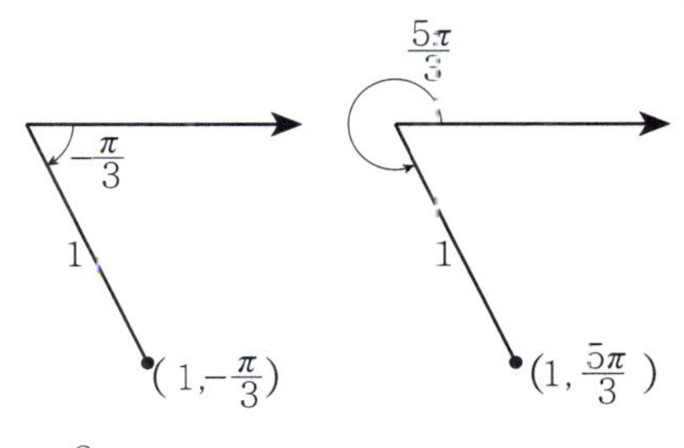

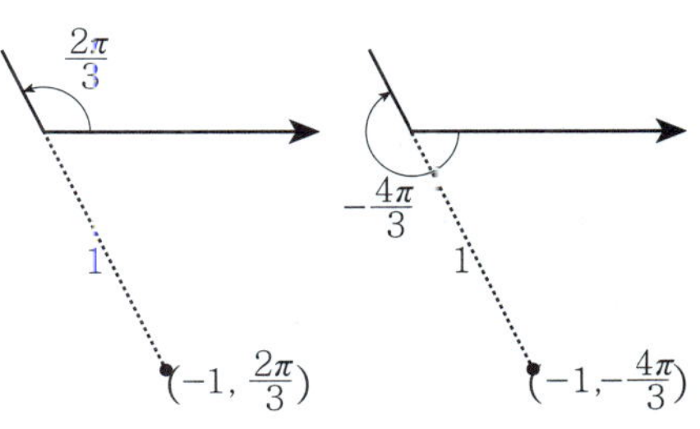

$\left(1,\ \frac{5\pi}{3}\right)$, $\left(-1,\ \frac{2\pi}{3}\right)$, and $\left(-1,\ -\frac{4\pi}{3}\right)$

Check Point 3

① $x=r\cos\theta=2\cos\left(\frac{3\pi}{4}\right)=-\sqrt{2}$ and

$y=r\sin\theta=2\sin\left(\frac{3\pi}{4}\right)=\sqrt{2}$.

So the rectangular coordinate is $(-\sqrt{2},\ \sqrt{2})$.

$\left(2,\ \frac{3\pi}{4}\right)\rightarrow(-\sqrt{2},\ \sqrt{2})$

② $x=r\cos\theta=4\cos\left(-\frac{\pi}{6}\right)=2\sqrt{3}$ and

$y=r\sin\theta=4\sin\left(-\frac{\pi}{6}\right)=-2$.

So the rectangular coordinate is $(2\sqrt{3},\ -2)$.

$\left(4,\ -\frac{\pi}{6}\right)\rightarrow(2\sqrt{3},\ -2)$

Check Point 4

①

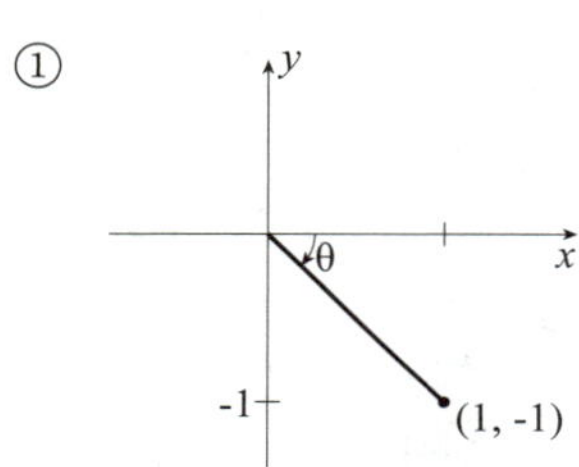

$\tan\theta=\frac{-1}{1}=-1,\ \theta=\tan^{-1}(-1)=-\frac{\pi}{4}$ and $r=\sqrt{1^2+(-1)^2}=\sqrt{2}$. So the polar coordinate is $\left(\sqrt{2},\ -\frac{\pi}{4}\right)$.

$(1,-1)\rightarrow\left(\sqrt{2},\ -\frac{\pi}{4}\right)$

②

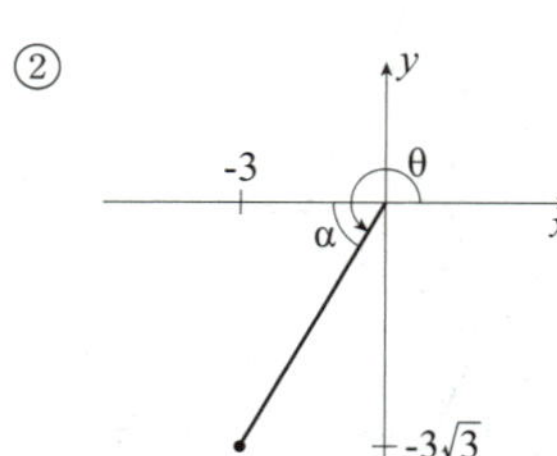

$\tan\alpha=\left(\frac{3\sqrt{3}}{3}\right),\ \alpha=\tan^{-1}\left(\frac{3\sqrt{3}}{3}\right)=\frac{\pi}{3}$ and $\theta=\alpha+\pi=\frac{\pi}{3}+\pi=\frac{4\pi}{3}$. Since $r=\sqrt{(-3)^2+(-3\sqrt{3})^2}=6$, the polar coordinate is $\left(6,\ \frac{4\pi}{3}\right)$.

$(-3,-3\sqrt{3})\rightarrow\left(6,\ \frac{4\pi}{3}\right)$

Check Point 5

① Since $x=r\cos\theta$, $r\cos\theta=2$,

$r=\frac{2}{\cos\theta}=2\sec\theta$.

$r=2\sec\theta$

② Since $x=r\cos\theta$ and $y=r\sin\theta$,

$r\cos\theta-4(r\sin\theta)+8=0$

$r(\cos\theta-4\sin\theta)=-8,\ r=\frac{8}{4\sin\theta-\cos\theta}$

$r=\frac{8}{4\sin\theta-\cos\theta}$

Check Point 6

① $r=2\sin\theta$

$(r=2\sin\theta)\cdot r$

$r^2=2r\sin\theta$

Since $x^2+y^2=r^2$ and $r\sin\theta=y$,

$x^2+y^2=2y,\ x^2+y^2-2y=0$.

$x^2+y^2-2y=0$

② $r=\frac{1}{1+\cos\theta},\ r+r\cos\theta=1,\ r+x=1$

$r=1-x$

$r^2=(1-x)^2$ → Square both sides

$x^2+y^2=1-2x+x^2,\ y^2+2x-1=0$

$y^2+2x-1=0$

Check Point 7

① $r=2,\ r^2=2^2$

$x^2+y^2=4$

The graph of $r=2$ is a circle with center at the origin and radius 2.

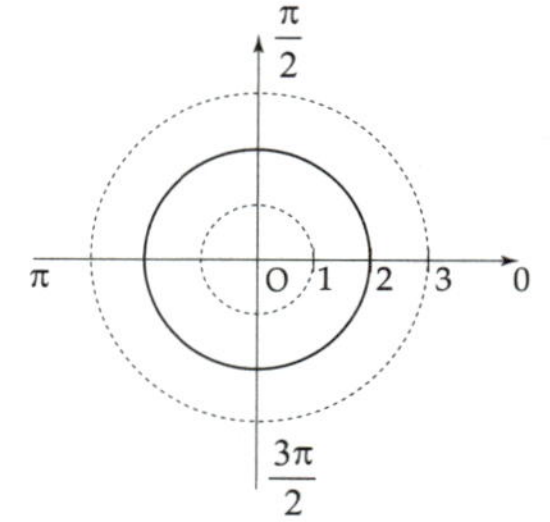

② $\theta=\frac{\pi}{3}$, $\tan\theta=\tan\frac{\pi}{3}$

$\frac{y}{x}=\sqrt{3}$, $y=\sqrt{3}x$

The graph of $\theta=\frac{\pi}{3}$ is a line passing through the pole with slope $\sqrt{3}$.

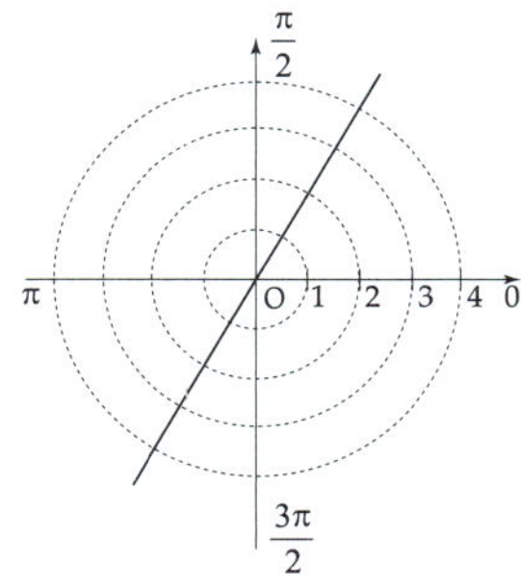

③ $r=-\frac{2}{\sin\theta}$

$r\sin\theta=-2$, $y=-2$

The graph of $r=-\frac{2}{\sin\theta}$ is a horizontal line 2 units below the x-axis.

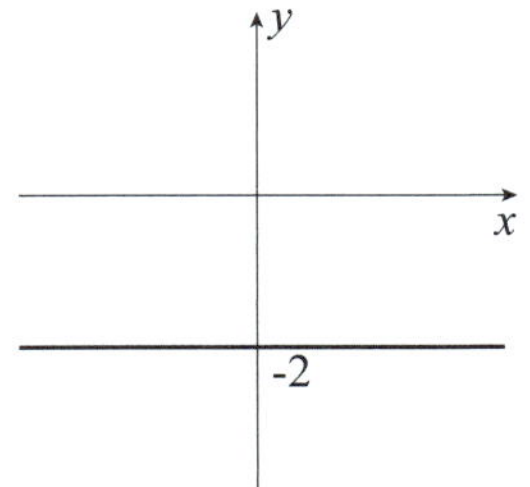

④ $\tan\theta=-1$, $\frac{y}{x}=-1$

$y=-x$

The graph of $\tan\theta=-1$ is a line passing through the origin with slope -1.

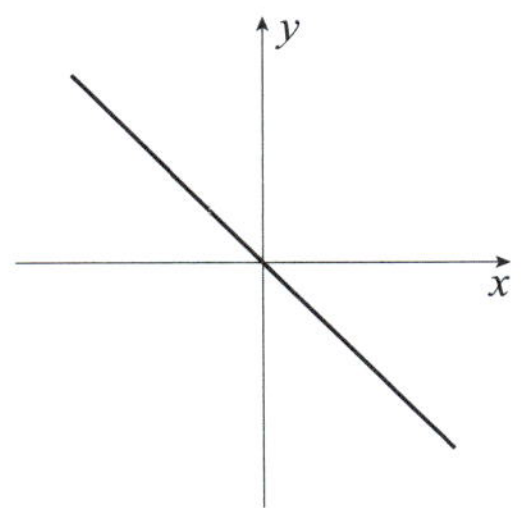

Check Point 8

① $r=2\sin\theta$

θ	r	θ	r
0	0	$\frac{\pi}{2}$	2
$\frac{\pi}{6}$	1	$\frac{2\pi}{3}$	$\sqrt{3}$
$\frac{\pi}{4}$	$\sqrt{2}$	$\frac{3\pi}{4}$	$\sqrt{2}$
$\frac{\pi}{3}$	$\sqrt{3}$	$\frac{5\pi}{6}$	1

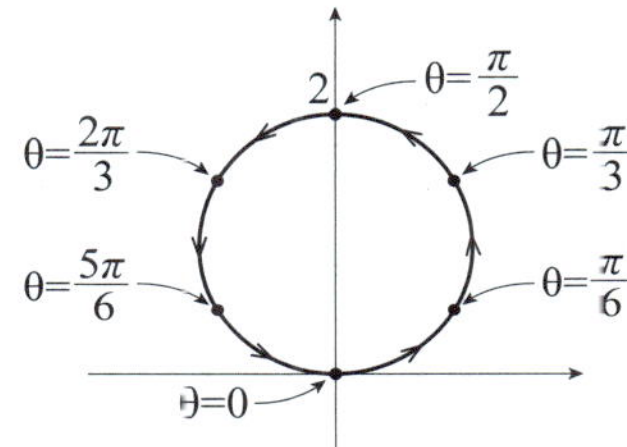

② $r=2+2\cos\theta$

θ	r	θ	r
0	4	$\frac{\pi}{2}$	2
$\frac{\pi}{6}$	$2+\sqrt{3}$	$\frac{2\pi}{3}$	1
$\frac{\pi}{4}$	$2+\sqrt{2}$	$\frac{3\pi}{4}$	$2-\sqrt{2}$
$\frac{\pi}{3}$	3	π	0

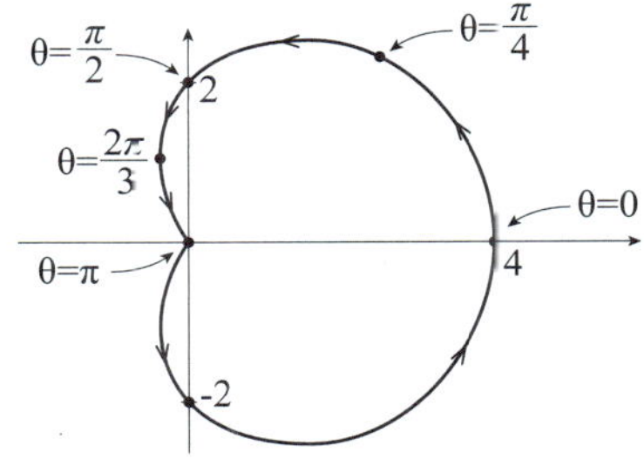

Check Point 9

① $r=-3\cos(2\theta)$

$r=-3\cos(2(-\theta))$ → Replace $(r,\ \theta)$ by $(r,\ -\theta)$

$r=-3\cos(2\theta)$ → $\cos(-\theta)=\cos\theta$

So $r=-3\cos(2\theta)$ is symmetric about the polar axis.

② $r=1+4\sin\theta$

$r=1+4\sin(\pi-\theta)$ → Replace $(r,\ \theta)$ by $(r,\ \pi-\theta)$

$r=1+4\sin\theta$ → $\sin(\pi-\theta)=\sin\theta$

So $r=1+4\sin\theta$ is symmetric about the line $\theta=\frac{\pi}{2}$.

Check Point 10

① $r=2+4\cos\theta$

Since $\frac{2}{4}<1$, the graph is limacon with an inner loop.

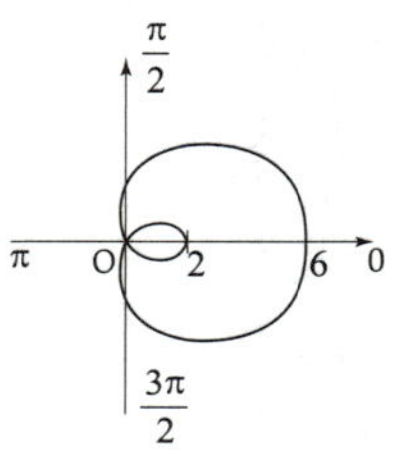

② $r=2-2\sin\theta$

Since $\frac{2}{2}=1$, the graph is cardioid.

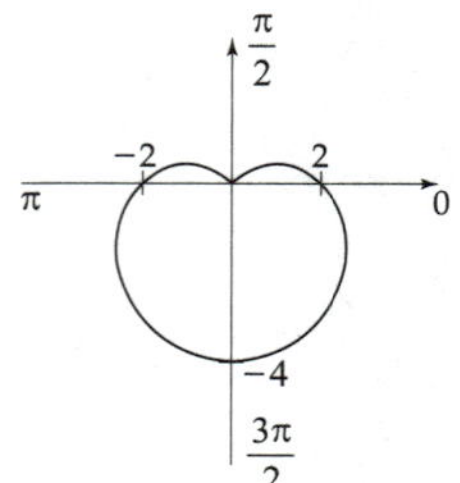

Check Point 11

① $r=3\sin(2\theta)$

This is a rose curve and since $n=2$, there are $2n=4$ petals.

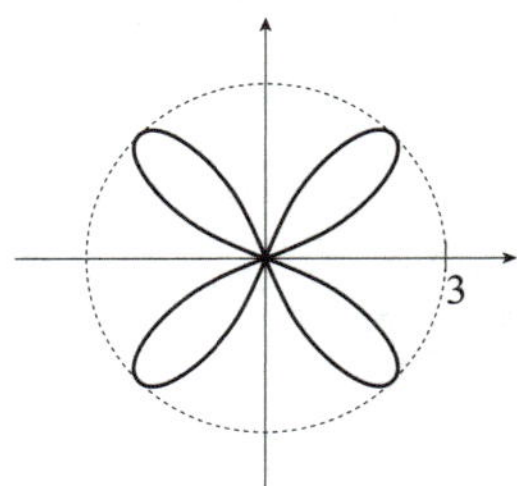

② $r=5\cos(3\theta)$

This is a rose curve and since $n=3$, there are 3 petals.

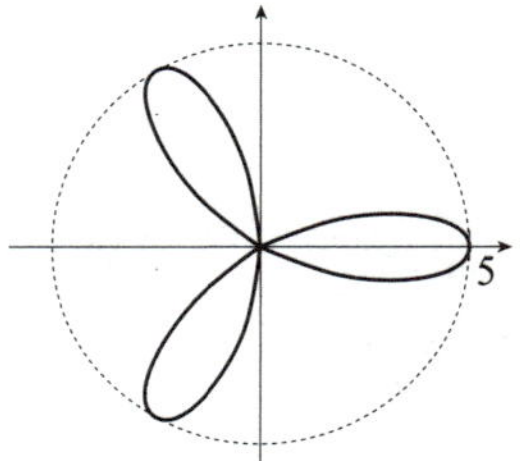

Review Exercises

01

(1) $x=r\cos\theta=4\cos\left(\frac{11\pi}{4}\right)=-2\sqrt{2}$ and $y=r\sin\theta=4\sin\left(\frac{11\pi}{4}\right)=2\sqrt{2}$. So the rectangular coordinate is $(-2\sqrt{2},\ 2\sqrt{2})$.

$\left(4,\ \frac{11\pi}{4}\right)\rightarrow(-2\sqrt{2},\ 2\sqrt{2})$

(2) $x=r\cos\theta=-1\cdot\cos\left(-\frac{2\pi}{3}\right)=\frac{1}{2}$ and

$y=r\sin\theta=-1\cdot\sin\left(-\frac{2\pi}{3}\right)=\frac{\sqrt{3}}{2}$

So the rectangular coordinate is $\left(\frac{1}{2},\ \frac{\sqrt{3}}{2}\right)$.

$\left(-1,-\frac{2\pi}{3}\right)\rightarrow\left(\frac{1}{2},\ \frac{\sqrt{3}}{2}\right)$

02

(1)

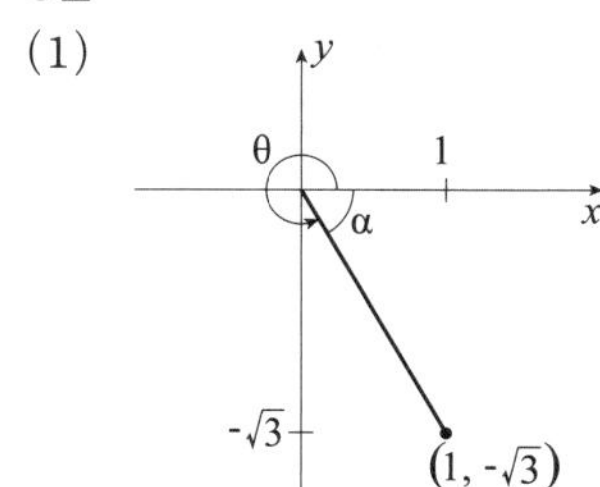

$\tan\alpha=\frac{\sqrt{3}}{1}=\sqrt{3}$, $\alpha=\tan^{-1}(\sqrt{3})=\frac{\pi}{3}$ and

$\theta=2\pi-\alpha=2\pi-\frac{\pi}{3}=\frac{5\pi}{3}$.

Since $r=\sqrt{1^2+(-\sqrt{3})^2}=2$, the polar coordinate is $\left(2,\ \frac{5\pi}{3}\right)$.

$(1,\ -\sqrt{3})\to\left(2,\ \frac{5\pi}{3}\right)$

Three addition polar points:

$\left(2,\ \frac{5\pi}{3}-2\pi\right)=\left(2,\ -\frac{\pi}{3}\right)$

$\left(-2,\ \frac{5\pi}{3}-\pi\right)=\left(-2,\ \frac{2\pi}{3}\right)$

$\left(-2,\frac{5\pi}{3}-3\pi\right)=\left(-2,-\frac{4\pi}{3}\right)$

(2)

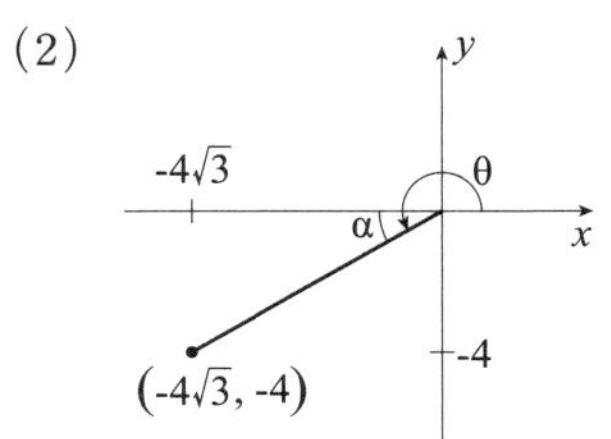

$\tan\alpha=\frac{-4}{-4\sqrt{3}}=\frac{1}{\sqrt{3}}$ $\alpha=\tan^{-1}\left(\frac{1}{\sqrt{3}}\right)=\frac{\pi}{6}$ and

$\theta=\alpha+\pi=\frac{\pi}{6}+\pi=\frac{7\pi}{6}$.

Since $r=\sqrt{(-4\sqrt{3})^2+(-4)^2}=8$, the polar coordinate is $\left(8,\ \frac{7\pi}{6}\right)$.

$(-4\sqrt{3},\ -4)\to\left(8,\ \frac{7\pi}{6}\right)$

Three addition polar points:

$\left(8,\ \frac{7\pi}{6}-2\pi\right)=\left(8,\ -\frac{5\pi}{6}\right)$

$\left(-8,\ \frac{7\pi}{6}-\pi\right)=\left(-8,\ \frac{\pi}{6}\right)$

$\left(-8,\ \frac{7\pi}{6}-3\pi\right)=\left(-8,\ -\frac{11\pi}{6}\right)$

03

(1) $y=5$

$r\sin\theta=5$, $r=\frac{5}{\sin\theta}=5\csc\theta$

$r=5\csc\theta$

(2) $y=-x+1$

$r\sin\theta=-r\cos\theta+1$, $r\sin\theta+r\cos\theta=1$

$r(\sin\theta+\cos\theta)=1$, $r=\frac{1}{\sin\theta+\cos\theta}$

$r=\frac{1}{\sin\theta+\cos\theta}$

(3) $x^2+y^2-4=0$

$r^2-4=0$, $r=2$

$r=2$

(4) $x^2+6x+y^2-4y=0$, $(x^2+y^2)+6x-4y=0$

$r^2+6r\cos\theta-4r\sin\theta=0$

$(r^2=4r\sin\theta-6r\cos\theta)\cdot\frac{1}{r}$,

$r=4\sin\theta-6\cos\theta$

$r=4\sin\theta-6\cos\theta$

(5) $2x+3y-9=0$,

$2r\cos\theta+3r\sin\theta=9$

$r(2\cos\theta+3\sin\theta)=9$, $r=\frac{9}{2\cos\theta+3\sin\theta}$

$r=\frac{9}{2\cos\theta+3\sin\theta}$

04

(1) $r=3$

$r^2=3^2$, $x^2+y^2=9$

$x^2+y^2=9$

(2) $r=6\sin\theta$

$(r=6\sin\theta)\cdot r$, $r^2=6r\sin\theta$

$x^2+y^2=6y$, $x^2+y^2-6y=0$

$x^2+y^2-6y=0$

(3) $r=-2\sec\theta$, $r=-\dfrac{2}{\cos\theta}$

$r\cos\theta=-2$, $x=-2$

$x=-2$

(4) $r=\dfrac{1}{1-\sin\theta}$, $r-r\sin\theta=1$, $r-y=1$

$r=y+1$, $r^2=(y+1)^2$

$x^2+y^2=y^2+2y+1$

$x^2-2y-1=0$

$x^2-2y-1=0$

(5) $r=\dfrac{1}{1+2\cos\theta}$, $r+2r\cos\theta=1$, $r+2x=1$

$r=1-2x$, $r^2=(1-2x)^2$

$x^2+y^2=1-4x+4x^2$

$3x^2-y^2-4x+1=0$

$3x^2-y^2-4x+1=0$

05

$r^2=4\sin(2\theta)$

$(-r)^2=4\sin(2\theta)$ → Replace (r, θ) by $(-r, \theta)$

$r^2=4\sin(2\theta)$ → $(-r)^2=r^2$

So $r^2=4\sin(2\theta)$ is symmetric about the pole.

06

$r=2-2\sec\theta$

$r=2-2\sec(-\theta)$ → Replace (r, θ) by $(r, -\theta)$

$r=2-2\sec\theta$ → $\sec(-\theta)=\sec\theta$

So $r=2-2\sec\theta$ is symmetric about the polar axis.

07

(1) The graph of $r=-4$ is a circle with center at the origin and radius of 4.

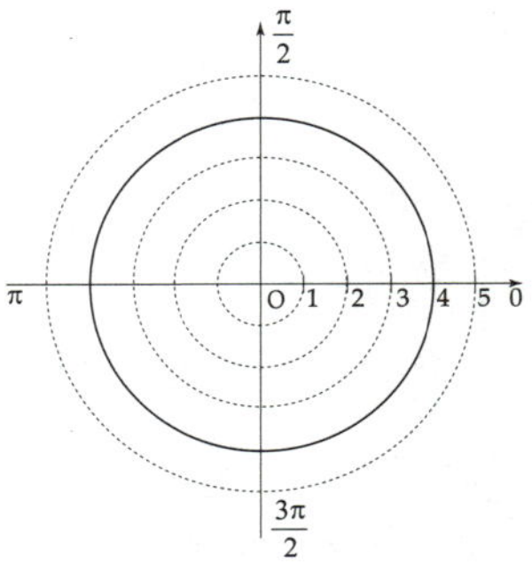

(2) $\theta=-\dfrac{7\pi}{6}$, $\tan\theta=\tan\left(-\dfrac{7\pi}{6}\right)$

$\dfrac{y}{x}=-\dfrac{1}{\sqrt{3}}$, $y=-\dfrac{1}{\sqrt{3}}x$

The graph of $\theta=-\dfrac{7\pi}{6}$ is a line passing through the origin with slope $-\dfrac{1}{\sqrt{3}}$.

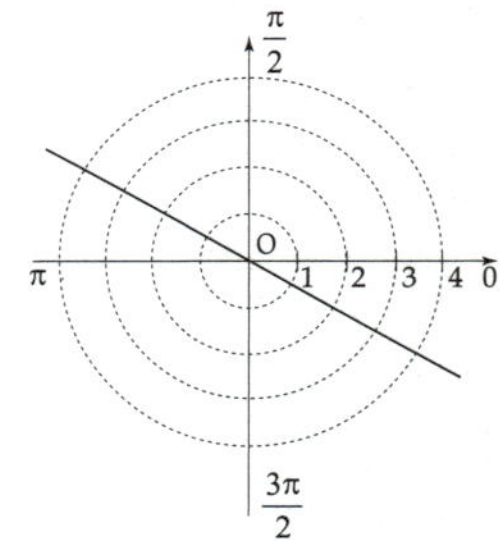

(3) $r=-4\sin\theta$

In a special polar graph, the graph of $r=a\sin\theta$ is a circle. So $r=-4\sin\theta$ is a circle with center at the $(0, -2)$ and radius of 2.

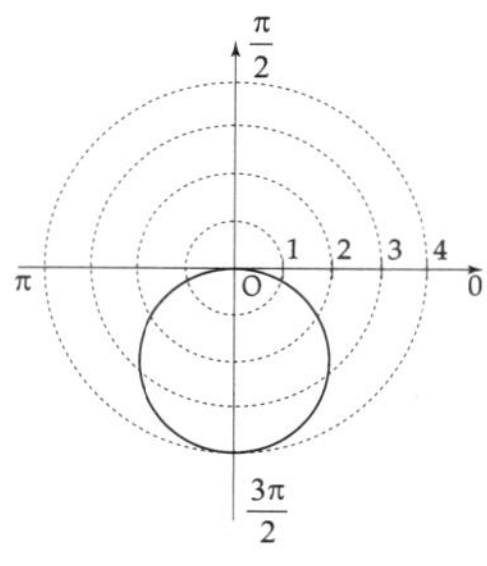

(4) $r=6\csc\theta$, $r=\dfrac{6}{\sin\theta}$

$r\sin\theta=6$, $y=6$

The graph of $r=6\csc\theta$ is a horizontal line 6 units above the $x-$axis.

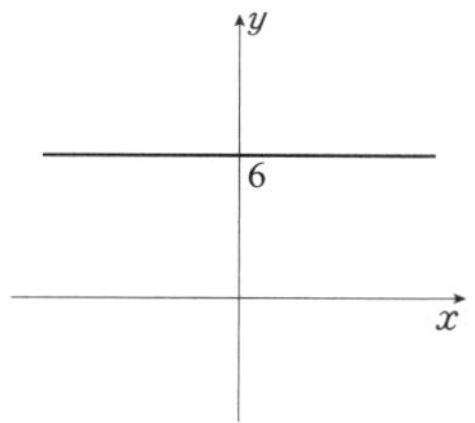

(5) $r=-1+3\sin\theta$

In a special polar graph, $r=a\pm b\sin\theta$ is a limacons. Since $\frac{1}{3}<1$, the graph is a limacon with an inner loop.

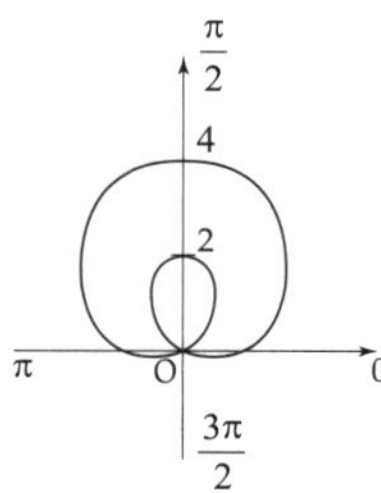

(6) $r=-3-2\cos\theta$

In a special polar graph, $r=a\pm b\cos\theta$ is a limacon. Since $\frac{3}{2}>1$, the graph is a dimpled limacon.

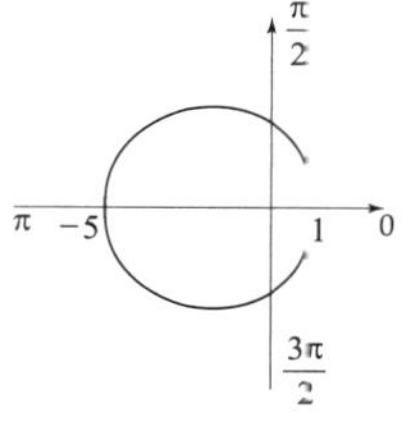

(7) $r=3\cos(2\theta)$

In a special polar graph, $r=a\cos(n\theta)$ is a rose curve. Since $n=2$, there are $2n=4$ petals.

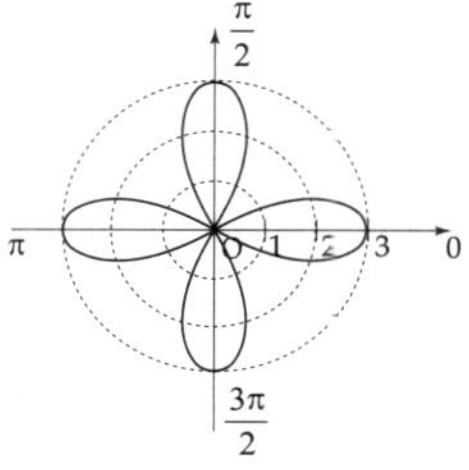

(8) $r=2\sin(5\theta)$

In a special polar graph, $r=a\sin(n\theta)$ is a rose curve. Since $n=5$, there are 5 petals.

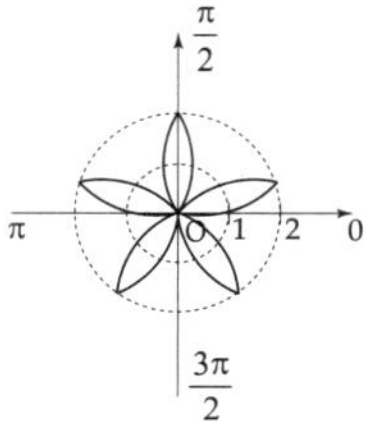

(9) $r^2=4\cos(2\theta)$

In a special polar graph, $r^2=a^2\cos(2\theta)$ is a lemniscate with $a=2$.

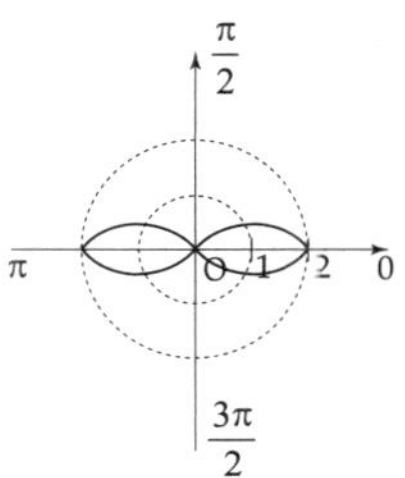

(10) $r^2=16\sin(2\theta)$

In a special polar graph, $r^2=a^2\sin(2\theta)$ is a lemniscate with $a=4$.

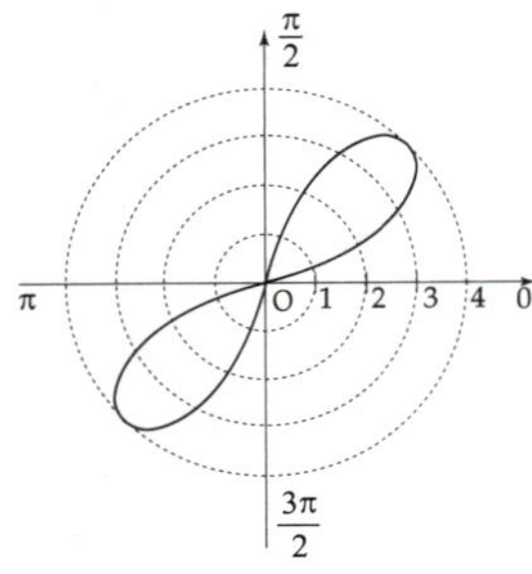

08

Polar coordinates: $\left(-4,\ \frac{\pi}{6}\right)$

Convert polar coordinates to rectangular coordinates:

$$x=r\cos\theta=-4\cos\left(\frac{\pi}{6}\right)=-4\cdot\frac{\sqrt{3}}{2}=-2\sqrt{3}$$

$$y=r\sin\theta=-4\sin\left(\frac{\pi}{6}\right)=-4\cdot\frac{1}{2}=-2$$

Therefore, the correct answer is (C).

09

(A) $\left(4,\ \frac{11\pi}{4}\right)=\left(4,\ \frac{3\pi}{4}+2\pi\right)$: Valid

(B) $\left(4,\ -\frac{5\pi}{4}\right)=\left(4,\ \frac{3\pi}{4}-2\pi\right)$: Valid

(C) $\left(-4,\ -\frac{\pi}{4}\right)=\left(-4,\ \frac{3\pi}{4}-\pi\right)$: Valid

(D) $\left(-4,\ \frac{5\pi}{4}\right)$: Not valid,

since $\left(4,\ \frac{3\pi}{4}+\pi\right)=\left(4,\ \frac{7\pi}{4}\right)$

Therefore, the correct answer is (D).

10

(A) $\left(-1,\ -\frac{4\pi}{3}\right)=\left(-1,\ \frac{2\pi}{3}-2\pi\right)$: Valid

(B) $\left(-1,\ -\frac{\pi}{3}\right)$: Not valid,

since $\left(-1,\ \frac{2\pi}{3}-2\pi\right)=\left(-1,\ -\frac{4\pi}{3}\right)$

(C) $\left(1,\ \frac{5\pi}{3}\right)=\left(1,\ \frac{2\pi}{3}+\pi\right)$: Valid

(D) $\left(1, -\frac{\pi}{3}\right)=\left(1,\ \frac{2\pi}{3}-\pi\right)$: Valid

Therefore, the correct answer is (B).

11

Since the circle has a radius $r=6$:

$(-3\sqrt{3})^2+k^2=6^2$

$k^2=36-27=9,\ k=3$

Since we are given that the coordinate is $(-3\sqrt{3},\ 3)$, the angle corresponds to $150°$.

12

Analyze the behavior of r in the given interval:

When $\theta=0$, $r=1-2\cos 0=-1$.

When θ approaches $\frac{\pi}{3}$,

$r=1-2\cos\frac{\pi}{3}=1-2\cdot\frac{1}{2}=0$.

Therefore, for $0\le\theta<\frac{\pi}{3}$, the graph is getting close to the origin, because r is negative and increasing. The correct answer is (B).

13

For $\frac{\pi}{2}\le\theta<\pi$, the angle 2θ ranges from π to 2π. In this interval, $\sin(2\theta)$ ranges from 0 to 0, going through negative values. Therefore, the graph shows in the fourth quadrant. The answer is (B).

14

The maximum distance from the origin will be at $\theta=\pi$:

$r=4\cos\pi-4=-4-4=-8$

The graph of the polar curve is at its maximum distance from the origin at $\theta=\pi$.

15

$\sin\theta$ increases from 0 to 1 in $0\le\theta<\frac{\pi}{2}$ and decreases from 1 to 0 in $\frac{\pi}{2}<\theta\le\pi$.

This fits the given behavior. Therefore, the answer is (A).

16

$r=\theta^2-\theta-12$

$=(\theta+3)(\theta-4)=0$, $\theta=-3$ and $\theta=4$

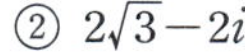

The distance between point on the graph of polar curve $r=f(\theta)$ and the origin is decreasing because the values of r are negative and increasing to 0. Therefore, the correct answer is (D).

10. Polar Form of a Complex Numbers

Check Point 1-1

$a+bi=r(\cos\theta+i\sin\theta)$

① $2i$

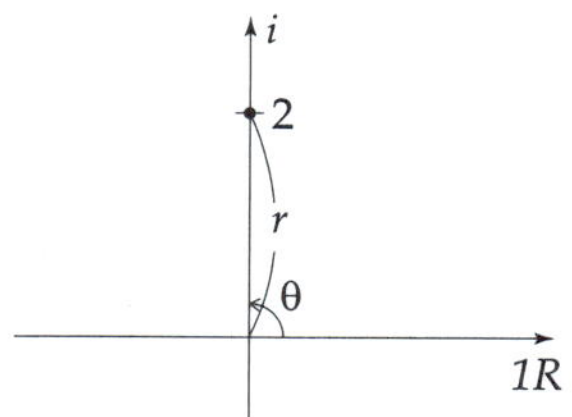

$r=\sqrt{0^2+2^2}=2$ and $\theta=\frac{\pi}{2}$. So we have $2i=2\left(\cos\frac{\pi}{2}+i\sin\frac{\pi}{2}\right)$.

② $2\sqrt{3}-2i$

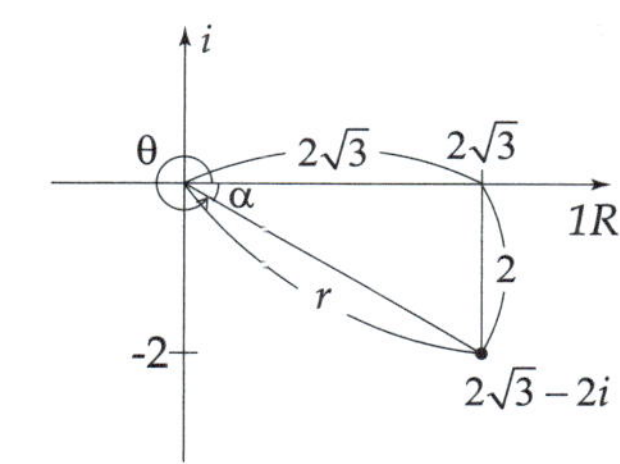

$r=\sqrt{(2\sqrt{3})^2+(2)^2}=4$

$\tan\alpha=\frac{2}{2\sqrt{3}}=\frac{1}{\sqrt{3}}$, $\alpha=\tan^{-1}\left(\frac{1}{\sqrt{3}}\right)=\frac{\pi}{6}$

$\theta=2\pi-\alpha=2\pi-\frac{\pi}{6}=\frac{11\pi}{6}$. So we have

$2\sqrt{3}-2i=4\left(\cos\frac{11\pi}{6}+i\sin\frac{11\pi}{6}\right)$

Check Point 1-2

① $4(\cos 225^\circ-i\sin 225^\circ)$

$=4\left(-\frac{\sqrt{2}}{2}-\frac{\sqrt{2}}{2}i\right)=-2\sqrt{2}-2\sqrt{2}i$

② $3\left(\cos\frac{3\pi}{2}-i\sin\frac{3\pi}{2}\right)=3(0-i)=-3i$

Check Point 2

① $z_1z_2=3\cdot 2(\cos(60°+30°)+i\sin(60°+30°))$
$=6(\cos 90°+i\sin 90°)=6(0+i)=6i$

$\frac{z_1}{z_2}=\frac{3}{2}(\cos(60°-30°)+i\sin(60°-30°))$
$=\frac{3}{2}(\cos 30+i\sin 30)$
$=\frac{3}{2}\left(\frac{\sqrt{3}}{2}+\frac{1}{2}i\right)=\frac{3\sqrt{3}}{4}+\frac{3}{4}i$

② $z_1z_2=6\cdot 3\left(\cos\left(\frac{3\pi}{4}+\pi\right)+i\sin\left(\frac{3\pi}{4}+\pi\right)\right)$
$=18\left(\cos\frac{7\pi}{4}+i\sin\frac{7\pi}{4}\right)$
$=18\left(\frac{\sqrt{2}}{2}-\frac{\sqrt{2}}{2}i\right)=9\sqrt{2}-9\sqrt{2}i$

$\frac{z_1}{z_2}=\frac{6}{3}\left(\cos\left(\frac{3\pi}{4}+\pi\right)+i\sin\left(\frac{3\pi}{4}+\pi\right)\right)$
$=2\left(\cos\left(-\frac{\pi}{4}\right)+i\sin\left(-\frac{\pi}{4}\right)\right)$
$=2\left(\frac{\sqrt{2}}{2}-\frac{\sqrt{2}}{2}i\right)=\sqrt{2}-\sqrt{2}i$

Check Point 3

① $\left(2\left(\cos\frac{\pi}{6}+i\sin\frac{\pi}{6}\right)\right)^4$
$=2^4\left(\cos\left(\frac{\pi}{6}\times 4\right)+i\sin\left(\frac{\pi}{6}\times 4\right)\right)$
$=16\left(\cos\frac{2\pi}{3}+i\sin\frac{2\pi}{3}\right)$
$=16\left(-\frac{1}{2}+\frac{\sqrt{3}}{2}i\right)=-8+8\sqrt{3}i$

② First, convert the complex number to polar form.

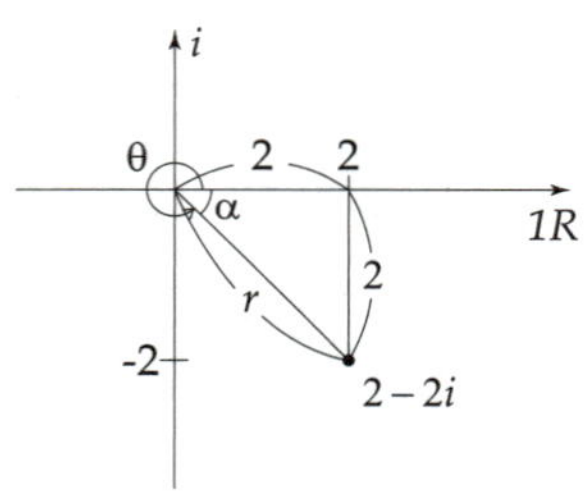

$r=\sqrt{2^2+2^2}=2\sqrt{2}$

$\tan\alpha=\frac{2}{2}=1,\ \alpha=\tan^{-1}1=\frac{\pi}{4}$

Since θ lies in Quadrant IV, $\theta=2\pi-\frac{\pi}{4}=\frac{7\pi}{4}$.

Now by the DeMoivre's Theorem,

$(2-2i)^5=\left(2\sqrt{2}\left(\cos\frac{7\pi}{4}+i\sin\frac{7\pi}{4}\right)\right)^5$
$=(2\sqrt{2})^5\left(\cos\left(\frac{7\pi}{4}\times 5\right)+i\sin\left(\frac{7\pi}{4}\times 5\right)\right)$
$=128\sqrt{2}\left(\cos\frac{35\pi}{4}+i\sin\frac{35\pi}{4}\right)$
$=128\sqrt{2}\left(-\frac{\sqrt{2}}{2}+\frac{\sqrt{2}}{2}i\right)=-128+128i$

Check Point 4

① The cube roots are given by

$\sqrt[3]{8}\left(\cos\left(\frac{\frac{\pi}{2}+2\pi k}{3}\right)+i\sin\left(\frac{\frac{\pi}{2}+2\pi k}{3}\right)\right),$

where $k=0$, 1, and 2.

$k=0$;

$\sqrt[3]{8}\left(\cos\left(\frac{\frac{\pi}{2}+2\pi(0)}{3}\right)+i\sin\left(\frac{\frac{\pi}{2}+2\pi(0)}{3}\right)\right)$
$=2\left(\cos\frac{\pi}{6}+i\sin\frac{\pi}{6}\right)=\sqrt{3}+i$

$k=1$;

$\sqrt[3]{8}\left(\cos\left(\frac{\frac{\pi}{2}+2\pi(1)}{3}\right)+i\sin\left(\frac{\frac{\pi}{2}+2\pi(1)}{3}\right)\right)$
$=2\left(\cos\frac{5\pi}{6}+i\sin\frac{5\pi}{6}\right)=-\sqrt{3}+i$

$k=2$;

$\sqrt[3]{8}\left(\cos\left(\frac{\frac{\pi}{2}+2\pi(2)}{3}\right)+i\sin\left(\frac{\frac{\pi}{2}+2\pi(2)}{3}\right)\right)$
$=2\left(\cos\frac{3\pi}{2}+i\sin\frac{3\pi}{2}\right)=-2i$

$\sqrt{3}+i,\ -\sqrt{3}+i,\ -2i$

② First, $-32i=32\left(\cos\frac{3\pi}{2}+i\sin\frac{3\pi}{2}\right)$.

The fifth roots are given by

$\sqrt[5]{32}\left(\cos\left(\frac{\frac{3\pi}{2}+2\pi k}{5}\right)+i\sin\left(\frac{\frac{3\pi}{2}+2\pi k}{5}\right)\right),$

wherek=0, 1, 2, 3 and 4.

$k=0$;

$$\sqrt[5]{32}\left(\cos\left(\frac{\frac{3\pi}{2}+2\pi(0)}{5}\right)+i\sin\left(\frac{\frac{3\pi}{2}+2\pi(0)}{5}\right)\right)$$

$$=2\left(\cos\frac{3\pi}{10}+i\sin\frac{3\pi}{10}\right)\approx 1.176+1.618i$$

$k=1$;

$$\sqrt[5]{32}\left(\cos\left(\frac{\frac{3\pi}{2}+2\pi(1)}{5}\right)+i\sin\left(\frac{\frac{3\pi}{2}+2\pi(1)}{5}\right)\right)$$

$$=2\left(\cos\frac{7\pi}{10}+i\sin\frac{7\pi}{10}\right)\approx -1.176+1.618i$$

$k=2$;

$$\sqrt[5]{32}\left(\cos\left(\frac{\frac{3\pi}{2}+2\pi(2)}{5}\right)+i\sin\left(\frac{\frac{3\pi}{2}+2\pi(2)}{5}\right)\right)$$

$$=2\left(\cos\frac{11\pi}{10}+i\sin\frac{11\pi}{10}\right)\approx -1.902-0.618i$$

$k=3$;

$$\sqrt[5]{32}\left(\cos\left(\frac{\frac{3\pi}{2}+2\pi(3)}{5}\right)+i\sin\left(\frac{\frac{3\pi}{2}+2\pi(3)}{5}\right)\right)$$

$$=2\left(\cos\frac{15\pi}{10}+i\sin\frac{15\pi}{10}\right)\approx -2i$$

$k=4$;

$$\sqrt[5]{32}\left(\cos\left(\frac{\frac{3\pi}{2}+2\pi(4)}{5}\right)+i\sin\left(\frac{\frac{3\pi}{2}+2\pi(4)}{5}\right)\right)$$

$$=2\left(\cos\frac{19\pi}{10}+i\sin\frac{19\pi}{10}\right)\approx 1.902-0.618\text{i}$$

$1.176+1.618i$, $-1.176+1.618i$, $-1.902-0.618i$, -2i, $1.902-0.618i$

Review Exercises

01

$a+bi=r(\cos\theta+i\sin\theta)$

(1) $-3i$

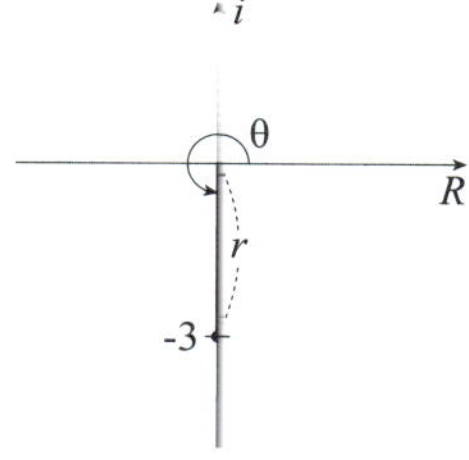

$r=\sqrt{(-3)^2+0^2}=3$ and $\theta=\frac{3\pi}{2}$

$-3i=3\left(\cos\frac{3\pi}{2}+i\sin\frac{3\pi}{2}\right)$

(2) $-3+3i$

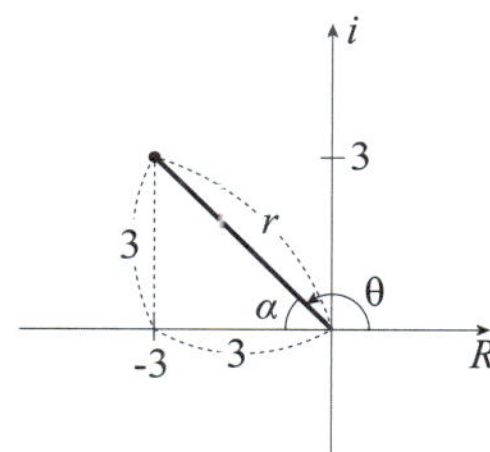

$r=\sqrt{(-3)^2+3^2}=3\sqrt{2}$

$\tan\alpha=\frac{3}{3}=1$, $\alpha=\tan^{-1}(1)$

$\theta=\pi-\tan^{-1}(1)=\pi-\frac{\pi}{4}=\frac{3\pi}{4}$

$-3+3i=3\sqrt{2}\left(\cos\frac{3\pi}{4}+i\sin\frac{3\pi}{4}\right)$

02

(1) $2(\cos 60°+i\sin 60°)=2\left(\frac{1}{2}+\frac{\sqrt{3}}{2}i\right)=1+\sqrt{3}i$

(2) $\sqrt{3}\left(\cos\frac{7\pi}{6}+i\sin\frac{7\pi}{6}\right)=\sqrt{3}\left(-\frac{\sqrt{3}}{2}-\frac{1}{2}i\right)$

$=-\frac{3}{2}-\frac{\sqrt{3}}{2}i$

03

(1) $z_1z_2=2\cdot4(\cos(120°+90°)+i\sin(120°+90°))$

$=8(\cos 210°+i\sin 210°)$

$=8\left(-\frac{\sqrt{3}}{2}-\frac{1}{2}i\right)=-4\sqrt{3}-4i$

$\frac{z_1}{z_2}=\frac{2}{4}(\cos(120°-90°)+i\sin(120°-90°))$

$=\frac{1}{2}(\cos 30°+i\sin 30°)$

$=\frac{1}{2}\left(\frac{\sqrt{3}}{2}+\frac{1}{2}i\right)=\frac{\sqrt{3}}{4}+\frac{1}{4}i$

(2) $z_1z_2=6\cdot2\left(\cos\left(\frac{4\pi}{3}+\frac{13\pi}{6}\right)+i\sin\left(\frac{4\pi}{3}+\frac{13\pi}{6}\right)\right)$

$=12\left(\cos\frac{7\pi}{2}+i\sin\frac{7\pi}{2}\right)$

$=12(0-i)=-12i$

$\frac{z_1}{z_2}=\frac{6}{2}\left(\cos\left(\frac{4\pi}{3}-\frac{13\pi}{6}\right)+i\sin\left(\frac{4\pi}{3}-\frac{13\pi}{6}\right)\right)$

$=3\left(\cos\left(-\frac{5\pi}{6}\right)+i\sin\left(-\frac{5\pi}{6}\right)\right)$

$=3\left(-\frac{\sqrt{3}}{2}-\frac{1}{2}i\right)=-\frac{3\sqrt{3}}{2}-\frac{3}{2}i$

04

(1) $\left(\cos\frac{5\pi}{3}+i\sin\frac{5\pi}{3}\right)^3$

$=\cos\left(\frac{5\pi}{3}\times3\right)+i\sin\left(\frac{5\pi}{3}\times3\right)$

$=\cos 5\pi+i\sin 5\pi=-1$

(2) First, convert the complex number to trigonometric form.

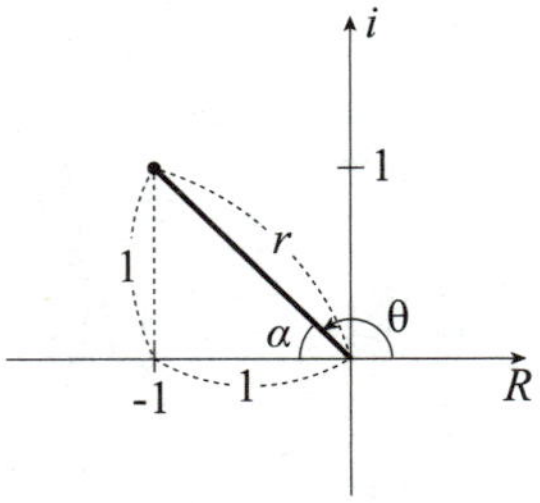

$-1+i \rightarrow r=\sqrt{(-1)^2+1^2}=\sqrt{2}$

$\tan\alpha=\frac{1}{1}=1,\ \alpha=\tan^{-1}(1)$

$\theta=\pi-\tan^{-1}(1)=\pi-\frac{\pi}{4}=\frac{3\pi}{4}$

So, $(-1+i)^6=\left(\sqrt{2}\left(\cos\frac{3\pi}{4}+i\sin\frac{3\pi}{4}\right)\right)^6$

$=(\sqrt{2})^6\left(\cos\left(\frac{3\pi}{4}\times6\right)+i\sin\left(\frac{3\pi}{4}\times6\right)\right)$

$=8\left(\cos\frac{9\pi}{2}+i\sin\frac{9\pi}{2}\right)$

$=8(0+i)=8i$

05

(1) The square roots are given by

$$\cos\left(\frac{\frac{5\pi}{4}+2\pi k}{2}\right)+i\sin\left(\frac{\frac{5\pi}{4}+2\pi k}{2}\right),$$

where $k=0$ and 1.

$k=0$;

$\left(\cos\left(\frac{\frac{5\pi}{4}+2\pi(0)}{2}\right)+i\sin\left(\frac{\frac{5\pi}{4}+2\pi(0)}{2}\right)\right)$

$=\cos\left(\frac{5\pi}{8}\right)+i\sin\left(\frac{5\pi}{8}\right)$

$=-\frac{\sqrt{2-\sqrt{2}}}{2}+\frac{\sqrt{2+\sqrt{2}}}{2}i$

$k=1$;

$\left(\cos\left(\frac{\frac{5\pi}{4}+2\pi(1)}{2}\right)+i\sin\left(\frac{\frac{5\pi}{4}+2\pi(1)}{2}\right)\right)$

$=\cos\left(\frac{13\pi}{8}\right)+i\sin\left(\frac{13\pi}{8}\right)$

$=\frac{\sqrt{2-\sqrt{2}}}{2}-\frac{\sqrt{2+\sqrt{2}}}{2}i$

$-\frac{\sqrt{2-\sqrt{2}}}{2}+\frac{\sqrt{2+\sqrt{2}}}{2}i,\ \frac{\sqrt{2-\sqrt{2}}}{2}-\frac{\sqrt{2+\sqrt{2}}}{2}i$

(2) First, $-\frac{1}{2}+\frac{\sqrt{3}}{2}i=\cos\frac{2\pi}{3}+i\sin\frac{2\pi}{3}$.

The fourth roots are given by

$$\cos\left(\frac{\frac{2\pi}{3}+2\pi k}{4}\right)+i\sin\left(\frac{\frac{2\pi}{3}+2\pi k}{4}\right)$$

where $k=0$, 1, 2, and 3.

$k=0$;

$\cos\left(\frac{\frac{2\pi}{3}+2\pi(0)}{4}\right)+i\sin\left(\frac{\frac{2\pi}{3}+2\pi(0)}{4}\right)$

$=\cos\frac{\pi}{6}+i\sin\frac{\pi}{6}=\frac{\sqrt{3}}{2}+\frac{1}{2}i$

$k=1$;

$$\cos\left(\frac{\frac{2\pi}{3}+2\pi(1)}{4}\right)+i\sin\left(\frac{\frac{2\pi}{3}+2\pi(1)}{4}\right)$$

$$=\cos\frac{2\pi}{3}+i\sin\frac{2\pi}{3}=-\frac{1}{2}+\frac{\sqrt{3}}{2}i$$

$k=2$;

$$\cos\left(\frac{\frac{2\pi}{3}+2\pi(2)}{4}\right)+i\sin\left(\frac{\frac{2\pi}{3}+2\pi(2)}{4}\right)$$

$$=\cos\frac{7\pi}{6}+i\sin\frac{7\pi}{6}=-\frac{\sqrt{3}}{2}-\frac{1}{2}i$$

$k=3$;

$$\cos\left(\frac{\frac{2\pi}{3}+2\pi(3)}{4}\right)+i\sin\left(\frac{\frac{2\pi}{4}+2\pi(3)}{4}\right)$$

$$=\cos\frac{5\pi}{3}+i\sin\frac{5\pi}{3}=\frac{1}{2}-\frac{\sqrt{3}}{2}i$$

$\frac{\sqrt{3}}{2}+\frac{1}{2}i,\ -\frac{1}{2}+\frac{\sqrt{3}}{2}i,\ -\frac{\sqrt{3}}{2}-\frac{1}{2}i,\ \frac{1}{2}-\frac{\sqrt{3}}{2}i$

Unit Ⅲ Test

01

(1) $-840°\times\frac{\pi}{180°}=-\frac{14\pi}{3}$

(2) $28°45'=\left(28+\frac{45}{60}\right)^{°}=28.75°$

$28.75°\times\frac{\pi}{180°}=\frac{23\pi}{144}$

02

(1) $-2.4\pi\times\frac{180°}{\pi}=-432°$

(2) $0.75\times\frac{180°}{\pi}=\left(\frac{135}{\pi}\right)^{°}$

03

(1) $180°+360°=540°,\ 180°-360°=-180°$

(2) $\frac{7\pi}{3}-2\pi=\frac{\pi}{3},\ \frac{7\pi}{3}-2(2\pi)=-\frac{5\pi}{3}$

04

The area of the sector is $A=\frac{1}{2}r^2\theta$.

$12\pi=\frac{1}{2}r^2\left(\frac{3\pi}{4}\right),\ r^2=32,\ r=4\sqrt{2}$

So the arc length of the circle is

$l=r\theta=4\sqrt{2}\left(\frac{3\pi}{4}\right)=3\sqrt{2}\pi$

05

$120°\times\frac{\pi}{180°}=\frac{2\pi}{3}$

The arc length of the circle is $l=r\theta$.

$4\pi=r\left(\frac{2\pi}{3}\right),\ r=6$

So the area of the sector is

$A=\frac{1}{2}r^2\theta=\frac{1}{2}rl=\frac{1}{2}(6)(4\pi)=12\pi$

06

(1) The linear speed of a tire in miles per min is

$$v=\frac{25\text{ mi}}{\text{hr}}\times\frac{1\text{ hr}}{60\text{ min}}=\frac{5}{12}\text{ mi/min}.$$

(2) First, the circumference of the circle is $C=2\pi(9)=18\pi\ in$. In miles,

$$18\pi\text{ in}\times\frac{1\text{ ft}}{12\text{ in}}\times\frac{1\text{ mi}}{5280\text{ ft}}=\frac{\pi}{3520}\text{ mi}.$$

Now, using the linear speed we found above, $\dfrac{5\text{ mi}}{12\text{ min}}\times\dfrac{1\text{ rev}}{\frac{\pi}{3520}\text{ mi}}=466.85\text{ rev/min}.$

The tire rotates about 467 revolutions per minutes.

07

(1)

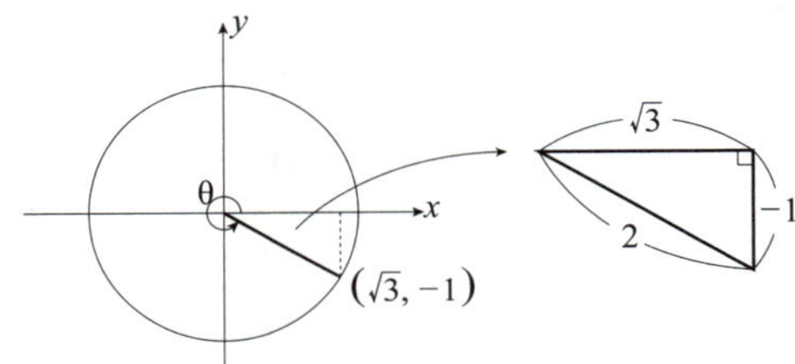

$\sin\theta=-\frac{1}{2}$ $\qquad$ $\csc\theta=-2$

$\cos\theta=\frac{\sqrt{3}}{2}$ $\qquad$ $\sec\theta=\frac{2}{\sqrt{3}}=\frac{2\sqrt{3}}{3}$

$\tan\theta=-\frac{1}{\sqrt{3}}=-\frac{\sqrt{3}}{3}$

$\cot\theta=-\sqrt{3}$

(2)

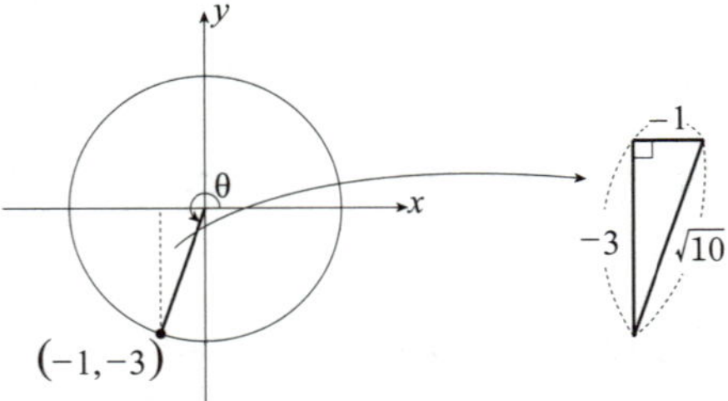

$\sin\theta=-\frac{3}{\sqrt{10}}=-\frac{3\sqrt{10}}{10}$ $\qquad$ $\csc\theta=-\frac{\sqrt{10}}{3}$

$\cos\theta=-\frac{1}{\sqrt{10}}=-\frac{\sqrt{10}}{10}$

$\sec\theta=-\sqrt{10}$

$\tan\theta=\frac{-3}{-1}=3$ $\qquad$ $\cot\theta=\frac{1}{3}$

08

(1)

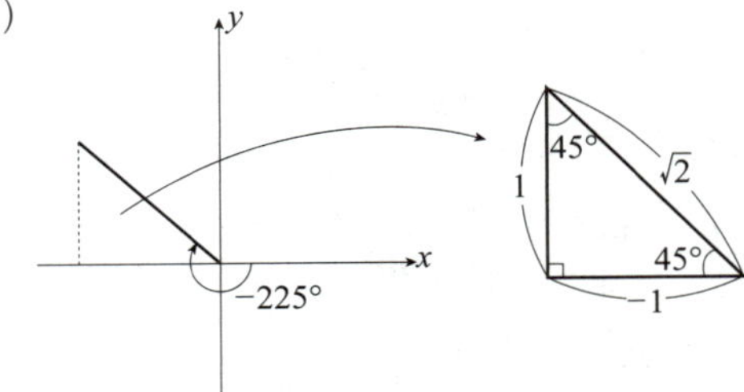

$\sin(-225^\circ)=\frac{1}{\sqrt{2}}=\frac{\sqrt{2}}{2}$

$\csc(-225^\circ)=\sqrt{2}$

$\cos(-225^\circ)=-\frac{1}{\sqrt{2}}=-\frac{\sqrt{2}}{2}$

$\sec(-225^\circ)=-\sqrt{2}$

$\tan(-225^\circ)=-\frac{1}{1}=-1$

$\cot(-225^\circ)=-1$

(2)

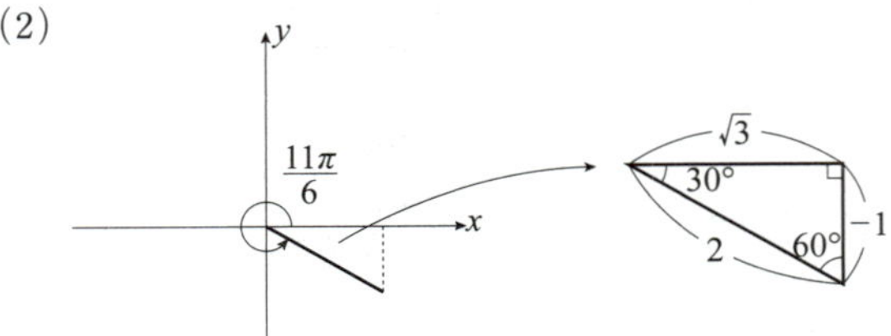

$\sin\frac{11\pi}{6}=-\frac{1}{2}$ $\qquad$ $\csc\frac{11\pi}{6}=-2$

$\cos\frac{11\pi}{6}=\frac{\sqrt{3}}{2}$ $\qquad$ $\sec\frac{11\pi}{6}=\frac{2}{\sqrt{3}}=\frac{2\sqrt{3}}{3}$

$\tan\frac{11\pi}{6}=-\frac{1}{\sqrt{3}}=-\frac{\sqrt{3}}{3}$

$\cot\frac{11\pi}{6}=-\sqrt{3}$

09

(1) $\tan\theta=-\frac{2}{5} \rightarrow \cot\theta=-\frac{5}{2}$, $\cos\theta>0$

Since $\tan\theta<0$ and $\cos\theta>0$, θ lies in Quadrant IV.

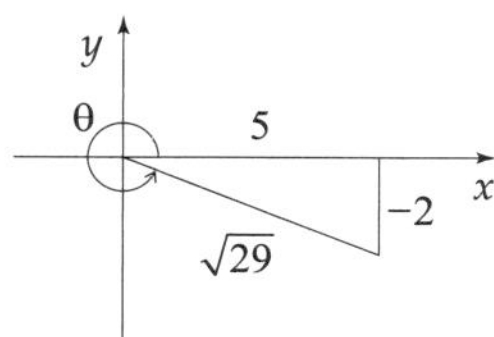

$\sin\theta=-\frac{2}{\sqrt{29}}=-\frac{2\sqrt{29}}{29}$ $\csc\theta=-\frac{\sqrt{29}}{2}$

$\cos\theta=\frac{5}{\sqrt{29}}=\frac{5\sqrt{29}}{29}$ $\sec\theta=\frac{\sqrt{29}}{5}$

(2) $\csc=-\frac{\sqrt{17}}{4} \rightarrow \sin\theta=-\frac{4}{\sqrt{17}}=-\frac{4\sqrt{17}}{17}$, $\sec<0$

Since both $\csc\theta<0$ and $\sec\theta<0$, θ lies in Quadrant III.

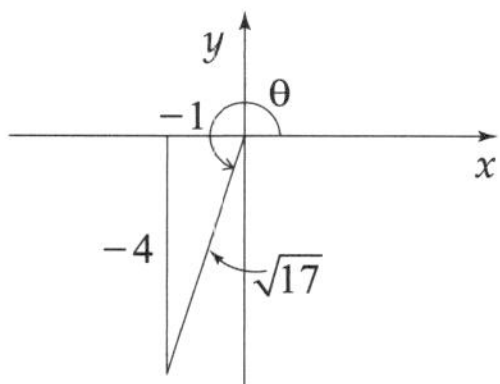

$\cos\theta=-\frac{1}{\sqrt{17}}=-\frac{\sqrt{17}}{17}$ $\sec\theta=-\sqrt{17}$

$\tan\theta=\frac{-4}{-1}=4$ $\cot\theta=\frac{1}{4}$

10

$y=\frac{2}{3}\tan\left(\frac{2x-1}{3}\right)+1=\frac{2}{3}\tan\left(\frac{2x}{3}-\frac{1}{3}\right)+1$

$=\frac{2}{3}\tan\frac{2}{3}\left(x-\frac{1}{2}\right)+1$

The period is $\frac{\pi}{\frac{2}{3}}=\frac{3\pi}{2}$.

11

The function $y=2\cos\left(\frac{\pi}{3}-2x\right)$ has an amplitude of $|2|=2$. So the range of $y=2\cos\left(\frac{\pi}{3}-2x\right)$ is $-2\leq y\leq 2$. Since the graph of $y=2\cos\left(\frac{\pi}{3}-2x\right)-2$ is shifted 2 units down from $y=2\cos\left(\frac{\pi}{3}-2x\right)$, the range is

$-2-2\leq y\leq 2-2$

$-4\leq y\leq 0$

12

The amplitude of the graph is 4 and the period is

$\frac{3\pi}{4}-\left(-\frac{\pi}{4}\right)=\pi$. Since $a<0$, the graph can be thought of as shifting $\frac{\pi}{4}$ units to the left from $y=-4\sin(2x)$. So, the function is $y=-4\sin 2\left(x+\frac{\pi}{4}\right)$.

13

In the interval $\frac{\pi}{2}<x<\pi$, both the graph of sine and tangent are bending downwards, indicating concave down behavior. Therefore, the correct answer is (A).

14

In the interval $\frac{\pi}{4}<x<\frac{3\pi}{4}$, $\cos(2x)$ first decreases and then increases. Also, the graph of f is concave up during this interval. Therefore, the correct answer is (B).

15

$f(x)=g(h(x)) \Rightarrow \cos x=\sin(h(x)+\pi)$

We need to find $h(x)$ such that $\cos x=\sin(h(x)+\pi)$. Using the co−function identity:

$$x+h(x)+\pi=\frac{\pi}{2}$$

$$h(x)=-x-\frac{\pi}{2}$$

Therefore, the correct answer is (C).

16

(1) $\cos^{-1}\left(\sin\left(-\frac{5\pi}{4}\right)\right)$

First, $\sin\left(-\frac{5\pi}{4}\right)=\frac{\sqrt{2}}{2}$. If $\cos^{-1}\frac{\sqrt{2}}{2}=y$, then $\cos y=\frac{\sqrt{2}}{2}$ in the range of $[0, \pi]$.

Since $\cos\frac{\pi}{4}=\frac{\sqrt{2}}{2}$, $\frac{\pi}{4}=\cos^{-1}\frac{\sqrt{2}}{2}$.

Thus, $\cos^{-1}\left(\sin\left(-\frac{5\pi}{4}\right)\right)=\cos^{-1}\frac{\sqrt{2}}{2}=\frac{\pi}{4}$.

(2) $\cos\left(\arctan\frac{5}{2}\right)$

If $\arctan\frac{5}{2}=y$, then $\tan y=\frac{5}{2}$ in the range of $\left(-\frac{\pi}{2}, \frac{\pi}{2}\right)$.

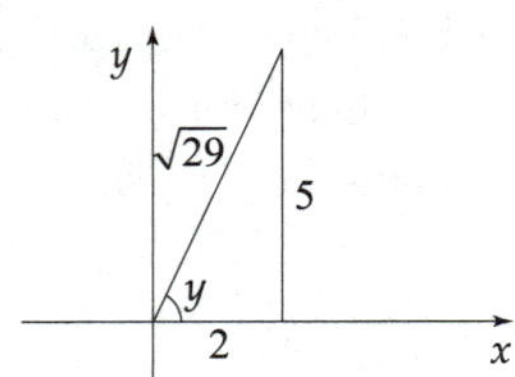

Thus, $\cos\left(\arctan\frac{5}{2}\right)=\cos y=\frac{2}{\sqrt{29}}=\frac{2\sqrt{29}}{29}$.

17

(1) $\tan(\sin^{-1}(3x)) \rightarrow$ If $\sin^{-1}(3x)=y$, then $\sin y=3x$.

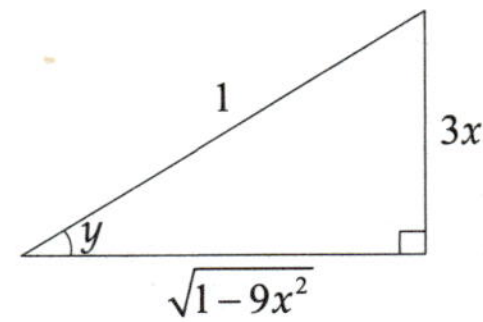

Thus, $\tan(\sin^{-1}(3x))=\tan y=\frac{3x}{\sqrt{1-9x^2}}$.

(2) $\sec(\arcsin(x-1))$

If $\arcsin(x-1)=y$, then $\sin y=x-1$.

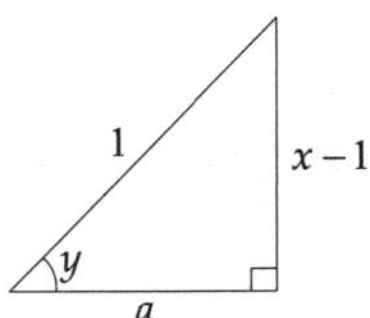

$(x-1)^2+a^2=1$, $x^2-2x+1+a^2=1$

$a^2=2x-x^2$, $a=\sqrt{2x-x^2}$

Thus, $\sec(\arcsin(x-1))=\sec y=\frac{1}{\sqrt{2x-x^2}}$.

18

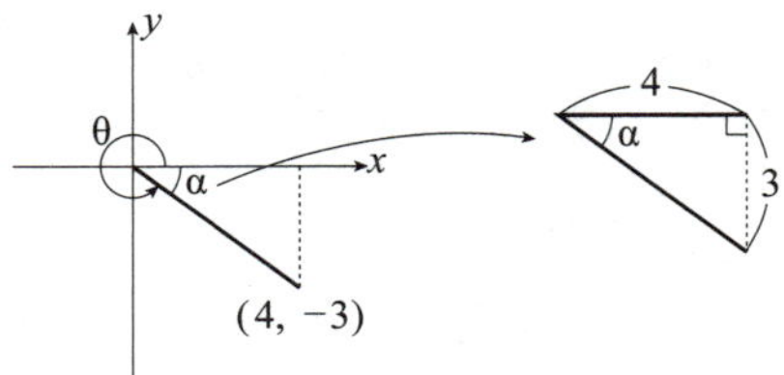

$\tan\alpha=\frac{3}{4}$, $\alpha=\tan^{-1}\left(\frac{3}{4}\right)$. Since $\alpha+\theta=2\pi$, $\theta=2\pi-\alpha=2\pi-\tan^{-1}\left(\frac{3}{4}\right)$.

So the answer is (E).

19

(1) If $\cos\theta=\frac{3m}{4}$ and $0<\theta<\frac{\pi}{2}$, we could have the following triangle :

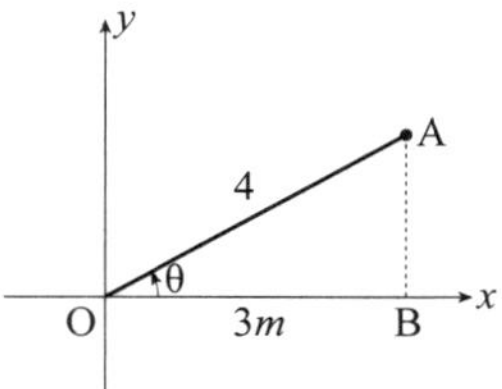

By the Pythagorean theorem,
$\overline{AB}^2+(3m)^2=4^2$
$\overline{AB}^2=16-9m^2$, $\overline{AB}=\sqrt{16-9m^2}$
Therefore, $\csc\theta=\frac{4}{\sqrt{16-9m^2}}$.

(2) If the angle is $\pi-\theta$, we have the following triangle :

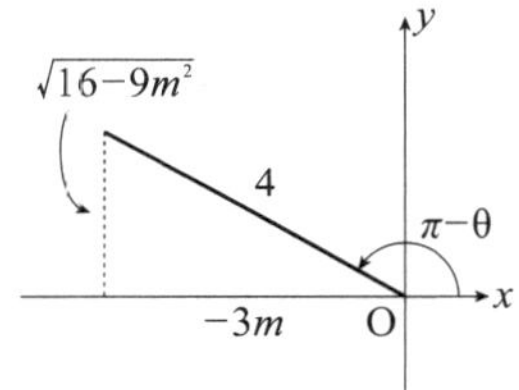

$\sin(\pi-\theta)=\frac{\sqrt{16-9m^2}}{4}$

(3) If the angle is $\theta+\pi$, we have the following triangle :

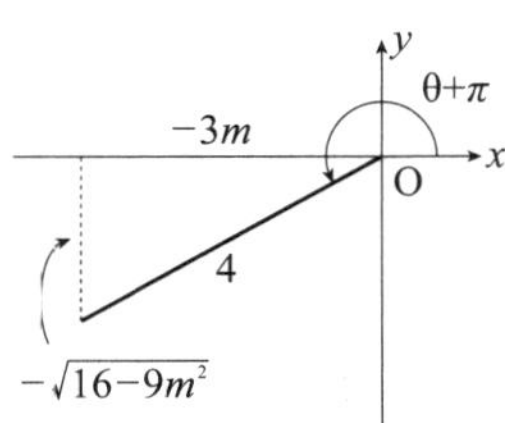

$\sec(\theta+\pi)=-\frac{4}{3m}$

(4) If the angle is $2\pi-\theta$, we have the following triangle :

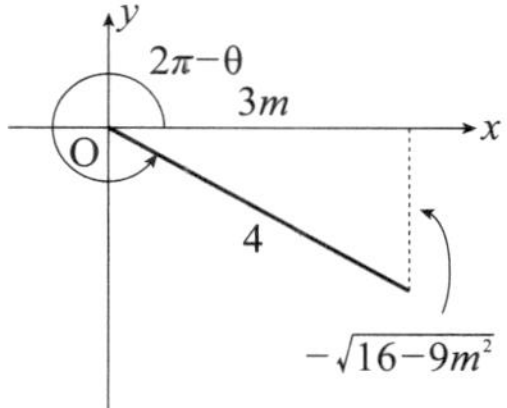

$\tan(2\pi-\theta)=-\frac{\sqrt{16-9m^2}}{3m}$

20

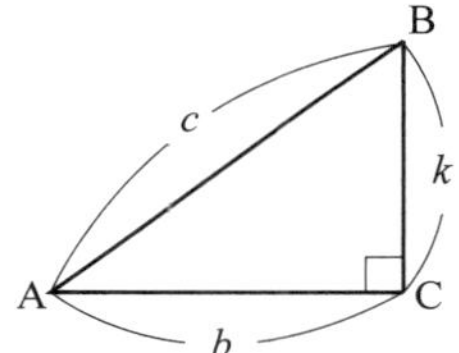

$\sin A=\frac{k}{c}=\frac{2}{3}$, $2c=3k$, $c=\frac{3k}{2}$

Using the Pythagorean theorem,
$b^2+k^2=c^2$, $b=\sqrt{c^2-k^2}$

$\overline{AC}=b=\sqrt{\left(\frac{3k}{2}\right)^2-k^2}=\sqrt{\frac{9k^2}{4}-k^2}$

$=\sqrt{\frac{5k^2}{4}}=\frac{\sqrt{5}k}{2}$

21

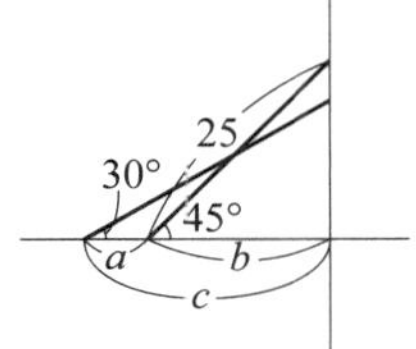

The distance the ladder traveled on the

ground is $a=c-b$.

$\cos 45°=\frac{b}{25}$, $b=25\cos 45°=25\cdot\frac{\sqrt{2}}{2}=\frac{25\sqrt{2}}{2}$

$\cos 30°=\frac{c}{25}$, $c=25\cos 30°=25\cdot\frac{\sqrt{3}}{2}=\frac{25\sqrt{3}}{2}$

$a=c-b=\frac{25\sqrt{3}}{2}-\frac{25\sqrt{2}}{2}=\frac{25}{2}(\sqrt{3}-\sqrt{2})$.

The ladder traveled $\frac{25}{2}(\sqrt{3}-\sqrt{2})$ feet.

22

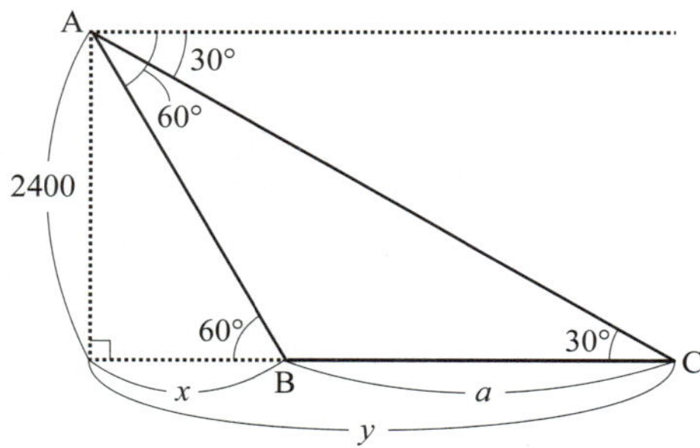

A represents the airplane and B and C represent two mountains. The distance between two mountains is $a=y-x$.

$\tan 60°=\frac{2400}{x}$, $x=\frac{2400}{\tan 60°}=\frac{2400}{\sqrt{3}}=800\sqrt{3}$

$\tan 30°=\frac{2400}{y}$, $y=\frac{2400}{\tan 30°}=2400\sqrt{3}$

$a=y-x=2400\sqrt{3}-800\sqrt{3}=1600\sqrt{3}$.

The distance between two mountains is $1600\sqrt{3}$.

23

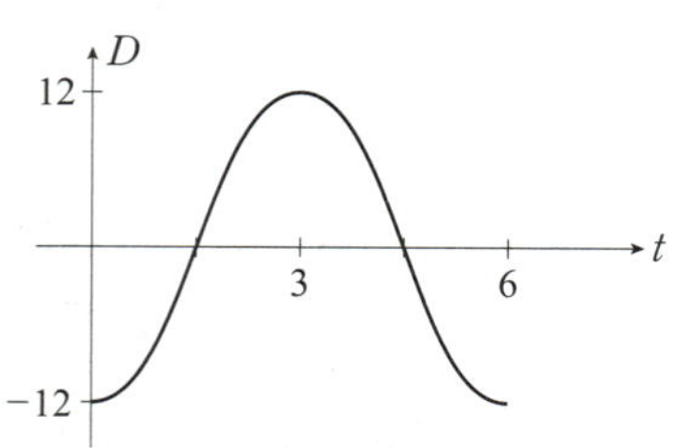

The amplitude is $12(a=-12)$ and the period is $6\left(\frac{2\pi}{w}=6,\ w=\frac{\pi}{3}\right)$. So the equation is $y=-12\cos\left(\frac{\pi}{3}t\right)$.

24

$\csc(-\theta)=\frac{3}{2}$, $-\csc\theta=\frac{3}{2}$, $\csc\theta=-\frac{3}{2}$ and $\cot\theta>0$. → θ is in Quadrant III.

From $1+\cot^2\theta=\csc^2\theta$,

$1+\cot^2\theta=\left(-\frac{3}{2}\right)^2$, $\cot^2\theta=\frac{5}{4}$, $\cot\theta=\frac{\sqrt{5}}{2}$

$\sin\theta=\frac{1}{\csc\theta}=-\frac{2}{3}$, $\tan\theta=\frac{1}{\cot\theta}=\frac{2}{\sqrt{5}}=\frac{2\sqrt{5}}{5}$

$\tan\theta=\frac{\sin\theta}{\cos\theta}$, $\cos\theta=\frac{\sin\theta}{\tan\theta}=\frac{-\frac{2}{3}}{\frac{2}{\sqrt{5}}}=-\frac{\sqrt{5}}{3}$

$\sec\theta=\frac{1}{\cos\theta}=\frac{1}{-\frac{\sqrt{5}}{3}}=-\frac{3}{\sqrt{5}}=-\frac{3\sqrt{5}}{5}$

$\sin\theta=-\frac{2}{3}$, $\cos\theta=-\frac{\sqrt{5}}{3}$, $\tan\theta=\frac{2\sqrt{5}}{5}$

$\csc\theta=-\frac{3}{2}$, $\sec\theta=-\frac{3\sqrt{5}}{5}$, $\cot\theta=\frac{\sqrt{5}}{2}$

25

(1) $(\sin\theta+\cos\theta)(\sin\theta-\cos\theta)+1$

$=\sin^2\theta-\cos^2\theta+\sin^2\theta+\cos^2\theta=2\sin^2\theta$

(2) $\frac{\sin\theta-\cos\theta}{\cos\theta+\sin\theta}+\frac{1-\tan\theta}{1+\tan\theta}$

$$=\frac{\sin\theta-\cos\theta}{\cos\theta+\sin\theta}+\frac{\frac{\cos\theta}{\cos\theta}-\frac{\sin\theta}{\cos\theta}}{\frac{\cos\theta}{\cos\theta}+\frac{\sin\theta}{\cos\theta}}$$

$$=\frac{\sin\theta-\cos\theta}{\cos\theta+\sin\theta}+\frac{\frac{\cos\theta-\sin\theta}{\cos\theta}}{\frac{\cos\theta+\sin\theta}{\cos\theta}}$$

$$=\frac{\sin\theta-\cos\theta}{\cos\theta+\sin\theta}+\frac{\cos\theta-\sin\theta}{\cos\theta+\sin\theta}=0$$

26

(1) $1+\cos^2\theta-\sin\theta$

$=1+(1-\sin^2\theta)-\sin\theta=-(\sin^2\theta+\sin\theta-2)$

$=-(\sin\theta+2)(\sin\theta-1)$

(2) $\tan^2\theta+\sec^2\theta-\sec\theta$

$=(\sec^2\theta-1)+\sec^2\theta-\sec\theta=2\sec^2\theta-\sec\theta-1$

$=(2\sec\theta+1)(\sec\theta-1)$

27

(1) $\dfrac{1+\cos\theta}{1-\cos\theta}-\dfrac{1-\cos\theta}{1+\cos\theta}=4\cot\theta\csc\theta$

Work on left side to reach right side.

$$\frac{1+\cos\theta}{1-\cos\theta}-\frac{1-\cos\theta}{1+\cos\theta}$$

$$=\frac{(1+\cos\theta)^2-(1-\cos\theta)^2}{(1-\cos\theta)(1+\cos\theta)}$$

$$=\frac{1+2\cos\theta+\cos^2\theta-(1-2\cos\theta+\cos^2\theta)}{1-\cos^2\theta}$$

$$=\frac{4\cos\theta}{\sin^2\theta}=\frac{4\cos\theta}{\sin\theta}\cdot\frac{1}{\sin\theta}=4\cot\theta\csc\theta$$

(2) $\cos^2\theta+1=\dfrac{1+\sec^2\theta}{1+\tan^2\theta}$

Work on right side to reach left side.

$$\frac{1+\sec^2\theta}{1+\tan^2\theta}=\frac{1+\sec^2\theta}{\sec^2\theta}$$

$$=\frac{1}{\sec^2\theta}+\frac{\sec^2\theta}{\sec^2\theta}=\cos^2\theta+1$$

28

$$\frac{x^2}{\sqrt{16-x^2}}=\frac{(4\sin\theta)^2}{\sqrt{16-(4\sin\theta)^2}}=\frac{16\sin^2\theta}{\sqrt{16-16\sin^2\theta}}$$

$$=\frac{16\sin^2\theta}{\sqrt{16(1-\sin^2\theta)}}=\frac{16\sin^2\theta}{\sqrt{4^2\cos^2\theta}}$$

$$=\frac{16\sin^2\theta}{4\cos\theta}=\frac{4\sin\theta}{1}\cdot\frac{\sin\theta}{\cos\theta}$$

$=4\sin\theta\tan\theta$

29

(1) $\tan\left(\dfrac{x}{3}\right)-1=0$, $\tan\left(\dfrac{x}{3}\right)=1$

$\dfrac{x}{3}=\dfrac{\pi}{4}\ \rightarrow\ x=\dfrac{3\pi}{4}$

The solutions is $x=\dfrac{3\pi}{4}$

(2) $\cos^2x-6=\cos x$, $\cos^2x-\cos x-6=0$

$(\cos x-3)(\cos x+2)=0$

$\cos x=3$ or $\cos x=-2$

Since $-1\le\cos x\le1$, there is

NO solution to the equation.

(3) $\csc^2x-4=0$, $\csc^2x=4$, $\csc x=\pm2$

$\csc x=2$, $\sin x=\dfrac{1}{2}\ \rightarrow\ x=\dfrac{\pi}{6}$ and $x=\dfrac{5\pi}{6}$

$\csc x=-2$, $\sin x=-\dfrac{1}{2}$

$\rightarrow\ x=\dfrac{7\pi}{6}$ and $x=\dfrac{11\pi}{6}$

The solutions are $x=\dfrac{\pi}{6}$, $x=\dfrac{5\pi}{6}$, $\dfrac{7\pi}{6}$

and $\dfrac{11\pi}{6}$

(4) $\sin x+2\cos^2x=1$, $\sin x+2(1-\sin^2x)=1$

$\sin x+2-2\sin^2x-1=0$, $2\sin^2x-\sin x-1=0$

$(2\sin x+1)(\sin x-1)=0$

$\sin x=-\dfrac{1}{2}\ \rightarrow\ x=\dfrac{7\pi}{6}$ and $x=\dfrac{11\pi}{6}$

$\sin x=1\ \rightarrow\ x=\dfrac{\pi}{2}$

The solutions are $x=\dfrac{\pi}{2}$, $x=\dfrac{7\pi}{6}$ and

$x=\dfrac{11\pi}{6}$

30

(1) $\cos(-15^\circ)=\cos(30^\circ-45^\circ)$

$=\cos30^\circ\cos45^\circ+\sin30^\circ\sin45^\circ$

$=\dfrac{\sqrt3}{2}\dfrac{\sqrt2}{2}+\dfrac{1}{2}\dfrac{\sqrt2}{2}=\dfrac{\sqrt6+\sqrt2}{4}$

(2) $\sin\left(\frac{5\pi}{12}\right)=\sin\left(\frac{\pi}{4}+\frac{\pi}{6}\right)$

$=\sin\left(\frac{\pi}{4}\right)\cos\left(\frac{\pi}{6}\right)+\cos\left(\frac{\pi}{4}\right)\sin\left(\frac{\pi}{6}\right)$

$=\frac{\sqrt{2}}{2}\frac{\sqrt{3}}{2}+\frac{\sqrt{2}}{2}\frac{1}{2}=\frac{\sqrt{6}+\sqrt{2}}{4}$

(3) $\cos 70^\circ \cos 80^\circ-\sin 70^\circ \sin 80^\circ$

$=\cos(70+80)^\circ=\cos 150^\circ=-\frac{\sqrt{3}}{2}$

(4) $\dfrac{\tan\left(\frac{\pi}{8}\right)-\tan\left(\frac{3\pi}{8}\right)}{1+\tan\left(\frac{\pi}{8}\right)\tan\left(\frac{3\pi}{8}\right)}=\tan\left(\frac{\pi}{8}-\frac{3\pi}{8}\right)$

$=\tan\left(-\frac{\pi}{4}\right)=-1$

(5) $\sin\left(\arctan 2-\arcsin\frac{5}{13}\right)$

Let $\alpha=\arctan 2$ and $\beta=\arcsin\frac{5}{13}$.

Then we have $\tan\alpha=2$ and $\sin\beta=\frac{5}{13}$.

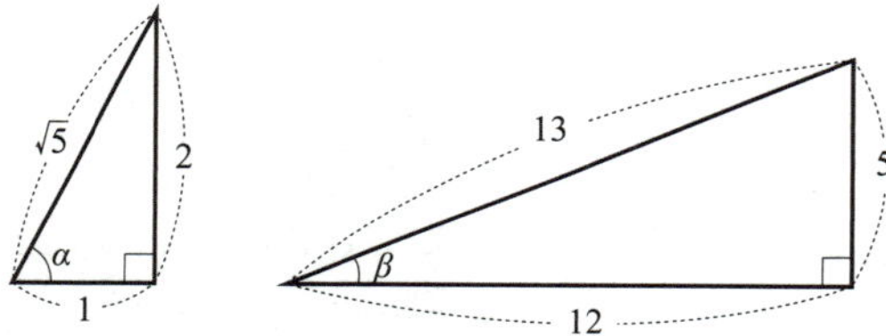

$\sin\left(\arctan 2-\arcsin\frac{5}{13}\right)$
$=\sin(\alpha-\beta)=\sin\alpha\cos\beta-\cos\alpha\sin\beta$

$=\frac{2}{\sqrt{5}}\cdot\frac{12}{13}-\frac{1}{\sqrt{5}}\cdot\frac{5}{13}=\frac{19}{13\sqrt{5}}=\frac{19\sqrt{5}}{65}$

(6) $\cos\left(2\sin^{-1}\left(\frac{4}{5}\right)\right)$

Let $\alpha=\sin^{-1}\left(\frac{4}{5}\right)$. Then, $\sin\alpha=\frac{4}{5}$.

$\cos\left(2\sin^{-1}\left(\frac{4}{5}\right)\right)=\cos(2\alpha)=1-2\sin^2\alpha$

$=1-2\left(\frac{4}{5}\right)^2=1-\frac{32}{25}=-\frac{7}{25}$

31

$\sin\alpha=-\frac{5}{13}$, $\cos\beta=\frac{\sqrt{3}}{2}$

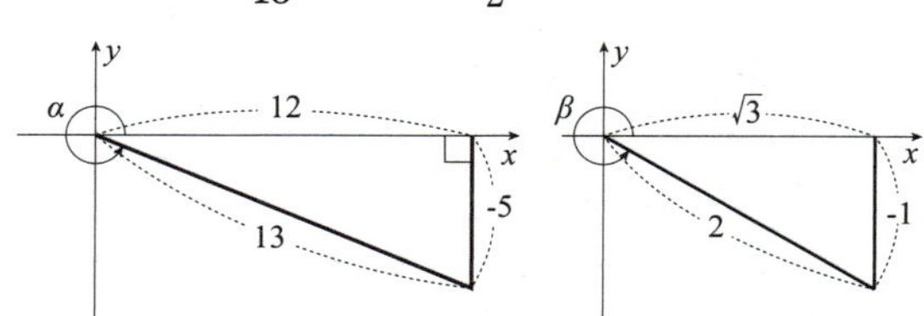

(1) $\sin(\alpha-\beta)=\sin\alpha\cos\beta-\cos\alpha\sin\beta$

$=\left(-\frac{5}{13}\right)\left(\frac{\sqrt{3}}{2}\right)-\left(\frac{12}{13}\right)\left(-\frac{1}{2}\right)$

$=\frac{12-5\sqrt{3}}{26}$

(2) $\cos(\alpha+\beta)=\cos\alpha\cos\beta-\sin\alpha\sin\beta$

$=\left(\frac{12}{13}\right)\left(\frac{\sqrt{3}}{2}\right)-\left(-\frac{5}{13}\right)\left(-\frac{1}{2}\right)$

$=\frac{12\sqrt{3}-5}{26}$

(3) $\tan(\alpha-\beta)=\dfrac{\tan\alpha-\tan\beta}{1+\tan\alpha\tan\beta}$

$=\dfrac{-\frac{5}{12}-\left(-\frac{1}{\sqrt{3}}\right)}{1+\left(-\frac{5}{12}\right)\left(-\frac{1}{\sqrt{3}}\right)}=\dfrac{\frac{4\sqrt{3}-5}{12}}{1+\frac{5\sqrt{3}}{36}}$

$=\frac{169\sqrt{3}-240}{407}$

32

$\sin\left(\frac{\pi}{2}+x\right)+\cos\left(\frac{\pi}{2}+x\right)$

$=\sin\frac{\pi}{2}\cos x+\cos\frac{\pi}{2}\sin x+\cos\frac{\pi}{2}\cos x$

$-\sin\frac{\pi}{2}\sin x$

$=1\cdot\cos x+0\cdot\sin x+0\cdot\cos x-1\cdot\sin x$

$=\cos x-\sin x$

33

(1) $\sin(2x)-2\sin x=0$

$2\sin x\cos x-2\sin x=0$

$2\sin x(\cos x-1)=0$

$\sin x=0 \rightarrow x=0$ and $x=\pi$

$\cos x=1 \rightarrow x=0$

The solutions are $x=0$ and $x=\pi$

(2) $\cos(2x)+3\sin x=-1$

$1-2\sin^2 x+3\sin x=-1$

$2\sin^2 x-3\sin x-2=0$

$(\sin x-2)(2\sin x+1)=0$

$\sin x=2 \rightarrow$ No Solution

$\sin x=-\frac{1}{2} \rightarrow x=\frac{7\pi}{6}$ and $x=\frac{11\pi}{6}$

The solutions are $x=\frac{7\pi}{6}$ and $x=\frac{11\pi}{6}$

34

$\csc\theta=-\frac{5}{2}$, $\sin\theta=-\frac{2}{5}$ and θ is in Quadrant III.

From $\sin^2\theta+\cos^2\theta=1$,

$\cos^2\theta=1-\sin^2\theta=1-\left(-\frac{2}{5}\right)^2=\frac{21}{25}$,

$\cos\theta=-\frac{\sqrt{21}}{5}$

$$\tan\theta=\frac{\sin\theta}{\cos\theta}=\frac{-\frac{2}{5}}{-\frac{\sqrt{21}}{5}}=\frac{2}{\sqrt{21}}=\frac{2\sqrt{21}}{21}$$

$$\sin(2\theta)=2\sin\theta\cos\theta=2\left(\frac{-2}{5}\right)\left(-\frac{\sqrt{21}}{5}\right)=\frac{4\sqrt{21}}{25}$$

$$\cos(2\theta)=1-2\sin^2\theta=1-2\left(-\frac{2}{5}\right)^2=\frac{17}{25}$$

$$\tan(2\theta)=\frac{2\tan\theta}{1-\tan^2\theta}=\frac{2\left(\frac{2}{\sqrt{21}}\right)}{1-\left(\frac{2}{\sqrt{21}}\right)^2}=\frac{4\sqrt{21}}{17}$$

35

$\tan\theta=4$ and $\pi<\theta<\frac{3\pi}{2}$, $\frac{\pi}{2}<\frac{\theta}{2}<\frac{3\pi}{4}$.

$\frac{\theta}{2}$ is in Quadrant II.

From $1+\tan^2\theta=\sec^2\theta$,

$\sec^2\theta=1+\tan^2\theta=1+4^2=17$, $\sec\theta=-\sqrt{17}$.

$$\cos\theta=-\frac{1}{\sqrt{17}}=-\frac{\sqrt{17}}{17}$$

$$\sin\left(\frac{\theta}{2}\right)=\sqrt{\frac{1-\cos\theta}{2}}=\sqrt{\frac{1-\left(-\frac{\sqrt{17}}{17}\right)}{2}}$$

$$=\sqrt{\frac{17+\sqrt{17}}{34}}$$

$$\cos\left(\frac{\theta}{2}\right)=-\sqrt{\frac{1+\cos\theta}{2}}=-\sqrt{\frac{1+\left(-\frac{\sqrt{17}}{17}\right)}{2}}$$

$$=-\sqrt{\frac{17-\sqrt{17}}{34}}$$

$$\tan\left(\frac{\theta}{2}\right)=\frac{\sin\left(\frac{\theta}{2}\right)}{\cos\left(\frac{\theta}{2}\right)}=-\sqrt{\frac{1-\left(-\frac{\sqrt{17}}{17}\right)}{1+\left(-\frac{\sqrt{17}}{17}\right)}}$$

$$=-\sqrt{\frac{17+\sqrt{17}}{17-\sqrt{17}}}$$

36

$\cos(3x)=\cos(2x+x)$

$=\cos(2x)\cos x-\sin(2x)\sin x$

$=\cos(x+x)\cos x-\sin(x+x)\sin x$

$=(\cos x\cos x-\sin x\sin x)\cos x$

$\qquad -(\sin x\cos x+\cos x\sin x)\sin x$

$=\cos^3 x-\sin^2 x\cos x-2\sin^2 x\cos x$

37

$\cos(2x+x)+\cos x=0$

$\cos(2x)\cos x-\sin(2x)\sin x+\cos x=0$

$(1-2\sin^2 x)\cos x-2\sin x\cos x\sin x+\cos x=0$

$\cos x-2\sin^2 x\cos x-2\sin^2 x\cos x+\cos x=0$

$2\cos x-4\sin^2 x\cos x=0$

$2\cos x(1-2\sin^2 x)=0$

$\cos x=0 \rightarrow x=\frac{\pi}{2}$ and $x=\frac{3\pi}{2}$

$\sin x=\frac{1}{\sqrt{2}} \rightarrow x=\frac{\pi}{4}$ and $x=\frac{3\pi}{4}$

$\sin x=-\frac{1}{\sqrt{2}} \rightarrow x=\frac{5\pi}{4}$ and $x=\frac{7\pi}{4}$

The solutions are $x=\frac{\pi}{4}$, $x=\frac{3\pi}{4}$, $x=\frac{\pi}{2}$, $x=\frac{5\pi}{4}$, $x=\frac{3\pi}{2}$ and $x=\frac{7\pi}{4}$

38

$\sin(2x)\cos(3x)$

$=\frac{1}{2}[\sin(2x+3x)+\sin(2x-3x)]$

$=\frac{1}{2}[\sin(5x)+\sin(-x)]$

$=\frac{1}{2}[\sin(5x)-\sin x]$

39

$\sin(5x)+\sin(2x)$

$=2\sin\left(\frac{5x+2x}{2}\right)\cos\left(\frac{5x-2x}{2}\right)$

$=2\sin\left(\frac{7x}{2}\right)\cos\left(\frac{3x}{2}\right)$

40

(1)

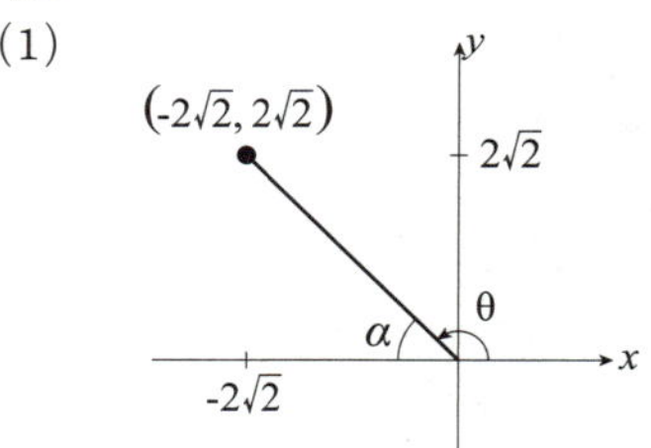

$\tan\alpha=\frac{2\sqrt{2}}{2\sqrt{2}}=1$, $\alpha=\tan^{-1}(1)=\frac{\pi}{4}$ and $\theta=\pi-\alpha=\pi-\frac{\pi}{4}=\frac{3\pi}{4}$.

Since $r=\sqrt{(2\sqrt{2})^2+(2\sqrt{2})^2}=4$, the polar coordinate is $\left(4, \frac{3\pi}{4}\right)$.

$\left(-2\sqrt{2}, 2\sqrt{2}\right) \rightarrow \left(4, \frac{3\pi}{4}\right)$

Two addition polar points:

$\left(4, \frac{3\pi}{4}-2\pi\right)=\left(4, -\frac{5\pi}{4}\right)$

$\left(-4, \frac{3\pi}{4}+\pi\right)=\left(-4, \frac{7\pi}{4}\right)$

(2)

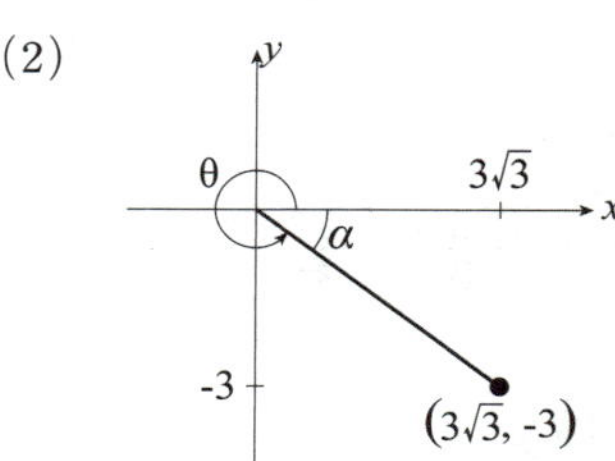

$\tan\alpha=\frac{3}{3\sqrt{3}}=\frac{1}{\sqrt{3}}$, $\alpha=\tan^{-1}\left(\frac{1}{\sqrt{3}}\right)=\frac{\pi}{6}$ and $\theta=2\pi-\alpha=2\pi-\frac{\pi}{6}=\frac{11\pi}{6}$.

Since $r=\sqrt{(3\sqrt{3})^2+(3)^2}=6$, the polar coordinate is $\left(6, \frac{11\pi}{6}\right)$.

$(3\sqrt{3}, -3) \rightarrow \left(6, \frac{11\pi}{6}\right)$

Two addition polar points:

$\left(6, \frac{11\pi}{6}-2\pi\right)=\left(6, -\frac{\pi}{6}\right)$

$\left(-6, \frac{11\pi}{6}-\pi\right)=\left(-6, \frac{5\pi}{6}\right)$

41

(1) $x^2-2y^2-16=0$

$(r\cos\theta)^2-2(r\sin\theta)^2-16=0$

$r^2\cos^2\theta-2r^2\sin^2\theta=16$

$r^2(\cos^2\theta-2\sin^2\theta)=16$

$r^2=\dfrac{16}{\cos^2\theta-2\sin^2\theta}$, $r=\dfrac{4}{\sqrt{\cos^2\theta-2\sin^2\theta}}$

(2) $2x^2-3x+2y^2+2y=0$

$2(x^2+y^2)-3x+2y=0$

$2r^2-3r\cos\theta+2r\sin\theta=0$

$(2r^2-3r\cos\theta+2r\sin\theta=0)\cdot\dfrac{1}{r}$

$2r-3\cos\theta+2\sin\theta=0$

$2r=3\cos\theta-2\sin\theta$, $r=\dfrac{3\cos\theta-2\sin\theta}{2}$

42

(1) Since $\tan\theta=\dfrac{y}{x}$, $\cot\theta=\dfrac{x}{y}$.

$r=4\cot\theta$, $r^2=(4\cot\theta)^2$

$x^2+y^2=\dfrac{16x^2}{y^2}$, $x^2y^2+y^4=16x^2$

$y^4+x^2y^2-16x^2=0$

(2) $r=\dfrac{1}{4-6\sin\theta}$, $4r-6r\sin\theta=1$

$4r-6y=1$, $r=\dfrac{1+6y}{4}$

$r^2=\left(\dfrac{1+6y}{4}\right)^2$, $x^2+y^2=\dfrac{1+12y+36y^2}{16}$

$16x^2+16y^2=1+12y+36y^2$

$16x^2-20y^2-12y-1=0$

43

$r=-4\sin(3\theta)$

$r=-4\sin(3(\pi-\theta))$ → Replace (r,θ) by $(r,\pi-\theta)$

$r=-4\sin(3\theta)$ → $\sin(\pi-\theta)=\sin\theta$

So $r=-4\sin(3\theta)$ is symmetric about the line $\theta=\dfrac{\pi}{2}$.

44

$r=1-\cos\theta$

$r=1-\cos(-\theta)$ → Replace (r,θ) by $(r,-\theta)$

$r=1-\cos\theta$ → $\cos(-\theta)=\cos\theta$

So $r=1-\cos\theta$ is symmetric about the polar axis.

45

(1) $r=-3\cos(3\theta)$

In a special polar graph, $r=a\cos(n\theta)$ is a rose curve. Since $n=3$, there are 3 petals.

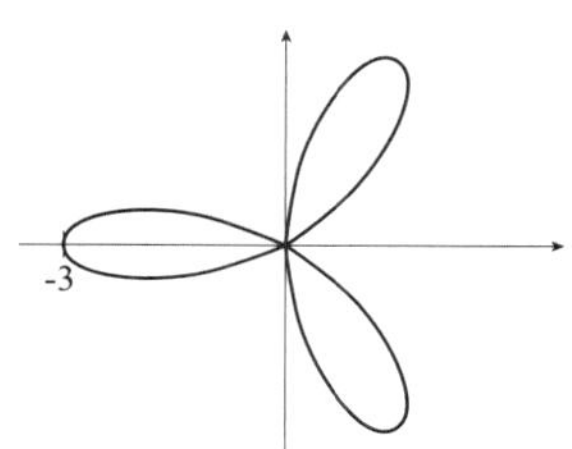

(2) $r=4+4\sin\theta$

In a special polar graph, $r=a\pm b\sin\theta$ is a limagons. Since $\dfrac{4}{4}=1$, the graph is a cardioid.

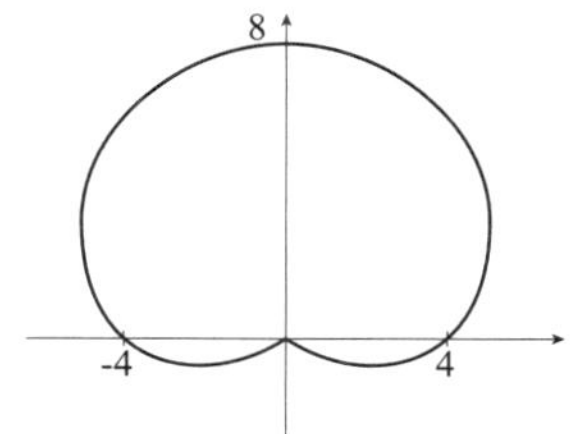

46

(1) $\sqrt{3}-i$

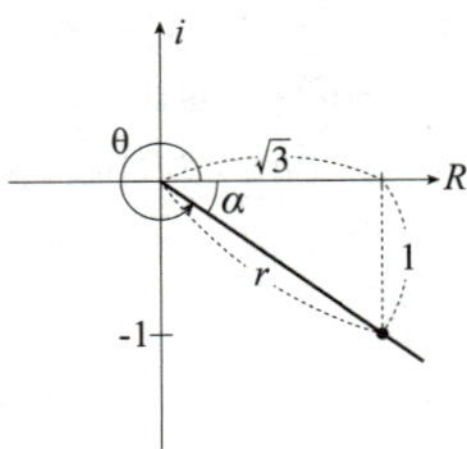

$r=\sqrt{(\sqrt{3})^2+(-1)^2}=2$ and

$\tan\alpha=\frac{1}{\sqrt{3}}$, $\alpha=\tan^{-1}\left(\frac{1}{\sqrt{3}}\right)=\frac{\pi}{6}$

$\theta=2\pi-\alpha=2\pi-\frac{\pi}{6}=\frac{11\pi}{6}$. So we have

$\sqrt{3}-i=2\left(\cos\frac{11\pi}{6}+i\sin\frac{11\pi}{6}\right)$

(2) $-2-2\sqrt{3}\,i$

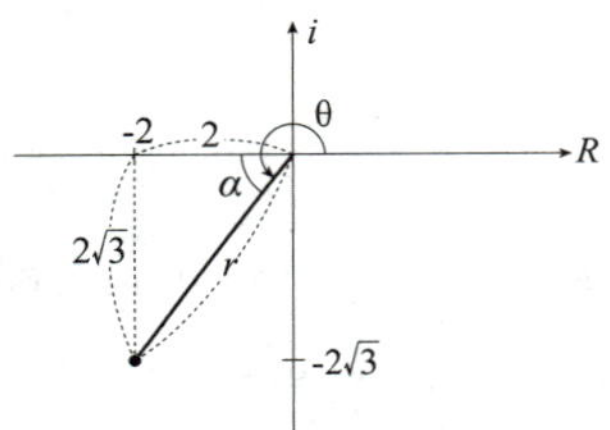

$r=\sqrt{(-2)^2+(-2\sqrt{3})^2}=4$ and

$\tan\alpha=\frac{2\sqrt{3}}{3}=\sqrt{3}$, $\alpha=\tan^{-1}(\sqrt{3})=\frac{\pi}{3}$

$\theta=\pi+\alpha=\pi+\frac{\pi}{3}=\frac{4\pi}{3}$. So we have

$-2-2\sqrt{3}\,i=4\left(\cos\frac{4\pi}{3}+i\sin\frac{4\pi}{3}\right)$

47

$$z_1z_2=2\cdot\sqrt{2}\left(\cos\left(\frac{7\pi}{4}+\frac{\pi}{2}\right)+i\sin\left(\frac{7\pi}{4}+\frac{\pi}{2}\right)\right)$$
$$=2\sqrt{2}\left(\cos\frac{9\pi}{4}+i\sin\frac{9\pi}{4}\right)$$
$$=2\sqrt{2}\left(\frac{\sqrt{2}}{2}+\frac{\sqrt{2}}{2}i\right)=2+2i$$

$$\frac{z_1}{z_2}=\frac{2}{\sqrt{2}}\left(\cos\left(\frac{7\pi}{4}-\frac{\pi}{2}\right)+i\sin\left(\frac{7\pi}{4}-\frac{\pi}{2}\right)\right)$$
$$=\sqrt{2}\left(\cos\frac{5\pi}{4}+i\sin\frac{5\pi}{4}\right)$$
$$=\sqrt{2}\left(-\frac{\sqrt{2}}{2}-\frac{\sqrt{2}}{2}i\right)=-1-i$$

48

$(-3\sqrt{3}-3i)^4$

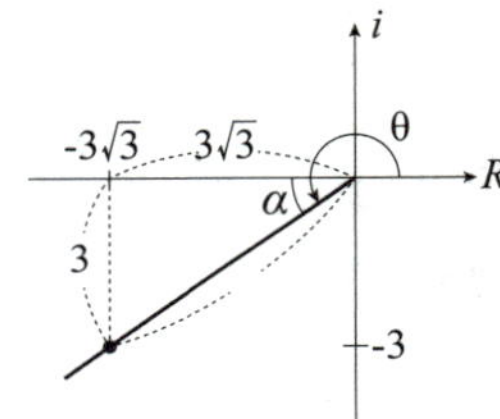

$r=\sqrt{(-3\sqrt{3})^2+(-3)^2}=6$ and

$\tan\alpha=\frac{3}{3\sqrt{3}}=\frac{1}{\sqrt{3}}$, $\alpha=\tan^{-1}\left(\frac{1}{\sqrt{3}}\right)=\frac{\pi}{6}$.

$\theta=\pi+\alpha=\pi+\frac{\pi}{6}=\frac{7\pi}{6}$. So we have

$-3\sqrt{3}-3i=6\left(\cos\frac{7\pi}{6}+i\sin\frac{7\pi}{6}\right)$ and

$(-3\sqrt{3}-3i)^4=\left(6\left(\cos\frac{7\pi}{6}+i\sin\frac{7\pi}{6}\right)\right)^4$

$=6^4\left(\cos\left(\frac{7\pi}{6}\times4\right)+i\sin\left(\frac{7\pi}{6}\times4\right)\right)$

$=6^4\left(\cos\frac{14\pi}{3}+i\sin\frac{14\pi}{3}\right)$

$=6^4\left(-\frac{1}{2}+\frac{\sqrt{3}}{2}i\right)=-648+648\sqrt{3}\,i$

49

The fourth roots are given by

$$\sqrt[4]{16}\cos\left(\frac{\frac{2\pi}{3}+2\pi k}{4}\right)+i\sin\left(\frac{\frac{2\pi}{3}+2\pi k}{4}\right),$$

where $k=0$, 1, 2 and 3.

$k=0$;

$$\sqrt[4]{16}\left(\cos\left(\frac{\frac{2\pi}{3}+2\pi(0)}{4}\right)+i\sin\left(\frac{\frac{2\pi}{3}+2\pi(0)}{4}\right)\right)$$

$$=2\left(\cos\frac{\pi}{6}+i\sin\frac{\pi}{6}\right)=\sqrt{3}+i$$

$k=1$;

$$\sqrt[4]{16}\left(\cos\left(\frac{\frac{2\pi}{3}+2\pi(1)}{4}\right)+i\sin\left(\frac{\frac{2\pi}{3}+2\pi(1)}{4}\right)\right)$$

$$=2\left(\cos\frac{2\pi}{3}+i\sin\frac{2\pi}{3}\right)=-1+\sqrt{3}i$$

$k=2$;

$$\sqrt[4]{16}\left(\cos\left(\frac{\frac{2\pi}{3}+2\pi(2)}{4}\right)+i\sin\left(\frac{\frac{2\pi}{3}+2\pi(2)}{4}\right)\right)$$

$$=2\left(\cos\frac{7\pi}{6}+i\sin\frac{7\pi}{6}\right)=-\sqrt{3}-i$$

$k=3$;

$$\sqrt[4]{16}\left(\cos\left(\frac{\frac{2\pi}{3}+2\pi(3)}{4}\right)+i\sin\left(\frac{\frac{2\pi}{3}+2\pi(3)}{4}\right)\right)$$

$$=2\left(\cos\frac{5\pi}{3}+i\sin\frac{5\pi}{3}\right)=1-\sqrt{3}i$$

$\sqrt{3}+i,\ -1+\sqrt{3}i,\ -\sqrt{3}-i,\ 1-\sqrt{3}i$

memo

Functions Involving Parameters, Vectors, and Matrices

1. Parametric Equation

Check Point 1

① Solve x for t.

$x=t-2,\ t=x+2$

Substitute t into the equation y.

$y=t^3,\ y=(x+2)^3$

$y=(x+2)^3$

t	x	y
0	-2	0
1	-1	1
2	0	8

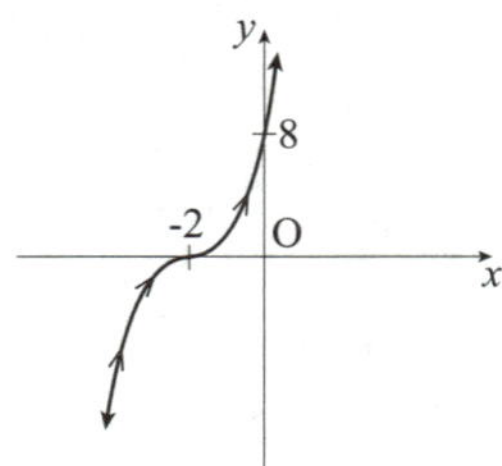

② Solve x for t.

$x=2t+1,\ t=\frac{x-1}{2}$

Substitute t into the equation y.

$$y=\frac{t}{2}-3,\ y=\frac{\frac{x-1}{2}}{2}-3=\frac{x-1}{4}-3$$

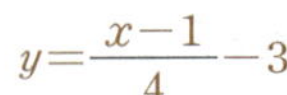

t	x	y
0	1	-3
2	5	-2
4	9	-1

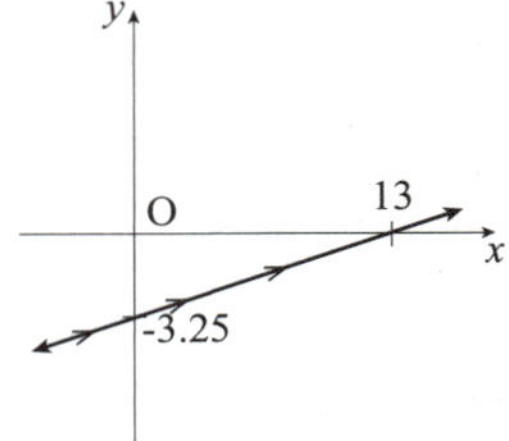

③ Solve x for t.

$x=t-1,\ t=x+1$ where $x\neq0$

Substitute t into the equation y.

$$y=\frac{t}{t-1},\ y=\frac{(x+1)}{(x+1)-1}=\frac{x+1}{x}=1+\frac{1}{x}$$

$y=1+\frac{1}{x}$ where $x\neq0$

t	x	y
-1	-2	0.5
0	-1	0
2	1	2
3	2	1.5

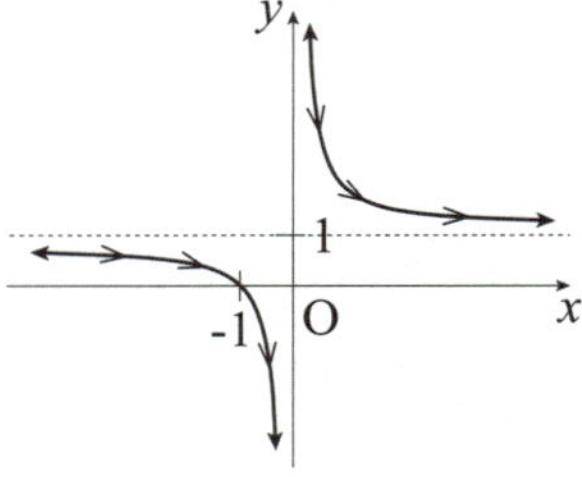

④ Solve x for t.

$x=\sqrt{t}+1,\ t=(x-1)^2$ where $x\geq1$

Substitute t into the equation y.

$y=4t-3,\ y=4(x-1)^2-3$

$y=4(x-1)^2-3$ where $x\geq1$

t	x	y
0	1	-3
1	2	1
4	3	13

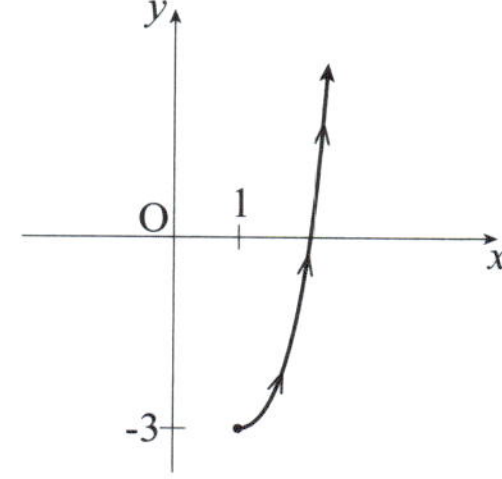

This is the equation of the ellipse centered at the origin;

$t=0 \to (0,\ -5)$ and $t=\frac{\pi}{2} \to (-3,\ 0)$

The curve starts at $(0,\ -5)$ rotates clockwise.

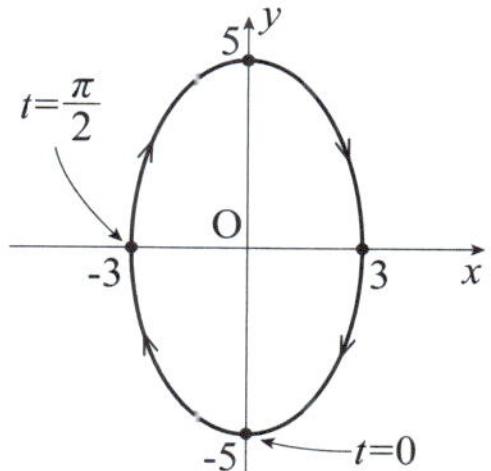

Check Point 2

① $x=3\cos t$, $\cos t=\frac{x}{3}$

$y=5\sin t$, $\sin t=\frac{y}{5}$

Using the Pythagorean Identity,

$\sin^2 t+\cos^2 t=1$

$\left(\frac{y}{5}\right)^2+\left(\frac{x}{3}\right)^2=1$, $\frac{x^2}{9}+\frac{y^2}{25}=1$

This is the equation of the ellipse centered at the origin; $t=0 \to (3,\ 0)$ and $t=\frac{\pi}{2} \to (0,\ 5)$

The curve starts at $(3,\ 0)$ rotates counterclockwise.

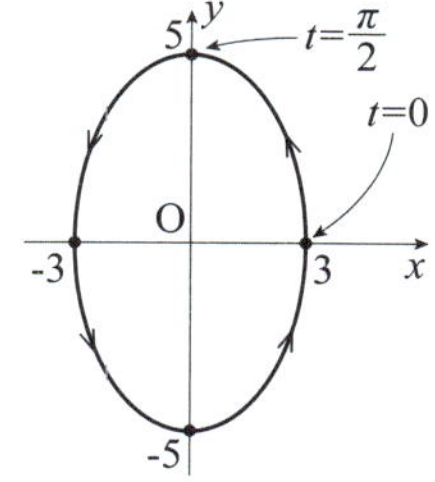

② $x=-3\sin t$, $\sin t=-\frac{x}{3}$

$y=-5\cos t$, $\cos t=-\frac{y}{5}$

Using the Pythagorean Identity,

$\sin^2 t+\cos^2 t=1$

$\left(-\frac{x}{3}\right)^2+\left(-\frac{y}{5}\right)^2=1$, $\frac{x^2}{9}+\frac{y^2}{25}=1$

Check Point 3

① Let $x=t$. Then

$y=-4x-5$, $y=-4t-5$

Let $x=t+1$. Then

$y=-4x-5$, $y=-4(t+1)-5$, $y=-4t-9$

$x=t$, $y=-4t-5$

$x=t+1$, $y=-4t-9$

② Let $x=t$. Then

$y=\sqrt{2x+1}$, $y=\sqrt{2t+1}$

Let $x=t+1$. Then

$y=\sqrt{2x+1}$, $y=\sqrt{2(t+1)+1}$, $y=\sqrt{2t+3}$

$x=t$, $y=\sqrt{2x+1}$

$x=t+1$, $y=\sqrt{2t+3}$

Check Point 4

We have $h=\frac{1}{2}m$, $\theta=45°$, $v_0=8$ m/sec, and $g=9.8$ m/sec^2.

① $x(t)=(v_0\cos\theta)t$

$=(8\cos 45°)t=\left(8\cdot\frac{\sqrt{2}}{2}\right)t=4\sqrt{2}\,t$

$y(t)=-\frac{1}{2}gt^2+(v_0\sin\theta)t+h$

$=-\frac{1}{2}(9.8)t^2+(8\sin 45°)t+\frac{1}{2}$

$$=-4.9t^2+\left(8\cdot\frac{\sqrt{2}}{2}\right)t+\frac{1}{2}$$
$$=-4.9t^2+4\sqrt{2}t+\frac{1}{2}$$

$$\begin{cases} x(t)=4\sqrt{2}t \\ y(t)=-4.9t^2+4\sqrt{2}t+\frac{1}{2} \end{cases}$$

② $y=-4.9t^2+4\sqrt{2}t+\frac{1}{2}$

$0=-4.9t^2+4\sqrt{2}t+\frac{1}{2}$, $0=9.8t^2-8\sqrt{2}t-1$

$$t=\frac{8\sqrt{2}\pm\sqrt{6(-8\sqrt{2})^2-4(9.8)(-1)}}{2(9.8)}$$

$$=\frac{8\sqrt{2}\pm\sqrt{167.2}}{2(9.8)}$$

$t=-0.082$ or $t=1.237$

Since $t\geq0$, the ball is in the air for about 1.237 seconds

③ $y=-4.9t^2+4\sqrt{2}t+\frac{1}{2}$

The maximum height of the ball can be found when

$$t=-\frac{b}{2a}=-\frac{4\sqrt{2}}{2(-4.9)}=0.577 \text{ sec.}$$

The ball is at its maximum height after 0.577 seconds

④ The maximum height of the ball is $y(0.577)$.

$y=-4.9t^2+4\sqrt{2}t+\frac{1}{2}$

$y(0.577)=-4.9(0.577)^2+4\sqrt{2}(0.577)+\frac{1}{2}$

$=2.133$

The maximum height of the ball is approximately 2.133 meters

⑤ $x(t)=4\sqrt{2}t$

The ball is in the air for 1.237 seconds. So the horizontal distance that the ball travels is

$x(1.237)=4\sqrt{2}\times1.237=6.998$ meters

The horizontal distance that the ball travels is approximately 6.998 meters

Review Exercises

01

(1) Solve y for t.

$y=\frac{t}{3}$, $t=3y$

Substitute t into the equation x.

$x=t^2-1$, $x=(3y)^2-1=9y^2-1$

$x=9y^2-1$

t	y	x
-3	-1	8
0	0	-1
3	1	8

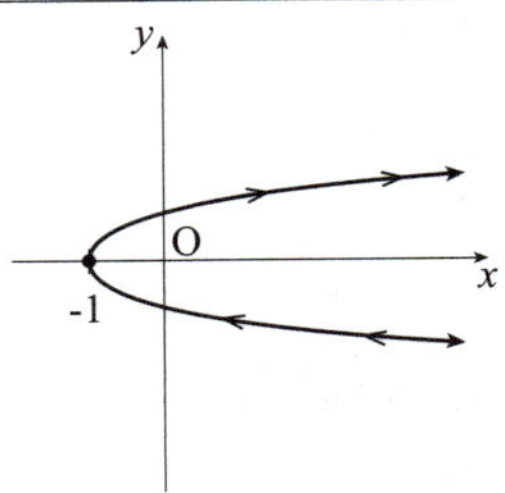

(2) $x=\cos t$ where $-1\leq x\leq1$

$y=\cos^2 t-\cos t-6$, $y=x^2-x-6$,

$y=(x-3)(x+2)$

$y=(x-3)(x+2)$, $-1\leq x\leq1$

t	x	y
0	1	-6
$\frac{\pi}{2}$	0	-6
π	-1	-4

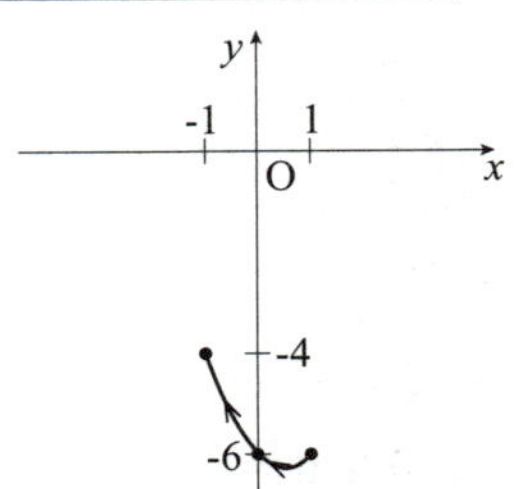

(3) $x=\sin t-1$, $x+1=\sin t$

$y=2\cos t+2$, $\frac{y-2}{2}=\cos t$

Using the Pythagorean Identity,
$\sin^2 t+\cos^2 t=1$

$(x+1)^2+\left(\frac{y-2}{2}\right)^2=1$

$$(x+1)^2+\frac{(y-2)^2}{4}=1$$

This is the equation of the ellipse centered at $(-1, 2)$; $t=0 \to (-1, 4)$ and $t=\frac{\pi}{2} \to (0, 2)$ The curve starts at $(-1, 4)$ rotates clockwise.

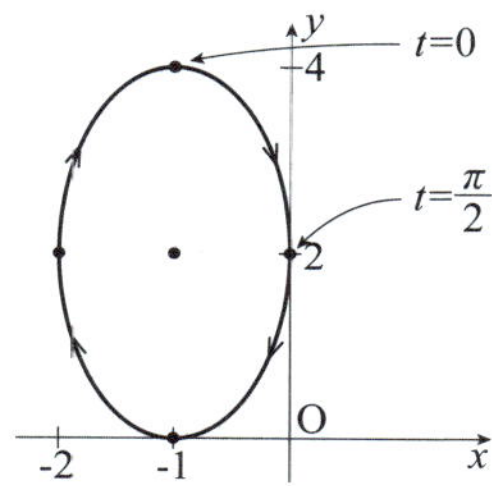

(4) $x=2\cos^2 t$, $\frac{x}{2}=\cos^2 t$, $y=\sin^2 t$

Using the Pythagorean Identity,
$\sin^2 t+\cos^2 t=1$

$y+\frac{x}{2}=1$, $y=-\frac{x}{2}+1$

$$y=-\frac{x}{2}+1,\ 0\le x\le 2$$

t	x	y
0	2	0
$\frac{\pi}{2}$	0	1
π	2	0

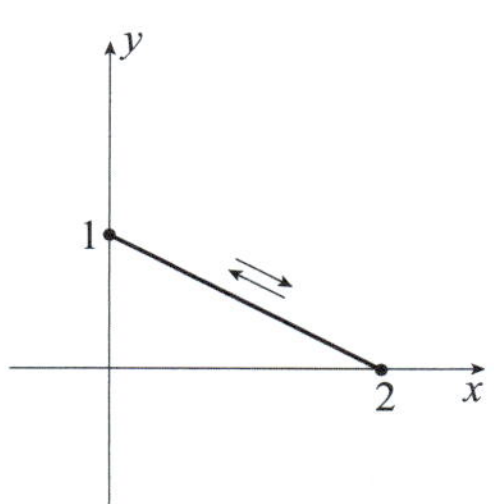

02

(1) Let $x=t$. Then $y=\frac{x+1}{x-1}=\frac{t+1}{t-1}$.

$$x=t,\ y=\frac{t+1}{t-1}$$

(2) Let $y=t$. Then $x=y+\sqrt{2}y$, $x=t+\sqrt{2}t$.

$$x=t+\sqrt{2}t,\ y=t$$

03

(1) The equation for the line is $y=mx+b$. The slope of the line is $2 \to y=2x+b$ and passes through $(-3, 6) \to 6=2(-3)+b$, $b=12$. So the equation for the line is $y=2x+12$. Now, if we let $x=t$, then $y=2t+12$.

$$x=t,\ y=2t+12$$

(2) The equation for the line is $y=mx+b$. Since the line passes through $(2, 1)$ and $(0, -4)$, we have

$$\begin{cases} 1=m(2)+b \\ -4=m(0)+b \end{cases} \to m=\frac{5}{2},\ b=-4.$$

So the equation for the line is $y=\frac{5}{2}x-4$.

Now, if we let $x=t$, then $y=\frac{5}{2}t-4$.

$$x=t,\ y=\frac{5}{2}t-4$$

04

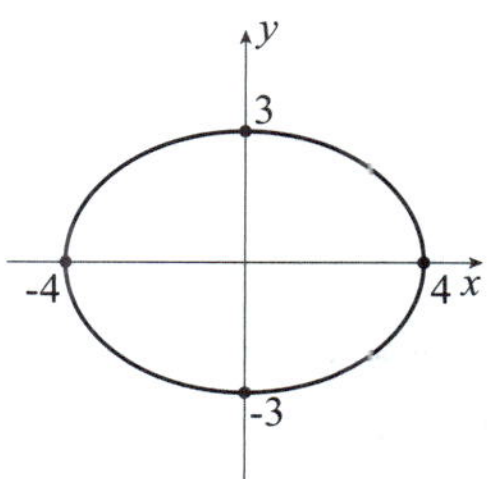

(1) Since the particle starts to move clockwise at $(4, 0)$, we must have following values:

t	x	y
0	4	0
$\frac{1}{4}$	0	-3
$\frac{1}{2}$	-4	0

$\frac{x^2}{16}+\frac{y^2}{9}=1$, $\left(\frac{x}{4}\right)^2+\left(\frac{y}{3}\right)^2=1$

Using the identity, $(\sin bt)^2+(\cos bt)^2=1$, the period is $1 \to P=\frac{2\pi}{b}=1$, $b=2\pi$ and

we must have $\begin{cases}\cos(2\pi t)=\frac{x}{4}, & 4\cos(2\pi t)=x \\ -\sin(2\pi t)=\frac{y}{3}, & -3\sin(2\pi t)=y\end{cases}$

$x=4\cos(2\pi t)$, $y=-3\sin(2\pi t)$

(2) Since the particle starts to move counterclockwise at $(0, 3)$, we must have following values:

t	x	y
0	0	3
$\frac{1}{2}$	-4	0
1	0	-3

$\frac{x^2}{16}+\frac{y^2}{9}=1$, $\left(\frac{x}{4}\right)^2+\left(\frac{y}{3}\right)^2=1$

Using the identity, $(\sin bt)^2+(\cos bt)^2=1$, the period is $2 \to P=\frac{2\pi}{b}=2$, $b=\pi$ and

we must have $\begin{cases}-\sin(\pi t)=\frac{x}{4}, & -4\sin(\pi t)=x \\ \cos(\pi t)=\frac{y}{3}, & 3\cos(\pi t)=y\end{cases}$

$x=-4\sin(\pi t)$, $y=3\cos(\pi t)$

(3) Since the particle starts to move counterclockwise at $(-4, 0)$, we must have following values:

t	x	y
0	-4	0
1	0	-3
2	4	0

$\frac{x^2}{16}+\frac{y^2}{9}=1$, $\left(\frac{x}{4}\right)^2+\left(\frac{y}{3}\right)^2=1$

Using the identity, $(\sin bt)^2+(\cos bt)^2=1$, the period is $4 \to P=\frac{2\pi}{b}=4$, $b=\frac{\pi}{2}$ and

we must have $\begin{cases}-\cos\left(\frac{\pi t}{2}\right)=\frac{x}{4}, & -4\cos\left(\frac{\pi t}{2}\right)=x \\ -\sin\left(\frac{\pi t}{2}\right)=\frac{y}{3}, & -3\sin\left(\frac{\pi t}{2}\right)=y\end{cases}$

$x=-4\cos\left(\frac{\pi t}{2}\right)$, $y=-3\sin\left(\frac{\pi t}{2}\right)$

(4) Since the particle starts to move clockwise at $(0, 3)$, we must have following values:

t	x	y
0	0	3
$\frac{1}{8}$	4	0
$\frac{1}{4}$	0	-3

$\frac{x^2}{16}+\frac{y^2}{9}=1$, $\left(\frac{x}{4}\right)^2+\left(\frac{y}{3}\right)^2=1$

Using the identity, $(\sin bt)^2+(\cos bt)^2=1$, the period is $0.5 \to P=\frac{2\pi}{b}=0.5$, $b=4\pi$ and

we must have $\begin{cases}\sin(4\pi t)=\frac{x}{4}, & 4\sin(4\pi t)=x \\ \cos(4\pi t)=\frac{y}{3}, & 3\cos(4\pi t)=y\end{cases}$

$x=4\sin(4\pi t)$, $y=3\cos(4\pi t)$

05

We have $h=6$ ft, $\theta=60°$, $v_0=110$ ft/sec, and $g=32$ ft/sec^2.

First, find the parametric equations that describe the position.

$$x(t)=(v_0\cos\theta)t$$
$$=(110\cos 60°)t=\left(110\cdot\frac{1}{2}\right)t=55t$$
$$y(t)=-\frac{1}{2}gt^2+(v_0\sin\theta)t+h$$
$$=-\frac{1}{2}(32)t^2+(110\sin 60°)t+6$$
$$=-16t^2+\left(110\cdot\frac{\sqrt{3}}{2}\right)t+6$$

$=-16t^2+55\sqrt{3}t+6$

(1) $y=-16t^2+55\sqrt{3}\ t+6$

$0=-16t^2+55\sqrt{3}\ t+6$

$t=\frac{-55\sqrt{3}\pm\sqrt{(55\sqrt{3})^2-4(-16)(6)}}{2(-16)}$

$=\frac{-55\sqrt{3}\pm\sqrt{9459}}{-32}$

$t=-0.062$ or $t=6.016$

Since $t\geq0$, the ball is in the air for about 6.016 seconds

(2) $y=-16t^2+55\sqrt{3}t+6$

The maximum height of the ball can be found when $t=-\frac{b}{2a}=-\frac{55\sqrt{3}}{2(-16)}$

$=2.977$ seconds.

So the maximum height of the ball is

$y(2.977)=-16(2.977)^2+55\sqrt{3}\ (2.977)+6$

$=147.797$

The maximum height of the ball is approximately 147.797 feet

(3) $x(t)=55t$

The ball is in the air for 6.016 seconds. So the horizontal distance that the ball travels is $x(6.016)=55(6.016)=330.88$

The horizontal distance that the ball travels is approximately 330.88 feet

06

We have $h=4\ ft$, $\theta=90°$, $v_0=240\ ft/\text{sec}$, and $g=32\ ft/\text{sec}^2$. When the ball returns to the ground, the height $y=0$.

$y(t)=-\frac{1}{2}gt^2+(v_0\sin\theta)t+h$

$=-\frac{1}{2}(32)t^2+(240\sin 90°)t+4$

$=-16t^2+240t+4$

$0=-16t^2+240t+4$, $0=4t^2-60t-1$

$t=\frac{60\pm\sqrt{(-60)^2-4(4)(-1)}}{2(4)}$

$=\frac{60\pm\sqrt{3616}}{8}$

$t=-0.017$ or $t=15.017$

Since $t\geq0$, the ball returns to the ground after 15.017 seconds

07

$x(t)=\cos t$ and $y(t)=2\sin t$, $\frac{y}{2}=\sin t$

Using the trigonometric identity

$\sin^2 t+\cos^2 t=1$

$\left(\frac{y}{2}\right)^2+x^2=1$, $\frac{y^2}{4}+x^2=1$

Therefore, the correct answer is (C).

08

We need to identify the graph that lies entirely in the first quadrant, where both x and y are positive. Therefore, the correct answer is (A).

09

(1) To find the point $A(a, a)$, we set $x=a$ and $y=a$.

$a=4t+3$ and $a=t^2-2$

Set the two equations equal to each other and solve for t.

$4t+3=t^2-2$

$t^2-4t-5=0$, $(t-5)(t+1)=0$

Since $t\geq0$, $t=5$. For $t=5$, $a=4(5)+3=23$.

Therefore, the value of a is 23.

(2) As t increases, both $x(t)$ and $y(t)$ clearly increases because both the terms $4t$ and t^2 grows positively with t. This indicates that the particle is moving to the right and up. Therefore, the correct answer is (A).

10

(1) Substitute $t=2$ into the parametric equations:

$$x(2)=-4(2)^2+8(2)-3=-3$$
$$y(2)=2(2)-1=3$$

This point lies in Quadrant II where x is negative and y is positive. Therefore, the correct answer is (B).

(2) To find the time when $x(t)$ is at its maximum(farthest point to the right), we need to find the vertex of the quadratic function $x(t)=-4t^2+8t-3$. The vertex of a parabola occurs at

$$t=-\frac{b}{2a}=-\frac{8}{2(-4)}=1$$

So, the particle is at its farthest point to the right at $t=1$.

(3) The x-intercept occurs when $y(t)=0$.

$$y(t)=2t-1=0,\ t=\frac{1}{2}$$

Now, find $x(t)$ at $t=\frac{1}{2}$.

$$x\left(\frac{1}{2}\right)=-4\left(\frac{1}{2}\right)^2+8\left(\frac{1}{2}\right)-3=0$$

Therefore, the x-intercept is at $x=0$.

(4) Analyze the behavior of x and y for $t>2$.
$x(t)$: Since the coefficient of t^2 is negative, $x(t)$ is a downward-opening parabola. Thus, $x(t)$ decreases for $t>1$, which means it is decreasing for $t>2$.
$y(t)$: Since the coefficient of t is positive, $y(t)$ increases as t increases.
Therefore, the particle is moving to the left and up for $t>2$. The correct answer is (D).

11

$$x(t)=2\sin t-1,\ \sin t=\frac{x+1}{2}$$

$$y(t)=\cos^2 t+2,\ \cos^2 t=y-2$$

Using the trigonometric identity:

$$\sin^2 t+\cos^2 t=1$$

$$\left(\frac{x+1}{2}\right)^2+(y-2)=1$$

$$y-2=-\frac{(x+1)^2}{4}+1$$

$$y=-\frac{1}{4}(x+1)^2+3$$

Thus, the vertex of the graph f in the xy-plane is $(-1,\ 3)$. Therefore, the correct answer is (A).

12

$$x(t)=a+b\sin t,\ \sin t=\frac{x-a}{b}$$

$$y(t)=c+d\cos t,\ \cos t=\frac{y-c}{d}$$

Using the trigonometric identity:

$$\sin^2 t+\cos^2 t=1$$

$$\left(\frac{x-a}{b}\right)^2+\left(\frac{y-c}{d}\right)^2=1$$

$$\frac{(x-a)^2}{b^2}+\frac{(y-c)^2}{d^2}=1$$

The center of the ellipse is given as $(1,\ -2)$:
$a=1$ and $c=-2$.

The lengths of major and minor axis of 8 and 4, respectively:

$$b=\frac{8}{2}=4 \text{ and } d=\frac{4}{2}=2$$

Reference: (The values of b and d may be interchanged). Therefore, the value $a+b+c+d$ is

$$1+4-2+2=5$$

2. Conic Sections: Parabola

Check Point 1

① The standard equation :

$x^2=4py \rightarrow$ Vertex$(0,\ 0)$

$x^2+12y=0,\ x^2=-12y$

$\rightarrow 4p=-12,\ p=-3$

Since p is negative, the graph opens downward.

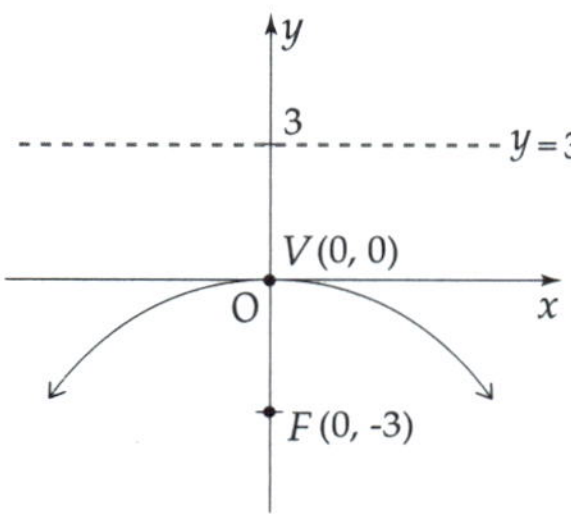

Vertex : $(0,\ 0)$ Focus : $(0,\ p)=(0,\ -3)$

Equation of directrix : $y=-p=3$

Focal diameter : $|4p|=|4\cdot(-3)|=12$

② The standard equation :

$y^2=4px \rightarrow$ Vertex $(0,0)$

$-\frac{1}{4}y^2-6x=0,\ y^2=-24x$

$\rightarrow 4p=-24,\ p=-6$

Since p is negative, the graph opens to the left.

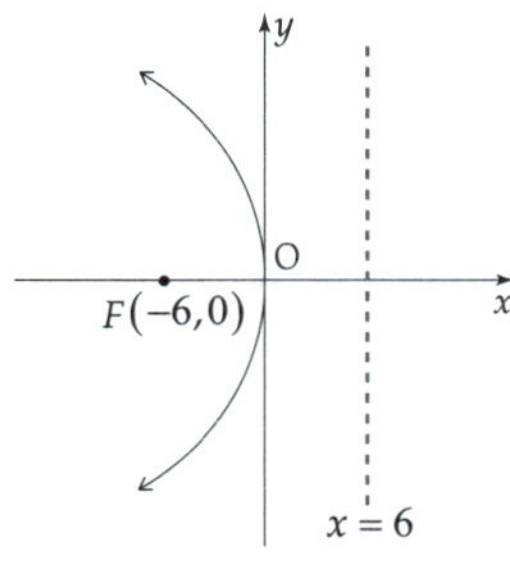

Vertex : $(0,\ 0)$ Focus : $(p,\ 0)=(-6,\ 0)$

Equation of directrix : $x=-p=6$

Focal diameter : $|4p|=|4\cdot(-6)|=24$

Check Point 2

①

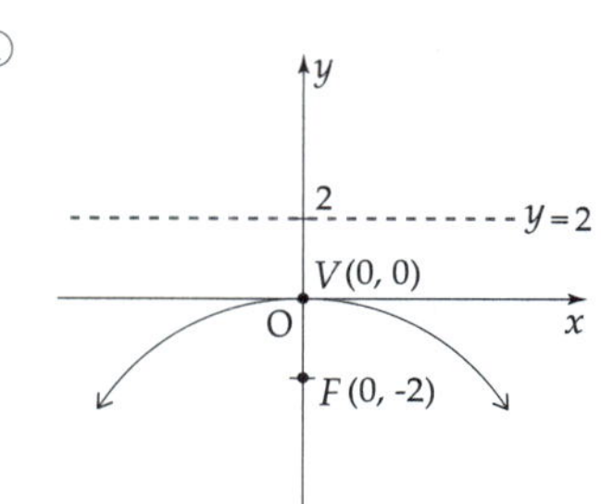

The standard equation is $x^2=4py$.

Since the parabola opens downward, $p=-2$.

So the equation is $x^2=4(-2)y,\ x^2=-8y$.

$x^2=-8y$

②

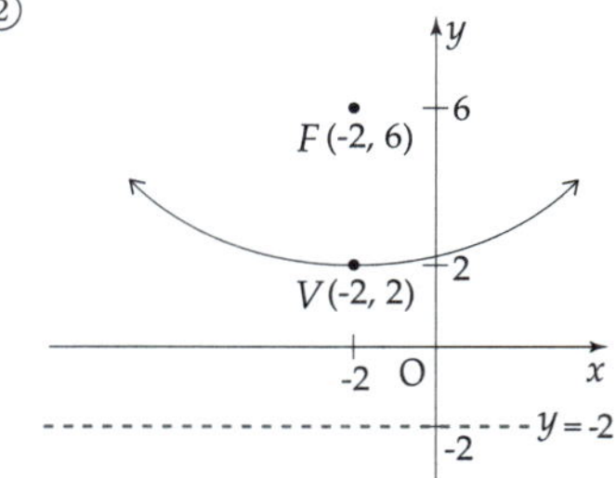

The standard equation is

$(x-h)^2=4p(y-k)$.

Since the parabola opens upward, $p=4$.

So the equation is

$(x+2)^2=4(4)(y-2),\ (x+2)^2=16(y-2)$.

$(x+2)^2=16(y-2)$

Check Point 3

① $2x^2+12x+3y=0,\ 2x^2+12x=-3y$

$2(x^2+6x+9-9)=-3y$

$2(x+3)^2-18=-3y,\ 2(x+3)^2=-3y+18$

$(x+3)^2=-\frac{3}{2}(y-6)$

Comparing this equation with

$(x-h)^2=4p(y-k) \rightarrow 4p=-\frac{3}{2},\ p=-\frac{3}{8}$

Since p is negative, the graph opens downward.

Vertex : $(h,\ k)=(-3,\ 6)$

Focus : $(h,\ k+p)=\left(-3,\ 6+\left(-\frac{3}{8}\right)\right)$

$=\left(-3,\ \frac{45}{8}\right)$

Equation of directrix :

$y=-p+k=-\left(-\frac{3}{8}\right)+6=\frac{51}{8}$

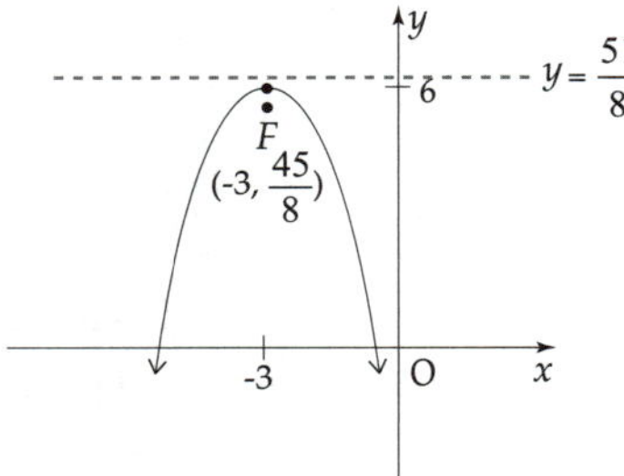

② $y^2+4y-2x=0,\ y^2+4y=2x$

$y^2+4y+4-4=2x$

$(y+2)^2=2x+4,\ (y+2)^2=2(x+2)$

Comparing this equation with

$(y-k)^2=4p(x-h) \rightarrow 4p=2,\ p=\frac{1}{2}$

Since p is positive, the graph opens to the right.

Vertex : $(h,\ k)=(-2,\ -2)$

Focus : $(h+p,\ k)=\left(-2+\frac{1}{2},\ -2\right)=\left(-\frac{3}{2},\ -2\right)$

Equation of directrix :

$x=-p+h=-\frac{1}{2}-2=-\frac{5}{2}$

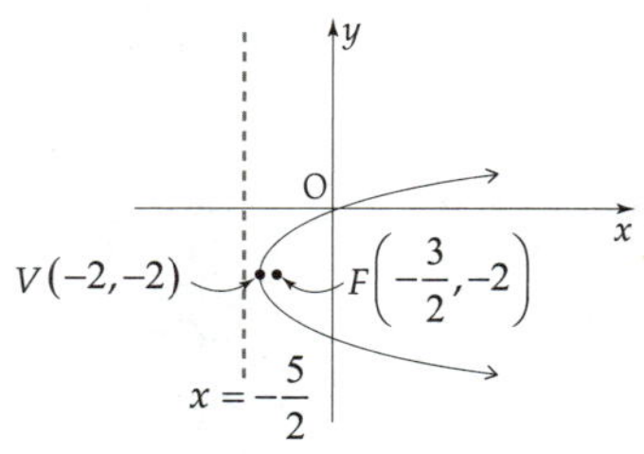

Review Exercises

01

(1) $x^2-6y+4x-8=0,\ x^2+4x=6y+8$

$x^2+4x+4-4=6y+8,\ (x+2)^2=6y+12$

$(x+2)^2=6(y+2) \rightarrow 4p=6,\ p=\frac{3}{2}$

Since p is positive, the graph opens upward.

Vertex : $(h,\ k)=(-2, -2)$

Focus : $(h,\ k+p)=\left(-2, -2+\frac{3}{2}\right)=\left(-2, -\frac{1}{2}\right)$

Equation of directrix :

$y=-p+k=-\frac{3}{2}-2=-\frac{7}{2}$

Focal diameter : $|4p|=\left|4\cdot\frac{3}{2}\right|=6$

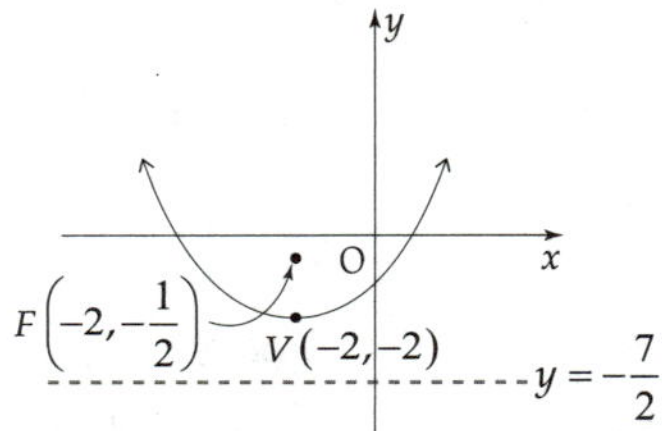

(2) $-y^2+4y-x=5,\ y^2-4y=-x-5$

$y^2-4y+4-4=-x-5,\ (y-2)^2=-x-1$

$(y-2)^2=-(x+1) \rightarrow 4p=-1,\ p=-\frac{1}{4}$

Since p is negative, the graph opens to the left.

Vertex : $(h,\ k)=(-1,\ 2)$

Focus : $(h+p,\ k)=\left(-1-\frac{1}{4},\ 2\right)=\left(-\frac{5}{4},\ 2\right)$

Equation of directrix :

$x=-p+h=-\left(-\frac{1}{4}\right)-1=-\frac{3}{4}$

Focal diameter : $|4p|=|4\cdot-\frac{1}{4}|=1$

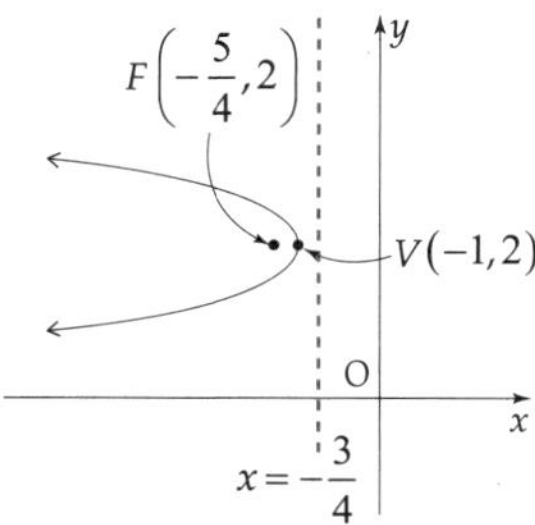

02

(1)

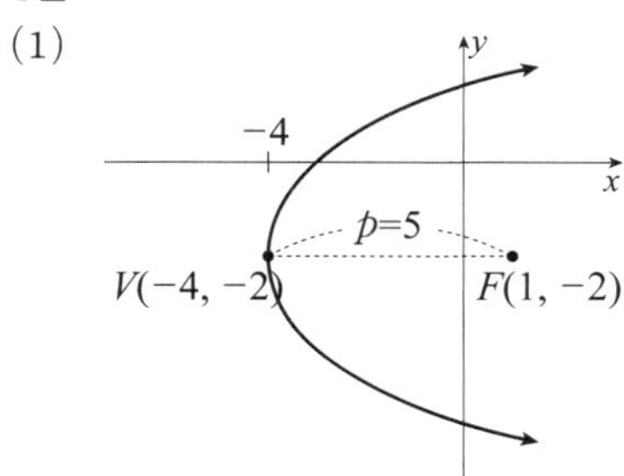

The standard equation is $(y+2)^2=4p(x+4)$ and $p=1-(-4)=5$. So we have $(y+2)^2=4(5)(x+4)$, $(y+2)^2=20(x+4)$.

$(y+2)^2=20(x+4)$

(2)

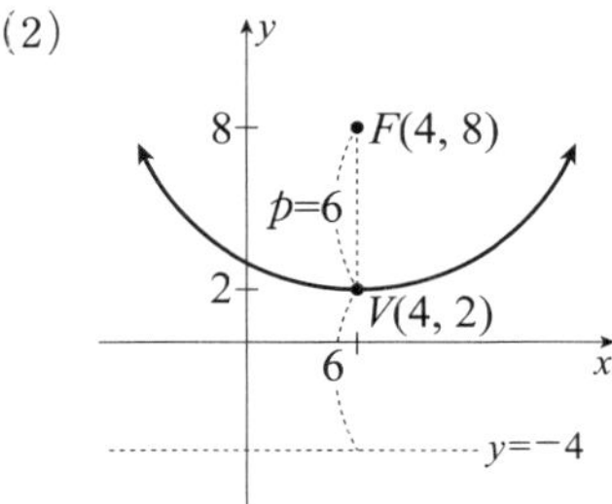

The standard equation is $(x-4)^2=4p(y-2)$ and $p=2-(-4)=6$. So we have $(x-4)^2=4(6)(y-2)$, $(x-4)^2=24(y-2)$.

$(x-4)^2=24(y-2)$

(3)

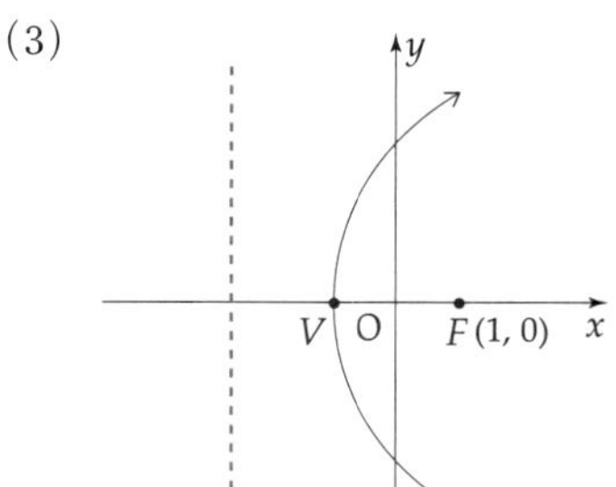

The standard equation is $(y-k)^2=4p(x-h)$.

The vertex is $(-1,0)$ because it is the midpoint of the focus and directrix.

$p=1-(-1)=2$. So the equation is $(y-0)^2=4(2)(x+1)$, $y^2=8(x+1)$

$y^2=8(x+1)$

(4)

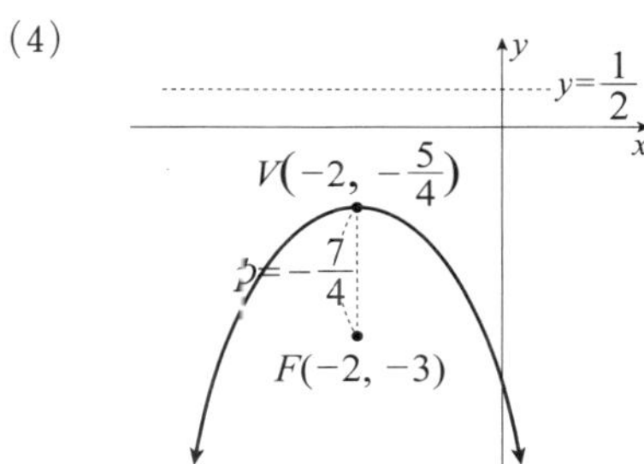

The standard equation is $(x-h)^2=4p(y-k)$.

The vertex is $\left(-2,-\frac{5}{4}\right)$ because it is midpoint of the focus and directrix.

$p=-3-\left(-\frac{5}{4}\right)=-\frac{7}{4}$. So the equation is

$(x+2)^2=4\left(-\frac{7}{4}\right)\left(y+\frac{5}{4}\right)$,

$(x+2)^2=-7\left(y+\frac{5}{4}\right)$

$(x+2)^2=-7\left(y+\frac{5}{4}\right)$

03

(1) Since the parabola opens to the left, the standard equation is $(y-k)^2=4p(x-h)$ and $p=-2-1=-3$. So we have
$(y-2)^2=4(-3)(x-1)$, $(y-2)^2=-12(x-1)$

$(y-2)^2=-12(x-1)$

(2) Since the parabola opens upward the standard equation is $(x-h)^2=4p(y-k)$. The vertex is $(2, -3)$ because it is the midpoint of the focus and directrix. $p=-2-(-3)=1$. So the equation is
$(x-2)^2=4(1)(y+3)$, $(x-2)^2=4(y+3)$

$(x-2)^2=4(y+3)$

04

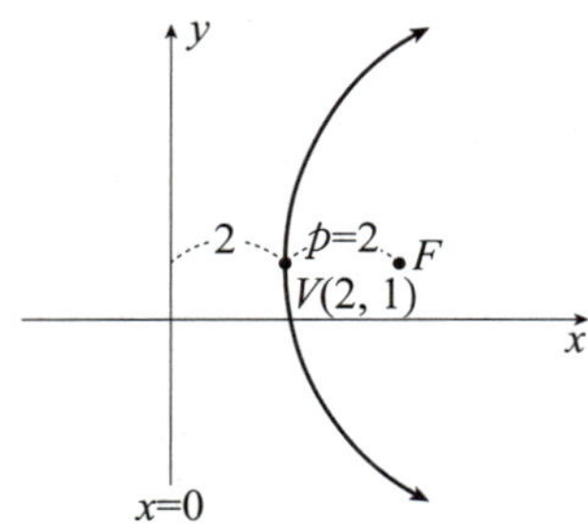

The standard equation is $(y-k)^2=4p(x-h)$ with $p=2$. So the equation is
$(y-1)^2=4(2)(x-2)$, $(y-1)^2=8(x-2)$

$(y-1)^2=8(x-2)$

05

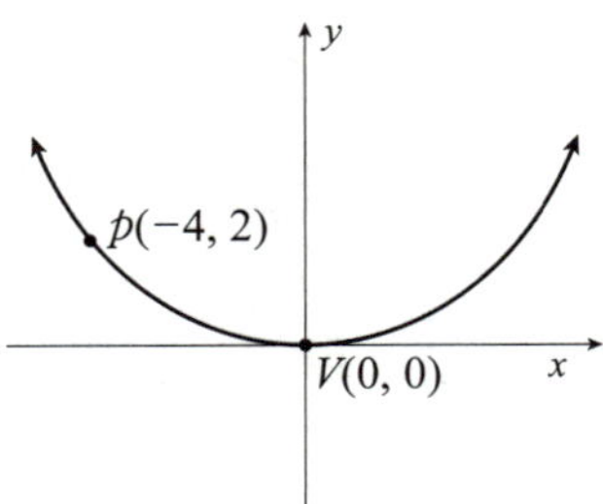

The standard equation is $(x-h)^2=4p(y-k)$ with the vertex $(0, 0)$. So the equation is
$(x-0)^2=4p(y-0)$, $x^2=4py$
Since the parabola passes through the point $(-4, 2)$, we have
$x^2=4py$, $(-4)^2=4p(2)$
$16=8p$, $p=2$
Therefore, the equation is
$x^2=4(2)y$, $x^2=8y$

$x^2=8y$

06

$(y-k)^2=4p(x-h) \rightarrow (y+1)^2=4(x-4)$
The parabola opens to the right. The vertex is $(h, k)=(4, -1)$ and $p=1$.

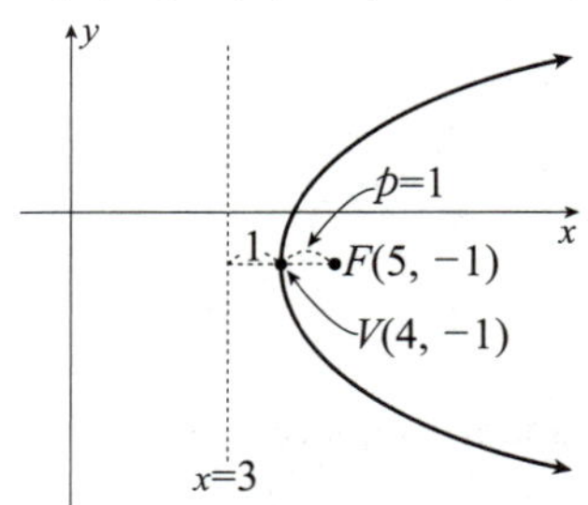

So the answer is (B).

07

The vertex of the parabola is halfway between the focus and the directrix. Thus, the vertex is at (2, 0). The distance p is the distance between the vertex and the focus: $p=4-2=2$

Since the directrix is vertical ($x=0$), this indicates a horizontal parabola, which has the general form $(y-k)^2=4p(x-h)$.

Therefore, the equation of the parabola is:

$(y-0)^2=4(2)(x-2)$, $y^2=8(x-2)$

The correct answer is (D).

3. Conic Sections: Ellipse

Check Point 1

① The standard equation is $\frac{y^2}{a^2}+\frac{x^2}{b^2}=1$

The center is (0,0).

$\frac{x^2}{4}+\frac{y^2}{16}=1$, $\frac{y^2}{16}+\frac{x^2}{4}=1$

$a^2=16$, $a=4$; $b^2=4$, $b=2$

$c=\sqrt{a^2-b^2}=\sqrt{16-4}=2\sqrt{3}$

Center: (0, 0), Vertices: $(0, \pm a)=(0, \pm 4)$

Foci: $(0, \pm c)=(0, \pm 2\sqrt{3})$

Major Axis: $2a=2\cdot 4=8$

Minor Axis: $2b=2\cdot 2=4$

Eccentricity: $\frac{c}{a}=\frac{2\sqrt{3}}{4}=\frac{\sqrt{3}}{2}$

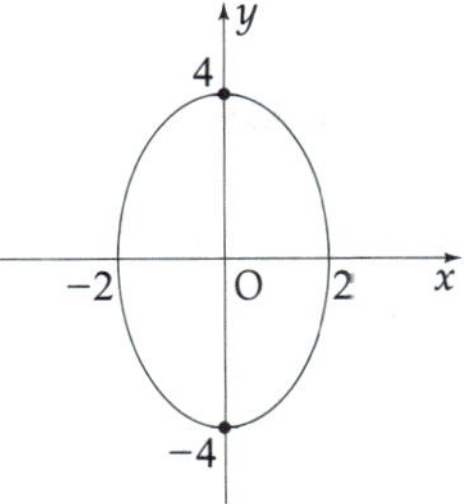

② $3x^2+12y^2=36$

$(3x^2+12y^2=36)\frac{1}{36}$, $\frac{x^2}{12}+\frac{y^2}{3}=1$

The standard equation is $\frac{x^2}{a^2}+\frac{y^2}{b^2}=1$

The center is (0, 0).

$a^2=12$, $a=\sqrt{12}=2\sqrt{3}$; $b^2=3$, $b=\sqrt{3}$

$c=\sqrt{a^2-b^2}=\sqrt{12-3}=\sqrt{9}=3$

Center: (0, 0), Vertices: $(\pm a, 0)=(\pm 2\sqrt{3}, 0)$

Foci: $(\pm c, 0)=(\pm 3, 0)$

Major Axis: $2a=2\cdot 2\sqrt{3}=4\sqrt{3}$

Minor Axis: $2b=2\cdot\sqrt{3}=2\sqrt{3}$

Eccentricity: $\frac{c}{a}=\frac{3}{2\sqrt{3}}=\frac{3\sqrt{3}}{6}=\frac{\sqrt{3}}{2}$

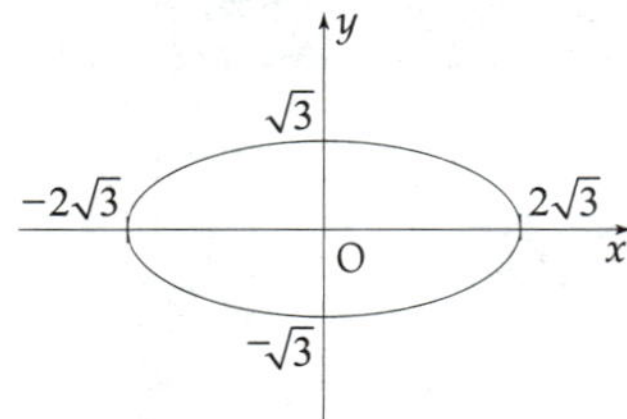

Check Point2

①

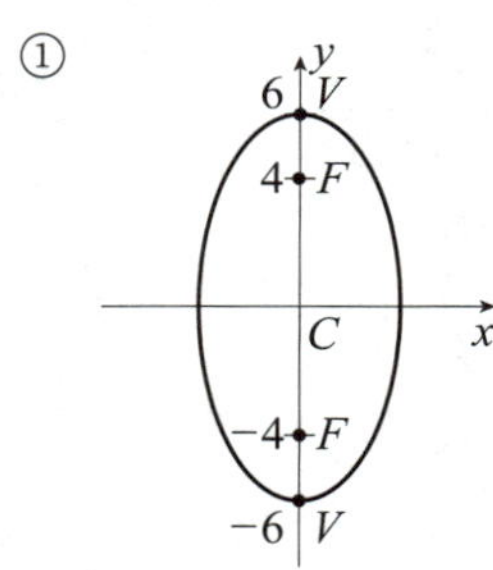

The standard equation is $\frac{y^2}{a^2}+\frac{x^2}{b^2}=1$.

The center is $\left(0,\ \frac{6-6}{2}\right)=(0,\ 0)$. $a=6,\ c=4$,

and $b=\sqrt{a^2-c^2}=\sqrt{6^2-4^2}=2\sqrt{5}$.

So the equation is

$\frac{y^2}{6^2}+\frac{x^2}{(2\sqrt{5})^2}=1,\ \frac{y^2}{36}+\frac{x^2}{20}=1.$

$\frac{y^2}{36}+\frac{x^2}{20}=1$

②

The standard equation is $\frac{(x-h)^2}{a^2}+\frac{y^2}{b^2}=1$.

The center is

$\left(\frac{0+4}{2},\ 0\right)=(2,\ 0)$. $a=\frac{12}{2}=6,\ c=2,$

and $b=\sqrt{a^2-c^2}=\sqrt{6^2-4^2}=4\sqrt{2}$.

So the equation is

$\frac{(x-2)^2}{6^2}+\frac{y^2}{(4\sqrt{2})^2}=1,\ \frac{(x-2)^2}{36}+\frac{y^2}{32}=1$

$\frac{(x-2)^2}{36}+\frac{y^2}{32}=1$

Check Poin3

① $x^2+4y^2+6x-8y+9=0$

$x^2+6x+4(y^2-2y)=-9$

$x^2+6x+9-9+4(y^2-2y+1-1)=-9$

$(x+3)^2-9+4(y-1)^2-4=-9$

$(x+3)^2+4(y-1)^2=4,\ \frac{(x+3)^2}{4}+\frac{(y-1)^2}{1}=1$

$a^2=4,\ a=2;\ b^2=1,\ b=1$

$c=\sqrt{a^2-c^2}=\sqrt{6^2-4^2}=\sqrt{3}.$

Center: $(h,\ k)=(-3,\ 1)$

Vertices: $(h\pm a,k)=(-3\pm 2,\ 1)$

$=(-1,\ 1),(-5,\ 1)$

Foci: $(h\pm c,k)=(-3\pm\sqrt{3},\ 1)$

Major Axis: $2a=2\cdot 2=4$

Minor Axis: $2b=2\cdot 1=2$

Eccentricity: $\frac{c}{a}=\frac{\sqrt{3}}{2}$

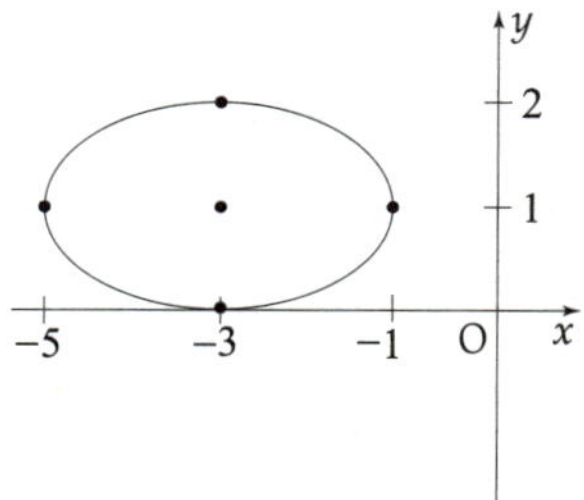

② $9x^2+4y^2+36x-24y+36=0$

$9(x^2+4x)+4(y^2-6y)=-36$

$9(x^2+4x+4-4)+4(y^2-6y+9-9)=-36$

$9(x+2)^2-36+4(y-3)^2-36=-36$

$9(x+2)^2+4(y-3)^2=36,\ \frac{(y-3)^2}{9}+\frac{(x+2)^2}{4}=1$

$a^2=9,\ a=3;\ b^2=4,\ b=2$

$c=\sqrt{a^2-b^2}=\sqrt{9-4}=\sqrt{5}$

Center: $(h,k)=(-2,3)$

Vertices: $(h,k\pm a)=(-2,3\pm 3)$

$=(-2,6),(-2,0)$

Foci: $(h,\ k\pm c)=(-2,\ 3\pm\sqrt{5})$

Major Axis: $2a=2\cdot 3=6$

Minor Axis: $2b=2\cdot 2=4$

Eccentricity: $\frac{c}{a}=\frac{\sqrt{5}}{3}$

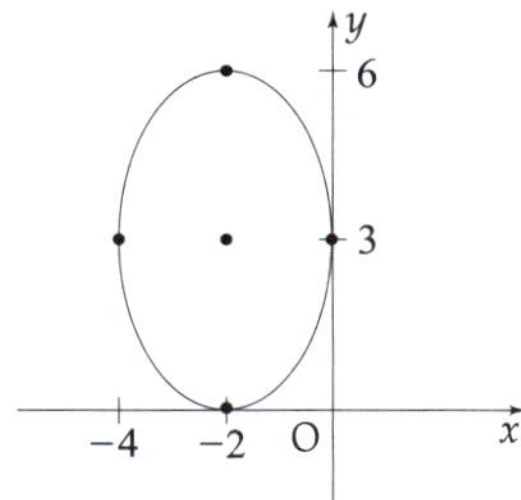

Review Exercises

01

$\frac{(x-2)^2}{9}+\frac{(y+4)^2}{12}=1$

$a^2=12,\ a=\sqrt{12}=2\sqrt{3}$

The length of the major axis is $2a=2\cdot 2\sqrt{3}=4\sqrt{3}$.

02

$8x^2+4y^2-8y=8,\ 2x^2-y^2-2y=2$

$2x^2+(y^2+2y)=2$

$2x^2+(y^2+2y+1-1)=2$

$2x^2+(y+1)^2-1=2,\ 2x^2+(y+1)^2=3$

$\frac{x^2}{\frac{3}{2}}+\frac{(y+1)^2}{3}=1$

$a^2=\frac{3}{2},\ a=\frac{\sqrt{3}}{\sqrt{2}}=\frac{\sqrt{6}}{2};\ b^2=3,\ b=\sqrt{3}$

So the answer is (C).

03

(1) $4x^2+y^2=20,\ (4x^2+y^2=20)\cdot\frac{1}{20}$

$\frac{x^2}{5}+\frac{y^2}{20}=1,\ \frac{y^2}{20}+\frac{x^2}{5}=1$

$a^2=20,\ a=2\sqrt{5};\ b^2=5,\ b=\sqrt{5}$

$c=\sqrt{a^2-b^2}=\sqrt{20-5}=\sqrt{15}$

Center: $(0\ \ 0)$,

Vertices: $(0,\ \pm a)=(0,\ \pm 2\sqrt{5})$

Foci: $(0,\ \pm c)=(0,\ \pm\sqrt{15})$

Major Axis: $2a=4\sqrt{5}$,

Minor Axis: $2b=2\sqrt{5}$

Eccentricity: $\frac{c}{a}=\frac{\sqrt{15}}{2\sqrt{5}}=\frac{\sqrt{3}}{2}$

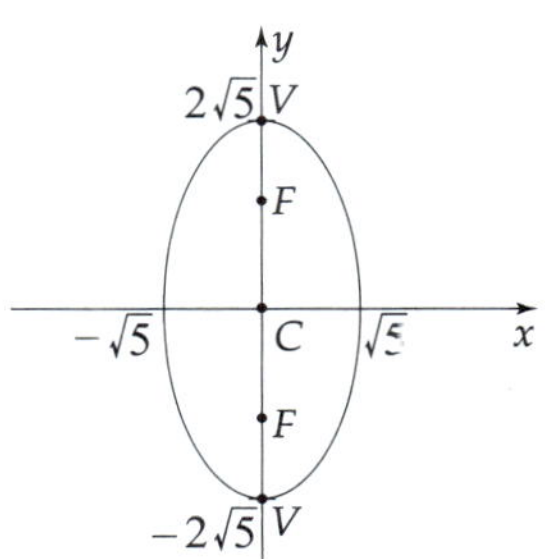

(2) $x^2+2y^2+2x-12y+9=0$

$(x^2+2x)-2(y^2-6y)=-9$

$(x^2+2x+1-1)+2(y^2-6y+9-9)=-9$

$(x+1)^2-1+2(y-3)^2-18=-9$

$(x+1)^2+2(y-3)^2=10,\ \frac{(x+1)^2}{10}+\frac{(y-3)^2}{5}=1$

$a^2=10,\ a=\sqrt{10};\ b^2=5,\ b=\sqrt{5}$

$c=\sqrt{a^2-b^2}=\sqrt{10-5}=\sqrt{5}$

Center: $(h,k)=(-1,3)$

Vertices: $(h\pm a,k)=(-1\pm\sqrt{10},3)$

Foci: $(h\pm c,\ k)=(-1\pm\sqrt{5},\ 3)$

Major Axis: $2a=2\sqrt{10}$,

Minor Axis: $2b=2\sqrt{5}$

Eccentricity: $\frac{c}{a}=\frac{\sqrt{5}}{\sqrt{10}}=\frac{1}{\sqrt{2}}=\frac{\sqrt{2}}{2}$

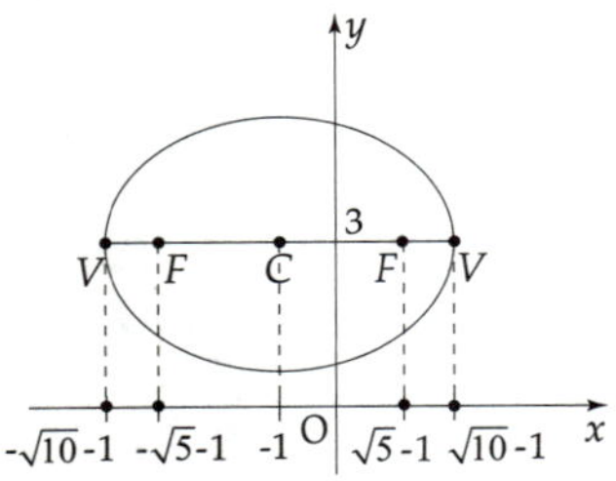

04

(1)

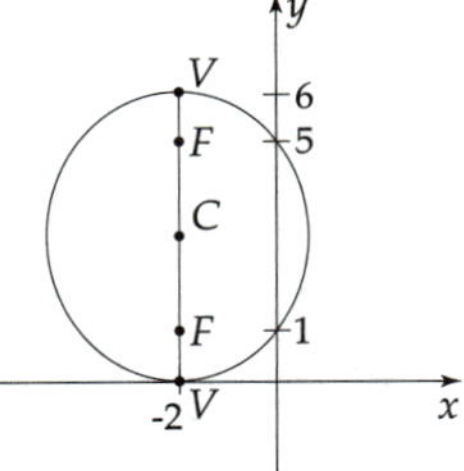

The standard equation is

$$\frac{(y-k)^2}{a^2}+\frac{(x-h)^2}{b^2}=1$$

The center is $\left(-2,\ \frac{0+6}{2}\right)=(-2,\ 3)$.

$a=3$, $c=2$, and $b=\sqrt{a^2-b^2}=\sqrt{9-4}=\sqrt{5}$.

So the equation is

$$\frac{(y-3)^2}{3^2}+\frac{(x+2)^2}{(\sqrt{5})^2}=1,$$

$$\frac{(y-3)^2}{9}+\frac{(x+2)^2}{5}=1.$$

$$\frac{(y-3)^2}{9}+\frac{(x+2)^2}{5}=1$$

(2)

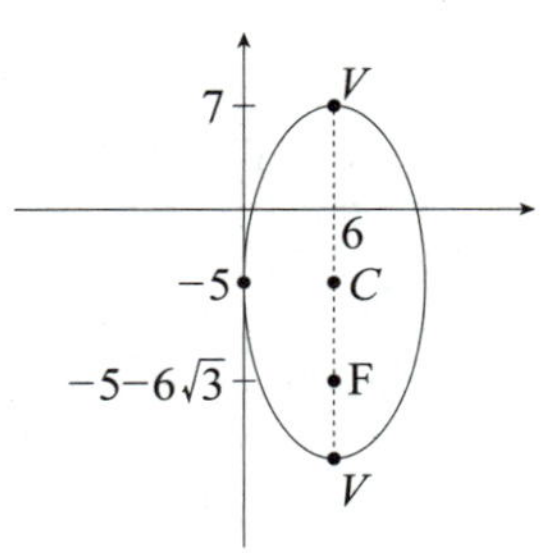

The standard equation is

$$\frac{(y-k)^2}{a^2}+\frac{(x-h)^2}{b^2}=1.$$

$a=7-(-5)=12$, $c=-5-(-5-6\sqrt{3})=6\sqrt{3}$,

and $b=\sqrt{a^2-c^2}=\sqrt{(12^2-(6\sqrt{3})^2}=6$.

So the equation is

$$\frac{(y+5)^2}{12^2}+\frac{(x-6)^2}{6^2}=1,\ \frac{(y+5)^2}{144}+\frac{(x-6)^2}{36}=1.$$

$$\frac{(y+5)^2}{144}+\frac{(x-6)^2}{36}=1$$

(3)

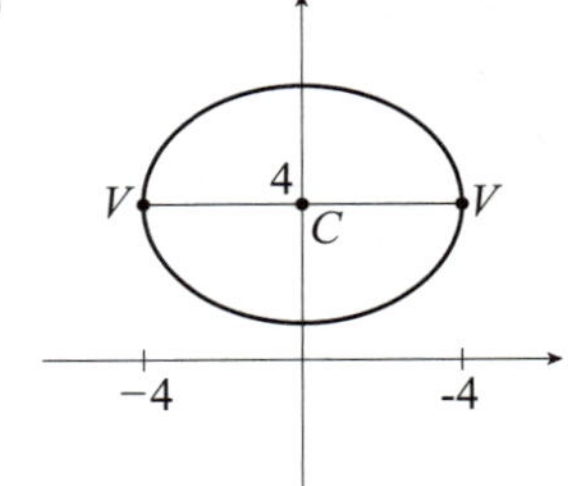

The standard equation is

$\frac{(x-h)^2}{a^2}+\frac{(y-k)^2}{b^2}=1$ and $a=4$.

Since eccentricity is $\frac{1}{2}$, $\frac{c}{a}=\frac{1}{2}$, $a=2c$,

$c=2$.

and $b=\sqrt{a^2-c^2}=\sqrt{4^2-2^2}=2\sqrt{3}$.

So the equation is

$$\frac{(x-0)^2}{4^2}+\frac{(y-4)^2}{(2\sqrt{3})^2}=1,$$

$$\frac{x^2}{16}+\frac{(y-4)^2}{12}=1.$$

$$\frac{x^2}{16}+\frac{(y-4)^2}{12}=1$$

05

$x^2+4y^2=9$, $(x^2+4y^2=9)\cdot\frac{1}{9}$

$$\frac{x^2}{9}+\frac{y^2}{\frac{9}{4}}=1$$

$a^2=9$, $a=3$; $b^2=\frac{9}{4}$, $b=\frac{3}{2}$

So we have the following graph.

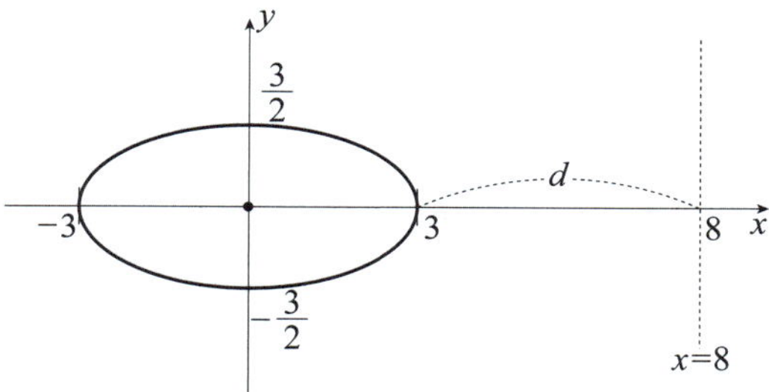

Therefore, the shortest distance between the line $x=8$ and the ellipse is $d=8-3=5$.

06

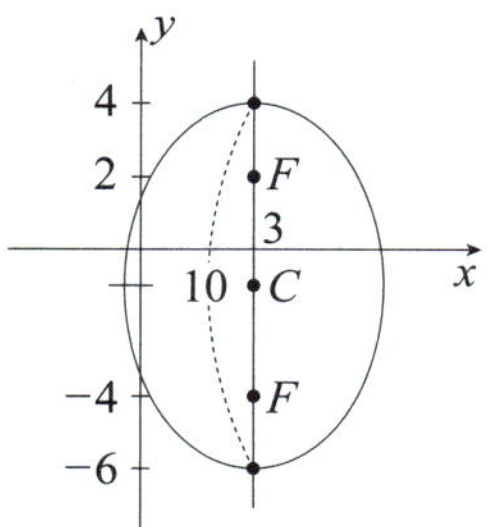

The standard equation is
$\frac{(y-k)^2}{a^2}+\frac{(x-h)^2}{b^2}=1.$

The center is $\left(3,\ \frac{2+(-4)}{2}\right)=(3,-1)$.

Since the length of major axis is $2a=10$, $a=5$, and $c=2-(-1)=3$.

So $b=\sqrt{a^2-c^2}=\sqrt{25-9}=4$.

So the equation is

$\frac{(y+1)^2}{5^2}+\frac{(x-3)^2}{4^2}=1,\ \frac{(y+1)^2}{25}+\frac{(x-3)^2}{16}=1.$

$\frac{(y+1)^2}{25}+\frac{(x-3)^2}{16}=1$

07

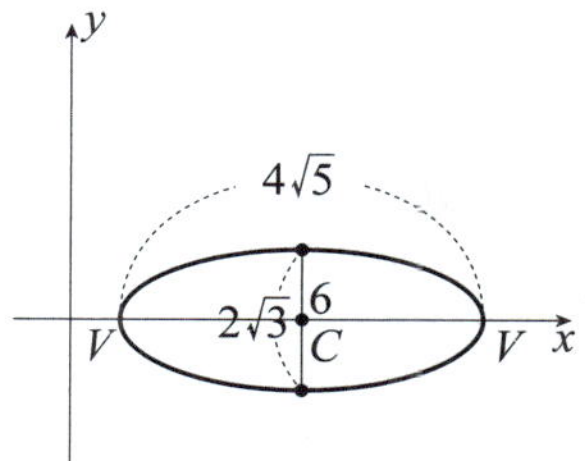

The standard equation is
$\frac{(x-h)^2}{a^2}+\frac{(y-k)^2}{b^2}=1.$

The length of major axis is
$2a=4\sqrt{5}$, $a=2\sqrt{5}$ and
the length of minor axis is $2b=2\sqrt{3}$, $b=\sqrt{3}$.

So the equation is

$\frac{(x-6)^2}{(2\sqrt{5})^2}+\frac{(y-0)^2}{(\sqrt{3})^2}=1,\ \frac{(x-6)^2}{20}+\frac{y^2}{3}=1.$

$\frac{(x-6)^2}{20}+\frac{y^2}{3}=1$

08

Rewrite the Equation in Standard Form:

$$3x^2+2y^2+6x-12y+9=0$$
$$3(x^2+2x-1^2-1^2)+2(y^2-6y+3^2-3^2)+9=0$$
$$3(x+1)^2-3+2(y-3)^2-18+9=0$$
$$3(x+1)^2+2(y-3)^2=12$$
$$\frac{(x+1)^2}{2^2}+\frac{(y-3)^2}{(\sqrt{6})^2}=1$$

Therefore, the length of the major axis is $2\sqrt{6}$.

$2\sqrt{6}$

4. Conic Sections: Hyperbola

Check Point 1

① $\frac{x^2}{9}-\frac{y^2}{25}=1$

The standard equation is $\frac{x^2}{a^2}-\frac{y^2}{b^2}=1$ and the center is $(0,\ 0)$. $a^2=9$, $a=3$; $b^2=25$, $b=5$, and the $c=\sqrt{a^2+b^2}=\sqrt{9+25}=\sqrt{34}$.

Center: $(0,\ 0)$, Vertices: $(\pm a,\ 0)=(\pm 3,\ 0)$

Foci: $(\pm c,\ 0)=(\pm\sqrt{34},\ 0)$

Transverse Axis: $2a=2\cdot 3=6$

Conjugate Axis: $2b=2\cdot 5=10$

Equation of Aysmptote: $y=\pm\frac{b}{a}x=\pm\frac{5}{3}x$

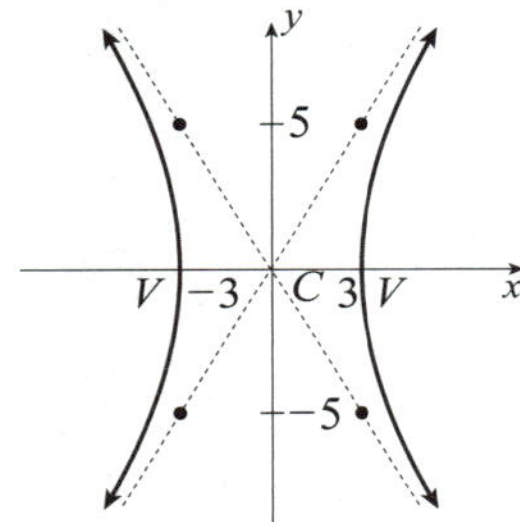

② $12y^2-24x^2=96$

$(12y^2-24x^2=96)\cdot\frac{1}{96}$, $\frac{y^2}{8}-\frac{x^2}{4}=1$

The standard equation is $\frac{y^2}{a^2}-\frac{x^2}{b^2}=1$ and the center is $a^2=8$, $a=2\sqrt{2}$; $b^2=4$, $b=2$, and $c=\sqrt{a^2+b^2}=\sqrt{8+4}=2\sqrt{3}$

Center: $(0,0)$, Vertices: $(0,\pm a)=(0,\pm 2\sqrt{2})$

Foci: $(0,\pm c)=(0,\pm 2\sqrt{3})$

Transverse Axis: $2a=2\cdot 2\sqrt{2}=4\sqrt{2}$

Conjugate Axis: $2b=2\cdot 2=4$

Equation of Aysmptote:

$y=\pm\frac{a}{b}x$, $y=\pm\frac{2\sqrt{2}}{2}x=\pm\sqrt{2}x$

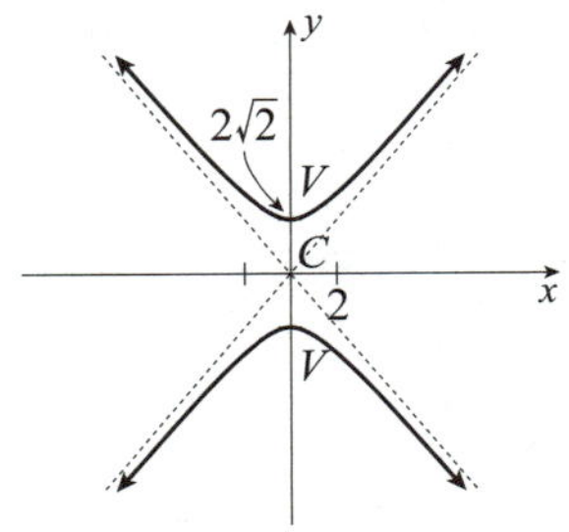

Check Point 2

①

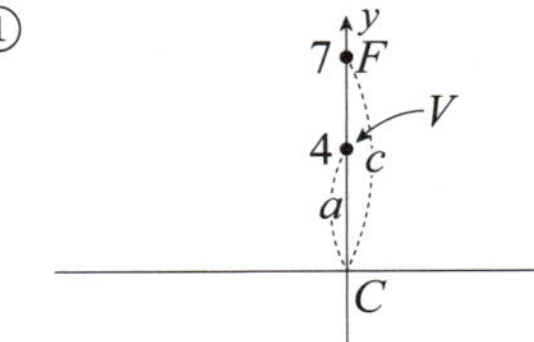

The standard equation is $\frac{y^2}{a^2}-\frac{x^2}{b^2}=1$.

The center is $\left(0,\ \frac{4-4}{2}\right)=(0,\ 0)$.

$a=4$, $c=7$, and $b=\sqrt{c^2-a^2}=\sqrt{49-16}=\sqrt{33}$.

So the equation is

$\frac{y^2}{4^2}-\frac{x^2}{(\sqrt{33})}=1$, $\frac{y^2}{16}-\frac{x^2}{33}=1$.

$\frac{y^2}{16}-\frac{x^2}{33}=1$

②

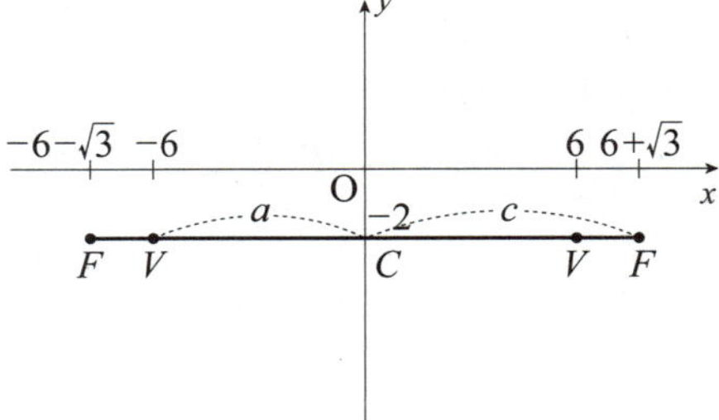

The standard equation is

$\frac{(x-h)^2}{a^2}-\frac{(y-k)^2}{b^2}=1$.

The center is $\left(\frac{-6+6}{2},\ -2\right)=(0,\ -2)$.

$a=6,\ c=6+\sqrt{3}$,

and $b=\sqrt{c^2-a^2}=\sqrt{(6+\sqrt{3})^2-6^2}=\sqrt{12\sqrt{3}+3}$.

So the equation is

$\frac{x^2}{6^2}-\frac{(y+2)^2}{(\sqrt{12\sqrt{3}+3})^2}=1,\ \frac{x^2}{36}-\frac{(y+2)^2}{12\sqrt{3}+3}=1.$

$\frac{x^2}{36}-\frac{(y+2)^2}{12\sqrt{3}+3}=1$

Check Point 3

① $x^2-2y^2+12y-26=0,\ x^2-2(y^2-6y)=26$

$x^2-2(y^2-6y+9-9)=26$

$x^2-2(y-3)^2+18=26$

$x^2-2(y-3)^2=8,\ \frac{x^2}{8}-\frac{(y-3)^2}{4}=1$

$a^2=8,\ a=2\sqrt{2}\,;\ b^2=4,\ b=2$

$c=\sqrt{a^2+b^2}=\sqrt{8+4}=2\sqrt{3}$

Center: $(h,k)=(0,\ 3)$

Vertices: $(h\pm a,k)=(\pm 2\sqrt{2},\ 3)$

Foci: $(h\pm c,k)=(\pm 2\sqrt{3},\ 3)$

Equation of Aysmptote: $y=\pm\frac{b}{a}(x-h)+k$,

$y=\pm\frac{2}{2\sqrt{2}}x+3$

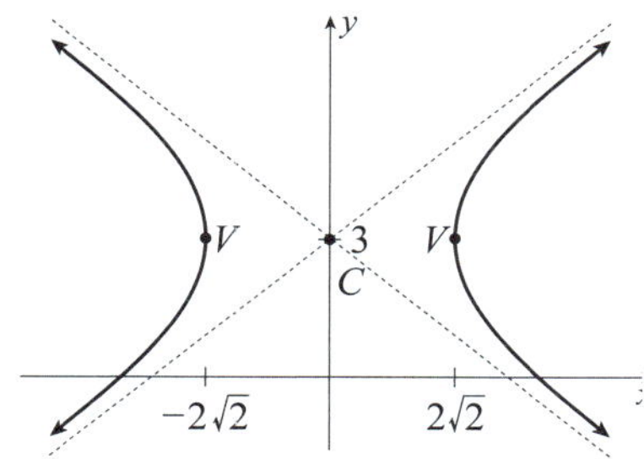

② $x^2-2y^2-6x-16y-15=0$

$(x^2-6x)-2(y^2+8y)=15$

$(x^2-6x+9-9)-2(y^2+8y+16-16)=15$

$(x-3)^2-9-2(y+4)^2+32=15$

$(x-3)^2-2(y+4)^2=-8$

$\frac{(y+4)^2}{4}-\frac{(x-3)^2}{8}=1$

$a^2=4,\ a=2;\ b^2=8,\ b=2\sqrt{2}$

$c=\sqrt{a^2+b^2}=\sqrt{4+8}=2\sqrt{3}$

Center: $(h,k)=(3,-4)$

Vertices: $(h,k\pm a)=(3,\ -4\pm 2)$

$=(3,\ -2),(3,\ -6)$

Foci: $(h,k\pm c)=(3,-4\pm 2\sqrt{3})$

Equation of Aysmptote:

$y=\pm\frac{a}{b}(x-h)+k,\ y=\pm\frac{2}{2\sqrt{2}}(x-3)-4$

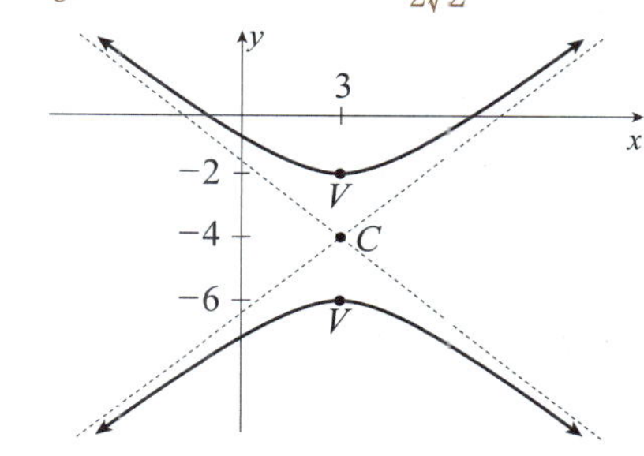

Review Exercises

01

(1) $y^2-2x^2=6$

$(y^2-2x^2=6)\cdot\frac{1}{6},\ \frac{y^2}{6}-\frac{x^2}{3}=1$

$a^2=6,\ a=\sqrt{6}\,;\ b^2=3,\ b=\sqrt{3}$

$c=\sqrt{a^2+b^2}=\sqrt{6+3}=3$

Center: $(0,\ 0)$

Vertices: $(0,\pm a)=(0,\pm\sqrt{6})$

Foci: $(0,\ \pm c)=(0,\ \pm 3)$

Equation of Aysmptote:

$y=\pm\frac{a}{b}x,\ y=\pm\frac{\sqrt{6}}{\sqrt{3}}x=\pm\sqrt{2}x$

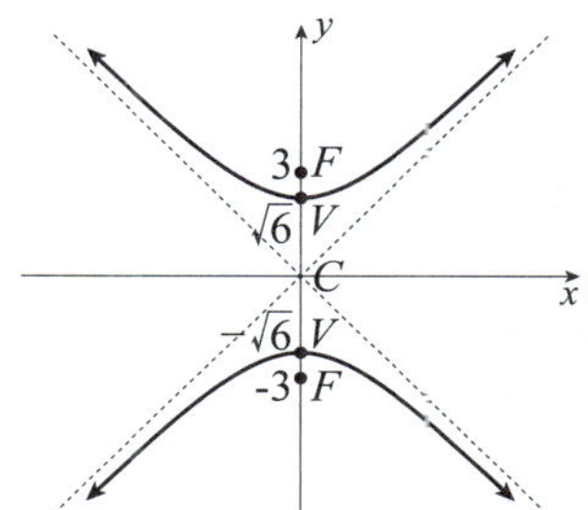

(2) $3x^2-2y^2-6x-8y-17=0$

$3(x^2-2x)-2(y^2+4y)=17$

$3(x^2-2x+1-1)-2(y^2+4y+4-4)=17$

$3(x-1)^2-3-2(y+2)^2+8=17$

$3(x-1)^2-2(y+2)^2=12$

$\frac{(x-1)^2}{4}-\frac{(y+2)^2}{6}=1$

$a^2=4,\ a=2;\ b^2=6,\ b=\sqrt{6}$

$c=\sqrt{a^2+b^2}=\sqrt{4+6}=\sqrt{10}$

Center: $(h,\ k)=(1,\ -2)$

Vertices: $(h\pm a,\ k)=(1\pm 2,\ -2)$
$=(-1,\ -2),(3,\ -2)$

Foci: $(h\pm c, k)=(1\pm\sqrt{10}, -2)$

Equation of Aysmptote:

$y=\pm\frac{b}{a}(x-h)+k,\ y=\pm\frac{\sqrt{6}}{2}(x-1)-2$

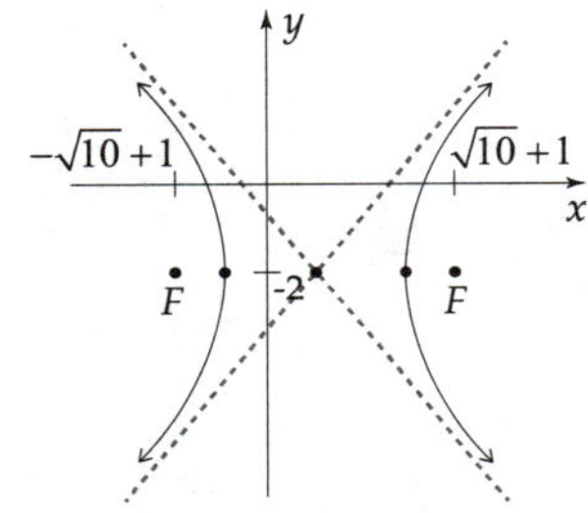

02

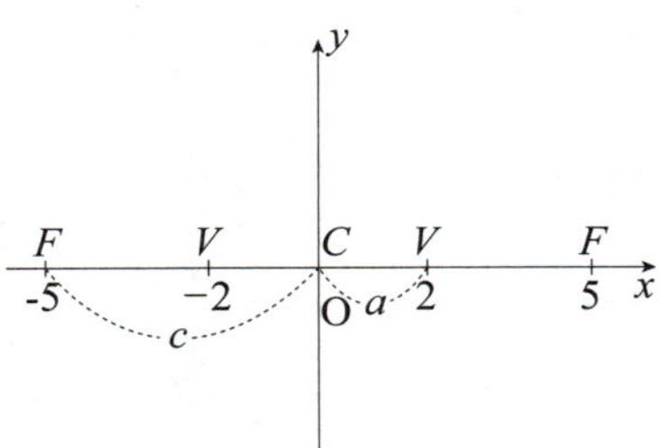

The standard equation is $\frac{x^2}{a^2}-\frac{y^2}{b^2}=1$

The center is $(0,\ 0)$. $a=2,\ c=5,$
and $b=\sqrt{c^2-a^2}=\sqrt{25-4}=\sqrt{21}$

So the equation is

$\frac{x^2}{2^2}-\frac{y^2}{(\sqrt{21})^2}=1,\ \frac{x^2}{4}-\frac{y^2}{21}=1.$

$\frac{x^2}{4}-\frac{y^2}{21}=1$

03

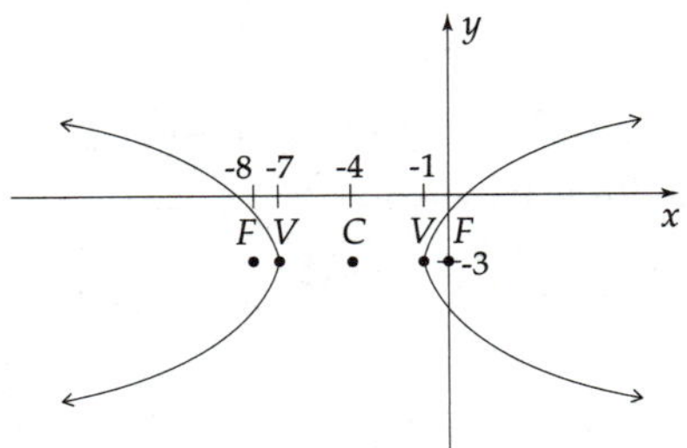

The standard equation is
$\frac{(x-h)^2}{a^2}-\frac{(y-k)^2}{b^2}=1.$

The center is $\left(\frac{-1+(-7)}{2},\ -3\right)=(-4,\ -3).$

$a=3,\ c=4,$ and $b=\sqrt{c^2-a^2}=\sqrt{16-9}=\sqrt{7}$

So the equation is

$\frac{(x+4)^2}{3^2}-\frac{(y+3)^2}{(\sqrt{7})^2}=1,\ \frac{(x+4)^2}{9}-\frac{(y+3)^2}{7}=1.$

$\frac{(x+4)^2}{9}-\frac{(y+3)^2}{7}=1$

04

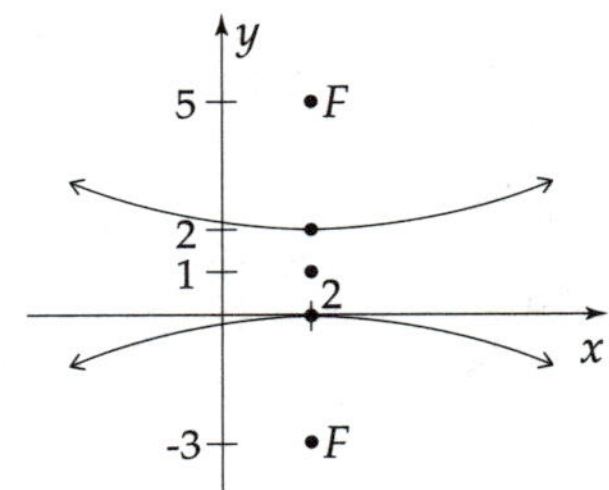

The standard equation is
$\frac{(y-k)^2}{a^2}-\frac{(x-h)^2}{b^2}=1.$

The center is $\left(2,\ \frac{-3+5}{2}\right)=(2,\ 1).$

$a=1,\ c=4,$
and $b=\sqrt{c^2-a^2}=\sqrt{16-1}=\sqrt{15}$

So the equation is

$\frac{(y-1)^2}{1^2}-\frac{(x-2)^2}{(\sqrt{15})^2}=1,\ (y-1)^2-\frac{(x-2)^2}{15}=1$

$(y-1)^2-\frac{(x-2)^2}{15}=1$

05

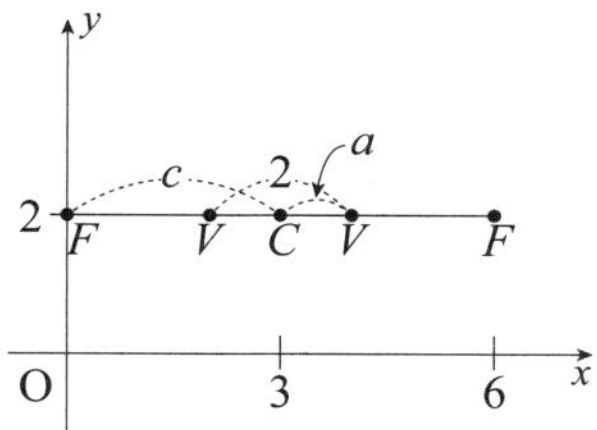

The standard equation is
$\frac{(x-h)^2}{a^2}-\frac{(y-k)^2}{b^2}=1$.

The center is $\left(\frac{0+6}{2},\ 2\right)=(3,\ 2)$.

Since the length of transverse axis is 2, $2a=2$, $a=1$. $c=6-3=3$ and $b=\sqrt{c^2-a^2}=\sqrt{9-1}=2\sqrt{2}$.
So the equation is
$\frac{(x-3)^2}{1^2}-\frac{(y-2)^2}{(2\sqrt{2})^2}=1$, $(x-3)^2-\frac{(y-2)^2}{8}=1$.

$(x-3)^2-\frac{(y-2)^2}{8}=1$

06

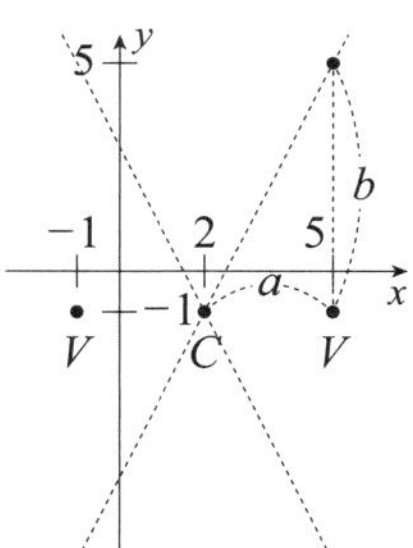

The standard equation is
$\frac{(x-h)^2}{a^2}-\frac{(y-k)^2}{b^2}=1$.

The center is $\left(\frac{-1+5}{2},\ -1\right)=(2,\ -1)$.

$a=5-2=3$ from the graph above. Since the slope of the asymptotes are ± 2, we have $\pm\frac{b}{a}=\pm 2$, $\frac{b}{3}=2$, $b=6$. So the equation is
$\frac{(x-2)^2}{3^2}-\frac{(y+1)^2}{6^2}=1$, $\frac{(x-2)^2}{9}-\frac{(y+1)^2}{36}=1$.

$\frac{(x-2)^2}{9}-\frac{(y+1)^2}{36}=1$

07

Rewrite the Equation in Standard Form:

$$x^2-y^2+2x-4y=10$$
$$(x^2+2x+1^2-1^2)-(y^2+4y+2^2-2^2)=10$$
$$(x+1)^2-1-(y+2)^2+4=10$$
$$(x+1)^2-(y+2)^2=7$$
$$\frac{(x+1)^2}{7}-\frac{(y+2)^2}{7}=1$$

The center of the hyperbola is at the point $(-1,\ -2)$. Therefore, the correct answer is (B).

08

$\frac{(y-2)^2}{4}-\frac{x^2}{9}=1 \Rightarrow a=2,\ b=3$

For a hyperbola in the form
$\frac{(y-k)^2}{a^2}-\frac{(x-h)^2}{b^2}=1$, the equations of the asymptotes are given by:

$y-k=\pm\frac{a}{b}(x-h)$

$y-2=\pm\frac{2}{3}(x-0)$, $y=\pm\frac{2}{3}x+2$

Therefore, the correct answer is (D).

Solutions Manual

5. Introduction to Vectors

Check Point 1

The component form of $\overrightarrow{AB}$ is
$\overrightarrow{AB}=\langle -2-1,\ 2-4\rangle=\langle -3,-2\rangle$.
The magnitude is
$|\overrightarrow{AB}|=\sqrt{(-3)^2+(-2)^2}=\sqrt{13}$.

Check Point 2

① $\vec{v}-\vec{w}=\langle 2,\ 3\rangle-\langle -2,\ 1\rangle=\langle 2-(-2),\ 3-1\rangle$
$=\langle 4,\ 2\rangle$

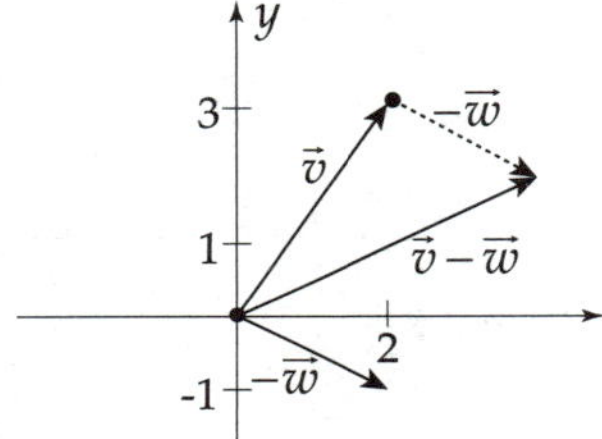

② $3\vec{v}-2\vec{x}=3\langle 2,\ 3\rangle-2\langle 4,\ 0\rangle$
$=\langle 6,\ 9\rangle-\langle 8,\ 0\rangle$
$=\langle 6-8,\ 9-0\rangle=\langle -2,\ 9\rangle$

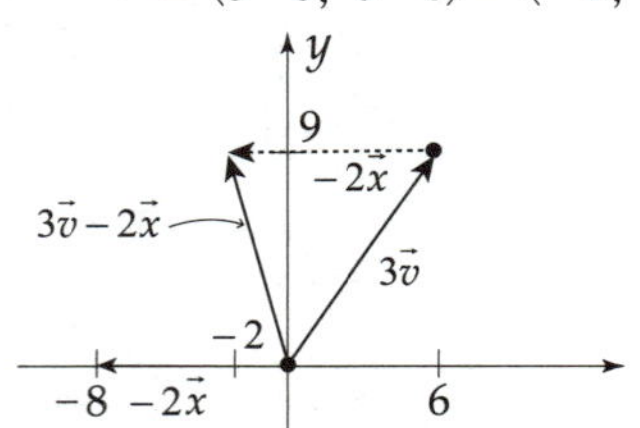

Check Point 3

① The unit vector in the direction of $\vec{v}$ is

$$\vec{u}=\frac{\vec{v}}{|\vec{v}|}=\frac{\langle -6,\ 8\rangle}{\sqrt{(-6)^2+8^2}}=\frac{\langle -6,\ 8\rangle}{10}=\left\langle -\frac{3}{5},\ \frac{4}{5}\right\rangle.$$

② The vector $\vec{w}=5i-12j$ can be written as $5i-12j=\langle 5,\ -12\rangle$. So the unit vector in the direction of $\vec{w}$ is

$$\vec{u}=\frac{\vec{w}}{|\vec{w}|}=\frac{\langle 5,\ -12\rangle}{\sqrt{5^2+(-12)^2}}=\frac{\langle 5,\ -12\rangle}{13}$$
$$=\left\langle \frac{5}{13},\ -\frac{12}{13}\right\rangle.$$

Also, note that

$$\vec{u}=\left\langle \frac{5}{13},\ -\frac{12}{13}\right\rangle=\frac{5}{13}i-\frac{12}{13}j.$$

Check Point 4

① $\vec{v}=|\vec{v}|\langle\cos\theta,\ \sin\theta\rangle$
$=12\langle\cos 60°,\ \sin 60°\rangle$
$=12\left\langle\frac{1}{2},\ \frac{\sqrt{3}}{2}\right\rangle=\langle 6,\ 6\sqrt{3}\rangle$

$\vec{v}=\langle 6,\ 6\sqrt{3}\rangle$

② $\vec{v}=|\vec{v}|\langle\cos\theta,\ \sin\theta\rangle$
$=8\langle\cos 225°,\ \sin 225°\rangle$
$=8\left\langle-\frac{\sqrt{2}}{2},\ -\frac{\sqrt{2}}{2}\right\rangle=\langle -4\sqrt{2},\ -4\sqrt{2}\rangle$

$\vec{v}=\langle -4\sqrt{2},\ -4\sqrt{2}\rangle$

Check Point 5

①

θ = 360° − α

$\tan\alpha=\frac{3}{5}$, $\alpha=\tan^{-1}\left(\frac{3}{5}\right)\approx 30.964°$

The direction angle is
$\theta=360°-30.964°=329.036°$.

②

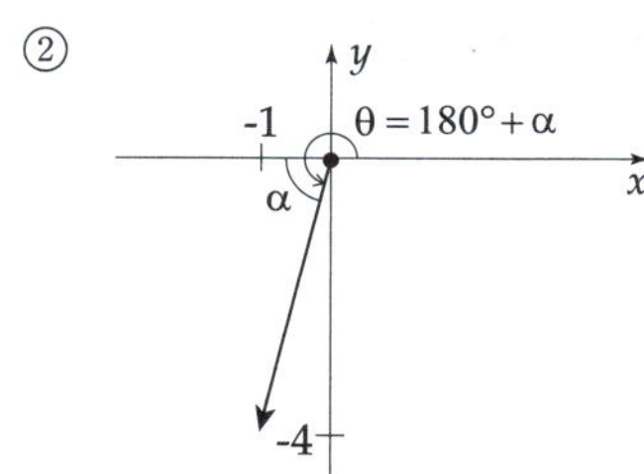

$\tan\alpha = \frac{4}{1}$, $\alpha = \tan^{-1}4 \approx 75.964°$

The direction angle is

$\theta = 180° + 75.964° = 255.964°$.

Review Exercises

01

The component form of $\vec{v}$ is

$\vec{v} = \langle 0-(-2),\ -1-2 \rangle = \langle 2,\ -3 \rangle$.

So the magnitude of

$\vec{v}$ is $|\vec{v}| = \sqrt{2^2+(-3)^2} = \sqrt{13}$.

02

(1) $\vec{w} - \vec{x} = \langle 5,\ 3 \rangle - \langle -2,\ -3 \rangle = \langle 7,\ 6 \rangle$

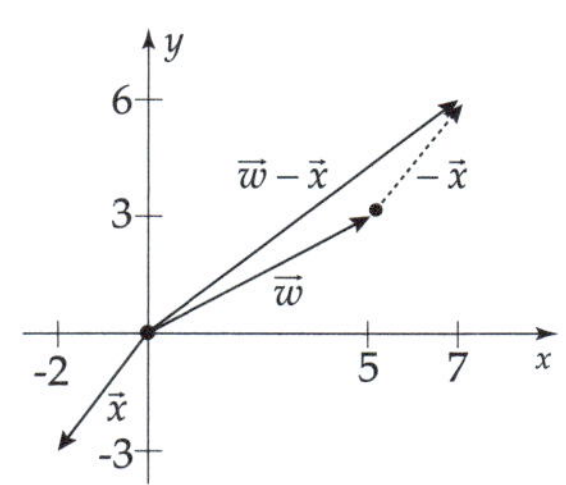

(2) $2\vec{v} + 3\vec{x} = 2\langle 3,\ -1 \rangle + 3\langle -2,\ -3 \rangle$

$= \langle 6,\ -2 \rangle + \langle -6,\ -9 \rangle = \langle 0,\ -11 \rangle$

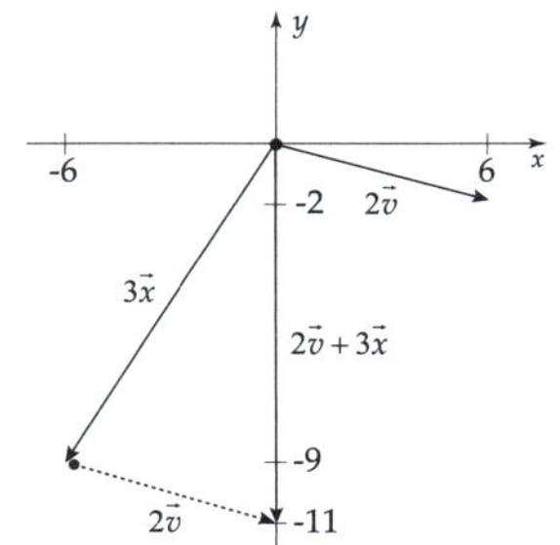

03

By Triangle Method, $\vec{a} + \vec{c} = \vec{b}$.

So the answer is (D)

04

(A)

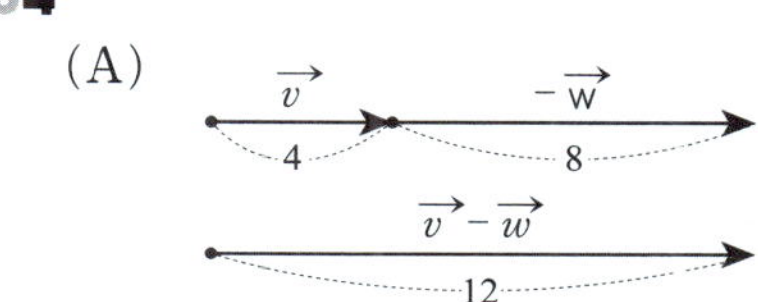

(B)

$\vec{v}$

4

$-\vec{w}$

8

(A) : The maximum magnitude of vector $\vec{v} - \vec{w}$ is $8+4=12$.

(B) : The minimum magnitude of vector $\vec{v} - \vec{w}$ is $8-4=4$.

So the magnitude of vector $\vec{v} - \vec{w}$ must be between 4 and 12, inclusive. Therefore, the answer is (E).

05

(1) $\vec{u} = \frac{\vec{v}}{|\vec{v}|} = \frac{\langle -3,\ 4 \rangle}{\sqrt{(-3)^2+4^2}} = \frac{\langle -3,\ 4 \rangle}{5}$

$= \left\langle -\frac{3}{5},\ \frac{4}{5} \right\rangle$.

(2) $\vec{x} = -4i - 5j = \langle -4,\ -5 \rangle$

$\vec{u} = \frac{\vec{x}}{|\vec{x}|} = \frac{\langle -4,\ -5 \rangle}{\sqrt{(-4)^2+(-5)^2}}$

$= \frac{\langle -4,\ -5 \rangle}{\sqrt{41}} = \left\langle -\frac{4}{\sqrt{41}},\ -\frac{5}{\sqrt{41}} \right\rangle$

06

Using the direction angle and magnitude of the vector, it can be written as

$\vec{v} = |\vec{v}| \langle \cos\theta,\ \sin\theta \rangle$.

(1) $\vec{v} = |\vec{v}| \langle \cos\theta,\ \sin\theta \rangle$

$=5\langle \cos 45°, \ \sin 45° \rangle$

$=5\left\langle \frac{\sqrt{2}}{2}, \ \frac{\sqrt{2}}{2} \right\rangle = \left\langle \frac{5\sqrt{2}}{2}, \ \frac{5\sqrt{2}}{2} \right\rangle$

(2) $\vec{v}=|\vec{v}|\langle \cos\theta, \ \sin\theta \rangle = 7\langle \cos 270°, \ \sin 270° \rangle$

$=7\langle 0, \ -1 \rangle = \langle 0, \ -7 \rangle$

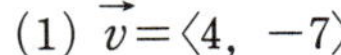

07

(1) $\vec{v}=\langle 4, \ -7 \rangle$

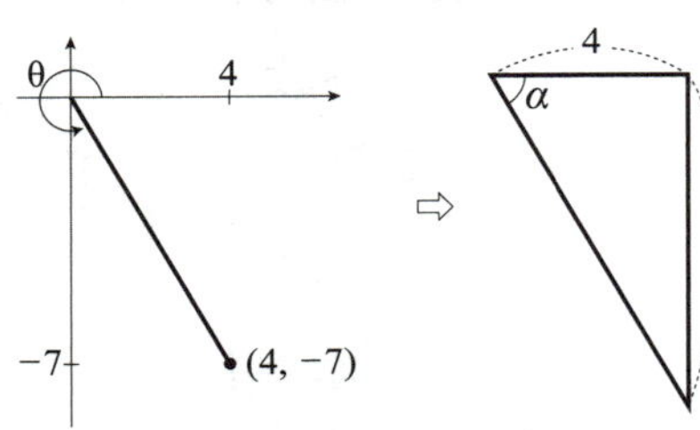

$\tan\alpha=\frac{7}{4}, \ \alpha=\tan^{-1}\left(\frac{7}{4}\right) \approx 60.255°$

The angle is $\theta=360°-60.255°=299.745°$

(2) $\vec{w}=-5i+4j=\langle -5, \ 4 \rangle$

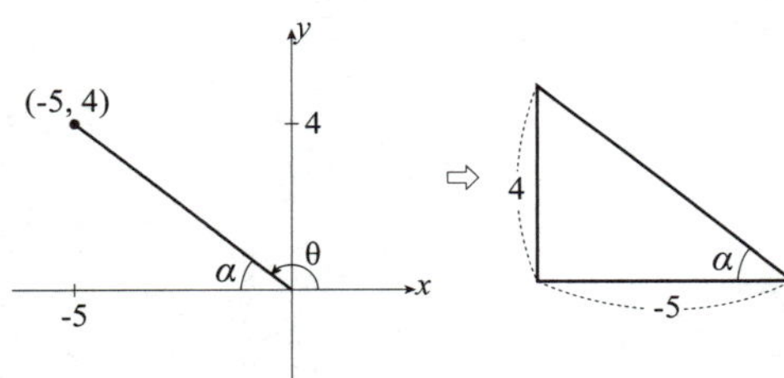

$\tan\alpha=\frac{4}{5}, \ \alpha=\tan^{-1}\left(\frac{4}{5}\right) \approx 38.660°$

The angle is $\theta=180°-33.660°=141.340°$

08

$\vec{v}=|\vec{v}|\langle \cos\theta, \sin\theta \rangle = 6\langle \cos 40°, \sin 40° \rangle$

$=\langle 6\cos 40°, 6\sin 40° \rangle$

$\vec{w}=|\vec{w}|\langle \cos\theta, \ \sin\theta \rangle = 2\langle \cos 100°, \sin 100° \rangle$

$=\langle 2 \ \cos 100°, 2 \ \sin 100° \rangle$

$\vec{v}-\vec{w}=\langle 6\cos 40°-2\cos 100°,$

$6\sin 40°-2 \ \sin 100° \rangle$

$=\langle 4.944, 1,887 \rangle$

$|\vec{v}-\vec{w}|=\sqrt{(4.944)^2+(1.887)^2}=5.292$

6. Dot Product of the Vectors

Check Point 1

① $\vec{v}\cdot\vec{w}=\left\langle -2, \ \frac{5}{2} \right\rangle \cdot \langle 5, \ 4 \rangle$

$=(-2)(5)+\left(\frac{5}{2}\right)(4)=-10+10=0$

② $\vec{v}\cdot\vec{w}=(3i-4j)\cdot(-2i-j)$

$=\langle 3, \ -4 \rangle \cdot \langle -2, \ -1 \rangle$

$=(3)(-2)+(-4)(-1)$

$=-6+4=-2$

Check Point 2

① $\cos\theta=\frac{\vec{v}\cdot\vec{w}}{|\vec{v}||\vec{w}|}=\frac{\langle 2, \ 5 \rangle \cdot \langle 4, \ -1 \rangle}{\sqrt{2^2+5^2}\sqrt{4^2+(-1)^2}}$

$=\frac{8-5}{\sqrt{29}\sqrt{17}}=\frac{3}{\sqrt{29}\sqrt{17}}$

$\theta=\cos^{-1}\left(\frac{3}{\sqrt{29}\sqrt{17}}\right) \approx 82.235°$

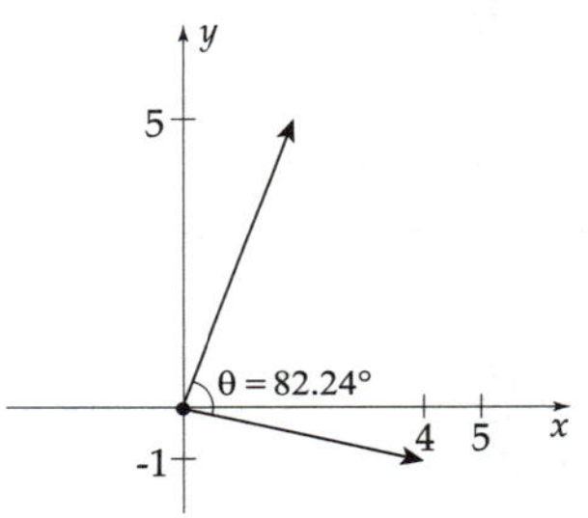

② $\cos\theta=\frac{\vec{v}\cdot\vec{w}}{|\vec{v}||\vec{w}|}=\frac{\langle -4, \ -2 \rangle \cdot \langle 3, \ -2 \rangle}{\sqrt{(-4)^2+(-2)^2}\sqrt{3^2+(-2)^2}}$

$=\frac{-12+4}{\sqrt{20}\sqrt{13}}=\frac{-8}{\sqrt{20}\sqrt{13}}$

$\theta=\cos^{-1}\left(\frac{-8}{\sqrt{20}\sqrt{13}}\right) \approx 119.745°.$

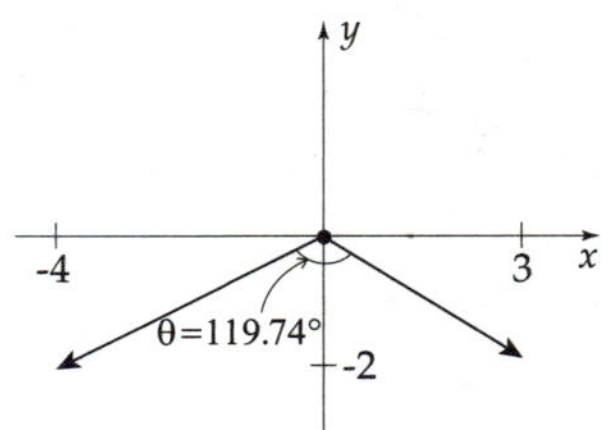

Check Point 3

① $\vec{v}\cdot\vec{w}=(-2)\left(-\frac{1}{4}\right)+(-4)\left(\frac{2}{3}\right)$

$$=\frac{1}{2}+\left(-\frac{8}{3}\right)=-\frac{13}{6}\neq 0$$

$\vec{v}$ and $\vec{w}$ are NOT orthogonal.

② $\vec{v}=5j=\langle 0,\ 5\rangle$, $\vec{w}=-4i=\langle -4,\ 0\rangle$

$\vec{v}\cdot\vec{w}=(0)(-4)+(5)(0)=0+0=0$

$\vec{v}$ and $\vec{w}$ are orthogonal.

Check Point 4

Let $\vec{v}=\vec{x_1}+\vec{x_2}$, where $\vec{x_1}=\text{proj}_w\, v$ and $\vec{x_2}=\vec{v}-\vec{x_1}$.

① $x_1=\text{proj}_w\, v=\dfrac{\vec{v}\cdot\vec{w}}{|\vec{w}|^2}\vec{w}$

$$=\frac{\langle 4,\ 1\rangle\cdot\langle 3,\ -4\rangle}{(\sqrt{3^2+(-4)^2})^2}\langle 3,\ -4\rangle=\frac{12-4}{(\sqrt{25})^2}$$

$$=\frac{8}{25}\langle 3,\ -4\rangle=\left\langle\frac{24}{25},\ -\frac{32}{25}\right\rangle$$

$$\vec{x_2}=\vec{v}-\vec{x_1}=\langle 4,\ 1\rangle-\left\langle\frac{24}{25},\ -\frac{32}{25}\right\rangle=\left\langle\frac{76}{25},\ \frac{57}{25}\right\rangle$$

$$\vec{v}=\vec{x_1}+\vec{x_2}=\left\langle\frac{24}{25},\ -\frac{32}{25}\right\rangle+\left\langle\frac{76}{25},\ \frac{57}{25}\right\rangle$$

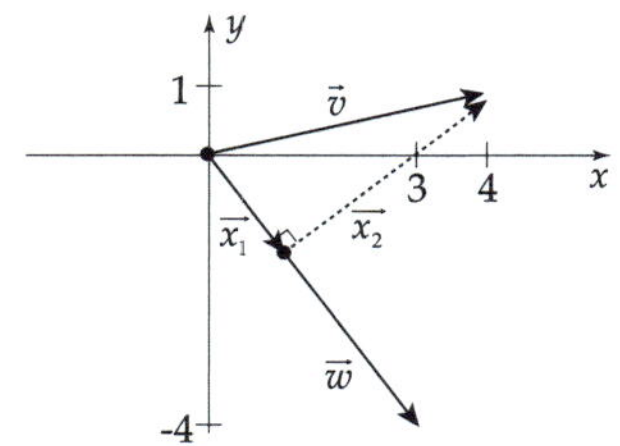

② $\vec{x_1}=\text{proj}_w\, v=\dfrac{\vec{v}\cdot\vec{w}}{|\vec{w}|^2}\vec{w}$

$$=\frac{\langle -6,\ 2\rangle\cdot\langle -4,\ 5\rangle}{(\sqrt{(-4)^2+5^2})^2}\langle -4,\ 5\rangle$$

$$=\frac{24+10}{(\sqrt{41})^2}\langle -4,\ 5\rangle$$

$$=\frac{34}{41}\langle -4,\ 5\rangle=\left\langle -\frac{136}{41},\ \frac{170}{41}\right\rangle$$

$$\vec{x_2}=\vec{v}-\vec{x_1}=\langle -6,\ 2\rangle-\left\langle -\frac{136}{41},\ \frac{170}{41}\right\rangle$$

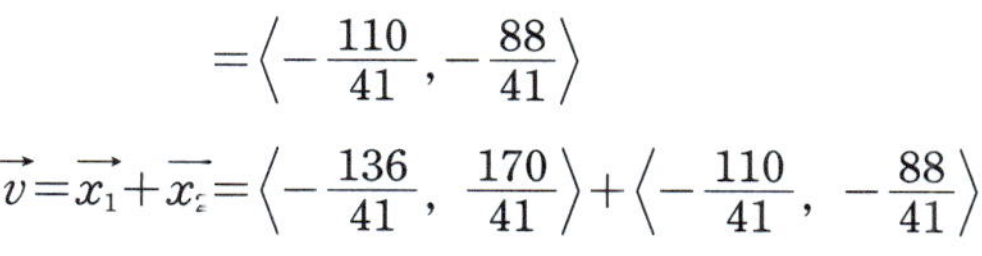

$$=\left\langle -\frac{110}{41},\ -\frac{88}{41}\right\rangle$$

$$\vec{v}=\vec{x_1}+\vec{x_2}=\left\langle -\frac{136}{41},\ \frac{170}{41}\right\rangle+\left\langle -\frac{110}{41},\ -\frac{88}{41}\right\rangle$$

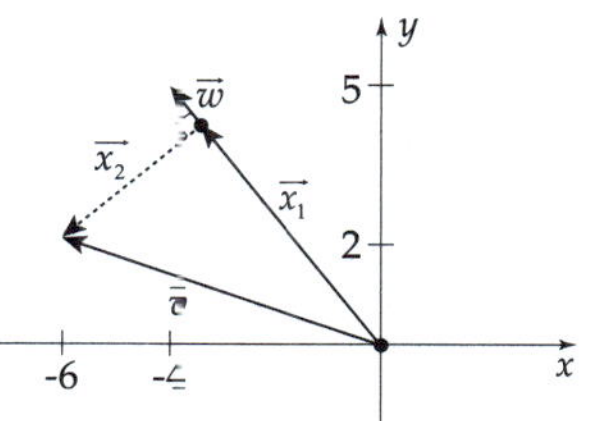

Review Exercises

01

(1) $\vec{v}\cdot\vec{w}=\langle 3,\ 4\rangle\cdot\langle -1,\ 2\rangle$

$=(3)(-1)+(4)(2)=5\neq 0$

$\vec{v}$ and $\vec{w}$ are NOT orthogonal.

(2) $\vec{v}=-2i-3j=\langle -2,\ -3\rangle$,

$\vec{w}=6i-4j=\langle 6,\ -4\rangle$

$\vec{v}\cdot\vec{w}=\langle -2,\ -3\rangle\cdot\langle 6,-4\rangle$

$=(-2)(6)+(-3)(-4)=0$

$\vec{v}$ and $\vec{w}$ are orthogonal.

02

(1) $2\vec{v}\cdot\vec{w}=2(\vec{v}\cdot\vec{w})=2((2)(-1)+(1)(4))=4.$

(2) $\vec{x}\cdot\vec{x}=|\vec{x}|^2=(\sqrt{2^2+(-3)^2})^2=13$

(3) $(\vec{v}\cdot 3\vec{w})\vec{x}=3(\vec{v}\cdot\vec{w})\vec{x}$

$=3((2)(-1)+(1)(4))\langle 2,\ -3\rangle$

$=6\langle 2,\ -3\rangle=\langle 12,\ -18\rangle$

(4) Know that

$\vec{w}-\vec{x}=\langle -1,\ 4\rangle-\langle 2,\ -3\rangle=\langle -3,\ 7\rangle$.

So $(\vec{v}\cdot\vec{w})-(\vec{v}\cdot\vec{x})=\vec{v}\cdot(\vec{w}-\vec{x})$

$=\langle 2,\ 1\rangle\cdot\langle -3,\ 7\rangle=(2)(-3)+(1)(7)=1.$

03

(1) $\cos\theta=\dfrac{\vec{v}\cdot\vec{w}}{|\vec{v}||\vec{w}|}=\dfrac{\langle 1,\ 3\rangle\cdot\langle 3,\ -2\rangle}{\sqrt{1^2+3^2}\sqrt{3^2+(-2)^2}}$

$=\dfrac{3-6}{\sqrt{10}\sqrt{13}}=\dfrac{-3}{\sqrt{10}\sqrt{13}}$

$\theta=\cos^{-1}\left(\dfrac{-3}{\sqrt{10}\sqrt{13}}\right)\approx 105.255°$

(2) $\cos\theta=\dfrac{\vec{v}\cdot\vec{w}}{|\vec{v}||\vec{w}|}=\dfrac{\langle 4,\ -5\rangle\cdot\langle 7,\ 0\rangle}{\sqrt{4^2+(-5)^2}\sqrt{7^2+0^2}}$

$=\dfrac{28+0}{\sqrt{41}\sqrt{49}}=\dfrac{28}{7\sqrt{41}}=\dfrac{4}{\sqrt{41}}$

$\theta=\cos^{-1}\left(\dfrac{4}{\sqrt{41}}\right)\approx 51.340°$

04

Let $\vec{v}=\vec{x_1}+\vec{x_2}$, where $\vec{x_1}=\text{proj}_w\ v$ and $\vec{x_2}=\vec{v}-\vec{x_1}$.

(1) $\vec{x_1}=\text{proj}_w\ v=\dfrac{\vec{v}\cdot\vec{w}}{|\vec{w}|^2}\vec{w}$

$=\dfrac{\langle 5,\ 3\rangle\cdot\langle 3,\ -3\rangle}{(\sqrt{3^2+(-3)^2})^2}\langle 3,\ -3\rangle$

$=\dfrac{15-9}{(\sqrt{18})^2}\langle 3,\ -3\rangle$

$=\dfrac{6}{18}\langle 3,\ -3\rangle=\dfrac{1}{3}\langle 3,\ -3\rangle=\langle 1,\ -1\rangle$

$\vec{x_2}=\vec{v}-\vec{x_1}=\langle 5,\ 3\rangle-\langle 1,\ -1\rangle=\langle 4,\ 4\rangle$

$\vec{v}=\vec{x_1}+\vec{x_2}=\langle 1,\ -1\rangle+\langle 4,\ 4\rangle$

(2) $\vec{v}=-4i+4j=\langle -4,\ 4\rangle$, $\vec{w}=i+2j=\langle 1,\ 2\rangle$

$\vec{x_1}=\text{proj}_w\ v=\dfrac{\vec{v}\cdot\vec{w}}{|\vec{w}|^2}\vec{w}$

$=\dfrac{\langle -4,\ 4\rangle\cdot\langle 1,\ 2\rangle}{(\sqrt{1^2+2^2})^2}\langle 1,\ 2\rangle$

$=\dfrac{-4+8}{(\sqrt{5})^2}\langle 1,\ 2\rangle$

$=\dfrac{4}{5}\langle 1,\ 2\rangle=\left\langle \dfrac{4}{5},\ \dfrac{8}{5}\right\rangle$

$\vec{x_1}=\vec{v}-\vec{x_1}=\langle -4,\ 4\rangle-\left\langle \dfrac{4}{5},\ \dfrac{8}{5}\right\rangle=\left\langle -\dfrac{24}{5},\ \dfrac{12}{5}\right\rangle$

$\vec{v}=\vec{x_1}+\vec{x_2}=\left\langle \dfrac{4}{5},\ \dfrac{8}{5}\right\rangle+\left\langle -\dfrac{24}{5},\ \dfrac{12}{5}\right\rangle$

7. Application of Vectors

Check Point 1

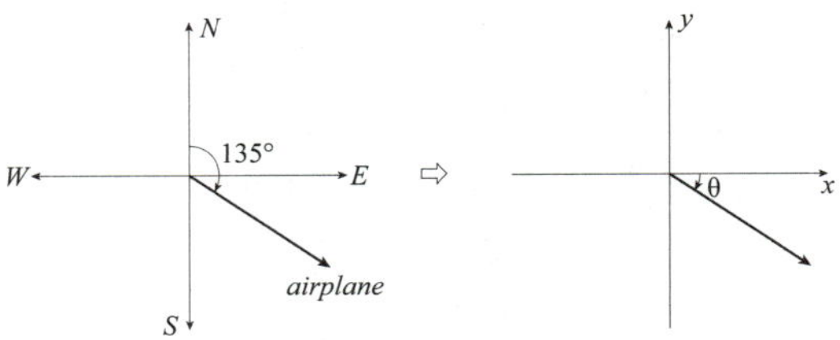

Bearing of 135° is equal to $\theta=-45°$.

$\vec{v}=|\vec{v}|\langle\cos\theta,\ \sin\theta\rangle$

$=380\langle\cos(-45°),\ \sin(-45°)\rangle$

$\vec{v}=\langle 190\sqrt{2},\ -190\sqrt{2}\rangle$

Check Point 2

Velocity of the airplane :

The direction angle is 220°.

$\vec{v}=|\vec{v}|\langle\cos\theta,\ \sin\theta\rangle=540\langle\cos 220°,\ \sin 220°\rangle$

$=\langle 540\cos 220°,\ 540\sin 220°\rangle$

Velocity of the wind :

The direction angle is 215°.

$\vec{w}=|\vec{w}|\langle\cos\theta,\ \sin\theta\rangle=38\langle\cos 215°,\ \sin 215°\rangle$

$=\langle 38\cos 215°,\ 38\sin 215°\rangle$

Velocity of the airplane+wind :

$\vec{v}+\vec{w}=\left\langle \begin{matrix}540\cos 220°+38\cos 215°,\\ 540\sin 220°+38\sin 215°\end{matrix}\right\rangle$

$\approx\langle -444.792,\ -368.901\rangle$

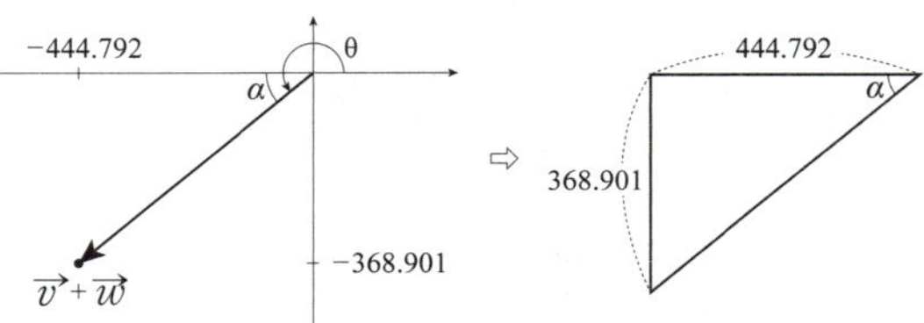

So the actual speed of the airplane is

$|\vec{v}+\vec{w}|=\sqrt{(-444.792)^2+(-368.901)^2}\approx 577.865$

and the direction is

$\tan\alpha=\dfrac{368.901}{444.792}$, $\alpha=\tan^{-1}\left(\dfrac{368.901}{444.792}\right)$

$\theta=180°+\tan^{-1}\left(\dfrac{368.901}{444.792}\right)\approx 219.672°$

577.865 mph in the direction of 219.672°

Check Point 3

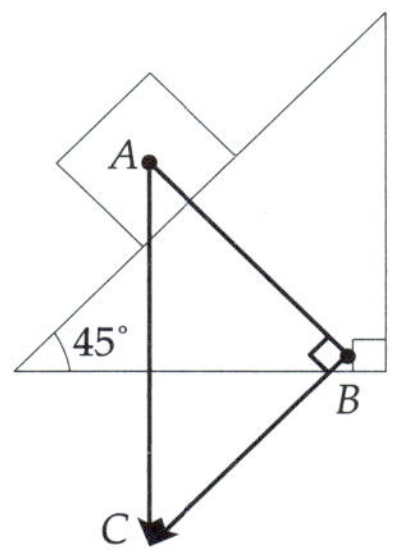

$\overrightarrow{BC}=\overrightarrow{AC}\sin 45°=75\sin 45°=\dfrac{75\sqrt{2}}{2}$

The magnitude of the force needed is $\dfrac{75\sqrt{2}}{2}$

Check Point 4

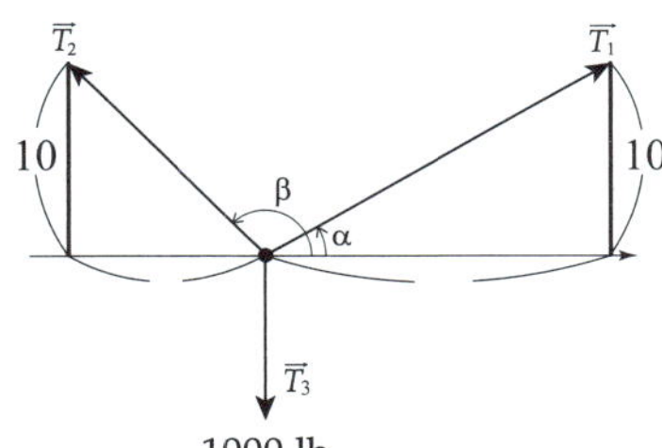

$\alpha=\tan^{-1}\left(\dfrac{10}{12}\right)\approx 39.806°$

$\beta=180°-\tan^{-1}\left(\dfrac{10}{5}\right)\approx 116.565°$

$\overrightarrow{T_1}=|\overrightarrow{T_1}|\langle\cos 39.806°,\ \sin 39.806°\rangle$

$\overrightarrow{T_2}=|\overrightarrow{T_2}|\langle\cos 116.565°,\ \sin 116.565°\rangle$

Because $\overrightarrow{T_1}+\overrightarrow{T_2}+\overrightarrow{T_3}=0$, and $\overrightarrow{T_3}=\langle 0,-1000\rangle$,
$\overrightarrow{T_1}+\overrightarrow{T_2}=\langle 0,1000\rangle$.
$|\overrightarrow{T_1}|\cos 39.806°+|\overrightarrow{T_2}|\cos 116.565°=0$ and
$|\overrightarrow{T_1}|\sin 39.806°+|\overrightarrow{T_2}|\sin 116.565°=1000$
By solving the system above, we have
$|\overrightarrow{T_1}|\approx 459.427$ and $|\overrightarrow{T_2}|\approx 789.197$.

$|\overrightarrow{T_1}|=459.427$, $|\overrightarrow{T_2}|=789.197$

Check Point 5

The work done is
$W=\overrightarrow{F}\cdot\overrightarrow{d}=1200\cdot 7=8400\ ft-lb$.

Review Exercises

01

The velocity of the airplane is
$\vec{v}=|\vec{v}|\langle\cos\theta,\ \sin\theta\rangle$
$=600\langle\cos(90°-48°),\ \sin(90°-48°)\rangle$
$=600\langle\cos 42°,\ \sin 42°\rangle=\langle 445.887,\ 401.487\rangle$

02

Velocity of the ship :
The direction angle is 130°.
$\vec{v}=|\vec{v}|\langle\cos\theta,\ \sin\theta\rangle=45\langle\cos 130°,\ \sin 130°\rangle$
$=\langle 45\cos 130°,\ 45\sin 130°\rangle$

Velocity of the current :
The direction angle is 45°.
$\vec{w}=|\vec{w}|\langle\cos\theta,\ \sin\theta\rangle=5\langle\cos 45°,\ \sin 45°\rangle$
$=\langle 5\cos 45°,\ 5\sin 45°\rangle$

Velocity of the ship+current :
$\vec{v}+\vec{w}=\left\langle\begin{matrix}45\cos 130°+5\cos 45°\\ 45\sin 130°+5\sin 45°\end{matrix}\right\rangle$
$\approx\langle -25.390,\ 38.008\rangle$

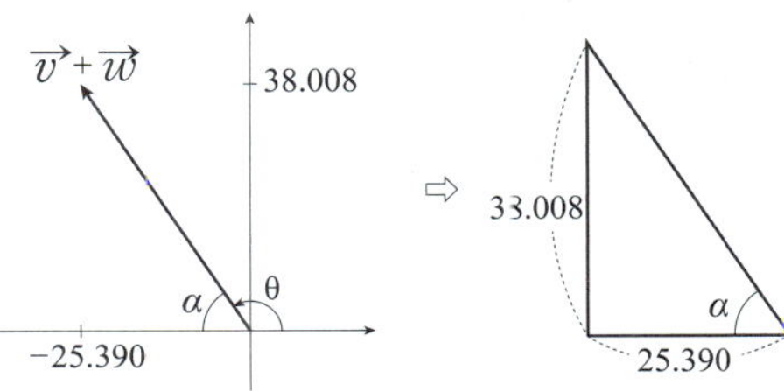

So the actual speed of the ship is
$|\vec{v}+\vec{w}|=\sqrt{(-25.390)^2+38.008^2}\approx 45.708$
and the direction is

$$\theta = 180° - \tan^{-1}\left(\frac{38.008}{25.390}\right) \approx 123.744°$$

45.708 mph in the direction of 123.744°

03

Velocity of the motorcycle :

$\vec{v} = |\vec{v}|\langle\cos\theta,\ \sin\theta\rangle = 85\langle\cos 70°,\ \sin 70°\rangle$

$= \langle 85\cos 70°,\ 85\sin 70°\rangle$

Velocity of the wind : $\vec{w} = |\vec{w}|\langle\cos\theta,\ \sin\theta\rangle$

Velocity of the motorcycle+wind :

$\vec{v} + \vec{w} = 82\langle\cos 68°,\ \sin 68°\rangle$

$= \langle 82\cos 68°,\ 82\sin 68°\rangle$

Now, we have

$\langle 85\cos 70°,\ 85\sin 70°\rangle + \vec{w}$

$= \langle 82\cos 68°,\ 82\sin 68°\rangle$

$\vec{w} = \langle 82\cos 68°,\ 82\sin 68°\rangle - \langle 85\cos 70°,\ 85\sin 70°\rangle$

$= \langle 82\cos 68° - 85\cos 70°,\ 82\sin 68° - 85\sin 70°\rangle$

$\approx \langle 1.646, -3.845\rangle$

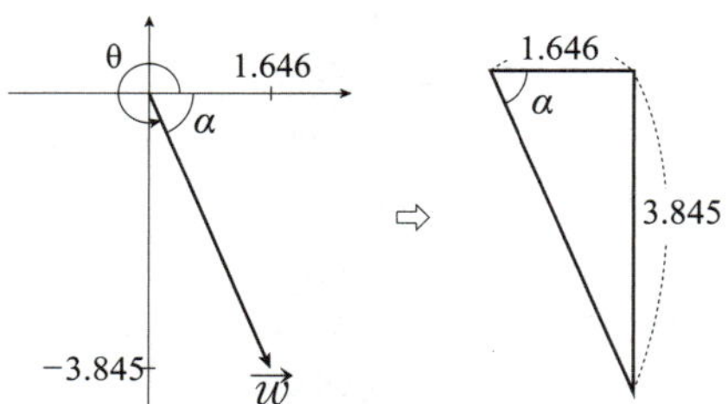

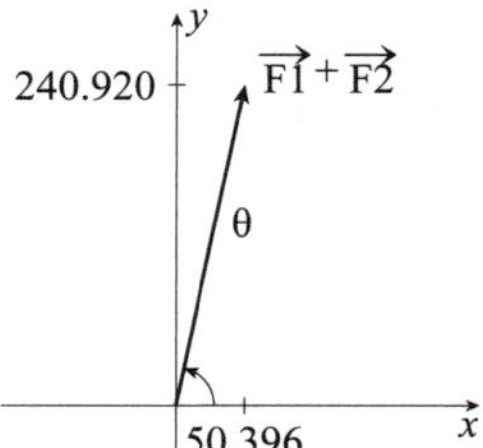

So the speed of the wind is

$|\vec{w}| = \sqrt{1.646^2 + (-3.845)^2} \approx 4.183$

and the direction is

$$\theta = 360° - \tan^{-1}\left(\frac{3.845}{1.646}\right) = 293.175°$$

4.183 mph in the direction of 293.175°

04

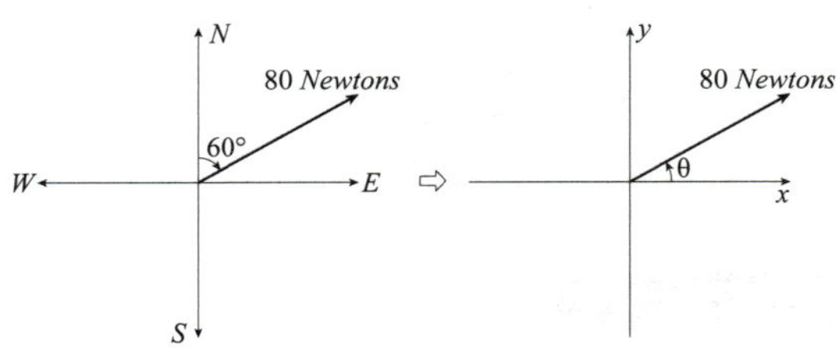

$\theta = 90° - 60° = 30°$

$\vec{F} = 80\langle\cos 30°,\ \sin 30°\rangle$

$= \langle 80\cos 30°,\ 80\sin 30°\rangle = \langle 40\sqrt{3},\ 40\rangle$

Horizontal component : $40\sqrt{3}$ Newton

Vertical component : 40 Newton

05

$\vec{F_1} = 150\langle\cos(180-28)°,\ \sin(180-28)°\rangle$

$= \langle 150\cos 152°,\ 150\sin 152°\rangle$

$\vec{F_2} = 250\langle\cos 43°,\ \sin 43°\rangle$

$= \langle 250\cos 43°,\ 250\sin 43°\rangle$

$\vec{F_1} + \vec{F_2} = \langle 150\cos 152° + 250\cos 43°,\ 150\sin 152° + 250\sin 43°\rangle$

$\approx \langle 50.396,\ 240.920\rangle$

240.920
F1+F2
θ
50.396
y
x

The magnitude of the resultant force is

$|\vec{F_1} + \vec{F_2}| = \sqrt{50.396^2 + 240.920^2} \approx 246.135$

and direction is $\theta = \tan^{-1}\left(\frac{240.920}{50.396}\right) \approx 78.185°$

The resultant force is 246.135 lb and the direction is 78.185°.

06

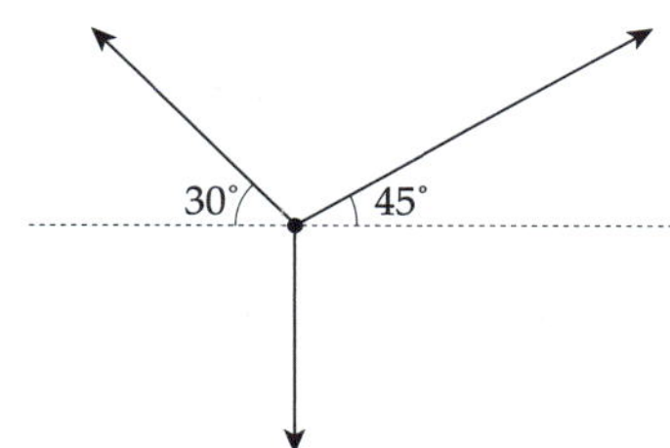

Since the longer cable has a tension 200 lb, $|\vec{T_1}|=200$. So, we have

$\vec{T_1}=200\langle\cos(180-30)°,\ \sin(180-30)°\rangle$

$=\langle 200\cos 150°,\ 200\sin 150°\rangle$

$=\langle -100\sqrt{3},\ 100\rangle$

$\vec{T_2}=|\vec{T_2}|\langle\cos 45°,\ \sin 45°\rangle$

$=\langle|\vec{T_2}|\cos 45°, |\vec{T_2}|\sin 45°\rangle=\left\langle\frac{|\vec{T_2}|}{\sqrt{2}},\ \frac{|\vec{T_2}|}{\sqrt{2}}\right\rangle$

Since the ball is in a state of equilibrium, the horizontal tension is 0.

So, $-100\sqrt{3}+\frac{|\vec{T_2}|}{\sqrt{2}}=0$.

$\rightarrow \frac{|\vec{T_2}|}{\sqrt{2}}=100\sqrt{3},\ |\vec{T_2}|=100\sqrt{6}$

Now, the vertical tension(ball's weight) is

$100+\frac{|\vec{T_2}|}{\sqrt{2}}=100+\frac{100\sqrt{6}}{\sqrt{2}}$

$=100+100\sqrt{3}\approx 273.205.$

The heaviest ball that can be supported by the cables is approximately 273.205 lb

07

The horizontal force acting on the wagon is $\vec{F}=|\vec{F}|\cos\theta$. So the work done is

$W=|\vec{F}|\cos\theta\cdot\vec{d}=40\cos 25°\cdot 65=2356.4\,ft-lb$

$W=2356.4\,ft-lb$

8. The Algebra of Matrices

Check Point 1

① $3A=3\begin{bmatrix}1 & -2\\ 3 & 2\end{bmatrix}=\begin{bmatrix}1\times3 & -2\times3\\ 3\times3 & 2\times3\end{bmatrix}=\begin{bmatrix}3 & -6\\ 9 & 6\end{bmatrix}$

$3A=\begin{bmatrix}3 & -6\\ 9 & 6\end{bmatrix}$

② $A+B=\begin{bmatrix}1 & -2\\ 3 & 2\end{bmatrix}+\begin{bmatrix}0 & 4\\ -4 & 1\end{bmatrix}$

$=\begin{bmatrix}1+0 & -2+4\\ 3-4 & 2+1\end{bmatrix}=\begin{bmatrix}1 & 2\\ -1 & 3\end{bmatrix}$

$A+B=\begin{bmatrix}1 & 2\\ -1 & 3\end{bmatrix}$

③ Since A is 2×2 matrix and C is 3×2 matrix $A-C$ is not defined.

④ $2B-A=2\begin{bmatrix}0 & 4\\ -4 & 1\end{bmatrix}-\begin{bmatrix}1 & -2\\ 3 & 2\end{bmatrix}$

$=\begin{bmatrix}0 & 8\\ -8 & 2\end{bmatrix}-\begin{bmatrix}1 & -2\\ 3 & 2\end{bmatrix}=\begin{bmatrix}-1 & 10\\ -11 & 0\end{bmatrix}$

$2B-A=\begin{bmatrix}-1 & 10\\ -11 & 0\end{bmatrix}$

Check Point 2

① $AB=\underbrace{\begin{bmatrix}3 & 1\\ 2 & -1\end{bmatrix}}_{2\times2}\underbrace{\begin{bmatrix}2 & -1 & 4\\ -3 & 0 & 5\end{bmatrix}}_{2\times3}$

$=\begin{bmatrix}(3)(2)+(1)(-3) & (3)(-1)+(1)(0) & (3)(4)+(1)(5)\\ (2)(2)+(-1)(-3) & (2)(-1)+(-1)(0) & (2)(4)+(-1)(5)\end{bmatrix}$

$=\underbrace{\begin{bmatrix}3 & -3 & 17\\ 7 & -2 & 3\end{bmatrix}}_{2\times3}$

$AB=\begin{bmatrix}3 & -3 & 17\\ 7 & -2 & 3\end{bmatrix}$

② $BC=\underbrace{\begin{bmatrix} 2 & -1 & 4 \\ -3 & 0 & 5 \end{bmatrix}}_{2\times3}\underbrace{\begin{bmatrix} 4 & 0 \\ 3 & -1 \\ -2 & 3 \end{bmatrix}}_{3\times2}$

$=\begin{bmatrix} (2)(4)+(-1)(3)+(4)(-2) & (2)(0)+(-1)(-1)+(4)(3) \\ (-3)(4)+(0)(3)+(5)(-2) & (-3)(0)+(0)(-1)+(5)(3) \end{bmatrix}$

$=\underbrace{\begin{bmatrix} -3 & 13 \\ -22 & 15 \end{bmatrix}}_{2\times2}$

$BC=\begin{bmatrix} -3 & 13 \\ -22 & 15 \end{bmatrix}$

③ Since the number of columns of matrix A is NOT equal to the number of rows of matrix C, the product AC is NOT defined.

④ $CA=\underbrace{\begin{bmatrix} 4 & 0 \\ 3 & -1 \\ -2 & 3 \end{bmatrix}}_{3\times2}\underbrace{\begin{bmatrix} 3 & 1 \\ 2 & -1 \end{bmatrix}}_{2\times2}$

$=\begin{bmatrix} (4)(3)+(0)(2) & (4)(1)+(0)(-1) \\ (3)(3)+(-1)(2) & (3)(1)+(-1)(-1) \\ (-2)(3)+(3)(2) & (-2)(1)+(3)(-1) \end{bmatrix}$

$=\underbrace{\begin{bmatrix} 12 & 4 \\ 7 & 4 \\ 0 & -5 \end{bmatrix}}_{3\times2}$

$CA=\begin{bmatrix} 12 & 4 \\ 7 & 4 \\ 0 & -5 \end{bmatrix}$

Check Point 3

① $\begin{cases} x-2y+3z=6 \\ 2x+4y-5z=-7 \\ 3x+4z=7 \end{cases} \rightarrow \begin{bmatrix} 1 & -2 & 3 & 6 \\ 2 & 4 & -5 & -7 \\ 3 & 0 & 4 & 7 \end{bmatrix}$

$\begin{matrix} \\ 2R_1-R_3 \\ 3R_1-R_3 \end{matrix}\begin{bmatrix} 1 & -2 & 3 & 6 \\ 0 & -8 & 11 & 19 \\ 0 & -6 & 5 & 11 \end{bmatrix}$

$-\left(\frac{1}{8}\right)R_2\begin{bmatrix} 1 & -2 & 3 & 6 \\ 0 & 1 & -\frac{11}{8} & -\frac{19}{8} \\ 0 & -6 & 5 & 11 \end{bmatrix}$

$6R_2+R_3\begin{bmatrix} 1 & -2 & 3 & 6 \\ 0 & 1 & -\frac{11}{8} & -\frac{19}{8} \\ 0 & 0 & -\frac{13}{4} & -\frac{13}{4} \end{bmatrix}$

$-\left(\frac{4}{13}\right)R_3\begin{bmatrix} 1 & -2 & 3 & 6 \\ 0 & 1 & -\frac{11}{8} & -\frac{19}{8} \\ 0 & 0 & 1 & 1 \end{bmatrix}$

Therefore,

$z=1$

$y-\frac{11}{8}z=-\frac{19}{8},\ y-\frac{11}{8}(1)=-\frac{19}{8},\ y=-1$

$x-2y+3z=6,\ x-2(-1)+3(1)=6,\ x=1$

$x=1,\ y=-1,$ and $z=1$

② $\begin{cases} x-4y+3z=6 \\ 2x-2y+5z=-6 \end{cases} \rightarrow \begin{bmatrix} 1 & -4 & 3 & 6 \\ 2 & -2 & 5 & -6 \end{bmatrix}$

$2R_1-R_2\begin{bmatrix} 1 & -4 & 3 & 6 \\ 0 & -6 & 1 & 18 \end{bmatrix}$

$-\left(\frac{1}{6}\right)R_2\begin{bmatrix} 1 & -4 & 3 & 6 \\ 0 & 1 & -\frac{1}{6} & -3 \end{bmatrix}$

The corresponding system is

$\begin{cases} x-4y+3z=6 \\ y-\frac{1}{6}z=-3 \end{cases}$

To write a solution to the system, let $z=k$, where k is any real number. Then the solutions can be written as in terms of k.

$y-\frac{1}{6}k=-3,\ y=-3+\frac{1}{6}k$ and

$x-4\left(-3+\frac{1}{6}k\right)+3k=6,\ x=-6-\frac{7}{3}k$

$x=-6-\frac{7k}{3},\ y=-3+\frac{k}{6},$ and $z=k.$

Review Exercises

01

$$A=\begin{bmatrix}1 & 4\\ 3 & -2\end{bmatrix},\ B=\begin{bmatrix}6 & 8\\ -4 & -1\end{bmatrix}$$

(a) $\frac{1}{2}B=\begin{bmatrix}6 & 8\\ -4 & -1\end{bmatrix}=\begin{bmatrix}3 & 4\\ -2 & -\frac{1}{2}\end{bmatrix}$

(b) $A+B=\begin{bmatrix}1 & 4\\ 3 & -2\end{bmatrix}+\begin{bmatrix}6 & 8\\ -4 & -1\end{bmatrix}=\begin{bmatrix}7 & 12\\ -1 & -3\end{bmatrix}$

(c) $2B-3A=2\begin{bmatrix}6 & 8\\ -4 & -1\end{bmatrix}-3\begin{bmatrix}1 & 4\\ 3 & -2\end{bmatrix}$

$$=\begin{bmatrix}12 & 16\\ -8 & -2\end{bmatrix}-\begin{bmatrix}3 & 12\\ 9 & -6\end{bmatrix}=\begin{bmatrix}9 & 4\\ -17 & 4\end{bmatrix}$$

02

$$A=\begin{bmatrix}\frac{3}{2}\\ 4\\ -\frac{1}{2}\end{bmatrix},\ B=\begin{bmatrix}-2\\ 1\\ \frac{5}{2}\end{bmatrix}$$

(a) $\frac{1}{2}B=\frac{1}{2}\begin{bmatrix}-2\\ 1\\ \frac{5}{2}\end{bmatrix}=\begin{bmatrix}-1\\ \frac{1}{2}\\ \frac{5}{4}\end{bmatrix}$

(b) $A+B=\begin{bmatrix}\frac{3}{2}\\ 4\\ -\frac{1}{2}\end{bmatrix}+\begin{bmatrix}-2\\ 1\\ \frac{5}{2}\end{bmatrix}=\begin{bmatrix}-\frac{1}{2}\\ 5\\ 2\end{bmatrix}$

(c) $2B-3A=2\begin{bmatrix}-2\\ 1\\ \frac{5}{2}\end{bmatrix}-3\begin{bmatrix}\frac{3}{2}\\ 4\\ -\frac{1}{2}\end{bmatrix}$

$$=\begin{bmatrix}-4\\ 2\\ 5\end{bmatrix}-\begin{bmatrix}\frac{9}{2}\\ 12\\ -\frac{3}{2}\end{bmatrix}=\begin{bmatrix}-\frac{17}{2}\\ -10\\ \frac{13}{2}\end{bmatrix}$$

03

$$A=\begin{bmatrix}-2 & 0 & 4\\ 0 & -3 & -1\\ 2 & \frac{1}{3} & -\frac{3}{4}\end{bmatrix},\ B=\begin{bmatrix}4 & -5\\ 1 & 4\\ -3 & \frac{1}{2}\end{bmatrix}$$

(a) $\frac{1}{2}B=\frac{1}{2}\begin{bmatrix}4 & -5\\ 1 & 4\\ -3 & \frac{1}{2}\end{bmatrix}=\begin{bmatrix}2 & -\frac{5}{2}\\ \frac{1}{2} & 2\\ -\frac{3}{2} & \frac{1}{4}\end{bmatrix}$

(b) Not Possible

(c) Not Possible

04

$$A=\begin{bmatrix}\frac{1}{3} & 1 & -2\\ 3 & 0 & 2\\ -5 & 4 & -\frac{5}{3}\end{bmatrix},\ B=\begin{bmatrix}4 & -2 & 0\\ -1 & 4 & 6\\ 3 & -2 & 12\end{bmatrix}$$

(a) $\frac{1}{2}B=\frac{1}{2}\begin{bmatrix}4 & -2 & 0\\ -1 & 4 & 6\\ 3 & -2 & 12\end{bmatrix}=\begin{bmatrix}2 & -1 & 0\\ -\frac{1}{2} & 2 & 3\\ \frac{3}{2} & -1 & 6\end{bmatrix}$

(b) $A+B=\begin{bmatrix}\frac{1}{3} & 1 & -2\\ 3 & 0 & 2\\ -5 & 4 & -\frac{5}{3}\end{bmatrix}+\begin{bmatrix}4 & -2 & 0\\ -1 & 4 & 6\\ 3 & -2 & 12\end{bmatrix}$

$$=\begin{bmatrix}\frac{13}{3} & -1 & -2\\ 2 & 4 & 8\\ -2 & 2 & \frac{31}{3}\end{bmatrix}$$

(c) $2B-3A=2\begin{bmatrix}4 & -2 & 0\\ -1 & 4 & 6\\ 3 & -2 & 12\end{bmatrix}-3\begin{bmatrix}\frac{1}{3} & 1 & -2\\ 3 & 0 & 2\\ -5 & 4 & -\frac{5}{3}\end{bmatrix}$

$$=\begin{bmatrix}8 & -4 & 0\\ -2 & 8 & 12\\ 6 & -4 & 24\end{bmatrix}-\begin{bmatrix}1 & 3 & -6\\ 9 & 0 & 6\\ -15 & 12 & -5\end{bmatrix}$$

$$=\begin{bmatrix}7 & -7 & 6\\ -11 & 8 & 6\\ 21 & -16 & 29\end{bmatrix}$$

05

$A=\begin{bmatrix} -2 & 0 \\ 3 & 4 \end{bmatrix}$, $B=\begin{bmatrix} 4 & 2 \\ -1 & -3 \end{bmatrix}$

(a) $AB=\begin{bmatrix} -2 & 0 \\ 3 & 4 \end{bmatrix}\begin{bmatrix} 4 & 2 \\ -1 & -3 \end{bmatrix}$

$=\begin{bmatrix} -8+0 & -4+0 \\ 12-4 & 6-12 \end{bmatrix}$

$=\begin{bmatrix} -8 & -4 \\ 8 & -6 \end{bmatrix}$

(b) $BA=\begin{bmatrix} 4 & 2 \\ -1 & -3 \end{bmatrix}\begin{bmatrix} -2 & 0 \\ 3 & 4 \end{bmatrix}$

$=\begin{bmatrix} -8+6 & 0+8 \\ 2-9 & 0-12 \end{bmatrix}$

$=\begin{bmatrix} -2 & 8 \\ -7 & -12 \end{bmatrix}$

(c) $B^2=\begin{bmatrix} 4 & 2 \\ -1 & -3 \end{bmatrix}\begin{bmatrix} 4 & 2 \\ -1 & -3 \end{bmatrix}$

$=\begin{bmatrix} 16-2 & 8-6 \\ -4+3 & -2+9 \end{bmatrix}$

$=\begin{bmatrix} 14 & 2 \\ -1 & 7 \end{bmatrix}$

06

$A=\begin{bmatrix} 1 & 4 & \frac{2}{3} \end{bmatrix}$, $B=\begin{bmatrix} 2 \\ 5 \\ -3 \end{bmatrix}$

(a) $AB=\begin{bmatrix} 1 & 4 & \frac{2}{3} \end{bmatrix}\begin{bmatrix} 2 \\ 5 \\ -3 \end{bmatrix}=[2+20-2]=[20]$

(b) $BA=\begin{bmatrix} 2 \\ 5 \\ -3 \end{bmatrix}\begin{bmatrix} 1 & 4 & \frac{2}{3} \end{bmatrix}=\begin{bmatrix} 2 & 8 & \frac{4}{3} \\ 5 & 20 & \frac{10}{3} \\ -3 & -12 & -2 \end{bmatrix}$

(c) $B^2=\begin{bmatrix} 2 \\ 5 \\ -3 \end{bmatrix}\begin{bmatrix} 2 \\ 5 \\ -3 \end{bmatrix}=$Not Possible

07

$A=\begin{bmatrix} 3 & 2 \\ -2 & 0 \\ 4 & 1 \end{bmatrix}$, $B=\begin{bmatrix} 3 & \frac{1}{2} \\ -2 & \frac{1}{4} \end{bmatrix}$

(a) $AB=\begin{bmatrix} 3 & 2 \\ -2 & 0 \\ 4 & 1 \end{bmatrix}\begin{bmatrix} 3 & \frac{1}{2} \\ -2 & \frac{1}{4} \end{bmatrix}=\begin{bmatrix} 9-4 & \frac{3}{2}+\frac{1}{2} \\ -6+0 & -1+0 \\ 12-2 & 2+\frac{1}{4} \end{bmatrix}$

$=\begin{bmatrix} 5 & 2 \\ -6 & -1 \\ 10 & \frac{9}{4} \end{bmatrix}$

(b) $BA=\begin{bmatrix} 3 & \frac{1}{2} \\ -2 & \frac{1}{4} \end{bmatrix}\begin{bmatrix} 3 & 2 \\ -2 & 0 \\ 4 & 1 \end{bmatrix}=$Not Possible

(c) $B^2=\begin{bmatrix} 3 & \frac{1}{2} \\ -2 & \frac{1}{4} \end{bmatrix}\begin{bmatrix} 3 & \frac{1}{2} \\ -2 & \frac{1}{4} \end{bmatrix}$

$=\begin{bmatrix} 9-1 & \frac{3}{2}+\frac{1}{8} \\ -6-\frac{1}{2} & -1+\frac{1}{16} \end{bmatrix}$

$=\begin{bmatrix} 8 & \frac{13}{8} \\ -\frac{13}{2} & -\frac{15}{16} \end{bmatrix}$

08

$A=\begin{bmatrix} 1 & 0 & 2 \\ \frac{1}{2} & 4 & 6 \end{bmatrix}$, $B=\begin{bmatrix} 0 & 3 & 5 \\ 3 & -2 & 0 \\ -4 & 1 & -1 \end{bmatrix}$

(a) $AB=\begin{bmatrix} 1 & 0 & 2 \\ \frac{1}{2} & 4 & 6 \end{bmatrix}\begin{bmatrix} 0 & 3 & 5 \\ 3 & -2 & 0 \\ -4 & 1 & -1 \end{bmatrix}$

$=\begin{bmatrix} 0+0-8 & 3+0+2 & 5+0-2 \\ 0+12-24 & \frac{3}{2}-8+6 & \frac{5}{2}+0-6 \end{bmatrix}$

$=\begin{bmatrix} -8 & 5 & 3 \\ -12 & -\frac{1}{2} & -\frac{7}{2} \end{bmatrix}$

(b) $BA=\begin{bmatrix} 0 & 3 & 5 \\ 3 & -2 & 0 \\ -4 & 1 & -1 \end{bmatrix}\begin{bmatrix} 1 & 0 & 2 \\ \frac{1}{2} & 4 & 6 \end{bmatrix}$

=Not Possible

(c) $B^2=\begin{bmatrix} 0 & 3 & 5 \\ 3 & -2 & 0 \\ -4 & 1 & -1 \end{bmatrix}\begin{bmatrix} 0 & 3 & 5 \\ 3 & -2 & 0 \\ -4 & 1 & -1 \end{bmatrix}$

$=\begin{bmatrix} 0+9-20 & 0-6+5 & 0+0-5 \\ 0-6+0 & 9+4+0 & 15+0+0 \\ 0+3+4 & -12-2-1 & -20+0+1 \end{bmatrix}$

$=\begin{bmatrix} -11 & -1 & -5 \\ -6 & 13 & 15 \\ 7 & -15 & -19 \end{bmatrix}$

09

$\begin{cases} x+4y-3z=0 \\ -x-2y-2z=-4 \\ -2x+6y+7z=8 \end{cases} \rightarrow \begin{bmatrix} 1 & 4 & -3 & 0 \\ -1 & -2 & -2 & -4 \\ -2 & 6 & 7 & 8 \end{bmatrix}$

$\rightarrow \begin{matrix} R_1+R_2 \\ 2R_1+R_3 \end{matrix} \begin{bmatrix} 1 & 4 & -3 & 0 \\ 0 & 2 & -5 & -4 \\ 0 & 14 & 1 & 8 \end{bmatrix}$

$\rightarrow \left(\frac{1}{2}\right)R_2 \begin{bmatrix} 1 & 4 & -3 & 0 \\ 0 & 1 & -\frac{5}{2} & -2 \\ 0 & 14 & 1 & 8 \end{bmatrix}$

$\rightarrow 14R_2-R_3 \begin{bmatrix} 1 & 4 & -3 & 0 \\ 0 & 1 & -\frac{5}{2} & -2 \\ 0 & 0 & -36 & -36 \end{bmatrix}$

$\rightarrow \left(-\frac{1}{36}\right)R_2 \begin{bmatrix} 1 & 4 & -3 & 0 \\ 0 & 1 & -\frac{5}{2} & -2 \\ 0 & 0 & 1 & 1 \end{bmatrix}$

$z=1$

$y-\frac{5}{2}z=-2 \rightarrow y-\frac{5}{2}(1)=-2 \rightarrow y=\frac{1}{2}$

$x+4y-3z=0 \rightarrow x+4\left(\frac{1}{2}\right)-3(1)=0 \rightarrow x=1$

The solution is $x=1$, $y=\frac{1}{2}$, and $z=1$

10

$\begin{cases} x-2y-z=-4 \\ 2x+3y-z=9 \\ 4x-4y-3z=-1 \end{cases} \rightarrow \begin{bmatrix} 1 & -2 & -1 & -4 \\ 2 & 3 & 1 & 9 \\ 4 & -4 & 3 & -1 \end{bmatrix}$

$\rightarrow \begin{matrix} 2R_1-R_2 \\ 4R_1-R_3 \end{matrix} \begin{bmatrix} 1 & -2 & -1 & -4 \\ 0 & -7 & -3 & -17 \\ 0 & -4 & -7 & -15 \end{bmatrix}$

$\rightarrow -\left(\frac{1}{7}\right)R_2 \begin{bmatrix} 1 & -2 & -1 & -4 \\ 0 & 1 & \frac{3}{7} & \frac{17}{7} \\ 0 & -4 & -7 & -15 \end{bmatrix}$

$\rightarrow 4R_2+R_3 \begin{bmatrix} 1 & -2 & -1 & -4 \\ 0 & 1 & \frac{3}{7} & \frac{17}{7} \\ 0 & 0 & -\frac{37}{7} & -\frac{37}{7} \end{bmatrix}$

$\rightarrow -\left(\frac{7}{37}\right)R_3 \begin{bmatrix} 1 & -2 & -1 & -4 \\ 0 & 1 & \frac{3}{7} & \frac{17}{7} \\ 0 & 0 & 1 & 1 \end{bmatrix}$

$z=1$

$y+\frac{3}{7}z=\frac{17}{7} \rightarrow y+\frac{3}{7}(1)=\frac{17}{7} \rightarrow y=2$

$x-2y-z=-4 \rightarrow x-2(2)-(1)=-4 \rightarrow x=1$

The solution is $x=1$, $y=2$, and $z=1$

11

$\begin{cases} 3x-2y-z=-5 \\ 2x+3y+z=7 \\ 4x-4y+3z=-5 \end{cases} \rightarrow \begin{bmatrix} 3 & -2 & -1 & -5 \\ 2 & 3 & 1 & 7 \\ 4 & -4 & 3 & -5 \end{bmatrix}$

$\rightarrow \begin{matrix} \left(\frac{1}{4}\right)R_3 \\ R_2 \\ R_1 \end{matrix} \begin{bmatrix} 1 & -1 & \frac{3}{4} & -\frac{5}{4} \\ 2 & 3 & 1 & 7 \\ 3 & -2 & -1 & -5 \end{bmatrix}$

$\rightarrow \begin{matrix} 2R_1-R_2 \\ 3R_1-R_3 \end{matrix} \begin{bmatrix} 1 & -1 & \frac{3}{4} & -\frac{5}{4} \\ 0 & -5 & \frac{1}{2} & -\frac{19}{2} \\ 0 & -1 & \frac{13}{4} & \frac{5}{4} \end{bmatrix}$

$\rightarrow \begin{matrix} -R_3 \\ R_2 \end{matrix} \begin{bmatrix} 1 & -1 & \frac{3}{4} & -\frac{5}{4} \\ 0 & 1 & -\frac{13}{4} & -\frac{5}{4} \\ 0 & -5 & \frac{1}{2} & -\frac{19}{2} \end{bmatrix}$

$$\rightarrow 5R_2+R_3 \begin{bmatrix} 1 & -1 & \frac{3}{4} & -\frac{5}{4} \\ 0 & 1 & -\frac{13}{4} & -\frac{5}{4} \\ 0 & 0 & -\frac{63}{4} & -\frac{63}{4} \end{bmatrix}$$

$$\rightarrow -\left(\frac{4}{63}\right)R_3 \begin{bmatrix} 1 & -1 & \frac{3}{4} & -\frac{5}{4} \\ 0 & 1 & -\frac{13}{4} & -\frac{5}{4} \\ 0 & 0 & 1 & 1 \end{bmatrix}$$

$z=1$

$y-\frac{13}{4}z=-\frac{5}{4} \rightarrow y-\frac{13}{4}(1)=-\frac{5}{4} \rightarrow y=2$

$x-y+\frac{3}{4}z=-\frac{5}{4}$

$\rightarrow x-(2)+\frac{3}{4}(1)=-\frac{5}{4} \rightarrow x=0$

The solution is $x=0$, $y=2$, and $z=1$

12

$$\begin{cases} 2x+y-z=3 \\ x-2y+z=2 \\ 2x-4y+2z=-1 \end{cases} \rightarrow \begin{bmatrix} 2 & 1 & -1 & 3 \\ 1 & -2 & 1 & 2 \\ 2 & -4 & 2 & -1 \end{bmatrix}$$

$$\rightarrow \begin{matrix} R_2 \\ R_1 \\ R_3 \end{matrix} \begin{bmatrix} 1 & -2 & 1 & 2 \\ 2 & 1 & -1 & 3 \\ 2 & -4 & 2 & -1 \end{bmatrix}$$

$$\rightarrow \begin{matrix} \\ 2R_1-R_2 \\ 2R_1-R_3 \end{matrix} \begin{bmatrix} 1 & -2 & 1 & 2 \\ 0 & -5 & 3 & 1 \\ 0 & 0 & 0 & 5 \end{bmatrix}$$

Since $0z=5$, no solution exists

13

$$\begin{cases} 2x+4y-2z=3 \\ 3x-2y-4z=1 \end{cases} \rightarrow \begin{bmatrix} 2 & 4 & -2 & 3 \\ 3 & -2 & -4 & 1 \end{bmatrix}$$

$$\rightarrow \left(\frac{1}{2}\right)R_1 \begin{bmatrix} 1 & 2 & -1 & \frac{3}{2} \\ 3 & -2 & -4 & 1 \end{bmatrix}$$

$$\rightarrow 3R_1-R_2 \begin{bmatrix} 1 & 2 & -1 & \frac{3}{2} \\ 0 & 8 & 1 & \frac{7}{2} \end{bmatrix}$$

$$\rightarrow \left(\frac{1}{8}\right)R_2 \begin{bmatrix} 1 & 2 & -1 & \frac{3}{2} \\ 0 & 1 & \frac{1}{8} & \frac{7}{16} \end{bmatrix}$$

Let $z=k$, where k is any real number. Then,

$y+\frac{z}{8}=\frac{7}{16} \rightarrow y=\frac{7}{16}-\frac{k}{8}$

$x+2y-z=\frac{3}{2} \rightarrow x=\frac{3}{2}-2\left(\frac{7}{16}-\frac{k}{8}\right)+k$

$\rightarrow x=\frac{5}{8}+\frac{5k}{4}$

The solution is $x=\frac{5}{8}+\frac{5k}{4}$, and $y=\frac{7}{16}-\frac{k}{8}$

14

$$\begin{cases} x-3y-\frac{1}{2}z=-1 \\ \frac{1}{3}x+z=-3 \end{cases} \rightarrow \begin{bmatrix} 1 & -3 & -\frac{1}{2} & -1 \\ \frac{1}{3} & 0 & 1 & -3 \end{bmatrix}$$

$$\rightarrow 3R_2 \begin{bmatrix} 1 & -3 & -\frac{1}{2} & -1 \\ 1 & 0 & 3 & -9 \end{bmatrix}$$

$$\rightarrow R_1-R_2 \begin{bmatrix} 1 & -3 & -\frac{1}{2} & -1 \\ 0 & -3 & -\frac{7}{2} & 8 \end{bmatrix}$$

$$\rightarrow -\left(\frac{1}{3}\right)R_2 \begin{bmatrix} 1 & -3 & -\frac{1}{2} & -1 \\ 0 & 1 & \frac{7}{6} & -\frac{8}{3} \end{bmatrix}$$

Let $z=k$, where k is any real number. Then,

$y+\frac{7z}{6}=-\frac{8}{3} \rightarrow y=-\frac{8}{3}-\frac{7k}{6}$

$x-3y-\frac{z}{2}=-1 \rightarrow x=-1+3\left(-\frac{8}{3}-\frac{7k}{6}\right)+\frac{k}{2}$

$\rightarrow x=-9-3k$

The solution is $x=-9-3k$, and $y=-\frac{8}{3}-\frac{7k}{6}$

15

If $x=-2$, we have

$$\begin{bmatrix} 1 & -2 & 3 \\ 2 & -2 & 4 \end{bmatrix}+\begin{bmatrix} -4 & -1 & 0 \\ -1 & -3 & 5 \end{bmatrix}=\begin{bmatrix} -3 & -1 & 3 \\ 1 & y & 9 \end{bmatrix}$$

Therefore, $-2-3=y$, $y=-5$. So the correct answer is (B).

16

$$A_{r\times m}\cdot B_{m\times n}=C_{r\times n} \rightarrow A_{3\times 4}\cdot B_{m\times n}=C_{3\times 2}$$

Therefore, the dimensions of B must be 4×2. The correct answer is (D).

17

I. True. Matrix A has 2 columns and matrix B has 3 rows. Since these numbers are not equal, the product AB does not exist.

II. False

III. True. $B_{3\times 3}\cdot A_{3\times 2}=C_{3\times 2}$

I and III are true. Therefore, the correct answer is (C).

9. The Inverse of Matrices

Check Point 1

① $AB=\begin{bmatrix} -2 & -1 \\ 6 & 4 \end{bmatrix}\begin{bmatrix} -2 & -\frac{1}{2} \\ 3 & 1 \end{bmatrix}$

$=\begin{bmatrix} 4-3 & 1-1 \\ -12+12 & -3+4 \end{bmatrix}=\begin{bmatrix} 1 & 0 \\ 0 & 1 \end{bmatrix}=I_2$

$BA=\begin{bmatrix} -2 & -\frac{1}{2} \\ 3 & 1 \end{bmatrix}\begin{bmatrix} -2 & -1 \\ 6 & 4 \end{bmatrix}$

$=\begin{bmatrix} 4-3 & 2-2 \\ -6+6 & -3+4 \end{bmatrix}=\begin{bmatrix} 1 & 0 \\ 0 & 1 \end{bmatrix}=I_2$

② $AB=\begin{bmatrix} 3 & 2 & 2 \\ 4 & 3 & 5 \\ 0 & 0 & 2 \end{bmatrix}\begin{bmatrix} 3 & -2 & 2 \\ -4 & 3 & -\frac{7}{2} \\ 0 & 0 & \frac{1}{2} \end{bmatrix}$

$=\begin{bmatrix} 9-8+0 & -6-6+0 & 6-7+1 \\ 12-12+0 & -8+9+0 & 8-\frac{21}{2}+\frac{5}{2} \\ 0+0+0 & 0+0+0 & 0+0+1 \end{bmatrix}$

$=\begin{bmatrix} 1 & 0 & 0 \\ 0 & 1 & 0 \\ 0 & 0 & 1 \end{bmatrix}=I_3$

$BA=\begin{bmatrix} 3 & -2 & 2 \\ -4 & 3 & -\frac{7}{2} \\ 0 & 0 & \frac{1}{2} \end{bmatrix}\begin{bmatrix} 3 & 2 & 2 \\ 4 & 3 & 5 \\ 0 & 0 & 2 \end{bmatrix}$

$=\begin{bmatrix} 9-8+0 & 6-6+0 & 6-10+4 \\ -12+12+0 & -8+9+0 & -8+15-7 \\ 0+0+0 & 0+0+0 & 0+0+1 \end{bmatrix}$

$=\begin{bmatrix} 1 & 0 & 0 \\ 0 & 1 & 0 \\ 0 & 0 & 1 \end{bmatrix}=I_3$

Check Point 2

① Using the formula, given $A=\begin{bmatrix} 3 & 4 \\ -1 & 2 \end{bmatrix}$,

$$A^{-1}=\frac{1}{(3)(2)-(-1)(4)}\begin{bmatrix} 2 & -4 \\ 1 & 3 \end{bmatrix}$$

$$=\frac{1}{10}\begin{bmatrix} 2 & -4 \\ 1 & 3 \end{bmatrix}=\begin{bmatrix} \frac{1}{5} & -\frac{2}{5} \\ \frac{1}{10} & \frac{3}{10} \end{bmatrix}$$

Therefore, the inverse of A is

$$A^{-1}=\begin{bmatrix} \frac{1}{5} & -\frac{2}{5} \\ \frac{1}{10} & \frac{3}{10} \end{bmatrix}$$

② Using Gauss−Jordan elimination,

$$\left[\begin{array}{ccc|ccc} 2 & 2 & 1 & 1 & 0 & 0 \\ -2 & -1 & 1 & 0 & 1 & 0 \\ -1 & -3 & -3 & 0 & 0 & 1 \end{array}\right] \to [(A|I)]$$

$$\begin{array}{r} -R_3 \\ \\ R_1 \end{array}\left[\begin{array}{ccc|ccc} 1 & 3 & 3 & 0 & 0 & -1 \\ -2 & -1 & 1 & 0 & 1 & 0 \\ 2 & 2 & 1 & 1 & 0 & 0 \end{array}\right]$$

$$\begin{array}{r} \\ 2R_1+R_2 \\ 2R_1-R_3 \end{array}\left[\begin{array}{ccc|ccc} 1 & 3 & 3 & 0 & 0 & -1 \\ 0 & 5 & 7 & 0 & 1 & -2 \\ 0 & 4 & 5 & -1 & 0 & -2 \end{array}\right]$$

$$\begin{array}{r} \\ \left(\frac{1}{5}\right)R_2 \\ \\ \end{array}\left[\begin{array}{ccc|ccc} 1 & 3 & 3 & 0 & 0 & -1 \\ 0 & 1 & \frac{7}{5} & 0 & \frac{1}{5} & -\frac{2}{5} \\ 0 & 4 & 5 & -1 & 0 & -2 \end{array}\right]$$

$$\begin{array}{r} -3R_2+R_1 \\ \\ 4R_2-R_3 \end{array}\left[\begin{array}{ccc|ccc} 1 & 0 & -\frac{6}{5} & 0 & -\frac{3}{5} & \frac{1}{5} \\ 0 & 1 & \frac{7}{5} & 0 & \frac{1}{5} & -\frac{2}{5} \\ 0 & 0 & \frac{3}{5} & 1 & \frac{4}{5} & \frac{2}{5} \end{array}\right]$$

$$\begin{array}{r} \\ \\ \left(\frac{5}{3}\right)R_3 \end{array}\left[\begin{array}{ccc|ccc} 1 & 0 & -\frac{6}{5} & 0 & -\frac{3}{5} & \frac{1}{5} \\ 0 & 1 & \frac{7}{5} & 0 & \frac{1}{5} & -\frac{2}{5} \\ 0 & 0 & 1 & \frac{5}{3} & \frac{4}{3} & \frac{2}{3} \end{array}\right]$$

$$\begin{array}{r} \left(\frac{6}{5}\right)R_3+R_1 \\ -\left(\frac{7}{5}\right)R_3+R_2 \\ \\ \end{array}\left[\begin{array}{ccc|ccc} 1 & 0 & 0 & 2 & 1 & 1 \\ 0 & 1 & 0 & -\frac{7}{3} & -\frac{5}{3} & -\frac{4}{3} \\ 0 & 0 & 1 & \frac{5}{3} & \frac{4}{3} & \frac{2}{3} \end{array}\right]$$

$$\to [I\,|\,A^{-1}]$$

So the inverse of A is

$$A^{-1}=\begin{bmatrix} 2 & 1 & 1 \\ -\frac{7}{3} & -\frac{5}{3} & -\frac{4}{3} \\ \frac{5}{3} & \frac{4}{3} & \frac{2}{3} \end{bmatrix}$$

Review Exercises

01

$$AB=\begin{bmatrix} 1 & 0 \\ 3 & 2 \end{bmatrix}\begin{bmatrix} 1 & 0 \\ -\frac{3}{2} & \frac{1}{2} \end{bmatrix}$$

$$=\begin{bmatrix} 1+0 & 0+0 \\ 3-3 & 0+1 \end{bmatrix}$$

$$=\begin{bmatrix} 1 & 0 \\ 0 & 1 \end{bmatrix}=I_2$$

02

$$AB=\begin{bmatrix} -5 & 4 \\ 2 & -2 \end{bmatrix}\begin{bmatrix} -1 & -2 \\ -1 & -\frac{5}{2} \end{bmatrix}$$

$$=\begin{bmatrix} 5-4 & 10-10 \\ -2+2 & -4+5 \end{bmatrix}$$

$$=\begin{bmatrix} 1 & 0 \\ 0 & 1 \end{bmatrix}=I_2$$

03

$$AB=\begin{bmatrix}4 & 1 & 2\\ 2 & 0 & 1\\ -1 & -2 & 0\end{bmatrix}\begin{bmatrix}-2 & 4 & -1\\ 1 & -2 & 0\\ 4 & -7 & 2\end{bmatrix}$$

$$=\begin{bmatrix}-8+1+8 & 16-2-14 & -4+0+4\\ -4+0+4 & 8+0-7 & -2+0+2\\ 2-2+0 & -4+4+0 & 1+0+0\end{bmatrix}$$

$$=\begin{bmatrix}1 & 0 & 0\\ 0 & 1 & 0\\ 0 & 0 & 1\end{bmatrix}=I_3$$

04

$$AB=\begin{bmatrix}1 & -4 & 0\\ 1 & 2 & 0\\ 1 & 2 & 1\end{bmatrix}\begin{bmatrix}\frac{1}{3} & \frac{2}{3} & 0\\ -\frac{1}{6} & \frac{1}{6} & 0\\ 0 & -1 & 1\end{bmatrix}$$

$$=\begin{bmatrix}\frac{1}{3}+\frac{2}{3}+0 & \frac{2}{3}-\frac{2}{3}+0 & 0+0+0\\ \frac{1}{3}-\frac{1}{3}+0 & \frac{2}{3}+\frac{1}{3}+0 & 0+0+0\\ \frac{1}{3}-\frac{1}{3}+0 & \frac{2}{3}+\frac{1}{3}-1 & 0+0+1\end{bmatrix}$$

$$=\begin{bmatrix}1 & 0 & 0\\ 0 & 1 & 0\\ 0 & 0 & 1\end{bmatrix}=I_3$$

05

$$\begin{bmatrix}-2 & 3\\ -1 & 2\end{bmatrix}$$

$$A^{-1}=\frac{1}{(-2)(2)-(3)(-1)}\begin{bmatrix}2 & -3\\ 1 & -2\end{bmatrix}=\begin{bmatrix}-2 & 3\\ -1 & 2\end{bmatrix}$$

06

$$\begin{bmatrix}-2 & 4\\ -1 & 1\end{bmatrix}$$

$$A^{-1}=\frac{1}{(-2)(1)-(4)(-1)}\begin{bmatrix}1 & -4\\ 1 & -2\end{bmatrix}$$

$$=\begin{bmatrix}\frac{1}{2} & -2\\ \frac{1}{2} & -1\end{bmatrix}$$

07

$$\begin{bmatrix}1 & 0 & 1\\ 3 & 2 & -1\\ 0 & -1 & 4\end{bmatrix}$$

$$\left[\begin{array}{ccc|ccc}1 & 0 & 1 & 1 & 0 & 0\\ 3 & 2 & -1 & 0 & 1 & 0\\ 0 & -1 & 4 & 0 & 0 & 1\end{array}\right] \rightarrow [(A|I)]$$

$$3R_1-R_2\left[\begin{array}{ccc|ccc}1 & 0 & 1 & 1 & 0 & 0\\ 0 & -2 & 4 & 3 & -1 & 0\\ 0 & -1 & 4 & 0 & 0 & 1\end{array}\right]$$

$$\begin{matrix}\\ -R_3\\ R_2\end{matrix}\left[\begin{array}{ccc|ccc}1 & 0 & 1 & 1 & 0 & 0\\ 0 & 1 & -4 & 0 & 0 & -1\\ 0 & -2 & 4 & 3 & -1 & 0\end{array}\right]$$

$$\begin{matrix}\\ \\ 2R_2+R_3\end{matrix}\left[\begin{array}{ccc|ccc}1 & 0 & 1 & 1 & 0 & 0\\ 0 & 1 & -4 & 0 & 0 & -1\\ 0 & 0 & -4 & 3 & -1 & -2\end{array}\right]$$

$$\begin{matrix}\\ \\ -\left(\frac{1}{4}\right)R_3\end{matrix}\left[\begin{array}{ccc|ccc}1 & 0 & 1 & 1 & 0 & 0\\ 0 & 1 & -4 & 0 & 0 & -1\\ 0 & 0 & 1 & -\frac{3}{4} & \frac{1}{4} & \frac{1}{2}\end{array}\right]$$

$$\begin{matrix}-R_3+R_1\\ 4R_3+R_2\\ \\ \end{matrix}\left[\begin{array}{ccc|ccc}1 & 0 & 0 & \frac{7}{4} & -\frac{1}{4} & -\frac{1}{2}\\ 0 & 1 & 0 & -3 & 1 & 1\\ 0 & 0 & 1 & -\frac{3}{4} & \frac{1}{4} & \frac{1}{2}\end{array}\right]$$

$\rightarrow [I \mid A^{-1}]$

So, $A^{-1}=\begin{bmatrix} \frac{7}{4} & -\frac{1}{4} & -\frac{1}{2} \\ -3 & 1 & 1 \\ -\frac{3}{4} & \frac{1}{4} & \frac{1}{2} \end{bmatrix}$

08

$\begin{cases} -2x+4y=2 \\ x+y=2 \end{cases} \to \begin{bmatrix} -2 & 4 \\ 1 & 1 \end{bmatrix}\begin{bmatrix} x \\ y \end{bmatrix}=\begin{bmatrix} 2 \\ 2 \end{bmatrix}$

$\to \begin{bmatrix} x \\ y \end{bmatrix}=\begin{bmatrix} -2 & 4 \\ 1 & 1 \end{bmatrix}^{-1}\begin{bmatrix} 2 \\ 2 \end{bmatrix}$

Because $\begin{bmatrix} -2 & 4 \\ 1 & 1 \end{bmatrix}^{-1}=\begin{bmatrix} -\frac{1}{6} & \frac{2}{3} \\ \frac{1}{6} & \frac{1}{3} \end{bmatrix}$,

$\begin{bmatrix} x \\ y \end{bmatrix}=\begin{bmatrix} -\frac{1}{6} & \frac{2}{3} \\ \frac{1}{6} & \frac{1}{3} \end{bmatrix}\begin{bmatrix} 2 \\ 2 \end{bmatrix}=\begin{bmatrix} 1 \\ 1 \end{bmatrix}$

The solution is $x=1$ and $y=1$

09

$\begin{cases} -3x-2y=1 \\ -x+4y=-9 \end{cases} \to \begin{bmatrix} -3 & -2 \\ -1 & 4 \end{bmatrix}\begin{bmatrix} x \\ y \end{bmatrix}=\begin{bmatrix} 1 \\ -9 \end{bmatrix}$

$\to \begin{bmatrix} x \\ y \end{bmatrix}=\begin{bmatrix} -3 & -2 \\ -1 & 4 \end{bmatrix}^{-1}\begin{bmatrix} 1 \\ -9 \end{bmatrix}$

Because $\begin{bmatrix} -3 & -2 \\ -1 & 4 \end{bmatrix}^{-1}=\begin{bmatrix} -\frac{2}{7} & -\frac{1}{7} \\ -\frac{1}{14} & \frac{3}{14} \end{bmatrix}$

$\begin{bmatrix} x \\ y \end{bmatrix}=\begin{bmatrix} -\frac{2}{7} & -\frac{1}{7} \\ -\frac{1}{14} & \frac{3}{14} \end{bmatrix}\begin{bmatrix} 1 \\ -9 \end{bmatrix}=\begin{bmatrix} 1 \\ -2 \end{bmatrix}$

The solution is $x=1$ and $y=-2$

10

$\begin{cases} x+z=2 \\ 3x+2y-z=-2 \\ -y+4z=10 \end{cases} \to \begin{bmatrix} 1 & 0 & 1 \\ 3 & 2 & -1 \\ 0 & -1 & 4 \end{bmatrix}\begin{bmatrix} x \\ y \\ z \end{bmatrix}=\begin{bmatrix} 2 \\ -2 \\ 10 \end{bmatrix}$

$\to \begin{bmatrix} x \\ y \\ z \end{bmatrix}=\begin{bmatrix} 1 & 0 & 1 \\ 3 & 2 & -1 \\ 0 & -1 & 4 \end{bmatrix}^{-1}\begin{bmatrix} 2 \\ -2 \\ 10 \end{bmatrix}$

Because $\begin{bmatrix} 1 & 0 & 1 \\ 3 & 2 & -1 \\ 0 & -1 & 4 \end{bmatrix}^{-1}=\begin{bmatrix} \frac{7}{4} & -\frac{1}{4} & -\frac{1}{2} \\ -3 & 1 & 1 \\ -\frac{3}{4} & \frac{1}{4} & \frac{1}{2} \end{bmatrix}$,

$\begin{bmatrix} x \\ y \\ z \end{bmatrix}=\begin{bmatrix} \frac{7}{4} & -\frac{1}{4} & -\frac{1}{2} \\ -3 & 1 & 1 \\ -\frac{3}{4} & \frac{1}{4} & \frac{1}{2} \end{bmatrix}\begin{bmatrix} 2 \\ -2 \\ 10 \end{bmatrix}=\begin{bmatrix} -1 \\ 2 \\ 3 \end{bmatrix}$

The solution is $x=-1$, $y=2$, and $z=3$

11

$\begin{cases} 2x+2y+z=-2 \\ -2x-y+z=5 \\ -x-3y-3z=-2 \end{cases}$

$\to \begin{bmatrix} 2 & 2 & 1 \\ -2 & -1 & 1 \\ -1 & -3 & -3 \end{bmatrix}\begin{bmatrix} x \\ y \\ z \end{bmatrix}=\begin{bmatrix} -2 \\ 5 \\ -2 \end{bmatrix}$

$\to \begin{bmatrix} x \\ y \\ z \end{bmatrix}=\begin{bmatrix} 2 & 2 & 1 \\ -2 & -1 & 1 \\ -1 & -3 & -3 \end{bmatrix}^{-1}\begin{bmatrix} -2 \\ 5 \\ -2 \end{bmatrix}$

Because $\begin{bmatrix} 2 & 2 & 1 \\ -2 & -1 & 1 \\ -1 & -3 & -3 \end{bmatrix}^{-1}$

$=\begin{bmatrix} 2 & 1 & 1 \\ -\frac{7}{3} & -\frac{5}{3} & -\frac{4}{3} \\ \frac{5}{3} & \frac{4}{3} & \frac{2}{3} \end{bmatrix}$,

$\begin{bmatrix} x \\ y \\ z \end{bmatrix}=\begin{bmatrix} 2 & 1 & 1 \\ -\frac{7}{3} & -\frac{5}{3} & -\frac{4}{3} \\ \frac{5}{3} & \frac{4}{3} & \frac{2}{3} \end{bmatrix}\begin{bmatrix} -2 \\ 5 \\ -2 \end{bmatrix}=\begin{bmatrix} -1 \\ -1 \\ 2 \end{bmatrix}$

The solution is $x=-1$, $y=-1$, and $z=2$

12

Write the system of equations in matrix form $AX=B$, where A is the coefficient matrix, X is the variable matrix, and B is the constant matrix.

$$\begin{bmatrix} 1 & -2 & 3 \\ 2 & 4 & -5 \\ 3 & 0 & 4 \end{bmatrix}\begin{bmatrix} x \\ y \\ z \end{bmatrix}=\begin{bmatrix} 6 \\ -7 \\ 7 \end{bmatrix}$$

Then

$$\begin{bmatrix} x \\ y \\ z \end{bmatrix}=\underbrace{\begin{bmatrix} 1 & -2 & 3 \\ 2 & 4 & -5 \\ 3 & 0 & 4 \end{bmatrix}^{-1}}_{3\times 3}\underbrace{\begin{bmatrix} 6 \\ -7 \\ 7 \end{bmatrix}}_{3\times 1}$$

Therefore, the correct answer is (D).

13

We need to create a matrix that represents the quantities of each item purchased by the students and multiply it by a matrix representing the prices of each item to find the total cost for each student. Therefore, the correct matrix is

$$\underbrace{\begin{bmatrix} 5 & 12 & 4 \\ 8 & 6 & 5 \end{bmatrix}}_{2\times 3}\underbrace{\begin{bmatrix} 1.5 \\ 2.5 \\ 3 \end{bmatrix}}_{3\times 1}$$

The correct answer is (C).

10. Determinants and Cramer's Rule

Check Point 1

① $\begin{vmatrix} 5 & 4 \\ -3 & -2 \end{vmatrix}=(5)(-2)-(4)(-3)=2$

② $\begin{vmatrix} -2 & 3 \\ -1 & 2 \end{vmatrix}=(-2)(2)-(3)(-1)=-1$

Check Point 2

① By deleting 1st row and 1st column of $\begin{bmatrix} -2 & 1 \\ 6 & 3 \end{bmatrix}$,

$M_{11}=|3|=3$ and

$C_{11}=(-1)^{1+1}M_{11}=(-1)^2\cdot 3=3$

$C_{11}=3$

② By deleting 2nd row and 3rd column of $\begin{bmatrix} 2 & 3 & 0 \\ 3 & 5 & -2 \\ -1 & -2 & 4 \end{bmatrix}$,

$M_{23}=\begin{vmatrix} 2 & 3 \\ -1 & -2 \end{vmatrix}=(2)(-2)-(3)(-1)=-1$

and $C_{23}=(-1)^{2+3}M_{23}=(-1)^5\cdot(-1)=1$

$C_{23}=1$

Check Point 3

① By expanding along the first row,

$$\begin{vmatrix} 2 & -2 & 3 \\ -1 & 3 & 6 \\ -1 & 1 & 2 \end{vmatrix}$$

$$=2(-1)^{1+1}\begin{vmatrix} 3 & 6 \\ 1 & 2 \end{vmatrix}+(-2)(-1)^{1+2}\begin{vmatrix} -1 & 6 \\ -1 & 2 \end{vmatrix}$$

$$+3(-1)^{1+3}\begin{vmatrix} -1 & 3 \\ -1 & 1 \end{vmatrix}$$

$$=2(6-6)+2(-2+6)+3(-1+3)=14$$

$\begin{vmatrix} 2 & -2 & 3 \\ -1 & 3 & 6 \\ -1 & 1 & 2 \end{vmatrix}=14$

② By expanding along the second row,

$$\begin{vmatrix} 6 & 1 & 5 \\ 2 & -4 & 0 \\ -3 & -2 & 0 \end{vmatrix}$$

$$=2(-1)^{2+1}\begin{vmatrix} 1 & 5 \\ -2 & 0 \end{vmatrix}+(-4)(-1)^{2+2}\begin{vmatrix} 6 & 5 \\ -3 & 0 \end{vmatrix}$$

$$+(0)(-1)^{2+3}\begin{vmatrix} 6 & 1 \\ -3 & -2 \end{vmatrix}$$

$$=-2(0+10)-4(0+15)+0=-80$$

$$\begin{vmatrix} 6 & 1 & 5 \\ 2 & -4 & 0 \\ -3 & -2 & 0 \end{vmatrix}=-80$$

Check Point 4

① We need to find D, D_x, and D_y.

$$D=\begin{vmatrix} -2 & 3 \\ -1 & 2 \end{vmatrix}=-4+3=-1$$

$$D_x=\begin{vmatrix} -3 & 3 \\ -1 & 2 \end{vmatrix}=-6+3=-3$$

$$D_y=\begin{vmatrix} -2 & -3 \\ -1 & -1 \end{vmatrix}=2-3=-1$$

$$x=\frac{D_x}{D}=\frac{-3}{-1}=3,\ y=\frac{D_y}{D}=\frac{-1}{-1}=1$$

The solution is $x=3$ and $y=1$

② We need to find D, D_x, D_y, and D_z.
By expanding along the *first row*,

$$D=\begin{vmatrix} 1 & 0 & 1 \\ 3 & 2 & -1 \\ 0 & -1 & 4 \end{vmatrix}=(1)(-1)^{1+1}\begin{vmatrix} 2 & -1 \\ -1 & 4 \end{vmatrix}$$

$$+(0)(-1)^{1+2}\begin{vmatrix} 3 & -1 \\ 0 & 4 \end{vmatrix}$$

$$+(1)(-1)^{1+3}\begin{vmatrix} 3 & 2 \\ 0 & -1 \end{vmatrix}$$

$$=(8-1)+0+(-3-0)=4$$

$$D_x=\begin{vmatrix} 4 & 0 & 1 \\ 4 & 2 & -1 \\ 6 & -1 & 4 \end{vmatrix}=(4)(-1)^{1+1}\begin{vmatrix} 2 & -1 \\ -1 & 4 \end{vmatrix}$$

$$+(0)(-1)^{1+2}\begin{vmatrix} 4 & -1 \\ 6 & 4 \end{vmatrix}$$

$$+(1)(-1)^{1+3}\begin{vmatrix} 4 & 2 \\ 6 & -1 \end{vmatrix}$$

$$=(4)(8-1)-(0)(16+6)+(1)(-4-12)=12$$

$$D_y=\begin{vmatrix} 1 & 4 & 1 \\ 3 & 4 & -1 \\ 0 & 6 & 4 \end{vmatrix}=(1)(-1)^{1+1}\begin{vmatrix} 4 & -1 \\ 6 & 4 \end{vmatrix}$$

$$+(4)(-1)^{1+2}\begin{vmatrix} 3 & -1 \\ 0 & 4 \end{vmatrix}+(1)(-1)^{1+3}\begin{vmatrix} 3 & 4 \\ 0 & 6 \end{vmatrix}$$

$$=(1)(16+6)-(4)(12-0)+(1)(18-0)=-8$$

$$D_z=\begin{vmatrix} 1 & 0 & 4 \\ 3 & 2 & 4 \\ 0 & -1 & 6 \end{vmatrix}=(1)(-1)^{1+1}\begin{vmatrix} 2 & 4 \\ -1 & 6 \end{vmatrix}$$

$$+(0)(-1)^{1+2}\begin{vmatrix} 3 & 4 \\ 0 & 6 \end{vmatrix}+(4)(-1)^{1+3}\begin{vmatrix} 3 & 2 \\ 0 & -1 \end{vmatrix}$$

$$=(1)(12+4)-(0)(18-0)+(4)(-3-0)=4$$

$$x=\frac{D_x}{D}=\frac{12}{4}=3,\ y=\frac{D_y}{D}=\frac{-8}{4}=-2,$$

and $z=\frac{D_z}{D}=\frac{4}{4}=1$

The solution is $x=3$, $y=-2$, and $z=1$

Review Exercises

01

$\begin{bmatrix} -2 & 0 \\ 3 & 4 \end{bmatrix}$; C_{11}

$M_{11}=|4|=4$ and

$C_{11}=(-1)^{1+1}M_{11}=(-1)^2\cdot 4=4$

02

$\begin{bmatrix} 6 & 8 \\ -4 & -1 \end{bmatrix}$; C_{12}

$M_{12}=|-4|=-4$ and

$C_{12}=(-1)^{1+2}M_{12}=(-1)^3\cdot(-4)=4$

03

$\begin{bmatrix} -2 & 4 \\ 1 & 1 \end{bmatrix}$; C_{22}

$M_{22}=|-2|=-2$ and

$C_{22}=(-1)^{2+2}M_{22}=(-1)^4\cdot(-2)=-2$

04

$$\begin{bmatrix} 0 & 3 & 5 \\ 3 & -2 & 0 \\ -4 & 1 & -1 \end{bmatrix};\ C_{21}$$

$M_{21}=\begin{vmatrix} 3 & 5 \\ 1 & -1 \end{vmatrix}=(3)(-1)-(5)(1)=-8$ and

$C_{21}=(-1)^{2+1}M_{21}=(-1)^3\cdot(-8)=8$

05

$$\begin{bmatrix} 3 & 2 & 2 \\ 4 & 3 & 5 \\ 0 & 0 & 2 \end{bmatrix};\ C_{32}$$

$M_{32}=\begin{vmatrix} 3 & 2 \\ 4 & 5 \end{vmatrix}=(3)(5)-(2)(4)=7$ and

$C_{32}=(-1)^{3+2}M_{32}=(-1)^5\cdot 7=-7$

06

$$\begin{bmatrix} -2 & 0 & 4 \\ 0 & -3 & -1 \\ \frac{3}{2} & \frac{1}{3} & -\frac{3}{4} \end{bmatrix};\ C_{13}$$

$M_{13}=\begin{vmatrix} 0 & -3 \\ \frac{3}{2} & \frac{1}{3} \end{vmatrix}=(0)\left(\frac{1}{3}\right)-(-3)\left(\frac{3}{2}\right)=\frac{9}{2}$

and $C_{13}=(-1)^{1+3}M_{13}=(-1)^4\cdot\frac{9}{2}=\frac{9}{2}$

07

$$\begin{bmatrix} 4 & -2 \\ -2 & 1 \end{bmatrix}$$

$\begin{vmatrix} 4 & -2 \\ -2 & 1 \end{vmatrix}=(4)(1)-(-2)(-2)=0$

08

$$\begin{bmatrix} -3 & -2 \\ -1 & 4 \end{bmatrix}$$

$\begin{vmatrix} -3 & -2 \\ -1 & 4 \end{vmatrix}=(-3)(4)-(-2)(-1)=-14$

09

$$\begin{bmatrix} 1 & 0 & 1 \\ 3 & 2 & -1 \\ 0 & -1 & 4 \end{bmatrix}$$

Expanded along the *first row*

$$\begin{vmatrix} 1 & 0 & 1 \\ 3 & 2 & -1 \\ 0 & -1 & 4 \end{vmatrix}$$

$=(1)(-1)^{1+1}\begin{vmatrix} 2 & -1 \\ -1 & 4 \end{vmatrix}+(0)(-1)^{1+2}\begin{vmatrix} 3 & -1 \\ 0 & 4 \end{vmatrix}$

$+(1)(-1)^{1+3}\begin{vmatrix} 3 & 2 \\ 0 & -1 \end{vmatrix}$

$=(8-1)+(-3-0)=4$

10

$$\begin{bmatrix} 3 & 0 & 1 \\ 0 & 2 & 0 \\ 2 & 4 & 1 \end{bmatrix}$$

Expanded along the *first row*

$$\begin{vmatrix} 3 & 0 & 1 \\ 0 & 2 & 0 \\ 2 & 4 & 1 \end{vmatrix}$$

$=(3)(-1)^{1+1}\begin{vmatrix} 2 & 0 \\ 4 & 1 \end{vmatrix}+(0)(-1)^{1+2}\begin{vmatrix} 0 & 0 \\ 2 & 1 \end{vmatrix}$

$+(1)(-1)^{1+3}\begin{vmatrix} 0 & 2 \\ 2 & 4 \end{vmatrix}$

$=3(2-0)+(0-4)=2$

11

$$\begin{bmatrix} 2 & 2 & 1 \\ -2 & -1 & 1 \\ -1 & -3 & -3 \end{bmatrix}$$

Expanded along the *first row*

$$\begin{bmatrix} 2 & 2 & 1 \\ -2 & -1 & 1 \\ -1 & -3 & -3 \end{bmatrix}$$

$=(2)(-1)^{1+1}\begin{vmatrix} -1 & 1 \\ -3 & -3 \end{vmatrix}+(2)(-1)^{1+2}\begin{vmatrix} -2 & 1 \\ -1 & -3 \end{vmatrix}$

$+(1)(-1)^{1+3}\begin{vmatrix} -2 & -1 \\ -1 & -3 \end{vmatrix}$

$=2(3+3)-2(6+1)+(6-1)=3$

12

$$\begin{cases}4x+2y=12\\-2x+y=-6\end{cases}$$

$$D=\begin{vmatrix}4 & 2\\-2 & 1\end{vmatrix}=4+4=8$$

$$D_x=\begin{vmatrix}12 & 2\\-6 & 1\end{vmatrix}=12+12=24$$

$$D_y=\begin{vmatrix}4 & 12\\-2 & -6\end{vmatrix}=-24+24=0$$

$$x=\frac{D_x}{D}=\frac{24}{8}=3,\ y=\frac{D_y}{D}=\frac{0}{8}=0$$

The solution is $x=3$ and $y=0$

13

$$\begin{cases}2x+2y+z=0\\-2x-y+z=-5\\-x-3y-3z=7\end{cases}$$

Expanded along the *first row*

$$D=\begin{vmatrix}2 & 2 & 1\\-2 & -1 & 1\\-1 & -3 & -3\end{vmatrix}$$

$$=(2)(3+3)-(2)(6+1)+(1)(6-1)=3$$

$$D_x=\begin{vmatrix}0 & 2 & 1\\-5 & -1 & 1\\7 & -3 & -3\end{vmatrix}$$

$$=(0)(3+3)-(2)(15-7)+(1)(15+7)=6$$

$$D_y=\begin{vmatrix}2 & 0 & 1\\-2 & -5 & 1\\-1 & 7 & -3\end{vmatrix}$$

$$=(2)(15-7)-(0)(6+1)+(1)(-14-5)=-3$$

$$D_z=\begin{vmatrix}2 & 2 & 0\\-2 & -1 & -5\\-1 & -3 & 7\end{vmatrix}$$

$$=(2)(-7-15)-(2)(-14-5)+(0)(6-1)$$

$$=-6$$

$x=\frac{D_x}{D}=\frac{6}{3}=2,\ y=\frac{D_y}{D}=\frac{-3}{3}=-1$, and

$$z=\frac{D_z}{D}=\frac{-6}{3}=-2$$

The solution is $x=2$, $y=-1$ and $z=-2$

Unit Ⅳ Test

01

(1) Solve y for t.

$y=3t-2,\ y+2=3t,\ t=\frac{y+2}{3}$

Substitute t into the equation x.

$x=2t^2+5$

$$x=2\left(\frac{y+2}{3}\right)^2+5=\frac{2(y+2)^2}{9}+5$$

$$\frac{2(y+2)^2}{9}+5$$

(2) $x=4\sin t-3,\ x+3=4\sin t,$

$\sin t=\frac{x+3}{4},\ \sin^2 t=\left(\frac{x+3}{4}\right)^2$

$y=2\cos^2 t+1,\ y-1=2\cos^2 t,\ \cos^2 t=\frac{y-1}{2}$

Using the Pythagorean Identity,

$\sin^2 t+\cos^2 t=1$

$$\left(\frac{x+3}{4}\right)^2+\frac{y-1}{2}=1,\ \frac{(x+3)^2}{16}+\frac{y-1}{2}=1$$

$$\frac{(x+3)^2}{16}+\frac{y-1}{2}=1$$

02

The equation for the line is $y=mx+b$.
Since the line passes through $(-1,\ 5)$ and $(1,\ 1)$, we have

$$\begin{cases}5=m(-1)+b\\1=m(1)+b)\end{cases}\rightarrow m=-2,\ b=3.$$

So the equation for the line is $y=-2x+3$.
Now, if we let $x=t$, then $y=-2t+3$.

$x=t,\ y=-2t+3$

03

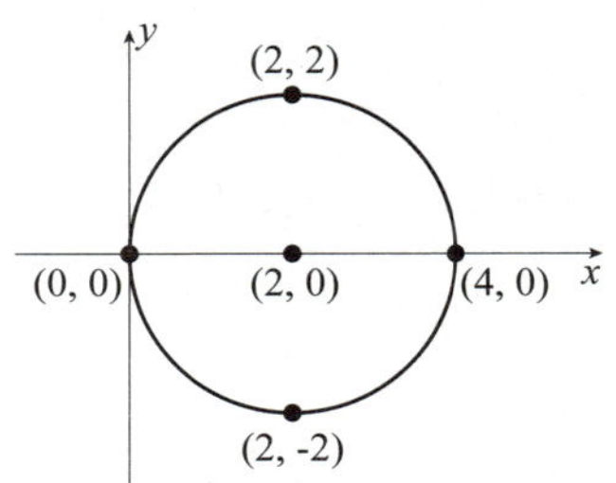

(1) Since the particle starts to move clockwise at (0, 0), we must have following values:

t	x	y
0	0	0
$\frac{3}{2}$	2	2
3	4	0

$(x-2)^2+y^2=4,\ \left(\frac{x-2}{2}\right)^2+\left(\frac{y}{2}\right)^2=1$

Using the identity, $(\sin bt)^2+(\cos bt)^2=1$, the period is 6 → $P=\frac{2\pi}{b}=6,\ b=\frac{\pi}{3}$ and we must have

$$\begin{cases} -\cos\left(\frac{\pi t}{3}\right)=\frac{x-2}{2},\ 2-2\cos\left(\frac{\pi t}{3}\right)=x \\ \sin\left(\frac{\pi t}{3}\right)=\frac{y}{2},\ 2\sin\left(\frac{\pi t}{3}\right)=y \end{cases}$$

$x=2-2\cos\left(\frac{\pi t}{3}\right),\ y=2\sin\left(\frac{\pi t}{3}\right)$

(2) Since the particle starts to move counterclockwise at (2, 2), we must have following values:

t	x	y
0	2	2
$\frac{1}{2}$	0	0
1	2	-2

$(x-2)^2+y^2=4,\ \left(\frac{x-2}{2}\right)^2+\left(\frac{y}{2}\right)^2=1$

Using the identity, $(\sin bt)^2+(\cos bt)^2=1$, the period is 2 → $P=\frac{2\pi}{b}=2,\ b=\pi$ and we must have

$$\begin{cases} -\sin(\pi t)=\frac{x-2}{2},\ 2-2\sin(\pi t)=x \\ \cos(\pi t)=\frac{y}{2},\ 2\cos(\pi t)=y \end{cases}$$

$x=2-2\sin(\pi t),\ y=2\cos(\pi t)$

04

We have $h=2\ ft$, $\theta=30°$, $v_0=40\ ft/\text{sec}$, and $g=32\ ft/\text{sec}^2$.

First, find parametric equations that describe the position.

$x(t)=(v_0\cos\theta)t$

$=(40\cos 30°)t=\left(40\cdot\frac{\sqrt{3}}{2}\right)t=20\sqrt{3}\,t$

$y(t)=-\frac{1}{2}gt^2+(v_0\sin\theta)t+h$

$=-\frac{1}{2}(32)t^2+(40\sin 30°)t+2$

$=-16t^2+\left(40\cdot\frac{1}{2}\right)t+2$

$=-16t^2+20t+2$

(1) $y(t)=-16t^2+20t+2$

$0=-16t^2+20t+2,\ 8t^2-10t-1=0$

$t=\frac{10\pm\sqrt{(-10)^2-4(8)(-1)}}{2(8)}=\frac{5\pm\sqrt{33}}{8}$

$t=-0.093$ or $t=1.343$

Since $t\geq 0$, the ball is in the air for about 1.343 seconds.

(2) $y(t)=-16t^2+20t+2$

The maximum height of the ball can be found when $t=-\frac{b}{2a}=-\frac{20}{2(-16)}=\frac{5}{8}$ seconds.

The ball is at its maximum height after $\frac{5}{8}$ seconds.

(3) The maximum height of the ball is

$y\left(\frac{5}{8}\right)=-16\left(\frac{5}{8}\right)^2+20\left(\frac{5}{8}\right)+2=\frac{33}{4}$

The maximum height of the ball is approximately $\frac{33}{4}$ feet.

(4) $x(t)=20\sqrt{3}t$

The ball is in the air for 1.343 seconds. So the horizontal distance that the ball travels is

$x(1.343)=20\sqrt{3}\ (1.343)=46.523$ feet.

The horizontal distance is approximately 46.523 feet.

05

(1) $4x^2+\frac{1}{2}y=0$, $4x^2=-\frac{1}{2}y$, $x^2=-\frac{1}{8}y$

$\rightarrow 4p=-\frac{1}{8}$, $p=-\frac{1}{32}$

Since p is negative, the graph opens downward.

Vertex: (0,0), Focus: $(0,-\frac{1}{32})$

Equation of directrix: $y=\frac{1}{32}$

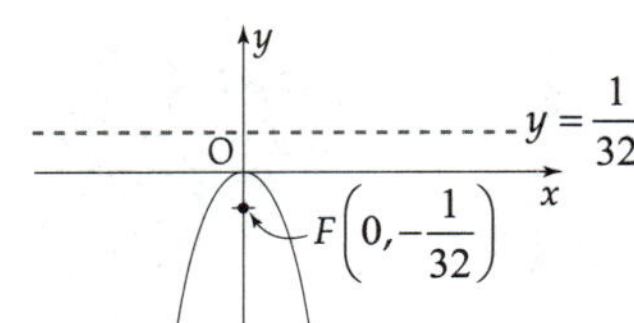

(2) $x^2+2y-6x=1$, $x^2-6x=1-2y$

$x^2-6x+9-9=1-2y$

$(x-3)^2=10-2y$, $(x-3)^2=-2(y-5)$

$\rightarrow 4p=-2$, $p=-\frac{1}{2}$

Since p is negative, the graph opens downward.

Vertex: (3, 5), Focus: $(3,\ 5-\frac{1}{2})=(3,\ \frac{9}{2})$

Equation of directrix: $y=\frac{1}{2}+5=\frac{11}{2}$

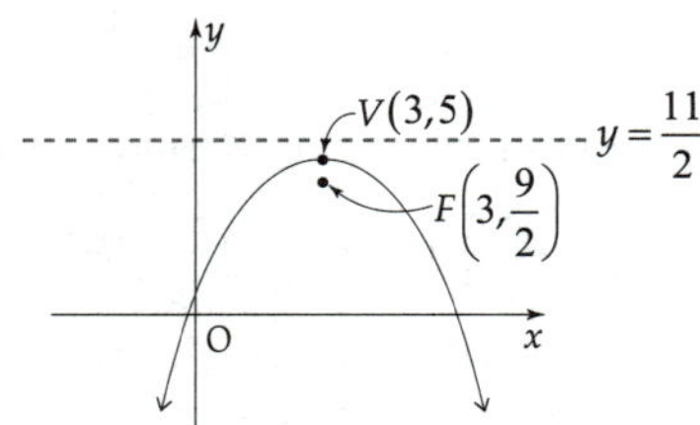

06

(1)

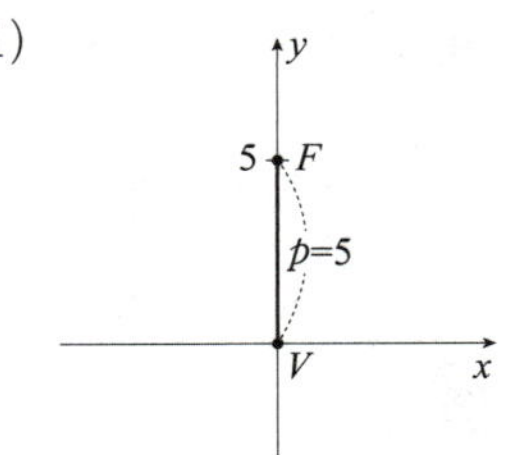

The standard equation is $x^2=4py$ and $p=5$. So we have $x^2=4(5)y$, $x^2=20y$

$x^2=20y$

(2)

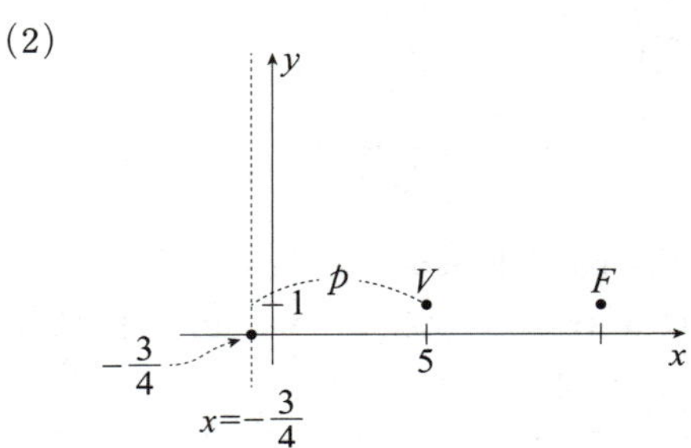

The standard equation is $(y-1)^2=4p(x-5)$ and $p=5-\left(-\frac{3}{4}\right)=\frac{23}{4}$. So we have $(y-1)^2=4\left(\frac{23}{4}\right)(x-5)$, $(y-1)^2=23(x-5)$.

$(y-1)^2=23(x-5)$

(3)

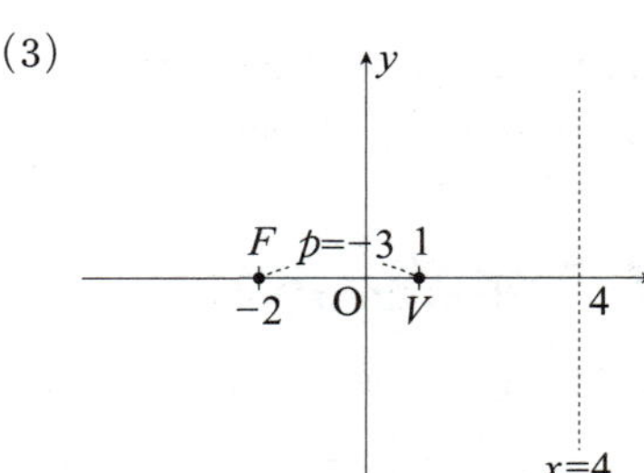

The standard equation is $(y-k)^2=4p(x-h)$. The vertex is (1, 0) because it is the midpoint of the focus and directrix.

$p=-2-1=-3$. So the equation is

$(y-0)^2=4(-3)(x-1)$, $y^2=-12(x-1)$

$y^2=-12(x-1)$

07

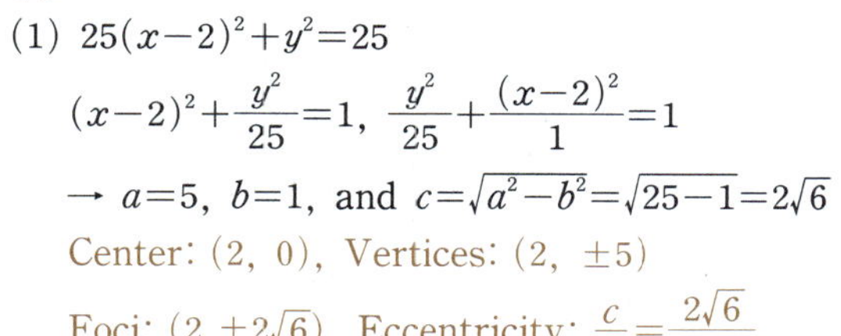

(1) $25(x-2)^2+y^2=25$

$(x-2)^2+\frac{y^2}{25}=1$, $\frac{y^2}{25}+\frac{(x-2)^2}{1}=1$

$\rightarrow a=5$, $b=1$, and $c=\sqrt{a^2-b^2}=\sqrt{25-1}=2\sqrt{6}$

Center: $(2,\ 0)$, Vertices: $(2,\ \pm5)$

Foci: $(2, \pm2\sqrt{6})$, Eccentricity: $\frac{c}{a}=\frac{2\sqrt{6}}{5}$

Major Axis: $2a=10$, Minor Axis: $2b=2$

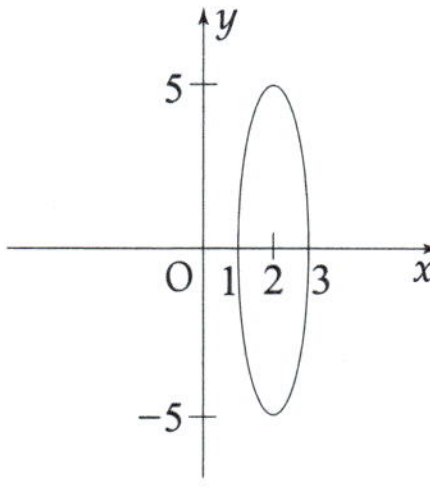

(2) $-2x^2-16x-\frac{1}{2}y^2+y=0$,

$2x^2+16x+\frac{1}{2}y^2-y=0$

$2(x^2+8x)+\frac{1}{2}\ (y^2-2y)=0$

$2(x^2+8x+16-16)+\frac{1}{2}(y^2-2y+1-1)=0$

$2(x+4)^2-32+\frac{1}{2}(y-1)^2-\frac{1}{2}=0$

$2(x+4)^2+\frac{1}{2}(y-1)^2=\frac{65}{2}$,

$\frac{(y-1)^2}{65}+\frac{(x+4)^2}{\frac{65}{4}}=1$

$\rightarrow a=\sqrt{65}$, $b=\frac{\sqrt{65}}{2}$, and

$c=\sqrt{a^2-b^2}=\sqrt{65-\frac{65}{4}}=\frac{\sqrt{195}}{2}$

Center: $(-4,1)$, Vertices: $(-4,1\pm\sqrt{65})$

Foci: $\left(-4,\ 1\pm\frac{\sqrt{195}}{2}\right)$

Eccentricity: $\frac{c}{a}=\frac{\frac{\sqrt{195}}{2}}{\sqrt{65}}=\frac{\sqrt{3}}{2}$

Major Axis: $2a=2\sqrt{65}$,

Minor Axis: $2b=\sqrt{65}$

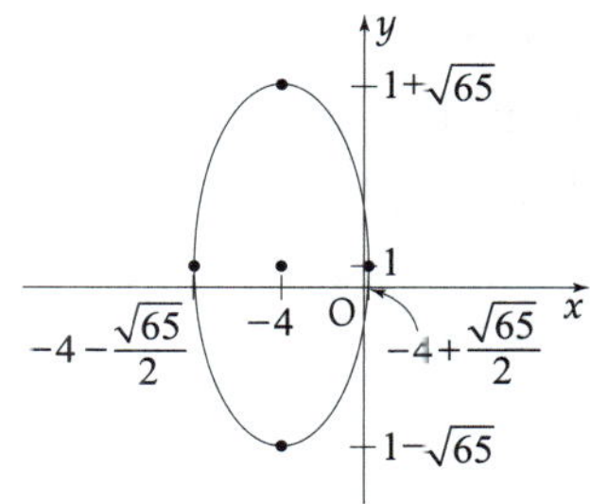

08

(1)

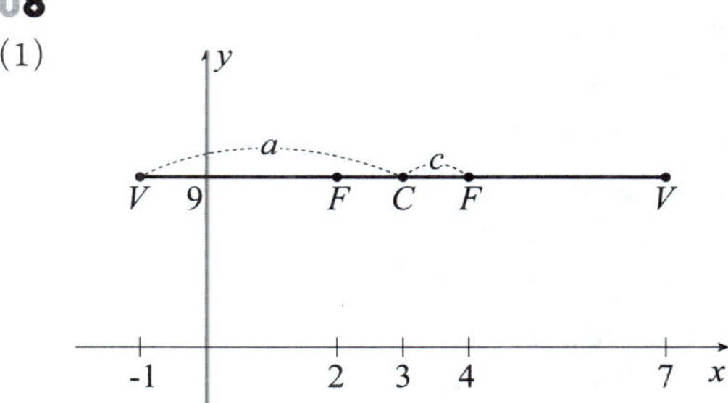

The standard equation is

$\frac{(x-h)^2}{a^2}+\frac{(y-k)^2}{b^2}=1$.

The center is $\left(\frac{-1+7}{2},\ 9\right)=(3,\ 9)$.

$a=4$, $c=1$, and $b=\sqrt{a^2-c^2}=\sqrt{16-1}=\sqrt{15}$.

So the equation is

$\frac{(x-3)^2}{4^2}+\frac{(y-9)^2}{(\sqrt{15})^2}=1$, $\frac{(x-3)^2}{16}+\frac{(y-9)^2}{15}=1$.

$\frac{(x-3)^2}{16}+\frac{(y-9)^2}{15}=1$

(2)

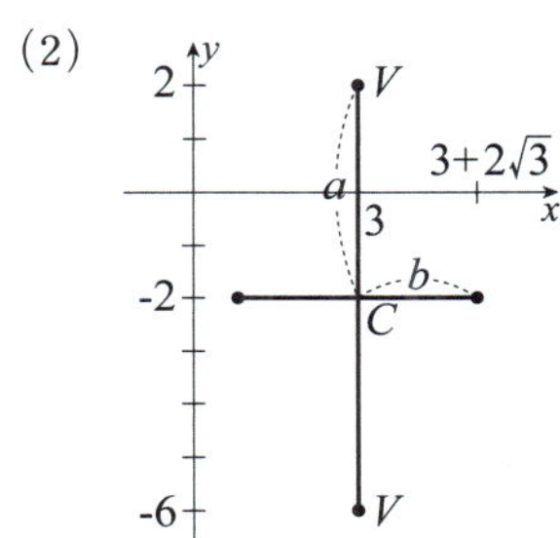

The standard equation is

$$\frac{(y-k)^2}{a^2}+\frac{(x-h)^2}{b^2}=1,$$

The center is

$$\left(3,\ \frac{2+(-6)}{2}\right)=(3,-2),\ a=4,\ b=2\sqrt{3}.$$

So the equation is

$$\frac{(y+2)^2}{4^2}+\frac{(x-3)^2}{(2\sqrt{3})^2}=1,\ \frac{(y+2)^2}{16}+\frac{(x-3)^2}{12}=1.$$

$$\frac{(y+2)^2}{16}+\frac{(x-3)^2}{12}=1$$

09

(1) $3x^2-4y^2-30x+8y+35=0$

$3(x^2-10x)-4(y^2-2y)=-35$

$3(x^2-10x+25-25)-4(y^2-2y+1-1)=-35$

$3(x^2-10x+25)-75-4(y^2-2y+1)+4=-35$

$3(x-5)^2-4(y-1)^2=36$

$\dfrac{(x-5)^2}{12}-\dfrac{(y-1)^2}{9}=1$

$\rightarrow a=2\sqrt{3},\ b=3,$ and $c=\sqrt{12+9}=\sqrt{21}$

Center: $(5,1)$, Vertices: $(5\pm2\sqrt{3},1)$

Foci: $(5\pm\sqrt{21},\ 1)$

Transverse Axis: $2a=4\sqrt{3}$

Conjugate Axis: $2b=6$

Equation of Asymptote:

$$y=\pm\frac{3}{2\sqrt{3}}(x-5)+1=\pm\frac{\sqrt{3}}{2}(x-5)+1$$

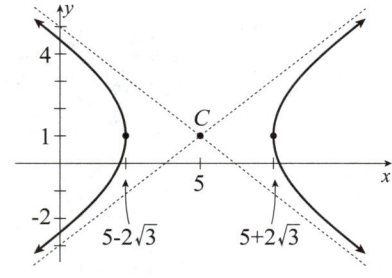

(2) $-2x^2+3y^2+4x-60y+268=0$

$-2(x^2-2x)+3(y^2-20y)=-268$

$-2(x^2-2x+1-1)+3(y^2-20y+100-100)=-268$

$-2(x^2-2x+1)+2+3(y^2-20y+100)-300=-268$

$3(y-10)^2-2(x-1)^2=30$

$\dfrac{(y-10)^2}{10}-\dfrac{(x-1)^2}{15}=1$

$\rightarrow a=\sqrt{10},\ b=\sqrt{15},$ and $c=\sqrt{10+15}=5$

Center: $(1,10)$, Vertices: $(1,10\pm\sqrt{10})$

Foci: $(1,10\pm5)=(1,15),(1,5)$

Transverse Axis: $2a=2\sqrt{10}$

Conjugate Axis: $2b=2\sqrt{15}$

Equation of Asymptote:

$$y=\pm\frac{\sqrt{10}}{\sqrt{15}}(x-1)+10=\pm\frac{\sqrt{6}}{3}(x-1)+10$$

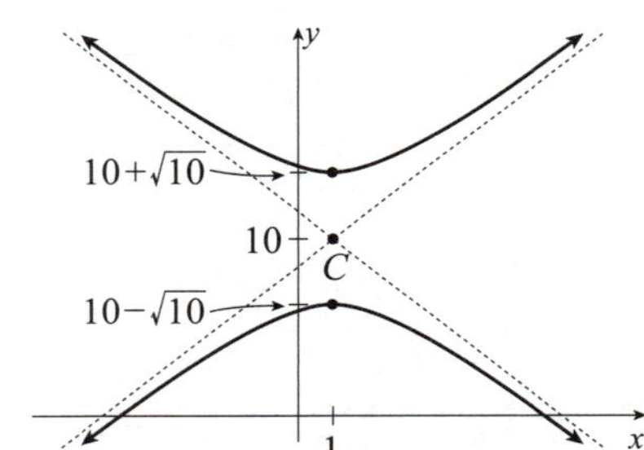

10

(1)

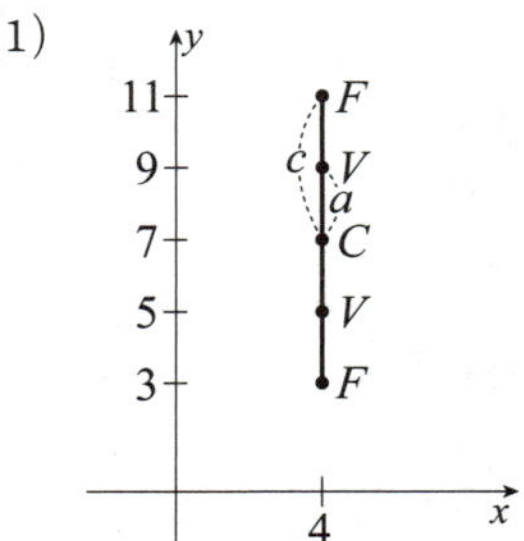

The standard equation is

$$\frac{(y-k)^2}{a^2}-\frac{(x-h)^2}{b^2}=1.$$

The center is $\left(4,\ \dfrac{3+11}{2}\right)=(4,\ 7)$,

So the equation is

$a=\dfrac{4}{2}=2$, $c=11-7=4$, and $b=\sqrt{4^2-2^2}=2\sqrt{3}$

$\dfrac{(y-7)^2}{2^2}-\dfrac{(x-4)^2}{(2\sqrt{3})^2}=1$, $\dfrac{(y-7)^2}{4}-\dfrac{(x-4)^2}{12}=1$

$\dfrac{(y-7)^2}{4}-\dfrac{(x-4)^2}{12}=1$

(2)

The standard equation is

$\dfrac{(x-h)^2}{a^2}-\dfrac{(y-k)^2}{b^2}=1.$

The center is

$\left(\dfrac{0+6}{2},\ 2\right)=(3,\ 2)$, $a=3$

Since the slope of the asymptotes are $\pm\dfrac{3}{2}$, we have

$\pm\dfrac{b}{a}=\pm\dfrac{2}{3}$, $\dfrac{b}{3}=\dfrac{2}{3}$, $b=2$

So the equation is

$\dfrac{(x-3)^2}{3^2}-\dfrac{(y-2)^2}{2^2}=1$, $\dfrac{(x-3)^2}{9}-\dfrac{(y-2)^2}{4}=1$

$\dfrac{(x-3)^2}{9}-\dfrac{(y-2)^2}{4}=1$

11

$x=2\sin t$, $\sin t=\dfrac{x}{2}$

$y=\cos t-1$, $\cos t=y+1$

Using the trigonometric identity:

$\sin^2 t+\cos^2 t=1$

$\left(\dfrac{x}{2}\right)^2+(y+1)^2=1$, $\dfrac{x^2}{4}+(y+1)^2=1$

Therefore, the correct answer is (C).

12

Since the coefficient of $x^2>0$ and the coefficient of $y^2<0$, the given equation represents a hyperbola. Therefore, the correct answer is (D).

13

(1) $\overrightarrow{AB}=\langle 2-(-1),\ 5-3\rangle=\langle 3,\ 2\rangle$

$|\overrightarrow{AB}|=\sqrt{3^2+2^2}=\sqrt{13}$

(2) $\overrightarrow{CB}=\langle 2-4,\ 5-(-2)\rangle=\langle -2,\ 7\rangle$

$\overrightarrow{AB}+\overrightarrow{CB}=\langle 3,\ 2\rangle+\langle -2,\ 7\rangle=\langle 1,\ 9\rangle$

$|\overrightarrow{AB}+\overrightarrow{CB}|=\sqrt{1^2+9^2}=\sqrt{82}$

(3) $\overrightarrow{BC}=\langle 4-2,\ -2-5\rangle=\langle 2,\ -7\rangle$

$\overrightarrow{BA}=\langle -1-2,\ 3-5\rangle=\langle -3,\ -2\rangle$

$\overrightarrow{BC}-2\overrightarrow{BA}=\langle 2,\ -7\rangle-2\langle -3,\ -2\rangle$

$=\langle 2,\ -7\rangle+\langle 6,\ 4\rangle$

$=\langle 2+6,\ -7+4\rangle=\langle 8,\ -3\rangle$

$|\overrightarrow{BC}-2\overrightarrow{BA}|=\sqrt{8^2+(-3)^2}=\sqrt{73}$

14

(1) $\vec{v}+\vec{w}=\langle 3,\ -1\rangle+\langle 5,\ 3\rangle=\langle 8,\ 2\rangle$

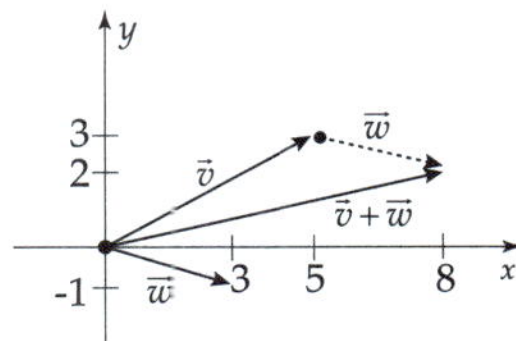

(2) $\vec{x}+2\vec{w}-\vec{v}=\langle -2,\ -3\rangle+2\langle 5,\ 3\rangle-\langle 3,\ -1\rangle$

$=\langle -2,\ -3\rangle+\langle 10,\ 6\rangle-\langle 3,\ -1\rangle=\langle 5,\ 4\rangle$

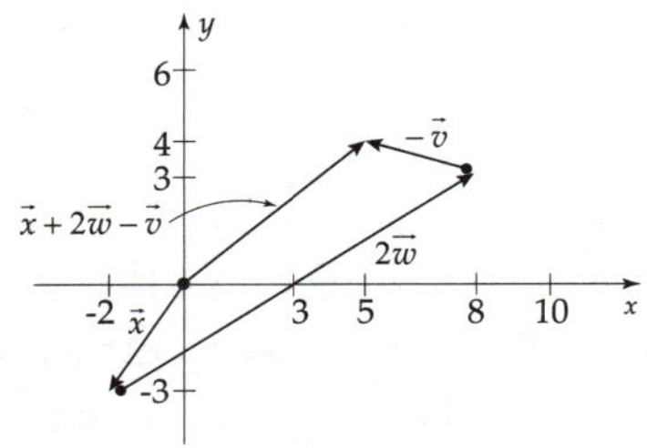

15

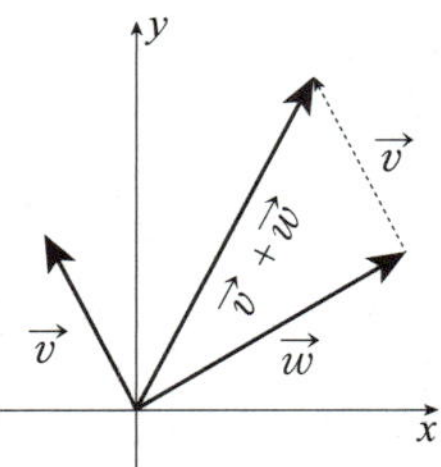

16

Since $|\vec{a}|=7$ and $|\vec{b}|=11$, $|3\vec{a}|=21$ and $|2\vec{b}|=22$.

(1)

$2\vec{b}$ 22 $3\vec{a}$ 21

$2\vec{b}+3\vec{a}$ 43

(2)

$2\vec{b}$ 22

$3\vec{a}$ 21

1 $2\vec{b}+3\vec{a}$

(1) : The maximum magnitude of vector $2\vec{b}+3\vec{a}$ is $22+21=43$.

(2) : The minimum magnitude of vector $2\vec{b}+3\vec{a}$ is $22-21=1$.

So the magnitude of vector $2\vec{b}+3\vec{a}$ must be between 1 and 43, inclusive. The answer is (D).

17

(1) $\vec{v}=\langle 2,\ 5\rangle$

$$\vec{u}=\frac{\vec{v}}{|\vec{v}|}=\frac{\langle 2,\ 5\rangle}{\sqrt{2^2+5^2}}=\left\langle \frac{2}{\sqrt{29}},\ \frac{5}{\sqrt{29}}\right\rangle$$
$$=\left\langle \frac{2\sqrt{29}}{29},\ \frac{5\sqrt{29}}{29}\right\rangle$$

(2) $\vec{w}=i-j=\langle 1,\ -1\rangle$

$$\vec{u}=\frac{\vec{w}}{|\vec{w}|}=\frac{\langle 1,\ -1\rangle}{\sqrt{1^2+(-1)^2}}=\left\langle \frac{1}{\sqrt{2}},\ -\frac{1}{\sqrt{2}}\right\rangle$$
$$=\left\langle \frac{\sqrt{2}}{2},\ -\frac{\sqrt{2}}{2}\right\rangle$$

18

Using the direction angle and magnitude of the vector, it can be written as $\vec{v}=|\vec{v}|\langle\cos\theta,\ \sin\theta\rangle$.

(1) $\vec{v}=|\vec{v}|\langle\cos\theta,\ \sin\theta\rangle=10\langle\cos 150°,\ \sin 150°\rangle$

$$=10\left\langle -\frac{\sqrt{3}}{2},\ \frac{1}{2}\right\rangle=\langle -5\sqrt{3},\ 5\rangle$$

(2) $\vec{v}=|\vec{v}|\langle\cos\theta,\ \sin\theta\rangle$

$$=4\langle\cos(-60°),\ \sin(-60°)\ \rangle$$
$$=4\left\langle \frac{1}{2},\ -\frac{\sqrt{3}}{2}\right\rangle=\langle 2,\ -2\sqrt{3}\rangle$$

19

(1) $\vec{v}=\langle 2,\ 1\rangle$

y 1 θ 2 2 1 x

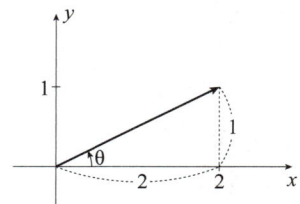

$\tan\theta=\frac{1}{2}$, $\theta=\tan^{-1}\left(\frac{1}{2}\right)=26.565°$

(2) $\vec{x}=3i-j=\langle 3,\ -1\rangle$

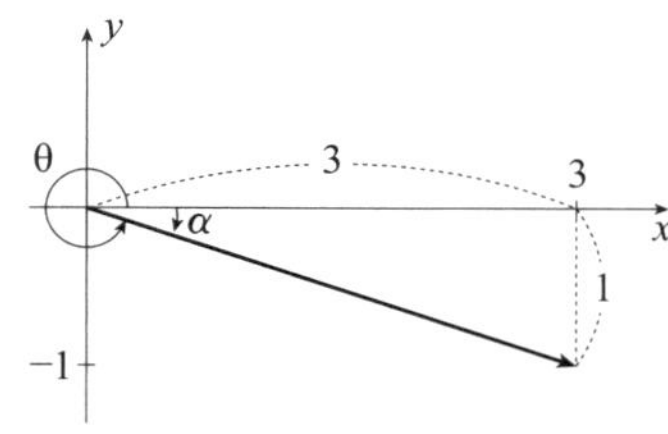

$\tan\alpha=\frac{1}{3},\ \alpha=\tan^{-1}\left(\frac{1}{3}\right)$

$\theta=360°-\alpha=360°-\tan^{-1}\left(\frac{1}{3}\right)=341.565°$

20

(1) $\vec{v}=\langle -2,\ -4\rangle,\ \vec{w}=\left\langle -\frac{1}{4},\ \frac{2}{3}\right\rangle$

$\vec{v}\cdot\vec{w}=(-2)\left(-\frac{1}{4}\right)+(-4)\left(\frac{2}{3}\right)$

$=\frac{1}{2}+\left(-\frac{8}{3}\right)=-\frac{13}{6}\neq 0$

$\vec{v}$ and $\vec{w}$ are NOT orthogonal.

(2) $\vec{v}=-\frac{4}{3}i+6j=\left\langle -\frac{4}{3},\ 6\right\rangle,$

$\vec{w}=9i+\frac{3}{4}j=\left\langle 9,\ \frac{3}{4}\right\rangle$

$\vec{v}\cdot\vec{w}=\left(-\frac{4}{3}\right)(9)+(6)\left(\frac{3}{4}\right)$

$=-12+\frac{9}{2}=-\frac{15}{2}\neq 0$

$\vec{v}$ and $\vec{w}$ NOT orthogonal.

21

(1) $\vec{v}\cdot\vec{v}=|\vec{v}|^2=(\sqrt{4^2+(-3)^2})^2=25$

(2) $(\vec{x}\cdot\vec{w})\vec{v}$

$\vec{x}\cdot\vec{w}=(-2)(-3)+(4)(1)=6+4=10$

$(\vec{x}\cdot\vec{w})\vec{v}=10\langle 4,\ -3\rangle=\langle 40,\ -30\rangle$

(3) $(\vec{w}\cdot\vec{x})+(\vec{w}\cdot\vec{v})=\vec{w}(\vec{x}+\vec{v})$

$\vec{x}+\vec{v}=\langle -2,\ 4\rangle+\langle 4,\ -3\rangle=\langle 2,\ 1\rangle$

$\vec{w}(\vec{x}+\vec{v})=(-3)(2)+(1)(1)=-6+1=-5$

22

(1) $\vec{v}=\langle -4,\ 2\rangle,\ \vec{w}=\langle -3,\ -4\rangle$

$\cos\theta=\frac{\vec{v}\cdot\vec{w}}{|\vec{v}|\,|\vec{w}|}=\frac{\langle -4,\ 2\rangle\cdot\langle -3,\ -4\rangle}{\sqrt{(-4)^2+2^2}\sqrt{(-3)^2+(-4)^2}}$

$=\frac{12-8}{\sqrt{20}\sqrt{25}}=\frac{4}{10\sqrt{5}}=\frac{2}{5\sqrt{5}}$

$\theta=\cos^{-1}\left(\frac{2}{5\sqrt{5}}\right)=79.695°$

(2) $\vec{v}=2i+2j,\ \vec{w}=-5i-3j$

$\cos\theta=\frac{\vec{v}\cdot\vec{w}}{|\vec{v}|\,|\vec{w}|}=\frac{\langle 2,\ 2\rangle\cdot\langle -5,\ -3\rangle}{\sqrt{2^2+2^2}\sqrt{(-5)^2+(-3)^2}}$

$=\frac{-10-6}{\sqrt{8}\sqrt{34}}=\frac{-16}{4\sqrt{17}}=-\frac{4}{\sqrt{17}}$

$\theta=\cos^{-1}\left(-\frac{4}{\sqrt{17}}\right)=165.964°$

23

Let $\vec{v}=\vec{x_1}+\vec{x_2}$,

where $\vec{x_1}=\text{proj}_w\, v$ and $\vec{x_2}=\vec{v}-\vec{x_1}$.

(1) $\vec{x_1}=\text{proj}_w\, v=\frac{\vec{v}\cdot\vec{w}}{|\vec{w}|^2}\vec{w}$

$=\frac{\langle -7,\ 2\rangle\cdot\langle -4,\ -5\rangle}{(\sqrt{(-4)^2+(-5)^2})^2}\langle -4,\ -5\rangle$

$=\frac{18}{41}\langle -4,\ -5\rangle=\left\langle -\frac{72}{41},\ -\frac{90}{41}\right\rangle$

$\vec{x_2}=\vec{v}-\vec{x_1}=\langle -7,\ 2\rangle-\left\langle -\frac{72}{41},\ -\frac{90}{41}\right\rangle$

$=\left\langle -\frac{215}{41},\ \frac{172}{41}\right\rangle$

$\vec{v}=\vec{x_1}+\vec{x_2}=\left\langle -\frac{72}{41},\ -\frac{90}{41}\right\rangle+\left\langle -\frac{215}{41},\ \frac{172}{41}\right\rangle$

(2) $\vec{x_1}=\text{proj}_w\, v=\frac{\vec{v}\cdot\vec{w}}{|\vec{w}|^2}\vec{w}$

$=\frac{\langle -1,\ -7\rangle\cdot\langle -5,\ -2\rangle}{(\sqrt{(-5)^2+(-2)^2})^2}\langle -5,\ -2\rangle$

$=\frac{19}{29}\langle -5,\ -2\rangle=\left\langle -\frac{95}{29},\ -\frac{38}{29}\right\rangle$

$\vec{x_2}=\vec{v}-\vec{x_1}=\langle -1,-7\rangle-\left\langle -\frac{95}{29},\ -\frac{38}{29}\right\rangle$

$$=\left\langle \frac{66}{29},\ -\frac{165}{29} \right\rangle$$

$$\vec{v}=\vec{x_1}+\vec{x_2}=\left\langle -\frac{95}{29},\ -\frac{38}{29} \right\rangle+\left\langle \frac{66}{29},\ -\frac{165}{29} \right\rangle$$

24

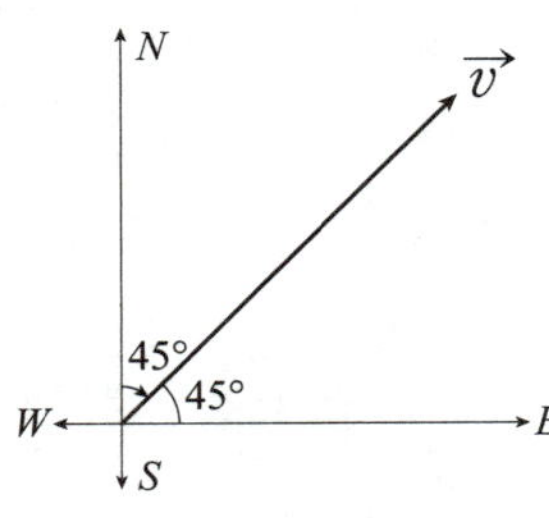

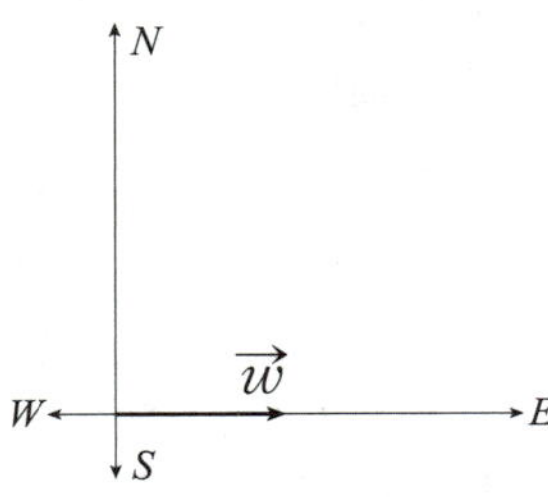

Velocity of the airplane :

$\vec{v}=|\vec{v}|\langle\cos\theta,\ \sin\theta\rangle=500\langle\cos 45°,\ \sin 45°\rangle$

$=500\left\langle \frac{\sqrt{2}}{2},\ \frac{\sqrt{2}}{2} \right\rangle=\langle 250\sqrt{2},\ 250\sqrt{2}\rangle$

Velocity of the wind :

$\vec{w}=|\vec{w}|\langle\cos\theta,\ \sin\theta\rangle=30\langle\cos 0°,\ \sin 0°\rangle$

$=30\langle 1,\ 0\rangle=\langle 30,\ 0\rangle$

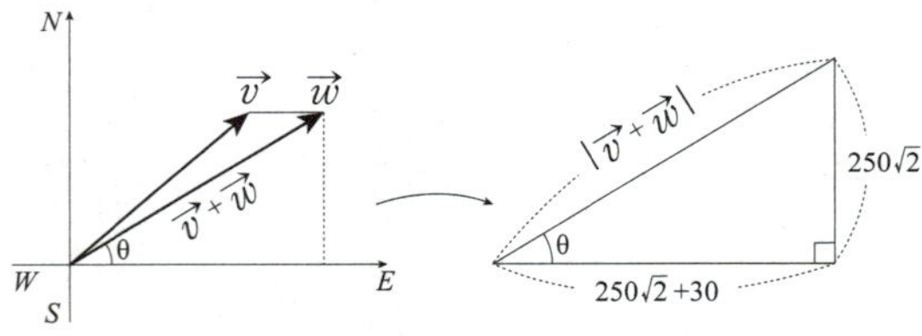

Velocity of the airplane+wind :

$\vec{v}+\vec{w}=\langle 250\sqrt{2}+30,\ 250\sqrt{2}\rangle$

So the actual speed of the airplane is

$|\vec{v}+\vec{w}|=\sqrt{(250\sqrt{2}+30)^2+(250\sqrt{2})^2}\approx 521.645$

and the direction is

$$\tan\theta=\frac{250\sqrt{2}}{250\sqrt{2}+30}$$

$$\theta=\tan^{-1}\left(\frac{250\sqrt{2}}{250\sqrt{2}+30}\right)=42.669°$$

521.645 mhp in the direction of 42.669°.

25

Let $\vec{F_3}=\langle x,\ y\rangle$ be the force required for equilibrium. Then, $\vec{F_1}+\vec{F_2}+\vec{F_3}=\langle 0,\ 0\rangle$.

So we have

$\vec{F_1}+\vec{F_2}+\vec{F_3}$

$=\langle -2,\ 2\sqrt{3}\rangle+\langle -1, -5\sqrt{3}\rangle+\langle x,\ y\rangle=\langle 0,\ 0\rangle$

$-2-1+x=0,\ x=3$

$2\sqrt{3}-5\sqrt{3}+y=0,\ y=3\sqrt{3}\ \rightarrow\ \vec{F_3}=\langle 3,\ 3\sqrt{3}\rangle$

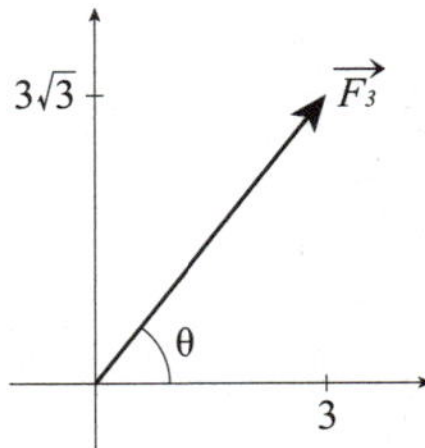

$|\vec{F_3}|=\sqrt{3^2+(3\sqrt{3})^2}=6$

$\tan\theta=\frac{3\sqrt{3}}{3}=\sqrt{3},\ \theta=\tan^{-1}\sqrt{3}=60°$

The magnitude of the force is 6 and the direction is 60°.

26

The work done is

$W=|\vec{F}|\cos\theta\cdot\vec{d}=40\cos 30°\cdot 100$

$=40\cdot\frac{\sqrt{3}}{2}\cdot 100=2000\sqrt{3}\ ft-lb$

$W=2000\sqrt{3}\ ft-lb$

27

(1) $AB=\begin{bmatrix}2&4\\1&3\end{bmatrix}\begin{bmatrix}5&1\\2&6\end{bmatrix}=\begin{bmatrix}2\cdot5+4\cdot2&2\cdot1+4\cdot6\\1\cdot5+3\cdot2&1\cdot1+3\cdot6\end{bmatrix}$

$=\begin{bmatrix}18&26\\11&19\end{bmatrix}$

$$AB=\begin{bmatrix}18 & 26\\11 & 19\end{bmatrix}$$

(2) $BA=\begin{bmatrix}5 & 1\\2 & 6\end{bmatrix}\begin{bmatrix}2 & 4\\1 & 3\end{bmatrix}=\begin{bmatrix}5\cdot2+1\cdot1 & 5\cdot4+1\cdot3\\2\cdot2+6\cdot1 & 2\cdot4+6\cdot3\end{bmatrix}$

$=\begin{bmatrix}11 & 23\\10 & 26\end{bmatrix}$

Therefore, $AB\neq BA$.

28

(1) $|C|=\begin{vmatrix}3 & 7\\2 & 5\end{vmatrix}=3\cdot5-7\cdot2=1$

$$|C|=1$$

(2) $C^{-1}=\frac{1}{|C|}\begin{bmatrix}5 & -7\\-2 & 3\end{bmatrix}=\frac{1}{1}\begin{bmatrix}5 & -7\\-2 & 3\end{bmatrix}$

$=\begin{bmatrix}5 & -7\\-2 & 3\end{bmatrix}$

$$C^{-1}=\begin{bmatrix}5 & -7\\-2 & 3\end{bmatrix}$$

29

The $A+B$ or $A-B$ exists only if both matrices have the same dimensions. So A and B cannot be added or subtracted. The product AB exists because the number of columns in A(which is k) matches the number of rows in B(which is also k). Given this, the product AB is defined and will have dimensions $m\times l$. Therefore, the correct answer is (C).

30

Let the quantities matrix be Q and the prices matrix be P. The total cost matrix for John and Eugene is obtained by multiplying the prices matrix by the quantities matrix:

$P\times Q=\underbrace{[\text{John Eugene}]}_{1\times2}$

$=\underbrace{[60\ 85\ 100]}_{1\times3}\times\underbrace{\begin{bmatrix}6 & 5\\8 & 10\\4 & 7\end{bmatrix}}_{3\times2}$

Therefore, the correct answer is (B).

31

Let the cost of each cookie be c, the cost of each brownie be b, and the cost of each chip be p. Using the data given, we can set up the following system of linear equations based on the total amounts collected by each student:

$24c+16b+15p=93$

$18c+22b+12p=87$

$20c+18b+16p=95$

Using the matrices,

$$\begin{bmatrix}24 & 16 & 15\\18 & 22 & 12\\20 & 18 & 16\end{bmatrix}\begin{bmatrix}c\\b\\p\end{bmatrix}=\begin{bmatrix}93\\87\\95\end{bmatrix}$$

$$\begin{bmatrix}c\\b\\p\end{bmatrix}=\begin{bmatrix}24 & 16 & 15\\18 & 22 & 12\\20 & 18 & 16\end{bmatrix}^{-1}\begin{bmatrix}93\\87\\95\end{bmatrix}$$

$$=\begin{bmatrix}1\\1.5\\3\end{bmatrix}$$

Therefore, the cost of each brownie is \$1.5. The correct answer is (B).

memo

memo

memo

JM EDU Workbook Series

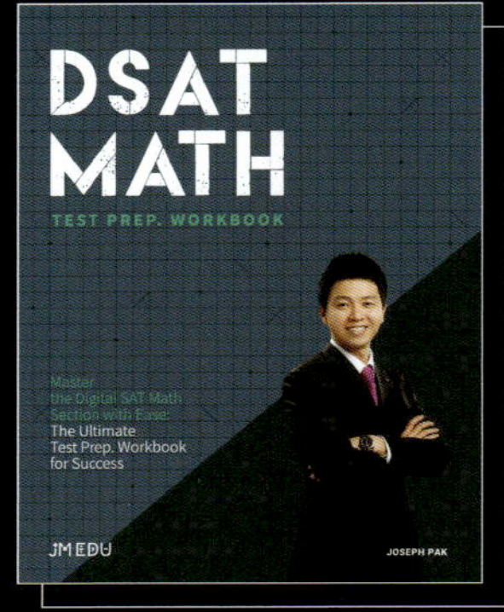

A well-structured workbook plays a critical role in students' learning experience!

CONCEPT & EXAMPLE ▸ CHECK POINT ▸ REVIEW EXERCISE ▸ CHAPTER TEST

Online Math Courses and Books
www.jmeducation.net

YouTube Channel: "Math-Up PLUS"
https://youtube.com/@math-upplus

53410
9791197067075
ISBN 979-11-970670-7-5

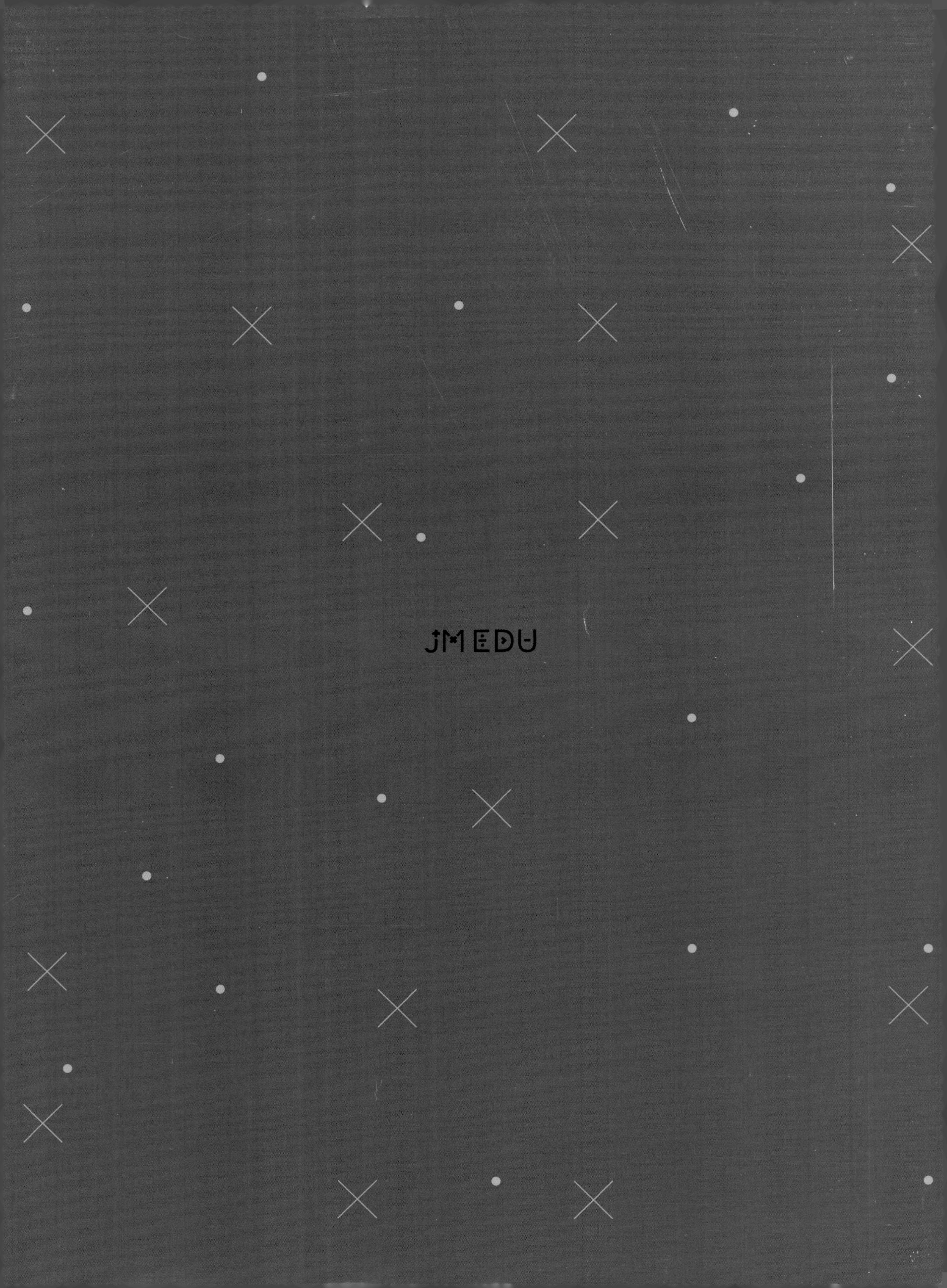
JMEDU